SOUTH-EAST ASIA

INVESTMENT RESOURCES AND CAPITAL FOR SOUTH-EAST ASIAN COUNTRIES HANDBOOK

STRATEGIC INFORMATION, OPPORTUNITIES, CONTACTS

International Business Publications, USA
Washington DC, USA

SOUTH-EAT ASIA

INVESTMENT RESOURCES AND CAPITAL FOR SOUTH-EAST ASIAN COUNTRIES HANDBOOK

STRATEGIC INFORMATION, OPPORTUNITIES, CONTACTS

UPDATED ANNUALLY

We express our sincere appreciation to all government agencies and international organizations which provided information and other materials for this directory

Cover Design: **International Business Publications, USA**

2017 Edition Updated Reprint International Business Publications, USA
ISBN 978-07397-2764-5

Printed in the USA

SOUTH-EAST ASIA

INVESTMENT RESOURCES AND CAPITAL FOR SOUTH-EAST ASIAN COUNTRIES HANDBOOK

STRATEGIC INFORMATION, OPPORTUNITIES, CONTACTS

SOUTH-EAST ASIAN COUNTRIES - STRATEGIC INFORMATION AND INVESTMENT CLIMATE

BASIC INFORMATION

Southeast Asia or **Southeastern Asia** is a subregion of Asia, consisting of the countries that are geographically south of China, east of India, west of New Guinea and north of Australia. The region lies near the intersection of geological plates, with heavy seismic and volcanic activity. Southeast Asia consists of two geographic regions:

1. **Maritime Southeast Asia**, comprising Indonesia, East Malaysia, Singapore, Philippines, East Timor, Brunei, and Christmas Island.
2. **Mainland Southeast Asia**, also known historically as **Indochina**, comprising Cambodia, Laos, Myanmar (Burma), Thailand, Vietnam, and West Malaysia;

Definitions of "Southeast Asia" vary, but most definitions include the area represented by the countries (sovereign states and dependent territories) listed below. All of the states except for East Timor are members of the Association of Southeast Asian Nations (ASEAN). The area, together with part of South Asia, was widely known as the East Indies or simply the Indies until the 20th century. Christmas Island and the Cocos (Keeling) Islands are considered part of Southeast Asia though they are governed by Australia. Sovereignty issues exist over some territories in the South China Sea. Papua New Guinea has stated that it might join ASEAN, and is currently an observer.

SOVEREIGN STATES

State	Area (km^2)	Population	Density ($/km^2$)	GDP (nominal), USD (2016)	GDP (nominal) per capita, USD (2016)	HDI	Capital
Brunei	5,765	453,000	78	17,105,000,000	$37,759	0.852	Bandar Seri Begawan
Cambodia	181,035	15,561,000	85	17,291,000,000	$1,111	0.584	Phnom Penh
East Timor	14,874	1,172,000	75	4,382,000,000	$3,239	0.620	Dili
Indonesia	1,904,569	251,490,000	132	895,677,000,000	$3,511	0.684	Jakarta
Laos	236,800	6,557,000	30	11,206,000,000	$1,709	0.569	Vientiane
Malaysia	329,847	30,034,000	91	367,712,000,000	$13,123	0.773	Kuala Lumpur*
Myanmar	676,000	51,419,000	98	63,881,000,000	$1,419	0.524	Nay Pyi Daw
Philippines	342,353	101,649,000	338	369,188,000,000	$3,568	0.668	Manila
Singapore	724	5,554,000	7,671	289,086,000,000	$52,049	0.901	Singapore (city-state)
Thailand	513,120	65,236,000	127	437,344,000,000	$5,697	0.722	Bangkok
Vietnam	331,210	92,571,000	279	187,848,000,000	$2,370	0.638	Hanoi

Dependent territoriesTerritory	Area (km^2)	Population	Density ($/km^2$)	Capital
Christmas Island	135	1,402[14]	10.4	Flying Fish Cove
Cocos (Keeling) Islands	14	596[15]	42.6	West Island (Pulau Panjang)

ADMINISTRATIVE SUBDIVISIONS

Territory	Area (km^2)	Population	Density ($/km^2$)	Capital
Andaman and Nicobar Islands	8,250	379,944[16]	46	Port Blair

BRUNEI INVESTMENT AND BUSINESS CLIMATE - STRATEGIC INFORMATION AND CONTACTS FOR STARTING BUSINESS

Brunei Darussalam is an energy-rich Sultanate on the northern coast of Borneo in Southeast Asia. Brunei boasts a well-educated, largely English-speaking population, excellent infrastructure, and a government intent on attracting foreign investment and projects. In parallel with Brunei's efforts to attract foreign investment, the country has improved its protections for Intellectual Property Rights (IPR).

Despite repeated calls for diversification, Brunei's economy remains dependent on the income derived from sales of oil and gas. Substantial revenue from overseas investment supplements income from domestic hydrocarbon production. These two revenue streams provide a comfortable quality of life for Brunei's population. Citizens are not required to pay taxe, have access to free education through to the university level,free medical care and, frequently, subsidized housing.

Brunei has a stable political climate and is generally sheltered from natural disasters. Brunei's central location in Southeast Asia, with good telecommunications, numerous airline connections, business tax credits in specified sectors, and no income, sales or export taxes offers a welcoming climate for would-be investors. Brunei is a founding member of the Trans-Pacific Partnership (TPP) trade negotiations. Sectors offering U.S. business opportunities in Brunei include Aerospace & Defense, Agribusiness, Construction, Petrochemicals, Energy & Mining, Environmental Technologies, Food Processing & Packaging, Franchising, Health Technologies, Information & Communication, Islamic Finance, and Services. In 2014 Brunei released an Energy White Paper outlining its vision of leveraging its oil wealth to diversify its economy, create local employment, increase foreign direct investment (FDI), and sharply increase the use of renewable energy by 2035.

The Export-Import Bank of the United States (EXIM) and the Energy Department of Brunei's Prime Minister's Office signed a Memorandum of Understanding (MOU) that calls for expanded information sharing regarding trade and energy business opportunities in the Asia-Pacific region, as well as exploring options for utilizing up to USD 1 billion EXIM Bank loans to finance U.S. exports in support of selected projects in the region. The MOU creates significant new opportunities for U.S. energy companies in Brunei and the Asia-Pacific region while advancing the goals set out by the United States-Asia Pacific Comprehensive Energy Partnership (USACEP).

In 2014 Brunei began supplementing the existing common law-based penal system with a penal code based on Islamic law, which will carry Sharia punishments. The Islamic Penal Code is applicable across the board. The first phase became effective on May 1, 2014. It expands restrictions regarding the drinking of alcohol, eating in public during the fasting hours in the month of Ramadan, and indecent behavior. Two subsequent phases, the timing of which is not yet clear, are expected to introduce severe punishments such as; stoning to death for certain sex-related offenses and the amputating of limbs. Brunei officials say the most severe punishments will rarely if ever be implemented given the very high standard of proof required under the Sharia Penal Code. While the law does not specifically address business-related matters, potential investors should be aware that there is controversy surrounding the Sharia Penal Code issue.

1. OPENNESS TO, AND RESTRICTIONS UPON, FOREIGN INVESTMENT

Attitude toward Foreign Direct Investment

Brunei has an open economy favorable to foreign trade and foreign direct investment (FDI) as it continues its economic diversification efforts away from its long reliance on oil and gas exports.

FDI is important to Brunei as it plays a key role in economic and technological development. Brunei encourages FDI in the domestic economy through various investment incentives offered by the Brunei Economic Development Board (BEDB) and the Ministry of Industry and Primary Resources (MIPR) and through activities by the Ministry of Foreign Affairs and Trade (MOFAT).

The 2015 World Bank and the International Finance Corporation report indicated that Brunei's ease of doing business ranking had dropped 3 spots to rank 101 out of 189 economies. The report attributed the drop less to any action by Brunei to make it harder to do business and more to inaction while other countries made positive changes. The one significant gain was a change in rank of 16 spots on dealing with construction permits, largely attributed to Brunei consolidating final inspections under a single agency. The Authority for Building and Construction Industry (ABCi) one-stop shop also issues all pre-construction approvals and building permits. The rankings for six of the ten indicators slipped, including: starting a business; registering property; getting credit; protecting minority investors; enforcing contracts; and resolving insolvency.

Responding to the report, Brunei's Minister of Industry and Primary Resources stated that the culture of business-as-usual was no longer relevant in the increasingly competitive world facing Brunei. Brunei also amended its laws to make it easier and quicker for entrepreneurs to establish businesses. The Miscellaneous License Act (Amendment) 2015 cuts down the wait time for new business registrants to start operations, with low-risk businesses like eateries and shops able to start operations immediately. Brunei fell from the number four country in the Association of Southeast Asian Nations (ASEAN) in terms of ease of doing business to number six.

Other Investment Policy Reviews

Not applicable.

Laws/Regulations of Foreign Direct Investment

The basic legislation on investment includes the Investment Incentive Order 2001 and Income Tax (As Amended) Order 2001. Brunei does not yet have a stock exchange, but the creation of a securities market is reportedly under development. Brunei's constitution does specifically provide for judicial independence, but in practice the court system operates without government interference. Brunei's legal system includes parallel systems; one based on Common Law and the other based on Islamic Law.

Brunei's national strategy, Wawasan (National Vision) 2035, emphasizes attracting FDI as an important driver of growth. The Brunei Economic Development Board (BEDB) seeks to diversify Brunei's economy and create employment opportunities for its people. The BEDB administers incentives and loans to encourage investment projects from abroad.

The Ministry of Industry and Primary Resources is the main coordinating agency for investment and industrial development in the primary sector, manufacturing, and tourism. The Ministry encourages and assists local and foreign investors to participate in ventures to produce goods and services for export and local markets and to satisfy national food security and employment needs.

Industrial Promotion

Through its Investment Incentives Order 2001, Brunei seeks to stimulate economic development by encouraging the establishment and expansion of specified industrial and economic enterprises. The authority to administer this legislation is currently vested in the Minister of Industry and Primary Resources, who is able to offer investment incentives in the form of tax relief for the following:

Pioneer Industries: Any limited company that has been granted a pioneer certificate will then be given pioneer incentives, including exemption from the 30 percent corporate tax for a period ranging from five years for a fixed capital expenditure of BND 500,000 to BND 2.5 million (USD 370,000 to USD 1,852,000); eight years for an expenditure over BND 2.5 million; and 11 years for a project located in a designated high-tech industrial park, with permitted extensions; exemption from taxes on imported duties on machinery, equipment, components parts, accessories or building structures; exemption from taxes on imported raw materials not available or produced in Brunei intended as feedstock for the production of Pioneer products; and carry forward losses and allowances.

Industries that have been declared as pioneer industries and pioneer products include: Agribusiness (fertilizers and pesticides); Agricultural, Construction, Building & Heavy Equipment (cement finishing mill, manufacture of electrical industrial machinery and apparatus, rolling mill plant, sheet metal-forming); Chemicals, Petrochemicals, Plastics & Composites (plastics and synthetic, manufacture of non-metallic mineral products, gas); Consumer Goods & Home Furnishings (furniture, ceramic and potteries, tissue paper, toys); Environmental Technologies (related waste industry); Food Processing & Packaging (slaughtering, preparing and preserving halal meat, canning, bottling and packaging); Health Technologies (pharmaceuticals); Information & Communication (manufacture of radio, television and communication equipment and apparatus); Industrial Equipment & Supplies (glass, wood base); Marine Technology (ship repair and maintenance, supporting services to water transport); Metal Manufacturing & Products (aluminum wall tile); Services (aircraft catering services); Textiles, Apparel & Sporting Goods (textiles). Additional details are available at**http://www.bedb.com.bn/doing_incentives_pioneer.html**

Pioneer Service Companies: Pioneer service companies may be eligible for tax relief, depending on the fixed capital expenditure, for a period of 8 years with given extension not exceeding 11 years in total.

Activities that have been declared as pioneer services include: Agribusiness (agriculture technology related services and activities); Architecture & Engineering (any engineering or technical services including laboratory, consultancy and research and development activities, development or production of any industrial design); Automotive & Ground Transportation (operation or management of any mass rapid transit system); Education (provision of education related services); Finance (business, management and professional consultancy services, financial services, venture capital fund activity); Health Technologies (medical services); Information & Communication (computer-based information and other computer related services, publishing services); Media & Entertainment (maintaining and operating a private museum, provision of leisure and recreation related services and activities); Services (services and activities related to warehousing facilities); Travel (services and activities relating to the organization or management of exhibitions and conferences). Additional details are available at **http://www.bedb.com.bn/doing_incentives_pioneerservice.html**.

Production For Export: The Minister of Industry and Primary Resources may approve a company proposing to engage in specified activities either wholly or partly for export as an export enterprise. Certified companies may be exempted from income tax; from import duties on machinery, equipment, component parts, accessories or building structures; and from import duties on raw materials for a period of six to 15 years depending on the company's fixed capital expenditure and pioneer status.

Qualified activities have included: Agribusiness (agriculture, forestry and fishery activities). Additional details are available at **http://www.bedb.com.bn/doing_incentives_production.html**.

Service For Export: Specified services may be eligible for exemption from income tax and deduction of allowance and losses. The tax relief period of an export service company shall begin on its day of commencement and shall not exceed 11 years. Any given extension shall not exceed 3 years at one time and not exceed 20 years in total.

Qualified services have included: Architecture & Engineering (technical services including construction, distribution, design and engineering services); Education (educational and training service); Industrial Equipment & Supplies (fabrication of machinery and equipment, and procurement of materials, components and equipment); Information & Communication (data processing, programming, computer software development, telecommunications and other related ICT services); Services (consultancy, management supervisory or advisory services relating to any technical matter or to any trade or business; professional services including accounting, legal, medical and architectural services.) Additional details are available at **http://www.bedb.com.bn/doing_incentives_service.html**

Foreign Loan for Product Equipment: There is a 20% withholding tax for interest paid to non-resident lenders. However the government may grant a tax exemption for any approved foreign loan if the loan is utilized for the purchase of production equipment. Additional information is available at **http://www.bedb.com.bn/doing_incentives_foreign.html**. Information on additional forms of business and investment incentives is available at **http://www.bedb.com.bn/doing_incentives.html**.

Limits on Foreign Control

There has been no restriction on total foreign ownership of companies incorporated in Brunei Darussalam. The Companies Act requires locally incorporated companies to have at least one of the two directors—or if more than two directors, at least two of them—to be ordinarily resident in Brunei Darussalam. The Companies Act allows the board to be totally non-resident; however, the company concerned would have to apply to the appropriate authorities for permission and show justifications for such decisions. Notwithstanding whether the company is locally or foreign owned and managed, the rate of corporate income tax is the same.

Privatization Program

Brunei's Ministry of Communication has made corporatization and privatization part of its Strategic Plans 2008-2017, which call for the Ministry to shift its role from a service provider to a regulatory body with policy-setting responsibility. In that role, the Ministry will develop specific policies through corporatization and privatization; establish a regulatory framework and business facilitation. Currently, the Ministry is studying initiatives to privatize and corporatize four state-owned agencies: the Ports Department, the Maritime and Port Authority of Brunei

Darussalam, the Postal Services Department, and Brunei International Airport management. These services are not yet completely privatized and there is no timeline for privatization, as the Ministry is still in the process of considering the initiative. Guidelines regarding the role of foreign investors and the bidding process are not yet available. The strategy can be found in www.mincom.gov.bn.

Screening of FDI

Post is informed that Brunei, through BEDB, has one or more processes to screen, review or approve foreign investments. The processes are kept confidential. Post has received no complaints from U.S. businesses about the screening process.

Competition Law

Brunei does not have any general competition legislation pertaining to the regulation of competition issues. Brunei formally started the process of drafting the Brunei Competition Order in May 2012, which reportedly emulates the legislation and best practices in the international jurisdiction including prohibitions against anti-competitive agreements, abuse of dominance, and anti-competitive mergers. It is not known when the law will be approved and implemented.

Investment Trends

Brunei is a founding member in the Trans-Pacific Partnership (TPP) negotiations, through which the United States and 10 other Asia-Pacific partners are seeking to establish a comprehensive, next-generation regional agreement to liberalize trade and investment. This agreement will advance U.S. economic and trade policies within fast-growing economies, and aid in the economic integration across the Asia-Pacific region. The TPP agreement will include commitments on goods, services, intellectual property rights, labor, and other traditional trade and investment issues. It will also address a range of emerging issues not covered by past agreements. In addition to the United States and Brunei, the TPP negotiating partners currently include Australia, Canada, Chile, Japan, Malaysia, Mexico, New Zealand, Peru, Singapore, and Vietnam. Brunei is also a negotiating party to the Regional Comprehensive Economic Partnership (RCEP).

According to the U.S. Trade Representative, Brunei's annual trade balance decreased by 16.8 per cent from BND 11,765.5 million (USD 9,488.31 million) in 2012 to BND 9,788.4 million (USD 7,830.72 million) in 2013. Meanwhile the total trade showed a decline of 8.9 per cent from BND 20,675.9 million (USD 16,672.11 million) in 2012 to BND 18,829.6 million (USD 15,063.68 million) in 2013. The U.S. goods trade surplus with Brunei was BND 676 million (USD 541 million) in 2013, a decrease of USD 470 million (BND 587 million) from 2012. U.S. goods exports in 2013 were USD 559 million (BND 699 million), up 254.4 percent from the previous year. Corresponding U.S. imports from Brunei were USD 17 million (BND 21 million), down 81 percent. Brunei is currently the 100th largest export market for U.S. goods. The stock of U.S. foreign direct investment (FDI) in Brunei was USD 116 million (BND 160 million) in 2012 (latest data available), up 17.2% from 2011.

Table 1

Measure	Year	Index or Rank	Website Address
TI Corruption Perceptions index	2014	N/A	transparency.org/cpi2014/results
World Bank's Doing Business Report "Ease of Doing Business"	2015	101 of 189	doingbusiness.org/rankings
Global Innovation Index	2014	88 of 143	globalinnovationindex.org/content.aspx?page=data-analysis
World Bank GNI per capita	2013	n/a	data.worldbank.org/indicator/NY.GNP.PCAP.CD

2. Conversion and Transfer Policies

Foreign Exchange

In June 2013 the Financial Action Task Force (FATF) announced that Brunei Darussalam is no longer subject to FATF's monitoring process under its on-going global Anti-Money Laundering/Countering the Financing of Terrorism (AML/CFT) compliance process. Brunei Darussalam will work with the Asia-Pacific Group (APG) as it continues to address the full range of AML/CFT issues identified in its Mutual Evaluation Report. The report cited Brunei's significant progress in improving its AML/CFT regime and noted that Brunei had established the legal and regulatory framework to meet its commitments in its Action Plan regarding the strategic deficiencies that the FATF had identified in June 2011.

Remittance Policies

Not applicable/information not available.

3. Expropriation and Compensation

There is no history of expropriation of foreign owned property in Brunei. There have been cases of domestically owned private property being expropriated for infrastructure development. Compensation was provided in such cases, and claimants were provided with due process regarding their disputes.

4. DISPUTE SETTLEMENT

Legal System, Specialized Courts, Judicial Independence, Judgments of Foreign Courts

Onshore companies are governed by the Companies Act while offshore companies are governed by the International Business Companies Order of 2000. There are no specialized commercial courts. Brunei's constitution does not provide for judicial independence but in practice the court system operates without government interference. Post has received no complaints from companies regarding the judicial system.

The use of Alternative Dispute Mechanisms (ADR) is not new to Brunei. Both mediation and conciliation as a means of settling disputes has been deep rooted in Brunei's traditions and were originally carried out community leaders and important social figures

Bankruptcy

Brunei's bankruptcy act is available at http://www.agc.gov.bn/agc1/images/LAWS/ACT_PDF/cap067.pdf. Recent amendments to the act increased the minimum threshold for declaring bankruptcy from BND 500 to BND 10,000 (USD 370 to USD 7,407) and enabled the trustee to direct the Controller of Immigration to impound and retain the bankrupt's passport, certificate of identity or travel document to prevent him from leaving Brunei Darussalam. The amendments also saw the imposition of a number of duties on the bankrupt to deliver all his property under his possession, books, paper etc. to the trustee.

Information not available.

ICSID Convention and New York Convention

Brunei is a member state to the convention on the International Centre for Settlement of Investment Disputes (ICSID Convention) and a signatory to the Recognition and Enforcement of Foreign Arbitral Awards (1958 New York Convention.

5. PERFORMANCE REQUIREMENTS AND INVESTMENT INCENTIVES

WTO/TRIMS

Brunei became a World Trade Organization (WTO) member in 1995 and a signtory to the General Agreement on Tariffs and Trade (GATT) in 1993.

Investment Incentives

Companies producing goods and services for export can apply for a renewable 10-year tax exemption. Corporate tax relief of up to 5 years is available for companies that invest between BND 500,000 to BND 2.5 million (USD 370,000 to USD 1.85million), and up to 8 years for amounts exceeding BND 2.5million (USD 1.85 million) in approved ventures. An 11-year tax break is offered if the venture is located in a high-tech industrial park. Businesses wishing to compete in domestic markets can qualify for tax breaks for up to eight years. Sole proprietorships and partnerships are not subject to tax. Individuals do not pay any capital gains tax and profits arising from the sale of capital assets are not taxable. Brunei has double-taxation agreements with Britain, Indonesia, China, Singapore, Vietnam, Bahrain, Oman, Japan, and Pakistan. Tax on petroleum operations is codified in the 1960 Income Tax enactment, which is similar to tax policies in other oil-producing nations.

Performance Requirements

The Brunei government is actively seeking to increase the number of Bruneians working in the private sector. Brunei's 2014 Energy White Paper calls for the number of persons employed in the energy sector to increase from 20,000 in 2010 to 50,000 in 2035, and for the number of locals employed in the sector to increase from 10,000 to 40,000 in the same period. To advance this goal, all companies competing for a tender in the oil and gas industry are required to have at least half of their employees Bruneians.

Expatriate employment is controlled by a Labor Quota system from the Labor Department and the issuance of employment passes, by the Immigration Department. Brunei allows for new companies to apply for "special approval" to expedite the recruitment of expatriate workers in select positions for essential jobs. According to the Ministry of Home

Affairs, this approval is only available to new companies operating in the urban and suburban areas for six months, and covers businesses such as restaurants and shops. The "special approval" cuts the waiting time down from 21 days to 7.

6. RIGHT TO PRIVATE OWNERSHIP AND ESTABLISHMENT

All businesses in Brunei must be registered with the Registrar of Companies within the Attorney General's Chambers. Except for sole proprietorships, foreign investors can fully own incorporated companies, foreign company branches or representative offices. Partnerships generally require the participation of citizens. Foreign direct investments by multi-national corporations may not require local partnership in setting up a subsidiary of their parent company in Brunei. However, at least one company director must be a Brunei citizen or permanent resident in Brunei Darussalam. A multinational company with an operating plant on an MIPR industrial park is required to have 30% of the companies' board represented by Brunei citizens and permanent residents.

7. PROTECTION OF PROPERTY RIGHTS

Real Property

Mortgages are recognized and enforced in Brunei, however only Bruneians can own land property in Brunei. Foreigners and permanent residents can only hold properties under strata tiles or long-term leasehold rights. Most banks have stopped granting housing loans to foreigners and permanent residents. The 2011 data from the International Monetary Fund (IMF) showed no foreign direct investment (FDI) for real estate, rentals and business activity. In 2009 and 2010, the sector saw BND 3 million in FDI per year while in 2007 and 2008 it logged BND 2 million of FDI value.

Amendments to the Land Code are in the works to ban past practices of proxy sale of land to foreigners and permanent residents using the power of attorney (PA) and Trust Deeds (TD). PA and TD are no longer recognized as viable mechanisms in land deals involving non-citizens. The move to ban the PA and TD was announced at the 8th Legislative Council meeting on March 12, 2012. The proposed laws will also have retroactive effect, converting all existing property owned through PA and TD into 60-year leases. The rationale for the restriction is to ensure sufficient land ownership by citizens. PA's are still in land development transactions allowing for only 5-year ownership for land developers and 25-year ownership for banks. The PA in these cases was allowed to be used as collateral.

Intellectual Property Rights

Brunei's IP protection and enforcement regime is still in development but is increasingly strong and effective. The country was removed from the Special 301 report in 2013, and stayed off the list in 2014 and 2015, in recognition of its improving IPR protections, increasing enforcement, and efforts to educate the public about the importance of IPR.

Brunei's long-gestating Copyright (Amendment) Order 2013 was finalized and adopted in December 2013, a development long requested by the U.S. government. The change further enhanced enforcement provisions for copyright infringement by increasing penalties for offences; adding new offenses; strengthening the enforcement powers of the Royal Brunei Police Force and the Ministry of Finance Customs and Excise Department; and allowing for sanctioned private prosecution. The amendments are designed to deter copyright infringements with fines of BND 10,000 (USD 7,400) to BND 20,000 (USD 14,800) per infringing copy, imprisonment for a term up to five years or both. The new penalty is up to four times more severe than the previously existing penalty. Enforcement agencies are authorized to enter premises and arrest without warrant, to stop, search and board vehicles and also to access computerized and digitized data. The amendments further allow for admissibility of evidence obtained covertly and protect the identity of informants. Statistics on seizures of counterfeit goods are unavailable.

Brunei transferred its Registry of Trademarks from the Attorney General's Chambers (AGC) to the BEDB effective June 2013. The transfer expanded the BEDB Patents Registry Office's (PRO) capabilities to accept applications for the registration of trademarks in addition to patents and industrial designs. The office's name officially changed the Brunei Intellectual Property Office (BruIPO). The change created a national IP office, making policy coordination easier. The World Intellectual Property Organization's Singapore office described the move as a very positive step in terms of strengthening the IP protection efforts, because it provides comprehensive management of IP. In 2014, BruIPO reported that local trademark applications more than doubled in comparison to 2013, rising from 41 to 101.

In September 2013, Brunei acceded to the Geneva (1999) Act of the Hague Agreement Concerning the International Registration of Industrial Designs to protect IP from industrial designs, making it the second ASEAN Member country, following Singapore, to accede. The accession emphasized Brunei's commitment under the ASEAN Intellectual Property Rights Action Plan 2011 – 2015. Brunei also plans and has publicly committed to acceding to other World Intellectual Property Organization's (WIPO) treaties including the Madrid Protocol for the International Registration of Marks, the WIPO Performances and Phonograms Treaty

(WPPT), and the UPOV Convention 1991 for the protection of New Varieties of Plants (PV). In addition, Brunei is actively negotiating the Trans-Pacific Partnership's IPR chapter with the United States and other TPP participants. The Recording Industry Association of Malaysia, which in the past had criticized Brunei for a lack of support for IPR protection, opened its own office in Brunei in 2013. For additional information about treaty obligations and points of contact at local IP offices, please see WIPO's country profiles at http://www.wipo.int/directory/en/.

Resources for Rights Holders

Contact at Mission:

Allison M. Carragher

Political/Economic/Consular Officer

+673 238-4616 ext. 2165

CarragherAM@state.gov

Country/Economy resources:

The United States Embassy in Bandar Seri Begawan maintains a list of local attorneys at**http://brunei.usembassy.gov/list-of-attorneys.html**

8. TRANSPARENCY OF THE REGULATORY SYSTEM

Brunei's foreign direct investment policies are not fully transparent, particularly with respect to limits on foreign equity participation, partnership requirements, and the identification of sectors in which foreign direct investment is restricted.

9. EFFICIENT CAPITAL MARKETS AND PORTFOLIO INVESTMENT

Brunei recently signed a Memorandum of Understanding (MOU) with the Securities

Commission Malaysia (SCM) to boost cooperation in the capital markets. The MOU was designed to strengthen collaboration in the development of fair and efficient capital markets in the two countries. It also provided a framework to facilitate greater cross-border capital market activities and cooperation in the areas of regulation as well as capacity building and human capital development, particularly in the area of Islamic capital markets.

10. COMPETITION FROM STATE-OWNED ENTERPRISES

Brunei's state-owned enterprises are involved in key sectors of the economy, such as oil and gas, telecommunications, transport, and energy generation and distribution. However, Brunei has not yet notified its state trading enterprises to the WTO Working Party on State Trading Enterprises. There is no published list of SOE's, but specific examples include:

Semaun Holdings, incorporated as a private limited company, is wholly owned by the Brunei Government. Its emphasis is on joint ventures with foreign investors, mainly in aquaculture, food processing, glass crystal, and hi-tech manufacturing industries which are currently not open for 100% foreign ownership.

Under the Telecommunications Order 2001, the Authority for Info-communications Technology Industry (AiTi) regulates the licensing of the telecommunications industry. The establishment, installation, maintenance, provision or operation of unlicensed telecommunication systems or services within Brunei is a punishable offence, resulting in imprisonment, and large fines. AiTi has not opened up the telecommunications industry for foreign participation. The telecommunications industry is dominated by Telekom Brunei (TelBru) and Data Stream Technologies (DST) Communications both privatized state companies. Telbru is the sole provider of fixed lines. Its subsidiary company, B-mobile, provides 3G mobile services together with DST. DST is also the sole provider of Global Systems for Mobile communication (GSM) mobile phone service and the sole pay-television service provider.

Royal Brunei Technical Services (RBTS), established in 1988 as a wholly-government owned corporation, is responsible for managing the acquisition of a wide range of systems and equipment and maintaining those acquired systems and equipment.

Brunei National Petroleum Sendirian Berhad (PB) is the national oil company. PB is wholly owned by the Brunei Government and was incorporated on January 14, 2001 as a private limited company. The company was granted all the mineral rights in eight prime onshore and offshore petroleum blocks comprised of the deepwater offshore Blocks CA1 & CA2, inboard offshore Blocks N, P, Q, & B and onshore Blocks L & M totaling 20,552 sq. km. Currently, the company manages the production sharing contractors exploring the onshore and deepwater offshore blocks. The company is also working with the Block B operator in the development of the Maharaja Lela/Jamalulam Field.

OECD Guidelines on Corporate Governance of SOEs

Brunei does not adhere to the OECD guidelines on corporate governance of SOE's.

Sovereign Wealth Funds

The Brunei Investment Agency (BIA) manages the Government of Brunei's General Reserve Fund, and their external assets. Established in 1983, its assets are reportedly worth USD 30 billion. It has holdings in corporations, real estate, and currencies. BIA's activities are not publicly disclosed. It is ranked the lowest in transparency ratings by The Sovereign Wealth Fund Institute.

11. Corporate Social Responsibility

Corporate social responsibility (CSR) is still a relatively new concept in Brunei, and there are no specific government programs encouraging foreign and local enterprises to follow generally accepted CSR principles. However there is a broad awareness of corporate social responsibility among both producers and consumers, and individual private and public sector organizations have formalized CSR programs and policies. There are no reporting requirements and no independent NGOs in Brunei that promote or monitor CSR.

OECD Guidelines for Multinational Enterprises

Brunei does not adhere to the OECD guidelines for multinational enterprises.

12. POLITICAL VIOLENCE

Brunei has no recent history of political violence. The country experienced an uprising in 1962, when it was a British protectorate, which ended through the intervention of British troops. The country has been ruled peacefully under emergency law ever since.

13. CORRUPTION

Since January 1, 1982, Brunei has enforced the Emergency (Prevention of Corruption) Act. In1984, the Act was renamed the Prevention of Corruption Act (Chapter 131). The Anti-Corruption Bureau (ACB) was established on February 1, 1982 for the purpose of enforcing the Act. The Prevention of Corruption Act provides specific powers to the ACB for the purpose of investigating accusations of corruption. The Act also provides power for ACB to investigate certain offences under the Penal Code and offences under other written laws, provided such offences were disclosed during the course of ACB investigation into offences under the Prevention of Corruption Act.

The ACB strives to ensure a corruption-free public service. Corrupt practices are punishable under the Prevention of Corruption Act. The Act also applies to Brunei citizens abroad. There are perceptions that corruption in the private sector is more prevalent than in the public sector. This has prompted the ACB to focus on the private sector, as the private sector plays a critical role in Brunei's economic diversification. Brunei is a member of the International Association of Anti-Corruption Authorities.

In Transparency International's Corruption Perception Index (CPI) 2014, Brunei is ranked 38 out of 175 countries.

No U.S. Company has identified corruption as an obstacle to conduct business in Brunei.

UN Anticorruption Convention, OECD Convention on Combatting Bribery

Brunei has signed and ratified the UN Anticorruption Convention.

Resources to Report Corruption

Government Point of Contact:

Name: Hj Md Juanda Hj A. Rashid

Title: Director

Organization: Anti-Corruption Bureau Brunei Darussalam

Address: Old Airport Berakas, BB 3510 Brunei Darussalam

Tel: +673 238-3575 / +673 238-3197

Fax: +673-2383193

Mobile: +673 8721002

Email: **info.bmr@acb.gov.bn**

There are no international, regional, local or nongovernmental organizations operating in the country/economy that monitor corruption.

14. BILATERAL INVESTMENT AGREEMENTS

Brunei is a member of the Association of Southeast Asian Nations (ASEAN), which has Free Trade Agreements (FTA) with Australia, New Zealand, China, India, and South Korea, and a Comprehensive Economic Partnership Agreement with Japan.

Brunei currently has Bilateral Investment Treaties with China, Germany, India, the Republic of Korea, Oman, and South Africa.

Brunei was the ASEAN Coordinator in negotiations for the ASEAN-Australia-New Zealand Free Trade Agreement (AANZFTA), which was signed in Thailand on 27 February 2009 and entered into force on 1 January 2010. Brunei is a negotiating party to the TPP and the Regional Comprehensive Economic Partnership (RCEP).

Brunei was one of the original members of the Trans-Pacific Strategic Economic Partnership Agreement (P4), a Free Trade Agreement between Brunei Darussalam, Chile, Singapore, and New Zealand signed on 18 July 2005. The P4 later evolved into the Trans-Pacific Partnership (TPP) with the addition of new members, namely the United States, Australia, Canada, Japan, Peru, Malaysia, Mexico, and Vietnam, The TPP negotiations are currently ongoing.

Bilateral Taxation Treaties

Brunei does not have a bilateral taxation treaty with the United States.

15. OPIC AND OTHER INVESTMENT INSURANCE PROGRAMS

Overseas Private Investment Corporation (OPIC) programs are not available in Brunei given the country's affluence.

16. LABOR

The 2011 labor force estimate was 185,900 persons with an unemployment rate of 1.7 percent, according to the Brunei Darussalam Statistical Yearbook 2011 (latest data available), though unofficial estimates place the unemployment figures higher.

Brunei relies heavily on foreign labor in lower-skill and lower-paying positions, with approximately 120,000 guest workers brought in to fulfill specific contracts. The largest percentage of those work in construction, followed by wholesale and retail trade and then professional, technical, administrative and support services. Most unskilled laborers in Brunei are immigrants from Indonesia, Malaysia and the Philippines on renewable two year contracts.

The skilled labor pool includes both immigrants on short term visas and Bruneian citizens and permanent residents, who often are well educated but who often prefer to work for the government, with its better benefits such as bonuses, education allowance, interest-free loans, housing allowance, and other benefits, rather than the private sector. Approximately 25% of the total Brunei citizen workforce is employed in the public sector.

Matters relating to labor conditions are covered under the Labor Act, Employment Order 2009 and Workmen's Compensation Act. Expatriate employment is controlled by a Labor Quota system from the Labor Department and the issuance of employment passes, by the Immigration Department. Brunei allows for new companies to apply for "special approval" to expedite the recruitment of expatriate workers in select positions for essential jobs. According to the Ministry of Home Affairs, this approval is only available to new companies operating in the urban and suburban areas for six months, and covers businesses such as restaurants and shops. The special approval cuts the waiting time down from 21 days to 7.

The Brunei government is actively seeking to increase the number of Bruneians working in the private sector. Brunei's 2014 Energy White Paper calls for the number of persons employed in the energy sector to increase from 20,000 in 2010 to 50,000 in 2035, and for the number of locals employed in the sector to increase from 10,000 to 40,000 in the same period. To advance this goal, all companies competing for a tender in the oil and gas industry are required to have at least half of their employees Bruneians.

The law, including related regulations and statutory instruments, protects the right of workers to form and join unions. Under the Trade Unions Act, unions must be registered with the government. All workers, including civil servants other than those serving in the military and those working as prison guards or police officers, may form and join trade unions of their choice without previous authorization or excessive requirements. The only union in the country, which was composed of Brunei Shell Petroleum workers, dissolved in 2014. There are no other active unions or worker organizations.

While the law permits the formation of trade union federations, it forbids affiliation with international labor organizations unless there is consent from the minister of home affairs and the Department of Labor. The government prohibits strikes, and the law makes no explicit provision for the right to collective bargaining. The law prohibits employers from discriminating against workers in connection with union activities, but it does not provide for reinstatement for dismissal related to union activity.

Various domestic laws prohibit the employment of children under age 16. Parental consent and approval by the Labor Commission are required for those under age 18. Female workers under age 18 may not work at night or on offshore oil platforms. The Department of Labor, which is part of the Ministry of Home Affairs, effectively enforced laws related to the employment of children. There were no reports of violations of child labor laws.

The law does not set a minimum wage, but most employed citizens commanded good salaries. The public sector pay scale covers all workers in government jobs. Wages for employed foreign residents were wide ranging. Some foreign embassies set minimum wage requirements for their nationals working in the country.

The standard workweek is Monday through Thursday and Saturday, with Friday and Sunday off, allowing for two rest periods of 24 hours each week. The law provides for paid annual holidays, overtime for work in excess of 48 hours per week, and double time for work performed on legal holidays. The law also stipulates that an employee may not work more than 72 hours of overtime a month. Laws regarding hours were frequently not observed in practice. Occupational health and safety standards were established by government regulations. The Labor Department inspected working conditions both on a routine basis and in response to complaints. There were approximately 40 labor inspectors in the Labor Department in 2014. The government usually moved quickly to investigate abuses, and abusive employers faced criminal and civil penalties. All employment agencies have to be endorsed by the government and have to undergo government vetting and training before operating. In 2014, there were three cases of Employment Agencies operating without a license. Two of the cases were forwarded to the Law and Prosecution Division of the Department of Labor, while one case is still under investigation. The Labor Department had the power to terminate the license of abusive employers and revoke their foreign labor quota. The majority of abuse cases were settled out of court through agreements where the employer paid financial compensation to the worker.

The government generally enforced labor, health, and safety regulations effectively, but enforcement in the unskilled labor sector was lax. This was true especially for foreign laborers at construction sites, where wage arrears and inadequate safety and living conditions were reported. The government may close a workplace where health, safety, or working conditions are unsatisfactory, but this did not happen during the year.

Government data from 2011, the most recent available, indicated approximately 85,000 foreigners lived in the country temporarily. The law protected the rights of foreign workers through inspections of facilities and a telephone hotline for worker complaints. Immigration law allows for prison sentences and caning for workers who overstay their work permits, for workers who fall into irregular status due to their employers' negligence, for irregular immigrants seeking work, as well as for foreign workers employed by companies other than their initial sponsor. The law also requires recruiting agencies to be registered.

Government mediation by the Labor Department continued to be the most common means used to resolve labor disputes. The commissioner responsible for labor had the additional authority to protect foreign worker rights. The government prosecuted employers who employed irregular immigrants or did not process workers' documents, rendering them irregular. When grievances could not be resolved, regulations require employers to pay for the repatriation of the foreign workers and all outstanding wages. By custom, particularly for low-skilled workers, some employers held employee passports and restricted employee activities during non-work hours. Foreign workers who filed grievances sometimes did not receive their back wages. Foreign migrant workers often signed contracts with employment agents or other sponsors in their home countries that reduced their promised salaries through payments to the agencies or sponsors. The government forbade wage deductions to agencies or sponsors and mandated that employees receive their full salaries; nevertheless, foreign workers continued to pay high fees to manpower agents to obtain work in the country.

There were cases reported of nonpayment of salaries. The majority of cases involved domestic and construction workers. In many cases courts levied judicial penalties including convictions and fines against employers found guilty of nonpayment of wages.

17. FOREIGN TRADE ZONES/FREE PORTS/TRADE FACILITATION

Muara Port is Brunei's main seaport with an established Free Trade Zone called the Muara Export Zone (MEZ), which was established to promote and develop Brunei Darussalam as a trade hub of the region. The establishment of the MEZ was an initial step towards developing other Free Trade Zones in the country.

18. Foreign Direct Investment and Foreign Portfolio Investment Statistics

Table 2: Key Macroeconomic Data, U.S. FDI in Host Country/Economy

	Host Country Statistical source*		USG or international statistical source		USG or International Source of Data: BEA; IMF; Eurostat; UNCTAD, Other
Economic Data	Year	Amount	Year	Amount	
Host Country Gross Domestic Product (GDP) ($M USD)	2012	16,950	2014	14,914	www.worldbank.org/en/country
Foreign Direct Investment	Host Country Statistical source*		USG or international statistical source		USG or international Source of data: BEA; IMF; Eurostat; UNCTAD, Other
U.S. FDI in partner country ($M USD, stock positions)	N/A	N/A	2013	132	BEA
Host country's FDI in the United States ($M USD, stock positions)	N/A	N/A	N/A	N/A	
Total inbound stock of FDI as % host GDP	N/A	N/A	2013	Less than 1%	

*Host country GDP data available from Brunei Economic Development Board (BEDB)

CONTACT FOR MORE INFORMATION

U.S. Embassy Bandar Seri Begawan
Simpang 336-52-16-9
Jalan Duta BC 4115
(+673) 238-4616
BSBCommercial@state.gov

LEGAL CONTACTS

FATHAN, RUDI LEE, ANNIE KON & ASSOCIATES
Advocates & Solicitors / Commissioners For Oaths
Unit A1-1 & A2-1, 1st Floor, Block A Shakirin Complex
Simpang 88, Kampung Kiulap, BSB BE1518
Tel: +673.223.5111
Fax: +673.223.4206
Email: *fralaw2@gmail.com*

***Services Provided**: adoptions, commercial/business law, foreign investments, trademarks, civil law, criminal law, damages, narcotics, collections, commerical law, contracts, corporations, foreign claims, estates, labor relations, immigration, auto/accidents*

PENGIRAN IZAD & LEE
Advocates & Solicitors / Commissioners For Oaths
6th Floor, Bangunan Hj. Ahmad Laksamana Othman
38-39, Jalan Sultan, BSB BS8811
Tel: +673.223.2945/6/7/8
Fax: +673.223.2944
Email: *pial@brunet.bn*

***Services Provided**: family law, insurance, banking/financial, commercial/business law, foreign investments, marketing agreements, patents/trademarks/copyrights, civil law, criminal law, damages, collections, commerical law, contracts, corporations, aeronautical/maritime, foreign claims, estates, taxes, government relations, labor relations, immigration, auto/accidents*

SANDHU & COMPANY
Advocates & Solicitors
Unit 3, 4 & 5, Block A, Simpang 150, Bangunan Habza
Kg. Kiarong, BSB BE1518
Tel: +673.222.0783
Fax: +673.224.1237
Email: *sandhuco@brunet.bn*

***Services Provided**: insurance, commercial/business law, patents/trademarks/copyrights, civil law, damages, commerical law, contracts, foreign claims, auto/accidents*

CAMBODIA INVESTMENT AND BUSINESS CLIMATE - STRATEGIC INFORMATION AND CONTACTS FOR STARTING BUSINESS

Cambodia has experienced rapid economic growth over the last decade. Cambodian gross domestic product (GDP) grew at an average annual rate of over eight percent between 2000 and 2010 and over seven percent since 2011. The tourism, garment, construction & real estate, and agriculture sectors accounted for the bulk of growth. The percentage of the population living in poverty also decreased to approximately 17.7 percent in 2012, the latest figures available. GDP per capita increased to an estimated USD 1,130 in 2014.

Cambodia has an open and liberal foreign investment regime with relatively pro-investor legal and policy framework. Investment incentives available to foreign investors include 100 percent foreign ownership of companies, corporate tax holidays of up to eight years, a 20 percent corporate tax rate after the incentive period ends, duty-free import of capital goods, and no restrictions on capital repatriation.

Historically, these incentives have not been able to attract significant U.S. capital due to various factors including high levels of corruption, a limited supply of skilled labor, inadequate infrastructure (including high energy costs), and a lack of transparency in government approval processes. The political impasse and labor unrest that followed the 2013 national elections were additional deterrents to investment. Recently, however, the Phnom Penh Special Economic Zone has attracted more than USD 100 million in investments from several large American companies, including Coca-Cola, Tiffany & Co., and American Licorice.

Following the 2013 national elections, the government announced a variety of economic and business reforms. The government is also moving forward with new legislation to meet the 2015 deadline for the Association of Southeast Asian Nations (ASEAN) Economic Community.

1. OPENNESS TO, AND RESTRICTIONS UPON, FOREIGN INVESTMENT

Attitude toward Foreign Direct Investment

Cambodia began its transformation from a command economy to a free market economy in the late 1980s. It is now integrating into the regional and world trading framework. Cambodia joined ASEAN in 1999 and served as ASEAN chair in 2012. In 2001, the country joined the World Customs Organization, and in September 2004, it became a member of the World Trade Organization (WTO).

Cambodia's 1994 Law on Investment established an open and liberal foreign investment regime. All sectors of the economy are open to foreign investment and the government permits 100 percent foreign ownership of companies in most sectors. In a few sectors, such as cigarette manufacturing, movie production, rice milling, gemstone mining and processing, publishing and printing, radio and television, wood and stone carving production, and silk weaving, foreign investment is subject to local equity participation or prior authorization from authorities. There is little or no discrimination against foreign investors either at the time of initial investment or after investment. Some foreign businesses, however, have reported that they are at a disadvantage vis-a-vis Cambodian or other foreign rivals that engage in acts of corruption or tax evasion or take advantage of Cambodia's poor enforcement of laws and regulations.

More information about investment and investment incentives in Cambodia may be found on the Council for the Development of Cambodia's website via the following link: **http://www.cambodiainvestment.gov.kh**.

Other Investment Policy Reviews

In compliance with WTO requirements, Cambodia conducted its first review of trade policies and practices in November 2011. The next review will be conducted in 2017. Cambodia's full trade policy review report can be found at:**http://www.wto.org/english/tratop_e/tpr_e/tp353_e.htm**.

In response to the trade policy review recommendations, Cambodia has undertaken the following reforms:

Elimination of the Certificate of Origin requirement for exports to countries where a certificate is not required;

Implementation of online business registration;

Adoption of competitive hiring process for Ministry of Commerce staff;

Implementation of risk evaluation measures for the Cambodia Import-Export Inspection and Fraud Repression Directorate General (CamControl) and creation of a CamControl risk management unit;

Enactment of Law on Public Procurement. In February 2015, the Ministry of Economy and Finance issue a sub-decree on the establishment, organization, and functioning of a procurement commission and unit;

Creation of the Commercial Court as a specialized Court of First Instance

Ongoing or planned reforms include the following:

Amendment to the Law on Standards.

Laws/Regulations of Foreign Direct Investment

As described more fully in Section 4 below, Cambodian courts are ostensibly independent, and the government has no right to intervene in private commercial disputes. Foreign investors, however, are generally reluctant to resort to the Cambodian judicial system to resolve commercial disputes because the courts are perceived as unreliable and susceptible to external political influence or bribery. To address these concerns, the Cambodian government has enacted the Law on Court Structure in July 2014 under which the Commercial Court was created, which it hopes will increase the judiciary's professionalism and discourage corruption and external political influence.

Cambodia's 1994 Law on Investment created an investment licensing scheme to regulate the approval process for foreign direct investment and provide incentives to potential investors. In March 2003, the government simplified the licensing scheme and increased transparency and predictability by enacting the Law on the Amendment to the Law on Investment (Amended Law on Investment). The licensing scheme for investments of less than USD 2 million was clarified in a sub-decree on the Establishment of the Sub-Committee on Investment in the Provinces-Municipalities of the Kingdom of Cambodia in February 2005. Sub-decree No. 111 on the Implementation of the Law on the Amendment to the Law on Investment, issued in September 2005, lays out detailed procedures for registering a Qualified Investment Project with the Council for the Development of Cambodia and provincial/municipal investment sub-committees.

Cambodia is currently reviewing its investment laws and regulations in connection with the formation of the ASEAN Economic Community in 2015.

Industrial Promotion

The agricultural sector, which contributed an estimated 29.7 percent to Cambodia's GDP in 2014, is a key driver of the country's economy. As part of the government's policy to support the agriculture industry, materials and equipment used in agricultural production are exempt from import duties. While the government hopes these policies will increase milled rice exports to one million tons per year by 2015, exports were only 379,000 tons in 2014. On March 6, 2015, the Council of Ministers approved a new industrial policy, which is expected to launch in 2015, to further boost rice exports.

Limits on Foreign Control

There are few limitations on foreign control in Cambodia. Foreign investors may own 100 percent of their investment projects except in the sectors of cigarette manufacturing, movie production, rice milling, gemstone mining and processing, publishing and printing, radio and television, wood and stone carving production, and silk weaving. According to Cambodia's Amended Law on Investment and related sub-decrees, there are no limitations based on shareholder nationality or discrimination against foreign investors except in relation to investments in real property or state-owned enterprises. The Law on Investment and the Amended Law on Investment state that the majority interest in land must be held by one or more Cambodian citizens. Pursuant to the Law on Public Enterprise, the Cambodian government must directly or indirectly hold more than 51 percent of the capital or the right to vote in state-owned enterprises.

Screening of FDI

Foreign direct investment must be registered at the Ministry of Commerce, and investors must obtain operating permits from the relevant line ministries. If a foreign investor seeks investment incentives as a Qualified Investment Project, he/she must register and receive approval from the Council for the Development of Cambodia or the Provincial-Municipal Investment Sub-Committee. The application to the Council for the Development of Cambodia may be made either before or after registration at the Ministry of Commerce. More information about the Qualified Investment Project process may be found at **http://www.cambodiainvestment.gov.kh/investment-scheme/investment-application-procedures.html**.

Competition Law

The government is in the process of drafting a competition law. The Ministry of Commerce expects to submit a draft Law on Competition to the Council of Ministers in May 2015.

Investment Trends

The total stocks of foreign direct investment registered capital and fixed assets in Cambodia from 1994 to 2014 were USD 5.5 billion and USD 29 billion, respectively. The average annual foreign direct investment inflow based on fixed assets during the last three years (2012 -2014) amounted to approximately USD 1.2 billion. Annual foreign direct investment inflow based on fixed assets decreased by about 15 percent to USD 1 billion in 2014.

Table 1

Measure	Year	Index or Rank	Website Address
TI Corruption Perceptions index	2014	156 of 175	transparency.org/cpi2014/results
World Bank's Doing Business Report "Ease of Doing Business"	2015	135 of 189	doingbusiness.org/rankings
Global Innovation Index	2014	106 of 143	globalinnovationindex.org/content.aspx?page=data-analysis
World Bank GNI per capita	2013	USD 950	data.worldbank.org/indicator/NY.GNP.PCAP.CD

Millennium Challenge Corporation Country Scorecard

Table 1B: Scorecards

Measure	Year	Score
MCC Government Effectiveness	FY2015	-0.01/49 percent
MCC Rule of Law	FY2015	-0.1/40 percent
MCC Control of Corruption	FY2015	-0.16/42 percent
MCC Fiscal Policy	FY2015	-3.5/39 percent
MCC Trade Policy	FY2015	72.2/62 percent
MCC Regulatory Quality	FY2015	0.42/83 percent
MCC Business Start-Up	FY2015	0.367/2 percent
MCC Land Rights and Access	FY2015	0.69/65 percent
MCC Natural Resource Protection	FY2015	100.0/100 percent
MCC Access to Credit	FY2015	74/98 percent

The Millennium Challenge Corporation, a U.S. Government entity charged with delivering development grants to countries that have demonstrated a commitment to reform, produced scorecards for countries with a per capita gross national income (GNI) of USD 4,125 or less. A list of countries/economies with MCC scorecards and links to those scorecards is available here: **http://www.mcc.gov/pages/selection/scorecards**. Details on each of the MCC's indicators and a guide to reading the scorecards are available here: **http://www.mcc.gov/pages/docs/doc/report-guide-to-the-indicators-and-the-selection-process-fy-2015**.

2. CONVERSION AND TRANSFER POLICIES

Foreign Exchange

There are no restrictions on the conversion of capital for investors. Cambodia's 1997 Law on Foreign Exchange states that there shall be no restrictions on foreign exchange operations through authorized banks. Authorized banks are required, however, to report the amount of any transfer equaling or exceeding USD 100,000 to the National Bank of Cambodia on a regular basis.

Loans and borrowings, including trade credits, are freely contracted between residents and nonresidents, provided that loan disbursements and repayments are made through an authorized intermediary.

The Foreign Exchange Law allows the National Bank to implement exchange controls in the event of a foreign exchange crisis. In the event of such a crisis, the National Bank may impose certain temporary restrictions for a maximum period of three months on the activity or foreign exchange position of authorized intermediaries or on any loans in domestic currency extended to nonresidents. The Department of State is not aware of any cases in which investors have encountered obstacles in converting local currency to foreign currency or in sending capital out of the country.

Remittance Policies

Article 11 of the Law on the Amendment to the Law on Investment of 2003 states that Qualified Investment Projects can freely remit foreign currencies abroad, purchased through authorized banks, for the discharge of financial obligations incurred in connection with their investments. These financial obligations include:

Payment for imports and repayment of principal and interest on international loans;

Payment of royalties and management fees;

Remittance of profits; and

Repatriation of invested capital in case of dissolution.

Financial Action Task Force (FATF) status

Cambodia has committed to work with FATF and the Asia Pacific Group (APG) to address its strategic Anti-Money Laundering/Combating the Financing of Terrorism (AML/CFT) deficiencies. The FATF's website states that Cambodia has made significant progress in improving its AML/CFT regime and notes that Cambodia has established the legal and regulatory framework to meet its commitments in its action plan regarding the strategic deficiencies that the FATF had identified in June 2011. Cambodia is therefore no longer subject to the FATF's monitoring process under its on-going global AML/CFT compliance process. Cambodia will work with APG as it continues to address the full range of AML/CFT issues identified in its mutual evaluation report.

3. EXPROPRIATION AND COMPENSATION

Land rights are a contentious issue in Cambodia, complicated by the fact that most property holders do not have legal documentation of their ownership rights as a result of the Khmer Rouge era. Numerous cases have been reported of influential individuals or groups acquiring land titles or concessions through political and/or financial connections, and then using force to displace communities to make way for commercial enterprises. In late 2009, the National Assembly approved the Law on Expropriation, which sets broad guidelines on land-taking procedures for public interest purposes. It defines public interest activities to include construction, rehabilitation, preservation, or expansion of infrastructure projects, and development of buildings for national defense and civil security. These provisions include construction of border crossing posts, construction of facilities for research and exploitation of natural resources, and construction of oil pipeline and gas networks. Property can also be expropriated for natural disasters and emergencies, as determined by the government. Legal procedures regarding compensation and appeals are expected to be established in a forthcoming sub-decree, which is expected to be submitted to the legal affair council of the Ministry of Economy and Finance by mid-2015. The Department of State is not aware of any cases in which Cambodia has expropriated a U.S. investment.

4. DISPUTE SETTLEMENT

Legal System, Specialized Courts, Judicial Independence, Judgments of Foreign Courts

Most investors are generally reluctant to resort to the Cambodian judicial system to resolve commercial disputes because the courts are perceived as unreliable and susceptible to external political influence or bribery. Both local and foreign businesses report frequent problems with inconsistent judicial rulings, corruption, and difficulty enforcing judgments. For these reasons, most commercial disputes are currently resolved through negotiations facilitated by the Ministry of Commerce, the Council for the Development of Cambodia, the Cambodian Chamber of Commerce, or other concerned institutions.

Cambodia adopted a Commercial Arbitration Law in 2006. In 2010, the government provided for the establishment of the National Commercial Arbitration Center (NCAC), Cambodia's first alternative dispute resolution mechanism, to enable companies to resolve commercial disputes more quickly and inexpensively than through the court system. The NCAC was officially launched in March 2013 and is now ready to accept cases. Three laws related to the judicial system were enacted in July 2014: the Law on Court Structures, the Law on the Duties and Discipline of Judges and Prosecutors, and the Law on the Organization and Functioning of the Supreme Council of Magistracy. Under the Law on Court Structure, the Commercial Court, established as one of the four specialized Courts of First Instance, will have jurisdiction over all commercial matters, including insolvency cases. The Commercial Chambers will hear all appeals arising out of the Commercial Court.

Bankruptcy

Cambodia's 2007 Law on Insolvency was intended to provide collective, orderly, and fair satisfaction of creditor claims from debtor properties and, where appropriate, the rehabilitation of the debtor's business. The Law on Insolvency applies to the assets of all business people and legal entities in Cambodia. The 2015 World Bank's Doing Business Report ranks Cambodia 84 out of 189 in terms of the ease of resolving insolvency, a dramatic increase from 2014 when it was ranked 163 out of 189.

International Arbitration

International arbitration is available for Cambodian commercial disputes. In March 2014, the Supreme Court of Cambodia confirmed a decision of the Cambodian Court of Appeal, which had ruled in favor of the recognition and enforcement of an arbitral award issued by the Korean Commercial Arbitration Board (KCAB) of Seoul, South Korea. Cambodia became a member of the World Bank's International Center for Settlement of Investment Disputes in January 2005. In 2009, the International Center approved a U.S. investor's request for arbitration in a case against the Cambodian government, and in 2013 the tribunal rendered an award in favor of Cambodia.

Domestically, commercial disputes could also be resolved through the National Commercial Arbitration Center (NCAC), Cambodia's first alternative dispute resolution mechanism, which was officially launched in March 2013.

ICSID Convention and New York Convention

Cambodia is a member of the International Center for Settlement of Investment Disputes (ICSID). Cambodia is also a signatory to the New York Convention on the Recognition and Enforcement of Foreign Arbitral Awards 1958 (the New York Convention) since 1960. In 2001, Cambodia passed the Law on Agreement and Implementation of the United National Convention on the Recognition and Enforcement of Foreign Arbitral Awards.

Duration of Dispute Resolution

Due to corruption and an overly bureaucratic system, investment/commercial disputes may take years to resolve.

5. PERFORMANCE REQUIREMENTS AND INVESTMENT INCENTIVES

WTO/TRIMS

To date, Cambodia has not notified the WTO of any measurements that were inconsistent with the Trade Related Investment Measure (TRIMs) requirements.

Investment Incentives

All investments need to be registered with the Ministry of Commerce. Cambodia's Law on Investment and Amended Law on Investment also provide a mechanism for investment incentives (there are varying types of incentives) that meet specified criteria. Investors seeking an investment incentive must submit an application to the Cambodian Investment Board, the division of the Council for the Development of Cambodia charged with reviewing investment applications. Investment activities excluded from incentives are detailed in the September 2005 Sub-Decree on the Implementation of the Amendment to the Law on Investment. These include the following sectors: retail, wholesale, and duty-free stores; entertainment establishments (including restaurants, bars, nightclubs, massage parlors, and casinos); tourism service providers; currency and financial services; press and media-related activities; professional services; and production and processing of tobacco and wood products.

Incentives also may not be applied to investments in the production of certain products if the investment is less than USD 500,000. This includes food and beverages; textiles, garments, and footwear; and plastic, rubber, and paper products. Investors are not required to place a deposit guaranteeing their investment except in cases involving a concession contract or real estate development project. Investors who wish to apply are required to pay an application fee of seven million riel (approximately USD 1,750), which represents the administrative fees for securing necessary approvals, authorizations, licenses, or registrations from all relevant ministries and entities, including stamp duties. Under a 2008 sub-decree, the Council for the Development of Cambodia is required to seek approval from the Council of Ministers for investment proposals that involve an investment of capital of USD 50 million or more, politically sensitive issues, the exploration and exploitation of mineral or natural resources, or infrastructure concessions. The Council for the Development of Cambodia is also required to seek approval from the Council of Ministers for investment proposals that will have a negative impact on the environment or the government's long-term strategy.

Qualified Investment Projects are entitled to receive different incentives such as profit tax exemptions, special depreciation, and duty-free import of production equipment and construction materials. Investment projects located in designated special promotion zones or export processing zones are also entitled to the same incentives. Industry-specific investment incentives, such as a three-year profit tax exemption, may be available in the agriculture and agro-industry sectors. Agricultural materials used as inputs in export industries may be exempt from the value-added tax. More information about the criteria and investment areas eligible for incentives may be found at the following link:**http://www.cambodiainvestment.gov.kh/investment-scheme/investment-incentives.html**

Research and Development

The government does not have any restrictions on foreign firms participating in government financed and subsidized research and development programs. The government has public procurement procedures that companies can follow.

Performance Requirements

Under Cambodian law, most foreign investments and foreign investors will be affected by the following taxes: corporate profits tax (20 percent), tax on individual salaries (0 to 20 percent), withholding taxes (4 to 15 percent), value-added taxes (0 to 10 percent), and import duties (0 to 35 percent).

The Law on Investment permits investors to hire foreign nationals for employment as managers, technicians, or skilled workers if the qualifications and/or expertise are not available in Cambodia.

Data Storage

Cambodia does not have any forced localization policy that obligates foreign investors to use domestic contents in goods or technology. Cambodia also does not have any requirements for foreign IT providers to turn over source code.

The General Department of ICT in the Ministry of Post and Telecommunications oversees ICT related policy in Cambodia.

6. RIGHT TO PRIVATE OWNERSHIP AND ESTABLISHMENT

There are no limits on the rights of foreign and domestic entities to establish and own business enterprises or to compete with public enterprises. Only Cambodian citizens or legal entities, however, have the right to own land. Under the 2001 Land Law, foreign investors may secure control over land through Economic Land Concessions (ELCs), long-term leases, or renewable short-term leases. In May 2012, the government issued a moratorium on granting new ELCs. Since that time, however, there have been several new ELCs granted, which the government justified by stating that any ELC in which the parties were in private negotiations or had reached an agreement "in principle" prior to the directive could continue through to issuance. In October 2012, Prime Minister Hun Sen reiterated his support for the moratorium on new ELCs. In 2014, the Minister of the Environment canceled 23 ELCs totaling approximately 90,000 hectares of land, ostensibly for failing to develop the land pursuant to the terms of the ELC.

Qualified investors approved by the Council for the Development of Cambodia have the right to own buildings built on leased property. The law, however, is unclear as to whether buildings from qualified projects can be transferred between foreign investors or whether foreign investors can own buildings built through projects not approved by the Council for the Development of Cambodia.

In 2010, Cambodia adopted a law allowing limited foreign ownership in multi-story buildings from the second floor up, such that ownership may not exceed 70 percent of the area of all private units of the co-owned building. Foreigners are not authorized to acquire ownership rights in buildings located within 30 kilometers of the land borders of Cambodia, except in Special Economic Zones or other areas, as determined by the government.

7. PROTECTION OF PROPERTY RIGHTS

Real Property

Mortgages exist and the banks often require certificates of property ownership as collateral before approving loans. The mortgages recording system, which is handled by private banks, is generally considered reliable.

The 2001 Land Law provides a framework for real property security and a system for recording titles and ownership. Land titles issued prior to the end of the Khmer Rouge regime in 1979 are not recognized due to the severe dislocations that occurred during the Khmer Rouge period. The government is making efforts to accelerate the issuance of land titles, but in practice the titling system is cumbersome, expensive, and subject to corruption. The majority of property owners lack documentation proving ownership. Even where title records exist, recognition of legal title to land has not been uniform, and there are reports of court cases in which judges have sought additional proof of ownership. Although foreigners are constitutionally forbidden to own land, the 2001 law allows long- or short-term leases to foreigners. As noted above, Cambodia also allows foreign ownership in multi-story buildings from the second floor up. Cambodia was ranked 100th out of 189 economies for ease of registering property in the 2015 World Bank Doing Business Report.

Intellectual Property Rights

Cambodia has adopted legislation concerning the protection of intellectual property rights, including the Law on Copyrights and the Law on Patent and Industrial Design. Cambodia is a member of the World Intellectual Property Organization and the Paris Convention for the Protection of Industrial Property, and is a party to the ASEAN Framework Agreement on Intellectual Property Cooperation. Cambodia has also concluded bilateral agreements on intellectual property protection and cooperation with the United States, China, Thailand, Japan, and South Korea.

Cambodia has enacted several laws pursuant to its WTO commitments on intellectual property. Copyrights are governed by the Law on Copyrights and Related Rights, which was enacted in January 2003. Trademarks are governed by the Law Concerning Marks, Trade Names and Acts of Unfair Competition, which was enacted in 2002. A patent law has been in place since 2003. Some gaps in intellectual property protection remain, however, and outstanding legislation includes a draft law for protecting trade secrets, a law on integrated circuit protection, and legislation on protecting encrypted satellite signals required by the World Intellectual Property Organization. In January 2014, Cambodia enacted the Law on Geographical Indications, recognizing geographical indications of local and foreign products. Infringement of IPR is pervasive, particularly related to software, compact discs and music, books, cigarettes, alcohol, and pharmaceuticals. In March 2015, the Cambodian government submitted its instrument of accession to the Madrid Protocol for International Registration of Marks at the World Intellectual Property Organization.

Although Cambodia is not a major center for the production and export of pirated compact discs, digital video discs (DVD), or other copyrighted materials, local businesses report Cambodia is growing as a source of pirated material due to weak enforcement. An inter-ministerial committee was established to combat piracy of compact discs and DVDs in the domestic market. Infringement complaints may be made to the Economic Police, Customs, the Cambodia Import-Export Inspection and Fraud Repression Directorate General, or the Ministry of Commerce. The division of responsibility among each agency, however, is not clearly defined. The National Intellectual Property Rights Committee is planning to create two new sub-committees: a sub-committee on IPR enforcement and a sub-committee on the education and dissemination of IPR rules and regulations. The sub-decree on the establishment of the two sub-committees is under review by the Council of Ministers.

Cambodia was not listed in the U.S. Trade Representative (USTR)'s Special 301 report or notorious markets report.

For additional information about treaty obligations and points of contact at local IP offices, please see the World Intellectual Property Organization's country profiles at: **http://www.wipo.int/directory/en/details.jsp?country_code=KH**.

Resources for Rights Holders

Contact at Mission:

Mr. Peter N. Fowler
Regional IP Attaché
Telephone number: (662) 205-5913
Email address: **Peter.Fowler@trade.gov**

Country resources:

American Chamber of Commerce Cambodia
Email address: **ed@amchamcambodia.net**
Website: **www.amchamcambodia.net**

8. TRANSPARENCY OF THE REGULATORY SYSTEM

There is no pattern of systematic discrimination by the government against foreign investors in Cambodia. Numerous issues of transparency in the regulatory regime arise, however, from the lack of legislation and capacity of key institutions. Investors often complain that the decisions of Cambodian regulatory agencies are inconsistent, arbitrary, or corrupt. Cambodia has indicated a desire to discourage monopolistic trading arrangements in most sectors, but it has yet to pass the Law on Competition as part of its WTO accession obligations. The Ministry of Commerce expects Cambodia to enact competition legislation by 2015. Under the most recent draft, a National Committee on Competition would be established.

9. EFFICIENT CAPITAL MARKETS AND PORTFOLIO INVESTMENT

The Cambodian government does not use regulation of capital markets to restrict foreign investment. Banks have been free to set their own interest rates since 1995, and increased competition between local institutions has led to a gradual lowering of interest rates from year to year. Domestic financing, however, is still difficult to obtain at competitive interest rates. The average annual interest rate on loans in U.S. dollars stood at 12.45 percent in August 2014. A law addressing secured transactions, which includes a system for registering such secured interests, was promulgated in May 2007. Most loans are secured by real property mortgages or deposits of cash or other liquid assets, as provided for in existing contract and real property laws. In 2013, loans and deposits grew by 25.8 percent and 12.2 percent, respectively. The ratio of non-performing loans stood at 2.7 percent at the end of 2013, an increase of 0.3 percent compared to 2012. Figures for 2014 are not yet available.

As of June 2014, the banking system in Cambodia consisted of 35 commercial banks; nine specialized banks (banks set up to finance specific turn-key projects such as real estate development); 40 licensed microfinance institutions, of which seven were licensed microfinance deposit taking institutions; and 35 registered rural credit operators. The National Bank has also granted licenses to three financial leasing companies, four third-party processor companies (Wing, Western Union, Money Gram, and AM GSM), and one Credit Bureau Company to improve transparency and credit risk management and encourage more lending to small-and medium-sized enterprise customers.

In a move designed to address the need for capital markets in Cambodia, the Cambodian Securities Exchange (CSX) was launched on July 11, 2011. In April 2012, the Phnom Penh Water Supply Authority, a state-owned enterprise, was the first domestically registered company on the CSX. In June 2014, Grand Twins International (Cambodia) Plc, a garment factory from Taiwan, became the second company to list on the CSX. Two other state-owned enterprises, the Autonomous Port of Sihanoukville and Telecom Cambodia, and a private local company, Express Food Group Co., Ltd, are preparing for initial public offerings, but listing dates have yet to be announced. In November 2006, the National Assembly passed legislation to permit the government to issue bonds to address the country's budget deficits. No bonds, however, have been issued since 2007, and Prime Minister Hun Sen said in 2008 that the government did not plan to issue bonds in the near future. In 2007, the government also passed the Law on the Issuance and Trading of Non-government Securities.

Money and Banking System, Hostile Takeovers

In March 2014, Moody's Investors Service affirmed Cambodia's government issuer rating at B2 with a stable outlook. The rating was based on Cambodia's healthy economic growth outlook and a stable external payment position, which balanced structural weaknesses.

In 2008, the National Bank raised the minimum capital reserve requirements for banks from USD 13 million to USD 37.5 million. By the end of 2013, total assets in the banking system (commercial and specialized banks) had reached USD 12.7 billion, an increase of 17 percent compared with 2012 and equivalent to 75 percent of GDP. The infusion of capital from newly created banks and additional customer deposits were the primary drivers underlying the growth.

10. COMPETITION FROM STATE-OWNED ENTERPRISES

Cambodia has four main state-owned enterprises: Electricité du Cambodge, which is in charge of producing and distributing power nationwide; Phnom Penh Water Supply Authority, which is responsible for water treatment and supply; Rural Development Bank, which services and refinances loans to licensed financial institutions, commercial banks, specialized banks, micro-finance institutions, associations, development communities, and small- and medium-sized enterprises that take part in rural development in Cambodia; and Green Trade Company, which manages Cambodia's national reserve of rice through purchases and sales made at market prices. In March 2015, the Cambodian government, through the Ministry of Mines and Energy, announced that the government is exploring a possibility of establishing a national oil company to invest in the oil and gas sector.

OECD Guidelines on Corporate Governance of SOEs

Each state-owned enterprise is under the supervision of a line ministry or government institution and is overseen by a board of directors drawn from among senior government officials. Private enterprises are generally allowed to compete with state-owned enterprises under equal terms and conditions. These entities are also subject to the same taxes and value-added tax rebate policies as private-sector enterprises. State-owned enterprises are covered under the law on public procurement, which was promulgated in January 2012, and their financial reports are audited by the appropriate line ministry, Ministry of Economy and Finance, and the National Audit Authority.

Sovereign Wealth Funds

Cambodia does not have a sovereign wealth fund.

11. CORPORATE SOCIAL RESPONSIBILITY

Corporate social responsibility is a new concept to Cambodia and is not widely understood by local businesses or consumers. The vast majority of corporate social responsibility programs in Cambodia are run by U.S., European, or Australian companies.

OECD Guidelines for Multinational Enterprises

The government neither encourages nor discourages foreign and local enterprises to follow corporate social responsibility principles. Although Cambodia has a number of laws related to labor and employment rights, consumer protection, and environmental protection, enforcement is often inadequate and corruption remains a significant issue for many companies.

The Cambodian government has not enacted any laws or adopted any regulations concerning corporate governance, accounting, and executive compensation standards to protect the interests of shareholders. Companies operating in Cambodia are not required to publicly disclose information related to corporate governance, accounting, or executive compensation, and Embassy Phnom Penh is unaware of any NGOs in Cambodia that focus on private sector public disclosure.

12. POLITICAL VIOLENCE

The risk of political violence directed at foreign companies operating in Cambodia is low. Foreign companies have been the targets of violent protests in the past, such as the 2003 anti-Thai riots against the Embassy of Thailand and Thai-owned commercial establishments. More recently, there were reports that Vietnamese-owned establishments were looted during a January 2014 labor protest. Authorities have also used force, including truncheons, electric cattle prods, fire hoses, and even gunfire, to disperse protestors. Incidents of violence directed at businesses, however, are rare. Embassy Phnom Penh is unaware of any incidents of political violence directed at American or other Western interests.

Following the July 2013 national elections, the opposition Cambodia National Rescue Party (CNRP) refused to take its seats in the National Assembly due to electoral irregularities. In July 2014, the CNRP reached an agreement with the ruling Cambodian People's Party to enter the National Assembly, ending a tense year marked by numerous protests in Phnom Penh, including the largest peaceful political demonstrations ever held in the country, but also labor protest violence that left up to six dead and scores injured. In February 2015, after months of closed-door discussions, the two sides reached formal agreement on specific changes to the country's key electoral laws. The proposed changes and the opacity of the deal-making, however, disappointed many CNRP supporters and civil society. The electoral amendments were signed into law by King Sihamoni on March 26.

13. CORRUPTION

The Anti-Corruption Law was adopted in 2010 to combat corruption through education, prevention, and more effective enforcement. Under this law, all civil servants are obligated to declare their financial assets to the government every two years. The fourth round of asset and debt declaration took place during January 2015. The Anti-Corruption Unit (ACU), which was formed in 2010, has launched several high-profile prosecutions against public officials, including members of the police and judiciary.

UN Anticorruption Convention, OECD Convention on Combatting Bribery

Cambodia ratified the UN Convention against Corruption in 2007 and endorsed the Action Plan of the Asian Development Bank/Organization for Economic Co-operation and Development (OECD) Anti-Corruption Initiative for Asia and the Pacific in 2003. Cambodia is not a party to the OECD Convention on Combating Bribery.

Despite the passage of the Anti-Corruption Law and creation of the ACU, business people, both local and foreign (including U.S. companies), have identified corruption, particularly within the judiciary, customs service, and tax authorities, as the single greatest deterrent to investment in Cambodia. Corruption was cited by a plurality of respondents to the World Economic Forum survey as the most problematic factor for doing business in Cambodia. The government plans to increase the average base salary for all civil servants from about USD 105 per month to around USD 135 per month, starting from the second quarter of 2015. Although salaries have increased by 20 percent annually over the last few years, these wages remain below the level required to maintain a suitable quality of life in Cambodia, and as a result, public employees are susceptible to corruption and conflicts of interest. Local and foreign businesses report that they must often pay facilitation fees to expedite any business transaction. Even though the Cambodian government has published the official fees of public services since early 2013, the practice of paying additional fees remains common. Furthermore, the process for awarding government contracts is not transparent and is susceptible to corruption.

The ACU, in collaboration with the private sector, has been developing guidelines encouraging private companies to establish internal codes of conduct prohibiting bribery and corrupt practices. The ACU expects to publish the guidelines before the end of 2015.

Resources to Report Corruption

Government point of contact:

Om Yentieng
President
Anti-Corruption Unit
Building No. 54, Preah Norodom Blvd, Sangkat Phsar Thmey 3, Khan Daun Penh, Phnom Penh
Telephone number: +855-23-223954
Email address: **info@acu.gov.kh**

NGO point of contact:

Preap Kol
Executive Director
Transparency International Cambodia
Telephone number: +855-23-214430
Email address: **info@ticambodia.org**

14. BILATERAL INVESTMENT AGREEMENTS

Bilateral investment treaties provide reciprocal national treatment to investors, excluding benefits deriving from membership in future customs unions or free trade areas and agreements relating to taxation. These agreements preclude expropriations except those that are non-discriminatory, undertaken for a lawful or public purpose, and accompanied by prompt, adequate, and effective compensation at the fair market value of the property prior to expropriation. The agreements also guarantee repatriation of investments and provide for settlement of investment disputes via arbitration. Cambodia has signed bilateral investment agreements with Austria, Australia, China, Croatia, Cuba, Czech Republic, France, Germany, Indonesia, Kuwait, Japan, Laos, Malaysia, the Netherlands, Democratic People's Republic of Korea, Pakistan, the Philippines, Singapore, Republic of Korea, Switzerland, Thailand, Vietnam, and the Organization of the Petroleum Exporting Countries (OPEC). Future agreements are planned with Algeria, Bangladesh, Belarus, Belgium-Luxembourg Economic Union, Bulgaria, Myanmar, Egypt, Hungary, Israel, Iran, Libya, Macedonia, Malta, Qatar, Russia, Turkey, the United Kingdom, and Ukraine.

In July 2006, Cambodia signed a Trade and Investment Framework Agreement with the United States to promote greater trade and investment in both countries and provide a forum to address bilateral trade and investment issues. In August 2012, the United States and Cambodia agreed to begin exploratory discussions on a potential bilateral investment treaty. Those negotiations are ongoing.

Bilateral Taxation Treaties

Cambodia does not have a bilateral taxation treaty with the United States.

15. OPIC AND OTHER INVESTMENT INSURANCE PROGRAMS

Cambodia has an agreement with the Overseas Private Investment Corporation (OPIC) to encourage investment and is eligible for the Quick Cover Program under which OPIC offers financing and political risk insurance coverage for projects on an expedited basis. With most investment contracts written in U.S. dollars, there is little exchange rate risk. Even for riel-denominated transactions, the fact that Cambodia has adopted a managed floating exchange rate regime based on the U.S. dollar means that exchange rates are likely to remain stable. Cambodia is a member of the Multilateral Investment Guarantee Agency of the World Bank, which offers political-risk insurance to foreign investors. The Export-Import Bank of the United States (Ex-Im Bank) provides financing for purchases of U.S. exports by private-sector buyers in Cambodia on repayment terms of up to seven years. Ex-Im Bank support typically will be limited to transactions with a commercial bank functioning as an obligor or guarantor. The Ex-Im Bank will, however, consider transactions without a bank undertaking on a case-by-case basis.

16. LABOR

Approximately 65- 70 percent of the labor force is engaged in agriculture. Around 600,000 people, the majority of whom are women, are employed in the garment and footwear sector. An additional 500,000 Cambodians are employed in the tourism sector, and a further 50,000 people in construction. According to the 2013 Inter-Censal Population Survey of Cambodia, the latest survey available, the country's annual population growth rate was 1.46 percent from 2008 to 2013. Around 55 percent of the population is under the age of 25. The United Nations has estimated that around 300,000 new job seekers enter the labor market each year.

Given the severe disruption to the Cambodian education system and loss of skilled Cambodians during the 1975-79 Khmer Rouge period, workers with higher education or specialized skills are few and in high demand. The Cambodia Socio-Economic Survey conducted in 2013 found that about 27 percent of the labor force had completed an elementary education. Only 3.65 percent of the labor force had completed post-secondary education. The 2014-2015 Global Competitiveness Report of the World Economic Forum identified an inadequately educated workforce as one of the most serious problems to doing business in Cambodia.

Cambodia's 1997 Labor Code protects the right of association and the right to organize and bargain collectively. Specifically, the law provides for the right of private-sector workers to form and join trade unions of their own choice without prior authorization, the right to strike, and the right to bargain collectively. While unions may affiliate freely, the law does not explicitly address their right to affiliate internationally. The Cambodian government does not prohibit hiring foreign nationals. According to the Ministry of Labor and Vocational Training (MOLVT), the number of foreign workers should not exceed ten percent of the total number of Cambodian workers.

Unresolved labor disputes may be brought to the Arbitration Council, an independent state body that interprets labor regulations in collective disputes, such as when multiple employees are dismissed. The parties may choose whether to consider the council's decisions as binding. If neither party objects to the arbitral award within eight days of its issuance, it automatically becomes binding. Individual disputes may be brought before the courts, although the judicial system is neither impartial nor transparent.

The law requires trade unions to file their charters and lists of their officials with the MOLVT. The Bureau of Labor Relations is responsible for facilitating the process of union registration and certification of "most representative status" for unions, which entitles a union representing a majority of workers in a given enterprise to represent all the workers in that establishment.

Civil servants, including teachers, judges, and military personnel, as well as household workers, do not have the right to form or join a trade union. Personnel in the air and maritime transportation industries are free to form unions but are not entitled to social security and pension benefits and are exempt from the limitations on work hours prescribed by the labor law.

The law stipulates that workers can strike only after several requirements have been met, including the failure of other methods of dispute resolution (such as negotiation, conciliation, or arbitration), a secret-ballot vote of the union membership, and seven-days advance notice to the employer and the MOLVT. There is no law prohibiting strikes by civil servants, workers in public sectors, or workers in essential services. Legal protections are in place to guard strikers from reprisal.

The labor code prohibits forced or compulsory labor, establishes 15 as the minimum allowable age for paid work, and sets 18 as the minimum age for anyone engaged in work that is hazardous, unhealthy, or unsafe. The statute also guarantees an eight-hour workday and 48-hour work week, and provides for time-and-a-half pay for overtime or work on an employee's day off. To increase competitiveness of garment manufacturers, the labor code was amended in 2007 to establish a night shift wage of 130 percent of daytime wages.

As of October 2010, the minimum wage for garment and footwear workers was officially set at USD 61 per month. There is no minimum wage for any other industry. In November 2011, to help workers meet basic needs like healthcare, the government approved an increase of USD 5 per month starting in January 2012. More recently, garment workers pushed for an increase to USD 160 per month. In December 2013, the tripartite Labor Advisory Committee agreed to raise the minimum wage to USD 100, effective February 1, 2014. Following the Labor Advisory Committee's decision, violent clashes broke out in early January 2014, resulting in the deaths of at least four protesters. Labor leaders continue to advocate for an increase to USD 160, and the government has established a commission to review the minimum-wage level and report to the Labor Advisory Committee. In October 2014, the Committee decided to increase the minimum wage to USD 128, effective from January 1, 2015.

The labor law stipulates that a worker is entitled to indemnity if he/she is laid off for reasons of health or if the contract is terminated by the employer alone, except in the case of a serious offense by the worker.

Enforcement of many aspects of the labor code is poor, and many labor disputes involve workers simply demanding conditions to which they are legally entitled. Poor enforcement is due to a lack of capacity, corruption and a lack of political will on the part of the government. As a result, strikes are common in some sectors. Unions, for their part almost never observe the legally required prerequisites before initiating strikes. Collective labor disputes between employers and employees may be resolved through conciliation and arbitration by the Arbitration Council, which is an independent, national institution with quasi-judicial authority under Cambodian labor law.

The U.S. government, the International Labor Organization, and others have been working closely with Cambodia to improve enforcement of the labor code and workers' rights in general. The 1999 U.S.-Cambodia Bilateral Textile Agreement linked Cambodian compliance with internationally recognized core labor standards with the level of textile quota the United States granted to Cambodia. Under the terms of that agreement, the U.S. government committed to increase the size of Cambodia's textile export quota if the country demonstrated improvements in labor standards. This was the first bilateral trade agreement to positively link market access with progress in compliance with labor obligations. The International Labor Organization, which works with the government to monitor adherence to international labor standards in the garment sector, succeeded in improving compliance with workplace standards, virtually eliminating the worst labor abuses, such as forced labor and child labor. While the quota regime ended on January 1, 2005 following Cambodia's accession to the WTO, the International Labor Organization's Better Factories Cambodia program continues to monitor and report on working conditions in garment factories. All export garment factories in Cambodia must agree to be monitored by the program in order to receive an export license. Since March 2014, monitoring reports summarizing compliance issues, tracking trends, and analyzing progress in Cambodia's garment and footwear industries are available online.

17. FOREIGN TRADE ZONES/FREE PORTS/TRADE FACILITATION

To facilitate the country's development, the Cambodian government has shown great interest in increasing exports via geographically defined special economic zones. In December 2005, the government adopted the Sub-Decree on Special Economic Zones to speed up the creation of the zones by detailing the procedures, conditions, and incentives for investors. Since issuing the sub-decree, the Cambodia Special Economic Zones Board has approved 36 special economic zones, which are located in Phnom Penh, Koh Kong, Kandal, Kampot, Sihanoukville, and near the borders of Thailand and Vietnam. The main investment sectors in these zones include garments, shoes, bicycles, food processing, car and motorcycle assembly, and electrical equipment manufacturing.

18. Foreign Direct Investment and Foreign Portfolio Investment Statistics

Table 2: Key Macroeconomic Data, U.S. FDI in Host Country/Economy

	Host Country Statistical source*		USG or international statistical source		USG or International Source of Data: BEA; IMF; Eurostat; UNCTAD, Other
Economic Data	Year	Amount	Year	Amount	
Host Country Gross Domestic Product (GDP) ($M USD)	2014	16,911	2014	16, 367	www.worldbank.org/en/country
Foreign Direct Investment	Host Country Statistical source*		USG or international statistical source		USG or international Source of data: BEA; IMF; Eurostat; UNCTAD, Other
U.S. FDI in partner country ($M USD, stock positions)	2014	84.5	2013	63	http://bea.gov/international/factsheet/ factsheet.cfm?Area=607
Host country's	N/A	N/A	2013	-1	http://bea.gov/international/factsheet/

FDI in the United States ($M USD, stock positions)					factsheet.cfm?Area=607
Total inbound stock of FDI as % host GDP	2014	0.5%	2012	0.38%	U.S. FDI stock in Cambodia: USD 54 million (USTR source). GDP in 2012: USD 14,038 million (ADB source)

Local Source: Ministry of Economy and Finance (MEF), Council for the Development of Cambodia (CDC)

Table 3: Sources and Destination of FDI

According to International Monetary Fund data, total foreign direct investment in Cambodia amounted to USD 2.69 billion in 2013, with the Republic of Korea remaining the largest proportion (44 percent of total investment). The other top four foreign direct investment countries in Cambodia were Malaysia, Thailand, France, and Denmark. The number of Cambodian investments outside the country was quite small compared to inward foreign direct investment. In 2013, outward foreign direct investment was USD 475 million, with 71 percent of the total investment going to China. Two other major countries were Singapore (USD 97 million), which has increased by 26 percent compared to 2012, and the Philippines (USD 26 million).

Direct Investment from/in Counterpart Economy Data					
From Top Five Sources/To Top Five Destinations (US Dollars, Millions)					
Inward Direct Investment			Outward Direct Investment		
Total Inward	2,694	100%	Total Outward	475	100%
Republic of Korea	1,183	44%	China, P.R.: Mainland	337	71%
Malaysia	577	21%	Singapore	97	20%
Thailand	500	19%	Philippines	26	5%
France	222	8%	Czech Republic	6	1%
Denmark	137	5%	Thailand	6	1%
"0" reflects amounts rounded to +/- USD 500,000.					

Source: IMF Coordinated Direct Investment Survey

Table 4: Sources of Portfolio Investment

All the figures in the below tables are provided by the country of origin of the investments. Official data are not available.

The total value of portfolio investment assets was USD 2.42 billion in 2013, the latest figures available. Among the top five partners, Korea remained the largest holder of equity securities with 31 percent and debt securities with 71 percent. Thailand and France were still the second and third largest holders of equity securities and debt securities.

Portfolio Investment Assets								
Top Five Partners (Millions, US Dollars)								
Total			Equity Securities			Total Debt Securities		
All Countries	2,422	100%	All Countries	1,335	100%	All Countries	1,087	100%
Republic of Korea	1,186	49%	Republic of Korea	414	31%	Republic of Korea	772	71%
Thailand	506	21%	Thailand	244	18%	Thailand	262	24%
France	222	9%	France	195	15%	France	27	2%
China	337	14%	China	337	25%	Philippines	26	2%
Denmark	137	6%	Denmark	137	10%	N/A	N/A	N/A

Source: IMF Coordinated Portfolio Investment Survey

BUSINESS AND LEGAL CONTACTS

David Myers

Economic Officer

No. 1, Street 96, Sangkat Wat Phnom, Phnom Penh, Cambodia

Phone: (855) 23 – 728 401

Email: **CamInvestment@state.gov**

LIST OF LAWYERS

The Embassy of the United States of America in Phnom Penh assumes no responsibility for the professional ability or reputation of the persons whose names appear below:

BNG Legal
#64, Street 111, Sangkat Boeung Pralit, Khan 7 Makara, Phnom Penh, Cambodia
P.O. Box No. 172
Tel: (855)(23)212-740; (855)(23)212-671
Fax: (855)(23)212-840
E-mail: info@bnglegal.com
Website: http://www.bnglegal.com/
Services Provided: Full-service Commercial Law Firm

Bou Nou OUK & Partners/Advocates & Solicitors
#74, Street 136, Phsar Kandal I, Daun Penh, Phnom Penh, Cambodia
Tel/Fax: (855)(23)-220-823
H/P: (855)(12)952-211
Email: chapkeo.bno@online.com.kh
Services Provided: Family and General Practice

Bun & Associates
#29 Street 294, Phnom Penh, Cambodia
P.O. Box 2326
Tel: (855) 23-999-567
Fax: (855) 23-999-566
H/P: (855) 12-817-817
Email: bun@bun-associates.com
Website: http://www.bun-associates.com/
Services Provided: Business and General Practice

Cambodia International Law Firm
#254 Monivong Blvd, Phnom Penh, Cambodia
Tel: (855)(23) 221-843 ext: 1501
Direct call: (855)(23) 212-966
Mobile: (855)(12) 813-531; (855) (12) 555-911
Fax: (855)(23) 219-077
Email: cilf@online.com.kh
Services Provided: Criminal and Business

DFDL Mekong (Cambodia) Co LTD
#45 Soramarith (Street 268), Phnom Penh, Cambodia
Tel: (855)(23)210-400
Fax: (855)(23)428-227
Email: Cambodia@dfdlmekong.com
Services Provided: Business and General Practice

Dun Vibol Law Office
#141E0 Street 348, Sangkat Tuol Svay Prey 2, Chamkar Morn, Phnom Penh

Tel: (855)12-775-533
Tel: (855)16-593-007
Services Provided: Criminal

HBS Law Firm & Consultants
Level 4 & 5, SOMA TOWER, St.120, Sangkat Psar Thmey 2, Khan Daun Penh, Phnom Penh
Mobile: (855)77-777-893
Office Phone: (855)23-224-337
Fax: (855)23-224-136
Email: info@hbslaw.asia
Website: http://www.hbs.com.kh/
Services Provided: Criminal, International and Business

HML Law Firm & Consultants
#11 Mao Tse Tung Blvd
Sangkat BKK I, Khan Chamkarmorn, Phnom Penh, Cambodia
Tel: (855)23-220-900
Fax: (855)23-220-100
E-mail: info@hmllawfirm.com
Services Provided: Criminal and Business

Legal Aid of Cambodia
Lawyers Serving Cambodia's Poor
#18 Street 604 corner street 311, Phnom Penh, Cambodia
Tel: (855)(23)884-262; (855)(12)606-101
Fax: (855)(23)884-263
E-mail: lac@online.com.kh
Services Provided: Criminal and General Practice

P&A Asia
#7 Street 222, Sangkat Boeung Raing, Khan Daun Penh
Phnom Penh, Cambodia
Tel: (855) 23-223-391
H/P: (855) 97-992-6603; (855) 99-841-478
Email: allen@paasia.net
Webpage: http://www.paasia.net/
Services Provided: International and Business

Sciaroni & Associates
#56 Samdech Sothearos (Street 3), Phnom Penh, Cambodia
Tel: (855)(23) 210-225
Fax: (855)(23) 213-089
Email: info@sa-Cambodia.com
Services Provided: International and Business

So Dara Law Office
#136E0E1 Street 6, Sangkat Toul Sangke, Russey Keo, Phnom Penh
Tel:(855)12-400-708
Tel:(855)16-852-388
Services Provided: Criminal and General Practice

U.S. Immigration Consultants
P.O. Box:1430
Tel: (855) 12 949-421; (855) 12 604-698 in Cambodia

Tel: (66) 8-7-131-8621
USA Fax Number: (1) 202 470-5759
Email: wayne@thevisacenter.com
Services Provided: Immigration

VDB Loi
Level 6, Phnom Penh Tower
#445 Monivong Boulevard, Sangkat Boeung Pralit
Khan 7 Makara, Phnom Penh, 12250
Tel: (855) 23 964 430
Email: info@vdb-loi.com
Website: http://www.vdb-loi.com/
Services Provided: Specialized legal and tax advisory for foreign investors

INDONESIA INVESTMENT AND BUSINESS CLIMATE - STRATEGIC INFORMATION AND CONTACTS FOR STARTING BUSINESS

Contact for More Information

Phil Nervig
First Secretary and Economic Officer
U.S. Embassy Jakarta
+62-21-3435-9000

While Indonesia's population of 245 million, growing middle class, and stable economy remain attractive to U.S. investors, investing in Indonesia remains challenging. This report focuses on challenges foreign investors face rather than the range of investment opportunities.

Since October 2014, the Indonesian government under President Joko Widodo has prioritized boosting investment, including foreign investment, to support Indonesia's economic growth goals, and has committed to reducing bureaucratic barriers to investment, including announcing the creation of a "one stop shop" for permits and licenses at the Investment Coordination Board. However, factors such as a decentralized decision-making process, legal uncertainty, economic nationalism, and powerful domestic vested interests create a complex and difficult investment climate. The Indonesian government's requirements, both formal and informal, to partner with Indonesian companies and purchase goods and services locally, restrictions on some imports and exports, and pressure to make substantial, long-term investment commitments, also factor into foreign investors' plans. While the Indonesian Corruption Eradication Commission continues to investigate and prosecute high-profile corruption cases, a recent case involving the National Police has led some to question the Commission's future influence. Investors continue to cite corruption as an obstacle to pursuing opportunities in Indonesia.

Other barriers include poor government coordination, the slow rate of land acquisition for infrastructure projects, poor enforcement of contracts, an uncertain regulatory environment, and lack of transparency in the development of laws and regulations. New regulations are at times difficult to decipher and often lack sufficient notice and socialization for those impacted. The lack of coordination among ministries creates redundant and slow processes, such as for securing business licenses and import permits, and at times, conflicting regulations.

Indonesia restricts foreign investment in some sectors with a negative investment list. The latest version, issued in 2014, details the sectors in which foreign investment is restricted and outlines the foreign equity limits in a number of sectors. Some of the restricted sectors include: telecommunications, pharmaceuticals, e-commerce, film and creative industries, and construction. Of note, the energy and mining sector face significant investment barriers.

Indonesia began to abrogate its more than 60 existing Bilateral Investment Treaty agreements (BITs) in February 2014, allowing the agreements to expire as soon as they allow. While the United States does not have a BIT with Indonesia, the Indonesian government's action reminds foreign investors of the unpredictability of Indonesia's investment climate.

Despite these challenges, Indonesia continues to attract foreign investment. Private consumption is the backbone of the economy and the middle class is growing, making Indonesia a promising place for consumer product companies. Indonesia has ambitious plans to improve its infrastructure with a focus on strengthening its maritime transport corridors, which includes building roads, ports, railways and airports, as well as improving agricultural production, telecommunications, and broadband networks throughout the country. Indonesia continues to attract U.S. franchises and consumer product manufacturers. For many companies, Indonesia's investment grade rating, growing middle class, and young population make the country an attractive destination for long term investment.

1. OPENNESS TO, AND RESTRICTIONS UPON, FOREIGN INVESTMENT

Attitude toward Foreign Direct Investment

While Indonesia's GDP growth slowed to just over 5 percent in 2014, Indonesia's growing middle class, strong domestic demand, stable political situation, and conservative macroeconomic policy make Indonesia an attractive destination for Foreign Direct Investment (FDI). Indonesian government officials welcome increased FDI, aiming to create jobs and spur economic growth, and court foreign investors, notably focusing on infrastructure development and export-oriented manufacturing. However, vague and conflicting regulations, poor existing infrastructure, rigid labor laws, and corruption continued to be significant concerns for foreign investors. U.S. firms have expressed hope that better coordination under Indonesia's new Administration will help to improve the investment climate.

Other Investment Policy Reviews

The April 2013 World Trade Organization (WTO) Investment Policy Review (IPR) of Indonesia can be found here: **http://www.wto.org/english/tratop_e/tpr_e/tp378_e.htm**

The most recent OECD Investment Policy Review (IPR) of Indonesia can be found here: **http://www.oecd.org/daf/inv/investmentfordevelopment/indonesia-investmentpolicyreview-oecd.htm**

Laws/Regulations of Foreign Direct Investment

Foreign Direct Investment in Indonesia is regulated by Law 25/2007 (The Investment Law). Under the law, any form of Foreign Direct Investment in Indonesia must be in the form of a limited liability company, with the foreign investor holding shares in the company. In addition, the government outlines restrictions on FDI in presidential decree 39/2014, commonly referred to as the Negative List. The Negative List aims to consolidate FDI restrictions in certain sectors from numerous decrees and regulations to create greater certainty for foreign and domestic investors.

Industrial Promotion

Natural Resources

Indonesia's vast natural resource wealth has attracted significant foreign investment over the last century and continues to offer significant prospects. But a variety of government regulations have made doing business in the resources sector increasingly difficult, and Indonesia now ranks near the bottom (112th) among the world's 122 mining countries in the Fraser Institute's Mining Policy Perception Index. In 2012, the Government of Indonesia (GOI) banned the export of raw minerals, dramatically increased the divestment requirements for foreign mining companies, and required major mining companies to renegotiate their contracts of work with the government. The ban on exportation of raw minerals went into effect in January 2014. The 2009 mining law devolved mining license issuing authority to local governments, who have responded by issuing more than 10,000 licenses, many of which overlap or are unclearly mapped.In the oil and gas sector, Indonesia's Constitutional Court disbanded the upstream regulator, injecting confusion and more uncertainty into the natural resources sector.

Infrastructure

Since taking office in October 2014, President Jokowi and his Administration have made infrastructure development a top priority. The government announced plans to add 35,000 megawatts of electricity capacity and create a maritime nexus, to include the development and/or expansion of 24 ports and other transportation infrastructure. Indonesia's 15-year, USD 1 trillion Master Plan for Acceleration and Economic Development (MP3EI), launched in 2011, remains active but has received less public attention since the new Administration took office. Through August 2014, 383 projects valued at USD 69.4 billion have been launched under the MP3EI

Limits on Foreign Control

Restrictions on FDI are, for the most part, outlined in presidential decree 39/2014, commonly referred to as the Negative List. The Negative List aims to consolidate FDI restrictions from numerous decrees and regulations to create greater certainty for foreign and domestic investors. In 2014, the share of foreign ownership permitted was increased in pharmaceutical manufacturing, venture capital companies, land transportation facilities, certain agricultural activities larger than 25 hectares, and certain power sector investments, but decreased in warehousing, distribution and cold storage, certain oil & gas services, e-commerce, telecommunication network services, certain retail sales, and power plants with less than 10 megawatts of installed capacity. For investment in certain sectors, such as mining and higher education, the Negative List is useful only as a starting point, as additional licenses and permits are required by individual ministries. Foreign capital investment, through the stock market, is not governed by the Negative List. Foreigners may purchase equity in state-owned firms through initial public offerings. Capital investments in publicly listed companies through the stock exchange are not subject to Indonesia's Negative List unless an investor is buying a controlling interest.

Privatization Program

While some state-owned enterprises have offered shares on the stock market, Indonesia does not have an active privatization program.

Screening of FDI

The Investment Coordinating Board (BKPM) is responsible for issuing investment licenses to foreign entities and has taken steps to simplify the application process through better coordination between various government institutions. BKPM has launched an online portal for its National Single Window for Investment which allows foreign investors to apply for and track the status of licenses and other services online. In an effort to streamline the investment licensing and permitting process, BKPM launched a national one-stop shop to coordinate many of the permits issued by more than a dozen ministries and agencies required for investment approval. While the BKPM one-stop shop's goal is to help ease investment approvals, investments in the mining, oil and gas, plantation, and most other sectors still require multiple licenses from related ministries and authorities. Likewise, certain tax and land permits, among others, typically must be obtained from local government authorities. Though Indonesian companies only require one approval at the local level, businesses report that foreign companies often must obtain both administrative and de facto legislative approval in order to establish a business.

The Coordinating Ministry of Home Affairs, Ministry of Administrative Reform and Bureaucracy Reform, and BKPM issued a circulating letter on September 15, 2010, to clarify investment that crosses provincial and regional boundaries. Investment in a regency is managed by the regency government; investment that lies in two or more regencies is managed by the provincial government; and investment that lies in two or more provinces is managed by central government, or central BKPM. BKPM has plans to roll out its one-stop shop structure to the provincial and regency level to streamline local permitting processes at more than 500 sites around the country.

Competition Law

The Indonesian Competition Authority (KPPU) implements and enforces the 1999 Indonesia Competition Law. The KPPU reviews agreements, business practices and mergers that may be deemed anti-competitive, advises the government on policies that may affect competition, and issues guidelines relating to the Competition Law.

Investment Trends

Not applicable/information not available.

Table 1

Measure	Year	Index or Rank	Website Address
TI Corruption Perceptions index	2014	107 of 175	transparency.org/cpi2014/results
World Bank's Doing Business Report "Ease of Doing Business"	2014	114 of 189	doingbusiness.org/rankings
Global Innovation Index	2014	87 of 143	globalinnovationindex.org/content.aspx?page=data-analysis
World Bank GNI per capita	2013	USD 3,580	data.worldbank.org/indicator/NY.GNP.PCAP.CD

Millennium Challenge Corporation Country Scorecard

The Millennium Challenge Corporation, a U.S. Government entity charged with delivering development grants to countries that have demonstrated a commitment to reform, produced scorecards for countries with a per capita gross national income (GNI) or USD 4,125 or less. A list of countries/economies with MCC scorecards and links to those scorecards is available here: **http://www.mcc.gov/pages/selection/scorecards**. Details on each of the MCC's indicators and a guide to reading the scorecards are available here: **http://www.mcc.gov/pages/docs/doc/report-guide-to-the-indicators-and-the-selection-process-fy-2015**.

2. CONVERSION AND TRANSFER POLICIES

Foreign Exchange

The rupiah (IDR), the local currency, is freely convertible. Currently, banks must report all foreign exchange transactions and foreign obligations to the Bank of Indonesia (BI). With respect to the physical movement of currency, any person taking cash into or out of Indonesia in the amount of IDR 100 million (USD 8,700) or more, or the equivalent in another currency, must report the amount to the Director General of Customs and Excise.

Banks on their own behalf or for customers may conduct derivative transactions related to derivatives of foreign currency rates, interest rates, and/or a combination thereof. BI requires borrowers to conduct their foreign currency borrowing through domestic banks registered with BI. The regulations apply to borrowing in cash, non-revolving loan agreements, and debt securities.

Under the 2007 Investment Law, the GOI gives assurance to investors relating to the transfer and repatriation of funds, in foreign currency, on capital, profit, interest, dividends and other income, funds required for (i) purchasing raw material, intermediate goods or final goods, and (ii) replacing capital goods for continuation of business operations, additional funds required for investment, funds for debt payment, royalties, income of foreign individuals working on the investment, earnings from selling or liquidation of the invested company, compensation for losses, and compensation for expropriation. U.S. firms report no difficulties in obtaining foreign exchange.

Bank Indonesia began in 2012 to require exporters to repatriate their export earnings through domestic banks within three months of the date of the export declaration form. Once repatriated, there are currently no restrictions on re-transferring export earnings abroad. Some companies report this requirement is not enforced.

Remittance Policies

The Indonesian government places no restrictions or time limitations on investment remittances. However, certain reporting requirements exist. Any transfer of funds in excess of USD 10,000, whether incoming or outgoing, must be reported to Bank Indonesia (BI) along with the reason for the transfer.

Carrying more than IDR 100 million in cash out of Indonesia requires prior approval from Bank BI, while any person carrying IDR 100 million or more into the country must verify the funds with Indonesian Customs upon arrival. Indonesia does not engage in currency manipulation.

The Financial Action Task Force (FATF) upgraded Indonesia to the Improved Compliance-Ongoing Monitoring or gray list at the February 2015 plenary meeting, though Indonesia remains a State Of Concern. The GOI is working towards the goal of an International Cooperation Review Group (ICRG) process exit this June.

3. EXPROPRIATION AND COMPENSATION

The GOI generally recognizes and upholds property rights of foreign and domestic investors, and the 2007 Investment Law opened major sectors of the economy to foreign investment while assuring investors' protection from nationalization, except where corporate crime is involved. However, Indonesia's rising economic nationalism has manifested itself through negotiations, policies, regulations, and laws that erode investor value. These include local content requirements, requirements to divest equity shares to Indonesia stakeholders, and requirements to set up manufacturing or processing facilities in Indonesia.

In 2012, the GOI issued a regulation requiring foreign-owned mining operations to divest majority equity to Indonesian shareholders within 10 years of operational startup. That regulation relies upon cost of investment incurred, rather than market value, for purposes of divestment valuation. In October 2014, with Regulation 77/2014, the Indonesian government eased the foreign ownership restrictions to 60 percent for companies that smelt domestically (40 percent divestment) and 70 percent for companies that operate underground mines (30 percent divestment). The GOI is requiring that mining contracts of work be renegotiated to alter terms in favor of the GOI, including royalty and tax rates, local content levels, domestic processing of minerals, and reduced mine areas. Some mining companies have had to reduce the size of their original mining work area without compensation.

In general, Indonesia's rising resource nationalism supports the idea that domestic interests should not have to pay prevailing market prices for domestic resources. In the oil and gas sector, the GOI is increasingly explicit in its policy that expiring production sharing contracts operated by foreign companies be transferred to domestic interests rather than extended. While there is no obligation of compensation under the production sharing contract, this policy has begun to affect the Indonesian business interests of foreign companies.

The Law on Land Acquisition Procedures for Public Interest Development passed in December 2011 sought to streamline GOI acquisition of land for much-needed infrastructure projects. The law seeks to clarify roles, reduce the time frame for each phase of the land acquisition process, deter land speculation, and curtail obstructionist litigation, while still ensuring safeguards for land-right holders. The implementing regulations, first approved in 2012, went into effect on January 1 2015. The law has neither led to significantly reduced land acquisition timelines nor resulted in accusations of GOI expropriation of land.

4. DISPUTE SETTLEMENT

Legal System, Specialized Courts, Judicial Independence, Judgments of Foreign Courts

Indonesia's legal system is based on civil law. The court system consists of District Courts (primary courts of original jurisdiction), High Courts (courts of appeal), and the Supreme Court (the court of last resort). Indonesia also has a Constitutional Court. The Constitutional Court has the same legal standing as the Supreme Court, and its role is to review the constitutionality of legislation. Both the Supreme and Constitutional Courts have authority to conduct judicial review.

The court system often does not provide effective recourse for resolving property and contractual disputes. Cases that would be adjudicated in civil courts in other jurisdictions sometimes result in criminal charges in Indonesia. Judges are not bound by precedent and many laws are open to various interpretations.

A lack of clear land titles has plagued Indonesia for decades, although the land acquisition law enacted in December 2011 included legal mechanisms designed to resolve some past land ownership issues. Indonesia also has a poor track record on contract sanctity. Government Regulation 79 of 2010 opened the door for the GOI to remove recoverable costs from production sharing contracts. The GOI is also requiring mining companies to renegotiate their contracts of work to require higher royalties, more divestment, more local content, and domestic processing of mineral ore.

Indonesia's commercial code, grounded in colonial Dutch law, has been updated to include provisions on bankruptcy, intellectual property rights, incorporation and dissolution of businesses, banking, and capital markets. Application of the commercial code, including the bankruptcy provisions, remains uneven, in large part due to corruption and training deficits for judges, prosecutors, and defense lawyers.

Bankruptcy

The bankruptcy law is decidedly pro-creditor and the law makes no distinction between domestic and foreign creditors. As a result, foreign creditors have the same rights as all potential creditors in a bankruptcy case, as long as foreign claims are submitted in compliance with underlying regulations and procedures. Monetary judgments in Indonesia are made in local currency.

Investment Disputes

Judicial handling of investment disputes remains mixed. Indonesia's legal code recognizes the right of parties to apply agreed upon rules of arbitration. Some arbitration but not all is handled by Indonesia's domestic arbitration agency, the Indonesian National Arbitration Body.

Companies have resorted to ad hoc arbitrations in Indonesia using the UN Commission on International Trade Laws (UNCITRAL model law) arbitration rules. Though doing business in Indonesia remains challenging, there is not a clear pattern of investment disputes involving U.S. or other foreign investors.

International Arbitration

In early 2014, Indonesia began to terminate its Bilateral Investment Treaty agreements (BITs) by allowing more than 60 outstanding agreements to expire. Indonesia is developing its own model Bilateral Investment Treaty (BIT) but has not yet announced when it would be finalized. The United States does not have a BIT with Indonesia. On-going international arbitration cases involving Indonesia may have played a role in Indonesia's decision to abrogate its BITs.

ICSID Convention and New York Convention

Indonesia is a Member of the International Center for Settlement of Investment Disputes (ICSID) and the New York Convention of 1958 on the Recognition and Enforcement of Foreign Arbitral Awards. Thus, foreign arbitral awards are legally recognized and enforceable in the Indonesian courts, but, in practice, are not always enforced. The 2012 ICSID arbitration case of British firm Churchill Mining vs. Indonesia is on-going as of April 2015.

Duration of Dispute Resolution

The court system in Indonesia works slowly. International arbitration awards, when enforced, may take years from original judgment to payment.

5. PERFORMANCE REQUIREMENTS AND INVESTMENT INCENTIVES

WTO/TRIMS

The Indonesian government notified the WTO of its compliance with Trade-Related Investment Measures (TRIMS) on August 26, 1998. The 2007 Investment Law states that the GOI shall provide the same treatment to both domestic and foreign investors originating from any country. The Indonesian government pursues policies to promote local manufacturing that could be inconsistent with TRIMS requirements, such as linking import approvals to investment pledges and local content requirements in some sectors.

Investment Incentives

The GOI offers a tax holiday scheme to exempt certain businesses from paying corporate income taxes for up to ten years under Ministry of Finance Decree No. 130/PMK.011/2011. Businesses must have operated as a legal entity in Indonesia for at least 12 months prior to the issuance of the tax holiday regulation, among other requirements. Priority is given to investment in resource extraction, resource refinement, industrial machinery, renewable resources, telecommunications equipment, or pioneer sectors. Government Regulation No. 62 of 2008 provides a tax incentive program for projects conducted in national high-priority sectors which encompass 128 different fields. Businesses may only apply for one tax incentive: either the tax holiday or the tax incentive program.

Research and Development

At present, Indonesia does not have formal regulations granting national treatment to U.S. and other foreign firms participating in Government-financed or subsidized research and development programs. The State Ministry for Research and Technology handles applications on a case-by-case basis.

Performance Requirements

The GOI expects foreign investors to contribute to the training and development of Indonesian nationals, allowing the transfer of skills and technology required for their effective participation in the management of foreign companies. As a general rule, a company can hire foreigners only for positions that the government has deemed open to non-Indonesians. Employers must have manpower-training programs aimed at replacing foreign workers with Indonesians. If a direct investment enterprise wants to employ foreigners, the enterprise should submit an Expatriate Placement Plan to BKPM to get a Limited Stay Visa or Semi-Permanent Residence Visa (VITAS/VBS). Expatriates are issued a Limited Stay Permit (KITAS) and a blue book, valid for two years and renewable for up to two extensions without leaving the country. The foreign worker must meet education, work experience, and Indonesian language requirements and commit to transfer knowledge to an Indonesian counterpart. Under Ministry of Manpower regulations, any expatriate who holds a work and residence permit must contribute USD 1,200 per year to a fund for local manpower training at regional manpower offices. Some U.S. firms report difficulty in renewing KITASs for their foreign executives. In 2013, the government issued new regulations on the employment of foreigners, including an age cap of 55 years on foreign executives for oil and gas firms. In December 2013, the Ministry of Manpower and Transmigration issued Regulation 12 on Procedures for Employing Foreign Manpower. The new regulation made some changes to the previous 2008 regulation, including the introduction of a new mechanism to hire temporary foreign workers and simplification of the permit process for foreigners married to Indonesians.

With the passage of the defense law in October 2012 and subsequent implementing regulations in October 2014, the GOI established a policy that imposes offset requirements for procurements from foreign defense suppliers. Currently, U.S. defense equipment suppliers are still competing for contracts with local partners on the basis of an exception in the law that indicates that purchases may be made from non-state owned enterprise (SOE) sources if not readily available on the local market. The 2014 implementing regulations did little to clarify how offsets would be applied. According to the legislation and subsequent implementing regulations, an initial 35 percent of any foreign defense procurement or contract must be offset through local content, counter-trade agreements, transfer of technology agreements, or a variety of other mechanisms. The offset amount must increase by 10 percent every five years until a maximum of 85 percent of a contract or procurement value is reached. The implementing regulations also refer to a "multiplier factor" that can be applied to increase a given offset valuation depending on "the impact on the development of the national economy." Decisions regarding multiplier values, authorized local content, and other key aspects of the new law are in the hands of the Defense Industry Policy Committee (KKIP), an entity comprising GOI interagency representatives and defense industry leadership, further increasing issues with transparency and predictability of how the regulations will be applied.

Data Storage

The Indonesian government issued Government Regulation 82 in 2012 requiring certain "public service providers" to establish data storage and disaster recovery centers on Indonesian soil. The government continues to contemplate how broadly to apply the definition of "public service providers" under Regulation 82/2012, but it is possible that data localization rules will affect financial and other service delivery companies.

6. Right to Private Ownership and Establishment

The Ministry of Law and Human Rights' implementation of an electronic business registration filing and notification system has dramatically reduced the number of days needed to register a company. Foreign firms are not required to disclose proprietary information to the government before investing.

To establish a business, one must: obtain the standard form of the company deed; arrange for a notary electronically; obtain clearance for the Indonesian company's name at the Ministry of Law and Human Rights; notarize company documents; obtain a certificate of company domicile from the local municipality; pay the State Treasury for the non-tax state revenue fees for legal services; apply to the Ministry of Law and Human Rights for approval of the deed of establishment; apply at the one stop service for the permanent business trading license and company registration certificate; register with the Ministry of Manpower; apply for the workers' social security and health program; and, obtain a taxpayer registration number and a value added tax (VAT) collector number. The process takes an average of 52 days.

7. PROTECTION OF PROPERTY RIGHTS

Real Property

The Basic Agrarian Law of 1960, the predominant body of law governing land rights, recognizes the right of private ownership. Indonesia's 1945 Constitution states that all natural resources are owned by the GOI for the benefit of the people. This principle was augmented by the passage of a land acquisition bill in December 2011 that enshrined the concept of eminent domain and established mechanisms for fair market value compensation and appeals. The National Land Agency registers property under Regulation No. 24 of 1997, though the Ministry of Forestry administers all 'forest land'. Registration is sometimes complicated by local government requirements and claims as a result of decentralization. Registration is also not conclusive evidence of ownership, but rather strong evidence of such. Foreigners are not allowed to own land in Indonesia, but can acquire the rights to use, sell, lease, and mortgage land through an Indonesian entity. Indonesia ranks 117th on the World Bank's, Ease of Registering Property ranking.

Intellectual Property Rights

Indonesia is currently on the Special 301 priority watch list for intellectual property rights (IPR) protection. Indonesia's failure to effectively protect intellectual property and enforce IPR laws has resulted in high levels of physical and online piracy. The International Intellectual Property Alliance estimates that 86 percent of business software is unlicensed, while retail piracy rates are likely even higher. Harco Glodok, Indonesia's largest trade center for consumer electronics and related goods, remains on the Notorious Markets list in 2015.

Indonesia's intellectual property laws provide a solid foundation for enforcement efforts. In September 2014 Parliament amended Indonesia's 2002 Copyright Law. Changes to the law include extending copyright protection for most works to lifetime plus 70 years for individuals or 50 years for copyrights held by legal entities, strengthens the role of collective management organizations to streamline royalty collections, including for foreign copyrights through bilateral or multilateral agreement, criminalizing illegal upload or download of copyrighted material for commercial use, and creating landlord liability for "deliberately and knowingly" allowing the sale or duplication of copyright infringing material. Draft amendments to Indonesia's Trademark and Patent laws are on the 2015 legislative calendar and are scheduled to be submitted to Parliament this year. Currently, a standard trademark application process can take up to 24 months, and trademark holders report that claiming well-known mark status can be difficult. Patent applications can take up to 48 months.

Despite adequate intellectual property laws, enforcement remains limited. The Directorate General for Intellectual Property (DGIP) reported limited seizures in 2014, although BPOM, Indonesia's food and drug administration, reported the seizure of more than USD 7 million in counterfeit medicine during the year. Trademark and Copyright legislation requires a rights-holder complaint for investigations, and DGIP and BPOM investigators lack the authority to make arrests so must rely on police cooperation for any enforcement action. In 2012, the Supreme Court ruled that Customs may obtain rights for temporary injunctions to suspected counterfeit shipments at the border. However, Customs still cannot exercise ex officio powers, as intended in the 2006 amended customs law. The Indonesian Government is responsible for the storage and destruction of seized counterfeit goods, although rights-holders have contributed to the cost of destroying IP-infringing goods in the past.

Resources for Rights Holders

For additional information about treaty obligations and points of contact at local IP offices, please see WIPO's country profiles at **http://www.wipo.int/directory/en/**.

AmCham Indonesia: **http://www.amcham.or.id/**

8. TRANSPARENCY OF THE REGULATORY SYSTEM

Indonesia continues to bring its legal, regulatory, and accounting systems into compliance with international norms, but progress is slow. Recent successes include passage of a comprehensive anti-money laundering law in late 2010 and a land acquisition law in December 2011, both of which could have positive implications for foreign investment. Although Indonesia continues to move forward with regulatory system reforms, these efforts have not yet created a level playing field for foreign investors nor does the current regulatory system establish clear and transparent rules for all actors. Certain laws and policies, including the Negative List, establish sectors that are either fully off-limits to foreign investors or are subject to substantive conditions.

Bureaucratic reforms have slowed, and decentralization has introduced another layer of bureaucracy for firms to navigate, resulting in costly red tape. Ineffective management and corruption are among the challenges faced by the GOI in launching bureaucratic reform. U.S. businesses cite regulatory and transparency problems as ongoing factors hindering operations. Government ministries and agencies, including the Indonesian Parliament, continue to publish many proposed laws and regulations in draft form for public comment; however, not all draft laws and regulations are made available in public fora. Laws and regulations are often vague and require substantial interpretation by the implementers, leading to business uncertainty and rent-seeking opportunities. In short, investors remain interested but wary, as Indonesia is not currently making the longer-term regulatory changes to generate greater domestic or foreign investment.

9. EFFICIENT CAPITAL MARKETS AND PORTFOLIO INVESTMENT

The Indonesia Stock Exchange (IDX) index closed at 5226.9 on December 30, 2014, up 24 percent for the calendar year. In 2014, IDX had 503 listed companies and reached capitalization as high as (USD 512.82 billion) in May. There were 23 initial public offerings in 2014. Foreigners conducted more than half of total IDX stock trades in the last quarter of 2014 (65 percent in Q4 2014). In 2011, the IDX launched the Indonesian Sharia Stock Index (ISSI), its first index of sharia-compliant companies, primarily to attract greater investment from Middle East companies and investors. As of 2014 the ISSI is composed of 313 stocks listed on IDX's Jakarta Composite Index.

Government treasury bonds are the most liquid bonds offered by the GOI. Treasury bills are less liquid due to their small issue size. Liquidity in BI-issued Sertifikat Bank Indonesia (SBI) is also limited due to the three-month required holding period. The GOI also issued its first sukuk treasury bills as part of efforts to diversify Islamic debt instruments and increase their liquidity. Indonesia's sovereign debt is currently graded as BBB- by Fitch Ratings and baa3 grade by Moody's.

The Financial Services Supervisory Authority (OJK) assumed BI's supervisory role over commercial banks as of January 1, 2014 and began overseeing the capital markets and non-banking institutions on January 1, 2013, replacing the Capital Market and Financial Institution Supervisory Board.

Foreigners have good access to the Indonesian securities market and are a major source (33 percent in government securities) of portfolio investment. Foreign ownership of Indonesian companies may be limited in certain industries as determined by the Negative List.

Money and Banking System, Hostile Takeovers

Although there is some concern regarding the operations of the many small and medium family-owned banks, the banking system is generally considered sound with banks enjoying some of the widest interest rate margins in the region. The ten largest banks, with IDR 3,361 trillion for December 2014 (USD 272.6 billion) in total assets or 65.2 percent of the total, dominate the banking sector. Loans grew 12 percent as of December 31, 2014, (vis-à-vis 21.4 percent in 2013) while gross non-performing loans stood at 2.1 percent, up from 1.7 percent a year earlier.

Foreigners may purchase up to 99 percent of the total shares of a domestic bank through private placement or on the stock exchange. Purchases of 25 percent or more require BI approval. Foreign banks may establish branches if the foreign bank is ranked in the top 200 global banks by assets. To establish a representative office, the foreign bank must be ranked in the top 300 global banks by assets. A special operating license is required from BI in order to establish a foreign branch.

BI has limited bank ownership to no more than 40 percent by any single shareholder, applicable to foreign and domestic shareholders, and requiring foreign bank branches to become subsidiaries.

10. COMPETITION FROM STATE-OWNED ENTERPRISES

Indonesia had 119 SOEs at the end of 2014, 26 of which contributed more than 90 percent of the total SOE profit. Twenty are listed on the Indonesian stock exchange and 14 are special purpose entities under the SOE ministry with one under the Ministry of Finance (the Indonesian Infrastructure Guarantee Fund). SOEs are present in almost all sectors/industries including banking (finance), tourism (travel), agriculture, forestry, mining, construction, fishing, energy, and telecommunications (information and communications). In 2014, the profits fell by 3.5 percent YOY to IDR 148.6 trillion (USD 11.4 billion) compared to 2013. As of the end of 2014, SOEs employ around 781,760 people and contribute an estimated 40 percent of the country's gross domestic product. As of December 30, 2014, there are 20 state-owned companies with a market capitalization amounting to IDR 1,381 trillion or 26.41 percent of the total capitalization of shares listed on the Stock Exchange. Indonesian SOE R&D spending varies by sector.

Private enterprises can compete with SOEs under the same terms and conditions with respect to access to markets, credit, and other business operations. However, many sectors report that, in reality, SOEs receive strong preference for GOI projects. SOEs publish an annual report and are audited by the Supreme Audit Agency (BPK), the Financial and Development Supervisory Agency (BPKP), and external and internal auditors.

Indonesian SOEs adopt a two-tier Board structure with a Board of Commissioners (similar to an American company's board of directors) and a Board and Directors (similar to an American company's executive management team). Depending on the type of SOE, either the President or the Minister of SOEs has the right to make appointments and to dismiss members of either the Board of Commissioners or Board of Directors. With such control, board member appointments are subject to government interference. Hence, it is not uncommon for SOEs to have ministers, high-ranking bureaucrats, military generals, or member of political parties, either retired or still active, sitting as Board members. Some SOEs suffer from poor management, which has led to several cases of graft and corruption against former Commissioners and Directors.

OECD Guidelines on Corporate Governance of SOEs

State Owned Enterprises (SOEs) in Indonesia generally do not adhere to the OECD Guidelines on Corporate Governance for SOEs.

Sovereign Wealth Funds

The GOI established the Pusat Investasi Pemerintah (PIP) to act as a special purpose investment entity and eventually as a sovereign wealth fund. To date, it has limited its investments to the domestic market in strategic sectors with the goal of stimulating national economic growth. PIP can invest in a variety of asset classes such as equity, debt, infrastructure, and direct investments. PIP is in addition to other GOI SOEs that invest in domestic markets such as PT Sarana Multi Infrastructure, PT Indonesia Infrastructure Guarantee Facility, and Indonesia Infrastructure Finance.

11. CORPORATE SOCIAL RESPONSIBILITY

While international organizations like the OECD and UN envision corporate social responsibility (CSR) as a comprehensive management paradigm that includes concepts like human rights, employee relations, environment and science, bribery and corruption, consumer interests, and taxation, understanding of CSR in Indonesia tends to focus on community and economic development, and educational projects and programs. This is at least in part caused by the fact that such projects are often required in the environmental impact permits ("Amdal") of resource extraction companies, which undergo a good deal of domestic and international scrutiny of their operations. Because much resource extraction activity occurs in remote and rural areas where government services are limited or absent, these companies face very high community expectations to provide such services themselves. Despite significant investments – especially by large multinational firms – in CSR projects, there is limited general awareness of those projects, even among government regulators and officials.

OECD Guidelines for Multinational Enterprises

Indonesia is not an adherent to the OECD Guidelines for Multinational Enterprises.

12. POLITICAL VIOLENCE

As in other democracies, politically motivated demonstrations occasionally occur throughout Indonesia, but are not a major ongoing concern for most foreign investors.

Fighting terrorism remains a top priority for the Indonesian government, and President Jokowi Widodo has demonstrated a continued strong commitment to combating terrorism. Since the 2009 bombings of two international hotels in Jakarta, Indonesian police and security forces have disrupted a number of terrorist cells, including some affiliated with Jemaah Islamiyah (JI), a U.S. government-designated terrorist organization that carried out several bombings at various times since 2000. In response to terrorist threats and attacks, Indonesia has effectively pursued counterterrorism efforts through legislation and law enforcement. In 2014, the Attorney General's Office handled nearly 50 terrorism related cases. Though the Indonesian government's sustained counterterrorism campaign has significantly degraded the operational capabilities of violent extremist organizations in Indonesia, these groups continue to demonstrate a willingness and ability to carry out attacks with little or no warning. Although U.S. and Western-affiliated interests remain potential targets of terrorists, the focus of terrorists is increasingly on attacks against local governments and law enforcement entities, especially the police. There is also concern about Indonesians traveling to Syria or Iraq as foreign terrorist fighters; several hundred Indonesians are estimated to have traveled to the Middle East to join violent groups operating there.

Foreign investors in Papua face certain unique challenges. Indonesian security forces occasionally conduct operations against the Free Papua Movement, a small armed separatist group that is most active in the Central Highlands region. Low-intensity communal, tribal, and political conflict also exists in Papua and has caused deaths and injuries. Anti-government protests have resulted in deaths and injuries, and violence has been committed against employees and contractors of a U.S. company there.

13. CORRUPTION

President Jokowi was elected in 2014 on a strong good-governance platform. However, corruption remains a serious problem, preventing increased FDI, according to some U.S. companies. Although the government has issued detailed directions on combating corruption in targeted ministries and agencies, there has not been a concerted government-led effort to encourage or require companies to establish internal codes of conduct, or effective internal controls, ethics, and compliance programs to detect and prevent bribery of public officials.

Indonesia's ranking in Transparency International's Corruption Perceptions Index in 2014 is 107 out of 175 countries. Corruption remains pervasive despite laws to combat it. The independence and authority of the Corruption Eradication Commission (KPK) has been called into question following its announcement and subsequent deferral of its investigation into a candidate for National Police Chief. The KPK's purview in corruption cases is typically limited to law enforcement and other public officials, cases that exceed USD 100,000 in value and/or that represent significant loss to the state. Corruption cases are also handled by the Indonesian National Police and Attorney General's Office, neither of which have the same organizational capacity to investigate or prosecute corruption cases. Giving or accepting a bribe is a criminal act, with possible fines ranging from USD 3,850 to USD 77,000 and imprisonment up to a maximum of 20 years or life imprisonment, depending on the severity of the charge.

UN Anticorruption Convention, OECD Convention on Combatting Bribery

Indonesia ratified the UN Convention against Corruption in September 2006. Indonesia has not yet acceded to the OECD Anti-Bribery Convention, but attends meetings of the OECD Anti-Corruption Working Group. In 2014 Indonesia chaired the Open Government Partnership, a multilateral platform to promote transparency, empower citizens, fight corruption, and strengthen governance. Several civil society organizations function as vocal and competent corruption watchdogs, including Transparency International Indonesia and Indonesia Corruption Watch.

Resources to Report Corruption

Jln. HR Rasuna Said Kav. C1 Kuningan
Jakarta Selatan 12920
informasi@kpk.go.id

14. BILATERAL INVESTMENT AGREEMENTS

Indonesia has signed investment agreements with 60 countries, including: Algeria, Argentina, Australia, Bangladesh, Belgium, Bulgaria, Cambodia, Chile, Croatia, Cuba, Czech Republic, Denmark, Egypt, Finland, France, Germany, Hungary, India, Iran, Italy, Jamaica, Jordan, Kyrgyzstan, Laos, Malaysia, Mauritius, Mongolia, Morocco, Mozambique, North Korea, Norway, Pakistan, People's Republic of China, Peru, Philippines, Poland, Qatar, Romania, Saudi Arabia, Singapore, Slovak Republic, South Korea, Spain, Sri Lanka, Sudan, Suriname, Syria, Sweden, Switzerland, Thailand, The Netherlands, Tunisia, Turkey, Turkmenistan, Ukraine, United Kingdom, Uzbekistan, Vietnam, Yemen, and Zimbabwe. Indonesia does not have a bilateral investment treaty with the United States.

Since 2014, Indonesia began to abrogate its existing BITs, by allowing the agreements to expire. An updated Indonesian model BIT has been in development for some time, which the government could use in the future to renegotiate expiring agreements or negotiate new BITs.

Under the ASEAN Free Trade Agreement, duties on imports from ASEAN countries generally range from 0 percent to 5 percent, except for products specified on exclusion lists. Indonesia also provides preferential market access to Australia, China, Japan, Korea, India, Pakistan, and New Zealand under regional ASEAN agreements and to Japan under a bilateral agreement. In accordance with the ASEAN-China FTA, in August 2012 Indonesia increased the number of goods from China receiving duty-free access to 10,012 tariff lines. Indonesia is currently negotiating bilateral agreements with Iran, India, Australia, New Zealand, South Korea, and European Free Trade Association, studying potential FTAs with Chile, Turkey, Tunisia, Mexico, South Africa, and Egypt. The ASEAN Economic Community arrangement will come into effect on January 1, 2016, and is expected to reduce barriers for goods, services and some skilled employees across ASEAN. Indonesia is also participating in negotiations for the Regional Comprehensive Economic Partnership (RCEP), which includes the 10 ASEAN Member States and 6 additional countries (Australia, China, India, Japan, Korea and New Zealand).

Bilateral Taxation Treaties

Non double income taxation between the United States and Indonesia is granted in accordance with the Convention between the Government of the Republic of Indonesia and the Government of the United States of America for the Avoidance of Double Taxation and the Prevention of the Fiscal Evasion with Respect to Taxes on Income, signed at Jakarta July 11, 1988, and its amending Protocol, signed at Jakarta July 24, 1996.

15. OPIC AND OTHER INVESTMENT INSURANCE PROGRAMS

In 2010, the Overseas Private Investment Corporation (OPIC) updated its 1967 investment support agreement between the United States and Indonesia by adding OPIC products such as direct loans, coinsurance, and reinsurance to the means of OPIC support which U.S. companies may use to invest in Indonesia.

Indonesia has joined the Multilateral Investment Guarantee Agency (MIGA). MIGA, a part of the World Bank Group, is an investment guarantee agency to insure investors and lenders against losses relating to currency transfer restrictions, expropriation, war and civil disturbance, and breach of contract.

16. LABOR

The Indonesian labor market is generally open and flexible, although there are significant restrictions on the use of contract workers. Recent significant increases in the minimum wage for many provinces have made unskilled and semi-skilled labor more costly including a 44 percent increase in Jakarta in 2012.. Increases in the 2014 minimum wage were less dramatic, with a relatively modest 12.5 percent gain in the bellwether Jakarta area. Unions staged largely peaceful protests across Indonesia in December 2014 claiming that the wage increases are insufficient to offset the recent rise in fuel prices caused by the Jokowi administration's partial removal of fuel subsidies. While restrictions on the use of contract workers remain in place, continued labor protests focusing on this issue suggest that government enforcement continues to be lax. Unemployment has been declining in recent years and in 2014 was 5.9 percent. Unemployment tends to be higher than the national average among young people.

Indonesian labor is relatively low cost by world standards, but lack of adequate skills training and complicated labor laws combine to make Indonesia's competitiveness lag behind other Asian competitors. Investors frequently cite high severance payments to dismissed employees, restrictions on outsourcing and contract workers, and limitations on expatriate workers as significant obstacles to new investment in Indonesia. Employers also note that the skill base provided by the education system is lower than that of neighboring countries, and successive Labor Ministers have listed improved vocational training as a top priority. Labor contracts are relatively straightforward to negotiate but are subject to renegotiation, despite the existence of written agreements. Local courts often side with citizens in labor disputes, contracts notwithstanding. On the other hand, some foreign investors view Indonesia's labor regulatory framework, respect for freedom of association, and the right unionize as an advantage to investing in the country. [The GOI established in 2006 a new Labor Court as part of a broader labor dispute resolution system. U.S. companies expressed disappointment in the GOI's lack of mediation between labor groups and industry during 2012 minimum wage discussions]. Expert local human resources advice is essential for American companies doing business in Indonesia, even those only opening representative offices. Labor Minister Hanif Dhakiri announced in 2015 that he would like to make proficiency in the Indonesian language a requirement for expatriate employment, but it is not clear how or whether this will be implemented.

Minimum wages vary throughout the country as provincial governors set an annual minimum wage floor and district heads have the authority to set a higher rate. Indonesia's highly fractured and historically weak labor movement has gained strength in recent years, evidenced by significant increases in the minimum wage. Labor unions are independent of the government. The law, with some restrictions, protects the rights of workers to join independent unions, conduct legal strikes, and bargain collectively. Indonesia has ratified all eight of the core ILO conventions underpinning internationally accepted labor norms. The Ministry of Labor maintains an inspectorate to monitor labor norms, but enforcement is stronger in the formal than in the informal sector. In January 2014, Indonesia launched a national insurance plan. In October 2011, the Indonesian government passed a revised Social Security Law which took effect in January 2014 in which all formal sector workers must participate. Subject to a wage ceiling, employers' must contribute an amount equal to 4 percent of workers' salaries to this plan. Further, Indonesia is working toward establishing a national agency to support workers in the event of work accident, death, retirement, or old age.

A proposed revision to Indonesia's 2003 labor law may establish more stringent restrictions on outsourcing, currently used by many firms to circumvent some formal-sector job benefits.

17. FOREIGN TRADE ZONES/FREE PORTS/TRADE FACILITATION

The GOI offers incentives to over 1,500 foreign and domestic industrial companies that operate in bonded zones throughout Indonesia. The largest bonded zone is the free trade zone island of Batam, located just south of Singapore. Neighboring Bintan island and Karimun island also enjoy free trade zone areas. Investors in bonded zones are not required to apply for additional implementation licenses (location, construction, and nuisance act permits and land titles), and foreign companies are allowed 100 percent ownership. These companies do not pay import duty, income tax, VAT, and sales tax on imported capital goods, equipment, and raw materials until the portion of production destined for the domestic market is "exported" to Indonesia, in which case fees are owed only on that portion. Companies operating in bonded zones may lend machinery and equipment to subcontractors located outside of the bonded zone for a maximum two-year period.

Ministry of Finance Regulation No. 147/2011 stipulates that the delivery of products outside of bonded zones into the domestic market is set at a maximum of 25 percent (down from 50 percent) of export realization value of the previous year. If a bonded zone company exceeds the 25 percent limitation, its domestic quota for the next year will be reduced. The new regulation also restricts subcontract work and requires bonded zones less than 10,000 square meters in size to relocate to industrial estates.

As stipulated by the 2007 Investment Law, the Indonesian Legislature (DPR) passed regulations on special economic zones (SEZ) in 2009. At least 20 areas have submitted applications for SEZ status, but to date only two have been created -- Sei Mangke in North Sumatra and Tanjung Lesung in Banten. The new Administration has announced it will create 10 more zones by 2019 as a part of its economic growth strategy.

18. FOREIGN DIRECT INVESTMENT AND FOREIGN PORTFOLIO INVESTMENT STATISTICS

Table 2: Key Macroeconomic Data, U.S. FDI in Host Country/Economy

	Host Country Statistical source*		USG or international statistical source		USG or International Source of Data: BEA; IMF; Eurostat; UNCTAD, Other
Economic Data	Year	Amount	Year	Amount	
Host Country Gross Domestic Product (GDP) ($M USD)	2013	908,300	2013	868,345	www.worldbank.org/en/country
Foreign Direct Investment	Host Country Statistical source*		USG or international statistical source		USG or international Source of data: BEA; IMF; Eurostat; UNCTAD, Other
U.S. FDI in partner country ($M USD, stock positions)	2013	1,060	2013	12,777	http://www.bea.gov/international/factsheet/factsheet.cfm?Area=613
Host country's FDI in the United States ($M USD, stock positions)	N/A	N/A	2013	-55	http://www.bea.gov/international/factsheet/factsheet.cfm?Area=613
Total inbound stock of FDI as % host GDP	2013	2.0%	N/A	N/A	

*Bank of Indonesia

Table 3: Sources and Destination of FDI

Indonesia has two main sources for FDI statistics: BKPM, which issues permanent business licenses to domestic and foreign investors, and BI, which records international capital flows as part of balance of payments statistics. BKPM records FDI figures based on issued business licenses. Since licenses for oil and gas, mining, banking, non-bank financial institutions, insurance and leasing are issued by other government bodies, these sectors are not covered under the BKPM statistics. BKPM is expected to increase the sectorial coverage gradually while BI statistics cover all sectors.

BKPM categorizes all investments made into a foreign capital investment company as FDI, even if it is a joint venture with a local partner. This practice tends to inflate BKPM's FDI figures, which may additionally include equity contributions from domestic partners and investments financed from domestic sources. BI instead follows the standard FDI categorization of equity investment, retained earnings and other capital inflows.

Direct Investment from/in Counterpart Economy Data					
From Top Five Sources/To Top Five Destinations (US Dollars, Millions)					
Inward Direct Investment			Outward Direct Investment		
Total Inward	230,439	100%	Total Outward	N/A	100%
Singapore	53,367	23%			
Netherlands	45,731	20%			
Japan	25,983	11%			
Mauritius	15,746	7%			
United Kingdom	10,641	5%			
"0" reflects amounts rounded to +/- USD 500,000.					

Source: IMF Coordinated Direct Investment Survey

Table 4: Sources of Portfolio Investment

Portfolio Investment Assets								
Top Five Partners (Millions, US Dollars)								
Total			Equity Securities			Total Debt Securities		
All Countries	15,285	100%	All Countries	2,871	100%	All Countries	12,413	100%
United States	3,276	21%	Singapore	1,080	38%	United States	3,208	26%
China (PR Mainland)	1,501	10%	China (PR Mainland)	746	26%	Netherlands	1,101	9%
Singapore	1,358	9%	China (PR Hong Kong)	343	12%	Luxembourg	876	7%
Netherlands	1,101	7%	Cayman Islands	338	12%	China (PR Mainland)	756	6%
Luxembourg	876	6%	United States	69	2%	Singapore	278	2%

Source: IMF Coordinated Portfolio Investment Survey

LIST OF ATTORNEYS

The U.S. Embassy Jakarta, Indonesia assumes no responsibility or liability for the professional ability or reputation of, or the quality of services provided by, the following persons or firms. Inclusion on this list is in no way an endorsement by the Department of State or the U.S. Embassy/Consulate. Names are listed alphabetically, and the order in which they appear has no other significance. The information in the list on professional credentials, areas of expertise and language ability are provided directly by the lawyers.

ABRAHAM LAW OFFICE
Prince Centre 10th Floor, Jalan Jend. Sudirman Kav 3-4, Jakarta 10220
Telephone: (21) 573-8987, 5739123 or Prince Centre operator: 573-6706 or 573-7312 Ext. 1708, Fax: (62-21) 5738279; E-mail: david@abraham-lawfirm.com
Web site: www.abraham-lawfirm.com
Cell phone of Mr. David Abraham (head of the office): 816-801-806, 819-801-806
Member of The Global Justice Network
Affiliated with Lieff Global of San Francisco, USA
Member of Inter Pacific Bar Association
Expertise: civil and criminal law, foreign investment, marine, oil and gas as well as telecommunication. Also aviation cases, corporate and trading, criminal and civil litigations, class actions, legal opinion, mining, aviations and marines, administrative law, telecommunications, tax law, drafting of agreement, initial public offering, and corruption cases.

FRANS WINARTA & PARTNERS
Attorneys and Counsellors at Law
Kompleks Bukit Gading Mediterania (Florencia), Boulevard Bukit Gading Raya Blok A 15 - 17
Kelapa Gading Permai, Jakarta 14240, Indonesia
Telephone: (21) 4532143, 45854839, 45854840; Fax: (21) 4516605, 4520083
E-mail: fwp@cbn.net.id ; Website: www.franswinarta.com
Highly recommended Firm and a highly recommended Lawyer in Dispute Resolution – (PLC Which Lawyer 2008)
Leading Firm and a leading Lawyer in Dispute Resolution – (Chambers Asia 2008)
One of the top Litigation Experts in the world - (Expert Guides to the World's Leading Litigation Lawyers 2008)
Highly recommended Asia-Pacific Focused Lawyer in Intellectual Property – (Asialaw Leading Lawyers 2008)
Member of INTERLAW (an International Association of Independent Law Firms)
Appointed Lawyer of the Austrian Embassy in Jakarta since 2010

GEORGE WIDJOJO & PARTNERS
Address: Jalan Kali Besar Barat 5, Jakarta 11230 Indonesia; Telephone: (21) 690-1707, 691-2226, 692-4533; fax: 692-3648, 693-0712; E-mail: gwidjojo@indosat.net.id ; web site: www.widjojolaw.com ; Cell phone of Mr. George Widjojo: 8161903327
Expertise: This firm specializes in marriage/divorce collections, civil law, commercial law, commercial/business law, patents/trademarks/copyrights, and corporations.

HADROMI & PARTNERS LAW FIRM
Setiabudi Atrium, 2nd Floor, Suite 209A
Jl. H.R. Rasuna Said Kav. 62, Jakarta 12920, Indonesia
Telephone : (62-21) 520 7040 (hunting); Facsimile : (62-21) 520 7046, (62-21) 5290 7339
E-mail: hadromi@centrin.net.id ; info@hadromi.com ; Direct: iqbal@hadromi.com
Website : www.hadromi.com
Expertise: family law, adoptions, child custody, marriage/divorce collections, insurance contracts, civil law, commercial law, aeronautical/maritime, immigration, banking/financial, commercial/business law, foreign investments, patents/trademarks/copyrights, corporations, criminal law foreign claims, transportation law, labor relations.

HANAFIAH PONGGAWA & PARTNERS
Address: Wisma 46-Kota BNI 41st flr., Jl. Jend. Sudirman Kav. 1, Jakarta 10220.
Telephone: (21) 5701837; fax: 5701835; E-mail: fabianbp@hplaw.co.id ; Fabian@alum.calberkeley.org ; web site: www.hplaw.co.id ;
Expertise: commercial law, aeronautical/maritime, government relations, immigration, commercial/business law, foreign investments, marketing agreements, patents/trademarks/copyrights, corporations.

KUSNANDAR & ASSOCIATES
Address: Equity Tower, 25th flr., Jl. Jend. Sudirman Kav. 52-53, Jakarta 12190, Indonesia.
Telephone: (21) 5140 2020; fax: 5140 2021; E-mail kusnalaw@kusnandar.com ;
Web site: www.kusnandar.com ; Blog: www.kusnandarlaw.blogspot.com
Expertise: Full Fledged Service Law Firm, Establishment of Foreign Representative Office and Foreign Investment Company, Corporate Finance, Merger-Acquisition-Consolidation & Restructuring, Intellectual Property Right (IPR), Immigration, Capital Market & Securities, Licensing & Counterfeit, Maritime, Admiralty & Shipping Insurance, Natural Resources & Plantation, Legal Management, Financial & Tax Audit, Banking & Investment, Bankruptcy & Insolvency, Arbitration, Expert Witness, Mediation, Litigation & Debt Recovery, Conveyance, Recruitment & Human Resources, Labour, Tax & Accounting, Auction, Offshore Incorporation and Sworn Translation.
Language: English, German, Mandarin, French

LUBIS. SANTOSA & MAULANA
Address: Equity Tower, 12th Floor,l Sudirman Central Business District (SCBD),
Jl.Jend. Sudirman Kav. 52-53, Jakarta - 12190
Contact: Mr. Todung Mulya Lubis. Telephone: (21) 29035900; Fax: (21) 29035090
E-mail : mulyalubis@lsmlaw.co.id ; Website: www.lsmlaw.co.id

Expertise: commercial law, government relations, banking/financial, commercial/business law, foreign investments, marketing agreements, patents/trademarks/copyrights, corporations, media arbitration.
Language: fluently English.
This firm also provides certified/sworn translator and will take cases outside of Jakarta.

LUBIS GANIE SUROWIDJOJO (LGS)
Address: Menara Imperium, 30th floor, Jalan H.R. Rasuna Said Kav. 1, Jakarta, Indonesia
Telephone: (21) 831-5005, 831-5025; fax: 831-5015, 831-5018
E-mail: lubis@lgslaw.co.id ; ganie@lgslaw.co.id ; surowidjojo@lgslaw.co.id
Website: www.lgsonline.com
Expertise: This firm is qualified to practice law in Indonesia and to provide legal services to and represent foreign and Indonesian clients on commercial and corporate law matters, including acquisition, corporate reorganization, mergers, commercial litigation, capital markets, corporate finance and secured transactions, energy, foreign and domestic investment, maritime and shipping, aviation, mining, arbitration, banking, construction, international trade, lease financing, debt restructuring, bankruptcy/insolvency, intellectual proprietary rights including trademarks, copyrights and patents, real estate transactions, tax, telecommunications, venture capital, agency and distributorship, insurance and labor.

ANDRYAWAL SIMANJUNTAK & PARTNERS
Address: Komplek. Kejaksaan Agung, Blok : A1 No. 23, JL. Cipunagara I, Ciputat 15411.
Telephone: (62-21) 99560888, (62)81399960888; Web site: www.andryawal.blogspot.com
E-mail : andryawal@gmail.com
Expertise: This law firm's area practice include litigation, non litigation, bankruptcy, corporate, commercial, labour, capital & finance, banking, criminal law, family law, administration law, immigration, foreign investment, land matter.

VERITAS LEGAL SERVICES
Address: Gedung Total 2nd Flr., Jl. S. Parman Kav. 106A, Tomang, Grogol Petamburan, Jakarta Barat 11440;
Telephone: (62-21) 30000997; Fax: 30000998; Email: veritas@yahoo.co.id
Expertise: Litigation, civil rights, contracts, corporate law, business law, commercial law, capital market and M&A, finance law, insurance law, investment law, banking law, tax law, bankruptcy,
merger & acquisitions, debtor and creditor, alternative dispute resolution, labor and employment law, family law, immigration law, intellectual property rights.

GANI JEMAT AND ASSOCIATE
Address: Gani Jemat Plaza, 8th Fl.,Jl. Iman Bonjol 76-78,Jakarta Pusat
Telephone: (62-21) 390-3603; 390-3610; 390-2908; Fax: 3150386
Expertise: Perdata/civil & Pidana/criminal cases: Divorce, Adoption/Business maters

HADIPUTRANTO, HADINOTO,& PARTNERS
Address: The Jakarta Stock Exchange Building, Tower II, 21st Fl., Sudirman Central Business Distr., Jl. Jenderal Sudirman 52-53, Jakarta. Telephone: (62-21) 515-5091-3; Fax: 515-4840
Expertise: Perdata/civil cases: Business/Corporate cases 62-21 515-5090

MOCHTAR, KARUWIN & KOMAR
Address: Wisma Metropolitan II, 14th Fl. Jl. Jend. Sudirman 29, Jakarta Selatan
Telephone: (62-21) 571-1130; Fax: 571-1162
Expertise: Perdata/civil cases: Corporate/Business cases

O.C. KALIGIS & ASSOCIATES - Advocate & Legal Consultants
Address: Komp. Majapahit Permai Blok B-123, C101, Jakarta 10160
Telephone: (62-21) 345-3994; 385-3250; Fax: 380-8193
Expertise: Divorce, Adoption, Civil, Criminal, Commercial, and Capital Market Laws, Family Law - dissolution of marriage and, custody matters.
Linguistic Qualifications: Indonesian, German, English, Dutch, Italian

EFENDI LOD SIMANJUNTAK & PARTNERS LAW OFFICE
Address: Plaza Sentral 9th Floor, suite 914. Jl. Jend. Sudirman. No. 47 Jakarta 12930
Website: www.efendilaw.com ; Email: effendi@efendilaw.com or eldanalegal@yahoo.com
Telephone: (62-21) 570-8904; Fax: (62-21) 571-1635
Cell phone: (0815-1303-6010) / (0812-8282-6040). Contact: Efendi Lod Simanjuntak, SH., MH.
Practices area: Litigation for criminal, civil, corporate matters, mining, tax law and family law.

SOEWITO SUHARDIMAN EDDYMURTHY KARDONO (SSEK)
Address: Mayapada Tower, 14th Floor, Jl. Jend. Sudirman Kav. 28, Jakarta 12920
Telephone: (62-21) 521 2038/304 16700; Fax: (62-21) 521 2039; Website: Www.Ssek.Com
Contact: Darrell R. Johnson (Darrelljohnson@Ssek.Com)
Indonesian Law Firm Of The Year 2013, 2011 - Chambers Asia Pacific
Indonesian Law Firm Of The Year 2012, 2008, 2007, 2006 – Who's Who Legal

Indonesian Law Firm Of The Year 2011, 2010, 2009 – Asian-Counsel Magazine
Expertise: Banking & Finance, Corporate/Commercial, Foreign Investment, Infrastructure, Insurance, Labor & Employment, M&A, Mining, Oil & Gas, Real Estate, Shipping & Logistics, Tax Law
Languages: English, Indonesian

DAHANA & Rekan
Address: Suite I0-07, The Rasuna Epicentrum Office Park, Jl.H.R. Rasuna Said, Jakarta 12950
E-mail: sdahana@dahanarekan.com ; sdahana@cbn.co.id ; Web site: www.dahanarekan.com
Contact : Mr. Smara Dahana. Telephone: (62-21) 9390-2823; Fax: 9390-0845
Expertise: Criminal (Pidana), Civil (Perdata)

LAW OFFICES OF DYAH ERSITA & PARTNERS
Address: Graha Aktiva 3rd Fl.,Jl. H.R. Rasuna Said Blok X-1 Kav. 3 Kuningan Jakarta 12950
Mr. Andrew I. Sriro, BA, JD. Web site: www.sriro.com ; E-mail: depa@sriro.com
Telephone: (62-21) 520-3171; Fax: 520-3279

TOMAS LAW FIRM
Address: Plaza Great River Indonesia, 15th Fl. Jl. H.R. Rasuna SaidKav. X2 No.1, (Kuningan) Jakarta Selatan 12940
Contact: Tanjung Margono or Tomas Suwondo. Telephone: (62-21) 579-38942; Fax: 579- 38943
Expertise: Litigation, Civil & Criminal Arbitration; Corporate & Commercial; Family law

DANIEL & PARTNERS
Address: Artha Graha Building 6th Fl Jl Jend Sudirman Kav 52-5312190
Telephone: (62-21) 528-98048; Fax: 515-2362
Expertise: Full range legal services and provide counseling, advocacy in litigation and non-litigation issues which includes but not limited to Commercial, Civil, Criminal Laws; Labor Disputes and Arbitration, Family Law, State Administration and Trademark and Patent (Intellectual Property).
Linguistic Qualifications: Indonesian, English

LEMBAGA BANTUAN HUKUM JAKARTA (Indonesian Legal Aid Service)
Address: Jl Pangeran Diponegoro 74, Jakarta Pusat. Telephone: (62-21) 314- 5518(hunting); Fax: 391-2377; E-mail: lbhjakarta@bantuanhukum.or.id ; Web site: www.bantuanhukum.or.id
Expertise: Commercial, Civil, Criminal Laws; Labour and Land Disputes
Linguistic Qualifications: Indonesian, English

MAKARIM & TAIRA S
Summitmas Building, 17th Fl Jl Jend Sudirman Kav 61-62
Telephone: (62-21) 252-1272; Fax: 252-2750, 252-2751; Web site: www.makarim.com
Expertise: Legal Services for Australian and other multinational companies having actual or proposed business interest in Indonesia with particular emphasis on corporate and commercial law, securities regulations, joint ventures and property development and mining law matters.
Linguistic Qualifications: Indonesian and English (Indonesian, Australian, & American Staff).

SOEBAGJO, JATIM & JAROT
Address: Plaza DM 17th Fl., Jl Jend Sudirman Kav 25, Jakarta Selatan 12920
Telephone: (62-21) 522-9765 (Hunting); Fax: 522-9752-3; E-mail: dhefirm@sjdlawfirm.com
Expertise: Legal services including advice on banking, taxation, customs and imports, joint ventures, distribution and agency agreements, government contracts, mergers and acquisitions, capital markets, insurance, mining law, construction law, aviation and transport laws and technology transfer.

MR. SANGAP SIDAURUK - SANGAP & REKAN
Address: Jl Raya Basuki Rachmat No. 21, Jakarta 13410
Telephone: (62-21) 856-1186, 85901901; Fax: 8576596. E-mail: sangap_sidauruk@yahoo.com
Expertise: General, Commercial and Criminal Law, Family Law- dissolution of marriage and, custody matters.

SHOLEH, ADNAN & ASSOCIATES
Advocates & Counselors at Law
Address: Graha Pratama 18th Fl, Jl. MT. Haryono Kav 15, Jakarta 12810 Telephone: (62-21) 8379.3601; Fax: (62-21) 8379.3604; E-mail: aw_adnan@saa.co.id , saa_law@saa.co
Managing Partner : Wirawan Adnan; Senior Partner : Sholeh Amin; Senior Patner : Luthfie Hakim. Area of Practice : Criminal law, Civil and Commercial Litigation, Judicial Review in Supreme Court and Constitutional Court, Resolution of Disputes in the Oil Industry, Labor /Industrial Law

WIJAYA & COMPANY LAW FIRM
Suite 206, 2/F, Prestasi Building Jl Raya Sunan Giri No 5A, Rawamangun Jakarta 13220
Contact: Mr Asep Wijaya. Telephone: (62-21) 475-3173; 289-99218; Fax: 478-65463
E-mail: enquiries@wijayaco.com ; Web site: www.wijayaco.co

Full service Law Firm principally engaged in the provision of wide range legal services to international clients in Indonesia for businesses, families and individuals and for Indonesian-Expatriate Couples.

PT DFDL CONSULTING INDONESIA IN ASSOCIATION WITH MATARAM PARTNERS
Address: Wisma GKBI, 12th floor, Jalan Jenderal Sudirman no. 28, Jakarta 10210
William D. Greenlee, Jr.
Partner (Managing Director Indonesia and Laos, Head of China desk)
Telephone: (62) 811-909060; □ (0) 21 242 068-70; □ (0) 20 77 1000 11
E-mail: william.greenlee@dfdl.com ; web site: www.dfdl.com

BASTAMAN ENRICO BAGUS
Address: Plaza Asia, zone 12C, Jl. Jend. Sudirman Kav. 59, Jakarta 12190
Contact: Enrico Iskandar, Partner, E-mail: enrico@beblaw.co.id ; Bagus Nur Buwono, Parner,
E-mail: bagus@beblaw.co.id ; Meiny Meirany Rasmin, Partner, E-mail: Meiny@beblaw.co.id , web site: www.beblaw.co.id
Expertise: The firm specializes in the representation of foreign and local companies doing business in Indonesia and is supported with lawyers that has broad experience in all aspects of corporate/commercial law, banking, finance and insurance, mergers & acquisitions, capital markets, energy & resources, plantations, property and real estate, hospitality and entertainment, pharmaceutical, IT and telecommunications, intellectual property as well as infrastructure.
The firm has also been acknowledged in the international and highly respected UK based 2009/2010 Legal 500 publication for the last three years. The latest recognition of the firm in Corporate/M&A and Debt Restructuring & Insolvency is set out in the link to the Legal 500 website as follows: http://www.legal500.com/firms/31316-bastaman-enrico-bagus/34255-jakarta .
Language: English and Indonesian.

SINGGIH & PARTNERS LAW OFFICES
Address: Menara Batavia, 22nd Fl., Jl. K.H. Mas Mansyur 126, Jakarta Pusat 10220
Contact: Prasetyo Singgih, Mobile: 81386009989, E-mail: prasetyo.singgihlaw@gmail.com . Telephone: (62-21) 574-1135; Fax: 574-1158/391-6118.
Expertise: Singgih & Partners is a young (established 2001) and small law practice, and are organized for the sole purpose of providing effective services to address any issue in a short period of time. The Law office provides comprehensive legal services which include litigation, pre-litigation, corporate and commercial consultation as well as business advisory and special facilitation services for individuals and other legal entities alike.
Language: English and Indonesian.

AFDHAL & DEDY LAW FIRM
Address: Jl. KS Tubun III No. 20, Slipi, Jakarta Barat 11410
Telephone: (62-21) 5306885, Afdhal Muhammad 81381530266 or 87877823300; Fax: 21 53652210. E-mail: afdhal_sh@yahoo.co.id

MANULLANG & PUTRANTO
Address: Jl. Denpasar Raya blok C4 No. 23, Kompleks Menteri Kuningan, Jakarta Selatan 12950
Telephone: (62-21) 5204989; Fax: 5204990; E-mail: Putranto@wilamarta.com ; web site: www.manullang-putranto.com
Experienced in Family Law & Immigration issues, Mining & Agricultural Law, Commercial Litigation/Dispute Resolution, Intellectual Property Rights, Bankruptcy, Investment & General Corporate.
Language: English and Indonesian

MR SANTOSO H. TRAITMAN & ASSOCIATES
Address: Jl Kepatihan Barat A-5 (Jl Pemuda), Semarang
Telephone: (62-24) 354-6029, 0811-290943; Fax: 354-8679. E-mail: rohadish@hotmail.com
Expertise: Banking Affairs.
Linguistic Qualifications: Indonesian and some English

JACOB & ASSOCIATES
Address: Jl Kemasan 22 RT 07/RW 01, Kepatihan, Kulon Jebres, Solo 57129
Telephone: (62-271) 565-82
Associates: Mr Jacob Chris, SH, Mr Joni Laksito, SH, Mr Theo Wahyu Winarto, SH,
Mr Sunarto, SH
Expertise: Civil and Commercial Law, Estate and Trade Dispute cases. Does NOT handle Criminal cases.
Linguistic Qualifications: Indonesian and English.

MS TITIEK R DANUMIHARDJO, S.H.
Address: Jl Purwanggan (in front of Hero), Semarang 50121
Telephone: (62-274) 541-622. E-mail: titiekadp@yahoo.com
Associates: Mr Bastari Ilyas, SH, Mr Abdul Haris Semendawai, SH.
Expertise: Civil and Criminal Laws, Collection Cases, Estate and Trade Disputes.
Linguistic Qualifications: Indonesian and English.

LHS LAW FIRMS - Business Law Advocates & Legal Consultants

Address: Hotel Bugisan, Jl Sugeng Jeroni No 48, Yogyakarta. Telephone: (62) 0818 271155 Web site: www.kantorhukum-lhs.com ; E-mail: info@knatorhukum-lhs.com
Expertise: Business & Administrative Law, Accidents, Civil Litigation, Criminal Law, Debt Recovery, General Practice, Export Import, Personal Injury, Real Estate, Trade and Venture Capital.
Linguistic Qualifications: Indonesian and English.

LHS PARTNERS, ADVOCATERS & LEGAL CONSULTANTS
Business Law & Corporate Law Firm. Address: Jl Raya Yogya – Wonosari KM 7, Wiyorokidul No 1, Yogyakarta. Tel: (62) 0818 278386; Web site: www.kantorhukum-lhs.com ;
E-mail: info@knatorhukum-lhs.com
Expertise: Business & Administrative Law, Accidents, Civil Litigation, Criminal Law, Debt Recovery, General Practice, Export Import, Personal Injury, Real Estate, Trade and Venture Capital.
Linguistic Qualifications: Indonesian and English.

HENRY LIE A WENG SH
Address: Jl. Ir. H. Juanda No.35, Medan, North Sumatra
E-mail: leeaweng@indo.net.id ; Telephone: (62-61) 455-3290; 453-5577; Fax: 451-6555
Expertise: Busniess law; Family law; Permits

CHARLES TIGOR SILALAHI SH
Address: Jl. Prof. Moh. YaminKomp. Serdang Mas Blok C-3, Medan, North Sumatra
E-mail: charlessilalahi@telkom.net.id . Telephone: (62-61) 456-6427; Fax: 456-6427
Expertise: Criminal; Civil; Family law

A YAHYA AMIR SH, IWAN SEMBIRING SH
Address: Jl. Cut Nyak Din No.16, Medan, North Sumatra
Telephone: (62-61) 453-8955; Fax: 453-8933
Expertise: Criminal; Civil; Permits for foreigners

SAKTI HASIBUAN MD, SH
Address: Jl Sutomo No 160-BB, Medan, North Sumatra
Telephone: (62-61) 736-6100, 736-9503; Fax:719-503
Expertise: Civil and Corporate Laws, Family Law - dissolusion of marriage and, custody matters.
Linguistic Qualifications: Indonesian speaking only

AG JACOB MANURUNG SH & ASSOCIATES
Address: Kompleks Tasbi II Blok1 No 85, Medan
Telephone: (62-61) 821-0560; Fax: 821-0560; E-mail: advocate_jacm@yahoo.com

ZAIDUN & PARTNERS
World Trade Center, 4th. Fl., Suit 455–460, Jl. Pemuda No. 27–31, Surabaya 60271
Telephone: (62-31) 546-5740, 546-1835; Fax: 547-0077; E-mail: lawfirm@znp.co.id
Web site: www.znp.co.id
Expertise : Corporation, Business Transactions, Business & Corporate Structuring, Investment, Land & Real Property, Securities & Capital Market, Banking & Finance, International Trade, Employment, Patent and Trade Mark Law, Environmental & Maritime, Alternative Dispute Resolution.
Linguistic Qualifications: Indonesian and English.

MR TRIMOELJA D. SOERJADI
Address: Jl. Embong Sawo 16-18, Surabaya. Telephone: (62-31) 534-4842; Fax: 531-7240
E-mail: tridsoer@sby.dnet.net.id
Expertise: Criminal, Civil, and Commercial Laws; Land Disputes, Family Law - dissolution of marriage and, custody matters.
Linguistic Qualifications: Indonesian, English.

MARKUS SAJOGO & ASSOCIATES - Attorneys & Counselors at Law
Address: Jl. Untung Suropati No. 64, Surabaya 60264
Telephone: (62-31) 567-7140, 561-4624; Fax: 567-1915; E-mail: sajogo@law.com
Expertise : Civil & Criminal Litigation, Labour Law, Legal Aspects of Land and Property Rights, Finance and Banking Law, Investment and Capital Market Law, Legal Aspects of Business and Corporate Law, Alternative Dispute Resolution (A.D.R.), Intellectual Property Rights, Insurance and Collateral Law, Family Law, Auction and Execution of Court Judgment, Domestic and International Adoption, Bankruptcy/Insolvency Law (Receiver or Administrator).
Linguistic Qualifications: Indonesian, English, and Dutch.

AGUS SAPUTRA SH, MH& ASSOCIATION
Address: Komp. Sesetan Agung A-8, Jl. Raya Sesetan, Denpasar - Bali
Telephone: (62-361) 238-880; Fax: 239-996
Expertise: Civil & Commercial; personal injury; family law; commercial law; intellectual property

AMERTA JUSTISIA ADVOCATE OFFICE

Address: Jl. Pulau Tarakan 182nd Fl., Denpasar, Bali
E- mail: ketutsuwiga@yahoo.com ;Telephone: (62-361) 223-006; 0813-38775584; Fax: 223-006
Expertise: Criminal; private; religion; military; business; intellectual property

ANGGIA BROWNE & ASSOC. - Lawyers & Legal Consultants
Address: Jl. By Pass Ngurah Rai No.152, Sanur, Bali
E-mail: alblegal@indosat.net.id ; Telephone: (62-361) 287-960; 281-898; Fax: 361-281322

MR. ROBERT E. PARENGKUAN, SH - ADVOCATE & LEGAL CONSULTANT
Address: Jl. Sudirman No. 11, Manado 95122
Telephone: (62-431) 863-273, 851133; Fax: 851042; E-mail: robertparengkuan@yahoo.co.id
Expertise: Criminal, Civil, and Commercial Laws; Land Disputes, Family Law - dissolusion of marriage and, custody matters.
Linguistic Qualifications: Indonesian, English, and Dutch

I.J. ZEMELMAN, EA – TAXES FOR EXPATS
115 E34th Street, New York, NY 10036 USA
Tel: 646 EXPAT-US (397-2887); Web site: www.taxesforexpats.com ;
Email: questions@taxesforexpats.com

SIMBOLON & PARTNERS Advocates and Counselors at Law
Address: Menara Bidakara 1, 2nd Fl., Jl. Jend. Gatot Subroto Kav. 71-73, Jakarta Selatan 12870
Telephone: (62 21) 8379 3027; Fax: 8379 3014; E-mail: info@simbolon-lawfirm.com
Web: www.simbolon lawfirm.com
Expertise: Corporate & Commercial, Alternative Dispute Resolution and Litigation, Labor and Immigration, Intellectual Property Rights, Debt Recover/Collection, Research on Laws/Regulations; Company Search/Investigation.
Other Services: Court report, Company Search/Report, Establish Off Shore Companies, Corporate Secretary, Representative Office, Safe-Keeping, Notary, Tax Consultant, Appraisal Consultant, Appraisal Consultant, Human Resources Consultant.
Linguistic Qualifications: Indonesia, English

LAOS LAOS INVESTMENT AND BUSINESS CLIMATE - STRATEGIC INFORMATION AND CONTACTACT FOR STARTING BUSINESS IN LAOS

Contact Point
Matt Younger
Economic and Commercial Officer
American Embassy Vientiane, Rue Bartholonie, That Dam, Lao PDR
856-21-26-7156
youngermb@state.gov

After a decade-long experiment with a pure Marxist economy following the founding of the Lao People's Democratic Republic, the Lao PDR launched the "New Economic Mechanism" in 1986. Since that time, the country has gradually implemented the reforms and built the institutions necessary to a market economy. Over the last thirty years, the trend has been slow but steady progress, culminating in accession to the World Trade Organization in February, 2013. Since 2009, annual GPD growth has averaged approximately eight percent.

In order to meet the requirements for entry to the WTO, Laos engaged in major reforms of its economic and trade laws and regulations. The Lao government is now working to implement the commitments embodied in those laws, and to meet the 2015 goal for creation of the ASEAN Economic Community (AEC), which will further liberalize the trading environment and economy. Additionally, WTO and AEC requirements reinforce fuller implementation of the conditions of the 2005 U.S.-Laos Bilateral Trade Agreement.

Economic progress and trade expansion in Laos remain hampered by a low level of human resource development, weak education and health care systems, and a poor, although improving, transportation infrastructure. Institutions, especially in the justice sector, are a work in progress, and regulatory capacity is low. Additionally, increasing corruption has recently become a major concern, and the country has suffered through fiscal and monetary crises in the past year. The Lao economy is highly dependent on exploitation of natural resources, particularly in copper mining and hydropower. Although the services and industrial sectors have grown in recent years, the economy is in need of further diversification, and the majority of the Lao population is still employed in agriculture.

According to the 7th National Socio-Economic Development Plan (NSEDP) 2011-2015, Laos seeks to continue an annual economic growth rate in the neighborhood of 8%. To accomplish this, the government of Laos estimates that it needs approximately US$15 billion of total investment in the next five years, US$7 to US$8 billion of which it plans to source from foreign and domestic private investment. The plan directs the government to formulate "policies that would attract investments in addition to attracting Overseas Development Assistance; begin to implement public investment and investment promotion laws; and increase cooperation with friendly countries and international organizations."

1. OPENNESS TO, AND RESTRICTIONS UPON, FOREIGN INVESTMENT

The government of Lao PDR (GOL) officially welcomes both domestic and foreign investment as it seeks to graduate from Least Developed Country status by the year 2020. The pace of foreign investment has increased over the last several years. Mining and hydropower compose eighty percent of Foreign Direct Investment (FDI). China, Vietnam, Thailand Korea, and Japan are the largest sources of foreign investment.

The 2010 Law on Investment Promotion introduced uniform business registration requirements and tax incentives that apply equally to foreign and domestic investors. Foreigners may invest in any sector or business except those that the government deems to be detrimental to national security, health or national traditions, or to have a negative impact on the natural environment. There are no statutory limits on foreign ownership or control of commercial enterprises, but in practice, many companies seek a local partner. Companies involved in large FDI projects, especially in mining and hydropower, often either find it advantageous or are required to give the government partial ownership, frequently with money borrowed from the investor or multilateral institutions.

Foreign investors seeking to establish operations in Laos are typically required go through several steps prior to commencing operations. In addition to an investment license, foreign investors are required to obtain other permits, including; an annual business registration from the Ministry of Industry and Commerce; a tax registration from the Ministry of Finance; a business logo registration from the Ministry of Public Security; permits from each line ministry related to the investment (i.e., Ministry of Industry and Commerce for manufacturing; Ministry of Energy and Mines for power sector development); appropriate permits from local authorities; and an import-export license, if applicable. Obtaining the necessary permits can pose a challenge, especially in areas outside the capital. In 2013, the Lao government began allowing businesses to apply for tax registration at the time of incorporation, slightly simplifying the business registration process.

The Lao government has attempted to streamline business registration through the use of a "one-stop shop" model. For general business activities, this service is located in the Ministry of Industry and Commerce. For activities requiring a government concession, the service is located in the Ministry of Planning and Investment. For Special Economic Zones (SEZ), one-stop registration is run through the Secretariat to the Lao National Committee on Special Economic Zones (SNCSEZ) in the Office of the Prime Minister. According to PM Decree 177, the Savan-Seno SEZ authority is required to establish one-stop service to facilitate the issuing of investment licenses and improve the efficiency of business operations. In practice, it appears as though SEZ applications involve several different permissions and vary widely across SEZs. For clarification of one-stop shop procedures it is recommended that investors contact the SNCSEZ directly at: **sez@sncsez.gov.la**

Foreign partners in a joint venture must contribute at least thirty percent (30%) of the venture's registered capital. Capital contributed in foreign currency must be converted into kip based on the exchange rate of the Bank of the Lao People's Democratic Republic on the day of the capital contribution. Wholly foreign-owned companies may be either a new company or a branch of an existing foreign enterprise. Throughout the period of operation of a foreign investment enterprise, the assets of the enterprise must not be less than its registered capital.

Individual companies in the petrochemical industry are required to file an annual import plan. The government controls the retail price and profit margins of gasoline and diesel. Government documents articulating the restrictions and explaining the policy are difficult to obtain. Goods prohibited for import and export range from explosives and weapons, to literature that presents a negative view of the Lao government, to certain forestry products and wildlife. Agriculture production and most manufacturing production are private. State-owned enterprises (SOEs) currently account for only one percent of total employment. Over 90% of manufacturers have fewer than 10 employees. Equity in medium and large-sized SOEs can be obtained through a joint venture with the Lao government.

Although accurate statistics are difficult to obtain, there is no question that foreign investment has trended dramatically upward over the last several years, going from $1.2 billion in 2012 to $1.8 billion in 2013. There are also small but growing signs of growth in higher-quality FDI, focused on manufacturing, largely through one Special Economic Zone in the southern part of the country.

Measure	Year	Rank or value	Website Address
TI Corruption Perceptions index	2013	(140 of 177)	http://cpi.transparency.org/cpi2013/results/
Heritage Foundation's Economic Freedom index	2013	(144 of 178)	http://www.heritage.org/index/ranking
World Bank's Doing Business Report "Ease of Doing	2013	(159 of 189)	http//doingbusiness.org/rankings

Business"			
World Bank GNI per capita	2012	USD 1270	http://data.worldbank.org/indicator/NY.GNP.PCAP.CD

TABLE 1B – 2014 Lao PDR Millennium Challenge Scorecard:

MCC Scorecard Categories	Year	Percentage Score	Raw Score
MCC Government Effectiveness	FY 2014	56%	.04
MCC Rule of Law	FY 2014	60%	.07
MCC Control of Corruption	FY 2014	40%	-.13
MCC Fiscal Policy	FY 2014	49%	-3.1
MCC Trade Policy	FY 2014	12%	58.6
MCC Regulatory Quality	FY 2014	44%	-0.09
MCC Business Start-Up	FY 2014	23%	0.771
MCC Land Rights and Access	FY 2014	66%	0.68
MCC Natural Resource Protection	FY 2014	81%	93.9
MCC Access to Credit	FY 2014	36%	22
MCC Inflation	FY 2014	72%	4.3

The Millennium Challenge Corporation, a U.S. Government entity charged with delivering development grants to countries that have demonstrated a commitment to reform, produced scorecards for countries with a 2012 per capita gross national income (GNI) or $4,085 or less. A list of countries/economies with MCC scorecards and links to those scorecards is available here: **http://www.mcc.gov/pages/selection/scorecards**. Details on each of the MCC's indicators and a guide to reading the scorecards are available here: **http://www.mcc.gov/documents/reports/reference-2013001142401-fy14-guide-to-the-indicators.pdf**

2. CONVERSION AND TRANSFER POLICIES

In 2013, Laos suffered fiscal and monetary difficulties which resulted in low levels of foreign reserves. In response, the Bank of the Lao PDR (BOL) imposed daily limits on converting funds from Lao Kip into U.S. Dollars and Thai Baht, leading to difficulties in obtaining foreign exchange in Laos. The BOL also imposed restrictions on loans made in USD and Baht, limiting them to businesses which generated foreign currency. There were no reports of restrictions on, or difficulties in, repatriating or transferring funds associated with an investment.

In order to facilitate business transactions, foreign investors generally open commercial bank accounts in both local and foreign convertible currency at domestic and foreign banks in Laos. The Enterprise Accounting Law places no limitations on foreign investors transferring after-tax profits, income from technology transfer, initial capital, interest, wages and salaries, or other remittances to the company's home country or third countries provided that they request approval from the Lao government. Foreign enterprises must report on their performance annually and submit annual financial statements to the Ministry of Planning and Investment (MPI).

The Bank of Lao PDR manages the Lao currency, the kip, under a managed floating exchange rate in which it seeks to maintain its value in a band of plus or minus five percent around the nominal exchange rate with the U.S. dollar and Thai baht. Lao PDR is listed as a high-risk jurisdiction for money laundering/combating the financing of terrorism by the Financial Action Task Force (FATF) and has strategic deficiencies in its AML/CFT regime. In 2013, the Bank of Lao PDR agreed with the Asia Pacific Group, a regional FATF-body, to implement an action plan to address AML/CFT deficiencies.

3. EXPROPRIATION AND COMPENSATION

Foreign assets and investments in Laos are protected by laws and regulations against seizure, confiscation, or nationalization except when deemed necessary for a public purpose, in which case foreign investors are supposed to be compensated. Revocation of an investment license cannot be appealed to an independent body, and companies whose licenses are revoked must then quickly liquidate their assets.

Since 2012, Sanum Investments, a subsidiary of Lao Holdings, Inc., a company incorporated in Aruba and owned by American citizens, has been involved in a business dispute with its Lao partner. Thus far, court decisions in the case have been uniformly in favor of the Lao partner and could be construed as implicitly forcing local ownership. In addition, the company was subjected to audits and tax enforcement decisions that Sanum has alleged amount to expropriation. Sanum filed a case against the Lao PDR at the World Bank's International Center for the Settlement of Investment Disputes in 2012.

4. DISPUTE SETTLEMENT

The Lao judicial system is not independent and faces challenges in meeting the needs of a modern market economy. Contract law in Laos is lacking in many areas important to trade and commerce. While it does provide for sanctity of contracts, in practice contracts are subject to political interference and patronage. A contract can be voided if it is disadvantageous to one party, or if it conflicts with state or public interests. Foreign businessmen have described contracts in Laos as being considered "a framework for negotiation" rather than a binding agreement. Although a commercial court system exists, in practice most judges adjudicating commercial disputes have little training in commercial law. Those considering doing business in Laos are strongly urged to contact a reputable law firm for additional advice on contracts.

According to the Law on Investment Promotion, investors should resolve disputes in the following order: mediation; administrative dispute resolution; dispute resolution by the Committee for Economic Dispute Resolution; and finally, litigation. However, due to the poor state of the Lao legal system and low capacity of most Lao legal administrators, foreign investors are generally advised to seek arbitration outside the country.

Laos is not a member of the International Center for the Settlement of Investment Disputes. It became a party to the New York Convention of 1958 on the Recognition and Enforcement of Foreign Arbitral Awards on September 15, 1998, but Laos has never been asked to enforce a foreign arbitral award. Laos is a member of the United Nations Convention on International Trade Law.

In disputes involving the Ministry of Planning and Investment, decisions can only be appealed back to the Ministry itself. There is no separate independent body. Thus a company which feels it is receiving unfair treatment from the government has no independent recourse. Lao laws often contradict each other and lack implementing regulations. Some laws have been officially translated into English, including the business, tax, bankruptcy, customs, and secured transaction laws. The reliability of unofficial translations varies considerably. Application of Lao law remains inconsistent and knowledge of the laws themselves is often limited (especially outside the capital). The existence of a large number of government decrees, sometimes unpublished, further complicates the situation.

A commercial court does exist in Laos. Laos has no anti-trust statutes. The bankruptcy law permits either the business or creditor the right to petition the court for a bankruptcy judgment, and allows businesses the right to request mediation. There is no record of foreign-owned enterprises, whether as debtors or as creditors, petitioning the courts for a bankruptcy judgment.

5. PERFORMANCE REQUIREMENTS AND INVESTMENT INCENTIVES

Laos does not impose performance requirements and its regulations appear to be broadly consistent with WTO Trade Related Investment Measures (TRIMs), although it has notified the WTO that it will avail itself of transition periods for least-developed countries in completely phasing out local content and export performance requirements. Foreign investors are encouraged to give priority to Lao citizens in recruiting and hiring. Foreign personnel can be hired, although they may not normally exceed 10% of the enterprise's total labor force, with exceptions for skilled labor or politically important projects. Before bringing in foreign labor, foreign enterprises must apply for work permits from the Ministry of Labor and Social Welfare. A list of foreign personnel must also be submitted to MPI.

Laos grants incentives for foreign investment depending on industry sectors and activities promoted by the government, and the level of infrastructure and socio-economic development in specific geographic zones. Under Articles 49, 50 and 51 of the Law on Investment Promotion, the government defines agriculture, industry, handicraft and services as promoted activities.

Investment promotion is divided into 3 levels: Level 1 - high, Level 2 - medium and Level 3- low. Additionally, the country is divided into three promotion zones. Zone 1 is defined as areas lacking in socio-economic infrastructure – primarily mountainous and remote areas – and is assigned a high level of investment promotion. Zone 2 applies to areas with socio-economic infrastructure that is partially able to facilitate investments and is given medium priority. Zone 3 has infrastructure available to support investments and is assigned a low level of investment promotion.

In Zone 1, Level 1 investments receive profit tax exemptions for 10 years, Level 2 investments for 6 years and Level 3 investments for 4 years.

In Zone 2, Level 1 investments receive profit tax exemptions for 6 years, Level 2 investments for 4 years and Level 3 investments for 2 years.

In Zone 3, Level 1 investments receive profit tax exemptions for 4 years, Level 2 investments for two years and Level 3 investments for 1 year. Profit tax exemptions in all zones start from the date the enterprise commences operations.

Incentives related to customs duties, access to finance, and other taxes are described in Articles 52, 53 and 54 of the Law on Investment Promotion. As of 2011, foreign investors and workers must pay an income tax of 24% to the Lao Government, unless they are citizens of a country with which the Lao Government has signed a double-taxation agreement. Previously, this rate was 10%.

The United States does not have a double-taxation agreement with Laos. Article 67 of the Law on Investment Promotion stipulates that foreign investors and their families, including foreign professionals and foreign employees of an enterprise, may obtain multiple entry visas with a maximum term of five years. The government routinely approves long-term residence in the Lao PDR for foreign investors.

The government began replacing the turnover tax with a Value Added Tax (VAT) in 2010. Foreign investors are not required to pay import duty on equipment, spare parts and other materials used in the operation of their enterprises. Raw materials and intermediate goods imported for the purpose of processing and re-export are also exempt from import duties. Raw materials and intermediate goods imported for the purpose of import substitution are eligible for import duty reductions on a case-by-case basis.

Foreign enterprises are also eligible for profit tax and import duty reductions or exemptions on an individual basis, if the investment is determined by the GOL to benefit to Laos' socio-economic development. To date the Lao Government appears to have honored its incentives. Annual business license renewal is contingent upon certification that corporate income taxes have been paid. Investors report difficulties in obtaining tax certifications in a timely manner.

6. RIGHT TO PRIVATE OWNERSHIP AND ESTABLISHMENT

The GOL recognizes the right of private ownership, and foreigners may transfer shares of a foreign-invested company without prior government approval. However, the business law requires that all shareholders be listed in the articles of association, and changes in the articles of association of a foreign-invested company must be approved by Ministry of Planning and Investment. Thus, transferring shares in a foreign-invested company registered in Laos does require the indirect approval of the government.

7. PROTECTION OF PROPERTY RIGHTS

Foreign investors are not permitted to own land in fee-simple. However, Article 58 of the Law on Investment Promotion stipulates that foreign investors with registered investment capital of US$500,000 or above are entitled to purchase land use rights of less than 800 square meters in order to build housing or office buildings. The GOL grants long-term leases, and allows the ownership of leases and the right to transfer and improve leasehold interests. Government approval is not required to transfer property interests, but the transfer must be registered and a registration fee paid.

A creditor may enforce security rights against a debtor and the concept of a mortgage does exist. Although the GOL is engaged in a land parceling and titling project through the Ministry of Natural Resources and Environment, it remains difficult to determine if a piece of property is encumbered in Laos. Enforcement of mortgages is complicated by the legal protection given mortgagees against forfeiture of their sole place of residence.

Laos provides for secured interest in moveable and non-moveable property under the 2005 Law on Secured Transactions and a 2011 implementing decree from the Prime Minister. In 2013, the State Assets Management Authority at the Ministry of Finance launched a new Secured Transaction Registry (STR), intended to expand access to credit for individuals and smaller firms. The STR allows for registration of movable assets such as vehicles and equipment so that they may be easily verified by financial institutions and used as collateral for loans.

Intellectual Property: A government reorganization in 2011 created the Ministry of Science and Technology, which controls the issuance of patents, copyrights and trademarks. Laos is a member of the ASEAN Common Filing System on patents but lacks qualified patent examiners. Since Thailand and Laos have a bilateral Intellectual Property Rights (IPR) agreement, in principle a patent issued in Thailand would also be recognized in Laos.

Copyright protection in Laos is weak. There is no system to issue copyrights in Laos, only a certification of copyright information. Laos is a member of the World Intellectual Property Organization (WIPO) Convention and the Paris Convention on the Protection of Industrial Property but has not yet joined the Bern Convention on Copyrights.

In 2011 the National Assembly passed a comprehensive revision of the Law on Intellectual Property which brings it into compliance with WIPO and Trade-Related Aspects of Intellectual Property standards (TRIPS). The consolidation of responsibility for IPR under the Ministry of Science and Technology is a positive development, but it lacks enforcement capacity.

For additional information about treaty obligations and points of contact at local IP offices, please see WIPO's country profiles at **http://www.wipo.int/directory/en/**.

Embassy point of contact: Matt Younger **youngermb@state.gov**

8. TRANSPARENCY OF THE REGULATORY SYSTEM

Principal laws, regulations, decrees and guidelines governing international trade and investment are available to the public, although not all have been officially translated into English. Laws and their schedules for implementation are customarily published in Lao daily newspapers, and relevant line ministries are beginning to put laws and regulations on websites.

The National Assembly includes a step for public consultations in the legislative process prior to sending laws to the Prime Minister for consideration. However, a highly centralized decision-making process, combined with difficulties in obtaining information, can make the regulatory system appear arbitrary and inscrutable. The government purports to seek the advice given of the business community through the Lao Business Forum.

In 2012, the National Assembly passed the Law on Making Legislation, which requires 60-day periods for public comment and regulatory impact assessment notes of all new draft legislation. In 2013, the Lao Official Gazette opened online, a landmark achievement in legal transparency for the country. The gazette will facilitate the 60-day comment period, and the Ministry of Justice has committed to publishing all current Lao laws on the site. The gazette can be accessed here: **http://laoofficialgazette.gov.la/index.php?r=site/index**

9. EFFICIENT CAPITAL MARKETS AND PORTFOLIO INVESTMENT

Laos does not have a well-developed capital market, although government policies increasingly support the formation of capital and free flow of financial resources. Due to a monetary and fiscal crisis in 2013, there have been liquidity concerns, particularly related to foreign currency. The soundness of the banking system also appears to have suffered in the past year due to lending to off-budget infrastructure projects, and there are reports of some companies in the construction sector facing asset seizures by commercial banks.

The largest denomination of currency is 100,000 kip (about $12.50). Credit is generally not available on the local market for large capital investments, although letters of credit for export can sometimes be obtained locally. In January 2014, Laos issued a second round of government bonds denominated in Thai Baht, raising approximately $90 million. Its first foreign currency denominated bond sale, also in Thai Baht, raised $49 million in 2013.

The banking system is under the supervision of the Bank of Lao PDR, and includes 32 banks with assets of approximately US$6.8 billion. Private foreign banks can establish branches in all provinces of Laos. Domestic credit growth has been very high in the last decade and remained so at 31% year-over-year through September 2013. The BOL reports an increase in ATMs from 442 in 2012 to 622 through the middle of FY 2013. Technical assistance to Laos' financial sector has led to some reforms but overall capacity within the governance structure remains poor.

The Lao Securities Exchange (LSX) began operations in 2011 with two stocks listed, both of them state-owned – the Banque Pour l'Commerce Exterieur (BCEL), and electrical utility Electricity du Laos (EDL). In 2013, the LSX listed a third company that runs exhibitions and convention centers and appears to be largely privately-held. In 2012, the GOL increased the proportion of shares that foreigners can hold on the LSX from 10 to 20 percent.

10. COMPETITION FROM STATE-OWNED ENTERPRISES

The GOL maintains ownership stakes in key sectors of the economy such as telecommunications, energy, finance, and mining. Where state interests conflict with private ownership, the state is in a position of advantage.

In 2011, under the auspices of the Ministry of Post and Telecommunications, four large telecoms with high state ownership stakes cut service to a foreign-owned telecom in retaliation for alleged marketing violations. In 2012, private carrier Lao Central Airlines opened service on international and domestic routes, challenging the monopoly previously enjoyed by state-owned Lao Airlines.

There are reportedly 139 State-Owned Enterprises in Laos with $2.4 billion in assets. The government appears to be considering methods to increase private ownership in some SOE such as Lao Airlines, potentially through listing on the LSX.

11. CORPORATE SOCIAL RESPONSIBILITY

Corporate Social Responsibility is not yet well understood and recognized by Lao producers and consumers, but protection of the environment and mitigation of social impacts are stressed by some foreign companies, particularly in the natural resources and energy sectors.

12. POLITICAL VIOLENCE

Laos is a peaceful and politically stable country. The risk of political violence directed at foreign enterprises or businesspersons is low.

13. CORRUPTION

Corruption is a serious problem in Laos and appears to be growing alongside the economy. The GOL has developed several anti-corruption laws but enforcement remains weak, with no high-profile cases ever having been brought to trial. According to the State Inspection Authority, the Lao Government has prosecuted some individuals for corruption but it cannot publicize the information. In September 2009, Laos ratified the United Nations Convention Against Corruption.

The State Inspection Authority, located in the Prime Minister's Office, is charged with analyzing corruption at the national level and serves as a central office for gathering details and evidence of suspected corruption. Additionally, the State Inspection Department in each Ministry is responsible for combat internal ministry corruption. Laos is not a signatory to the OECD Convention on Combating Bribery. Both giving and accepting bribes are criminal acts punishable by fine and/or imprisonment. Foreign businesses frequently cite corruption as an obstacle to operating in Laos. Officials commonly accept bribes for the purpose of approving or expediting applications.

In 2014 an asset declaration regime entered into force for government officials requiring them to declare income, assets and debts for themselves and their family members. Assets over $2500 are required to be disclosed, including land, structures, vehicles and equipment, as well as cash, gold, and financial instruments. However, the effectiveness of this program has yet to be determined.

14. BILATERAL INVESTMENT AGREEMENTS

Laos has bilateral investment agreements with Australia, Burma, Cambodia, China, Cuba, Denmark, France, Germany, India, Indonesia, Japan, Kuwait, Malaysia, Mongolia, Netherlands, North Korea, Pakistan, Philippines, Russia, South Korea, Singapore, Sweden, Switzerland, Thailand, the United Kingdom, and Vietnam. On February 1, 2005 a Bilateral Trade Agreement (BTA) came into force between the U.S. and the Government of Laos. Laos and the United States do not have a bilateral taxation treaty.

15. OPIC AND OTHER INVESTMENT INSURANCE PROGRAMS

The United States and Laos signed an Overseas Private Investment Cooperation (OPIC) agreement in March 1996. OPIC does not have any projects ongoing in Laos but the potential exists in the Lao economy for OPIC involvement. In 1998 Laos signed an agreement with the Multilateral Investment Guarantee Agency (MIGA). The Lao kip is not an internationally traded currency and fluctuated in a narrow range against the U.S. dollar in 2012.

16. LABOR

70% of Laos' work force is engaged in subsistence agriculture. There are shortages in skilled labor across virtually the entire economy. The lack of a skilled workforce is consistently cited by foreign and domestic companies as the main constraint to growth. The estimated migration of Lao labor to Thailand numbers in the hundreds of thousands. At the same time, Laos has in recent years received a large influx of labor from China and Vietnam who largely come to work with Chinese and Vietnamese companies. Generally, the current extremely tight labor market places labor-management relations on a somewhat equal footing; if employees are not satisfied at their current job, they simply leave.

The 1994 labor law provides for the formation of trade unions; specifies working hours and compensation standards; allows for maternity leave and benefits; workers' compensation and retirement benefits; and establishes procedures for labor dispute resolution. There are, however, no unions independent of the Lao Federation of Trade Unions, a Communist Party organization. In January 2012, the Lao government raised the minimum wage for unskilled workers to US$78 per month based on a six-day, eight hour per day work week. Reforms to the labor law passed in 2014 contained the first mention in Lao law of collective bargaining, but the country still lacks freedom of association for labor, independent unions, or a detailed framework for independent collective bargaining. There is virtually no avenue for, or risk of, labor strikes in Laos currently. In 2014, Laos approved a national plan of action to combat the worst forms of child labor and the Ministry of Labor and Social Welfare is working to improve its capacity for labor inspections.

Laos has human resource deficiencies in virtually all sectors. English is not widely spoken. In 2012, about 16 percent of the population age 15 and above remained illiterate. The shortage of skilled labor is particularly acute in high-tech sectors. The country has a few technical colleges, one scientific research facility-- the National Institute of Hygiene and Epidemiology--and almost no effective post-graduate degree programs.

The Lao Government has dedicated few of its own resources to improve the country's education system and tends to rely heavily on international donors for support; there are a few state training programs and some foreign funded programs. Potential investors should note the need to dedicate substantial resources, both human and capital, to train employees. It is not unusual for foreign investors to bring in Thai managers due to a lack of skilled local personnel.

17. FOREIGN TRADE ZONES/FREE PORTS

The Foreign Investment Law allows for the establishment of Special Economic Zones (SEZ) and Specific Economic Zones as an investment incentive. Prime Ministerial Decree 443 on Special Economic Zones and Specific Economic Zones was issued in 2010 and provides guidance on the establishment of the zones.

Special Economic Zones are intended to support development of new infrastructure and commercial facilities and include incentives for investment. Specific Economic Zones are meant to develop existing infrastructure and facilities and provide a lower level of incentives and support than Special Economic Zones. Laos plans to construct 25 special and specific zones in the next ten years via foreign direct investment of US$3 billion.

There are currently 10 different economic zones across the country, including: Savan-Seno Special Economic Zone, Golden Triangle Special Economic Zone, Boten Beautiful Land Specific Economic Zone, Vientiane Industrial and Trade Zone, Saysettha Development Zone, Phoukyou Specific Economic Zone, Thatluang Lake Specific Economic Zone, Longthanh – Vientiane Specific Economic Zone, Dongphosy Specific Economic Zone and Thakhek Specific Economic Zone.

The Savan-Seno Special Economic Zone in Savannakhet province is legitimately developing as a production, supply, and distribution center with increasingly sophisticated manufacturing businesses and advanced infrastructure. Other SEZ's in the northern part of the country have experienced problems associated with casino gambling, prostitution and drug trafficking.

Lao laws pertaining to trade are supposedly applied uniformly across the entire customs territory of Laos, including all sub-central authorities, special economic zones, specific economic zones and border trade regions. In reality, however, customs practices vary widely at ports of entry in the provinces. Centralization of customs collection by the central government has led to more uniform practices and increased the flow of customs revenue to the central government. In order to comply with National Single Window requirements under the ASEAN Single Window, in 2012 Laos began operating the Automated System for Customs Data (ASYCUDA) at the busiest point of cross-border trade, the Lao-Thai Friendship Bridge linking Vientiane with Thailand and has slowly expanded the use of ASYCUDA at other border crossings as well.

18. FOREIGN DIRECT INVESTMENT AND FOREIGN PORTFOLIO INVESTMENT STATISTICS

Key Macroeconomic data, U.S. FDI in host country/economy

	Bank of the Lao PDR Annual Report	USG or international statistical source	USG or international

					Source of data (Source of Data: BEA; IMF; Eurostat; UNCTAD, Other)
Economic Data	Year	Amount	Year	Amount	
Host Country Gross Domestic Product (GDP) (Millions U.S. Dollars)	2012	9100	2012	9400	http://www.worldbank.org/en/country
Foreign Direct Investment	Ministry of Planning and Investment		USG or international statistical source		USG or international Source of data: BEA; IMF; Eurostat; UNCTAD, Other
U.S. FDI in partner country (Millions U.S. Dollars, stock positions)	3.513	NA	Insert 2012	Amount 0	(BEA) click selections to reach. Bureau of Economic Analysis Balance of Payments and Direct Investment Position Data U.S. Direct Investment Position Abroad on a Historical-Cost Basis By Country only (all countries) (Millions of Dollars)
Host country's FDI in the United States (Millions U.S. Dollars, stock positions)	NA	NA	NA	NA	(BEA) click selections to reach Balance of Payments and Direct Investment Position Data Foreign Direct Investment Position in the United States on a Historical-Cost Basis By Country only (all countries) (Millions of Dollars)
Total inbound stock of FDI as % host GDP (calculate)	Insert 2012	Amount 20.3%	Insert (Year)	Amount	

LAWYERS IN LAWS - IMPORTANT CONTACTS

There are a limited number of independent lawyers in Laos. A lawyer seeking to represent a foreign citizen in a criminal matter may need to obtain prior permission from the Ministry of Justice.

The U.S. Embassy in Vientiane, Laos assumes no responsibility or liability for the professional ability or reputation of, or the quality of services provided by, the following persons or firms. Inclusion on this list is in no way an endorsement by the Department of State or the U.S. Embassy. Names are listed alphabetically, and the order in which they appear has no other significance. The information in the list on professional credentials, areas of expertise and language ability are provided directly by the lawyers; the Embassy is not in a position to vouch for such information. You may receive additional information about the individuals on the list by contacting the local bar association or the local licensing authorities.

1. **Mr. William GREENLEE, Jr.**

Tel: 856-21-242-068

856-21-242-069

856-21-242-070

DFDL Mekong Law Group Fax: 856-21-218-422

PO Box 2920

Vientiane, Lao PDR Website:www.dfdl.com

Email: Laos@dfdl.com

William.Greenlee@dfdlmekong.com

Languages: English, Mandarin, Thai, Bahasa Indonesian

Areas of Expertise: Banking/Financial, Commercial/Business, Foreign Investments, Marketing, Patents/Trademarks/Copyrights, Damages, Collections, Contracts, Transportation, Corporations, Foreign Claims, Estates, Taxes, Government Relations, Labor

2. Mr. Brennan COLEMAN

Tel: 856-21-242-068

856-21-242-069

856-21-242-070

DFDL Mekong Law Group Fax: 856-21-218-422

PO Box 2920 Cell: 856-20-7878-7699

Vientiane, Lao PDR Website: www.dfdl.com

Email: Brennan.Coleman@dfdl.com

Languages: English

Areas of Expertise: Banking/Financial, Commercial/Business, Foreign Investments, Marketing, Patents/Trademarks/Copyrights, Damages, Collections, Contracts, Transportation, Corporations, Foreign Claims, Taxes, Government Relations, Labor

3. Mr. Somphou KEOMOUNMANY Tel: 856-21-454-300

Ban Naxay, Xaysettha District Cell: 856-20-5562-6676

Vientiane, Lao PDR Email:bearsomphou@yahoo.com

Languages (in addition to Lao): English

Areas of Expertise: Child Custody, Child Protection, Marriage/Divorce, Patents/Trademarks/Copyrights, Contracts, Labor

4. Mr. Viengsavanh PHANTHALY
Ban Phonpapao, Sisattanak District
Vientiane, Lao PDR
Tel: 856-21-330470
Cell: 856-20-5422-3377
Email: vlaw@live.com
v.phanthaly@vlaw.la
www.vlaw.la

Languages (in addition to Lao): English, Vietnamese, Thai, Japanese

Areas of Expertise: Family, Adoptions, Marriage/Divorce, Insurance, Banking/Financial, Commercial/Business, Foreign Investments, Marketing, Patents/Trademarks/Copyrights, Civil, Criminal, Damages, Contracts, Transportation, Corporations, Foreign Claims, Estates, Taxes, Government Relations, Labor, Immigration, Accidents

5. Mr. Sabh PHOMMARATH
Ban Anou, Chanthabury District
Vientiane, Lao PDR
Cell: 856-20-2220-2297
Email:sabhpr123@gmail.com
Languages (in addition to Lao): English, French, Thai
Areas of Expertise: Family, Marriage/Divorce, Foreign Investments, Marketing, Civil, Criminal, Contracts

6. Mr. Veng SAYSANA
Ban Naxay, Xaysettha District
Vientiane, Lao PDR
Cell: 856-20-5561-2883
Email:vengsaysana@yahoo.com
Languages (in addition to Lao): English, French
Areas of Expertise: Family, Adoption, Child Custody, Parental/Child Abduction, Child Protection, Marriage/Divorce, Banking/Financial, Commercial/Business, Foreign Investments, Marketing, Patents/Trademarks/Copyrights, Civil, Criminal, Damages, Narcotics, Collections, Contracts, Corporations, Aeronautical/Maritime, Estates, Government Relations, Labor

7. Mr. Vannloh SISOPHA
128 Saigon Rd.
Tel: 856-21-218-426
Cell: 856-20-5582-8178
Email:vannloh@gmail.com
Ban Anou, Chanthabury District
Vientiane, Lao PDR
Languages (in addition to Lao): English, French
Areas of Expertise: Family, Commercial/Business, Civil, Criminal

8. Mr. Douangsim SOUPHANTHONG
Cell: 856-20-5561-8379
Lao Bar Association, Ban Anou
Vientiane, Lao PDR
Languages (in addition to Lao): French, limited English
Areas of Expertise: Family, Adoption, Child Protection, Marriage/Divorce, Foreign Investment, Civil, Criminal, Damages, Contracts, Government Relations, Labor, Immigration, Accidents

9. Mr. Mixay THEPMANY
Ban Savang, Chanthabury District
Vientiane, Lao PDR
Cell: 856-20-5567-6383
Fax: 856-21-219051
Email: mthepmany@yahoo.com
Languages (in addition to Lao): English, French, Thai
Areas of Expertise: Family, Adoption, Child Custody, Child Protection, Marriage/Divorce, Commercial/Business, Foreign Investments, Civil, Criminal, Contracts, Labor

10. Mr. Sysavong VITHASAY
Ban Phayawath, Sisattanak District
Vientiane, Lao PDR
Fax: 856-21-353953
Cell: 856-20-5551-4259
Languages (in addition to Lao): French, Thai, limited English
Areas of Expertise: Family, Marriage/Divorce, Commercial/Business, Foreign Investments, Marketing, Civil, Criminal, Damages, Narcotics, Contracts, Labor

11. Mr. Manolin THEPKHAMVONG
Ban Sapanthong-kang, Sisattanak District

Vientiane, Lao PDR Email: m.thepkhamvong@vlaw.la
Languages (in addition to Lao): English, Thai
Areas of Expertise: Family, Civil, Criminal, Damages, Public Interest, land, environment protection, water and water recourses, narcotic, woman and children protection.

MALAYSIA INVESTMENT AND BUSINESS CLIMATE - STRATEGIC INFORMATION AND CONTACTS FOR STARTING BUSINESS

The Government of Malaysia encourages foreign direct investment (FDI), although it maintains restrictions or limits on investment in some sectors. It actively reaches out to targeted industries and negotiates incentive packages to attract FDI. Malaysia provides a number of incentives, particularly in export-oriented high-tech industries and "back office" service operations. Prime Minister Najib Razak has made generating new domestic and foreign investment a centerpiece of his economic reforms. Inbound FDI has been steady in nominal terms, and Malaysia's performance in attracting FDI relative to both earlier decades and the rest of the Association of Southeast Asian Nations (ASEAN) has slowed.

According to the 2013 Organization for Economic Cooperation and Development (OECD) Investment Policy Review of Malaysia, FDI to Malaysia began to decline in 1992, and private investment overall started to slide in 1997 following the Asian financial crisis. The OECD concludes that Malaysia's FDI levels are at record high levels in absolute terms, but at an all-time low as a percentage of GDP. Moreover, Malaysia's percentage of foreign direct investment into the ASEAN member states is now lower than its share of the group's GDP.

As a destination for FDI, Malaysia's attractiveness for lower-wage manufacturing has diminished as years of steady economic growth have increased average wage levels making Malaysia an upper middle-income country. The Malaysian Government seeks to move the economy further "up the value chain" to high income status by promoting investment in higher value added manufacturing and service sectors. The National Economic Advisory Council (NEAC) has been working since 2010 to improve Malaysia's competitiveness as a foreign investment destination to meet the country's goal of becoming a high-income economy by 2020.

Since Prime Minister Najib's ascension to power in 2009, his administration has progressively introduced a series of initiatives, including the 2010 Economic Transformation Program (ETP), focusing on policy measures to improve competitiveness and investment in 12 key economic area, including electrical and electronics (E&E), medical devices, green energy, machinery and equipment, oil and gas, and transportation, to accelerate economic growth. The ETP also targets investment into resource-based industries and some services sub-sectors, including logistics, though these are also subject to foreign investment conditions or restrictions. Another initiative, the Government Transformation Program (GTP) addresses governance and quality of life issues, and aims to reduce corruption and crime, to improve education, urban public transport and rural basic infrastructure, and to reduce the number of low-income households.

The climate has been conducive to U.S. investment. The largest U.S. investments are in the oil and gas sector, manufacturing, and financial services. Firms with significant investment in Malaysia's oil and gas and petrochemical sectors include: ExxonMobil, Caltex, ConocoPhillips, Murphy Oil, Hess Oil, Halliburton, Dow Chemical and Eastman Chemicals. Major semiconductor manufacturers, including Freescale, Texas Instruments, Intel, and others have substantial operations in Malaysia, as do electronics manufacturers Western Digital, Honeywell, Komag, Agilent, and Motorola. In recent years Malaysia has attracted significant investment in the production of solar panels, including from U.S. firms. Virtually all major Japanese consumer electronics firms (Sony, Fuji, Panasonic, Matsushita, Hitachi, etc.) have facilities in Malaysia.

1. OPENNESS TO, AND RESTRICTIONS UPON, FOREIGN INVESTMENT

Attitude toward Foreign Direct Investment

Malaysia has one of the world's most trade-dependent economies with trade reaching 165% of annual GDP according to the World Trade Organization. The Malaysian government values foreign investment as a powerful force for the continued economic development of the country, but is hampered by restrictions in some sectors and an at times burdensome regulatory regime. However, the government continues to liberalize and in some cases remove investment restrictions.

In 2009, Malaysia removed its former Foreign Investment Committee (FIC) investment guidelines, enabling transactions for acquisitions of interests, mergers, and takeovers of local companies by domestic or foreign parties without FIC approval. While the FIC itself still exists, it now only reviews the purchase by foreigners of commercial properties valued greater than at MYR 20 million (approximately USD 6.5 million) from the bumiputera (ethnic Malays and other indigenous ethnicities in Malaysia).

Since 2009, the government has liberalized the services sector to attract more foreign investment. Following liberalization of activities ranging from computer-related consultancies, tourism, and freight transportation, the government in 2011 began to allow 100% foreign ownership across the following sectors: healthcare, retail, education as well as professional, environmental, and courier services. Limits on foreign ownership remain in place across much of telecommunications, financial services, and transportation.

Foreign investments in services, whether in fully liberalized or controlled sub-sectors, remain subject to review and approval by ministries and agencies with jurisdiction over the relevant sectors. A key function of this review and approval process is to determine whether proposed investments meet the government's qualifications for the various incentives in place to promote economic development goals. Nevertheless, the Ministerial Functions Act grants relevant ministries broad discretionary powers over the approval of specific investment projects. Investors in industries targeted by the Malaysian government often can negotiate favorable terms with ministries, or other bodies, regulating the specific industry. This can include assistance in navigating a complex web of regulations and policies, some of which can be waived on a case-by-case basis. Foreign investors in non-targeted industries tend to receive less government assistance in obtaining the necessary approvals from the various regulatory bodies and therefore can face greater bureaucratic obstacles.

Other Investment Policy Reviews

Malaysia conducted an investment policy review through the Organization for Economic Cooperation and Development (OECD) in 2013. Although the review underscored the generally positive direction of economic reforms and efforts at liberalization, the recommendations emphasized the need for greater service sector liberalization, stronger intellectual property protections, enhanced guidance and support from Malaysia's Investment Development Authority (MIDA), and continued corporate governance reforms.

Malaysia also conducted a WTO Trade Policy Review in 2014, which incorporated a general overview of the country's investment policies. The WTO's review noted the Malaysian government's action to institute incentives to encourage investment as well as a number of agencies to guide prospective investors. Beyond attracting investment, Malaysia had made measurable progress on reforms to facilitate increased commercial activity. For example, the Malaysian Productivity Commission had simplified licensing requirements at the federal, state, and local levels, thus reducing business compliance costs. Construction permit procedures were also streamlined, as were processing times for construction contracts. The 2013 National Policy on the Development and Implementation of Regulations has increased the transparency of government rulemaking and made the process more inclusive of the private sector and the general public.

http://www.oecd.org/daf/inv/investment-policy/IPRMalaysia2013Summary.pdf
https://www.wto.org/english/tratop_e/tpr_e/s292_e.pdf

Laws/Regulations of Foreign Direct Investment

The Government of Malaysia established the Malaysia Investment Development Authority (MIDA) to attract foreign investment and to serve as a focal point for legal and regulatory questions. Organized as part of the Ministry of International Trade and Industry (MITI), MIDA serves as a guide to foreign investors interested in the manufacturing sector and in many services sectors. Regional bodies providing support to investors include: Invest Kuala Lumpur, Invest Penang, Koridor Utara Malaysia (Malaysia's Northern Corridor), the East Coast Economic Region Development Council, the Sabah Economic Development and Investment Authority (SEDIA), and the Sarawak Economic Development Corporation.

The principal law governing foreign investors' entry and practice in the Malaysian economy is the Companies Act of 1965 (CA). Incorporation requirements under the CA are relatively simple and are the same for domestic and foreign sole proprietorships, partnerships, as well as privately held and publicly traded corporations. In addition to registering with the Companies Commission of Malaysia, business entities must file: 1) Memorandum and Articles of Association (i.e., company charter); 2) a Declaration of Compliance (i.e., compliance with provisions of the Companies Act); and 3) a Statutory Declaration (i.e., no bankruptcies, no convictions).

Beyond these requirements, foreign investors must obtain licenses. Under the Industrial Coordination Act of 1975, an investor seeking to engage in manufacturing will need a license if the business claims capital of MYR 2.5 million (approximately USD 690,000) or employs at least 75 full-time staff. The Malaysian Government's guidelines for approving manufacturing investments, and by extension, manufacturing licenses, are generally based on capital-to-employee ratios. Projects below a threshold of MYR 55,000 (approximately USD 15,000) of capital per employee are deemed labor-intensive and will generally not qualify. Manufacturing investors seeking to expand or diversify their operations will need to apply through MIDA. As noted, the Ministerial Functions Act authorizes government ministries to oversee investments under their jurisdiction. Prospective investors in the services sector will need to follow requirements set by the relevant Malaysian Government ministry or agency over the sector in question.

Post is not aware of the Malaysian Government's interference in judicial proceedings involving foreign investors.

http://www.mida.gov.my/home/invest-in-malaysia/posts/ - The Malaysian Investment Development Authority's starting point for prospective foreign investors. Select the "General Guidelines and Facilities" tab.

http://www.ssm.com.my/en - The Malaysian Companies Commission homepage for registering sole proprietorships, partnerships, and companies.

http://www.mscmalaysia.my/ - The Multimedia Development Corporation (MDeC) is responsible for governing the Multimedia Super Corridor (MSC), the initiative to attract investment in information and communications technologies.

http://www.skmm.gov.my/Sectors/Broadcasting.aspx - The Malaysian Communications and Multimedia Commission's page for requirements in the communications sector.

http://www.moh.gov.my/english.php/pages/view/160 - The Ministry of Health's FAQs on liberalization of medical services.

Industrial Promotion

The Malaysian Government has codified the incentives available for investments in qualifying projects in target sectors and regions. Tax holidays, financing, and special deductions are among the measures generally available for domestic as well as foreign investors in the following sectors and geographic areas: information and communications technologies (ICT); biotechnology; halal products (e.g., food, cosmetics, pharmaceuticals); oil and gas storage and trading; Islamic finance; Kuala Lumpur; Labuan Island (off Eastern Malaysia); East Coast of Peninsular Malaysia; Sabah and Sarawak (Eastern Malaysia); Northern Corridor.

The lists of application procedures and incentives available to investors in these sectors and regions can be found at:**http://www.mida.gov.my/home/invest-in-malaysia/posts/**

Limits on Foreign Control

Despite the progress of reforms to open more of the economy to a greater share of foreign investment, limits on foreign ownership remain in place across many sectors.

Telecommunications

Malaysia began allowing 100% foreign equity participation in Applications Service Providers (ASP) in April 2012. However, for Network Facilities Providers (NFP) and Network Service Provider (NSP) licenses, a limit of 70% foreign participation remains in effect. In certain instances, Malaysia has allowed a greater share of foreign ownership, but the manner in which such exceptions are administered is non-transparent. Restrictions are still in force on foreign ownership allowed in Telekom Malaysia. The limitation on the aggregate foreign share is 30% or 5% for individual investors.

Oil and Gas

Under the terms of the Petroleum Development Act of 1974, the upstream oil and gas industry is controlled by Petroleum Nasional Berhad (PETRONAS), a wholly state-owned company and the sole entity with legal title to Malaysian crude oil and gas deposits. Foreign participation tends to take the form of production sharing contracts (PSCs). PETRONAS regularly requires its PSC partners to work with Malaysian firms for many tenders. Non-Malaysian firms are permitted to participate in oil services in partnership with local firms and are restricted to a 49% equity stake if the foreign party is the principal shareholder. PETRONAS sets the terms of upstream projects with foreign participation on a case-by-case basis.

Financial Services

Malaysia's 10-year Financial Sector Blueprint envisages further opening to foreign institutions and investors but does not contain specific market-opening commitments or timelines. For example, the services liberalization program that started in 2009 raised the limit of foreign ownership in insurance companies to 70%. However, the central bank, Bank Negara Malaysia (BNM) would allow a greater foreign ownership stake if the investment is determined to facilitate the consolidation of the industry. The latest Blueprint, 2011-2020, helped to codify the case-by-case approach. Under the Financial Services Act passed in late 2012, issuance of new licenses will be guided by prudential criteria and the "best interests of Malaysia." Prudential criteria include consideration of the financial strength, business record, experience, character and integrity of the prospective foreign investor, soundness and feasibility of the business plan for the institution in Malaysia, transparency and complexity of the group structure, and the extent of supervision of the foreign investor in its home country. In determining the "best interests of Malaysia," BNM will consider the contribution of the investment in promoting new high value-added economic activities, addressing demand for financial services where there are gaps, enhancing trade and investment linkages, and providing high-skilled employment opportunities.

BNM currently allows foreign banks to open four additional branches throughout Malaysia, subject to restrictions, which include designating where the branches can be set up (i.e.., in market centers, semi-urban areas and non-urban areas). The policies do not allow foreign banks to set up new branches within 1.5 km of an existing local bank. BNM also has conditioned foreign banks' ability to offer certain services on commitments to undertake certain back office activities in Malaysia..

Privatization Program

In several key sectors, including transportation, agriculture, utilities, financial services, manufacturing, and construction, Government Linked Corporations (GLCs) continue to dominate the market. However, the Malaysian Government remains publicly committed to the continued, eventual privatization, though it has not set a timeline for the process and faces substantial political pressure to preserve the roles of the GLCs. Malaysia revised its privatization program in 2006, and in 2009 established the Public-Private Partnership Unit (UKAS). As part of the Office of the Prime Minister, UKAS oversees transactions ranging from contracts and concessions to sales and transfers of ownership from the public sector to the private sector.

Foreign investors may participate in privatization programs, but foreign ownership is limited to 25% of the privatized entity's equity. The National Development Policy confers preferential treatment to the bumiputera (i.e., ethnic Malays and other indigenous groups), which are entitled to at least 30% of the privatized entity's equity.

The privatization process is formally subject to public bidding. However, the lack of transparency has led to criticism that the government's decisions tend to favor individuals and businesses with close ties to high-ranking officials.

Screening of FDI

The Malaysian Government has authority to review and approve all investments, foreign and domestic. Documents subject to the government's review include those mentioned in the section of this statement on Law/Regulations of Foreign Direct Investment as well as the investor's business plans, financial statements, and staffing projections. The investment review is connected to the government's responsibilities for granting the licenses required for the business to engage in its intended activity, whether in the provision of goods or services. This process also serves as a means for the government to assess whether the proposed investment meets the criteria for the various incentives available in target sectors and regions. Although U.S. businesses have, albeit rarely, raised concerns about delays in the government's review process, none has characterized the process itself as a barrier.

Competition Law

Malaysia's Competition Commission, established in 2010, has responsibility for determining whether a company's "conduct" constitutes an abuse of dominant market position or otherwise distorts, or restricts competition. As a matter of law, the Competition Commission does not have separate standards for foreign and domestic companies.

Investment Trends

Investment in the services sector has increased steadily in the last 10 years. Constituting 42% of private investment in 2005, services now capture more than 51% of total private investment each year. During the same period, manufacturing has declined from 40% of total private investment in 2005 to 25% in 2014. According to BNM, foreign direct investment has decreased as a share of total private investment from 35% in 2007 to an estimated 19% in 2014.

Table 1

Measure	Year	Index or Rank	Website Address
TI Corruption Perceptions index	2014	50 of 175	transparency.org/cpi2014/results
World Bank's Doing Business Report "Ease	2015	18 of 189	doingbusiness.org/rankings

of Doing Business"			
Global Innovation Index	2014	33 of 143	globalinnovationindex.org/content.aspx?page=data-analysis
World Bank GNI per capita	2013	USD 10,430t	data.worldbank.org/indicator/NY.GNP.PCAP.CD

2. CONVERSION AND TRANSFER POLICIES

Foreign Exchange

Bank Negara Malaysia (BNM), the central bank, states that Malaysia maintains liberal foreign exchange administration policies. A series of sequenced and progressive liberalization initiatives gradually relaxed controls on foreign direct investment flows, wages, dividends, interest, and rental income earned in Malaysia. Financial capital now moves freely in and out of the country.

The government continues to control the use of Malaysian ringgit outside of Malaysia for settlement. However, there are no longer restrictions on resident companies with export earnings from paying in foreign currencies to another resident company for the purchase of goods and services. Foreign investors are allowed to buy or sell Malaysian ringgit on a forward or spot basis with licensed onshore banks to facilitate the settlement of investments in Ringgit. In June 2011, BNM removed limits on outbound investment, non-bank inter-company loans, and trade financing.

BNM manages a floating exchange rate against a trade-weighted basket of currencies. The exchange rate against the USD stood at 3.49 on December 31, 2014. All payments to other countries must be made through authorized foreign exchange dealers. Banks must record the amount and purpose of each cross-border transfer over MYR 200,000 (approximately USD 58,000).

More information on Malaysia's regulation of foreign exchange can be found at **http://www.bnm.gov.my/index.php?ch=fea_adm&pg=fea_adm&lang=enA**.

Remittance Policies

Malaysia imposes few investment remittance rules on resident companies. Foreign exchange administration policies place no foreign currency asset limits on firms that have no ringgit-denominated debt. Companies that fund their purchases of foreign exchange assets with either onshore or offshore foreign exchange holdings, whether or not such companies have ringgit-denominated debt, face no limits in making remittances. However, a company with ringgit-denominated debt will need approval from BNM for conversions of MYR 50 million or more into foreign exchange assets in a calendar year.

Malaysia has not been identified in Treasury Department reports on currency manipulation.*

3. EXPROPRIATION AND COMPENSATION

The Embassy is not aware of any cases of uncompensated expropriation of U.S.-held assets by the Malaysian government. The government's stated policy is that all investors, both foreign and domestic, are entitled to fair compensation in the event that their private property is required for public purposes. Should the investor and the government disagree on the amount of compensation, the issue is then referred to the Malaysian judicial system.

4. DISPUTE SETTLEMENT

Legal System, Specialized Courts, Judicial Independence, Judgments of Foreign Courts

Malaysia has signed and ratified the Convention on the Settlement of Investment Disputes between States and Nationals of Other States. Malaysia became a Contracting State on October 14, 1966 when the Convention entered into force, granting jurisdiction over investment disputes between the Government of Malaysia and non-Malaysian citizens to the International Center for Settlement of Investment Disputes (ICSID). Malaysia also is a signatory to the Convention on the Recognition and Enforcement of Foreign Arbitral Awards. The domestic legal system is accessible but generally requires any non-Malaysian citizen to make a large deposit before pursuing a case in the Malaysian courts (i.e., USD 100,000), and can be slow and bureaucratic. Though post is unaware of any recent complaints by U.S. investors, some observers regard the courts as politically influenced.

Many firms choose to include mandatory arbitration clauses in their contracts. The government actively promotes use of the Kuala Lumpur Regional Center for Arbitration (http://www.klrca.org.my), established under the auspices of the Asian-African Legal Consultative Committee to offer international arbitration, mediation, and conciliation for trade disputes. The KLRCA is the only recognized center for arbitration in Malaysia. Arbitration held in a foreign jurisdiction under the rules of the Convention on the Settlement of Investment Disputes between States and Nationals of Other States 1965 or under the United Nations Commission on International trade Law Arbitration Rules 1976 and the Rules of the Regional Centre for Arbitration at Kuala Lumpur can be enforceable in Malaysia.

Bankruptcy

Malaysia's Department of Insolvency (MdI) is the lead agency implementing the Bankruptcy Act of 1967. The distribution of proceeds from the liquidation of a bankrupt company's assets generally adheres to the "priority matters and persons" identified by the Companies Act of 1965. After the bankruptcy process legal costs are covered, recipients of proceeds are: employees, secured creditors (i.e., creditors of real assets), unsecured creditors (i.e., creditors of financial instruments), and shareholders. Bankruptcy is not criminalized in Malaysia. The country ranks 36th on the World Bank Group's Doing Business Rankings for Ease of Resolving Insolvency, just behind F.Y.R. Macedonia and just ahead of Estonia.

Investment Disputes

Post has little data concerning the government's general handling of investment disputes. In 2004, a U.S. investor filed a case against the directors of the firm, who constituted the majority shareholders. The case involves allegations by the U.S. investor of embezzlement by the other directors. The case remains in the appeals process.

The Malaysian government has been involved in three ICSID cases -- in 1994, 1999, and 2005. The first case was settled out of court. The second, filed under the Malaysia-Belgo-Luxembourg Investment Guarantee Agreement (IGA), was concluded in 2000 in Malaysia's favor. The 2005 case, filed under the Malaysia-UK Bilateral Investment Treaty, was concluded in 2007, ultimately in favor of the investor.

International Arbitration

Many firms choose to include mandatory arbitration clauses in their contracts. The government actively promotes use of the Kuala Lumpur Regional Center for Arbitration (http://www.rcakl.org.my), established under the auspices of the Asian-African Legal Consultative Committee to offer international arbitration, mediation, and conciliation for trade disputes. The KLRCA is the only recognized center for arbitration in Malaysia. Arbitration held in a foreign jurisdiction under the rules of the Convention on the Settlement of Investment Disputes between States and Nationals of Other States 1965 or under the United Nations Commission on International trade Law Arbitration Rules 1976 and the Rules of the Regional Centre for Arbitration at Kuala Lumpur can be enforceable in Malaysia.

ICSID Convention and New York Convention

Malaysia has signed and ratified the Convention on the Settlement of Investment Disputes between States and Nationals of Other States. Malaysia became a Contracting State on October 14, 1966 when the Convention entered into force, granting jurisdiction over investment disputes between the Government of Malaysia and non-Malaysian citizens to the International Center for Settlement of Investment Disputes (ICSID). Malaysia also is a signatory to the Convention on the Recognition and Enforcement of Foreign Arbitral Awards. The domestic legal system is accessible but generally requires any non-Malaysian citizen to make a large deposit before pursuing a case in the Malaysian courts (i.e., USD 100,000), and can be slow and bureaucratic. Though post is unaware of any recent complaints by U.S. investors, some observers regard the courts as politically influenced.

Duration of Dispute Resolution

The World Bank Group's 2015 "Doing Business" indicators reflect that contract enforcement cases average 425 days, require 29 different procedures and filings, and cost approximately 37% of the amount at issue. The "Investing Across Borders" rankings state that parties to an arbitration process can expect to wait 24 weeks for resolution.

5. PERFORMANCE REQUIREMENTS AND INVESTMENT INCENTIVES

WTO/TRIMS

The Malaysian employs a variety of tax incentives to attract investment in various sectors and regions of the country. The most notable example of investment promotion efforts in tension with TRIMS is the National Automotive Policy (NAP).

Under the 2014 policy, the government eased manufacturing licensing restrictions for investors and manufacturers seeking to produce commercial and hybrid vehicles. However, the current policy on contract assembly and the freezing of licenses for reconditioning and reassembling activities remain in place. Moreover, the policy introduced higher tax exemptions for exported goods with a significant portion of value added in Malaysia. The tax exemptions on statutory income will be based on the percentage of increase in the value add to the exported goods. Specifically, tax exemptions have been increased:1) to 30 per cent of the value of increased exports (from a previous 10 per cent), provided the goods attain at least 30% value added; and 2) to 50 per cent of the value of increased exports (from a previous 15 per cent), provided that the goods attain at least 50 per cent value added. The NAP is currently under review.

Investment Incentives

The lists of application procedures and incentives available to investors in these sectors and regions can be found at:**http://www.mida.gov.my/home/invest-in-malaysia/posts**

Research and Development

Government-funded research and development programs are open to participation by U.S. and other foreign firms.

Performance Requirements

Fiscal incentives granted to both foreign and domestic investors historically have been subject to performance requirements, usually in the form of export targets, local content requirements and technology transfer requirements. Performance requirements are usually written into the individual manufacturing licenses of local and foreign investors.

The Malaysian government extends a full tax exemption incentive of fifteen years for firms with "Pioneer Status" (companies promoting products or activities in industries or parts of Malaysia to which the government places a high priority), and ten years for companies with "Investment Tax Allowance" status (those on which the government places a priority, but not as high as Pioneer Status). However, the government appears to have some flexibility with respect to the expiry of these periods, and some firms reportedly have had their pioneer status renewed. Government priorities generally include the levels of value-added, technology used, and industrial linkages. If a firm (foreign or domestic) fails to meet the terms of its license, it risks losing any tax benefits it may have been awarded. Potentially, a firm could lose its manufacturing license. The New Economic Model stated that in the long term, the government intends gradually to eliminate most of the fiscal incentives now offered to foreign and domestic manufacturing investors. More information on specific incentives for various sectors can be found at **www.mida.gov.my**.

Malaysia also seeks to attract foreign investment in the information technology industry, particularly in the Multimedia Super Corridor (MSC), a government scheme to foster the growth of research, development, and other high technology activities in Malaysia. Foreign investors who obtain MSC status receive tax and regulatory exemptions as well as public service commitments in exchange for a commitment of substantial technology transfer. For further details on incentives, see www.mdec.my. The Multimedia Development Corporation (MDeC) approves all applications for MSC status.

In the services sector, the government's stated goal is to attract foreign investment in regional distribution centers, international procurement centers, operational headquarter research and development, university and graduate education, integrated market and logistics support services, cold chain facilities, central utility facilities, industrial training, and environmental management. To date, Malaysia has had some success in attracting regional distribution centers and local campuses of foreign universities. For example, GE and Honeywell maintain regional offices for ASEAN in Malaysia, and First Solar, Motorola, Huntsman and Abbott all announced new or expanded investments in 2014.

Malaysia seeks to attract foreign investment in biotechnology, but sends a mixed message on agricultural and food biotechnology. On July 8, 2010, the Malaysian Ministry of Health posted amendments to the Food Regulations 1985 [P.U. (A) 437/1985] that require strict mandatory labeling of food and food ingredients obtained through modern biotechnology. The amendments also included a requirement that no person shall import, prepare or advertise for sale, or sell any food or food ingredients obtained through modern biotechnology without the prior written approval of the Director. There is no 'threshold' level on the labeling requirement. Labeling of "GMO Free" or "Non-GMO" is not permitted. The labeling requirements only apply to foods and food ingredients obtained through modern biotechnology but not to food produced with GMO feed. The labeling regulation was originally scheduled to be enforced beginning in July 2012. However, a Ministry of Health circular published on August 27, 2012 announced that enforcement would be deferred until July 8, 2014. However, there has not been any announcement to date of its enforcement. A copy of the law and regulations respectively can be found at: **http://www.biosafety.nre.gov.my/BiosafetyAct2007.shtml**, and**http://www.biosafety.nre.gov.my/BIOSAFETY%20REGULATIONS%202010.pdf**.

Data Storage

Malaysia has not implemented measures amounting to "forced localization" for data storage. The government has provided inducements to attract foreign and domestic investors to the Multimedia Super Corridor but does not mandate use of onshore providers. Companies in the information and communications technology sector are not required to hand over source code.

6. Right to Private Ownership and Establishment

Malaysian law allows foreign and domestic entities to establish and own business enterprises. Various requirements, such as registration and licensing, guide the government's supervision and regulation of business activity. Business owners and operators are able to compensate employees in the form of wages, salaries, leave pay, commissions, bonuses, allowances, housing accommodations, and securities.

7. PROTECTION OF PROPERTY RIGHTS

Real Property

Land administration is shared among federal, state, and local government. State governments have their own rules about land ownership, including foreign ownership. Malaysian law affords strong protections to real property owners. Real property titles are recorded in public records and attorneys review transfer documentation to ensure efficacy of a title transfer. There is no title insurance available in Malaysia. Malaysian courts protect property ownership rights. Foreign investors are allowed to borrow using real property as collateral. Foreign and domestic lenders are able to record mortgages with competent authorities and execute foreclosure in the event of loan default.

Intellectual Property Rights

Malaysia was removed from the U.S. Special 301 Watch List in 2012 following improvements in recent years in protecting IPR. In December 2011, the Malaysian Parliament passed amendments to the copyright law designed to, inter alia, bring the country into compliance with the WIPO Copyright Treaty and the WIPO Performance and Phonogram Treaty, define Internet Service Provider (ISP) liabilities, and prohibit unauthorized camcording of motion pictures in theaters. Malaysia subsequently acceded to the WIPO Copyright Treaty and the WIPO Performance and Phonogram Treaty in September 2012. In addition, the Ministry of Domestic Trade, Cooperatives, and Consumerism (MDTCC) took steps to enhance Malaysia's enforcement regime, including active cooperation with rights holders on matters pertaining to IPR enforcement, ongoing training of prosecutors for specialized IPR courts, and the 2013 reestablishment of a Special Anti-Piracy Taskforce.

In response to trends of rising internet piracy, the interagency Special Anti-Piracy Task Force established a Special Internet Forensics Unit (SIFU) within MDTCC. The SIFU presently consists of four officials whose responsibilities include monitoring for sites suspected of being, or known as, purveyors of infringing content. This new organization will also follow MDTCC's practice of launching investigations based on information and complaints from legitimate host sites and content providers. Near-term priorities for this new enforcement arm center on capacity building training, which includes orientation meetings with the Malaysian Communications and Multimedia Commission (MCMC), which has responsibility for overall regulation of internet content, and a short-term practicum with a firm that distributes online content. Our contacts at MDTCC have told Post they were not prepared to share details of enforcement actions related to suspected online piracy, but indicated that a "substantial number of cases" had been investigated. Officials plan to hire three additional officers to work in the SIFU by the end of 2015.

Despite Malaysia's success in improving IPR enforcement, key issues remain, including relatively widespread availability of pirated and counterfeit products in Malaysia, high rates of piracy over the Internet, and continued problems with book piracy. The United States continues to encourage Malaysia to accede to the WIPO Budapest Treaty on the International Recognition of the Deposit of Microorganisms for the Purposes of Patent Procedure. In addition, the United States continues to urge Malaysia to provide effective protection against unfair commercial use, as well as unauthorized disclosure, of undisclosed test or other data generated to obtain marketing approval for pharmaceutical products, and to provide an effective system to address patent issues expeditiously in connection with applications to market pharmaceutical products.

Resources for Rights Holders

Clayton Hays

Deputy Economic Counselor

+6-03-2168-5092

hayscp@state.gov

http://www.amcham.com.my/ - The American-Malaysian Chamber of Commerce
http://www.myipo.gov.my/ - The Intellectual Property Corporation of Malaysia - a government body to aid in registration and protection of patents, trademarks, copyrights, and designs.
http://www.wipo.int/directory/en - Additional information about treaty obligations and points of contact at local IP offices.

8. TRANSPARENCY OF THE REGULATORY SYSTEM

In July 2013, the Malaysian Government initiated a National Policy on Development and Implementation of Regulations (NPDIR). Under this policy, the federal government embarked on a comprehensive approach to minimize redundancies in the country's regulatory framework. The benefits to the private sector thus far have largely been reduced licensing requirements, fees, and approval wait-times for construction projects. The main components of the policy have been: 1) a regulatory impact assessment (a cost-benefit analysis of all newly proposed regulations); and 2) the creation of a regulations guide, PEMUDAH (similar to the role MIDA plays for prospective investors), to aid businesses and civil society organizations in understanding regulatory requirements affecting their organizations' activities. Under the NPDIR, the government has committed to reviewing all new regulations every five years to determine with the new regulations need to be adjusted or eliminated.

Despite this effort to make government more accountable for its rules and to make the process more inclusive, many foreign investors continue to criticize the lack of transparency in government decision making. The implementation of rules on government procurement contracts are a recurring concern. Non-Malaysian pharmaceutical companies claim to have lost bids against bumiputera-owned companies despite offering more effective medicines at lower cost. An example that adds to suspicions of an informal set of rules relates to a contract for providing medical devices to public hospitals. In October 2014, a group of Malaysian medical device manufacturers launched a public relations campaign with the intent of reversing a Ministry of Health contract awarded earlier in the year. The company that won the contract was started by a former senior-level Ministry of Health official and was alleged to be merely a front company for foreign-produced medical devices. The ministry began an investigation but has not made public either its findings or information about the contract awardee.

9. EFFICIENT CAPITAL MARKETS AND PORTFOLIO INVESTMENT

Foreigners may trade in securities and derivatives. Malaysia houses Asia's third largest corporate bond market, behind only Japan and Korea in market capitalization. Both domestic and foreign companies regularly access capital in Malaysia's bond market. Malaysia, which is the largest sukuk (Islamic bond) market in East Asia, provides tax incentives for foreign companies issuing Islamic bonds and financial instruments in Malaysia.

Malaysia's stock market (Bursa Malaysia) is open to foreign investment and foreign corporation issuing shares. However, foreign issuers remain subject to bumiputera ownership requirements of 12.5% if the majority of their operations are in Malaysia. Listing requirements for foreign companies are similar to that of local companies. There are additional criteria for foreign companies wanting to list in Malaysia including, among others: approval of regulatory authorities of the foreign jurisdiction where the company was incorporated, valuation of assets with standards applied in Malaysia or International Valuation Standards, and the company must have been registered with the Registrar of Companies under the Companies Act 1965.

Malaysia has taken steps to promote good corporate governance by listed companies. Publicly listed companies must submit quarterly reports that include a balance sheet and income statement within two months of each financial quarter's end and audited annual accounts for public scrutiny within four months of each year's end. An individual may hold up to 25 corporate directorships. All public and private company directors are required to attend classes on corporate rules and regulations.

Legislation also regulates equity buybacks, mandates book entry of all securities transfers, and requires that all owners of securities accounts be identified. A Central Depository System (CDS) for stocks and bonds established in 1991 makes physical possession of certificates unnecessary. All shares traded on the Bursa Malaysia must be deposited in the CDS. Short selling of stocks is prohibited.

Money and Banking System, Hostile Takeovers

International investors generally regard Malaysia's banking sector as dynamic and well regulated. Although privately owned banks are competitive with state-owned banks, the state-owned banks dominate the market. The five largest banks - Maybank, CIMB, Public Bank, RHB, and Ambank - account for an estimated 75% of banking sector loans. According to the Ministry of Finance Report for 2014-2015, total banking sector lending in 2014 was 150% of GDP for 2014. According to the World Bank, 1.8% of the Malaysian banking sector's loans were non-performing for 2014.

Bank Negara prohibits hostile takeovers of banks, but the Securities Commission has established non-discriminatory rules and disclosure requirements for hostile takeovers of publicly traded companies.

10. COMPETITION FROM STATE-OWNED ENTERPRISES

On April 21, 2010, the Parliament of Malaysia approved two bills, the Competition Commission Act 2010 and the Competition Act 2010. The Acts took effect January 1, 2012. The Competition Act prohibits cartels and abuses of a dominant market position, but does not create any pre-transaction review of mergers or acquisitions. Violations are punishable by fines, as well as imprisonment for individual violations. The Acts established a Competition Commission with broad investigative and enforcement powers, as well as a Competition Appeals Tribunal (CAT) to hear all appeals of Commission decisions. The CAC has since completed investigations and issued rulings since the Competition Law took effect. In the largest case to date, on September 6, 2013, the CAC found national carrier Malaysian Airlines and budget airline AirAsia to have breached the Competition Act 2010 and fined both airlines of USD 3.33 million each. The airlines are appealing against the decision, which will be the first case brought before the CAT.

State-owned enterprises play a very significant role in the Malaysian economy. Such enterprises have been used to spearhead infrastructure and industrial projects. The government owns approximately 36% of the value of firms listed on the Bursa Malaysia through its seven Government-Linked Investment Corporations (GLICs), including a majority stake in a number of companies. Only a minority portion of stock is available for trading for some of the largest publicly listed local companies. The government has indicated increasing interest in restarting its privatization efforts through the New Economic Model reforms. Khazanah, often considered the government's sovereign wealth fund, owns stakes in companies competing in many of the country's major industries. The Prime Minister chairs Khazanah's Board of Directors. PETRONAS, the state-owned oil and gas company, is Malaysia's only Fortune Global 500 firm.

In July 2011, the Government stated that 33 government-linked companies were ready for divestment, but did not identify them by name. Under the plan to rationalize the portfolio of government-linked companies (GLCs) in Malaysia, the Government will reduce its stakes in some of these companies, list a few others and sell the rest. In the first quarter of 2012 Khazanah offloaded its stake in the national car company Proton to DRB-Hicom Bhd. In Sept 2013, Khazanah divested Time Engineering Bhd to private sector Bumiputera owned company Censof Holdings Bhd. Nonetheless, the majority of GLCs have not been affected by the divestment plan, and GLCs will retain a major role in Malaysia's economy. Khazanah continued its divestments in 2014 but has only specified "six divestments with a gain on divestment of MYR 3 billion."

OECD Guidelines on Corporate Governance of SOEs

State-owned enterprises (SOEs), which in Malaysia are called government-linked companies (GLCs), with publicly traded shares must produce audited financial statements every year. These SOEs must also submit filings related to changes in the organization's management. The SOEs that do not offer publicly traded shares are required to submit annual reports to the Companies Commission. The requirement for publicly reporting the financial standing and scope of activities of SOEs has increased their transparency. It is also consistent with the OECD's guideline for Transparency and Disclosure. Moreover, many SOEs prioritize operations that maximize their earnings. However, the often close connections that SOEs have with senior government officials blurs the line between strictly commercial activity pursued for its own sake and activity that has been directed to advance a policy interest. For example, Petroliam Nasional Berhad (Petronas) is both SOE in the oil and gas sector and the regulator of the industry. Malaysia Airlines (MAS), in which the government previously held 70% but now holds 100%, required periodic infusions of resources from the government to maintain the large numbers of the company's staff and senior executives. The airline is currently undergoing a restructuring, and the stated goal of the country's largest sovereign wealth fund, Khazanah, which holds all of the airline's shares, is to re-list MAS in the coming years.

Sovereign Wealth Funds

In 2004, the government began a 10-year SOE Transformation Program. Under this program, SOEs are defined as companies in which sovereign wealth funds (SWFs), referred to locally as government-linked investment companies (GLICs), held a majority ownership stake. During the period, the SWFs supervised the management, structural, and disclosure changes of the many companies in which they were shareholders. The transformation ultimately extended to the SWFs, which now provide annual financial statements and publish quarterly reports on their efforts to make SOEs more effective.

11. CORPORATE SOCIAL RESPONSIBILITY

The development of corporate social responsibility in Malaysia is moving to higher levels and many larger companies have CSR programs and activities. In 2006, Malaysian stock market regulator, the Securities Commission, published a CSR Framework for all publicly listed companies, which are required to disclose their CSR programs in their annual financial reports. In 2007 the Women, Family and Community Ministry launched the Prime Minister's CSR's Awards to recognize companies that have made a difference to the communities in which they are active through their CSR programs.

OECD Guidelines for Multinational Enterprises

The government encourages the private sector to implement corporate social responsibility (CSR) programs. For example, the Prime Minister's Office presents annual CSR awards for: community and social welfare; environment; support for small businesses; workplace best practices; women's empowerment; education; culture and heritage; family friendly workplaces; and opportunities for persons with disabilities.

12. POLITICAL VIOLENCE

Malaysia has experienced political stability since its independence in 1957, with the exception of ethnic riots that followed the 1969 national elections. Najib Razak peacefully took office as Malaysia's 6th Prime Minister on April 2, 2009. The government historically denied assembly permits for anti-government street demonstrations. In April 2012, the Peaceful Assembly Act took effect, which eliminates the need for permits for public assemblies but outlaws street protests and places other significant restrictions on public assemblies. On April 28, 2012, the police disrupted a large protest march that took place despite restrictions the government attempted to impose. Subsequent demonstrations and protest marches took place in 2013 and 2014 without disruption. Following the July 2014 Israeli incursion into Gaza, several Malaysian non-governmental entities organized a boycott of McDonalds. Over a several week period, protestors picketed at several McDonalds restaurants, at times taunting and harassing employees. Periodically, Malaysian groups will organize modest protests against U.S. policies, usually involving demonstrations outside the U.S. embassy. To date, these have remained peaceful and localized, with a strong police presence.

13. CORRUPTION

The Malaysian government has taken steps to address corruption, including through the establishment of the Malaysian Anti-Corruption Commission (MACC) in 2008, passage of legislation to make judicial appointments more transparent (the Judicial Appointments Commission Act) also in 2008, passage of a Whistleblower Protection Act in 2010, the introduction of procurement reforms and the launch of government initiatives to target corrupt practices. The Malaysian government considers bribery a criminal act and does not permit bribes to be deducted from taxes. Malaysia's anti-corruption law includes the criminal offense of bribery of foreign public officials, permits the prosecution of Malaysians for offense committed overseas, and also provides for the seizure of properties.

Critics have questioned the MACC's ability to effectively address high-level corruption, although a number of prosecutions are ongoing. The MACC conducts investigations but prosecutorial discretion remains with the Attorney General. A lack of capacity and technical skills in some areas hampers MACC's overall effectiveness. The MACC introduced a public database of those convicted of corruption offenses. There is no systematic public disclosure of assets by senior officials. Critics also note that the Whistleblower Act does not protect those who disclose allegations to the media.

Government officials cite a four point approach to reducing corruption in government procurement, a key area of focus: increasing the number and decreasing the size of government procurement contract subject to open tenders, introducing the Transparency International "Integrity Pact" concept to be signed by all vendors that they understand bidding rules and anti-corruption laws prior to engaging in contract negotiations, issuing rules against Ministerial "referral letters" recommending specific contractors for government contracts, and fully implementing the new Whistleblower Act.

UN Anticorruption Convention, OECD Convention on Combatting Bribery

Malaysia signed the UN Convention Against Corruption in 2003 and ratified it in 2008. However, Malaysia is not a party to the OECD's Anti-Bribery Convention.

Resources to Report Corruption
Contact at government agency or agencies are responsible for combating corruption:
Abu Kassim Mohamad
Chief Commissioner
Malaysia Anti-Corruption Commission
Block D6, Complex D, Pusat Pentadbiran
Kerajaan Persekutuan, Peti Surat 6000

62007 Putrajaya
+6-1800-88-6000
info@sprm.gov.my

Cynthia Gabriel
Director
The Center to Combat Corruption and Cronyism (C4)
C Four Consultancies Sdn Bhd
A-2-10, 8 Avenue,
Jalan Sg Jernih 8/1,
Seksyen 8,
46050 Petaling Jaya,
Selangor, Malaysia
Email: **info@c4center.org**

14. BILATERAL INVESTMENT AGREEMENTS

Malaysia has bilateral investment treaties with 36 countries, but not with the United States. Malaysia does have bilateral investment guarantee agreements with over 70 economies, including the United States. The Government reports that 65 of Malaysia's existing investment agreements contain Investor State Dispute Settlement (ISDS) provisions.

Bilateral Taxation Treaties

Malaysia has double taxation treaties with over 70 countries, though the double taxation agreement with the U.S. currently is limited to air and sea transportation

15. OPIC AND OTHER INVESTMENT INSURANCE PROGRAMS

Malaysia has a limited investment guarantee agreement with the U.S. under the U.S. Overseas Private Investment Corporation (OPIC) program, for which it has qualified since 1959. Few investors have sought OPIC insurance in Malaysia, though in mid-2013, the OPIC Board of Directors approved a USD 250 million loan to help build Malaysia's first fully-integrated private medical school. However, the U.S. participant has since withdrawn from the project.

16. LABOR

Malaysia's shortage of skilled labor is the most oft-cited impediment to economic growth cited in numerous studies. Malaysia has an acute shortage of highly qualified professionals, scientists, and academics. The Embassy has heard reports from some U.S. companies that the shortage of skilled labor is resulting in companies reconsidering future expansion or investment in Malaysia

The Malaysian labor market operates at essentially full employment, with unemployment for Malaysians averaging 3.1% in 2013. In an effort to improve the employability of local graduates, the GOM offers additional training modules at public universities in English language skills, presentation techniques, and entrepreneurship.

Malaysia is a member of the International Labor Organization (ILO). Labor relations in Malaysia are generally non-confrontational. A system of government controls strongly discourages strikes. Some labor disputes are settled through negotiation or arbitration by an industrial court, though cases can be backlogged for years. Once a case is referred to the industrial court, the union and management are barred from further industrial action.

While national unions are proscribed due to sovereignty issues within Malaysia, there are a number of territorial federations of unions (the three territories being Peninsular Malaysia, Sabah and Sarawak). The government has prevented some trade unions, such as those in the electronics and textile sectors, from forming territorial federations. Instead of allowing a federation for all of Peninsular Malaysia, the electronics sector is limited to forming four regional federations of unions, while the textile sector is limited to state-based federations of unions, for those states which have a textile industry. Employers and employees share the costs of the Social Security Organization (SOSCO), which covers an estimated 12.9 million workers. No systematic welfare programs or government unemployment benefits exist; however the Employee Provident Fund (EPF), which employers and employees are required to contribute to, provides retirement benefits for workers in the private sector. Civil servants receive pensions upon retirement.

The regulation of employment in Malaysia, specifically as it affects the hiring and redundancy of workers remains a notable impediment to employing workers in Malaysia. The high cost of terminating their employees, even in cases of wrongdoing, is a source of complaint for domestic and foreign employers. The World Bank estimates that the financial cost of firing an employee averages 75 weeks of salary for that worker.

The Embassy hears reports from some U.S. companies that the government monitors the ethnic balance among employees and enforces an ethnic quota system for hiring in certain areas. Race-based preferences in hiring and promotion are widespread in government, government-owned universities and government-linked corporations. Implementation of the Minimum Wage Order 2012 began on January 1, 2014 and fixed the rate at just under USD 300 per month in Peninsular Malaysia and about USD 260 for those in East Malaysia.

In 2014, the Department of Labor's Trafficking Victims Protection Reauthorization Act (TVPRA) listing of goods produced with child labor and forced labor included Malaysian palm oil (child labor) and electronics (forced labor). Senior officials across the Malaysian interagency have taken this listing seriously and have been working with the private sector and civil society to address the concerns as they pertain to palm oil and electronics as well as other sectors.

17. FOREIGN TRADE ZONES/FREE PORTS/TRADE FACILITATION

The Free Zone Act of 1990 authorized the Minister of Finance to designate any suitable area as either a Free Industrial Zone (FIZ), where manufacturing and assembly takes place, or a Free Commercial Zone (FCZ), generally for warehousing commercial stock. The Minister of Finance may appoint any federal, state, or local government agency or entity as an authority to administer, maintain and operate any free trade zone. Currently there are 13 FIZs and 12 FCZs in Malaysia. In June 2006, the Port Klang Free Zone opened as the nation's first fully integrated FIZ and FCZ, although the project has been dogged by corruption allegations related to the land acquisition for the site. The government launched a prosecution in 2009 of the former Transport Minister involved in the land purchase process, though he was later acquitted in October 2013

Raw materials, products and equipment may be imported duty-free into these zones with minimum customs formalities. Companies that export not less than 80% of their output and depend on imported goods, raw materials, and components may be located in these FZs. Ports, shipping and maritime-related services play an important role in Malaysia since 90% of its international trade by volume is seaborne. Malaysia is also a major transshipment center.

Goods sold into the Malaysian economy by companies within the FZs must pay import duties. If a company wants to enjoy Common External Preferential Tariff (CEPT) rates within the ASEAN Free Trade Area, 40% of a product's content must be ASEAN-sourced. In addition to the FZs, Malaysia permits the establishment of licensed manufacturing warehouses outside of free zones, which give companies greater freedom of location while allowing them to enjoy privileges similar to firms operating in an FZ. Companies operating in these zones require approval/license for each activity. The time needed to obtain licenses depends on the type of approval and ranges from 2-8 weeks.

18. FOREIGN DIRECT INVESTMENT AND FOREIGN PORTFOLIO INVESTMENT STATISTICS

Table 2: Key Macroeconomic Data, U.S. FDI in Host Country/Economy

	Host Country Statistical source*		USG or international statistical source		USG or International Source of Data: BEA; IMF; Eurostat; UNCTAD, Other
Economic Data	Year	Amount	Year	Amount	
Host Country Gross Domestic Product (GDP) ($M USD)	2013	302,000	2013	313,159	www.worldbank.org/en/country
Foreign Direct Investment	Host Country Statistical source*		USG or international statistical source		USG or international Source of data: BEA; IMF; Eurostat; UNCTAD, Other
U.S. FDI in partner country ($M USD, stock positions)	2013	11,600	2013	16,409	http://bea.gov/international/factsheet/factsheet.cfm?Area=617
Host country's FDI in the United States ($M USD, stock positions)	Not available	Not available	2013	635	http://bea.gov/international/factsheet/factsheet.cfm?Area=617
Total inbound stock of FDI as	2012	53.8%	2012	43%	

% host GDP					

*Bank Negara Malaysia (i.e., central bank), and Department of Statistics Malaysia

Table 3: Sources and Destination of FDI

Direct Investment from/in Counterpart Economy Data					
From Top Five Sources/To Top Five Destinations (US Dollars, Millions)					
Inward Direct Investment			Outward Direct Investment		
Total Inward	135,638	100%	Total Outward	127,566	100%
Singapore	24,600	18%	Singapore	20,413	16%
Japan	19,917	15%	Indonesia	14,203	11%
United States	11,647	9%	Australia	8,413	7%
Netherlands	10,708	8%	Mauritius	6,421	5%
Switzerland	6,525	5%	Cayman Islands	6,203	5%
"0" reflects amounts rounded to +/- USD 500,000.					

Source: IMF Coordinated Direct Investment Survey

Table 4: Sources of Portfolio Investment

The IMF's data on Malaysia's portfolio investment partners are generally consistent with figures that the central bank and the Malaysian Department of Statistics supply.

Portfolio Investment Assets								
Top Five Partners (Millions, US Dollars)								
Total			Equity Securities			Total Debt Securities		
All Countries	66,068	100%	All Countries	44,317	100%	All Countries	21,571	100%
Singapore	21,589	33%	United States	16,378	37%	Singapore	7,445	34%
United States	19,549	30%	Singapore	14,143	32%	United States	3,171	15%
UK	3,581	5%	UK	2,814	6%	Australia	1,300	6%
Hong Kong	3,576	5%	Hong Kong	2,478t	6%	S. Korea	1,236	6%
Australia	2,234	3%	Russia	1,077	2%	Hong Kong	1,098	5%

Source: IMF Coordinated Portfolio Investment Survey

IMPORTANT BUSINESS CONTACTS

Contact for More Information
Clayton Hays
Deputy Economic Counselor
376 Jalan Tun Razak, Kuala Lumpur 50400 Malaysia
+6-03-2168-5092
hayscp@state.gov

LAW FIRMS

Johor

Johor Legal Aid Centre
Tingkat 5, Mahkamah Sesyen & Majistret
Jalan Ayer Molek
80000 Johor Bahru
Johor

Tel: 07-223 5698
Fax: 07-226 9024
Email: lacjb15@gmail.com

Bar Council Legal Aid Centre, Muar
(Bilik Peguam) Kompleks Mahkamah Muar
Jalan Temenggong Ahmad
84000 Muar
Johor

Tel: 06-951 4700
Fax: 06-951 4700
Email: lacmuar@gmail.com

Kedah

Kedah Legal Aid Centre (Alor Setar)
Kedah Bar Committee
No. 54, Jalan Utama 3/1
Kompleks Perniagaan Utama
Jalan Sultanah Sambungan
05350 Alor Setar
Kedah

Tel: 04-733 3467
Fax: 04-730 8305
Email: kedahlac@gmail.com

Kelantan

Kelantan Legal Aid Centre
Tingkat Bawah, Bangunan Mahkamah Tinggi
Jalan Hospital
15000 Kota Bahru
Kelantan

Tel: 09-744 8660
Fax: 09-744 8660
Email: abbyklac@yahoo.com

Kuala Lumpur

Kuala Lumpur Legal Aid Centre
Level 2, Wisma Hang Sam
1, Jalan Hang Lekir
50050 Kuala Lumpur

Tel: 03-2072 2050 / 03-2072 2051 / 03-2072 2052
Fax: 03-2072 3005

Malacca

Malacca Legal Aid Centre
No. 9373, Jalan Indah 1
Taman Indah Section 1
Bukit Sebukor
75150 Melaka

Tel: 06-284 5519 / 06-284 3396
Fax: 06-283 0755
Email: mcca.legalaid@gmail.com

Negeri Sembilan

Negeri Sembilan Legal Aid Centre
No.3 Jalan S2 D38
Magistrate's Square Seremban 2
70300 Seremban
Negeri Sembilan
(Opposite Court Complex Seremban 2)

Tel : 06-601 3844 / 06-601 3843
Fax : 06-601 3845 / 06-601 3353

Pahang

Kuantan Legal Aid Centre
No. B64, Tingkat 1A, Lorong Tun Ismail 6
Off Jalan Tun Ismail

25000 Kuantan
Pahang

Tel: 09-515 9244
Fax: 09-515 9243
Email: lacktn@yahoo.com

Temerloh Legal Aid Centre
Bilik Peguam, Bangunan Mahkamah Tinggi
28000 Temerloh
Pahang

Tel: 09-296 9410
Fax: 09-296 9410
Email: pbgtloh@gmail.my

Penang

Penang Legal Aid Centre
No.21, Greenhall
Ground Floor
10200 Penang

Tel: 04-261 7451
Fax: 04-261 6840
Email: lacpg2011@gmail.com

Butterworth Legal Aid Centre
No. 11, 2nd Floor, Lorong Jermal Indah
Taman Jermal Indah
12300 Butterworth
Penang

Tel: 04-310 8451 / 04-310 8452
Fax: 04-3108453
Email: lacbwth@gmail.com

Perak

Perak Legal Aid Centre
No.39, Jalan Dato Maharajalela
30300 Ipoh
Perak

Tel: 05-255 0523
Fax: 05-243 1530
Email: PerakLAC@gmail.com

Perlis

Perlis Legal Aid Centre
No.15, Tingkat Atas
Taman Guru Jaya
01000 Kangar
Perlis

Tel: 04 9770272
Fax: 04 9770198
Email: lacperlis@gmail.com

Selangor

Selangor Legal Aid Centre
No. 41-A, Jalan Bola Jaring 13/15
Seksyen 13, 40100 Shah Alam
Selangor

Tel: 03-5510 7007
Fax: 03-5510 7009
Email: lacselangor@outlook.com

Kuala Selangor Legal Aid Centre
No. 32, Jalan Bendahara 1/1
Taman Bendahara
45000 Kuala Selangor
Selangor

Tel: 03-3281 2428
Fax: 03-3281 2427
Email: kualaselangorlac@yahoo.com

Terengganu
Terengganu Legal Aid Centre
Tingkat 5, Kompleks Mahkamah
Jalan Sultan Muhamad
21100 Kuala Terengganu
Terengganu

Tel: 09-622 0249
Fax: 09-622 0249
Email: lac_trg@yahoo.com

BALENDRAN CHONG
3RD FLOOR HSBC BANK BUILDING JALAN MAHKOTA
25000 KUANTAN
PAHANG

JK LIM Advocates & Solicitors
E-2-08 Neo Damansara, Jalan PJU 8/1, Damansara Perdana
47820 Petaling Jaya
Selangor, Malaysia

Low & Partners
42-B, Jalan SS 21/58, Damansara Utama (Uptown)
47400 Petaling Jaya
Selangor

S. RAVICHANDARAN & ANUAR
JALAN DESA KIARA
50480 MONT KIARA
KUALA LUMPUR

MYANMAR INVESTMENT AND BUSINESS CLIMATE - STRATEGIC INFORMATION AND CONTACTS FOR STARTING BUSINESS

Following years of isolation from the global economy, Burma in 2011 embarked on a new course and began implementing significant reforms to spur economic development and create an attractive business climate meant to generate more inward foreign investment. Over the past several years, the government has made good on its promise to take steps that address some of the challenges facing Burma's economy, including eliminating multiple exchange rates, passing a new foreign investment law, reducing trade restrictions, and reforming tax policy and administration. Consequently, the international business community's interest in Burma and the unique opportunities the country presents – including a rich natural resources base, a large market potential, a young labor force and a strategic location between India, China and the countries that make up the Association of South East Asian Nations (ASEAN) – continues to grow. The European Union and Australia, in response to ongoing political reform, have lifted their sanctions on Burma entirely (except for an arms/military embargo). Similarly, the United States Government has eased almost all of its economic sanctions on Burma, allowing U.S. investment, the importation of Burmese products into the U.S., and the export of financial services, although remaining U.S. sanctions prevent U.S. persons from dealing with Specially Designated Nationals and restrict the import of Burmese jade and rubies into the United States.

The reduced sanctions combined with Burma's move towards economic liberalization and a favorable external environment have brightened Burma's macroeconomic outlook. Real GDP growth rose from 7.3% in fiscal year (FY) 2012/13 to 8.3% in FY 2013/14 led by strong performances in the construction, manufacturing and services sectors. Growth is expected to decelerate slightly to 7.8% in FY 2014/15 (year ending in March) due to slower growth in the agricultural sector. Inflation is expected to pick up to around 6% year on year (y/y) in FY2014/15 from 5.8% in FY2013/14, due in part to increases in food prices and higher electricity tariffs. Per capita GDP jumped to over USD 1,000, putting the country on the cusp of graduating to lower-middle income status (although the increase is largely due to a recalibration based on census results that confirm Burma's population at 51 million rather than the 60 million previously estimated).

Despite the reforms undertaken and improving economic indicators, the government has more work to do in order to create the foundation for a healthy investment environment that contributes to economic development and attracts foreign interest. The government has limited capacity and must prioritize among its long list of desired reforms. Currently, the country has many laws and regulations that are outdated and inadequate. Property rights are not well-established and land confiscation is a major concern. Investor protection and the criteria for foreign investment are not well-defined, and in addition to weak rule of law there are no proper mechanisms and instruments for enforcing contracts and property rights and for settling disputes. A lack of reliable data and information adds to the frustration that many foreign investors experience when attempting to look up market and consumer base information as well as capital and financial indicators. Investment approval procedures are not transparent, overly bureaucratic and complex, and exclude foreign participation in certain sectors.

The government's efforts to date indicate tentative progress toward the goal of a sound investment framework but investors should come in with "eyes wide open."

1. OPENNESS TO, AND RESTRICTIONS UPON, FOREIGN INVESTMENT

Attitude toward Foreign Direct Investment

Since 2011, Burma has made significant reforms to improve its legal and regulatory framework in order to create an attractive business climate capable of generating more inward foreign investment. The government has embarked on an ambitious agenda to strengthen the economy, tackle poverty and promote sustainable and equitable growth, and international investors – including from the United States – are closely watching actions to further open the economy and attract investment. Over the past several years, Burma's attitude towards Foreign Direct Investment (FDI) has been positive, and recent measures undertaken by the government, including ongoing revision of the Foreign Investment Law and the Special Economic Zone Law and the award of certain tenders and licenses to foreign businesses, illustrate the government's commitment to further openness. Observers expect FDI to Burma to continue growing in the short-term, but they note that further liberalization will be critical for sustaining FDI growth in the medium- to long-term. As the Organization for Economic Co-operation and Development (OECD) notes, policy uncertainty or backtracking on reforms, inconsistent implementation of rules, investor-state disputes which have been shown to discourage other foreign investors, or reputational risks for foreign investors from the government's failure to enforce environmental or social legislation which calls into question the responsible business conduct of investors could dissuade further foreign investment in Burma. Indeed, many investors are looking to elections scheduled for late 2015 – the degree to which they are held in an open and transparent manner, as well as the government's actions after the elections – as a key indicator of the government's willingness to continue to push forward on reforms.

Other Investment Policy Reviews

The OECD conducted an investment policy review of Burma in March 2014. The entire report can be found at:**http://www.oecd.org/daf/inv/investment-policy/Myanmar-IPR-2014.pdf**.

The World Trade Organization (WTO) conducted a trade policy review of Burma in March 2014. The entire report can be found at: **https://www.wto.org/english/tratop_e/tpr_e/s293_e.pdf**.

The World Bank's Doing Business 2015 report includes an analysis of Burma's investment sectors and business environment, and can be found at:**http://www.doingbusiness.org/~/media/GIAWB/Doing%20Business/Documents/Annual-Reports/English/DB15-Full-Report.pdf**.

The World Bank also conducted an enterprise survey of Burma in 2014, the results of which can be found at:**http://www.enterprisesurveys.org/data/exploreeconomies/2014/myanmar**.

DICA has released its own investment guide which can be found at: **http://dica.gov.mm.x-aas.net/admin/Pages/DisplayPdf?path=MIC%20-%20Myanmar%20Investment%20Guide%202014%20%28MIG2014%29_web.pdf**.

Laws/Regulations of Foreign Direct Investment

The main law applicable to foreign investors is the Foreign Investment Law which was approved by President Thein Sein in November 2012. The stated objectives of the 2012 Foreign Investment Law are to support:

The extraction/export of the rich natural resources of the state for the benefit of the people;

The creation and accumulation of jobs for the people;

The development of human resources;

The development of infrastructure such as banking and finance, modern roads, interstate highways, production of electricity and energy, and modern information technology;

Transportation of rail, water and air via an international standard to enable citizens to do business throughout the world; and

The advent of businesses and investments which are in line with established international practices and norms.

The Foreign Investment Law continues to limit certain types of foreign investment (see below).

Although many foreign investors feel that the Foreign Investment Law's stated objectives point to a positive, forward-thinking approach by the government, the OECD notes that the Foreign Investment Law "still leaves many questions unanswered, notably with respect to investor protection and the procedures for admitting foreign investors." In addition, Burma's current regulatory investment framework remains complex, and can cause confusion for investors given the numerous laws that regulate the entry of investors depending on the sector and the location, and depending on whether the investor is local or foreign. Investors have complained that the government's investment approval process (outlined below) is opaque, complex, onerous with regard to the paperwork required, and lengthy. Investors have also noted that the increase of foreign investor scrutiny of the country and the increase of investment proposals have overburdened the government, thereby creating a bottleneck when it comes to investment approvals.

In February 2015, the government released for public comment a draft Investment Law of 2015 that, when ratified, will consolidate and replace The Myanmar Citizens Investment Law of July 2013 (i.e., local investment law) and the 2012 Foreign Investment Law. Parliament may take up the draft law in coming months, but it is difficult to predict when the legislature will conclude deliberations and pass the draft given the large number of draft laws currently being considered by Parliament, as well as the body's impending shift of focus to elections scheduled for the end of the year.

Industrial Promotion

Different ministries and agencies promote investment into different sectors (e.g., the Ministry of Hotels and Tourism promotes responsible tourism investment), although the Directorate of Investment and Company Administration (DICA) under the Ministry of National Planning and Economic Development is officially mandated to coordinate investment promotion under the Foreign Investment Law.

Limits on Foreign Control

The Foreign Investment Law continues to limit certain types of foreign investment. Specifically, under the Foreign Investment Law, foreign investments cannot be made in the following businesses and services:

administration and conservation of natural forests;
production of traditional medicines;
drilling of oil wells whose depth does not exceed 1,000 feet;
small and medium scale mining;
cultivation and production of traditional herbal plants;
wholesale trading of components and scrap-iron;
traditional food production;
production of religious items and wares;
production of traditional and cultural items and wares;
handicraft production;
private specialist traditional hospitals;
trading of raw materials used for traditional medicines;
medical research and operation of laboratories for traditional medicine;
ambulance services;
care centers for the elderly;
catering on trains, freight forwarding using trains, cleaning of coaches, management of trains;
agency services;
[erection and operation of] power plants with less than 10 megawatts; and
printing, publishing and distribution of periodicals in local languages spoken in Myanmar, including the Myanmar language.

The Foreign Investment Law restricts foreign investment in certain agriculture and farming businesses, certain animal husbandry businesses, and certain fishery businesses. In addition, the implementing rules list those sectors requiring a joint venture (with a maximum of 80 percent foreign equity), as well as other foreign equity limitations and joint ventures permitted only with the state. The Foreign Investment Law has no minimum capital requirement for foreign ownership, except for (as noted) joint ventures in restricted sectors, although individual ownership requirements can be established by the Myanmar Investment Commission (MIC), which is in charge of assessing business proposals, setting requirements and conditions for investment and interpreting and overseeing the implementation of the Foreign Investment Law.

In addition to the Foreign Investment Law, the State-Owned Economic Enterprises Law, enacted in March 1989 and still in effect today, also regulates certain investments and economic activities. Under this law, state-owned enterprises (SOEs) have the sole right to carry out the following economic activities:

extraction of teak and sale of the same in the country and abroad;
cultivation and conservation of forest plantations, with the exception of village-owned firewood plantations cultivated by the villagers for their personal use;
exploration, extraction, sale, and production of petroleum and natural gas;
exploration, extraction, and export of pearls, jade, and precious stones;
breeding and production of fish and prawns in fisheries that have been reserved for research by the government;
postal and telecommunications services;
air transport and railway transport services;
banking and insurance services;
broadcasting and television services;
exploration, extraction, and exports of metals;
electricity generating services, other than those permitted by law to private and cooperative electricity generating services; and
manufacturing of products relating to security and defense.

However, the MIC, "in the interest of the State," can make exceptions to this law. In the past, the MIC has routinely granted numerous exceptions including through joint ventures or special licenses in the areas of banking (for domestic investors only), mining, petroleum and natural gas extraction, telecommunications, radio and television broadcasting, and air transport services. The 2012 Foreign Investment Law and its implementing regulations continue to grant the MIC broad discretion with regard to its decisions on investments. This can at times be beneficial to investors wishing to engage in economic activities in certain prohibited economic sectors.

This level of discretion allowed to the MIC is concerning. Although, as the OECD 2014 IPR notes, the system gives the government flexibility "to open progressively and selectively to foreign investment and to try to maximize the potential benefits from that investment," the same flexibility also creates uncertainty for investors "concerning the criteria upon which the decision to admit them is based [and] creates opportunities for corruption when individual officials are given responsibility for deciding on what basis to admit an investment project."

The Burmese armed forces are involved in many commercial activities via the Union of Myanmar Economic Holdings, Ltd. (UMEHL) and the Myanmar Economic Corporation (MEC). Foreign firms have in the past reported that an affiliation with UMEHL or MEC helped them receive the proper business permits when setting up a joint venture. Nonetheless, entering into business with UMEHL or MEC does not guarantee success for foreign partners. Under General License No. 17 issued by the Department of Treasury's Office of Foreign Assets Control (OFAC) on July 11, 2012, U.S. businesses are not allowed to invest or enter into an agreement with the Burmese Ministry of Defense or any state or non-state armed group, or any entity in which any of the above own a 50 percent or greater interest.

Privatization Program

According to the Government of Burma, the private sector's share in GDP is over 90%, with the State participating in telecommunication services, social and public administration, energy, forestry, construction, and electricity. According to the International Monetary Fund (IMF), the private sector is estimated to be closer to 85% of current GDP, although this is also based on data provided by the government. Another informal estimates place the private sector share between 65-70%. Prior to 2011, foreign participation was not allowed in the privatization process, however, in 2012, President Thein Sein created a new Privatization Commission headed by a Vice President. The commission is currently working on plans to adopt new privatization procedures that will emphasize open tenders and private-public-partnerships.

Screening of FDI

The MIC plays a leading role in the regulation of foreign investment, and approves all investment projects receiving incentives except those in special economic zones which are handled by the Central Working Body set up under the existing Special Economic Zone Law and joint ventures between foreign investors and state-owned economic enterprises which are the responsibility of the relevant line ministries.

The Foreign Investment Law outlines the procedures the MIC must take in considering foreign investments. Investment approvals are made on a case-by-case basis. To obtain an investment permit, the investor must submit a proposal in the prescribed form to the MIC, together with supporting documentation including details of intended activities and the financial credibility of the company/individual; an undertaking not to engage in trading activities; and annual reports for the last two financial years, or copies of the company's Head Office's balance sheet and profit and loss account for the last two financial years, notarized by the Burmese Embassy in the country where the company is incorporated. The MIC accepts or rejects an application within 15 days, and decides whether to approve the proposal within 90 days. Final approval comes from U Zayar Aung, Chairman of the MIC (and currently the Union Minister of Energy). The MIC evaluates foreign investment proposals and stipulates the terms and conditions of investment permits. An investor must also register with the Directorate of Investment and. Company Administration (DICA) – the MIC's Secretariat - except for joint ventures with State equity formed under the Special Company Act 1950. After depositing a registration fee in Myanmar Economic Bank, a foreign investor obtains a temporary registration certificate, valid for six months, then a Company Incorporation Certificate.

Although the MIC has no power to protect foreign companies, there is no evidence that the MIC discriminates against foreign investors. It should be noted that the MIC does not record some foreign investments if they do not require MIC approval, particularly for investors forming a joint venture with a military-controlled enterprise. Many smaller investments may also go unrecorded. Once licensed, foreign firms may register their companies locally, use their permits to obtain resident visas, lease cars and real estate, and obtain import and export licenses from the Ministry of Commerce. Foreign companies may register locally without an MIC license, in which case they are not entitled to receive the benefits and incentives provided for in the Foreign Investment Law.

More information on the MIC and DICA can be found at: http://dica.gov.mm.x-aas.net/. In addition, please find below contact information for the MIC:

Chairman U Zayar Aung
Myanmar Investment Commission
Building No.1
Thit Sar Road,
Yankin Township
Yangon Myanmar
Contact: U Aung Naing Oo, Director General, Directorate of Investment and Company Administration (DICA)
Tel: 0-1657891

Competition Law

A new Competition Law came into force on February 24, 2015. The objective of the law is to protect public interest from monopolistic acts, limit unfair competition, and prevent abuse of dominant position and economic concentration which weakens competition. Specifically, the Competition Law sets a foundation for creation of a regulatory body with investigative and adjudicative powers, addresses the three standard pillars of competition law (agreements that restrain competition, abuse of dominance and mergers) as well unfair trade practices, and establishes a comprehensive penalty regime.

The law classifies four types of behavior as sanctionable violations: acts restricting competition (applicable to all persons): acts leading to monopolies (applicable only to entrepreneurs); unfair competitive acts (applicable only to entrepreneurs); and business combinations such as mergers. The law also restricts the production of goods, market penetration, technological development and investment, although the government may exempt restrictive agreements "if they are aimed at reducing production costs and benefit consumers" such as reshaping the organizational structure and business model of a business so as to improve its efficiency; enhancing technology and technological advances for the improvement of the quality of goods and service; and promoting competitiveness of small and medium sized enterprises.

The Competition Law prohibits efforts to monopolize markets by: controlling prices of goods or services; limiting the availability of a good or service with the aim of controlling prices; reducing the availability of a good or service without appropriate reasons or lowering the quality of a good to reduce market demand; controlling or restrict the geographic market for sales to prevent entry and control market share; and interfering in another business' operations in an unfair manner.

The Competition Law also prohibits mergers where the merger is intended to lead to excessive domination of the market; the merger will reduce competition in a market with few competitors; or the resulting market share exceeds the thresholds prescribed by the Competition Commission. However, the law permits an otherwise prohibited merger where the resulting enterprise remains a SME; one of the merging parties was, or was likely to become, bankrupt; or the merger promotes exports or development of technology, systems or innovation.

The Competition Law creates the Competition Commission, the principal regulatory authority under the law and the Investigation Committee which will investigate conduct that may infringe the law. The penalties provided for "acts restricting competition" in Burma range from imprisonment up to three years and/or a fine of up to USD 15,000.

Burma is not party to any bilateral or regional agreement on anti-trust cooperation.

Investment Trends

According to the OECD, Burma's potential to attract FDI remains largely unexploited. The majority of the investment that Burma received in past decades went into natural resource sectors, with only a small portion of that investment going to the manufacturing or services sectors. However, this has started to change in recent years. The sectors receiving the largest share of FDI since 2011 include the oil and gas, transport and communication, tourism and power sectors, whereas the mining, agriculture, and livestock and fisheries sectors have received the lowest share of FDI.

Moving forward, observers expect the manufacturing and tourism services sectors to continue growing and attracting more FDI, given Burma's re-entry into the global economy and the removal of the majority of sanctions by Western countries. Conversely, observers suggest that political uncertainty and the rising influence of civil society may temporarily have halted or deterred new large-scale investments in the power and mining sectors.

However, as the World Bank's 2014 Enterprise Services Report notes, reforms to improve Burma's investment climate are urgently needed across a number of areas, especially in access to finance, land, electricity and skilled workers, which were identified as the top constraints. In addition, private firms also indicate that the incidence of corruption as measured by bribe payments is one of the highest in the region. Addressing these key constraints is critical to ensuring a fair and transparent business environment in which all private enterprises can grow and create jobs.

Table 1

Measure	Year	Index or Rank	Website Address
TI Corruption Perceptions index	2014	156 of 175	transparency.org/cpi2014/results
World Bank's Doing Business Report "Ease of Doing Business"	2014	177 of 189	doingbusiness.org/rankings
Global Innovation Index	2014	140 of 143	globalinnovationindex.org/content.aspx?page=data-analysis
World Bank GNI per capita	2013	n/a	data.worldbank.org/indicator/NY.GNP.PCAP.CD

Millennium Challenge Corporation Country Scorecard

The Millennium Challenge Corporation, a U.S. Government entity charged with delivering development grants to countries that have demonstrated a commitment to reform, produced scorecards for countries with a per capita gross national income (GNI) or USD 4,125 or less. Burma's scorecard is available here: https://assets.mcc.gov/scorecards/score-fy15-english-mm-burma.pdf.

2. CONVERSION AND TRANSFER POLICIES

Foreign Exchange

On April 2, 2012, Burma's multiple exchange rates were abolished and the Central Bank of Myanmar established a managed float of the Burmese kyat with an initial auction at 818 kyat per one U.S. dollar. The kyat has appreciated gradually since then and the exchange rate during the first quarter of 2015 floated between 1000 to 1076 kyat to the dollar.

Remittance Policies

According to the Foreign Investment Law, foreign investors have the right of remittance of foreign currency. Foreign investors are allowed to remit foreign currency overseas through banks which are authorized to conduct foreign banking business at the prevailing exchange rate. Banks began introducing remittance services during 2012 and the volume of such formal transfer is low but growing, according to local bank managers.

Nevertheless, in practice, the transfer of money in or out of Burma has been difficult, as many international banks have been slow to update their internal prohibitions on conducting business in Burma given the long history of U.S. and European sanctions that had isolated the country. The majority of foreign currency transactions are conducted through banks in Singapore. Despite the absence of any legal impediment, it appears that some U.S. banks still refuse to conduct money transfers to and from Burma.

The difficulties presented by the formal banking system are reflected in the continued use of informal sources of finance for loans and remittances by both the public and businesses. Although these informal sources tend to have higher interest charges, they offer an alternative to the limited loan services offered by banks, which provide almost only short-term credit for trade on a limited basis and require collateral. Remittances are also often made through a well-developed informal network of money carriers (aka the "hundi" system). Many overseas workers continue to use the hundi system to remit their money home though the volume of these informal transfers is declining gradually.

Burma is a "country of primary concern" in the 2014 International Narcotics Control Strategy Report. According to the report, Burma is not a regional or offshore financial center, its economy is underdeveloped and its banking sector is still relatively isolated. The report notes, however, that Burma's "prolific drug production, the growing use of credit/debit cards connected to international financial institutions, and lack of transparency make it attractive for domestic, and possibly, international money laundering" as do "the low risk of enforcement and prosecution." Key concerns raised in the report include Burma's level of poppy cultivation, corruption business and government, state-owned enterprises' and military holding companies' significant influence over the economy, including control of a substantial portion of Burma's natural resources, and weak rule of law. Burma does not engage in currency manipulation tactics.

3. EXPROPRIATION AND COMPENSATION

According to the OECD's 2014 IPR, Burma's "expropriation regime . . . does not appear to protect investors against indirect expropriations." In addition, it reports that Burma has not incorporated the principle of non-discrimination into its investment framework. Other than a constitutional safeguard that states that the government will not nationalize economic enterprises, there is no specific provision in Burma's legislation against expropriation without compensation. The Foreign Investment Law prohibits nationalization and states that foreign investments approved by the MIC will not be nationalized during the term of their investment. Specifically, the law states that "the Union Government guarantees that a business formed under the law shall not be nationalized within the term of the contract or the extended term if such term is extended." In addition, the law guarantees that the Government of Burma will not terminate an investment enterprise without reasonable cause, and on upon expiry of the contract, the Government of Burma guarantees an investor the withdrawal of foreign capital in the foreign currency in which the investment was made. Finally, the law states that "the Union Government guarantees that it shall not cease an investment enterprise operating under a Permit of the Commission before the expiry of the permitted term without any sufficient reason." The new Investment Law currently being drafted, when enacted, is expected to further strengthen the government's commitments related to non-discrimination, expropriation and nationalization.

Aside from the possibility of outright expropriation by the Government of Burma, private businesses have been subject to predatory practices by regime-linked cronies. Given the weak rule of law in Burma and the pervasive and powerful system of patronage, larger and more well-connected entities have generally been able to muscle out smaller competitors by denying access to markets, forcing the sale of assets, or otherwise disrupting business operations. However, public scrutiny of businesses is beginning to increase due to a more free and vibrant local press and an increasingly energetic Parliament, and that scrutiny is beginning to limit – or at least reduce the overt exercise of –such practices.

4. DISPUTE SETTLEMENT

Legal System, Specialized Courts, Judicial Independence, Judgments of Foreign Courts

Burmese criminal and civil laws are modeled on British law introduced during the colonial period, which ended in 1948. Every township, state, and division has its own law officers and judges. Following the transfer of power to a civilian government in March 2011, the regional military commanders and military authorities at the township, state, and divisional level no longer have authority over judicial decisions at the local and state/division level, although they still wield considerable influence that varies from region to region. Foreign companies have the right to bring cases to and defend themselves in local courts, but this option is rarely exercised due to concern about the impartiality of the courts. Foreign investors involved in conflicts with the government are unlikely to receive a court ruling in their favor.

Courts are neither independent nor impartial, thereby making local arbitration unreliable. Companies facing adverse administrative decisions have no recourse. In addition, Burma is not a member of the International Center for the Settlement of Investment Disputes. The Attorney General's Office and the Supreme Court exercise nominal control over the legal system in Burma, but neither body is independent of the government.

In order to address the concerns of foreign investors about dispute settlement in Burma, the government did take the significant step of acceding, on April 16, 2013, to the Convention on the Recognition and Enforcement of Foreign Arbitral Awards ("New York Convention"). However, it has not yet drafted domestic legislation to implement the New York Convention.

Bankruptcy

There is no bankruptcy law in Burma, and antiquated insolvency laws – such as The Insolvency Act of 1910 and The Insolvency Act of 1920 – are rarely used.

Investment Disputes

To date, Burma has not been party to any investment dispute. In addition, Burma has not been party to any dispute settlement proceeding at the WTO, as complainant, respondent, or third party.

International Arbitration

It is unclear on what grounds access to alternative dispute resolution, such as international arbitration, is an available option for foreign investors. According to the Foreign Investment Law, when disputes cannot be settled amicably between the parties concerned, the dispute should be settled according to the dispute settlement provisions of the "agreement" or in accordance with Burmese law if the contact contains no dispute settlement provisions, and that investors will inform the MIC about the dispute's circumstances as well as which mechanisms will be used to settle the dispute. According to the OECD, however, the exact meaning in the law of the term "agreement" is not specified, and observers are confused if "agreement" refers to contracts concluded between state authorities and individual foreign investors, or whether it also refers to bilateral investment treaties containing an investor-state dispute settlement provision. The OECD notes that lack of clarity on this front makes the dispute settlement regulations "vague on what options are de facto made available to investors seeking to resolve their disputes."

In the past, private and foreign companies suffered major disadvantages in disputes with Government of Burma and quasi-governmental entities. Foreign investors generally prefer to use the 1944 Arbitration Act, which allows for international arbitration. The Burmese government usually tries to stipulate local arbitration in contracts it signs with foreign investors.

ICSID Convention and New York Convention

Burma is not a party to the 1965 Convention on the Settlement of Investment Disputes between States and Nationals of other States (ICSID).

In 2013 the government ratified The Convention on the Recognition and Enforcement of Foreign Arbitral Awards (New York Convention).

Duration of Dispute Resolution

The Foreign Investment Law does stipulate that a foreign investor is entitled to have its dispute settled by foreign arbitration, although it should be noted that there are no domestic laws in place to reinforce international arbitration. Foreign investors have the benefit of the Foreign Investment Law which guarantees certain investment protections to the foreign investor. Because the Foreign Investment Law was only promulgated in November 2012, there has been insufficient time to determine how the law will be implemented in practice, how the Burmese courts will interpret the provisions of the Foreign Investment Law to determine investment disputes, and how long it will take to resolve investment and commercial disputes under this current system. The new Investment Law currently being drafted is expected to allow for the settlement of disputes through international arbitration.

5. PERFORMANCE REQUIREMENTS AND INVESTMENT INCENTIVES

WTO/TRIMS

Burma is a World Trade Organization member. To date, no claims have been raised against Burma on its maintenance of any measures that are inconsistent with the WTO's Trade Related Investment Measures (TRIMs) requirements.

Investment Incentives

According to Article 27 of the Foreign Investment Law, in order to promote foreign investment, the Government of Burma will grant new investors a five year tax holiday with an option for further exemption if the enterprise is beneficial to the State. The Foreign Investment Law also details several other exemptions and avenues of relief such as a three year exemption on custom duties and the relief from commercial tax for goods produced for export. In addition, Article 27 (j) grants an exemption from customs duty or other internal taxes for any machinery or equipment, or materials imported in order to expand the business.

The Myanmar Economic Zones Law also contains certain investment incentives for investors. Under the law, investors located in a Special Economic Zone (SEZ) may apply for income tax exemption for the first five years from the date of commencement of commercial operations, followed by a reduction of the income tax rate by 50% for the proceeding five year period. Under the law, if profits during the next third five year period are re-invested within one year, investors can apply for a 50% reduction of the income tax rate for profits derived from such re-investment.

Research and Development

There is no data (anecdotal or otherwise) that indicates that foreign firms are able to participate in government/authority financed and/or subsidized research and development programs.

Performance Requirements

Foreign investors must recruit at least 25% of their employees from the local labor force in the first two years of their investment. The local employment ratio increases to 50% for the third and fourth years, and 75% for the fifth and sixth years.

Data Storage

The Government of Burma does not follow forced localization, and foreign investors are not yet required to use domestic content in goods or technology. The Government of Burma is currently developing laws, rules and regulations on information technology (IT), and does not have in place requirements for foreign IT providers to turn over source code and/or provide access to surveillance.

6. RIGHT TO PRIVATE OWNERSHIP AND ESTABLISHMENT

To date, foreigners cannot purchase and own land or condominiums in Burma and – until September 2011 – could only rent property on a short-term basis, with leases typically limited to one year. However, according to Article 31 of the Foreign Investment Law, foreigners can invest in real estate development through a joint venture or by 100% ownership through a build-operate-transfer (BOT) lease agreement with the government. Under the joint venture scheme, foreign participation is limited to 80% (i.e., local citizens or enterprises must own at least 20% of the equity). The BOT lease agreements provide full ownership to foreign investors, although they are limited to 70 years. The law also allows foreigners to take over BOT leases from locals.

The government is currently drafting and considering a condominium law that would allow foreigners to lease, buy, exchange, or give a condominium unit located on the sixth floor or above in condominium buildings. Under the draft law, the maximum share allocated for foreigner units in any given condominium building would be 40%. Real estate observers had expected the law to be passed in 2014, although the expected date of passage is now mid-2015.

Most real estate transactions in Burma require cash, although banks have begun limited introduction of a consumer lending product that resembles a mortgage loan. Regular bank loans are difficult to obtain and are not available to foreigners. In accordance with The Transfer of Immovable Property Restriction Law of 1987, mortgages of immovable property are prohibited if the mortgagee is a foreigner, foreign company or foreign bank.

7. PROTECTION OF PROPERTY RIGHTS

Real Property

On paper, Burma has a legal system which protects and facilitates the acquisition and disposition of property such as land and buildings. However, judicial decisions can often be influenced through government interference, personal relationships or bribes, resulting in a judicial process that is perceived as far from impartial and fair. Burma also suffers from an antiquated legal system and outdated legislation; many laws are vague and often subject to manipulation. A lack of rule of law and an ineffective, corrupt judiciary pose major challenges for U.S. private sector constituents looking to do business in Burma. Furthermore, local entities may engage in deceptive, coercive activities by bribing local judges or using personal connections to obtain favorable judgments. A continuing area of concern involves land acquisition for large-scale investment projects. Property rights are not well-established and populations living on the land have complained about inadequate consultation and compensation.

Intellectual Property Rights

Burma does not have adequate intellectual property rights protection. Patent, trademark, industrial design, and copyright laws and regulations are antiquated and deficient, and there is minimal regulation and enforcement of existing statutes. For example, the registration of patents and designs in Burma is still governed by the Indian Patents and Designs Act of 1911, enacted under British colonial rule. The British colonial government also published a Copyright Act in 1914, but neither the colonial government nor the Government of Burma ever instituted a means to register copyrights. Consequently, there is no legal protection in Burma for foreign copyrights. In addition, Burma has no trademark law, although trademark registration is possible. Some firms place caution notices in local newspapers to declare ownership of their trademarks. After publication, the owners can take criminal and/or civil action against trademark infringers. Title to a trademark depends on use of the trademark in connection with goods sold in Burma.

Burma does not have in place a judicial court specifically dealing with intellectual property rights. Disputes related to the infringement of intellectual property rights are governed by common rules of civil and criminal procedure. Similarly, there is no institution in charge of supervising the administration, registration and enforcement of intellectual property.

The lack of adequate intellectual property rights translates to piracy and other intellectual property rights violations in Burma. Piracy of music CDs, video CDs, CD-ROMS, DVDs, books, software, and product designs is evident nationwide, especially in border regions and in the two major urban centers of Rangoon and Mandalay. Most consumers of information technology products in Burma, both in the private sector and in government, use pirated software. Given the small number of local customers, poor state of the economy, and lack of infrastructure (e.g., unreliable electricity for manufacturing), piracy does not have a significant adverse impact on U.S. products.

The Government of Burma is attempting to address these legal deficiencies and the high level of piracy within Burma. After Burma joined ASEAN in 1997, it agreed to modernize its intellectual property laws in accordance with the ASEAN Framework Agreement on Intellectual Property Cooperation. The Ministry of Science and Technology has drafted four new intellectual property laws – on trademarks, copyrights, patents, and industrial design – with the aim of creating a modern, comprehensive legal framework for intellectual property rights and improving Burma's business climate. The Ministry of Science and Technology has received advice from external stakeholders and experts during the drafting process. It expects to submit the draft laws to Parliament by mid-2015 with the expectation that Parliament approve the draft laws by end-2015. The Government of Burma is also exploring the establishment of a single national Intellectual Property Office that would monitor compliance with intellectual property laws and be responsible for further developing intellectual policy and regulations. In addition, the WTO has delayed required implementation of the Trade Related Aspects of Intellectual Property (TRIPs) Agreement for Least Developed Nations – including Burma – until 2021.

Burma is not listed in USTR's Special 301 report and is not listed in USTR's notorious market report.

For additional information about treaty obligations and points of contact at local IP offices, please see WIPO's country profiles at **http://www.wipo.int/directory/en/**.

Resources for Rights Holders

For Intellectual Property Rights issues in Burma, please contact:

Peter N. Fowler
Regional IP Attaché
U.S. Patent and Trademark Office
American Embassy Bangkok, Thailand
Tel: (662) 205-5913
Email: **Peter.Fowler@trade.gov**

Information on the American Chamber of Commerce (AmCham) Myanmar Chapter can be found at:**http://www.amchammyanmar.com/**

8. TRANSPARENCY OF THE REGULATORY SYSTEM

Burma lacks regulatory and legal transparency. In the past all existing regulations, including those covering foreign investment, import-export procedures, licensing, and foreign exchange, were subject to change with no advance or written notice, and without opportunity for public comment. The government continues to issue new regulations or laws often with no advance notice and little if any opportunity for review or comment by domestic or foreign market participants. Draft bills are not always made available for public comment and there is no formal public consultation process to publish and seek comment on proposed laws and regulations.

The Government of Burma, however, is attempting to enhance transparency in the public sector by using websites to publish information online and by establishing websites through which businesses can access trade information. The Ministry of Commerce, for example, publishes a weekly Commerce Journal, and a monthly Trade News booklet, providing trade-related information. In the past three years, the Government of Burma has also published new regulations and laws in government-run newspapers and "The Burma Gazette" more frequently than in the past.

In 2014, the Government of Burma became a candidate country in the Extractive Industries Transparency Initiative (EITI) -- a global standard for the promotion of revenue transparency. EITI requires extractives-related companies to declare any payments made to the government, and the Government of Burma is required to declare its revenues from extractive sectors. The World Bank will assist Burma in the conditions it must fulfill as an EITI candidate country, including the creation of a report by January 2016 that discusses revenues from certain sub-sectors of Burma's extractives sector, including oil and gas and mineral industries.

9. EFFICIENT CAPITAL MARKETS AND PORTFOLIO INVESTMENT

Burma has extremely small equity and debt markets in which foreigners cannot engage, and average citizens do not have portfolio investments. Banks are the primary buyers of government bonds issued by the Central Bank of Myanmar, which has established a fledgling bond market auction system. The Central Bank of Myanmar issues government treasury bonds with maturities of two, three and five years. Several Burmese companies sell bonds privately on a very small scale.

Burma's stock exchange, the Myanmar Securities Exchange Center, a joint venture of Myanmar Economic Bank and Japan's Daiwa Institute of Research. Almost no activity takes place on this unregulated stock exchange except for over-the-counter trading of government treasury bonds. On July 30, 2013, the Securities Exchange Law came into effect. The law provides the framework for the establishment of a stock exchange and is meant to promote the development of a market-oriented system, safeguard the participants who take part in the securities exchange certificate market, and encourage more participation by the public in financial markets. Specifically, the new law establishes a securities and exchange commission, the main regulatory body to supervise the securities market, as well as sets out licenses available for securities businesses (such as dealing, brokerage, underwriting, investment advisory and company's representative). In addition, the law provides for the establishment of an over the counter market, specifies the prohibited acts relating to securities trading (e.g. insider trading) and the penalties, and provides for the establishment of a securities depository and clearing business.

Implementation of the Securities Exchange Law is a positive step toward the development of an equity market. In 2012, the Central Bank of Myanmar signed a Memorandum of Understanding with the Tokyo Stock Exchange and Daiwa Securities Group to establish a fully-operational stock exchange by the end of 2015. Observers had expressed concern that this target would be missed because of slow progress on establishing a regulatory framework and a securities regulator. Despite passage of the Securities Exchange Law, however, it is unclear whether it will be effectively implemented, including the establishment of a credible and securities regulatory commission, in 2015 and whether many Burmese companies will be ready to list on the new exchange.

Private companies, whether foreign or domestically controlled, are generally small in size. Usually, a small number of people or entities, often within the same family, closely hold the business shares.

Money and Banking System, Hostile Takeovers

The Central Bank of Myanmar (CBM) is empowered to assume supervisory and regulatory functions for the banking sector. The CBM's policy objectives include domestic price stability, financial stability, and efficient payment systems, and the CBM is responsible for approving new banks and supervising new and existing banks. In 2013, the CBM was separated from the Ministry of Finance with a view to making it an independent central bank with greater autonomy in accordance with the new Central Bank of Myanmar Law, which entered into force the same month. The CBM intends to develop the banking sector in three phases: (i) allowing domestic private banks to operate joint ventures with foreign banks; (ii) allowing foreign banks to establish wholly owned locally incorporated subsidiaries; and (iii) allowing foreign banks to open direct branches in Burma.

There are four state-owned banks: the Myanmar Economic Bank (MEB), the Myanmar Foreign Trade Bank (MFTB), the Myanmar Investment and Commercial Bank, and the Myanmar Agricultural Development Bank. The role of the MEB, the largest bank in Myanmar, is to provide domestic and international banking services. The MFTB specializes in international banking. The Myanmar Investment and Commercial Bank carries out domestic and international banking business and extends banking services to private companies, including foreign joint ventures. The MADB extends agricultural credits to farmers. According to the government, the regulatory regime is the same for state-owned banks and private banks

Currently the CBM allows 11 domestic banks to conduct international currency transactions. In October 2014, however, the government awarded limited banking licenses to nine foreign banks – all from the Asia-Pacific region – allowing each bank to set up one branch and to provide loans to foreign companies. Four of the nine banks will begin operations at the end of April. Government officials said the banks will be restricted to providing loans in foreign currency and be required to partner with local banks in order to lend to local companies. The limited licenses are a "preliminary approval" to set up operations, and the government will review individual banks' operations on October 2015 before deciding whether to grant permanent licenses.

Despite recent reforms, Burma's banks continue to face a number of significant regulatory restrictions that limit the growth of lending, though deposits have grown significantly over the past years, albeit from a low base. As these restrictions are eased in the coming months and years, prompting further growth, the Government of Burma will need to address weaknesses in the country's supervisory and regulatory framework and in the internal business practices of private and government-linked banks. According to official figures published by Burma's Central Statistical Organization, total bank deposits by the end of November 2014 were approximately USD 15.3 billion.

10. COMPETITION FROM STATE-OWNED ENTERPRISES

As noted, the Government of Burma reserves for state-owned enterprises (SOEs) many lucrative sectors and sectors deemed sensitive (see above for the full list). For example, according to the 1989 State-Owned Economic Enterprises Law, state-owned enterprises have the sole right to carry out certain economic activities (see above). For example, exploration of natural gas in inland areas as well as downstream operations is reserved for the Myanmar Oil and Gas Enterprise (MOGE), a state-owned enterprise. The Government of Burma also has the sole right over the exploration and extraction of pearl, jade, and precious stones and, exports thereof. Myanma Railways, another state-owned enterprise, owns the rail infrastructure and holds the monopoly over freight and passenger rail transport services. However, the government has in practice licensed private sector competitors to operate in these nominally restricted sectors. As a result, for example, state-owned operator Myanma Airways' former dominance of domestic air transport has been eroded by the entry of new privately owned airlines, and state-owned institutions no longer dominate the banking and non-banking financial sector due to the recent growth of privately owned banks.

Starting in 2012, the Government of Burma began taking steps to reduce state-owned enterprises' reliance on government support and to make them more competitive through joint ventures. This included reducing budget subsidies for financing the raw material requirements of state-owned enterprises. The Government of Burma also continued efforts to privatize or lease enterprises and real estate properties to both foreign and domestic investors. Additional tenders for the sale or lease of state-owned enterprises and properties are expected during 2015.

OECD Guidelines on Corporate Governance of SOEs

Corporate governance of state-owned enterprises (SOE's) is not transparent, and they not required by law to publicly release annual reports. In general, a regulatory framework for corporate governance, including both private sector companies and state-owned ones, is lacking. In addition, the Government of Burma requires that state-owned enterprises use only state-owned banks for their financial transactions. Private enterprises do not compete on the same terms and conditions as state-owned enterprises. As a result, Burmese state-owned enterprises are inefficient and are unlikely to be able to compete with the private sector, especially foreign companies, on a level playing field.

Sovereign Wealth Funds

Burma does not have a sovereign wealth fund.

11. CORPORATE SOCIAL RESPONSIBILITY

Burma does not have a deep awareness of corporate social responsibility (CSR). Many local companies (and some international firms) still equate CSR with in-kind donations or charitable contributions. Burma is a deeply religious country with the majority of its residents practicing the Buddhist religion which holds that one may increase one's standing in the cycle of reincarnation by "making merit" through acts of charity. As a result, most Burmese business owners, including so-called cronies, often donate money, build schools, hospitals, low-rent apartments or even pay above the market wage as a result of their Buddhist faith. However, in recent years the Union of Myanmar Chambers of Commerce and Industry (UMFCCI), Burma's largest private sector association, has been promoting the United Nations Global Compact and CSR principles in general.

Private companies owned by foreign nationals from China, South Korea, Japan or other ASEAN countries may practice some form of CSR, but such practices are largely absent in the Burmese market. Several U.S. companies are actively incorporating CSR as an integral part of their entry (or pre-entry) strategy for Burma.

The Government of Burma does not have in place corporate governance, accounting, or executive compensation standards. Nonetheless, since 2011, Burmese civil society organizations have become more vocal in protesting against companies or government sponsored projects which they view as violating social standards.

The United States remains concerned about the protection of human rights, corruption, and the role of the military in the Burmese economy and as such require all new U.S. investment in excess of USD 500,000 to be subject to certain reporting requirements available at **http://www.humanrights.gov/2012/07/11/burmaresponsibleinvestment/**. There are several components to these reporting requirements. Investors are required to file reports with the State Department on an annual basis, to include a version of the report that the Department will make publicly available, consistent with relevant U.S. law. Key information that companies report on include information regarding policies and procedures with respect to human rights, workers' rights, environmental stewardship, land acquisitions, arrangements with security service providers, and, aggregate annual payments exceeding USD 10,000 to Burmese government entities, including state-owned enterprises. The purpose of the public report is to promote greater transparency and encourage civil society to partner with our companies toward responsible investment. The above reporting requirements apply to any new investment, whatever corporate form it might take. In addition, individuals or entities undertaking new investment pursuant to an agreement or pursuant to the exercise of rights under such an agreement, that is entered into with the Myanma Oil and Gas Enterprise (MOGE) must notify the Department of State within 60 days of their new investment.

For more information on U.S. government policies on issues of corporate social responsibility, please see the U.S. Government Approach on Business and Human Rights, released in May 2013. The Approach can be found at:**http://www.humanrights.gov/2013/05/01/u-s-government-approach-on-business-and-human-rights/**.

OECD Guidelines for Multinational Enterprises

Burma has not yet implemented the OECD Guidelines for Multinational Enterprises and does not proactively encourage foreign and local enterprises to follow generally accepted CSR principles included within the guidelines. Burma does not proactively encourage adherence to the United Nations Guiding Principles on Business and Human Rights.

12. POLITICAL VIOLENCE

There were no instances of political violence against Americans in 2014. Although political demonstrations and rallies are normally peaceful, spontaneous rioting, and attacks on individuals can occur due to the density of most gatherings and the mob mentality of unaccountability/anonymity that often prevails. In February and March 2015, student demonstrators protesting a new education law and police forces clashed in Rangoon and in Letpadan, leading to some instances of violence. In February 2015, garment workers on strike in an industrial zone in Rangoon also clashed with police forces.

Burma experienced sporadic bombing attacks in 2010 and 2011. In October 2013, an improvised explosive device, one of several employed over a 24 hour period, went off in a downtown Rangoon hotel, wounding an American woman. There is no indication that these attacks targeted U.S. citizens or U.S. interests. Local authorities regularly claim to discover explosive devices at various locations throughout Burma. In most cases, no groups claim responsibility.

While violence or demonstrations rarely target American or other Western interests in Burma, several ethnic groups are engaged in ongoing civil conflict with the Government of Burma. For decades, there has been anti-government insurgent activity in various locations, particularly near Burma's borders. These border areas have seen sporadic fighting between government forces and insurgent groups throughout the past 50 years. Currently, most ethnic minority groups have signed cease fire agreements with the central government and a national ceasefire agreement is under negotiation. Nonetheless, in Kachin State, in northern Burma on the border of China, instances of armed clashes between the Kachin Independence Army (KIA) and the Burmese Army periodically have flared up since June 2011. More recently, in February 2015, an alliance of armed groups in Kokang (a self-administered zone in northern Shan State which borders China's southern Yunnan province) attacked multiple Burmese military positions in an effort to regain land lost in a 2009 conflict, consequently leading to a large scale offensive against rebel positions by the military. Burma's military declared martial law and a state of emergency in Kokang.

Certain states in Burma also experience inter-communal violence. Violence between Buddhists and Muslims has led to enhanced international scrutiny. In 2012, riots and associated violence in Rakhine State in the western part of Burma left nearly 200 people dead and thousands displaced. In March 2013, in Meiktila in central Burma, violence between Buddhists and Muslims left more than 40 people dead. More recently, in March 2014, riots and looting in the capital of Rakhine State led to the destruction of international non-governmental organizations' (INGO) properties and supplies, and led to the mass evacuation of INGO staff.

For the latest security information, U.S. citizens living and traveling abroad should regularly monitor the Department of State's Consular Affairs website at http://travel.state.gov, where the current Worldwide Caution, Travel Alerts, Travel Warnings and health-information resources can be found.

13. Corruption

There are high levels of corruption in Burma. Due to a complex and capricious regulatory/legal environment and extremely low government salaries, rent-seeking activities are ubiquitous. Bribes are expected – and given – to facilitate many official transactions, from the smallest to the largest. Most citizens view corruption as a normal practice and requirement for survival.

Many economists and businesspeople consider corruption one of the most serious barriers to investment and commerce in Burma. In its 2014 Corruption Perceptions Index, Transparency International rated Burma 156th out of 177 countries, a jump up from the 2013 ranking of 157 and the 2012 rating of 172nd out of 177. In their Doing Business 2015 report, the World Bank and the International Finance Corporation ranked Burma 177 out of 189 countries, a jump from the 2014 ranking of 182 out of 189 countries on ease of doing business. The report cites corruption as a major disruptive force in conducting business in the country, and that the major areas where investors run into corruption are when seeking investment permits, in the taxation process, when applying for import and export licenses, and when negotiating land and real estate leases. The World Bank's 2014 Myanmar Enterprise Survey, however, contained a surprising survey result that business owners and managers did not cite corruption as a major constraint for doing business in Burma. The survey – which included survey results from business owners and managers from 632 private firms in five urban areas in Burma - cited access to financing as the top constraint facing businesses. Less than one percent of businesses owners and managers cited corruption as the top business constraint facing their firms. World Bank officials stressed that the World Bank continues to view corruption as a serious problem in Burma, adding that perceptions among local businessmen of corruption as a "fact of life" may have contributed to the low figure.

The Government of Burma appears to recognize the international community's perception of corruption in the country. Consequently, on March 7, 2013, the Government of Burma enacted an Anti-Corruption Law (which stipulates the specific offenses and accompanying punishment in bribery cases as well as includes language on an anti-bribery enforcement mechanism), and followed implementation of the law with its February 25, 2014 formation of a national commission to address bribery and graft (as mandated under the law).

UN Anticorruption Convention, OECD Convention on Combatting Bribery

Burma signed the UN Anticorruption Convention in December 2005 and ratified the convention on December 20, 2012.

Burma is not party to the OECD Convention on Combating Bribery of Foreign Public Officials in International Business Transactions.

Resources to Report Corruption

NAME: James J. Shea
TITLE: Economic Officer
ADDRESS OF MISSION: U.S. Embassy/110 University Avenue/Kamayut Township 11041/Rangoon, Burma
TELEPHONE NUMBER: 95 (0)1 536 509 Ext. 4248
EMAIL ADDRESS: **BurmaBusiness@state.gov**

14. BILATERAL INVESTMENT AGREEMENTS

Burma has signed and ratified several bilateral investment agreements with China, India, Japan, Philippines, and Thailand. It has also signed bilateral investment agreements with Israel, Laos, and Vietnam although these have not yet entered into force. The most recent investment agreement is a 2014 Korea- Burma investment guarantee treaty. Burma has also engaged in investment treaty negotiations with Russia, Mongolia, Bangladesh, Iran, Serbia, and Hong Kong, China. Observers opine that these agreements have had little impact on enhancing incoming investment from other countries in the region and that it is still too early to tell what impact, if any, these agreements will have in enhancing investment in Burma. Texts of the agreements or treaties that have come into force are available on the UNCTAD website at: **http://investmentpolicyhub.unctad.org/IIA/CountryBits/144**.

In 2013, the United States and Burma signed a Trade and Investment Framework Agreement. The United States and Burma have not yet engaged in discussions on bilateral investment treaty or a free trade agreement. Burma does not have a bilateral taxation treaty with the United States.

Through its membership in ASEAN, Burma is also a party to the ASEAN Comprehensive Investment Agreement, as well as to the ASEAN-Australia-New Zealand Free Trade Agreement, the ASEAN-Korea Free Trade Agreement, and the China-ASEAN Free Trade Agreement, which all contain an investment chapter that provides protection standards to qualifying foreign investors.

Burma has bilateral trade agreements with Bangladesh, Sri Lanka, China, South Korea, Laos, Malaysia, the Philippines, Thailand, and Vietnam in the Asian region, as well as with a number of Eastern European countries.

Bilateral Taxation Treaties

Burma does not have a bilateral taxation treaty with the United States.

15. OPIC AND OTHER INVESTMENT INSURANCE PROGRAMS

On May 21, 2013, the Overseas Private Investment Corporation (OPIC) signed an Investment Incentive Agreement with Burma. In 2014, OPIC announced that its financing and insurance programs are available for Burma.

On February 6, 2014, the Export-Import Bank of the United States (Ex-Im Bank) announced that it would open for business in Burma to help finance short-term and medium-term U.S. export sales. Ex-Im Bank can now provide export-credit insurance, loan guarantees and direct loans for creditworthy export sales to Burma. Short-term insurance is available for sovereign transactions with repayment terms of 180 days or less, and up to 360 days for capital goods. Medium-term insurance, loan guarantees and loans are available for sovereign transactions with terms typically up to five years. The Ex-Im Bank is also able to provide long-term support in Burma, provided there are financing arrangements that eliminate or externalize country risks, such as asset-backed financings and structures that earn revenues offshore in a third country.

On December 17, 2013, Burma became a member of the World Bank's Multilateral Investment Guarantee Agency (MIGA), which means that direct foreign investment into the country is eligible for the agency's investment guarantees.

16. LABOR

Until March 2012, independent labor unions were illegal in Burma, and workers were not allowed to organize, negotiate, or in any other legal way exercise control over their working conditions. However, in October 2011, the Government of Burma passed the Labor Organization Law, which legalized the formation of trade unions and allows workers to go on strike for the first time in Burma's modern history. The Labor Organization Law took effect in March 2012 and as of January 2015 roughly 1100 enterprise level unions had been formed in a variety of industries ranging from garments/textiles to agriculture to heavy industry. Though the passage of the Labor Organization Law has engendered a nascent labor movement in Burma, there is a very low level of awareness of labor issues among workers, employers, and even government officials. Labor groups and unions as well as other civil society actors are devising awareness-raising campaigns in order to educate workers on their rights.

Burma's labor costs are very low, even when compared to most of its Southeast Asian neighbors. Older Burmese, particularly those over 65 years of age, are generally well-educated. Many studied English in mission schools during the British colonial and early independence period. The military's nationalization of schools in 1964, its discouragement of English language classes in favor of Burmese, the lack of investment in education by the Government of Burma, and the repeated closing of Burmese universities over the past 20 years have taken a toll on the country's young. Skilled labor and managerial staff are in high demand and short supply, leading to high turnover. Most in the 15-39 year old demographic group lack technical skills and English proficiency. In order to address this gap, the Government of Burma's Employment and Skill Development Law entered into effect in December 2013. Among other things, the law provides for compulsory contributions on the part of employers to a "skill development fund", although this provision has not been implemented yet.

Although government regulations set a minimum employment age, wage rate, and maximum work hours, managers do not uniformly observe these regulations, especially in the private sector. In 2009, the Ministry of Finance and Revenue set the minimum wage at 1000 kyat (roughly USD 1.17) per day. The Ministry of Finance and Revenue has raised government salaries regularly since 2010 but has not revised the minimum wage for other workers. An average worker in Burma earns about 1500 kyat (roughly USD 1.76) per day, although this amount can be more or less depending on the type of work and whether it is in urban or rural areas. On March 22, 2013, the Government of Burma's Minimum Wage Law came into effect. The law, however, does not update or specify Burma's minimum wage, and instead created a National Committee made up of government, private sector and civil society representatives to determine a minimum wage and it application. The committee is currently working on national minimum wage survey.

In the past, the Government of Burma has utilized forced labor in its construction of commercial enterprises and for porterage and military building. In addition, Burma has been condemned for recruitment and use of child soldiers in armed combat by the military and by non-state armed groups. These labor practices are inconsistent with Burma's obligations under several International Labor Organization (ILO) Conventions, leading to the imposition of sanctions against Burma in 2000. In 2012, the ILO suspended those actions because of recent progress in labor rights and reform.

In addition to passage of the Labor Organization Law (see above), in March 2012, the Government of Burma passed the Ward or Village Tract Administration Law which defines, prohibits and criminalizes the use of forced labor in Burma, and simultaneously repealed an old colonial era law that had sanctioned the practice. In December 2013, the Government of Burma ratified ILO Convention 182 on the elimination of the worst forms of child labor. The ILO continues to work with the Burmese Government on forced labor issues under the Supplementary Understanding on Forced Labor which was signed in February 2007 and renewed in January 2012, and will also engage with the Government of Burma on the issues of child soldiers and child labor. The United States strongly supports ILO activities in Burma.

Although the government does not publish unemployment figures, anecdotal evidence indicates a level of unemployment as high as 20% and underemployment in formal, non-agricultural sectors.

Although workers have held small strikes since the passage of the Labor Organization Law, the largest strikes to date occurred in February and March 2015. Approximately 900 garment workers from five Korean-owned garment factories in Rangoon's Shwe Pyi Thar industrial zone went on strike in early March, demanding higher wages. After three weeks of protests and sit-ins, several groups of workers began marching through downtown Rangoon in mid-March, leading to a confrontation with local police forces that ended with the arrest of several workers and union leaders. Several international labor groups and NGOs as well as local media criticized the police's actions and arrest as overly zealous. As of April, four union leaders remained in the jail awaiting their trial hearings.

The government is currently working on a mandate from President Thein Sein's office to abolish all antiquated labor laws and to introduce new labor laws and regulations by June 2015. The government expects to repeal the antiquated Dockworkers Act (1948) and introduce to Parliament new laws on occupational safety and health and alien workers by June 2015. The government also hopes to amend a range of labor-related laws, including those associated with factory labor, wage payments, and shops and establishments.

On November 13, 2014, the Governments of the United States, Burma, Japan, Denmark, and the ILO formally launched the Initiative to Promote Fundamental Labor Rights and Practices in Myanmar (Initiative). The overarching goal of the Initiative is to promote a culture of compliance with fundamental labor rights. The Initiative supports two main objectives: (i) improving Myanmar's system of labor administration through comprehensive labor law reform and government capacity building on enforcement and administration; and (ii) building stakeholder engagement and strengthening labor relations. The Initiative is intended to cultivate relationships between business, labor, and civil society stakeholders and the

Government of Burma. These relationships are expected to serve as the foundation for a strong system of institutionalized social dialogue, industrial relations (employers and workers), and effective government engagement with broader civil society going forward, as well as to facilitate the promotion of corporate social responsibility in Burma, drawing from the United Nations (UN) Guiding Principles on Business and Human Rights..

17. FOREIGN TRADE ZONES/FREE PORTS/TRADE FACILITATION

The government has set aside 19 industrial zones, large tracts of land surrounding Rangoon, Mandalay, and other major cities, and is exploring the creation of another seven industrial zones. However, all these areas are merely zoned for industrial use and none of them come with any special services or investment incentives.

Burma enacted a Special Economic Zone Law in January 2011 that was replaced by the Myanmar Economic Zones Law which President Thein Sein ratified in January 2014. Under the newer law, investors located in a Special Economic Zone (SEZ) may apply for income tax exemption for the first five years from the date of commencement of commercial operations, followed by a reduction of the income tax rate by 50% for the proceeding five year period. Under the law, if profits during the preceding five year period are re-invested within one year, investors can apply for a 50% reduction of the income tax rate for profits derived from such re-investment. The law also mandates the formation of an SEZ central authority and a management committee. The management committee will be responsible for setting wage levels and monitoring the ratio of local and foreign labor. Under the law, local skilled labor should compose at minimum 25 percent of the total workforce in the first year, 50 percent in the second year and 75 percent in the third year. The law also stipulates the conditions needed in order to establish new zones.

There are three SEZs in Burma: one in Dawei, Tanintharyi Division; one at Kyaukphyu off the western coast of Rakhine State, and one in Thilawa on the outskirts of Rangoon. The Dawei and Kyaukphyu SEZs are being developed as deep sea ports. Initially, Thailand-based Italian-Thai Development Public Company Limited (ITD) was the project developer of the Dawei SEZ. However, after ITD failed to raise sufficient financing, the Government of Burma took over the project, and the search for a new developer continues. The governments of Burma and Japan have established a joint venture (with 51 percent Burma ownership, including a private sector Burmese business consortium) to develop the Thilawa SEZ, and the Thilawa SEZ already hosts port facilities that can accommodate larger vessels. Construction of the first factories in the Thilawa SEZ began in 2014 and is expected to be complete by the end 2015. The government has yet to award a tender for the development of the Kyaukphyu SEZ.

18. Foreign Direct Investment and Foreign Portfolio Investment Statistics

Table 2: Key Macroeconomic Data, U.S. FDI in Host Country/Economy

	Host Country Statistical source*		USG or international statistical source		USG or International Source of Data: BEA; IMF; Eurostat; UNCTAD, Other
Economic Data	Year	Amount	Year	Amount	
Host Country Gross Domestic Product (GDP) ($M USD)	n/a	n/a	2013	5,000	IMF staff estimates/projections
Foreign Direct Investment	Host Country Statistical source*		USG or international statistical source		USG or international Source of data: BEA; IMF; Eurostat; UNCTAD, Other
U.S. FDI in partner country ($M USD, stock positions)	n/a	n/a	2013	1	http://bea.gov/international/factsheet/factsheet.cfm?Area=606
Host country's FDI in the United States ($M USD, stock positions)	n/a	n/a	2013	<1	http://bea.gov/international/factsheet/factsheet.cfm?Area=606
Total inbound stock of FDI as % host GDP	n/a	n/a	2013	<1%	

The data on inward direct investment presented below is sourced from the Government of Burma's Ministry of National Planning and Economic Development's Selected Monthly Economic Indicators (January 2015) publication. A disproportionately large percentage of inward direct investment appears to come from Singapore, and this can be explained by U.S., western and other international companies routing their investments to Burma through their presence/branches in Singapore for ease of logistics and transfer. Local contacts report that Hong Kong's large share of inward direct investment can be explained by Chinese companies routing their investments to Burma through Hong Kong, and they opine that Chinese companies engage in this routing behavior so that their investments are not immediately seen as coming directly from China. Of note is Vietnam's presence on the Top Five list of inward direct investment: this is a recent phenomenon and prior to 2013-2014, Vietnam was not a top foreign investor in Burma.

Burma did not present any data on outward direct investment in the Ministry of National Planning and Economic Development's Selected Monthly Economic Indicators (January 2015) publication.

Direct Investment from/in Counterpart Economy Data					
From Top Five Sources/To Top Five Destinations (US Dollars, Millions)					
Inward Direct Investment			Outward Direct Investment		
Total Inward	6615	100%	Total Outward	n/a	100%
Singapore	3814	57%			
Hong Kong	455	7%			
United Kingdom	434	6%			
China	256	4%			
Vietnam	175	3%			
"0" reflects amounts rounded to +/- USD 500,000.					

IMPORTANT CONTACTS

CONTACT FOR MORE INFORMATION

NAME: James J. Shea
TITLE: Economic Officer
ADDRESS OF MISSION: U.S. Embassy/110 University Avenue/Kamayut Township 11041/Rangoon, Burma
TELEPHONE NUMBER: 95 (0)1 536 509 Ext. 4248
EMAIL ADDRESS: **BurmaBusiness@state.gov**

LOCAL ATTORNEYS

Name	U Hla Pe, Advocate, B.A., HGP
Areas of Specialization	Criminal, Civil, Narcotic, Contracts, Trademarks/Copyright
Languages	Burmese, English
Address	Office: No. 50, A-1 1st Floor, Bank St Kyauktada Township Rangoon, Burma Residence: No.11, 2nd. Floor (left) Kyay Padein Dan Street Tandaung Ward, Mingalar Taung Nyunt Township Rangoon, Burma
Telephone	c/o 95-9-73032721

Name	U Hla Sein, Advocate, LL.B.
Areas of Specialization	Criminal, Civil, Estates, Narcotic
Languages	Burmese, English (limited)

Address	Office: : No. 561, Room 302, Third Floor, M.A.C Tower Merchant St & 35th St. (corner) Kyauktada Township Residence: No.561, Room 701, 7th. Floor, M.A.C Tower Merchant St & 35th. St. (corner) Rangoon, Burma
Telephone	95-09-73204553 95-1-374399/391394

Name	U Htin Zaw, Advocate, B.S.C., HGP, RL
Areas of Specialization	Civil, Criminal, Commercial/Business Law
Languages	Burmese, English
Address	Office: No.355, 3rd. Floor, U Wisara Rd Taw Win Company Limited Rangoon, Burma Residence: No.5/25, Aung Zeya Road

	Konemyint Yeiktha, Mayangone Township Rangoon, Burma
Telephone	95-9-50-00347 (Mobile) 663049 09-5000821/374399

Name	Jaime Casanova
Areas of Specialization	Energy Law, Mergers and Acquisitions, Intellectual Property Law and Foreign Direct Investments
Languages	English, Spanish, German, French, Mandarin
Address	Russin & Vecchi, Ltd #134 (A) Than Lwin Road Bahan Township (Box 729 GPO) Yangon, Myanmar
Telephone	+95 1540995
Email	Myanmar@dfdl.com

	Jaime.casanova@dfdl.com
Website	www.dfdl.com

Name	Selvam & Partners / Duane Morris & Selvam LL.P.
Areas of Specialization	Anticorruption Compliance and Investigations, Corporate Finance, Licensing/ Market Entry, Funds, Private Equity & Venture Capital, Project Financing and Mergers and Acquisitions
Languages	Myanmar, English
Address	No.10 Bo Yar Zar Street Kyaukkone Yankin Township Rangoon, Burma
Telephone	95-1-569522 Mobile: 95-9510-3041/95-9520-201363
Email	KRamachandra@SelvamAndPartners.com, BKheng@SelvamAndPartners.com, KRamachandra@DuaneMorrisSelvam.com, GMBulmash@DuaneMorrisSelvam.com

Name	Strohal Legal Group U Min Sein and Strohal Partnership
Areas of Specialization	Corporate law, Establishment of Companies, Businesses and Properties, International Commercial Law, International Taxation, Labor Law, Immigration Law, Dispute Settlement, Joint Ventures, Inheritance Law, Personal Rights Protection, Intellectual Property.
Languages	Myanmar, English
Address	7B. 189-195 Pansodan Tower Pansodan Street Rangoon, Burma
Telephone	951-253273 951 391528 951 377276 Mobile: +65 98756490

Email office@SLG-strohallegalgroup.com

Website www.slg-strohallegalgroup.comt

Name	William Greenlee
Areas of specialization	Commercial, Transactional, Finance, Securities, Corporate
Languages	English
Address	№ 134/A, Than Lwin Road, Golden Valley Ward (1) Bahan Township (Box 729 GPO) Yangon, Myanmar
Telephone	+95 1 526 180
Email	William.Greenlee@dfdl.com

Name	Daw Khin Khin
Qualifications	Advocate and Notary Public (only provide Notary service)
Languages	Myanmar, English
Address	No.7 Pyidaw Aye Road Pyithayar, Baukhtaw, Ward 16, Yankin Township Rangoon, Burma

Telephone	95-1-400080/95-9-73157714
Name	Daw Khin Kyi
Qualifications	Advocate and Notary Public (only provide Notary service)
Areas of Specialization	No.55 Maha Bandoola Garden Street Rangoon, Burma
Languages	Myanmar, English
Address	Room 29, 55 Mahabandoola Garden St.
Telephone	Office: 95-1-375599 Residence: 95-1-250861
Email	makhinkyi.law@mptmail.net.mm
Website	www.winmutinlaw.com
Name	U Tin Maung Kyu Supreme Court Advocate and Notary Public
Languages	Myanmar, English
Address	No.73 Pansodan Street, Kyauktada Township Rangoon, Burma
Telephone	Office: 95-1-376780 Residence: 95-1-373197

PHILIPPINES INVESTMENT AND BUSINESS CLIMATE - STRATEGIC INFORMATION AND CONTACTS FOR STARTING BUSINESS

The Philippines is an increasingly attractive destination for Foreign Direct Investment (FDI). The country's growing middle class quickly spends its disposable income in a stable political environment, helping gross domestic product soar to an average growth of 6.3% over the last five years. FDI reached a record-high of USD 6.2 billion in 2014 and it is projected to continue to grow in the near future. The United States contributed the most FDI of any country in 2014 (USD 1.2 billion USD). Thanks to a large, educated, English-speaking workforce, the Business Process Outsourcing (BPO) and tourism industries have experienced tremendous growth in recent years, with no signs of a slowdown. Under the administration of President Benigno Aquino III, the Philippines has improved the investment climate, making strides in good governance, transparency, and accountability. The three major international credit rating agencies all lifted the Philippines to an investment grade rating for the first time starting in 2013.

Restrictions on foreign ownership, poor infrastructure, including very high power costs, and corruption continue to be significant concerns for investors. Traffic and port congestion are a regular part of business. Manila's main airport operates at full capacity. With its high economic growth, the strain is only expected to increase. Strengthening the rule of law is important, because the country's complex and slow judicial system inhibits the timely and fair resolution of commercial disputes. The Philippines lags behind its Asian neighbors in attracting FDI because of limits on foreign investment in many sectors of the economy. The Philippines recently liberalized its banking laws to stimulate investments. Invest Philippines (www.investphilippines.gov.ph) is the GPH's main portal for investors.

Investors report that Philippine bureaucracy can be difficult and opaque, business registration and procedures are slow and burdensome. Many investors report a more predictable business environment within the special economic zones, particularly those run by the Philippine Economic Zone Authority (PEZA), which is known for its regulatory transparency, no red tape policy, and "one-stop shop" services for investors. Overall, the investment climate of the Philippines has improved in recent years. If the country can maintain its reform momentum, particularly after a new president takes office in 2016, and continue to improve its infrastructure, the prospects for investment into the Philippines will continue to brighten.

1. Openness To, and Restrictions Upon, Foreign Investment

Attitude toward Foreign Direct Investment

The Philippines actively seeks foreign investment to promote economic development. The Philippine investment landscape has noteworthy advantages, such as its free trade zones, including zones administered by the Philippine Economic Zone Authority (PEZA) (http://www.peza.gov.ph/), and its large, educated, English-speaking Filipino workforce. Philippine law treats foreign investors the same as their domestic counterparts, except in sectors reserved for Filipinos by the Philippine Constitution and Foreign Investment Act (detailed below). However, inadequate public investment in the physical and social infrastructure and lack of transparency hinder foreign investment. Philippine regulatory regimes remain ambiguous in many sectors of the economy, and corruption is a significant problem. A complex and slow judicial system is also a major disincentive to investment.

Other Investment Policy Reviews

The World Trade Organization conducted a Trade Policy Review of the Philippines in March 2012. It is available at:**http://www.wto.org/english/tratop_e/tpr_e/tp361_e.htm**.

Laws/Regulations of Foreign Direct Investment

The Board of Investments (BOI) (**http://www.boi.gov.ph/**) regulates and promotes investments in the Philippines. The Investment Priorities Plan (IPP), administered by the BOI, identifies preferred economic activities approved by the President. Government agencies are encouraged to adopt policies and implement programs consistent with the IPP.

The 1991 Philippine Foreign Investment Act (FIA) requires the publishing of the Foreign Investment Negative List (FINL), which outlines sectors in which foreign investment is restricted. The FINL consists of two parts. Part A details sectors in which foreign equity participation is restricted by the Philippine Constitution or laws. Part B lists areas in which foreign ownership is limited (generally to 40%) for reasons of national security, defense, public health, morals, and/or the protection of small and medium enterprises (SMEs). The current FINL was published in October 2012, and a revision is expected this year.

The 1995 Special Economic Zone Act allows PEZA to regulate and promote investments in export-oriented manufacturing and service facilities inside special economic zone, including grants of fiscal and non-fiscal incentives.

Industrial Promotion

The Investment Priorities Plan (IPP) enumerates priority investment areas entitled to incentives. The 2014-2016 IPP seeks to raise investments in infrastructure, agriculture, education and health. The IPP list includes: manufacturing (e.g. motor vehicles, shipbuilding, aerospace, etc.), agribusiness and fisheries; services (e.g. creative industries, integrated circuit design, charging stations for e-vehicles, etc.); public infrastructure and logistics (airports, seaports, transport, etc.); Public-Private Partnership (PPP) projects; energy (development of energy sources, power generation plants and ancillary services); low-cost housing; and hospitals. The BOI reviews projects, and then determines incentives.

The PPP program aims to spur private-sector participation in government development projects, specifically in infrastructure. The Build-Operate-Transfer (BOT) law provides the legal framework for the program, and a Public Private Partnership (PPP) Center (http://ppp.gov.ph/) works to promote transparency and oversee project development and approval. The PPP program has been slow to approve contracts, although the pace for approval and awarding has picked up of late. As of May 2015, only 9 out of 61 PPP projects/contracts had been awarded, with 16 contracts out for bid. In February 2015, the U.S. Department of Commerce and the Philippine National Economic Development Authority (NEDA) (**http://www.neda.gov.ph**) signed a Memorandum of Cooperation on infrastructure collaboration in which potential U.S. investors will receive notification and information about forthcoming PPP infrastructure projects.

Limits on Foreign Control

Foreigners are prohibited from fully owning land under the 1987 Constitution, although the 1993 Investors' Lease Act allows foreign investors to lease a contiguous parcel of up to 1,000 hectares for 50 years, renewable one time for 25 additional years. The 2003 Dual-Citizenship Act allows dual citizens full rights to possess land. Yet, ownership deeds continue to be difficult to establish, and the court system is slow to resolve land disputes.

The FINL bans foreign ownership in the following areas: mass media (except recording); small-scale mining; private security; marine resources, including the small-scale utilization of natural resources in rivers, lakes, and lagoons; and the manufacture of firecrackers and pyrotechnic devices. Only Philippine citizens can practice the following licensed professions: engineering, medicine, accounting, architecture, interior design, chemistry, environmental planning, social work, teaching, law, real estate services, respiratory therapy, and psychology.

Other areas that carry varying foreign ownership ceilings include: private radio communications networks (20%); private employee recruitment (25%); contracts for the construction and repair of locally funded public works (25%); advertising agencies (30%); natural resource exploration, development, and utilization (40%, with exceptions); educational institutions (40%); operation and management of public utilities (40%); operation of commercial deep sea fishing vessels (40%); Philippine government procurement contracts (40% for supply of goods and commodities); construction of locally funded public works (25% with some exceptions); adjustment companies (40%); operations of Build-Operate-Transfer (BOT) projects in public utilities (40%); ownership of private lands (40%); rice and corn processing (40%, with some exceptions); financing companies and investment houses (60%).

For reasons of national security, defense and public health, the Philippines limits foreign ownership to 40% in the following industries: manufacturing of explosives, firearms, military hardware, and massage clinics.

Retail trade enterprises with capital of less than USD 2.5 million, or less than USD 250,000 for retailers of luxury goods, are reserved for Filipinos. Foreign investors are prohibited from owning stock in lending, financing, or investment companies unless the investor's home country affords the same reciprocal rights to Filipino investors. Foreign ownership is capped at 60% for enterprises engaged in financing and securities underwriting, which are regulated by the Securities and Exchange Commission (SEC) (http://www.sec.gov.ph/).

A law signed on July 15, 2014 liberalized the entry of foreign banks into the Philippine market. If they can meet certain requirements, foreign banks are allowed to establish branches or own up to 100% of the voting stock of locally incorporated subsidiaries. However, banks cannot open more than six branch offices each. The new law also stipulates a minimum 60% of the total assets of the Philippine banking system should, at all times, remain controlled by majority Philippine-owned banks.

The 2007 Lending Company Regulation Act requires majority Philippine ownership for credit enterprises that do not clearly fall under the scope of existing laws.

Privatization Program

The GPH's privatization program is managed by the Privatization Management Office (PMO) (**http://www.pmo.gov.ph/**) under the Department of Finance (DOF) (**http://www.dof.gov.ph/**). Apart from restrictions in the FINL, there are no regulations that discriminate against foreign buyers and the bidding process appears to be transparent.

Screening of FDI

Corporations or partnerships wishing to invest in the Philippines must register with the Securities and Exchange Commission (SEC). Sole proprietorships must register with the Bureau of Trade Regulation and Consumer Protection (BTRCP) in the Department of Trade and Industry (DTI) (**http://www.dti.gov.ph/**). A foreign enterprise seeking incentives under the OIC must apply for registration with the BOI, while export-oriented manufacturing and service enterprises within the economic zones must register with PEZA or another authorized economic zone administrator (see Section 17 – Foreign Trade Zones). In addition, foreign investors must register with the Philippine Central Bank (**http://www.bsp.gov.ph**) if the foreign exchange for repatriation of capital and remittance of earnings will be sourced from authorized agent banks or their affiliate foreign exchange corporations.

Competition Law

The Philippines does not have a general competition law, but there are several laws dealing with competition. A Fair Competition Law is pending in Congress and is expected to be passed before the current session ends June 12. The Department of Justice (DOJ) (**http://www.doj.gov.ph/**) is responsible for enforcement of and the investigation of cases involving competition laws.

Investment Trends

The Philippine investment climate continues to improve due to reforms undertaken by the current government. In 2014, FDI in the Philippines reached USD 6.2 billion, a 65.9% increase from the USD 3.7 billion in 2013, and the highest to date. The majority of investment inflows are in finance and insurance, manufacturing, real estate, large-scale mining and quarrying, and wholesale and retail trade sectors. In 2013 and 2014, Fitch, Standard & Poor's, and Moody's upgraded the Philippines' sovereign credit ratings to investment grade, citing robust economic performance, continued fiscal and debt consolidation, and improved governance. The Philippines inched up 13 spots in the World Bank's Doing Business Report in 2014, almost reaching the top 50%.

Constitutional and legal restrictions, inadequate infrastructure, regulatory inconsistency, corruption, and a slow and complex judicial process remain major constraints. The Philippines has a poor record of attracting foreign investment compared to its ASEAN counterparts. According to the United Nations Conference on Trade and Development (UNCTAD), the Philippines ranked sixth among ASEAN's ten countries in terms of FDI flows in 2013.

Table 1

Measure	Year	Index or Rank	Website Address
TI Corruption Perceptions index	2014	85 of 175	transparency.org/cpi2014/results
World Bank's Doing Business Report "Ease of Doing Business"	2015	95 of 189	doingbusiness.org/rankings
Global Innovation Index	2014	100 of 143	globalinnovationindex.org/content.aspx?page=data-analysis
World Bank GNI per capita	2013	USD 3,270	data.worldbank.org/indicator/NY.GNP.PCAP.CD

Millennium Challenge Corporation Country Scorecard

The Millennium Challenge Corporation, a U.S. Government entity charged with delivering development grants to countries that have demonstrated a commitment to reform, produces scorecards for countries with a per capita gross national income (GNI) of USD 4,125 or less. A list of countries/economies with MCC scorecards and links to those scorecards is available here: **http://www.mcc.gov/pages/selection/scorecards**. Details on each of the MCC's indicators and a guide to reading the scorecards are available here: **http://www.mcc.gov/pages/docs/doc/report-guide-to-the-indicators-and-the-selection-process-fy-2015**.

2. Conversion and Transfer Policies

Foreign Exchange

Since 2007, the Central Bank has accelerated efforts to relax and streamline the Philippine foreign exchange regulatory framework. There are no restrictions on the full and immediate transfer of funds associated with foreign investments, foreign debt servicing, or payment of royalties, lease payments, and similar fees. The Central Bank follows a market-determined exchange rate policy, with scope for intervention to smooth excess foreign exchange volatility.

Remittance Policies

Central Bank regulations provide specific requirements for foreign exchange purchases from banks and from foreign exchange dealers, money changers, and remittance agents. No mandatory foreign exchange surrender requirement is imposed on export earners or other foreign currency earners, such as overseas workers.

In June 2013, the Financial Action Task Force (FATF) removed the Philippines from its "watch list" of countries with strategic deficiencies in countering money laundering and the financing of terrorism. The FATF continues to urge regulation of the country's growing casino industry for anti-money laundering/terrorism financing purposes and is monitoring progress of pending legislation in the Philippines.

3. Expropriation and Compensation

Philippine law allows expropriation of private property for public use or in the interest of national welfare or defense, and offers fair market value compensation. In the event of expropriation, foreign investors have the right to receive the compensation in the currency in which the investment was originally made and remit it at the equivalent exchange rate. However, the process of agreeing on a mutually acceptable price can be protracted in the Philippine courts.

There are no recent cases of actual expropriation involving U.S. companies in the Philippines.

4. Dispute Settlement

Legal System, Specialized Courts, Judicial Independence, Judgments of Foreign Courts

The Philippine judicial system is a separate and independent branch of the government, made up of the Supreme Court (http://sc.judiciary.gov.ph/) and lower courts. The Supreme Court is the highest court and sole constitutional body as specified by the Philippine Constitution. The lower courts consist of (a) trial courts with limited jurisdictions (i.e. Municipal Trial Courts, Metropolitan Trial Courts, etc.); (b) Regional Trial Courts (RTCs); (c) Shari'ah District Courts (Muslim courts); and (d) Court of Appeals (appellate courts). Special courts include the "Sandiganbayan" (anti-graft court for public officials) and Court of Tax Appeals. Several RTCs have been designated as Special Commercial Courts (SCC) to hear intellectual property (IP) cases, with four SCCs authorized to issue writs of search and seizure on IP violations enforceable nationwide.

Under Philippine law, a separate action must be filed for foreign judgments to be recognized or enforced. Philippine law also does not recognize or enforce foreign judgments that run counter to existing laws, particularly those relating to public order, public policy, and good customs.

Bankruptcy

The 2010 Philippine bankruptcy and insolvency law provides a predictable framework for the rehabilitation and liquidation of distressed companies. Rehabilitation may be initiated by debtors or creditors under court-supervised, pre-negotiated, or out-of-court proceedings. The law sets the conditions for voluntary (debtor-initiated) and involuntary (creditor-initiated) liquidation. It also recognizes cross-border insolvency proceedings in accordance with the UNCTAD Model Law on Cross-Border Insolvency, allowing courts to recognize proceedings in a foreign jurisdiction involving a foreign entity with assets in the Philippines. Regional trial courts designated by the Supreme Court have jurisdiction over insolvency and bankruptcy cases. According to the International Finance Corporation (IFC)'s 2015 Ease of Doing Business report, the Philippines ranks 50th of the 189 economies in resolving insolvency and bankruptcy cases**http://www.doingbusiness.org/data/exploreeconomies/philippines#resolving-insolvency**.

Investment Disputes

Foreign investors describe the inefficiency and uncertainty of the judicial system as a significant disincentive to investment. Many investors do not wish to file dispute cases in court because of slow and complex litigation processes and corruption among some personnel. Stakeholders also report an inexperienced judiciary when confronted with complex issues such as technology, science, trade, and intellectual property cases.

To decongest the court's clogged dockets, several laws on alternative dispute resolution (ADR) mechanisms (i.e., arbitration, mediation, negotiation, and conciliation) have been approved. Further, PPP contracts are required to include ADR provisions to make resolving disputes less expensive and time-consuming, particularly for large-scale capital-intensive infrastructure and development contracts.

ICSID Convention and New York Convention

The Philippines is a member of the International Center for the Settlement of Investment Disputes (ICSID) and has adopted the Convention on the Recognition and Enforcement of Foreign Arbitral Awards, or the "New York Convention." Foreign arbitral awards are enforceable upon application in writing to the regional trial court with jurisdiction. The petition may be filed any time after receipt of the award.

Duration of Dispute Resolution

Investment disputes can take years to resolve due to systemic problems in the Philippine judicial system. Lack of resources, understaffing, and corruption make the already complex court processes protracted and expensive.

5. PERFORMANCE REQUIREMENTS AND INVESTMENT INCENTIVES

WTO/TRIMS

The Philippines currently has no measures reportedly violating WTO-TRIMS commitments.

Investment Incentives

There are about 180 fiscal incentive laws in the Philippines. The IPP lists promoted investment areas entitled to incentives facilitated by BOI. Available fiscal incentives include: an income tax holiday; tax credits; and deductions from taxable income. Non-fiscal incentives include: employment of foreign nationals; simplified customs procedures; importation of consigned equipment; and operation of a bonded manufacturing warehouse.

BOI-registered enterprises which locate in less-developed areas are entitled to "pioneer" incentives and can deduct 100% of the cost of necessary infrastructure work and labor expenses from its taxable income. Pioneer status can be granted to enterprises producing new products or using new methods, producing goods deemed highly essential to the country's agricultural self-sufficiency program, or goods utilizing non-conventional fuel sources. Furthermore, an enterprise with more than 40% foreign equity that exports at least 70% of its production may be entitled to incentives even if the activity is not listed in the IPP. Export-oriented firms with at least 50% of their revenues derived from exports may register for additional incentives under the 1994 Export Development Act.

Philippine law also provides incentives for multinational enterprises to establish regional or area headquarters in the Philippines. Multinational entities that establish regional warehouses for the supply of spare parts, manufactured components, or raw materials for foreign markets also enjoy incentives on imports that are re-exported, including exemption from customs duties, internal revenue taxes, and local taxes.

Research and Development

The participation of foreign entities in research and development is limited by several laws and regulations that stem from the limiting of the practice of professions, including engineering and teaching, to Filipino citizens, except when otherwise prescribed by law. An example is the "Balik Scientist" Program of the Department of Science and Technology (DOST) (**http://bsp.dost.gov.ph/**), where Filipino-born scientists who have acquired foreign citizenship are encouraged to return to the Philippines to help accelerate scientific, agro-industrial and economic development of the country. The DOST secures a special/temporary permit from the Professional Regulatory Commission (PRC) (**http://www.prc.gov.ph/**) to allow these "foreign" scientists to practice their profession in the Philippines.

Performance Requirements

In general, only Filipino citizens are allowed to practice licensed professions but companies registered with BOI and PEZA may employ foreign nationals in supervisory, technical, or advisory positions for five years from the date of registration (possibly extendable upon request). Top positions and elective officers of majority foreign-owned BOI-registered enterprises (i.e., president, general manager, and treasurer, or their equivalents) are exempt from the five-year limitation. Foreigners intending to work locally must secure an Alien Employment Permit (AEP) from the Department of Labor and Employment (DOLE) (http://www.dole.gov.ph), renewable every year or co-terminus with the duration of employment (which in no case shall exceed five years). The BOI and PEZA can help facilitate a special Non-Immigrant Visa with Multiple Entry Privileges and extend Visa Facilitation Assistance to foreign nationals, their spouses and dependents.

The 2003 Government Procurement Reform Act (GPRA) requires the public sector to procure goods, supplies, and consulting services from enterprises at least 60% Filipino-owned and infrastructure services from enterprises with at least a 75% Filipino interest. Under Philippine law, a single portal electronic procurement system (the Philippine Government Electronic Procurement System [**http://philgeps.gov.ph/**]) exists to provide transparency and efficiency in procurement procedures, the U.S. and other countries continue to raise concerns about irregularities and inconsistent implementation of government procurement. The Philippines is not a signatory to the WTO Agreement on Government Procurement.

Data Storage

The Philippines has no data localization law and does not impose restrictions on cross-border data transfers. Sensitive personal information is protected under the 2012 Data Privacy Act that provides penalties for unauthorized processing and improper disposal of data even if processed outside the Philippines.

6. RIGHT TO PRIVATE OWNERSHIP AND ESTABLISHMENT

Philippine law recognizes the private right to acquire and dispose of property or business interests, subject to foreign nationality caps specified in the Constitution and other laws.

7. PROTECTION OF PROPERTY RIGHTS

Real Property

The Land Registration Authority (LRA) (http://www.lra.gov.ph/) and the Register of Deeds, which facilitates the registration and transfer of property titles, are responsible for land administration. The Philippines recognizes and protects property rights, but the laws are weakly implemented. Multiple agencies are involved in property administration, which results in overlapping procedures for land valuation and titling processes. Property registration is tedious and costly. Record management is weak due to a lack of funds and trained personnel. Corruption is also prevalent among land administration personnel and the court system is slow to resolve land disputes. The Philippines ranked 108 out of 189 economies in terms of ease of property registration in the 2015 World Bank Doing Business Report.

Intellectual Property Rights

The Philippines remains off the United States Trade Representative's (USTR) Special 301 Watch List, and has no physical markets listed in the 2014 Notorious Markets Report due to sustained efforts by the Philippine government to improve IPR protection and civil and administrative enforcement. That effort included amendments to the IP Code in 2013. Challenges, however, remain as U.S. rights holders report concerns about the availability of counterfeit items such as medicines, clothing and software, and judicial inexperience in IPR enforcement. Nevertheless, the Philippines is considered a leader in ASEAN for its IP enforcement efforts.

The Intellectual Property (IP) Code provides the legal framework for IPR protection, particularly in the key areas of patents, trademarks, and copyright. The Intellectual Property Office (IPOPHL) (**http://www.ipophil.gov.ph/**) is the implementing agency of the IP Code. The Philippines generally has strong patent and trademark laws.

IPOPHL seeks to expand cooperation between the government and rights-holders to strengthen enforcement. In 2014, the National Committee on Intellectual Property Rights (NCPIR) reported USD 302 million worth of seized goods – their highest to date. In addition, the amended IP Code created an IP Enforcement Office (IEO) under IPOPHL that reviews IPR-related complaints and conducts visits to establishments reportedly engaged in IPR-related violations. Stakeholders report that the IEO has been effective in streamlining the process of filing complaints, coordinating among enforcement agencies, and reducing possibilities for corrupt officers to request bribes.

Enforcement actions, however, are often not followed by successful prosecutions. IP infringement is not considered a major crime in the Philippines and takes lower priority in court proceedings. Many stakeholders opt for out-of-court settlements (such as ADRs) rather than filing a lawsuit that may take years to resolve in Philippine courts. IPOPHL has jurisdiction to resolve certain disputes concerning alleged infringement and licensing through its Arbitration and Mediation Center (AMC). IPOPHIL reported 51% of cases received in 2014 had successful mediation.

For additional information about treaty obligations and points of contact at local IP offices, please see WIPO's country profiles at **http://www.wipo.int/directory/en/**.

Resources for Rights Holders

Contact at Mission:

Brian Breuhaus, Economic Officer
Economic Section, U.S. Embassy Manila
Telephone: (+632) 301.2000
Email: **ManilaEcon@state.gov**

8. TRANSPARENCY OF THE REGULATORY SYSTEM

In general, regulatory enforcement in the Philippines is weak, inconsistent, and unpredictable. Regulatory agencies are generally not statutorily independent, but are attached to cabinet departments or the Office of the President and, therefore, subject to political pressure. Many U.S. investors describe business registration, customs, immigration, and visa procedures as burdensome and a source of frustration. To counter this, several government agencies have established express lanes or "one-stop shops" to reduce bureaucratic delays.

All proposed laws must undergo public comment and review. When laws are passed, concerned government agencies are also required to develop implementing rules and regulations (IRRs) through public consultation hearings. New regulations must be published in newspapers or in the government's official gazette before taking effect.

The Philippines follows the Philippine Financial Reporting Standards, patterned after the International Financial Reporting Standards (IFRSs) issued by the International Accounting Standards Board (IASB). Those standards also apply to Small and Medium-sized Entities.

The Philippine SEC requires an entity's Chairman of the Board, Chief Executive Officer, and Chief Financial Officer to assume management responsibility and accountability for financial statements. Financial statements are examined by independent auditors in accordance with Philippine Standards on Auditing, which are based on international auditing standards. Certain regulatory agencies, such as the Central Bank, Insurance Commission (**http://www.insurance.gov.ph/**), and Bureau of Internal Revenue (BIR) (**http://www.bir.gov.ph/**) enforce separate accreditation rules.

9. EFFICIENT CAPITAL MARKETS AND PORTFOLIO INVESTMENT

The Philippines supports the entry of foreign portfolio investments, including into local and foreign-issued equities listed on the Philippine Stock Exchange (PSE) (**http://www.pse.com.ph**). There are minimal requirements for the divestment of portfolio investments and the subsequent repatriation of capital.

There are generally no restrictions on outward portfolio investments by Philippine residents defined to include non-Filipino citizens who have been residing in the country for at least one year, foreign-controlled entities organized under Philippine laws, and branches/subsidiaries/affiliates of foreign enterprises organized under foreign laws that are operating in the country. However, foreign exchange purchases from banks and foreign exchange subsidiaries/affiliates above USD 60 million per investor or per fund per year require prior Central Bank approval.

Although growing, the 260-listed firm Philippine stock market lags behind many of its neighbors in size, product offerings, and trading activity. By mid-2015, the PSI plans to launch a new industry-leading trading system procured from NASDAQ OMX. The securities market is growing, but remains dominated by government bills/bonds.

The Central Bank does not restrict payments and transfers for current transactions, subject to the submission of specified documentary requirements.

Credit is generally granted on market terms and foreign firms are able to obtain credit from the domestic market. However, some laws require financial institutions to set aside loans for preferred sectors. To help promote lending at competitive rates to MSMEs, the Philippines enacted the Credit Information System Act, which established the legal and regulatory framework for a centralized credit information system that collects and disseminates information about the track record of borrowers and the credit activities of entities in the financial system. The system is in place, but not yet operational.

Money and Banking System, Hostile Takeovers

The banking system is stable. Since 2011, the Central Bank has broadly revised its risk-based capital framework in step with adjustments in the Basel Committee on Banking Supervision capital adequacy rules. Capital adequacy ratios are well above the 8% international standard and the Central Bank's 10% regulatory requirement. The non-performing loan ratio was under 2.5% as of end-2014. There is ample liquidity, with the liquid assets-to-deposits ratio estimated at more than 56%. Commercial banks constitute more than 90% of the total assets of the Philippine banking industry. As of 2014, the five largest commercial banks represented about 53% of the total resources of the commercial banking sector.

Foreign residents and non-residents may open foreign exchange and local currency bank accounts. Although non-residents may open local currency deposit accounts, they are subject to conditions on the funding sources specified under Central Bank regulations.

Hostile takeovers are not common because most companies' shares are not publicly listed and controlling interest tends to remain with a small group of parties. Cross-ownership and interlocking directorates among listed companies also decrease the number of hostile takeovers.

10. COMPETITION FROM STATE-OWNED ENTERPRISES

State-owned enterprises, known in the Philippines as government-owned and controlled corporations (GOCC), are predominant in the power, transport, infrastructure, communications, land and water resources, social services, housing and support services sectors. There were 142 operational GOCCs as of November 2014 (see list at http://gcg.gov.ph/site/goccclassification).

The Philippine government derives substantial revenues from GOCCs, which are required to remit at least 50% of their annual net earnings (e.g. cash, stock or property dividends) to the national government. In 2013, the total assets of all GOCCs were 5.7 trillion Philippine pesos (about USD 125.7 billion). GOCCs remitted 32.3 billion pesos (about USD 751 million) in dividends to the national government in 2014.

Private and state-owned enterprises generally compete equally, with some clear exceptions. In 2002, the National Food Authority (NFA) (http://www.nfa.gov.ph/) first allowed the private sector to import rice. The Government Service Insurance System (GSIS) (http://www.gsis.gov.ph) is the only agency, with limited exceptions, allowed to provide coverage for the government's insurance risks and interests, including those in BOT projects and privatized government corporations. Since the national government acts as the main guarantor of loans, stakeholders report that GOCCs often have an advantage in getting financing from government financial institutions and some private banks. Also, most GOCCs are not statutorily independent, but attached to cabinet departments, and, therefore, subject to political interference.

OECD Guidelines on Corporate Governance of SOEs

The Philippines is not an OECD member country. Problems experienced by GOCCs, including poor financial performance, weak governance structures, and unauthorized allowances, led to the passage in 2011 of the GOCC Governance Act. The law allows unrestricted access to GOCC account books and requires strict compliance with accounting and financial disclosure standards; establishes the power to privatize, abolish, or restructure GOCCs without legislative action; and sets performance standards and limits on compensation and allowances. The law also created the GOCC Commission on Governance (GCG) (http://gcg.gov.ph/) to formulate and implement GOCC policies. GOCC Board Members are now limited to one-year terms, subject to reappointment based on a performance rating set by the GCG, with final approval by the President of the Philippines.

Sovereign Wealth Funds

The Philippines does not have sovereign wealth funds.

11. CORPORATE SOCIAL RESPONSIBILITY

Corporate social responsibility (CSR) is regularly practiced in the Philippines, although no domestic laws require it. The Philippine Tax Code provides CSR-related incentives to corporations, such as tax exemptions and deductions. Various non-government organizations and business associations also promote CSR. The Philippine Business for Social Progress (PBSP) (http://www.pbsp.org.ph/) is the largest corporate-led social development foundation involved in advocating corporate citizenship practice in the Philippines. U.S. companies report strong and favorable responses to CSR programs among employees and within local communities.

OECD Guidelines for Multinational Enterprises

The Philippines is not an OECD member country. While the Philippine government strongly supports CSR practices among the business community, it has not endorsed the OECD Guidelines for Multinational Enterprises to its stakeholders.

12. POLITICAL VIOLENCE

Terrorist groups and criminal gangs operate in some regions of the country. The Department of State publishes a consular information sheet and advises all Americans living in or visiting the Philippines to review this information periodically. A travel warning is in place for those U.S. citizens contemplating travel to the Philippines: **http://travel.state.gov/content/passports/english/alertswarnings/philippines-travel-warning.html**.

The State Department strongly encourages Americans in the Philippines to register with the Consular Section of the U.S. Embassy through the State Department's travel registration website found at the Smart Traveler Enrollment Program (STEP) at **https://step.state.gov/step/**.

The Philippines' most significant human rights problems continued to be extrajudicial killings and disappearances at the hands of security forces; a dysfunctional criminal justice system notable for poor cooperation between police and investigators; few prosecutions and lengthy procedural delays; and improving but still widespread official corruption and abuse of power.

The Philippines will hold a national election in May 2016 for president, vice president, Senate, House of Representatives, provincial governorships and a range of local offices. Unofficial campaigning will begin in late 2015 and some election-related violence may occur.

In 2014, the Philippine government and the Muslim insurgency group Moro Islamic Liberation Front (MILF) signed the Comprehensive Agreement on the Bangsamoro (CAB) that seeks to create a new, autonomous political entity by 2016 replacing the existing Autonomous Region in Muslim Mindanao (ARMM). A draft Bangsamoro Basic Law implementing the CAB is still pending at Philippine Congress as of the reporting period.

The New People's Army (NPA), the military arm of the Communist Party of the Philippines, is responsible in some parts of the country, mostly in Mindanao, for civil disturbances through assassinations of public officials, sporadic attacks on military and police forces, bombings, and other attacks. It frequently demands "revolutionary taxes" from local and, at times, foreign businesses. To enforce its demands, the NPA attacks infrastructure such as power facilities, telecommunications towers, and bridges.

Terrorist groups, including the Abu Sayaaf Group (ASG), Jema'ah Islamiyah (JI), and including an MILF splinter group called the Bangsamoro Islamic Freedom Fighters BIFF, periodically attack civilian targets in Mindanao, kidnap civilians – including foreigners – for ransom, and engage in armed skirmishes with government security forces. So far these groups have mostly carried out these activities in the western and central regions of Mindanao, including the Sulu Archipelago and its surrounding waters.

13. CORRUPTION

Corruption is a pervasive and long-standing problem in the Philippines. Recent government efforts have improved the country's ranking in Transparency International's Corruption Perceptions Index from 94 in 2013 to 85 in 2014. Nevertheless, the World Economic Forum's 2014-2015 Global Competitiveness Report ranked corruption as the top problematic factor for doing business in the Philippines. Although President Aquino has made fighting corruption a central part of his presidency, the problem is too endemic to change in a short time. The Bureau of Customs, known widely as the most corrupt agency in the Philippines, is a particular concern. The previous commissioner, who resigned in late April, took steps to decrease opportunities for employees to take bribes, such as fully automating many of the procedures.

The Philippines continues to implement anti-corruption reforms outlined in the Philippine Development Plan 2011-2016. Its 2012-2016 Good Governance and Anti-Corruption Cluster Plan further identifies specific measures to curb corruption through greater transparency and accountability in government transactions. Several bills supporting anti-corruption efforts are currently pending in Congress. A private-sector group has pushed an "Integrity Initiative" for the past four years, seeking a system of certification for businesses that adhere to ethical standards. Since President Aquino took office in 2010, corruption charges have been filed against several high-profile public officials, with no convictions to date.

The Philippine Revised Penal Code, the Anti-Graft and Corrupt Practices Act, and the Code of Ethical Conduct for Public Officials aim to combat corruption and related anti-competitive business practices. The Office of the Ombudsman (**http://www.ombudsman.gov.ph/**) investigates and prosecutes cases of alleged graft and corruption involving public officials. Cases against high-ranking officials are brought before the special anti-corruption court, the "Sandiganbayan", while cases against low-ranking officials are filed before regional trial courts. The Office of the President can directly investigate and hear administrative cases involving presidential appointees in the executive branch and government-owned and controlled corporations. Soliciting, accepting and/or offering/giving a bribe are criminal offenses punishable by imprisonment, a fine, and/or disqualification from public office or business dealings with the government.

UN Anticorruption Convention, OECD Convention on Combatting Bribery

The Philippines ratified the United Nations Convention against Corruption in 2003. It is not a signatory to the OECD Convention on Combatting Bribery.

Resources to Report Corruption

Contact at government agency:

Office of the Ombudsman
Ombudsman Building
Agham Road, North Triangle, Diliman
Quezon City, Philippines 1101
Telephone: (+632) 479.7300

Email: **pab@ombudsman.gov.ph**
http://www.ombudsman.gov.ph/

Contact at Watchdog Organization:

Transparency International Philippines, Inc.
4/F Libran House Building
144 Legazpi St. cor. V.A. Rufino and Bolanos Sts., Legazpi Village
Makati City, Philippines
Telephone: (+632) 869.9702
Email: **info@transparency-ph.org**
http://www.transparency-ph.org/

14. BILATERAL INVESTMENT AGREEMENTS

The Philippines has neither a bilateral investment nor a free trade agreement with the United States. The Philippines has bilateral investment agreements with 38 countries: Argentina, Australia, Austria, Bangladesh, Belgium and Luxembourg, Cambodia, Canada, Chile, China, the Czech Republic, Denmark, Finland, France, Germany, India, Indonesia, Iran, Italy, Japan, Republic of Korea, Kuwait, Mongolia, Myanmar, Netherlands, Pakistan, Portugal, Romania, Russian Federation, Saudi Arabia, Spain, Sweden, Switzerland, Syria, Taiwan, Thailand, Turkey, United Kingdom, and Vietnam.

The Philippines is a member of four ASEAN free trade agreements that include an investment chapter with trading partners Australia, New Zealand, Republic of Korea and China.

Bilateral Taxation Treaties

U.S. – Philippines Tax Treaty

The Philippines has a tax treaty with the United States to avoid double taxation, provide procedures for resolving interpretative disputes, and enforce taxes in both countries. The treaty encourages bilateral trade and investment by allowing the exchange of capital, goods and services under clearly defined tax rules and, in some cases, preferential tax rates or tax exemptions.

U.S. recipients of royalty income qualify for preferential tax rates (currently 10%) under the most favored nation clause of the United States-Philippines tax treaty. A preferential tax treaty rate of 15% applies to dividends and interest income. An entity must obtain a tax treaty relief ruling from the BIR to qualify for preferential tax treaty rates and treatment; tax practitioners find the requirements burdensome. Although the Supreme Court ruled in October 2013 against stricter regulations issued by the BIR in 2010 disqualifying late filings from preferential tax rates, issues reportedly can arise during tax audits. The volume of tax treaty relief applications also has resulted in processing delays, with most applications reportedly pending for over a year. Concerns also exist about inconsistent taxation rulings.

The BIR rules and regulations for tax accounting have not been fully harmonized with the Philippine Financial Reporting Standards. The disparities between reports for financial accounting and tax accounting purposes are common issues in tax assessments and are an irritant between taxpayers and tax collectors. The BIR requires taxpayers to maintain records reconciling figures presented in financial statements and income tax returns.

15. OPIC AND OTHER INVESTMENT INSURANCE PROGRAMS

Pursuant to the U.S.-Philippines Investment Incentive Agreement, the Overseas Private Investment Corporation (OPIC) is able to offer the following:

Investment Insurance: The Philippine government does not provide guarantees against losses due to inconvertibility of currency, expropriation, or damage caused by war. OPIC can provide U.S. investors with political risk insurance.

Financing: OPIC financing is available for creditworthy projects and companies with substantial

U.S. investment or participation and where sufficient or appropriate financing is not available from local or other private sector financial institutions.

16. LABOR

Managers of U.S.-based companies report that Philippine labor costs are low, and the workers are highly motivated with strong English language skills. In 2014, the Philippine labor force reached 41.3 million, with an unemployment rate of 6% at the end of the year. This figure includes employment in the informal sector and does not capture the substantial rates of underemployment in the country. Youths between the age of 15 and 24 made up nearly 50% of the unemployed. More than half of all employed persons worked in services, with about 30% in agriculture and 15% in industry.

Multinational managers report that compensation packages in the Philippines tend to be comparable with neighboring countries. Regional Wage and Productivity Boards meet periodically in each of the country's 16 administrative regions to determine minimum wages. The non-agricultural daily minimum wage in Metro Manila is PhP493 (approximately USD 11), although some private sector workers receive less. Most regions set their minimum wage significantly lower than Metro Manila. Violation of minimum wage standards is common, especially non-payment of social security contributions, bonuses, and overtime. Philippine law also provides for a comprehensive set of occupational safety and health standards. The Department of Labor and Employment (DOLE) (http://www.dole.gov.ph/) has responsibility for safety inspection, but a shortage of inspectors has made enforcement difficult.

The Philippine Constitution enshrines the right of workers to form and join trade unions. The trend among firms of using temporary contract labor continues to grow. The DOLE Secretary has the authority to end strikes and mandate a settlement between parties in cases involving the national interest. In 2013, the DOLE amended its rules concerning disputes, specifying industries vital to national interest: hospitals, electric power industry, water supply services (excluding small bottle suppliers), air traffic control, and other industries as recommended by the National Tripartite Industrial Peace Council (NTIPC). Economic zones often offer on-site labor centers to assist investors with recruitment. Although labor laws apply equally to economic zones, unions have noted some difficulty organizing inside the zones.

The Philippines is a signatory to all International Labor Organization (ILO) core conventions but has faced challenges enforcing them. Unions allege that companies or local officials use illegal tactics to prevent them from organizing workers. The quasi-judicial National Labor Relations Commission reviews allegations of intimidation and discrimination in connection with union activities. Meanwhile, the Philippines National Tripartite Industrial Peace Council (NTIPC) monitors the application of international labor standards.

There have been some reports of forced labor in the Philippines in connection with human trafficking in the commercial sex, domestic service, agriculture, and fishing industries.

17. FOREIGN TRADE ZONES/FREE PORTS/TRADE FACILITATION

Businesses enjoy preferential tax treatment when located in export processing zones, free trade zones, and certain industrial estates, collectively known as economic zones, or "ecozones." Businesses located in ecozones are considered outside customs territory and are allowed to import capital equipment and raw material free of customs duties, taxes, and other import restrictions. Goods imported into ecozones may be stored, repacked, mixed, or otherwise manipulated without being subject to import duties and are exempt from the Selective Preshipment Advance Classification Scheme. While some ecozones are designated as both export processing zones and free trade zones, individual businesses within them are only permitted to receive incentives under a single category.

Philippine Economic Zone Authority (PEZA)

PEZA currently operates 300 ecozones, primarily in the manufacturing, IT, tourism, medical tourism, logistics/warehousing, and agro-industrial sectors. PEZA manages three government-owned export-processing zones (Mactan, Baguio, and Cavite) and administers incentives to enterprises located in the other 297 privately owned and operated ecozones. Any person, partnership, corporation, or business organization, regardless of nationality, control and/or ownership, may register as an export, IT, tourism, medical tourism, or agro-industrial enterprise with PEZA, provided that the enterprise physically locates its activity inside any of the proclaimed ecozones. PEZA administrators have earned a reputation for maintaining a clear and predictable investment environment within the zones of their authority.

Bases Conversion Development Authority (BCDA) and Subic Bay Metropolitan Authority (SBMA)

The ecozones located inside former U.S. military bases were established under the 1992 Bases Conversion and Development Act. The BCDA (http://www.bcda.gov.ph/) operates the Clark Freeport Zone (Angeles City, Pampanga), the John Hay Special Economic Zone (Baguio), the Poro Point Freeport Zone (La Union), and the Bataan Technology Park (Morong, Bataan). The SBMA operates the Subic Bay Freeport Zone (Subic Bay, Zambales). Clark and Subic have their own international airports, power plants, telecommunications networks, housing complexes, and tourist facilities. These ecozones are independent of PEZA, though they offer comparable incentives. Enterprises already receiving incentives under the BCDA law are disqualified to receive incentives and benefits offered by other laws.

Other Zones

The Phividec Industrial Estate (Misamis Oriental, Mindanao) is governed by the Phividec Industrial Authority (PIA) (http://www.piamo.gov.ph/pia/), a government-owned and controlled corporation. Two lesser-known ecozones are the Zamboanga City Economic Zone and Freeport (Zamboanga City, Mindanao) (http://www.zambofreeport.com.ph/) and the Cagayan Special Economic Zone and Freeport (Santa Ana, Cagayan Province) (http://ceza.gov.ph/). The incentives available to investors in these zones are similar to PEZA incentives but administered independently. In addition to offering export incentives, the Cagayan Economic Zone Authority (CEZA) is authorized to grant gaming licenses.

18. FOREIGN DIRECT INVESTMENT AND FOREIGN PORTFOLIO INVESTMENT STATISTICS

Table 2: Key Macroeconomic Data, U.S. FDI in Host Country/Economy

	Host Country Statistical source*		USG or international statistical source		USG or International Source of Data: BEA; IMF; Eurostat; UNCTAD, Other
Economic Data	Year	Amount	Year	Amount	
Host Country Gross Domestic Product (GDP) ($M USD)	2014	284,615	2013	272,066	www.worldbank.org/en/country
Foreign Direct Investment	Host Country Statistical source*		USG or international statistical source		USG or international Source of data: BEA; IMF; Eurostat; UNCTAD, Other
U.S. FDI in partner country ($M USD, stock positions)	2013	N/A	2013	4,376	http://bea.gov/international/factsheet/factsheet.cfm?Area=623
Host country's FDI in the United States ($M USD, stock positions)	2014	N/A	2013	268	http://bea.gov/international/factsheet/factsheet.cfm?Area=623
Total inbound stock of FDI as % host GDP	2013	18.8%	2013	11.9%	

Host Country Statistical Sources: **http://www.nscb.gov.ph/sna/DataCharts.asphttp://www.bsp.gov.ph/statistics/sdds/iip_bpm6_liabilities.htm**

Table 3: Sources and Destination of FDI

The Philippine Central Bank does not publish or post inward and outward FDI stock broken down by country. Total stock figures are reported under the "International Investment Position" data that the Central Bank publishes and submits to the International Monetary Fund's (IMF) Dissemination Standards Bulletin Board (DSBB) using BPM6 concept. As of 2013, inward direct investments (i.e. liabilities) are USD 51,497 million, while outward direct investments (assets) are USD 27,617 million.

Host Country Statistical Sources:

http://www.bsp.gov.ph/statistics/sdds/iip_bpm6_liabilities.htm

http://www.bsp.gov.ph/statistics/sdds/iip_bpm6_assets.htm

Direct Investment from/in Counterpart Economy Data					
From Top Five Sources/To Top Five Destinations (US Dollars, Millions)					
Inward Direct Investment			Outward Direct Investment		
Total Inward	33,238	100%	Total Outward	3,238	100%
Netherlands	6,917	21%	British Virgin Islands	919	28%
Japan	6,173	18%	China, P.R.: Mainland	845	26%
Singapore	6,124	18%	Cayman Islands	648	20%
United States	4,306	13%	China, P.R.: Hong Kong	257	8%

China, P.R.: Hong Kong	2,059	6%	United States	181	6%
"0" reflects amounts rounded to +/- USD 500,000.					

Table 4: Sources of Portfolio Investment

While it disaggregates data into equity and debt securities, the Philippine Central Bank does not publish or post the stock of portfolio investment assets broken down by country. Total foreign portfolio investment stock figures are reported under the "International Investment Position" data that the Central Bank publishes and submits for the International Monetary Fund's (IMF) Dissemination Standards Bulletin Board (DSBB) using BPM6 concept. As of 2013, outward portfolio investments (i.e., assets) are USD 7,851 million, of which USD 151 million are in equity securities and USD 7,699 million are in debt securities.

Host Country Statistical Sources: **http://www.bsp.gov.ph/statistics/sdds/iip_bpm6_assets.htm**

Portfolio Investment Assets								
Top Five Partners (Millions, US Dollars)								
Total			Equity Securities			Total Debt Securities		
All Countries	5,775	100%	All Countries	244	100%	All Countries	5,531	100%
United States	1,869	32%	United States	134	55%	United States	1,735	31%
Indonesia	932	16%	Luxembourg	40	16%	Indonesia	932	17%
Cayman Islands	292	5%	Hong Kong, PRC	15	6%	Cayman Islands	289	5%
Korea, Republic of	287	5%	Australia	14	6%	Korea, Republic of	281	5%
United Kingdom	254	4%	Singapore	14	6%	United Kingdom	253	5%

IMPORTANT BUSINESS AND LEGAL CONTACTS

CONTACT FOR MORE INFORMATION

Brian Breuhaus
Economic Officer
U.S. Embassy Manila
1201 Roxas Boulevard, Manila
Telephone: (+632) 301.2000
Email: **ManilaEcon@state.gov**

LIST OF LAWYERS

The U.S. Embassy in Manila, Philippines assumes no responsibility or liability for the professional ability or reputation of, or the quality of services provided by, the following persons or firms. Inclusion on this list is in no way an endorsement by the Department of State or the U.S. Embassy/Consulate. Names are listed alphabetically, and the order in which they appear has no other significance. The information in the list on professional credentials, areas of expertise and language ability are provided directly by the lawyers. You may receive additional information about the individuals by contacting the local bar association (or its equivalent) or the local licensing authorities.

SERVICE OF PROCESS

American consular officers are prohibited by regulations from serving legal process emanating from any court, whether in the United States or abroad, and are prohibited from appointing others to do so, except in certain cases in the United States Federal courts involving service of process on United States citizens abroad (28USC 1783 and 1784,)

Service of process in the Philippines may be accomplished by various methods (depending on the circumstances of the case, such as by registered mail at last known address, by publications, and personal service which may also be made by other officers of the court, including attorneys. Most American law firms have found it helpful, and in many cases necessary, to engage the service of Philippine attorneys to advise and assist them in effecting service of process in the Philippines.

** Updated as of April 3, 2014*

METRO MANILA

*** Arreza & Associates**

Atty Augusto Jose Y. Arreza	Address: Unit O, 10/F, Burgundy Corporate Tower 252 Sen. Gil J. Puyat Ave., Makati City 1200 Telephone: (63 2 844-2595, 844-5168 Fax number: 63 2 844 5249 E-mail: arlaw@pldt.net	General practice, Civil, criminal & administrative litigation. Family relations, Corporations, Intellectual property, Industrial arbitration,Immigration

*** Bernas Law Offices**

Atty. Jose A. Bernas	Address: 8/F, Raha Sulayman Bldg., 108 Benavides Street Legaspi Village, Makati City Telephone: (63 2)810-1814 or 812-8994 or 892-7470 Fax number: (63 2) 892-1770 E-mail address: jabernas@bernaslaw.com	General Law Practice in civil, commercial, property, securities, corporation, investment, finance, estate, planning, tax & private international law LANGUAGES: English, Pilipino, French & Mandarin

*** Conrado R. Ayuyao & Associates**

Atty. Nestor Mejia Atty. Elpidio G. Navarro Atty. Jose J. Ferrer, Jr. Atty. Ernesto O. Pua	Address: 899 Pres. Quirino Avenue, Malate Manila Telephone: (63 2) 526-7151, 526-7155, 526-7159, 526-7165 Telefax: (63 2) 522-2940 E-mail ayuyao@pacific.net.ph	General practice; insurance & negligence cases, drug dependency & related cases, labor, business & trade disputes, settlement of estate, a corporation law, large collection cases, & immigration matters. Notary public. LANGUAGES: English, Spanish, Pilipino

*** Ricardo T. Diaz**

Atty. Ricardo T. Diaz	Address: 9th Floor, Fedman Bldg., Salcedo St., Legaspi Village, Makati City Telephone: (63 2) 818-6654 / 892-4188 Fax number: (63 2) 894-4699 E-mail: ricardo_t_diaz@yahoo.com Provincial address: #117 Lealtad St., Balayan, Batangas 4213 Telephone: (63 43) 921-1565 / 211-4290 Fax number: (63 43) 921-1565 Cell Phone: 09175042605	General practice. Criminal law. LANGUAGES: Pilipino & English

*** Fajardo Law Offices**

Atty. Beda Fajardo Atty. Rafaelita Fajardo Atty. Jacinto Fajardo, Jr. Atty. Diana Franco Atty. Angelito R. Villarin Atty. Anthony Escobar	Address: 7/F Cityland Condominium 10, Tower 2 Ayala Avenue, Makati City Telephone: (63 2) 810-9595 or 810-1490 Telefax number: (63 2) 810-2490 or 913-8321 E-mail: fajarlaw@skyinet.net	Maritime, corporate, commercial, insurance, family law, construction, arbitration & immigration law. LANGUAGES: Pilipino & English

Formoso, Navaro & Formoso Law Offices

Atty. Benjamin Formoso Atty. Manuel Quimbo Atty. Patricia V. Formoso	Address: 32 J. Abad Santos Street, corner Ibañez Street Little Baguio, San Juan 1500, Metro Manila Telephone: (63 2) 724-3374, 725-5291, 722-4677 Fax number: (63 2) 725-5687 & 724-2490 Email: formoso@mozcom.com	General practice, Annulment of marriage & family relations, probate and settlement of estate, real estate transactions, taxation, admiralty, mining, adoption, banking, immigration, insurance, negligence cases, business and trade disputes, collection cases, labor, intellectual property rights, patents, copyrights and trademarks. LANGUAGES: English and Philippine dialects (Tagalog, Ilocano and Waray.

Gonzalez, Sinense, Jimenez & Associates Law Offices

Atty. Miguel V. Gonzalez Atty. Eduardo Sinense Atty. Diosdado B. Jimenez Atty. Aristeo San Agustin Atty. Augustus C. Azura Atty. Melvyn S. Jusrisprudencia	Address: Room 203 Samii Bldg., Annex 2, Aduana Street Intramuros 1002, Manila Telephone: (63 2) 527-8876 Fax number: (63 2) 527-2951	General practice; banking; corporation; civil; criminal; administrative; labor; mining patents; copyrights & trademarks; taxation; estates. Notary Public LANGUAGES: English, Spanish, Pilipino PRO BONO SERVICES: Subject to the availability of service time, thru referrals from the courts & the public service programs of the Integrated Bar of the Philippines & the Philippine Bar Association

Oben Ventura Ablola Law Office

Atty. Reginaldo A. Oben Atty. Eulalio A. Ventura Atty. Allan S. Jao Atty. Hindenburg Barrios Atty. Pablo Antonio Ventura	Address: 12th/Flr. Strata 2000 Emerald Avenue Ortigas Center, Pasig City Telephone: (63 2) 914 – 0287 up to 89 Fax number: (63 2) 914-0287 local 102 Email: obenlaw@gmail.com	Corporate & Litigation, Special assistance to Foreign investors, Immigration Law practice and criminal defense.

Ortega, Del Castillo, Bacorro, Odulio, Calma & Carbonell

Atty. Gregorio F. Ortega Atty. Tomas Del Castillo, Jr. Atty. Benjamin T. Bacorro Atty. Elizer A. Odulio Atty. Renato Calma Atty. Pedro M. Carbonell II	Address: 5/F Alpap Building, 140 Leviste Street Salcedo Village, Makati City 1227 Telephone: (63 2) 818-2321 to 25, 810-4390 Fax number: (63 2) 810-3153 or 750-2606 E-mail: ocbocc@philonline.com , ocbocc@pldt.com , low@ocbocc.com Website: www.ocbocc.com	General Practice, Foreign Investments, Corporation, Taxation, Patents, Trademarks, Copyrights and Technology Transfers, Civil and Criminal Litigation, Insurance, Securities, Labor Laws, Admiralty, Estates and Trusts, Aviation, Immigration, Banking and Finance, Oil and Mining, Media Law, Family Law, Notary Public.

Chato Eleazar Lagmay & Arreza Law Office

Atty. Wilfredo M. Chato Atty. Liwayway Vinzons-Chato Atty. Victor Y. Eleazar Atty. Esther R. Ibañez Atty. Romeo Raymond C. Santos Atty. Peter Paul S. Romero Atty. Rubi L. Mayor	Address: 8/F Strata 2000, Emerald Avenue, Ortigas Center, 1605 Pasig City Telephone: (63 2) 631-6561 to 64 Fax number: (63 2) 631-7634 E-mail: chalex@pldt.net	Corporate and commercial practice, counseling on and/or documentation of commercial transactions, in particular: corporate acquisitions & divestments; foreign investments & joint ventures; loan syndications & underwriting of securities; real estate acquisitions; conveyance & land-use conversions; build-operate-transfer arrangements, banking investments; corporate secretaryship; organizations & restructuring of business organizations; tax planning & consultancy; specialized practice information technology; intellectual property; civil aviation; administrative practice-representation & filings before regulatory wuasi-judicial agencies; litigation & arbitration practice-cases involving family civil commercial & labor laws.

Quasha, Ancheta, Pena & Nolasco

Atty. Alonzo Q. Ancheta Atty. Nilo B. Pena	Address: 6/F Don Pablo Building, 114 Amorsolo Street Legaspi Village, Makati City Telephone: (63 2) 892-	General practice; corporate investments; taxation; labor & employment; immigration; civil law, particularly property; succession; persons & family relations; contracts & intellectual property LANGUAGES: English, Spanish, Pilipino

Atty. Pompeyo Nolasco Atty. Felisa Baguilat	3011/892-5736 Fax number: (63 2) 817-6423/893-1356 Email: quasha@quasha-interlaw.com	

Quiason, Makalintal, Barot, Torres & Ibarra

Atty. Pociano G.A. Mathay Atty. Wilfredo E. Sanchez	Address: 21/F Robinson-Equitable PCI Bank Tower ADB Avenue corner Poveda Street Ortigas Center, Pasig City Telephone: (63 2) 631-0981 up to 85 Fax number: (63 2) 631-3847 qmbti@qmbti.com	Corporate (inclusive of banking & finance, investments & trade, securities regulation; energy & public utilities; immigration; intellectual property; labor; litigation & taxation LANGUAGES: English, Spanish, Pilipino

Reyes, Santayana, Tayao, Molo & Alegre

Atty. Pedro T. Molo Atty. Zosimo G. Alegre Atty. Gene B. Macalauing Atty. Solomon Reyes Atty. Silverio Dayao	Address: 3/F Zaragoza Building, 102 Gamboa Street Legaspi Village, Makati City Telephone: (63 2) 843-3976 up to 78 Fax number: (63 2) 843-3977	General practice & litigation, corporation, banking & finance, foreign investment, aviation, labor laws, taxation, patents, trademarks & copyrights, civil & commercial laws. Notary Public. LANGUAGES: English, Spanish, Pilipino

Riguera & Riguera Law Office

Atty. Manuel Riguera Atty. Hazel Riguera	Address: 2/F Azucena Arcade, 255 Alabang-Zapote Road Pamplona, Las Piñas City Telephone: (63 2) 871-5749 or 872 6216 Fax number: (63 2) 871-5749 or 872-6216 e-mail: riglaw@pacific.net.ph riglaw@smartbro.net	General practice & litigation with fields of expertise in real estate & property law; credit & banking law; marriage & family law; insurance law; corporate; securities & investment law

Rodrigo Berenguer & Guno

Atty. Raul C. Rabe	Address: 4/F, Phil. First Building, 6764 Ayala Avenue Makati City Telephone: (63 2) 840-3141 up to 43 or 840-2733 up to 34 Fax number: (63 2) 840-4047 E-mail: rchrabe@rbglaw.com Website: rbg.com.ph	Civil and criminal litigation, corporate practice, international trade and investments. LANGUAGE: English

Romulo, Mabanta, Buenaventura, Sayoc & De Los Angeles

Atty. Ricardo J. Romulo Atty. Roman Mabanta, Jr. Atty. Jose F. Buenaventura Atty. Jesus S. J. Sayoc Atty. Eduardo de los Angeles	Address: 30/F Citibank Tower, 8741 Paseo de Roxas, Makati City P.O. Box 2089, Makati Central Post Office, 1260 Makati City Telephone: (63 2) 848-0114 Fax number: (63 2) 815-3172 or 810-3110 or 813-0906 or 818-0260 or 761-4991 Website: www.rmbsa.com Email: Ricardo.romulo@romulo.com	Admiralty, alternative dispute resolution, banking & finance, corporate & commercial laws, energy & infrastructure, environmental laws, foreign investments, immigration, insurance, intellectual property, labor laws, litigation, securities & taxation. LANGUAGES: English, Spanish, Pilipino Note: change in address after September 2011.

SyCip, Salazar, Hernandez & Gatmaitan

Atty. Andres G. Gatmaitan Atty. Rafael A. Morales Atty. Cirilo T. Tolosa Atty. Llewelyn L. Llanillo Atty. Andres B. Sta. Maria, Jr. Atty. Emmanuel L. Pena, Jr.	Address: SSHG Law Centre, 105 Paseo de Roxas Makati City 1225 Telephone: (63 2) 982-3500 or 982-23700 or 982-3600 Fax number: (63 2) 817-3896 E-mail: syciplaw@globe.com.ph Sshg@syciplaw.com Website: www.syciplaw.com	General practice, patents, criminal, civil, estate, family laws, immigration, adoption, child custody, litigation, maritime & business cases, corporate & commercial law, banking, finance & securities, labor relations, mining, energy & natural resources law, intellectual property, shipping, taxation, real estate. Notary Public. LANGUAGES: English, Spanish, Pilipino

SyquiaPascual-Lopez Santos Law Offices

Atty. Enrique P. Syquia Atty. Cicero R. Cua Atty. Felix R. Torralba Atty. Emiliano Espiritu Atty. Ma. Editha A. Go-Binas	Address: Unit 1902 Security Bank Center, 6776 Ayala Ave., Legaspi Village, Makati City Telephone: (63 2) 817-1095 or 817-1096 or 817-1098 or 817-1742 Fax number: (63 2) 893-5400 E-mail: syquia@intlaw.com.ph	General practice. Security Law, International law, collection cases. Notary Public. LANGUAGES: English, Spanish, Pilipino

Velicaria Egenias Law Offices

Atty. Antonio Velicaria Atty. Francis Egenias Atty. Anthony Velicaria	Addres: 3/F, Adamson Center, 121 Lefiste Street Salcedo Village, Makati City Telephone: (63 2) 810-7799 or 810-8085 or 810-7820 816-4672 or 816-4677 Fax number: (63 2) 893-4091	Maritime law, patents & trademarks, corporate practice, immigration, labor laws.

PARANAQUE CITY

* Jeanie S. Pulido Law Office

Atty. Jeanie S. Pulido	Address: Unit G-07 Antel Seaview Tower A. 2626 Roxas Blvd, Pasig City, 1300 Telephone: (63 2) 8214103 Fax number: (63 2) 821-4106 Email: jsplaw@philonline.com jsplaw@gmail.com Website: www.philippinelegalservices.com	Personal and family law, Immigration, Real Estate transactions, Probate and estate, Corporate and Business law, Labor law, Service of summons and criminal law. Language: English and Filipino

BAGUIO CITY

Agranzamendez, Liceralde Gallardo & Associates (ALGA Law)

Atty. Reynaldo Agranzamendez Atty. Miguel Liceralde, Sr. Atty. Rigoberto Gallardo Atty. Miguel L. Liceralde, Jr. Atty. Cres Manuel L. Liceralde Atty. Samuel D. Gallardo Atty. Ray Glenn C. Agranzamendez	Address: 3/F Antipolo Annex Bldg, #83 Session Road, Baguio City 2600 Telefax: (63-74) 4438625 Email: agra716@yahoo.com mbl_53@yahoo.com rdgallardo65@yahoo.com	General practice. Criminal cases, corporation, labor cases, tax matters, agrarian cases, special proceedings, foreclosures & collection cases, family law cases, corporate cases, child & women protection cases.

CEBU CITY

Mercado Cordero Bael Acuna & Sepulveda Law Office

Atty. Jose Ray Bael Atty. Vicente Cordero Atty. Cornelio Mercado Atty. Auren Acuña Atty. Rory Jon Sipolvida Atty. Allan Orvien P. Geotina	Address: 3/F CAO Mercado Building Osmeña Boulevard, Cebu City Telephone: (63-32) 253-4941 or 253-5209 or 253-5730 Fax number: (63-32) 245-4786 or 255-4786 E-mail: mcbaselaw@yahoo.com or fermlaw@col.net.ph	General practice. Litigation work in all levels (trial and appellate courts, administrative matters, corporate, insurance, labor, immigration, family and estate matters.

J. Neri & Associates

Atty. Julius Neri Atty. Jerome Dennis Neri Atty. Thelma Jordan Atty. Evelyn Nuñez Atty. Florante Abad Atty. Renato Galeon Atty. Joven Francis Neri	Address: 7/F Ayala Life-FGU Center Mindanao Avenue, cor. Biliran Road, Cebu Business Park, Cebu City 6000 Telephone: (63-32) 232-2359; 232-2375 or 415-8463 Telefax number: (63-32) 232-2375 or 232-2359 E-mail: j.nerilawfirm@yahoo.com.ph	Labor, civil, corporate, maritime, patent, taxation, criminal, violation of the family code & family code & child & youth welfare code, land registration cases.

SyCip, Salazar, Hernandez & Gatmaitan

Atty. Danilo Ortiz Atty. Alan Fontanosa	Address: 4/F Room 406 Keppel Center, Cebu Business Park Ayala, Cebu City 6000	Corporate & commercial law, banking, finance & securities, litigation, labor relations, mining, energy & natural resources law,
Atty. Thaddeus Alvizo Atty. Joseph Trillana Gonzales Atty. May Aileen Lizares Atty. Karen B. Caparros-Arquillano Atty. Dennis R. Quiokeles	Telephone: (63-32) 233-1211 up to 13 or 233-1950 Fax number: (63-32) 233-1682 E-mail: sycipceb@syciplaw.com , or sshgcebu@syciplaw.com	intellectual property, shipping and maritime law, taxation, real estate, immigration law. Notary Public.

DAVAO CITY

SyCip, Salazar, Hernandez & Gatmaitan

Atty. Dominador Carillo Atty. Geraldine Kimosin-Tiu Atty. Aaron Philip Cruz	Address: The Penthouse, 17th Landco Corporate Center J.P. Laurel Avenue Bajada, Davao City 8000 Telephone: (63 82) 221-3917; (63 32) 224-2742 Fax number: (63 82) 224-2743 E-mail: sshgdavao@syciplaw.com	General practice, patents, criminal, civil, estate, family laws, immigration, adoption, child custody, litigation, maritime & business cases, corporate & commercial law, banking, finance & securities, labor relations, mining, energy & natural resources law, intellectual property, shipping, taxation, real estate. Notary Public. LANGUAGES: English, Spanish, Pilipino, Fukien, Cebuano

ILOILO CITY

Treñas, Treñas & Rubias Law Offices

Atty. Raul Rivero Atty. Gregorio Rubias Atty. Manuel Miraflores Atty. Aloysius De La Cruz, II Attv. Rodolfo	Address: 2/F Golden Commercial Center Iznart Street, Iloilo City Telephone: (63-33) 337-3021 or 337-9964 Fax number: (63-33) 335-1075	General practice, civil, commercial, corporate, labor, collection, trade disputes, criminal cases, estates. Notaries Public. LANGUAGE: English, Spanish, Tagalog & Visayan dialects

Pollentes, Jr. Atty. Lina Layson Atty. Jose Mari Treñas		

Giron & Giron Law Office (Will send a fax of additional information)

Atty. Joselito V. Giron Atty. Rachel Giron	Address: #710 Ermita Center Building 1350 Roxas Boulevard Ermita, Manila 1000 Telephone: (632) 567-3913 Fax number:: (632) 567-3914 Mobile: (63-917)700-7555 / (63-917) 700-8555 Email: attyjv@mac.com / attyrg@mac.com Website: www.gironimmigration.com	Also based in Bacolod Province United States Immigration & Nationality Law, U.S. Visa consultation and applications LANGUAGE: English, Tagalog, other dialects of Philippines

MINDORO PROVINCE

Public Defender's Office

Atty. Gilbert Matibag	Address: Public Attorney's Office, Hall of Justice Provincial Capitol Complex Calapan City, Oriental Mindoro Telefax number: (63-43) 286-7047	General Practice. Criminal & civil cases.

OLONGAPO CITY (ZAMBALES)

Lacambra Law Office

Atty. Leopoldo Lacambra, Jr.	Address: 2415 Lincoln Lodge, Arthur Street West Bajac-Bajac, Olongapo City 2200 Fax number: (63-47) 224-1788 Email: leolacambra@yahoo.com	General practice. Domestic and Inter-country adoption, annulment/declaration of nullity of marriage, correction/cancellation of entries not covered by R.A. 9048,civil cases

PAMPANGA PROVINCE

Mangiliman, Benoza & Associates

Atty. Wilfrido Mangiliman Atty. Aramis Benoza Atty. Federico Tolentino, Jr. Atty. Raul Macalino Atty. Ma. Lowela V. Cezar-Benoza Atty. Josep Jepri M. Miranda Atty. Roseller T. Logronio	Address: Unit 5, Calsa Arcade II Gapan, Olongapo Road, corner Lazatin Avenue, San Fernando, Pampanga Telephone: (63-45) 961-2572 or 961-6028 Fax: (63-45) 879-7246 Email: mallow_mis@yahoo.com	General Practice. Willing to handle pro bono cases for indigent but deserving litigants. They are incumbent officers of the Integrated Bar of the Philippines, Pampanga/Angeles City Chapter.

AMERICAN ASSOCIATION OF THE PHILIPPINES

Platon Martinez Flores San Pedro & Leano Offices

Atty. Saklolo Leano	6/F Tuscan Building, 114 Herrera Street Legaspi Village, Makati (63 2) 867-4696 or 867-4696 (63 2) 867-1304 Email: counsel@platonmartinez.com

Siguion Reyna Montecillo & Ongsiako Law Offices

Atty. Romarie Villonco Atty. Ishak V. Mastura	4 and 6/F Citibank Center, 8741 Paseo de Roxas, Makati City (63 2) 810-0281 up to 90 (63 2) 819-1498 Email: general@frmo-law.com Website: http://www.srmo-law.com

Sycip Salazar Hernandez & Gatmaitan Law Offices

Atty. Emmanuel Pena	Sycip Law All Asia Center, 105 Paseo de Roxas, Makati City (63 2) 982-3500, 982-3600, 982-3700 (63 2) 817-3896 or 818-7562 Website: www.syciplaw.com

Angara Abello Concepcion Regala & Cruz Law Offices

Atty. Avelino V. Cruz	22/F ACCRA Law Tower, Second Avenue corner 30th Street, Crescent Park West, Bonifacio Global City, 0399 Taguig, Metro Manila, Phllippines (63 2) 830-8000 (632) 403-7007; (632) 403-7009 e-mail: accra@accralaw.com Website: www.accralaw.com

AMERICAN CHAMBER OF COMMERCE

Angara Abello Concepcion Regala & Cruz Law Offices

Atty. Avelino V. Cruz	22/F ACCRA Law Tower, Second Avenue corner 30th Street, Crescent Park West, Bonifacio Global City, 0399 Taguig, Metro Manila, Philippines (63 2) 830-8000 (632) 403-7007; (632) 403-7009 e-mail: accra@accralaw.com Website: www.accralaw.com

Baniqued & Banuqued

Atty. Carlos G. Baniqued	8/F, Jollibee Center, San Miguel Avenue, Pasig City (63 2) 633-9418 (63 2) 633-1911 e-mail: baniqued@info.com.ph Website: www.baniquedlaw.com

Belo Gozon Parel Asuncion & Lucila

Atty. Enrique M. Belo	15/F Saguittarius Condominium, H.V. da la Costa Street, Salcedo Village, Makati City (63 2) 816-3716 up to 19/814-4806 up to 09 (63 2) 817-0696 or 812-0008 e-mail: bgelaw@pldtdsl.net or bgelaw@pworld.net.ph Website: www.bgepal.com

Carpio Villaraza & Cruz Law Offices

Atty. Arthur L. Villaraza	5/F, LTA Building 118 Perea Street, Legaspi, Metro Manila, Philippines (63 2) 818-9836/38 (63 2) 816-7057/894-4729 e-mail: villaraza.angangco@cvclaw.com or carpio.villaraza@cvclaw.com

Ortega Del Castillo Bacorro Odullo Calma & Carbonell

Atty. Gregorio E. Ortega	5-6/Fs, Alpap Building, 140 Alfaro Street, Salcedo Village, Makati City (63 2) 818-2321 up to 24 (63 2) 810-3153/750-2606 e-mail: ocbocc@philonline.com

Romulo Mabanta Buenaventura Sayoc & De Los Angeles

Atty. Aileen Sarah Tolosa-Lerma	30/F Citibank Tower, 8741 Paseo de Roxas, Makati City (63 2) 848-0114 (63 2) 813-0906/815-3172 e-mail: rmbsa@rmbsa.com or tolosa@rmbsa.com

Siguion Reyna Montecillo & Ongsiako Law Offices

Atty. Rolando Mario G. Villonco	4th and 6th Floors, Citibank Center, 8741 Paseo de Roxas, Makati City (63 2) 810-0281/810-0409 (63 2) 819-1498 e-mail: general@srmo-law.com or srmo@l-next.net Website: www.srmo-law.com

AMERICAN CHAMBER OF COMMERCE - CEBU
Abello Concepcion Regala & Cruz Law Offices

Atty. Danilo R. Deen	6/F Cebu Holdings Center Building, Cebu Business Park (Ayala), 6000 Cebu City, PHILIPPINES (63 32) 231-1449; (63 32) 231-4223 (63 32) 231-3614 e-mail: accra@accralaw.com , or accralawcebu@pldtdsl.net Website: www.accralaw.com

Sycip Salazar Hernandez & Gatmaitan Law Offices

Atty. Thad Alvizo	4/F Room 406 Keppel Center, Cebu Business Park Ayala, Cebu City 6000 (63 32) 233-1211 to 13; (63 32) 233-1950 (63 32) 233-1682 Email: sycipceb@syciplaw.com , or sshgcebu@syciplaw.com (Note: This is the same firm as the first firm, "Sycip", listed on page 11)

SINGAPORE INVESTMENT AND BUSINESS CLIMATE - STRATEGIC INFORMATION AND CONTACTS FOR STARTING BUSINESS

Foreign investments, combined with investments through government-linked corporations (GLCs), underpin Singapore's open, heavily trade-dependent economy. With the exception of restrictions in the financial services, professional services, and media sectors, Singapore maintains a predominantly open investment regime. The World Bank's, Doing Business 2015 report ranked Singapore as the easiest country in which to do business. The Global Competitiveness Report 2014-2015 by the World Economic Forum ranked Singapore as the second-most competitive economy globally and first on its enabling trade index. The U.S.-Singapore Free Trade Agreement (FTA), which came into force January 1, 2004, expanded U.S. market access in goods, services, investment, and government procurement, enhanced intellectual property protection, and provided for cooperation in promoting labor rights and the environment.

The Government of Singapore (GOS) is strongly committed to maintaining a free market but also takes a leadership role in planning Singapore's economic development. The government actively uses the public sector as both an investor and catalyst for development. As of the end of February 2015, the top four Singapore-listed GLCs accounted for about 14.4 percent of total capitalization of the Singapore Exchange (SGX). Some observers have criticized the dominant role of GLCs in the domestic economy, arguing that it has displaced or suppressed private sector entrepreneurship and investment.

Singapore's aggressive pursuit of foreign investment as another pillar of its overall economic strategy has enabled the country to evolve into a regional base for multinational corporations (MNCs). The Economic Development Board (EDB), Singapore's investment promotion agency, focuses on securing major investments in high value-added manufacturing and service activities as part of a strategy to replace labor-intensive, low value-added activities that have migrated offshore.

1. OPENNESS TO, AND RESTRICTIONS UPON, FOREIGN INVESTMENT

Attitude toward Foreign Direct Investment

Singapore's legal framework and public policies are generally favorable toward foreign investors. Foreign investors are not required to enter into joint ventures or cede management control to local interests, and local and foreign investors are subject to the same basic laws. Apart from regulatory requirements in some sectors (reference Limits on National Treatment and Other Restrictions), the government screens investment proposals only to determine eligibility for various incentive regimes (reference Annex). Singapore places no restrictions on reinvestment or repatriation of earnings or capital. The judicial system upholds the sanctity of contracts, and decisions are effectively enforced.

Limits on National Treatment and Other Restrictions: Exceptions to Singapore's general openness to foreign investment exist in telecommunications, broadcasting, the domestic news media, financial services, legal, and other professional services, and property ownership. Under Singapore law, Articles of Incorporation may include shareholding limits that restrict ownership in corporations by foreign persons.

Telecommunications:

The Telecoms Competition Code opened the industry in 2000 to foreign or domestic companies seeking to provide facilities-based (fixed line or mobile) or services-based (local, international, and callback) telecommunications services. Singapore Telecommunications (SingTel), the former monopoly which is currently 52-percent government-owned, faces competition in all market segments. Its main competitors, MobileOne and StarHub, are also GLCs. As of March 2015, Singapore has 54 facilities-based (group) and 254 services-based (individual) operators. Since 2007, SingTel has been exempted from dominant licensee obligations for the residential and commercial portions of the retail international telephone services. SingTel is also exempted from dominant licensee obligations for wholesale international telephone services, International Managed Data Services Terrestrial International Private Leased Circuit, and Backhaul.

U.S. and other companies remain concerned about the lack of transparency in some aspects of Singapore's telecommunications regulatory and rule-making process. In particular, there is no obligation to make information publicly available concerning a company's request for a stay of decision or the filing of an appeal, request public comments about such requests, or to publish a detailed explanation concerning final decisions made by the Infocomm Development Authority (IDA) or the Ministry of Communication and Information (MCI).

Infrastructure for the next generation access network, a national broadband all-fiber network, has been developed by OpenNet, a consortium formed by Canada's Axia Netmedia (which holds 30-percent ownership), SingTel (30 percent), Singapore Press Holdings (25 percent), and SP Telecommunications (15 percent). The network will be operated by Nucleus Connect, a wholly-owned subsidiary of StarHub. Operational separation is imposed on Nucleus Connect to maintain its independence from OpenNet, and to ensure that it provide services to all downstream operators on the same prices and terms and conditions, with the same processes and access to information. Nearly all homes and offices are connected to the fiber-optic broadband network.

Under an agreement in 2013, NetLink Trust -- a business trust that owns the ducts and manholes through which the optical fiber cables pass to reach homes and buildings -- purchased OpenNet, giving it control over all the steps involved in connecting users to the networks. Seven Singapore telecommunication firms, including M1 and StarHub, voiced their opposition to the consolidation, noting it would see SingTel becoming the 100 percent beneficial owner of the only other nationwide fixed telecommunications network in Singapore, apart from SingTel's own network, leading to discriminatory treatment and a lack of independence. In response, IDA established several conditions to allay concerns about anti-competitive practices, including establishing a monitoring board consisting of government representatives to ensure SingTel does not influence any decisions on service price as well as terms and conditions. SingTel must also divest its majority stake in NetLink Trust by April 2018.

In December 2014, NetLink Trust, formerly OpenNet, fell short of the Quality of Service (QoS) review conducted from January to June 2014, leading to a USD 39,460 (SGD 50,000) financial penalty imposed by the IDA. During the assessment period, NetLink Trust fulfilled 85.34 percent to 92.48 percent of the service orders within three business days or by Request for Activation (RFA) date, short of the minimum standard of 98 percent. It also fulfilled 89.1 percent to 94.85 percent of the service orders within seven business days, or by RFA plus four business days, short of the 100 percent standard. The company was fined in November 2013 and May 2014, with fines totaling USD 349,243 (SGD 440,000), for breaching its non-residential QoS standards for timely service provisioning. IDA reported, however, that NetLink displayed improvements in providing connection service to residential end-users during the six-month assessment period despite not meeting the mark.

In 2011, the GOS amended the Telecommunications Act, giving it more power to curb monopolistic behavior in the telecommunications sector and ensure continuity in services to ensure the sector remains competitive. The law allows GOSI to issue a Separation Order to a telecommunications company (Telco) that engages in anti-competitive behavior, and empowers the Minister of Communication and Information to issue Special Administrative Orders (SAOs) that ensure a key telecommunication network or service continues to be functional, for public and national interest and revised the maximum administrative financial penalty on Telco that breach regulations to 10 percent of the annual business turnover for licensable services of a licensee, or USD 790,514 (SGD 1 million), whichever is higher. Media: The local free-to-air broadcasting, cable and newspaper sectors are effectively closed to foreign firms. Section 44 of the Broadcasting Act restricts foreign equity ownership of companies broadcasting to the Singapore domestic market to 49 percent or less, although the Act does allow for exceptions. Individuals cannot hold more than five percent of the ordinary shares issued by a broadcasting company without the government's prior approval.

The Newspaper and Printing Presses Act restricts equity ownership (local or foreign) to five percent per shareholder and requires that directors be Singapore citizens. Newspaper companies must issue two classes of shares, ordinary and management, with the latter available only to Singapore citizens or corporations approved by the government. Holders of management shares have an effective veto over selected board decisions. The government controls distribution, importation and sale of any foreign newspaper, and significantly restricts freedom of the press, having curtailed or banned the circulation of some foreign publications. The government has also gazetted foreign newspapers, i.e., numerically limited their circulation. Singapore's leaders have brought defamation suits against foreign publishers. Such suits have resulted in the foreign publishers issuing apologies and paying damages.

While local media is heavily government influenced, in practice there are few restrictions on the internet, and Singaporeans generally have uncensored access to international media. However, the Media Development Authority (MDA), which is responsible for regulating Internet service providers, has blocked various websites containing objectionable material, such as pornography and racist and religious hatred sites.

Licensing scheme for news websites

The Media Development Authority implemented in 2013 a regulation requiring certain internet news sites to obtain a license. MDA asserts the new regulation was intended to put online news sites on a more consistent regulatory basis with traditional media such as print and television, which are also individually licensed, and with both subject to the same content standards. This requirement applies to sites, both commercial news and other sites, that publish on average over a two-month period one article per week relating to issues in Singapore and which receive a two-month average of at least 50,000 monthly site visits from unique addresses of Singapore-based internet providers. The license requires these sites to submit a bond of SGD 50,000 (USD 40,000) and to adhere to new requirements to remove prohibited content within 24 hours of notification from the MDA. Some citizens viewed this regulation as a way to censor online critics of the government. In June 2013 more than 2,500 persons participated in a protest against the new regulation. The Minister for Communications and Information publicly stated that the new regulation was not intended to target individual bloggers or blogs.

MediaCorp TV is the only free-to-air TV broadcaster; the government via Temasek Holdings (Temasek) owns 100 percent of it. Pay-TV providers StarHub Cable Vision (SCV) and MioTV are wholly-owned subsidiaries of StarHub and SingTel, respectively. Free-to-air radio broadcasters are mainly government-owned, with MediaCorp Radio Singapore being the largest operator. BBC World Services is the only foreign free-to-air broadcaster in Singapore.

To rectify the high degree of content fragmentation in the Singapore pay-TV market, and shift the focus of competition from an exclusivity-centric strategy to other aspects such as service differentiation and competitive packaging, he Media Development Authority (MDA) implemented cross-carriage measures in 2011 requiring pay TV companies designated by MDA to be Receiving Qualified Licensees (RQL) – currently SingTel and StarHub -- to cross carry content subject to exclusive carriage provisions. RQLs with an exclusive contract for a channel are required to share that content with other pay TV companies at their request Content providers consider the measures an unnecessary interference in a competitive market that would deny content holders the ability to negotiate freely in the marketplace, and an interference with their ability to manage and protect their intellectual property. More common content is now available across the different pay-TV platforms, and the operators are beginning to differentiate themselves by originating their own content, offering subscribed content online via PCs and tablet computers, and delivering content via fiber networks.

Banking

The Monetary Authority of Singapore (MAS) regulates all banking activities as provided for under the Banking Act. Singapore maintains legal distinctions between foreign and local banks, and the type of license (i.e., full service, wholesale, and offshore) held by foreign banks. As of March 16, 2015 28 foreign full service licensees, 57 wholesale licensees, and 37 offshore licensees operated in Singapore. All offshore banks are eligible to be upgraded to wholesale bank status based on MAS criteria to enable them to conduct a wider range of activities. Except in retail banking, Singapore laws do not distinguish operationally between foreign and domestic banks.

The government initiated a banking liberalization program in 1999 to ease restrictions on foreign banks and has supplemented this with phased-in provisions under the FTA, including removal of a 40-percent ceiling on foreign ownership of local banks and a 20-percent aggregate foreign shareholding limit on finance companies. The Minister in charge of the Monetary Authority of Singapore must approve the merger or takeover of a local bank or financial holding company, as well as the acquisition of voting shares in such institutions above specific thresholds of 5 percent, 12 percent or 20 percent of shareholdings. Although the GOS has lifted the formal ceilings on foreign ownership of local banks and finance companies, the approval of controllers of local banks ensures that this control rests with individuals or groups whose interests are aligned with the long term interests of the Singapore economy and Singapore's national interests. Of the 28 full service licenses granted to foreign banks, four have gone to U.S. banks. Ten of the 28 full service licensees (including one U.S. bank) have been granted qualifying full bank (QFB) status. U.S. financial institutions enjoy phased-in benefits under the FTA. Since 2006, U.S.-licensed full service banks that are also QFBs have been able to operate at an unlimited number of locations (branches or off-premises ATMs) versus 25 for non-U.S. full service foreign banks with QFB status. U.S. and foreign full-service banks with QFB status can freely relocate existing branches and share ATMs among themselves. They can also provide electronic funds transfer and point-of-sale debit services, and accept services related to Singapore's compulsory pension fund. In 2007, Singapore lifted the quota on new licenses for U.S. wholesale banks.

Locally and non-locally incorporated subsidiaries of U.S. full-service banks with QFB status can apply for access to local ATM networks. However, no U.S. bank has come to a commercial agreement to gain such access. Despite liberalization, U.S. and other foreign banks in the domestic retail banking sector still face barriers. Under the enhanced QFB program launched in 2012, MAS will require QFBs it deems systemically significant to incorporate locally. If those locally incorporated entities are deemed "significantly rooted" in Singapore, with a majority of Singaporean or permanent resident members, Singapore may grant approval for an additional 25 places of business, of which up to 10 may be branches. Local retail banks do not face similar constraints on customer service locations or access to the local ATM network. As noted above, U.S. banks are not subject to quotas on service locations under the terms of the FTA. Holders of credit cards issued locally by foreign banks or other financial institutions sometimes cannot access their accounts through the local ATM networks. They are also unable to access their accounts for cash withdrawals, transfers or bill payments at ATMs operated by banks other than those operated by their own bank or at foreign banks' shared ATM network. Nevertheless, full-service foreign banks have made significant inroads in other retail banking areas, with substantial market share in products like credit cards and personal and housing loans.

U.S. industry advocates enhancements to Singapore's credit bureau system, in particular, adoption of an open admission system for all lenders, including non-banks. There are currently two credit bureaus in Singapore, Credit Bureau (Singapore) Private Ltd. (CBS) and Credit Scan.

Securities and Asset Management

Singapore has no trading restrictions on foreign-owned stockbrokers. There is no cap on the aggregate investment by foreigners regarding the paid-up capital of dealers that are members of the SGX. Direct registration of foreign mutual funds is allowed, provided MAS approves the prospectus and the fund. The FTA has relaxed conditions that foreign asset managers must meet in order to offer products under the government-managed compulsory pension fund (Central Provident Fund Investment Scheme).

Legal Services

As of 2015, 15 out of the 113 foreign law firms operating in Singapore were from the United States. In December 2008, Singapore granted Qualifying Foreign Law Practice (QFLP) licenses to six foreign law firms (two U.S. firms) to practice domestic law. Restrictions remain in certain legal fields including; conveyance, penal law, and domestic relations. In the first quarter of 2013, Singapore awarded another four QFLP licenses, stemming from applications submitted in 2012. Three of these firms were U.S. professional practices.

Foreign investments, combined with investments through government-linked corporations (GLCs), underpin Singapore's open, heavily trade-dependent economy. With the exception of restrictions in the financial services, professional services, and media sectors, Singapore maintains a predominantly open investment regime. The World Bank's,Doing Business 2015 report ranked Singapore as the easiest country in which to do business. "The 2014-2015 Global Competitiveness Report ranks Singapore as the second-most competitive economy globally, and first on its enabling trade index.

The 2004 U.S.-Singapore Free Trade Agreement (FTA), expanded U.S. market access in goods, services, investment, and government procurement, enhanced intellectual property protection, and provided for cooperation in promoting labor rights and the environment.

The GOS is strongly committed to maintaining a free market but also takes a leadership role in planning Singapore's economic development. The government actively uses the public sector as both an investor and catalyst for development. As of February 2015, the top four Singapore-listed GLCs accounted for about 14.4 percent of total capitalization of the Singapore Exchange (SGX). Some observers have criticized the dominant role of GLCs in the domestic economy, arguing that it has displaced or suppressed private sector entrepreneurship and investment.

In accordance with current legislation, foreign law firms can provide legal services under Singapore law only through a Joint Law Venture (JLV) or Formal Law Alliance (FLA) with a domestic law firm. The Joint Law Venture is collaboration between a Foreign Law Practice and Singapore Law Practice. There is not a clear indication regarding how share percentages can be held in this type of partnership.The Attorney-General will consider all the relevant circumstances including the proposed structure and its overall suitability to achieve the objectives for which Joint law Ventures are permitted to be established in deciding on its approval. Currently, there are two U.S. law firms with Joint Law Ventures in Singapore. U.S. and foreign attorneys are allowed to represent parties in arbitration without the need for a Singapore attorney to be present. With the exception of law degrees from a handful of designated U.S., British, Australian, and New Zealand universities, no foreign university law degrees are recognized for purposes of admission to practice law in Singapore. Under the FTA, Singapore recognizes law degrees from Harvard University, Columbia University, New York University, and the University of Michigan. Singapore will admit to the Singapore professional bar- a citizen or permanent-resident law school graduates of those designated universities who are ranked among the top 70 percent of their graduating class or have obtained lower-second class honors (under the Britis system).

Engineering and Architectural Services

Engineering and architectural firms can be 100 percent foreign-owned. Only engineers and architects registered with the Professional Engineers Board and the Architects Board, respectively, can practice in Singapore. All applicants (both local and foreign) must have at least four years of practical experience in engineering or architectural works, and pass an examination set by the respective Board.

Accounting and Tax Services

The major international accounting firms operate in Singapore. Public accountants and at least one partner of a public accounting firm must reside in Singapore. Only public accountants who are members of the Institute of Certified Public Accountants of Singapore and registered with the Public Accountants Board may practice in Singapore. The Board recognizes U.S. accountants registered with the American Institute of Certified Public Accountants.

Energy

Singapore completed efforts to liberalize its gas market with the amendment of the Gas Act and implementation of a Gas Network Code in 2008, which were designed to give gas retailers and importers direct access to the onshore gas pipeline infrastructure. However, key parts of the local gas market, such as gas retailing and access to offshore gas pipelines, remain controlled by incumbent Singaporean firms. In the past, the dominance of Singaporean government-linked corporations in this sector proved challenging for American companies that tried to enter the power generation and gas import business.

Other Investment Policy Reviews

Singapore has not conducted an investment policy review through OECD or UNCTAD in the past three years. Singapore is a World Trade Organization (WTO) member since 1995. The last Trade Policy Review was conducted in 2012.

Laws/Regulations of Foreign Direct Investment

Singapore enacted the Competition Act in 2004 and established the Competition Commission of Singapore in January 2005. The Act contains provisions on anti-competitive agreements, decisions, and practices; abuse of dominance; enforcement and appeals process; and mergers and acquisitions. There are no reports of government interference in judicial proceedings affecting foreign investors.

Business registration sites in Singapore include:

www.psi.gov.sg
www.enterpriseone.gov.sg

Industrial Promotion

The Economic Development Board (EDB), Singapore's investment promotion agency, focuses on securing major investments in high value-added manufacturing and service activities as part of a strategy to replace labor-intensive, low value-added activities that have migrated offshore.

As part of the government's strategy to develop Singapore into a premier financial center, the GOS offers tax incentives for financial institutions looking to set up operations. Further information, details and guidelines are available at**http://www.mas.gov.sg/Singapore-Financial-Centre/Value-Propositions/Setting-Up.aspx**.

Limits on Foreign Control

Exceptions to Singapore's general openness to foreign investment exist in telecommunications, broadcasting, the domestic news media, financial services, legal, and other professional services, and property ownership. Under Singapore law, Articles of Incorporation may include shareholding limits that restrict ownership in corporations by foreign persons.

Privatization Program

Singapore's Government-linked corporations (GLCs) are active in many sectors of the economy, especially strategically important sectors including telecommunications, media, public transportation, defense, port, and airport operations. In addition, the GLCs are also present in many other sectors of the economy, including banking, shipping, airline, consumer/lifestyle, infrastructure, and real estate. GLCs operate on a commercial basis and have no specific advantage in competing with private enterprises based on their government ownership. The GLC's are fully or partially owned by Temasek, a holding company with the Singapore Ministry of Finance as its sole shareholder.

Screening of FDI

Singapore has a generally open investment regime, and no overarching screening process for foreign investment.

Competition Law

The U.S.-Singapore FTA contains specific conduct guarantees to ensure that GLCs will operate on a commercial and non-discriminatory basis towards U.S. firms. GLCs with substantial revenues or assets are also subject to enhanced transparency requirements under the FTA. In accordance with its FTA commitments, Singapore enacted the Competition Act in 2004 and established the Competition Commission of Singapore in January 2005. The Act contains provisions on anti-competitive agreements, decisions, and practices; abuse of dominance; enforcement and appeals process; and mergers and acquisitions.

Singapore has an extensive network of GLCs that are active in many sectors of the economy. Some sectors, notably telecommunications and financial services, are subject to sector-specific regulatory bodies and competition regulations typically less rigorous than those being implemented under the Competition Act.

Investment Trends

Singapore's aggressive pursuit of foreign investment as another pillar of its overall economic strategy has enabled the country to evolve into a regional base for multinational corporations (MNCs). The Economic Development Board (EDB), Singapore's investment promotion agency, focuses on securing major investments in high value-added manufacturing and service activities as part of a strategy to replace labor-intensive, low value-added activities that have migrated offshore.

As part of the government's strategy to develop Singapore into a premier financial center, the GOS offers tax incentives for financial institutions looking to set up operations. Further information, details and guidelines are available at**http://www.mas.gov.sg/Singapore-Financial-Centre/Value-Propositions/Setting-Up.aspx**.

Table 1

Measure	Year	Index or Rank	Website Address
TI Corruption Perceptions index	2014	7 of 175	transparency.org/cpi2014/results
World Bank's Doing Business Report "Ease of Doing Business"	2015	1 of 189	doingbusiness.org/rankings
Global Innovation Index	2014	7 of 143	globalinnovationindex.org/content.aspx?page=data-analysis
World Bank GNI per capita	2013	USD 76,860	data.worldbank.org/indicator/NY.GNP.PCAP.CD

2. CONVERSION AND TRANSFER POLICIES

Foreign Exchange

The FTA commits Singapore to the free transfer of capital, unimpeded by regulatory restrictions. Singapore places no restrictions on reinvestment or repatriation of earnings and capital, and maintains no significant restrictions on remittances, foreign exchange transactions and capital movements. (reference Efficient Capital Markets for a discussion of certain restrictions on the borrowing of Singapore Dollars (SGD) for use offshore.)

Remittance Policies

The FTA commits Singapore to the free transfer of capital, unimpeded by regulatory restrictions. Singapore places no restrictions on reinvestment or repatriation of earnings and capital, and maintains no significant restrictions on remittances, foreign exchange transactions and capital movements.

3. EXPROPRIATION AND COMPENSATION

The FTA contains strong investor protection provisions relating to expropriation of private property and the need to follow due process; provisions are in place for an owner to receive compensation based on fair market value.

Singapore has not expropriated foreign owned property and has no laws that force foreign investors to transfer ownership to local interests. No significant disputes are pending.

Singapore has signed investment promotion and protection agreements with a wide range of countries. These agreements mutually protect nationals or companies of either country against war and non-commercial risks of expropriation and nationalization for an initial period of 15 years and continue thereafter unless otherwise terminated.

4. DISPUTE SETTLEMENT

Legal System, Specialized Courts, Judicial Independence, Judgments of Foreign Courts

Singapore's legal system has its roots in English common law and practice. All core obligations of the FTA are subject to the dispute settlement provisions of the Agreement. The dispute settlement procedures promote compliance through consultation and trade-enhancing remedies, rather than relying solely on trade sanctions. The procedures also set higher standards of openness and transparency.

Singapore enacted and subsequently amended their 2001 Arbitration Act on domestic arbitration by basing their rules on the United Nations Commission on International Trade Law (UNCITRAL Model Law). In 1986, Singapore ratified the convention on the Recognition and Enforcement of Foreign Arbitration Awards (1958 New York Convention) and is a member state to the International Centre for Settlement of Investment Disputes (ICSID convention). The Singapore International Arbitration Center (SIAC) and the Singapore Mediation Center (SMC) actively promote alternative dispute mechanisms (ADR) for settling commercial disputes.

Bankruptcy

Singapore has strict bankruptcy laws, with both debtors and creditors able to file a bankruptcy claim. Singapore is ranked number 19 for resolving insolvency in the World Bank's Doing Business index.

Investment Disputes

Singapore amended their Arbitration Act of 2001 by adapting the rules of the United Nations Commission on International Trade Law (UNCITRAL) Model Law to their arbitration procedure. In 1986, Singapore ratified the convention on the Recognition and Enforcement of Foreign Arbitration Awards (1958 New York Convention) and in 1968 became a member state to the International Centre for Settlement of Investment Disputes (ICSID convention). The Singapore International Arbitration Center (SIAC) and the Singapore Mediation Center (SMC) actively promote mediation and reconciliation for settling commercial disputes. There are no outstanding investment disputes or expropriation claims involving U.S. citizens.

International Arbitration

Singapore is home to a number of alternative dispute resolution (ADR) institutions for the both investment and commercial disputes. Among them is the Singapore International Arbitration Centre (SIAC), the Singapore International Commercial Court (SICC), the Singapore International Mediation Institute (SIMI) and the Singapore International Mediation Centre (SIMC) established in November 2014, the Singapore Mediation Centre (SMC), the Primary Dispute Resolution Centre, and Maxwell Chambers, Asia's first integrated dispute resolution complex. Singapore's extensive arbitration centers have contributed to its development as a regional hub for alternative disputes mechanisms. Arbitral awards in Singapore, for either domestic or international arbitration, are legally binding and enforceable in local courts.

ICSID Convention and New York Convention

Singapore is a member of the International Centre for Settlement of Investment Disputes (ICSID convention). Singapore ratified the convention on the Recognition and Enforcement of Foreign Arbitral Awards (1958 New York Convention). These agreements have been fundamental in the development of Singapore's arbitration law.

Duration of Dispute Resolution

Mediation cases can be handled within a short period of time. Arbitration cases involve a lengthier process and therefore vary considerably in the time they take to obtain an award. Within Singapore, arbitral awards, for cases involving domestic or international arbitration, are legally binding and enforceable in domestic courts.

5. PERFORMANCE REQUIREMENTS AND INVESTMENT INCENTIVES

WTO/TRIMS

Singapore is a World Trade Organization member since 1995. Singapore complies with WTO Trade-Related Investment Measures (TRIMS) obligations. The FTA prohibits and removes certain performance-related restrictions on U.S. investors such as limitations on the number of customer service locations for the retail banking sector.

There are no discriminatory or preferential export or import policies affecting foreign investors. The government does not require investors to purchase from local sources or specify a percentage of output for export. The government also does not require local equity ownership in the investment. There are no rules forcing the transfer of technology. Foreign investors face no requirement to reduce equity over time and are free to obtain their necessary financing from any source. Employment of host country nationals is not required.

Investment Incentives

Singapore offers numerous incentives to encourage foreign investors to startup businesses; particularly in targeted growth sectors.

Research and Development

Singapore's Economic Development Board sponsors a Research Incentive Scheme for Companies (RISC) to award government grants to develop research and development capabilities in strategic areas of technology. The scheme targets businesses registered in Singapore, and encourage companies to set up R&D centers in Singapore.

Performance Requirements

There are no discriminatory or preferential export or import policies affecting foreign investors. The government does not require investors to purchase from local sources or specify a percentage of output for export. The government also does not require local equity ownership in the investment. There are no rules forcing the transfer of technology. Foreign investors face no requirement to reduce equity over time and are free to obtain their necessary financing from any source. Employment of host country nationals is not required.

Data Storage

Singapore has no forced localization policy requiring domestic content in goods or technology. Personal data is protected under the Personal Data Protection Act of 2012, covering electronic and non-electronic data.

6. RIGHT TO PRIVATE OWNERSHIP AND ESTABLISHMENT

Foreign and local entities may readily establish, operate, and dispose of their own enterprises in Singapore. Except for representative offices (where foreign firms maintain a local representative but do not conduct commercial transactions in Singapore), there are no restrictions on carrying out remunerative activities.

All businesses in Singapore must be registered with the Accounting and Corporate Regulatory Authority. Foreign investors can operate their businesses in one of the following forms: sole proprietorship, limited partnership, incorporated company, foreign company branch or representative office.

Private businesses, both local and foreign, compete on a generally equal basis with GLCs, although some observers have complained that GLCs benefit from cheaper financing due to an implicit government guarantee. Singapore officials reject such assertions, arguing that the government does not interfere with the operations of GLCs or grant them special privileges, preferential treatment or hidden subsidies, adding that GLCs are subject to the same regulatory regime and discipline of the market as private sector companies. Many observers, however, have been critical of cases where GLCs have entered into new lines of business or where government agencies have "corporatized" certain government functions, in both circumstances entering into competition with already-existing private businesses.

The FTA contains specific conduct guarantees to ensure that GLCs will operate on a commercial and non-discriminatory basis towards U.S. firms. GLCs with substantial revenues or assets are also subject to enhanced transparency requirements under the FTA. In accordance with its FTA commitments, Singapore enacted the Competition Act in 2004 and established the Competition Commission of Singapore in January 2005. The Act contains provisions on anti-competitive agreements, decisions, and practices; abuse of dominance; enforcement and appeals process; and mergers and acquisitions.

Singapore has an extensive network of GLCs that are active in many sectors of the economy. Some sectors, notably telecommunications and financial services, are subject to sector-specific regulatory bodies and competition regulations typically less rigorous than those being implemented under the Competition Act.

7. PROTECTION OF PROPERTY RIGHTS

Real Property

Real property interests are enforced in Singapore. Residents have access to mortgages and liens, with reliable recording of properties. In the 2015 World Bank's, Doing Business Report, Singapore ranks number 1 in enforcing contracts, and number 24 in registering property.

Foreigners are not allowed to purchase public housing (HDB) in Singapore. Under the Residential Property Act, foreigners are allowed to purchase private sector housing (condominiums or any unit within a building) without the need to obtain prior approval from the Singapore Land Authority. However, foreigners are not allowed to acquire all the apartments within a building or all the units in an approved condominium apartment without prior approval. For landed homes (houses) and vacant residential land, prior approval is required. There are no restrictions on foreign ownership of industrial and commercial real estate. In December 2011, the GOS enacted an additional effective 10 percent tax, or Additional Buyer's Stamp Duty (ABSD), on foreigners who purchase homes in Singapore. In January 2013, the GOS further raised the ABSD to 15 percent, however, U.S. citizens are accorded national treatment under the FTA, meaning only second and subsequent purchases of residential property will be subject to 7 and 18 percent ABSD accordingly, the same as Singaporean citizens.

Intellectual Property Rights

In line with its FTA commitments and obligations under international treaties and conventions, Singapore has developed one of the stronger intellectual property rights (IPR) regimes in Asia, although concerns remain in certain areas such as business software piracy, online piracy and enforcement. Singapore has taken steps to bring its IPR laws in line with international standards, including amending its Trademarks Act, Patents Act, the Layout Designs of Integrated Circuits Act, Registered Designs Act, and new Plant Varieties Protection Act. In accordance with its FTA obligations, Singapore has implemented Article 1 through Article 6 of the Joint Recommendation concerning Provisions on the Protection of Well-Known Marks of 1999. It has signed and ratified the International Convention for the Protection of New Varieties of Plants (1991) and the Convention Relating to the Distribution of Program-Carrying Signals Transmitted by Satellite (1974). Singapore is not listed in USTR's Special 301 report.

Singapore is a member of the WTO and a party to the Agreement on Trade-Related Aspects of Intellectual Property Rights (TRIPS). It is a signatory to other international copyright agreements, including the Paris Convention, the Berne Convention, the Patent Cooperation Treaty, the Madrid Protocol, and the Budapest Treaty. The World Intellectual Property Organization (WIPO) Secretariat opened offices in Singapore in 2005 (**http://www.wipo.int/about-wipo/en/offices/singapore/**). Amendments to the Trademark Act, which took effect in January 2007, fulfill Singapore's obligations in WIPO's revised Treaty on the Law of Trademarks.

Facing reports stating Singapore has the highest incidence of per-capita infringement in Asia, Parliament amended the Copyright Act in July 2014 to allow rights owners, or the exclusive licensees of copyrighted material, to directly apply to the high court for an injunction to block leading infringing websites. The changes to the law target websites, which clearly and blatantly infringe copyright, rather than search engines or websites based primarily on user-generated content, is designed to allow rights holders to more effectively protect online content. Music and film industry representatives remain concerned that Internet piracy will persist given the lack of effective enforcement against online peer-to-peer infringement and Singapore's expanding high-speed broadband network. The FTA ensures that government agencies will not grant approval to patent-violating products, but Singapore does allow parallel imports. Under the amended Patents Act, the patent owner has the right to bring an action to stop an importer of "grey market goods" from importing the patent owner's patented product if the product has not previously been sold or distributed in Singapore.

The FTA ensures protection of test data and trade secrets submitted to the government for product approval purposes. Disclosure of such information is prohibited for a period of five years for pharmaceuticals and ten years for agricultural chemicals. Singapore has no specific legislation concerning trade secrets. Instead, it protects investors' commercially valuable proprietary information under common law by the Law of Confidence. U.S. industry has expressed concern that this provision is inadequate.

For additional information about treaty obligations and points of contact at local IP offices, please see WIPO's country profiles at **http://www.wipo.int/directory/en/**.

Resources for Rights Holders

Mark Saavedra, Economic Officer
SaavedraMA@state.gov
American Chamber of Commerce in Singapore
1 Scotts Road, Shaw Centre #23-03/04/05
Singapore 228208
+65 6597 5730

8. TRANSPARENCY OF THE REGULATORY SYSTEM

The U.S.-Singapore FTA enhances transparency by requiring regulatory authorities, to the extent possible, to consult with interested parties before issuing regulations, to provide advance notice, and comment periods for proposed rules, and to publish all regulations.

The government has established a centralized Internet portal -- www.reach.gov.sg -- to solicit feedback on selected draft legislation and regulations, a process that is being used with increasing frequency. As noted in the "Openness to Foreign Investment" section, some U.S. companies, in particular, in the telecommunications and media sectors, are concerned about the government's lack of transparency in its regulatory and rule-making process.

Singapore strives to promote an efficient, business-friendly regulatory environment. Tax, labor, banking and finance, industrial health and safety, arbitration, wage and training rules and regulations are formulated and reviewed with the interests of both foreign investors and local enterprises in mind. Starting in 2005, a Rules Review Panel, comprising senior civil servants, began overseeing a review of all rules and regulations; this process will be repeated every five years. A Pro-Enterprise Panel of high-level public sector and private sector representatives examines feedback from businesses on regulatory issues and provides recommendations to the government.

Local laws give regulatory bodies' wide discretion to modify regulations and impose new conditions, but in practice agencies use this positively to adapt incentives or other services on a case-by-case basis to meet the needs of foreign as well as domestic companies.

Procedures for obtaining licenses and permits are generally transparent and not burdensome, but some exceptions apply. Procedures can be faster for investors in areas considered national priorities. Singapore has established an online licensing portal to provide a one-stop application point for multiple licenses -- **https://licences.business.gov.sg**.

Singapore has a private sector-led Council on Corporate Disclosure and Governance to implement the country's Code of Corporate Governance. Compliance with the Code is not mandatory but listed companies are required under the Singapore Exchange Listing Rules to disclose their corporate governance practices and give explanations for deviations from the Code in their annual reports.

Singapore's prescribed accounting standards (Financial Reporting Standards or FRS) are aligned with those of the International Accounting Standards Board. Companies can deviate from these standards when required to present a true and fair set of financial statements. Singapore-incorporated, publicly-listed companies can use certain alternative standards such as International Accounting Standards (IAS) or the U.S. Generally Accepted Accounting Principles (U.S. GAAP) if they are listed on foreign stock exchanges that require these standards. They do not need to reconcile their accounts with FRS. All other Singapore-incorporated companies must use FRS unless the Accounting and Corporate Regulatory Authority exempts them.

9. EFFICIENT CAPITAL MARKETS AND PORTFOLIO INVESTMENT

The Government of Singapore actively facilitates the free flow of financial resources. Credit is allocated on market terms and foreign investors can access credit, U.S. dollars, Singapore dollars (SGD), and other foreign currencies on the local market. The Monetary Authority of Singapore (MAS) formulates and implements the country's monetary and exchange rate policy, and supervises and regulates the country's sophisticated financial and capital markets.

Total assets under management in Singapore stood at USD 1.45 trillion at the end of 2013, a 11.8 percent year-on-year increment in view of strong inflows and higher market valuations. About 77 percent of the funds managed in Singapore are foreign sourced, with some 67 percent of these funds invested in the Asia-Pacific region. Singapore-based companies issued approximately USD 24.6 billion in bonds in 2014, up from USD 19.7 billion in 2013.

Money and Banking System, Hostile Takeovers

Singapore's banking system is sound and well-regulated. Total domestic banking assets were about USD 836.86 billion as of December 2014. Local Singapore banks are relatively small by regional standards, but are reasonably profitable and have stronger capital levels and credit ratings than many of their peers in the region. As of fourth quarter 2014, the non-performing loans (NPLs) ratio of the three local banks averaged 0.9 percent. Banks are statutorily prohibited from engaging in non-financial business. Banks can hold 10 percent or less in non-financial companies as an "equity portfolio investment."

The Securities and Futures Act (SFA) of 2002 moved Singapore's capital markets to a disclosure-based regime. The SFA allows for imposition of civil or criminal penalties against corporations listed on the Singapore Exchange (SGX) that fail to disclose material information on a continuous basis. Listed companies are required to prepare quarterly financial reporting. The SFA requires persons acquiring shareholdings of five percent or more of the voting shares of a listed company to disclose such acquisitions as well as any subsequent changes in their holdings directly to the SGX within two business days. The SFA also contains enhanced market misconduct provisions. The Act was further strengthened in 2009 to provide for stronger market misconduct enforcement with the courts empowered to order disgorgement of gains from illegal trades, and allowing the transfer of evidence between the Commercial Affairs Department of the police force and MAS.

U.S. financial regulations do not restrict foreign banks' ability to hold accounts for U.S. citizens. Anecdotal evidence suggests, however, that U.S. citizens may be constrained in their ability to open bank accounts at some institutions, as some Americans have been turned away by banks reportedly as a result of the additional reporting requirements associated with the U.S. Foreign Account Tax Compliance Act (FATCA) and other U.S. financial regulations. The U.S. Embassy routinely encounters U.S. citizens with complaints about not being allowed to open accounts. There have also been cases of U.S. citizens with existing accounts who have been asked by their banks to close them. U.S. Citizens are encouraged to alert the nearest U.S. Embassy of any practices they encounter with regard to the provision of financial services.

10. COMPETITION FROM STATE-OWNED ENTERPRISES

Singapore has an extensive network of government-linked corporations (GLC) that are fully or partially owned by Temasek, a holding company with the Singapore Ministry of Finance as its sole shareholder. As previously noted, Singapore GLCs are active in many sectors of the economy, especially strategically important sectors including telecommunications, media, public transportation, defense, port, and airport operations. In addition, the GLCs are also present in many other sectors of the economy, including banking, shipping, airline, consumer/lifestyle, infrastructure, and real estate.

GLCs operate on a commercial basis and have no specific advantage in competing with private enterprises based on their government ownership. However, some private sector companies have said they encountered unfair business practices and opaque bidding processes that appeared to favor incumbent, government-linked firms.

GLCs' corporate governance is guided by policies developed by Temasek. MTI asserts, however, that Temasek does not direct the business decisions or operations of its portfolio companies. There are differences in corporate governance disclosures and practices across them, and GLC boards are allowed to determine their own governance practices. GLC board seats are not specifically allocated to government officials, although retired officials are often represented on boards and fill senior management positions.

OECD Guidelines on Corporate Governance of SOEs

As of the end of February 2015, the top four Singapore-listed GLCs accounted for about 14.4 percent of total capitalization of the Singapore Exchange (SGX). Some observers have criticized the dominant role of GLCs in the domestic economy, arguing that it has displaced or suppressed private sector entrepreneurship and investment. GLCs funding decisions are often driven by goals emanating from the central government.

Sovereign Wealth Funds

There are two sovereign wealth funds (SWF) in Singapore, the Government of Singapore Investment Corporation (GIC) and the previously- mentioned Temasek Holdings. The government established the two SWFs to manage the Government of Singapore's substantial investments, fiscal, and foreign reserves, with the stated objective to achieve long-term returns and preserve the international purchasing power of the reserves.

GIC, Singapore's largest SWF, does not publish the size of its funds, but some industry observers estimate its assets exceed USD 300 billion. GIC does not invest domestically, but manages Singapore's international investments, which are generally passive (non-controlling) investments in publicly-traded entities. Its investment is entirely overseas, with the United States as its top destination, accounting for 34 percent of GIC's portfolio as of March 2014. Although not required by law, since 2008 GIC has published an annual report describing its management and governance, and how it invests Singapore's foreign reserves.

Temasek began as a holding company for Singapore's state-owned enterprises, but has since branched to other asset classes and generally focuses on holding significant (often controlling) stakes in companies. As of March 2014, Temasek's exposure to Singapore (based on underlying assets) was 31 percent, with the rest of Asia accounting for 41 percent of its portfolio. Temasek's stated goal is to hold and manage the government's investments in companies for the long-term benefit of Singapore, to create jobs, and contribute to Singapore's economic survival, progress and prosperity. Temasek formerly focused on managing industries to promote economic development, but has shifted emphasis to commercial objectives and principles. Temasek exercises its shareholder rights to influence the strategic directions of its companies but does not get involved in the day-to-day business and commercial decisions of its firms and subsidiaries. Temasek has published an annual report since 2004, but only provides consolidated financial statements, which aggregate all of Temasek's subsidiaries into a single financial report.

Other leading GLC investing entities include the Economic Development Board (EDB), which has its own private equity and venture capital arm in the form of EDB Investments Pte Ltd, Singapore's Housing Development Board, which has the power to incorporate private companies as part of its charter, and other GoS agencies, with funding decisions driven by goals emanating from the central government.

11. CORPORATE SOCIAL RESPONSIBILITY

The awareness and implementation of CSR in Singapore has been increasing since the government's formation of the Singapore Compact, a national society promoting CSR in Singapore. In May 2004, the National Tripartite Committee on CSR was established to study the issues holistically and address any gaps at the national level. The initiative provides strategic direction and overall coordination for various CSR programs, which include helping small and medium-sized enterprises (SMEs) adopt good CSR practices. In January 2005, the Singapore Compact for Corporate Social Responsibility was set up to provide a forum for collaboration, support, and information sharing on good CSR practices.

The Singapore Stock Exchange implemented a requirement in June 2011 that listed companies report on their sustainable business practices.

OECD Guidelines for Multinational Enterprises

The Government of Singapore encourages foreign and local enterprises to follow generally accepted CSR principles.

12. POLITICAL VIOLENCE

Singapore's political environment is stable and there is no history of incidents involving politically motivated damage to foreign investments in Singapore. The ruling People's Action Party (PAP) has dominated Singapore's parliamentary government since 1959, and currently controls 80 of the 87 regularly contested parliamentary seats. Singapore opposition parties, which currently hold seven regularly contested parliamentary seats and three additional seats reserved to the opposition by the constitution, do not usually espouse views that are radically different from the mainstream of Singapore political opinion.

13. CORRUPTION

Singapore typically ranks as the least corrupt country in Asia and one of the least corrupt in the world. Singapore was seventh (i.e., with one being least corrupt) on watchdog group Transparency International (TI)'s global index in 2014.

Singapore actively enforces its strong anti-corruption laws. The Prevention of Corruption Act, and the Drug Trafficking and Other Serious Crimes (Confiscation of Benefits) Act provide the legal basis for government action by the Corrupt Practices Investigation Bureau, an anti-corruption agency that reports to the Prime Minister. These laws cover acts of corruption both within Singapore as well as those committed by Singaporeans abroad. When cases of corruption are uncovered, whether in the public or private sector, the government deals with them firmly, swiftly and publicly, as they do in cases where public officials are involved in dishonest and illegal behavior.

UN Anticorruption Convention, OECD Convention on Combatting Bribery

Singapore is not a party to the OECD Convention on Combating Bribery, but the Prevention of Corruption Act makes it a crime for a Singapore citizen to bribe a foreign official or any other person, whether within or outside Singapore.

Resources to Report Corruption

Corrupt Practices Investigation Bureau
2 Lengkok Bahru, Singapore 159047
+65 6270 0141

14. BILATERAL INVESTMENT AGREEMENTS

Singapore has 41 bilateral investment treaties (BIT) currently in force, including a BIT and a Fre Trade Agreement (FTA) with the United States. These agreements mutually protect nationals or companies of either economy against war and non-commercial risks of expropriation and nationalization.

Singapore has signed free trade/economic cooperation agreements that include investment chapters with Australia, China, the European Free Trade Association (Switzerland, Norway, Lichtenstein, and Iceland), , India, Japan, New Zealand, Panama, Peru, South Korea, Costa Rica, the United States, and the separate customs territory of Taiwan, Penghu, Kinmen, and Matsu. Singapore has completed negotiations with the European Union and is negotiating FTAs with Canada, Mexico, Pakistan, Turkey, and Ukraine. Singapore also has agreements with Jordan and the Gulf Cooperation Council (comprising Bahrain, Kuwait, Oman, Qatar, Saudi Arabia and the United Arab Emirates), but these agreements do not contain investment chapters. Singapore is a member of the Association of Southeast Asian Nations (ASEAN), which has concluded FTAs with Australia and New Zealand, China, India, and South Korea, and a Comprehensive Economic Partnership Agreement with Japan. Singapore is also a party in the Transpacific Strategic Economic Partnership Agreement together with Chile, New Zealand, and Brunei. These four nations formed the basis for the Trans-Pacific Partnership, a multi-lateral free trade agreement currently in negotiations that now includes Singapore, the U.S. and ten other countries (Australia, Brunei Darussalam, Canada, Chile, Malaysia, Mexico, New Zealand, Peru, Japan and Viet Nam). Singapore is also leading the goods chapter's negotiations for the Regional Comprehensive Economic Partnership (RCEP) FTA which was launched in November 2012 and includes ASEAN members plus Australia, China, India, Japan, New Zealand, and South Korea. Singapore has signed Comprehensive Avoidance of Double Taxation Agreements with a number of economies, but not with the United States.

Bilateral Taxation Treaties

U.S. financial regulations do not restrict foreign banks' ability to hold accounts for U.S. citizens. Anecdotal evidence suggests, however, that U.S. citizens may be constrained in their ability to open bank accounts at some institutions, as some Americans have been turned away by banks reportedly as a result of the additional reporting requirements associated with the U.S. Foreign Account Tax Compliance Act (FATCA) and other U.S. financial regulations. The U.S. Embassy routinely encounters U.S. citizens with complaints about not being allowed to open accounts. There have also been cases of U.S. citizens with existing accounts who have been asked by their banks to close them. U.S. Citizens are encouraged to alert the nearest U.S. Embassy of any practices they encounter with regard to the provision of financial services.

15. OPIC AND OTHER INVESTMENT INSURANCE PROGRAMS

Under the 1966 Investment Guarantee Agreement with Singapore, the Overseas Private Investment Corporation (OPIC) offers insurance to U.S. investors in Singapore against currency inconvertibility, expropriation, and losses arising from war. Singapore became a member of the Multilateral Investment Guarantee Agency (MIGA) in 1998.

16. LABOR

As of December-2014, Singapore's labor market totaled 3.62 million workers; this includes about 1.36 million foreigners, of which about 85 percent are unskilled or semi-skilled workers. Local labor laws allow for relatively free hiring and firing practices. Either party can terminate employment by giving the other party the required notice. The Ministry of Manpower (MOM) must approve employment of foreigners. Since 2011 the Government has introduced policy measures to support productivity increases coupled with reduced dependence on foreign labor. The MOM has started tightening foreign labor approvals, resulting in many businesses in Singapore voicing discontent at not being able to access sufficient labor.

In order to tackle the growing concerns that many foreigners are displacing locals in the job market, as well as concerns that many foreign managers are hiring their own fellow countryman instead of recruiting based on merit, Singapore's Ministry on Manpower (MOM) announced a ruling in September 2013, requiring employers to consider Singaporeans fairly, before hiring skilled professional foreigners. The new rules, known as the Fair Consideration Framework (FCF) were implemented from August 2014 and affect employers who apply for Employment Passes (EP), the work pass for foreign professionals working in professional, manager and executive (PME) posts. Under the new rules, firms making new EP applications must first advertise the job vacancy in a new jobs bank administered by the Singapore Workforce and Development Agency (WDA) for at least 14 days. The jobs bank will be free for use by companies and job seekers and the job advertisement must be open to all Singaporeans. Employers are encouraged to keep records of their interview process as proof that they have done due diligence in trying to look for a Singaporean worker. If an EP is still needed, the employer will have to make a statutory declaration that a job advertisement with the national jobs bank had been made. Some exceptions have been made for smaller firms with 25 or fewer employees and jobs which pay a fixed monthly salary of USD 9,600 (SGD 12,000) or more will not be subjected to the advertising requirement. Consistent with Singapore's WTO obligations, intra-corporate transfers (ICT) are allowed for managers, executives, and specialists who had worked for at least one-year in the firm before being posted to Singapore. ICT would still be required to meet all EP criteria, but the requirement for an advertisement in the jobs data bank would be waived.

Singapore imposes a ceiling on the ratio of unskilled/semi-skilled foreign workers to local workers that a company can employ, and charges a monthly levy for each unskilled or semi-skilled foreign worker. The government also provides incentives and assistance to firms to automate and invest in labor-saving technology.

Labor-management relations in Singapore are generally amicable. About 23 percent of the workforce is unionized. The majority of unions are affiliated with the National Trades Union Congress (NTUC), which maintains a symbiotic relationship with the PAP ruling party. Although workers, other than those employed in the three essential services of water, gas and electricity, have the legal right to strike, no workers did so between 1986-2011. In November 2012, some 171 SMRT bus drivers from China held an illegal strike. The drivers complained about poor living conditions and lower wages compared to Malaysian drivers. The incident resulted in a total of 4 Chinese drivers being charged in a Singapore court and pleading guilty for instigating the strike and causing public inconvenience, resulting in jail terms between six and seven weeks. Another 29 Chinese SMRT bus drivers had their work permits revoked and were deported. Singapore has no minimum wage law; the government follows a policy of allowing free market forces to determine wage levels. Singapore has a system in which the National Wage Council (NWC) recommends non-binding wage adjustments on an annual basis. The NWC is a tripartite body comprising a Chairman and representatives from the Government, employers and unions. The NWC recommendations apply to all employees in both domestic and foreign firms, and across the private and public sectors. While the NWC wage guidelines are not mandatory, they are widely implemented. The level of implementation is generally higher among unionized companies compared to non-unionized companies

17. FOREIGN TRADE ZONES/FREE PORTS/TRADE FACILITATION

Singapore has nine free-trade zones (FTZs), seven for seaborne cargo and two for airfreight. The FTZs may be used for storage and repackaging of import and export cargo, and goods transiting Singapore for subsequent re-export. Manufacturing is not carried out within the zones. Foreign and local firms have equal access to the FTZ facilities.

18. FOREIGN DIRECT INVESTMENT AND FOREIGN PORTFOLIO INVESTMENT STATISTICS

Table 2: Key Macroeconomic Data, U.S. FDI in Host Country/Economy

	Host Country Statistical source*		USG or international statistical source		USG or International Source of Data: BEA; IMF; Eurostat; UNCTAD, Other
Economic Data	Year	Amount	Year	Amount	
Host Country Gross Domestic Product (GDP) ($M USD)		286,900	2013	297,900	www.worldbank.org/en/country
Foreign Direct Investment	Host Country Statistical source*		USG or international statistical source		USG or international Source of data: BEA; IMF; Eurostat; UNCTAD, Other
U.S. FDI in partner country ($M USD, stock positions)	2013	90,865	2013	154,438	http://bea.gov/international/factsheet/ factsheet.cfm?Area=625
Host country's	2013	7,985	2013	19,760	http://bea.gov/international/factsheet/

FDI in the United States ($M USD, stock positions)					factsheet.cfm?Area=625
Total inbound stock of FDI as % host GDP	2013	0.08	2013	0.22	

* Source: Singapore Department of Statistics, "Foreign Direct Investment in Singapore, 2013"

Table 3: Sources and Destination of FDI

Direct Investment from/in Counterpart Economy Data					
From Top Five Sources/To Top Five Destinations (US Dollars, Millions)					
Inward Direct Investment			Outward Direct Investment		
Total Inward	750,078	100%	Total Outward	N/A	100%
U.S.	97,417	13%			
Netherlands	69,052	9%			
Virgin Islands, British	57,611	8%			
Japan	55,433	7%			
Cayman Islands	44,619	6%			
"0" reflects amounts rounded to +/- USD 500,000.					

Source: IMF Coordinated Direct Investment Survey

Table 4: Sources of Portfolio Investment

Portfolio Investment Assets								
Top Five Partners (Millions, US Dollars)								
Total			Equity Securities			Total Debt Securities		
All Countries	452,432	100%	All Countries	435,125	100%	All Countries	434,708	100%
U.S.	119,850	26%	U.S.	122,548	28%	U.S.	115,504	27%
China	55,266	12%	China	52,568	12%	India	26,992	%
Korea	22,958	5%	Japan	24,812	6%	Korea	25,932	6%
Japan	21,500	5%	Korea	22,567	5%	Malaysia	25,677	6%
India	21,453	5%	UK	19,762	5%	UK	20,252	5%

Source: Coordinated Portfolio Investment Survey

IMPORTANT BUSINESS AND LEGAL CONTACTS

CONTACT FOR MORE INFORMATION

George Ward
Econ Chief
U.S. Embassy Singapore
+65-6476-9344
WardGL@state.gov

AMERICAN OFFSHORE FIRMS:

Morrison & Foerster LLP (Singapore)50 Collyer Quay
#12-01 QUE Bayfront
Singapore 049321
Tel: (65) 6922-2000
Fax: (65) 6922-2008
Email: eng@mofo.com
URL: http://www.mofo.com/
Managing Partner: Mr. Eric J. Piesner

Services provided: banking, finance, venture capital financing, foreign investment, mergers & acquisitions, corporations, joint venture

White & Case
8 Marina View
#27-01 Asia Square Tower 1
Singapore 0118960
Tel: (65) 6225-6000
Fax: (65) 6225-6009
Email: rvogl@whitecase.com
URL: http://www.whitecase.com/

Services provided: civil damages, banking, finance investment, mergers and acquisitions, joint ventures, capital markets, corporate law advice

Local Law Firms:

Abraham Low LLC
24 Raffles Place
#07-02 Clifford Centre
Singapore 048621
Tel: (65) 6535-6688
Fax: (65) 6534-3606
Contact: Mr. Aloysius LENG
Email: aloysius_leng@abrahamlow.com.sg; inquiries@abrahamlow.com.sg
URL: http://www.abrahamlow.com.sg/

Services provided: general civil litigation, trusts and estate planning, family and matrimonial law, conveyance and property law, employment law and intellectual property

Asia Law Corporation
Advocates & Solicitors
490 Lorong 6, Toa Payoh
03-17 HDB Hub (Lift Lobby: Biz3, Lobby 2)
Singapore 310490
Tel: (65) 6222 2966
Fax: (65) 6222 2977
Partner: Mr. Harry Sim
email: harry@asialawcorp.com
Tel: (65) 6350-2111
Website: www.asialawcorp.com; www.notarypublic.com.sg

Services provided: litigation, disputes & court matters, criminal law cases, divorce, custody, adoption, wills & deceased estate law (probate), notary witnessing & certifying of documents

Chia Wong LLP (Singapore)
6 Temasek Boulevard #38-02
Suntec Tower 4
Singapore 038986Tel: (65) 6342-0002
Fax: (65) 6348-0002
Email: info@chiawongllp.com
URL: http://www.chiawongllp.com/
Partners: Chia Boon Teck, Wong Kai Yun

Services provided: family law, adoptions, child custody, parental child abduction, child protection, marriage, divorce, civil law, criminal law, damages, taxes, foreign claims, immigration, government relations, commercial/business law, banking, financial, foreign investments, insurance, marketing agreements, commissioner for oaths, notary public

David Chong & Co.
6 Temasek Boulevard
#09-04 Suntec Tower Four
Singapore 038986
Tel:(65) 6224-0955

Fax: (65) 6538-6585
Email: info@davidchong.com.sg
Sole Proprietor: Chong Kok Kong David

Services provided: trust & estates, corporate company, law, adoptions, child custody, divorce, immigration

Dhillon & Partners
#171 Chin Swee Rd.,
#08-05/06, San Centre
Singapore 169877
Tele: (65) 6323-2320
Fax: (65) 6538-8815
Contact: Surinder Singh Dhillon
Email: dhillon@dhillonpartners.com.sg

Services provided: family law, adoptions, child custody, parental child abduction, child protection, marriage/divorce, civil law, criminal law, damages, narcotics, collections, contracts, estates, immigration, commercial/business law, insurance, marketing agreements, auto accidents, labor relations, corporations

Donaldson & Burkinshaw
24 Raffles Place
#15-00 Clifford Centre
Singapore 048621
Tel: (65) 6533-9422
Fax: (65) 6533-7806
enquiries@donburk.com.sg
URL: http://www.donburk.com.sg/

Services provided: adoptions, child custody, taxes insurance, estates, divorce, aeronautical, maritime, banking, investment, auto accidents, and civil damage

Drew & Napier
10 Collyer Quay
10th Floor Ocean Financial Center
Singapore 049315
Tel: (65) 6535-0733
Fax: (65) 6535-4906
Contact: Mr. Davinder Singh, Senior Counsel
Email: mail@drewnapier.com
URL: http://www.drewnapier.com/

Services provided: Full service firm providing all legal services.

Duane Morris & Selvam LLP
16 Collyer Quay, #17-00
Singapore 049318
Tel: (65) 6311-3654
Fax: (65) 6311-0058
Email: Gmbulmash@DuaneMorrisSelvam.com
Website: www.DuaneMorrisSelvam.com

Services provided: civil law, collections, contracts, transportation law, estates, taxes, foreign claims, immigration law, commercial/business law, banking/financial, foreign investments, insurance, marketing agreements, patents/trademarks/copyrights, aeronautical/maritime, labor relations, corporations

Farallon Law Corporation
10 Collyer Quay
Ocean Financial Centre #40-00
Singapore 049315
Contact: Nicolas Tang
Tel: (65) 6808-6147
Fax: 6808-6144

Email: info@fl.sg
Website: www.fl.sg

Services provided: insurance, banking/financial, commercial/ business law, foreign investments, marketing agreements, civil law, criminal law, damages, narcotics, collections, contracts, transportation law, corporations, government relations, labor relations, immigration, auto/accidents

Gloria James-Civetta & Co.
25 North Bridge Road #03-02
EFG Bank Building
Singapore 179104
Tel: 6337-0469
Fax: 6337-0463
Contact: Gloria James
HP: 9725-4455
Email: consult@gjclaw.com.sg
URL: http://www.gjclaw.com.sg/

Services provided: criminal law, family law, international/cross-border divorces, corporate law, civil & commercial law, employment law, coroner's court inquests, notary services, wills & estate law matters, dispute resolution services, general solicitors work & other litigation matters

Harry Elias Partnership
SGX Centre 2, #17-01
4 Shenton Way
Singapore 068807
Tel: 65 6535 0550
Fax: 65 6438 0550
Website: http://www.harryelias.com/
Email: info@harryelias.com.sg

Services provided: aviation, shipping, arbitration, mediation, criminal law, family and matrimonial, general civil litigation, insolvency and asset recovery, corporate and financial assets, insurance, private wealth management, intellectual property, sport law

K&L Gates LLP
10 Collyer Quay
#37-01 Ocean Financial Centre
Singapore 049315
Tel: (65) 6507-8100
Fax (65) 6507-8111
Contact: Nicholas M. Hanna
Email: nicholas.hanna@klgates.com
Website: http://klgates.com/

Services provided: K&L Gates is a global full-service law firm with 46 offices across 5 continents. The firm's Singapore office represents clients doing business in Singapore and across the region including Malaysia, Indonesia, Thailand, the Philippines, Vietnam, and Myanmar in matters relating to corporate transactions; mergers and acquisitions; banking and asset finance; energy infrastructure and resources; anti-corruption investigations and corporate compliance; litigation and international arbitration.

Kalco Law LLC
101A Upper Cross St
People's Park Centre #12-17
Singapore 058358
Tel: (65) 6533-4833
Fax: (65) 6532-7408
Contact: Ms. Nadia Moynihan
Email: nadia@kalco.com.sg
Webpage: www.kalco.com.sg

Services provided: family Law, adoptions, child custody, immigration, parental child abduction, child protection, commercial/business law, marriage/divorce, civil law, criminal law, insurance, damages, marketing agreements, narcotics, auto accidents, contracts, labor relations, estates, corporations, foreign claims (arbitration or SICC)

Khattar Wong (Singapore)
80 Raffles Place, #25-01 UOB Plaza 1
Singapore 048624
Subhas Anandan
Tel: (65) 6238-3310
Fax: (65) 6238-8240
URL: http://www.khattarwong.com/
Contact: Subhas Anandan

Services provided: criminal law, commissioner for oaths, notary public

Rodyk & Davidson LLP
80 Raffles Place
#33-00 UOB Plaza 1
Singapore 048624
Tel: (65) 6225-2626
Fax: (65) 6225-1838
Email: mail@rodyk.com
Contact: Woon Chooi Yeo
Managing Partner: Philip Jeyaretnam, SC
Email: philipjeyyaretnam@rodyk.com
URL: http://www.rodyk.com/

Services provided: adoptions, child custody, taxes estates, divorce, civil damages, claims, insurance, auto accidents, immigration, narcotics, theft, fraud, embezzlement, and banking

Salem Ibrahim
79 Robinson Road
#16-06 CPF Building
Singapore 068897
Tel: (65) 6226-1233
Fax: (65) 6226-0988
Contact: Iman Ibrahim
Director: Salem Ibrahim
Email: salem@salemlaw.org.sg
URL: http://www.salemlaw.org.sg/

Services provided: family law, adoptions, child custody, parental child abduction, child protection, marriage/divorce, civil law, criminal law, damages, taxes, foreign claims, immigration, commercial/business law, banking/financial, foreign investments, insurance, marketing agreements, collections, contracts, transportation law, estates, auto accidents, aeronautical, labor relations, corporations as in aircraft sales, purchase, finance, leasings, charter and advise on operational legal issues

Shook, Lin & Bok
1 Robinson Road
#18-00 AIA Tower
Singapore 048542
Tel: (65) 6535-1944
Fax: (65) 6535-8577
Email: slb@shooklin.com.sg
URL: http://www.shooklin.com/

Services provided: banking, trade, estates, intellectual property, finance, insurance and conveyance

Straits Law Advocates & Solicitors
Straits Law Practice LLC
36 Robinson Road,
18th Floor, City House
Singapore 068877

Tel: (65) 6538-1300
Fax: (65) 6538-1311
Email: ming@straitslaw.com.sg
URL: http://www.straitslaw.com.sg/

Services provided: family law, adoptions, child custody, parental child abduction, child protection, marriage/divorce, civil law, criminal law, damages, narcotics, collections, contracts, transportation law, estates, taxes, foreign claims, immigration, government relations, commercial/business law, banking/financial, foreign investments, insurance, marketing agreements, damages, auto accidents, patents/trademarks/copyrights, labor relations, corporations

Virtus Law
49 Amoy Street # 02-00
Singapore 069875
Tel: (65) 6737-1234
Fax: (65) 6339-4991
URL: www.arthurloke.com.sg
Email: arthurloke@arthurloke.com

Services provided: adoptions, family law, estates/banking/insurance, corporate criminal cases, conveyance, intellectual property (copyrights and trademarks)

THAILAND INVESTMENT AND BUSINESS CLIMATE - STRATEGIC INFORMATION AND CONTACTS FOR STARTING BUSINESS

Thailand, the second largest economy in ASEAN after Indonesia, is an upper middle-income country with pro-investment policies and a well-developed and growing infrastructure platform. In May 2014, Thailand's democratically elected government was overthrown in a bloodless military coup. Since then, the military has appointed an interim government, interim legislature, and other entities tasked with developing and implementing reforms. Despite the upheaval, Thailand continues to maintain an open, market-oriented economy and encourages foreign direct investment as a means of promoting economic development, employment, and technology transfer. In recent decades, Thailand has been a major destination for foreign direct investment, and hundreds of U.S. companies have invested in Thailand successfully. Thailand continues to welcome investment from all countries and seeks to avoid dependence on any one country as a source of investment. Economic recovery and growth will be important to maintaining investor confidence. Delays in infrastructure spending and increased concerns about Thailand's regional competitiveness continue to weigh on growth forecasts, but investors remain cautiously optimistic that the Thai economy will retain its well-known resiliency and resume more robust growth.

Reforms implemented after the 1997-98 Asian Financial Crisis were designed to foster a more competitive and transparent climate for foreign investors. The Foreign Business Act (FBA) of 1999 continues to govern most investment activity by non-Thai nationals. Many U.S. businesses also enjoy investment benefits through the U.S.-Thailand Treaty of Amity and Economic Relations (AER), originally signed in 1833. The Treaty allows U.S. citizens and businesses incorporated in the United States or in Thailand that are majority-owned by U.S. citizens to engage in business on the same basis as Thai companies (national treatment) and exempts them from most restrictions on foreign investment imposed by the Foreign Business Act, although some types of business remain excluded under the Treaty. Notwithstanding their Treaty rights, many U.S. investors also choose to form joint ventures with Thai partners who hold a majority stake in the company, leveraging their partner's knowledge of the Thai economy and local regulations.

The Board of Investment (BOI) is Thailand's central investment promotion authority and offers investment incentives uniformly to both qualified domestic and foreign investors through clearly articulated application procedures. Effective January 1, 2015, the Board of Investment (BOI) launched a new investment incentive policy that gives preferential benefits to investment projects based on the level of technology involved in the activities. Firms employing a high level of advanced technologies qualify for the maximum incentive package, including an eight-year exemption from corporate income taxes, while activities that do not employ advanced technology, but are nevertheless still important to the supply chain, no longer receive any exemption. All companies may be eligible for other privileges if they engage in activities otherwise considered valuable, such as R&D, advanced technology training, or acquiring licenses to commercialize technology. For detailed information, visit www.boi.go.th.

Consistent and predictable enforcement of government regulations remains problematic for investors in Thailand. Gratuity payments to civil servants responsible for regulatory oversight and enforcement remain a common and inefficient practice.

Firms that refuse to make such payments can be placed at a competitive disadvantage when compared to other firms in the same field.

The Thai government maintains a regulatory framework that broadly encourages investment and largely avoids market-distorting support for specific sectors. Government policies generally do not restrict the free flow of financial resources to support product and factor markets, and credit is generally allocated on market terms rather than by "directed lending." Legal, regulatory, and accounting systems are largely transparent, with the Thai government investing considerable effort to bring these systems in line with international norms and achieving significant progress.

1. OPENNESS TO, AND RESTRICTIONS UPON, FOREIGN INVESTMENT

Attitude toward Foreign Direct Investment

Despite the May 2014 coup and installation of an interim military-led government, Thailand continues to maintain an open market-oriented economy and encourages foreign direct investment as a means of promoting economic development, employment, and technology transfer. In recent decades, Thailand has been a major destination for foreign direct investment, and hundreds of U.S. companies have successfully invested in Thailand. Thailand continues to welcome investment from all countries and seeks to avoid dependence on any one country as a source of investment. Economic impacts to tourism and retail businesses resulting from months of political impasse leading up to the May 2014 coup eroded growth for the year, but public and private sector analysts forecast 2015 growth to be between 3-4%. Investors remain cautiously confident that the Thai economy will retain its well-known resiliency and resume growth; however, many companies are also carefully considering market factors, including the country's declining competitiveness, when making future investment decisions.

In the wake of the 1997-98 Asian Financial Crisis, Thailand embarked on an International Monetary Fund (IMF)-sponsored economic reform program designed to foster a more competitive and transparent climate for foreign investors. Legislation in 1999 established a new bankruptcy court, reformed bankruptcy and foreclosure procedures, and allowed creditors to pursue payment from loan guarantors. Other 1999 reforms include amendments to the Land Code, Condominium Act, and the Property Leasing Act, all of which liberalized restrictions on property ownership by non-Thais. The Foreign Business Act (FBA) of 1999 continues to govern most investment activity by non-Thai nationals. The FBA opened some additional business sectors to foreign investment; however, foreign investment in most service sectors is limited to 49 percent ownership. Other key laws governing foreign investment are the Alien Employment Act B.E. 2521 (1978) and the Investment Promotion Act B.E. 2520 (1977).

Foreign companies are free to open and maintain bank accounts in foreign currency. However, Thailand retains, to some extent, investment control, as under certain circumstances, foreign investors that were previously granted national treatment are subject to some reservations, particularly in the service sector.

Other Investment Policy Reviews

None within the last three years.

Laws/Regulations of Foreign Direct Investment

The Foreign Business Act (FBA) of 1999 continues to govern most investment activity by non-Thai nationals. The FBA opened some additional business sectors to foreign investment; however, foreign investment in most service sectors is limited to 49 percent ownership. Other key laws governing foreign investment are the Alien Employment Act B.E. 2521 (1978) and the Investment Promotion Act B.E. 2520 (1977).

U.S. Investment: Many U.S. businesses enjoy investment benefits through the U.S.-Thailand Treaty of Amity and Economic Relations (AER), originally signed in 1833. The 1966 iteration of the Treaty allows U.S. citizens and businesses incorporated in the United States, or in Thailand that are majority-owned by U.S. citizens, to engage in business on the same basis as Thai companies (national treatment), exempting them from most restrictions on foreign investment imposed by the Foreign Business Act.

Banking: The Financial Institutions Business Act, passed at the end of 2007, unified the legal framework and strengthened the Bank of Thailand's (the country's central bank) supervision and enforcement powers. The Act gave power to the Bank of Thailand to raise foreign ownership limits for local banks from 25 percent to 49 percent on a case-by-case basis. The Act also allows the Minister of Finance to authorize foreign ownership above 49 percent if recommended by the central bank.

Insurance: The 2008 Life Insurance Act and the 2008 Non-Life Insurance Act apply a 25 percent cap on foreign ownership of insurance companies and on foreign boards of directors. However, the Office of the Insurance Commission (OIC) may, at its discretion, permit foreign equity ownership up to 49 percent and foreign directorship up to 50 percent.

Business Registration: Any entity wishing to do business in Thailand must register with the Department of Business Development at the Ministry of Commerce, which generally takes three to six months to complete. Firms engaging in production activities need to register with the Ministries of Industry and Labor and Social Welfare. If the entity falls under the definition of non-Thai national, as defined by the Foreign Business Act, it must obtain a foreign business license, which must be approved by the Council of Ministers (Cabinet) or Director-General of Department of Business Development at the Ministry of Commerce, depending on the applicable category of restricted business.

Americans planning to invest in Thailand are advised to obtain qualified legal advice. Such advice is particularly important given that Thai business regulations are governed predominantly by criminal, not civil, law. While foreigners are rarely jailed for improper business activities, violation of Thai business regulations can carry heavy criminal penalties. Thailand has an independent judiciary and government authorities are generally not permitted to interfere in the court system once a case is in process.

For more information, visit: **http://export.gov/thailand/index.asp**

Industrial Promotion

The Thailand Board of Investment (BOI) introduced a new seven-year investment promotion policy beginning in 2015. The new BOI policy no longer supports activities that have low added value, are labor intensive, or involve low technology and/or uncomplicated production processes. The new BOI strategy focuses on 1) investment that helps enhance national competitiveness by encouraging research and development (R&D) , innovation, and value creation in the agricultural, industrial, and services sectors, and SMEs; 2) activities that are environmentally friendly, save energy, or use alternative energy; 3) industrial clusters to create investment concentration in accordance with regional potential and strengthens value chains; 4) investment in border provinces in southern Thailand to help develop the local economy, supporting efforts to enhance security in the area; 5) the development of planned special economic zones, especially in border areas, to create economic connectivity with neighboring countries, and to prepare for entry into the ASEAN Economic Community; and 6) the promotion of Thai overseas investment.

Activity-based incentives vary and are categorized from A1 to B2. The activities in the A1 field are those that the country wants to promote the most, and will receive the highest incentives, such as an eight-year corporate income tax exemption without a cap, exemption of import duty on machinery and raw materials, and other non-tax incentives.

A1 activities include electricity generation, creative product design, electronics design, and R&D. Merit-based incentives are meant to encourage investment that benefits the country. A 200% additional cap on corporate income tax incentives will be granted to a company that has a high ratio of expenditure on R&D.

Limits on Foreign Control

According to the Foreign Business Act 1999 (FBA), certain types of business activities are reserved for Thai nationals only. Foreign investment in those businesses must comprise less than 50% of share capital, unless specially permitted or otherwise exempt.

The following three lists, attached as annexes to the FBA, detail restricted businesses for foreigners:

List 1. This contains activities prohibited to non-nationals, including:

Newspaper or radio broadcasting stations and radio and television station businesses

Rice farming and growing plantations or crops

Livestock farming
Forestry and timber processing from a natural forest
Fishery in Thai territorial waters and specific economic zones
Extraction of Thai medicinal herbs
Trading and auctioning of antique objects or objects of historical value from Thailand
Making or casting of Buddha images and monk alms bowls
Land trading

List 2. This contains activities related to national safety or security, or those which affect arts and culture, tradition, folk handicrafts, or natural resources and the environment. Among other things, they include:
The production, sale and maintenance of firearms and armaments.
Domestic transportation by land, water, and air.
Trading of Thai antiques or art objects.
Mining, including rock blasting and rock crushing.
Timber processing for production of furniture and utensils.

Remark: A foreign majority-owned company can engage in List 2 activities if Thai nationals or legal persons hold not less than 40% of the total shares and the number of Thai directors is not less than two-fifths of the total number of directors.

Exceptions are those which receive:

Permission from the Minister of Commerce with approval by the Cabinet (if there is a reasonable cause, the Minister, with the approval of the Cabinet, may reduce the Thai shareholding requirement, which cannot be less than 25% of the total shares)

Investment promotion from the Board of Investment
Authorization by the Industrial Estate Authority of Thailand
Permission under a treaty to which Thailand is bound
List 3. This contains activities in which there are economic protections for Thai nationals. Among other things, they include:
Accounting, legal, architectural, or engineering services
Retail and wholesale
Advertising businesses
Hotels
Guided touring
Selling food or beverages
Any kind of service business
There are exceptions to List 3 for those which receive the following:

Permission from the Director-General of the Department of Business Development at the Ministry of Commerce, with approval by the Foreign Business Committee, on obtaining a Foreign Business License.

Investment promotion from the Board of Investment or from the Industrial Estate Authority of Thailand, on obtaining a Foreign Business Certificate from the Director-General of the Department of Business Development at the Ministry of Commerce.

Protection under a treaty or obligation to which Thailand is bound, including: US Treaty of Amity and Economic Relations; Thai-Australia Free Trade Agreement (TAFTA); Japan-Thailand Economic Partnership Agreement (JTEPA); and ASEAN Framework Agreement on Services (AFAS), on obtaining a Foreign Business Certificate from the Director-General of the Department of Business Development at the Ministry of Commerce.

Further restrictions on foreign ownership in specific sectors, such as telecommunications, banking, or insurance, are regulated in specific laws pertaining to these sectors, such as the Telecommunications Business Act (2006), the Financial Institution Business Act (2008), the Life Insurance Act (1992), and the Non-Life Insurance Act (1992).

The U.S.-Thai Treaty of Amity and Economic Relations of 1833, commonly referred to as the Treaty of Amity, is a special economic relationship between the United States of America and the Kingdom of Thailand that gives special rights and benefits to U.S. citizens who wish to establish their businesses in Thailand. The Treaty of Amity was amended in 1966 and provides two major benefits:

American companies are permitted to maintain a majority shareholding or to wholly own its company, branch office, or representative office located in Thailand.

American companies receive national treatment, meaning U.S. firms may engage in business on the same basis as Thai companies, and are exempt from most of the restrictions on foreign investment imposed by the Alien Business Law of 1972.

Despite the Treaty of Amity, there are still certain restrictions on U.S. investment as follows:
Owning land
Engaging in inland transportation and communication industries

Engaging in fiduciary functions
Engaging in banking involving depository functions
Engaging in domestic trade in indigenous agricultural products
Exploiting land or other natural resources

The U.S. Commercial Service, U.S. Embassy Bangkok, is responsible for issuing a certification letter to confirm that the applicant is qualified to apply for protection under the Treaty of Amity. The applicant must first obtain documents verifying that the company has been registered in compliance with Thai Law. Upon receipt of the required documents, the U.S. Commercial Service office will then certify to the Thai Department of Commercial Registration in the Ministry of Commerce that the applicant is seeking to register an American-owned and managed company or that that the applicant is an American citizen and is therefore entitled to national treatment under the provisions of the Treaty. For more information on how to apply for protection under the Treaty of Amity, please e-mail: **ktantisa@trade.gov**

Privatization Program

With the aim of encouraging capital inflows and relieving resource constraints in many key sectors of the economy, the government of Thaksin Shinawatra embarked on a privatization program for state-owned economic enterprises (SOEs) and state monopolies. The interim government that followed the September 2006 coup, as well as the former government of Abhisit Vejjajiva (Democrat party), considered privatization too controversial and put these plans on hold. Most privatization plans have remained on hold since 2006. Other than the Petroleum Authority of Thailand (PTT), the Airport Authority of Thailand (later renamed Airports of Thailand (AOT) and the Mass Communication Organization of Thailand (MCOT), few significant privatizations have occurred. The 1999 State Enterprise Corporatization Act provides the framework for the conversion of SOEs into stock companies, and corporatization is viewed as an intermediate step toward eventual privatization. (Note: "Corporatization" describes the process by which an SOE adjusts its internal structure to resemble a publicly-traded enterprise; "privatization" means that a majority of the SOE's shares is sold to the public, and "partial privatization" refers to a situation in which less than half of a company's shares are sold to the public.) Foreign investors are allowed to participate in the privatization, but certain restrictions are applied in certain sectors, which are mostly regulated by the Foreign Business Act of 1999 and the Act on Standards Qualifications for Directors and Employees of State Enterprises of 1975 and its series of amendments.

The new State Enterprises Policy Commission, or "superboard," was established in 2014 to oversee reform of the country's 56 SOEs. In March 2015, the superboard approved, in principle, to establish a holding firm to supervise SOEs listed on the Stock Exchange of Thailand, while the State Enterprise Policy Office will be retained to supervise state enterprises that have been established by specific laws, including the Electricity Generating Authority of Thailand, the Metropolitan Electricity Authority, and the Provincial Electricity Authority.

Screening of FDI

Thailand does not have any government agency to screen, review, or approve foreign direct investment. The Board of Investment (BOI), which operates under the Ministry of Industry, is the principal government agency for encouraging investment in the country. Foreign investment in Thailand does not require approval from the BOI, provided the necessary operating permits have been obtained. Investors should determine whether the incentives available through the BOI outweigh the various restrictions involved.

Two of the most significant privileges offered by the BOI for promoted projects are:

Tax privileges, such as corporate income tax exemptions, tariff exemptions, reductions on imported machinery and tariff exemptions, or reductions on imported raw material

Non-tax privileges, such as permission to own land, permission to bring foreign experts to work on the promoted projects, exemptions on foreign ownership of companies, and exemption from work permits and visa rules

The BOI also appointed a subcommittee, comprised of 15 members, including the BOI Secretary General as Chairman; BOI senior executives; and representatives from the public and private sectors, such as the Ministry of Finance, Ministry of Natural Resources and Environment, Office of Industrial Economics, Department of Industrial Works, National Science and Technology Development Agency, Bank of Thailand, Industrial Estate Authority of Thailand, Federation of Thai Industries, Thai Chamber of Commerce, and Board of Trade of Thailand. The subcommittee is responsible for approving investment projects with an investment value between 200 and 750 million baht (USD 6.1 and USD 23 million) and export-led projects with over 750 million baht (USD 23 million) in investment value. The sub-committee is also responsible for screening projects with an investment value of over 750 million baht (USD 23 million) and passes them on to the BOI Board for further consideration and approval.

Competition Law

The Thailand Trade Competition Act (hereafter called "the Competition Act") stems from the Price Fixing and Anti-Monopoly Act of 1979, which contains provisions regarding price fixing and monopolies. The monopolies section of the 1979 Act is aimed at promoting fair competition, and empowers the Central Committee to monitor business structures that may create monopolies and conduct restrictive business practices. Due to subsequent issues in enforcement, the Department of Internal Trade then separated the Act into two separate laws: the Price of Goods and Services Act and the Competition Act. The Competition Act went into effect on April 30, 1999.

According to the new law, the "Competition Commission," which consists of the Minister of Commerce as Chairman, the Permanent-Secretary of the Ministry of Commerce as Vice-Chairman, the Director-General of the Department of Internal Trade as Member and Secretary, and the Permanent-Secretary of the Ministry of Finance, and no more than twelve other qualified persons as members, shall be responsible for the enforcement of the Act. These qualified persons appointed as members must not be political members, holders of political positions, executive members, or holders of positions with the responsibilities in the administration of political parties. They shall hold office for a term of two years and not more than two consecutive terms in case they are re-appointed. The Commission shall have the powers and duties to consider complaints, to prescribe rules for dominant positions, to consider an application for permission to merge businesses, or to initiate the joint reduction or restriction of competition to give orders for suspension, cessation, correction, or variation of activities by business operations.

Anti-competitive behaviors under the Act have been defined and divided into categories as follows.

1. Section 25 prohibits businesses with dominant positions to abuse their market power by:

setting unfair prices for goods and services;

setting unfair trading conditions, directly or indirectly, to customers in order to restrict customers' normal business practices;

limiting supply of goods and services to create a shortage of supply; and

intervening in other businesses without proper reasons.

A business operator with market domination is defined under the Competition Act as one or more business operators in the market of any goods or services who have the market share and sales volume above the level that is prescribed by the Commission.

2. Section 26 prohibits any merger that may create monopolistic power or reduce competition, unless it obtains authorization from the Commission granting that it is a business necessity and beneficial to the economy.

3. Section 27 prohibits a business operator from conspiring, colluding, or collaborating with another business operator in order to create monopolistic power or reduce competition. In the case where it is reasonably necessary in the business and does no serious harm to the economy, the business operators shall submit an application for permission to the Commission. The Commission has already approved forms, rules, and procedures to apply for permission for any kind of anti-competitive agreement.

4. Section 28 of the Act deals with agreements between domestic and overseas business operators performing an activity that will restrict the freedom or opportunity of a person residing in the Kingdom from purchasing goods or services for his/her own use directly from business operators outside the Kingdom.

5. Section 29 of the Act also prohibits a business operator from performing any act which is not free and fair competition and which results in destroying, impairing, obstructing, impeding, or restricting business operations of other business operators, preventing other persons from carrying out business, or causing the cessation of business.

Penalties:

Failure to abide by the above provisions of the Competition Act could result in jail terms between one to three years and/or fines ranging from two to six million baht (USD 61,427 to USD 184,281). Note that under the Act, such penalties may be applied not only to the enterprises, but also to their managing partners or persons in charge of operations, unless the offense at stake was committed without his/her knowledge or consent and/or reasonable measures were taken to prevent such offense.

Investment Trends

Foreign direct investment has been an important element of Thailand's economic development process and the country is an important FDI destination. In terms of investment, the country offers an attractive and modern legal framework and its economy benefits from regional dynamism. According to the UNCTAD World Investment Report 2014, since 2012, Thailand has been among the eight priority destinations for foreign investment for the period 2014-2016. It is the 7th largest FDI recipient in East and South-East Asia. After having slowed due to unfavorable international conditions, FDI flows have again been rising, despite a series of natural disasters and political instability. In anticipation of the new investment policy and after political stability had been restored in the second half of 2014, demands recorded by the Board of Investment reached record levels: the number of registered projects increased by 73%, with an increase in value of 117% over 2013 levels. In 2015, the government's new seven-year strategy to stimulate investment should further encourage FDI.

Japanese firms remained at the top of the list among foreign investors applying for tax relief, followed by those from the United States and the European Union. Thailand's Board of Investment (BOI) is the government agency responsible for providing incentives to stimulate investment in Thailand and investment-related services to both foreign and Thai investors. Companies, foundations, or co-operatives established under Thai law (including those established by foreign investors) are eligible for BOI promotion. When examining some of the individual investment projects endorsed by BOI, it is interesting to see that eco-friendly activities dominated. In December 2014, BOI approved 13 investment projects worth 20 billion baht (USD 614.3 million) in investment value. Most of the approved projects were alternative energy businesses, including a power plant that generates energy from waste and biomass.

BOI has laid out a new strategy to promote foreign direct investment over a seven-year period commencing in January 2015. The strategy is intended to improve Thailand's competitiveness, reduce its reliance on low cost labor, and will focus on high technology to support the government's efforts to build a digital economy. The new strategy awards privileges based on types of projects, emphasizing those that support the digital economy, such as high technology, research and development, design, and other specific industries in the same designated sectors.

Table 1

Measure	Year	Index or Rank	Website Address
TI Corruption Perceptions index	2014	85 of 175	transparency.org/cpi2014/results
World Bank's Doing Business Report "Ease of Doing Business"	2014	26 of 189	doingbusiness.org/rankings
Global Innovation Index	2014	48 of 143	globalinnovationindex.org/content.aspx?page=data-analysis
World Bank GNI per capita	2013	USD 5,340	data.worldbank.org/indicator/NY.GNP.PCAP.CD

2. CONVERSION AND TRANSFER POLICIES

Foreign Exchange

There are no limitations placed on foreign investors for converting, transferring, or repatriating funds associated with an investment. Repatriation of investment funds and repayments of overseas loans can be remitted freely, but only upon submission of supporting documents to commercial banks, including evidence of sale or transfer in the case of investment funds and evidence of inward remittances supporting the loan agreement. Foreign currency must be converted to Thai baht or deposited with authorized banks within 360 days after the date of bringing the money into the country. There are some exceptions for foreigners staying in Thailand for less than three months and those working for foreign embassies and international organizations. In addition, any person who brings foreign currency into or out of Thailand exceeding USD 20,000 or the equivalent must declare the amount at a Customs checkpoint. Investment funds are allowed to be freely converted into any currency. The exchange rate is determined by the managed float system, with the central bank's intervention to smooth any abrupt fluctuations.

Remittance Policies

There are no time limitations on remittances. There are no limitations on the inflow or outflow of funds for remittances of profits or revenue.

Since Thailand, like most Asian countries, is the recipient of capital inflows, the Bank of Thailand (BOT) has maintained a managed-float exchange rate regime, which focuses on curbing short-term volatility and maintaining regional competitiveness. The exchange rate movements have also been determined by market fundamentals; however, during the period of excessive capital inflows (i.e. exchange rate speculation), the central bank has stepped in to prevent extreme movements in the currency and to reduce the duration and extent of the exchange rate's deviation from the equilibrium.

The BOT normally uses both verbal and actual intervention when the Thai baht does not move in line with BOT foreign exchange policy, as determined by the Monetary Policy Committee. The actual interventions are outright spot or outright forward USD/Baht transactions executed by selling or buying USD against the Thai Baht. The BOT intervenes in the interbank foreign exchange market, both onshore and offshore, using designated agent banks in order to maintain anonymity. In practice, the BOT generally intervenes during the Asian time zone of high market liquidity.

In some cases, where the capital inflows were huge but underlying Thai economic fundamentals were still sound, the BOT adjusted its intervention strategy accordingly, allowing the Thai Baht to strengthen gradually. Since 2010, the central bank has started relaxing regulations by encouraging capital outflows (promoting outward investment of Thai investors overseas) in order to restore the balance between capital inflows and outflows in the market.

Thailand was publicly identified by the Financial Action Task Force (FATF) in 2010 for its strategic AML/CFT deficiencies, for which it developed an action plan. In February 2013, the FATF removed Thailand from its Public Statement after concluding that Thailand had made significant progress and had completed all items in its action plan.

3. EXPROPRIATION AND COMPENSATION

Private property can be expropriated for public purposes in accordance with Thai law, which provides for due process and compensation. In practice, this process is seldom used and has been principally confined to real estate owned by Thai nationals and needed for public works projects. U.S. firms have not reported any problems with property appropriation in Thailand. However, the Embassy has received reports of conflicts over land title authenticity in areas that the government has designated as national park land.

4. DISPUTE SETTLEMENT

Legal System, Specialized Courts, Judicial Independence, Judgments of Foreign Courts

Thailand has a civil code, commercial code, and a bankruptcy law. Monetary judgments are calculated at the market exchange rate. Decisions of foreign courts are not accepted or enforceable in Thai courts. Disputes such as the enforcement of property or contract rights have generally been resolved through the Thai courts. Thailand has an independent judiciary that is generally effective in enforcing property and contractual rights. The legal process is slow in practice, however, and litigants or third parties sometimes affect judgments through extra-legal means.

In addition, companies may establish their own arbitration agreements. Thailand signed the Convention on the Settlement of Investment Disputes Between States and Nationals of Other States in 1985, but has not yet ratified the Convention. Thailand is a member of the New York Convention and enacted its own rules on conciliation and arbitration in the Arbitration Act of 2002. The 2002 Arbitration Act adopted the principles under the United Nations Commission on International Trade Law (UNCITRAL). The Arbitration Office of the Ministry of Justice administers these procedures.

Bankruptcy

Under Thailand's Bankruptcy Act, once the court approves a petition for liquidation, an official receiver will be appointed. The receiver will gather all of the debtor's assets, fix all of the creditors' claims, and submit a report to the court for final judgment. Until the final judgment for bankruptcy is rendered, a creditor can request the following ex parte applications from the court:

Request an examination by the receiver of all assets of the debtor and/or request the debtor to attend questioning on the existence of assets;

Require that the debtor provide satisfactory security to the court;

Request the court to take immediate custody of the debtor's assets and/or seize evidence in order to prevent the loss of destruction of such items.

The liability of the investor, who is a shareholder, is limited up to the amount, if any, unpaid on the shares respectively held by them. If the investor already made full payments for the shares they hold, no further liability will be charged to the investor.

Investment Disputes

There have been a couple notable cases of investor-state disputes in recent years. In 2003, the Civil Court of Thailand upheld a 6.2 billion baht (USD 190.4 million) international arbitration award against the Expressway and Rapid Transit Authority of Thailand (ETA, a Thai government agency), in favor of Bangkok Expressway, PLC (a Thai-foreign joint venture company). In 2009, Walter Bau AG (a foreign contractor) was awarded approximately 30 million Euros in an international arbitration case regarding construction of the Don Muang tollway. Subsequently, the Thai Cabinet issued a resolution prohibiting the inclusion of arbitration in public-private contracts without prior approval by the Cabinet. Since then, the Cabinet has granted approval in several cases for an arbitration clause to be included in contracts. Local law firms allege that Thai courts have refused, in some instances, to enforce international arbitration awards based on interpretations which are not in keeping with international norms.

International Arbitration

Thailand's national Arbitration Act of 2002, which was modeled in part after the UNCITRAL Model law, governs domestic and international arbitration proceedings and states that "in cases where an arbitral award was made in a foreign country, the award shall be enforced by the competent court only if it is subject to an international convention, treaty, or agreement to which Thailand is a party." The Thai Arbitration Institute of the Alternative Dispute Resolution Office, Office of the Judiciary, and the Office of the Arbitration Tribunal of the Board of Trade of Thailand provide arbitration services to proceedings held within Thailand. There are only very limited circumstances under which a court can set aside an arbitration award. Thailand does not have a Bilateral Investment Treaty (BIT) or a Free Trade Agreement (FTA) with the United States.

ICSID Convention and New York Convention

Thailand is a signatory to the New York Convention. Thailand also signed, but did not ratify, the 1985 ICSID Convention.

Duration of Dispute Resolution

Disputes settled through arbitration can be settled within 12-18 months; while disputes that are litigated in domestic court can take considerably longer (up to several years) and are subject to appeal. Since the official language in all domestic court proceedings is Thai, this can present a challenge for foreigners who do not speak the language. Domestic court rulings are not enforceable outside of Thailand. It is not customary for local judges to specialize in hearing only cases involving one type of law; therefore it is not uncommon for there not to be sufficient understanding regarding the legal nature of the dispute. The Thai legal system allows the application of the international long-arm statue in the service of process regarding defendants located outside of Thailand. Nevertheless, since Thailand's legal system is based on Civil law, in order for there to be proper service it requires that the notice be taken to the Thai Ministry of Foreign Affairs where it undergoes a bureaucratic process in order to validate its service abroad.

5. PERFORMANCE REQUIREMENTS AND INVESTMENT INCENTIVES

WTO/TRIMS

Thailand committed to implement all World Trade Organization (WTO) agreements, including Trade-Related Investment Measures (TRIMS). In its latest Trade Policy Review in November 2011, the WTO noted, "Thailand did not take any new measures to restrict trade since the 2008 global financial crisis. Indeed, it has made some important improvements to trading conditions in some areas, such as its adoption of paperless import procedures and its intention to move to a single [customs] window. Furthermore, an appeals system has been introduced by the Customs Department to cover many aspects of import procedures. As a member of ASEAN, Thailand has adopted the Association's harmonized tariff nomenclature which has also helped facilitate trade by standardizing the customs codes used to identify products."

The report also said that Thailand has committed to liberalize the regulatory regime with legislation governing key sectors such as transport, distribution, and telecommunications under review. However, the report observed that there are some areas of Thailand's import and domestic policies that could hamper trading opportunities and impede its development, including agriculture policies, such as domestic support and tariff quota administration, complex tariff structure, technical barriers to trade, Sanitary Phyto Sanitary (SPS) measures, and intellectual property. The report also underlined that despite progress in the liberalization of trade in some service sectors, there remain concerns over foreign ownership and market access restrictions in financial services (particularly the insurance sector), telecommunications, maritime, and professional services. The report noted that Thailand has yet to modify its General Agreement on Trade in Services (GATS) schedule following the negotiations on telecommunications in 1997.

Investment Incentives

The Board of Investment (BOI), established by the Investment Promotion Act of 1977, is Thailand's central investment promotion authority. The BOI offers investment incentives uniformly to both qualified domestic and foreign investors with a clear articulation of the application procedures. Good governance is one of the key factors to manage and supervise the application for tax and duty privileges. Complete information on BOI's updated policies, programs, incentives, and application procedures can be found on the BOI website at: www.boi.go.th.

Two of the most significant privileges offered by the BOI for promoted projects are:

Tax privileges, such as corporate income tax exemption, tariff exemption, reduction on import machinery and tariff exemption, or reduction on imported raw material

Non-tax privileges, such as permission to own land, permission to bring foreign experts to work on the promoted projects, exemption on foreign ownership of companies, and exemption from work permits and visa rules.

Research and Development

Foreign firms, including U.S. firms, are able to benefit from the Board of Investment's promotion incentives for investment projects that employ a high level of technology and R&D.

Performance Requirements

The employment of foreigners is governed by the Foreign Employment Act and the Foreign Business Act. Both laws set employment preferences in favor of Thai nationals. Though requirements may vary, generally, employers must hire four Thais for every one foreign employee. Without exception, foreign private sector employees require work permits, which are granted by the Ministry of Labor. When considering whether to grant a work permit, the Ministry considers:

Whether the job could be done by a Thai employee

Whether the foreigner is qualified for the job

Whether the job fits the present economic needs of the Kingdom

Different requirements apply to companies promoted by the BOI, which typically result in greater flexibility and ease in obtaining work permits for foreign nationals.

Such schemes apply equally to senior management and boards of directors. According to the Foreign Business Act, if a foreigner is the managing partner or the manager, the company is subject to the restrictions applicable to foreign businesses and the Foreign Business License application.

There are no excessively onerous visa, residence, work permit, or similar requirements inhibiting mobility of foreign investors and their employees.

Work Permits: Thai law requires foreign workers to have a work permit issued by the Ministry of Labor in order to work legally in Thailand; Thai law also reserves 39 occupations for Thai workers and will not grant work permits for foreigners to engage in these occupations, including lawyers, architects, and civil engineers. Foreigners found to be working without work permits could be imprisoned up to five years and/or fined between 2,000 and 100,000 Thai baht (approximately USD 60 to USD 3,000). Exceptions to the requirement for a work permit include officially recognized diplomatic and consular delegations, representatives of member countries and officials of the United Nations and specialized institutions, personal servants working for the above persons, and those who are performing duties or missions otherwise exempted by the Royal Thai Government. Volunteer or charity work can be considered work under Thai law, requiring a work permit.

Factors that influence the granting of work permits include the degree of specialization required by the position, the size of the firm in terms of number of employees and registered capitalization, and the ratio of Thai nationals to foreigners employed by the firm. Foreigners working for the Thai government or working on projects promoted by the Board of Investment (BOI) usually have little difficulty obtaining work permits and typically receive their permits within seven days of application. Work permits in other areas are sometimes difficult to obtain. The duration of work permits is generally tied to the length of stay permitted by the person's visa.

U.S. citizens can enter Thailand without a visa for visits of up to thirty days. In order to apply for a work permit, a foreigner must enter Thailand on a non-immigrant visa (issued at Thai embassies and consulates) for a stay of three months or, for foreigners with well-defined work or business plans, for a stay of one year. Issuance of the three-month visa is usually completed within two or three days; the one-year visa requires approval from the Immigration Bureau of the Royal Thai Police in Bangkok. Upon obtaining a work permit, a holder of a three-month visa may apply for a one-year visa, which generally can be extended every year. Foreigners holding nonimmigrant visas who have lived in Thailand for at least three consecutive years may apply for permanent residence in Thailand if they meet strict criteria regarding investment or professional skills.

Despite the fact that Thailand generally welcomes foreign investment, some sectors are subject to foreign equity restrictions.

While these restrictions are imposed through a variety of different rules, regulations, and cabinet policies, the main governing law for such restrictions is the Foreign Business Act 1999 (FBA). Under the FBA, there are 43 categories of business, divided into three lists, which are subject to different levels of restrictions for foreigners, unless the foreigner is able to obtain a Foreign Business License. A company is considered foreign under the FBA if half or more than half of its shares are held by non-Thai natural or juristic persons.

Foreigners are prohibited from operating a business from any of the nine business categories mentioned in List 1 of the FBA, and therefore, such businesses cannot obtain a Foreign Business

License under any circumstances. This includes businesses such as operating newspapers, radio or television stations, rice farming, fishery, forestry, and land trading.

For activities under List 2 of the FBA, a foreigner would require a license from the Minister of Commerce and approval from the Thai Cabinet. Additionally, the company would have to be at least 40% owned by Thais (only 25% if the Minister of Commerce and the Cabinet have given special approval) and at least two-fifths of its managing directors would have to be Thai nationals. Business categories under List 2 of the FBA are businesses in national safety or security, including domestic aviation businesses, businesses affecting arts, culture, traditional customs, and folk handicrafts, and businesses affecting natural resources or the environment.

For activities under List 3 of the FBA, a foreigner would require a license from the Director General of the Commercial Registration Department of the Ministry of Commerce and approval from the Foreign Business Committee. List 3 includes all service businesses (accounting, legal, architecture, engineering, and any other category of service business), as well as retail (unless the company's registered capital is 100 million baht or more (approximately USD 3 million or more), hotel businesses, advertising, selling food and beverages, construction (with some exceptions), and others.

Further restrictions on foreign ownership in specific sectors, such as telecommunications, banking, or insurance, are regulated in specific laws pertaining to these sectors, such as the Telecommunications Business Act of 2006, the Financial Institution Business Act of 2008, the Life Insurance Act of 1992, or the Non-Life Insurance Act of 1992.

Exceptions from the restrictions of the FBA can be granted as promotional privileges by the BOI or IEAT, or, as a temporary measure, in the form of government approval issued by the Thai government.

Exceptions can also be provided based on international treaties Thailand has entered into. U.S. companies or nationals under the Treaty of Amity and Economic Relations between Thailand and the United States (Treaty of Amity) can be eligible for "national treatment," where, with some exceptions, they are treated in the same way as Thai nationals. Other international treaties, such as the Thai-Australia Free Trade Agreement (TAFTA), the Japanese Thai Economic Partnership Agreement (JTEPA) or the ASEAN Comprehensive Investment Agreement (ACIA), also provide for future exceptions, but these have mostly not yet been implemented under Thai laws.

Under the laws regulating the exceptions (such as promotional privileges by the BOI or IEAT, Foreign Business Licenses) from foreign investment restrictions, the authorities issuing such exceptions have been provided with bureaucratic discretion as to whether the exception will be granted.

Data Storage

The Thai government does not currently have any specific statutory law governing "forced localization" policy in which foreign investors must use domestic content in goods or technology.

6. Right to Private Ownership and Establishment

Private entities may establish and own business enterprises. The principal forms of business organization under Thai law are sole proprietorships, partnerships, limited companies, and public limited companies. In addition, branches of foreign corporations are recognized, and a "representative" or "liaison" office of a foreign company may receive special recognition. Regardless of the form of business organization, most businesses must apply for business registration. Establishment of a business in certain sectors by a foreign entity may be restricted by the Foreign Business Act. U.S. investors may benefit from the Treaty of Amity and Economic Relations (AER), as discussed above.

A Thai public limited company is similar to a corporation in the United States, and may be wholly owned by a foreigner, unless the corporation is involved in a business activity reserved for Thai nationals. A public limited company is allowed to offer its shares to the public. Eight laws pertaining to individual industries limit foreign ownership of companies listed on the Stock Exchange of Thailand.

7. PROTECTION OF PROPERTY RIGHTS

Real Property

Property rights are guaranteed by the Constitution against condemnation or nationalization without fair compensation. Secured interests in property are recognized and enforced. Thailand has a civil law system under which all laws are embodied in statutes or codes promulgated by the government. This practice is in contrast to the common law system in many Western countries, where court interpretations of statutes serve as governing legal precedent. There is an independent judiciary that provides a forum for settlement of disputes. Agencies of the government, as parties to commercial contracts, may be sued in the courts, and cannot raise a defense of sovereign immunity. However, state property is not subject to execution. There are four basic codes: Civil and Commercial Code, Criminal Code, Civil Procedure Code, and the Criminal Procedure Code. When adopting these codes early in the twentieth century, Thailand selected features of the two major Western legal systems (common law and civil law), and adapted provisions drawn from Great Britain, Germany, Switzerland, France, Japan, Italy, India, and other foreign systems, to circumstances in Thailand. Decisions and rulings of the judiciary and civil service can have considerable force as precedents.

There are three levels to the judicial system in Thailand: the Court of First Instance, which handles most matters at inception, the Court of Appeals, and the Supreme Court. There are specialized courts such as the Labor Court, Family Court, Tax Court, the Central Intellectual Property and International Trade Court, and the Bankruptcy Court. However, real property rights are uncertain because the interim constitution does not state a deadline for the enactment of the new constitution, which may define and/or protect real property rights differently.

Intellectual Property Rights

Widespread counterfeiting and piracy continue to plague intellectual property (IP) rights owners in Thailand. Particular areas of concern include counterfeiting of pharmaceuticals, cosmetics, apparel, and accessories. Piracy rates are also high for motion pictures, music, business, and entertainment software. The lack of sustained and coordinated enforcement, and, in particular, the failure to prosecute and penalize high level offenders, remains a substantial problem. The vast majority of criminal IP cases in Thailand are brought against retailers caught with relatively little infringing product. In addition to problems with counterfeiting and piracy, rights holders cite concerns about long delays in the patent process due to the large backlog of unexamined patent applications. Due to these concerns, Thailand has been on the Special 301 Priority Watch List since 2007 and on the Notorious Markets List. The government continues to develop measures to improve protection and enforcement of intellectual property rights.

Thailand amended its legal regime to comply with the WTO Agreement on Trade Related Aspects of Intellectual Property (TRIPs) in the mid-1990s, but questions remain about Thailand's implementation of obligations to protect pharmaceutical and agricultural test data from unfair commercial use, treatment of conflicting trademarks, and geographical indications. Since that time, Thailand has not kept pace with international IP legal developments in areas such as broadcasting and digital copyright. Thailand is a signatory to long-standing IP agreements such as the Berne and Paris Conventions, but not the World Intellectual Property Organization Copyright Treaty (WCT) or the Performances and Phonograms Treaty (WPPT). Thailand acceded to the Patent Cooperation Treaty in 2009.

Under the current military-run government, Thailand recently enacted legislative amendments to the Trade Secret Act and the Copyright Act. The amendment to the Trade Secret Act changes the composition of the Trade Secret Board and substantially reduced the penalties for a trade secret disclosure by its officers. The amendments to the Copyright Act were enacted by the National Legislative Assembly as two separate amendments dealing with anti-camcording and right management information. The Anti-Camcording amendment criminalizes the unauthorized camcording in cinemas by making the act of recording an offence by itself with no exception as a fair use, as provided under the Copyright Act. The other amendment dealt with technological protection measures, right management information, exceptions, performers' rights, and ISP liability.

Currently, Thailand is considering an amendment to the Trademark Act to streamline the trademark registration process and enable Thailand to accede to the Madrid Protocol, as well as clarify the application of the Trademark Act to illegal refilling practices.

According to the Royal Thai Government, the latest enforcement statistics collected in 2013 shows that Thai's enforcement authorities have conducted 10,515 enforcement actions with 2,981,427 infringing items seized. The Royal Thai Government is responsible for paying for the storage and destruction of these goods. While Royal Thai Customs has ex officio authority to seize counterfeit goods, without rightholder confirmation on product identification, it is reluctant to pursue cases. The Department of Intellectual Property (DIP) is the agency responsible for registration of most intellectual property, including trademarks, patents and designs. However, due to limited resources, rightholders complain that they experience substantial delays in the registration process.

On the enforcement side, IPR infringement is commonly treated as a criminal offense in Thailand. The police unit tasked with IPR infringement cases is the Economic and Cyber Crime Division (ECD) of the Royal Thai Police. Larger cases are generally brought to the Department of Special Investigation. Penalties for IPR infringement can range from fines to imprisonment.

An IP owner may also pursue a civil case for IPR infringement. Civil enforcement of IP infringement can yield compensation, an interim injunction, or a permanent injunction. However, the burden of proof for the actual damages in a civil action is considerably higher than in the United States, and attorney's fees and litigation costs are rarely recoverable.

For additional information about treaty obligations and points of contact at local IP offices, please see WIPO's country profiles at **http://www.wipo.int/directory/en/**

Resources for Rights Holders

For additional information about treaty obligations and points of contact at local IP offices, please see WIPO's country profiles at **http://www.wipo.int/directory/en/**.

Resources for Rights Holders: Peter N. Fowler, Regional Intellectual Property Attaché for Southeast Asia, U.S. Embassy Bangkok, **Peter.Fowler@trade.gov**. The American Chamber of Commerce in Thailand,**http://www.amchamthailand.com**.

8. TRANSPARENCY OF THE REGULATORY SYSTEM

In 1999, Thailand enacted the Trade Competition Act together with the Price of Goods and Services Act to strengthen the government's ability to regulate market monopolies and price fixing. The Trade Competition Act applies to all business activities with the exception of state-owned enterprises, cooperatives, agricultural and cooperative groups, government agencies, and certain enterprises exempted by the law. The law established a Trade Competition Commission with the authority to place limitations on market share and revenues of firms with substantial control of individual market sectors, to block mergers, and other forms of business combinations, and to levy fines for price fixing and other proscribed activities. Since the law's implementation, several foreign motorcycle distributors were found guilty of violating the law by forcing sales agencies to sell only their brands.

The government continues to have the authority to control the price of specific products under the Price of Goods and Services Act. The Department of Internal Trade under the Ministry of Commerce administers this law and interacts with the affected companies, though only the Committee on Prices of Goods and Services makes the final decision on what products to add or remove from price controls. As of January 2015, out of 41 controlled commodities and services, only sugar is subject to a price ceiling. Besides the 41 controlled commodities, practically any producer of consumer products is prohibited from raising prices without first notifying the Committee of its intention to do so. The government also uses its controlling stakes in major suppliers of products and services such as Thai Airways and PTT to influence prices in the market. Thailand has extensive legislation aimed at the protection of the environment, including the National Environmental Quality Act, the Hazardous Substances Act, and the Factories Act. Food purity and drug efficacy are controlled and regulated by a Food and Drug Administration with authority similar to its U.S. counterpart. Likewise, labor and employment standards are set and administered by the Ministry of Labor.

U.S. businesses have repeatedly expressed concern about the lack of transparency of the Thai customs regime and the significant discretionary authority exercised by Customs Department officials. The U.S. government and private sector have also expressed concern about the inconsistent application of Thailand's transaction valuation methodology and repeated use of arbitrary values by the Customs Department. Since the May 2014 coup, the interim government has made an effort to speed up passage of legislation that was stalled by the political gridlock of the previous administration. Several amendments of laws and regulations were passed in late 2014, including: Authorization of Customs Officials on Examination, Search and Seizure of Goods in Transit and Transshipment; Advance Ruling on Customs Valuation; Advance Ruling on Tariff Classification; Advance Ruling on the Origin of Goods; and Use of Electronic System for Customs Documents. Thailand is also currently revising other laws and regulations in preparation for the launch of the ASEAN Economic Community (AEC) at the end of 2015 and for Thailand's acceptance of the protocol for the WTO Trade Facilitation Agreement, also expected by the end of the year. These developments may lead to improvements in the challenging customs environment that many companies cite as one of their main concerns with doing business in Thailand.

Consistent and predictable enforcement of government regulations remains problematic for investment in Thailand. Gratuity payments to civil servants responsible for regulatory oversight and enforcement remain a common practice. Firms that refuse to make such payments can be placed at a competitive disadvantage when compared to other firms in the same field.

9. EFFICIENT CAPITAL MARKETS AND PORTFOLIO INVESTMENT

The Thai government maintains a regulatory framework that broadly encourages investment and largely avoids market-distorting support for specific sectors. Thailand's regulatory system has encouraged and facilitated portfolio investment. There is sufficient liquidity in the markets to enter and exit sizeable positions. Government policies generally do not restrict the free flow of financial resources to support product and factor markets. The Bank of Thailand has respected IMF Article VIII by refraining from restrictions on payments and transfers for current international transactions. Credit is generally allocated on market terms rather than by "direct lending." Foreign investors are not restricted from borrowing on the local market, but there are a number of regulations that affect foreign portfolio investment. In theory, the private sector has access to a wide variety of credit instruments, ranging from fixed term lending to overdraft protection to bills of exchange and bonds. However, the private debt market is not well-developed, and most corporate financing, whether for short-term working capital needs, trade financing, or project financing, requires borrowing from commercial banks or other financial institutions.

Money and Banking System, Hostile Takeovers

In general, Thailand's banking sector, with 14 commercial banks, is healthy with low rates of non-performing loans (around 2.35%) and a high ratio of capital funds/risk assets (capital adequacy) of 16.67% in Q4 2014 (compared to 8.5% set by the Bank of International Settlements' Basel Committee). Thailand's largest commercial bank is Krung Thai Bank, with assets totaling USD 85.2 billion as of January 2015. For the five largest commercial banks, their combined assets totaled USD 362.7 billion.

Thailand's central bank is the Bank of Thailand (BOT) was established in 1942 and is governed by a Governor with a five-year term. The BOT has the following roles and responsibilities: print and issue banknotes and other security documents (i.e. the Bank of Thailand bonds), promote monetary stability and formulate monetary policies, manage the BOT's assets, provide banking facilities to the government, act as the registrar of government bonds, and provide banking facilities for financial institutions.

Non-residents can open and maintain foreign currency accounts without deposit and withdrawal ceilings with authorized banks in Thailand. However, such accounts must use funds that originate abroad. Meanwhile, any deposits in the Thai Baht currency must be derived from one of the following sources: conversion of foreign currencies, payment of goods and services, or a capital transfer of which BOT approval is not required. Any withdrawals are permitted, except the withdrawal of funds for credit to another non-resident person or purchase of foreign currency involving an overdraft.

The Thai banking industry does not have a history of hostile takeovers, and the BOT does not have clear rules governing hostile takeovers. The Financial Institutions Business Act, passed at the end of 2007, unified the legal framework and strengthened BOT supervision and enforcement powers. The Act gave powers to the BOT to raise the foreign ownership limit in a local bank from 25% to 49% on a case-by-case basis. The Act also allows the Ministry of Finance to authorize foreign ownership above 49% only if recommended by the central bank. These past practices by the BOT have suggested that it applies rules on a non-discriminatory basis.

10. COMPETITION FROM STATE-OWNED ENTERPRISES

State-owned enterprises (SOEs) operate primarily in the energy, telecommunications, transportation, and financial sectors. The full list of SOEs list is published under the website of the State Enterprise Policy Office of the Ministry of Finance: (www.sepo.go.th). Although precise definitions of SOEs vary slightly according to different pieces of legislation, in general, the government defines SOEs as special agencies established by precise laws for a particular purpose and 100% owned by the government (through the Ministry of Finance as a shareholder) or limited company/public company limited that is 50% or more owned by the government.

The government does not specify R&D allocations for SOEs in percentages, but has encouraged all SOEs to set aside some portion of their budgets for it. In general, SOEs do not receive a larger percentage of government contracts/business than their private sector competitors. However, in some industries, such the telecommunications sector, the government has assigned all 'fixed line' operations in the country to SOEs, as the private sector competitors are reluctant to conduct such unprofitable business.

SOEs purchase or supply goods or services from private sector/foreign firms. Some SOEs have established rules and regulations on procurement, but most are still under the Government Procurement Agreement. In general, SOEs , like government agencies, reserve the right to accept or reject any or all bids at any time and may also modify the technical requirements during the bidding process, if, according to regulations, corruption is suspected. The latter provision allows considerable leeway to SOEs in managing procurements. Private enterprises can compete with SOEs under the same terms and conditions with respect to market share, products/services, and incentives in most sectors, but there are some exceptions, such as the fixed line operation in the telecommunications sector.

According to the government regulations, all SOES must deposit money or purchase securities (bonds) from only state-owned banks or private banks that have been approved by the Ministry of Finance. Therefore, SOEs tend to receive better loan conditions from these financial institutions than private enterprises. The Ministry of Finance usually guarantee loans made by SOEs, resulting in lower interest rate charged from lower risk of loan default.

The tax burden of SOEs depends on the type of SOE. SOEs established by special laws (e.g. 100% owned by the Ministry of Finance) that are not listed on the stock market are not subject to corporate income tax. SOEs in the form of limited companies/public limited companies/listed companies are subject to corporate income tax. Each year, all SOEs, regardless of type, must return a certain percentage (ranging from 35% to 88%) of their net profits back to the Ministry of Finance.

SOEs are not afforded material advantages such as preferential access to land and raw materials. Each year, the government regularly allocates three to four percent of its annual budget expenditures to fund SOEs. All SOEs can also borrow directly with a guarantee from the Ministry of Finance, or can request that the Ministry of Finance grant an on-lending loan for them. Depending on the size of the loan, either the board of the SOE or the Cabinet has to approve such loans. In general, combined borrowing of all (non-bank) SOEs cannot be higher than 20% of the government's annual budget expenditures.

OECD Guidelines on Corporate Governance of SOEs

Thailand is one of the leaders in corporate governance in private enterprises among Asian economies and emerging economies. However, corporate governance within SOEs, except for publicly listed SOEs, is viewed as lagging behind the private sector. In June 2014, the government established "the State Enterprise Policy Committee" or "Superboard", chaired by the Prime Minister, as a new central body to supervise and regulate all SOEs. The Committee also established a subcommittee on corporate governance, chaired by the Bank of Thailand Governor, with the Ministry of Finance's State Enterprise Policy Office (SEPO) as a secretariat. The subcommittee is now the core body promoting corporate governance within SOEs and has responsibilities for studying, analyzing, and laying plans to prevent corruption by promoting transparency and disclosure. The Ministry of Finance's SEPO also established guidelines for SOE board members, including rules on board member nomination process, roles and duties, responsibilities, and good governance. In addition, all SOEs are required by law to submit annual financial reports to the Office of the Auditor General. Publicly listed SOEs, such as Thai Airways and PTT, are required to publish their financial reports.

According to the officials at the SEPO, SOEs do adhere to the OECD Guidelines on corporate governance, including the state acting as an owner. The current guidelines are not yet sufficient to ensure a level playing field between SOEs and private sector enterprises, but the subcommittee of corporate governance has realized the important of the issue, which is now under the process of consideration and review.

In general, SOE senior management reports directly to a line minister and to the Superboard.

Corporate board seats are typically allocated to senior government officials or other politically-affiliated individuals. The Superboard tries to eliminate political interference in board member appointments.

Third-party analysts view the SOEs as tools of the government to deliver policies. For example, the Bank of Agriculture and Agricultural Cooperatives (BAAC) was the core agency to execute the rice pledging scheme under the Yingluck Administration.

Sovereign Wealth Funds

Thailand currently does not have a sovereign wealth fund. However, the Bank of Thailand is studying a plan to use its surplus foreign reserves to establish what would be called a New Opportunity Fund, aimed at increasing returns as part of an effort to improve the central bank's balance sheet. The establishment of this fund is likely to be postponed from its current 2015 timeframe.

11. CORPORATE SOCIAL RESPONSIBILITY

There is wide recognition and awareness of the value of corporate social responsibility (CSR) initiatives among Thai producers and consumers, but many companies still lack a full understanding of generally accepted CSR principles, such as the OECD Guidelines for Multinational Enterprises. CSR is most often identified as individual philanthropic projects or community service of companies, rather than as an overall corporate strategy aimed to improve the community in which the companies operate. Companies that pursue CSR are viewed favorably by the public.

Many business associations, including the American Chamber of Commerce, are actively supporting the development of CSR programs in Thailand. Since 2007, the American Chamber of Commerce Corporate Social Responsibility Excellence Awards have encouraged the expansion of CSR programs by identifying best practices of companies in Thailand. Many CSR programs incorporate the Embassy's Thai-U.S. Creative Partnership to work directly with local partner organizations on long-term projects training and promoting opportunities in innovative sectors, such as renewable energy, IT, and microfinance. The AMCHAM ACE program also tracks continuous improvement.

Both the Thai Chamber of Commerce (TCC) and the Federation of Thai Industries (FTI) have undertaken several CSR projects over the past years. The FTI, in particular, incorporated CSR focused on health, safety and environment as part of their mission statement. The Joint Standing Committee on Commerce, Industry, and Banking of Thailand (JSCCIB) has also established a CSR committee that consolidates reports on activities from both TCC and FTI members.

In February 2015, a bill was proposed by the National Reform Council (NRC) Committee on Social Enterprise. The purpose of the social enterprise bill is to create a regulatory framework to encourage the development of social enterprises, promote participation of the private sector through CSR in social development, and provide tax incentives to private enterprises to encourage spending a percentage of their profits on addressing social problems. The bill establishes a new independent regulating body, the Office of the National Social Enterprise Promotion (ONSEP), to be formed under the Prime Minister's Office; a National Social Enterprise Promotion Commission to coordinate policy and supervise ONSEP; and a new Social Enterprise Fund designed to provide loans to social enterprises and subsidize state or private agencies to achieve social enterprise goals. The draft bill is currently with the Cabinet pending review.

OECD Guidelines for Multinational Enterprises

See above.

12. POLITICAL VIOLENCE

Thailand continues to experience political volatility. In May 2014, the Thai armed forces seized power in a bloodless coup d'état. The military intervention followed nearly nine months of sometimes violent anti-government protests, a dissolved parliament, and aborted national elections. Following the coup, the military government restricted freedoms of the press, speech, and assembly, and has to date briefly detained over 1,000 political leaders, academics, journalists, and others. Despite some pockets of resistance, protests against the coup have been rare, due in part to continuing significant security measures and the prohibition of political assemblies.

There has been very limited political violence since the military coup. On February 1, 2015, one person was injured after two bombs exploded near a train station and a shopping mall in downtown Bangkok. On March 7, 2015, suspects threw a hand grenade at the Bangkok Criminal Court and were apprehended at the scene. Authorities have arrested 16 persons for the Criminal Court bombing.

Ongoing violence related to an 11-year Malay-Muslim insurgency in Thailand's southernmost provinces continues. Efforts to end the ethno-nationalist insurgency, which has claimed over 6,000 lives and caused over 10,000 injuries – mostly civilians – since 2004, have so far been unsuccessful.

Thailand and Cambodia have disputed sections of their common border, which resulted in sporadic clashes in 2008-2011 that killed over 20 military personnel. In November 2013, the International Court of Justice (ICJ) ruled that land surrounding the 11th century temples at Preah Vihear belonged to Cambodia, and instructed Thailand to withdraw its troops from the area. Cambodia had sought clarification of a 1962 ICJ ruling that awarded sovereignty of the temples to Cambodia but left ambiguous the sovereignty over the surrounding land. The border has remained generally calm since the latest ruling, and both governments meet regularly to discuss border issues, including overlapping claims in the Gulf of Thailand that contain hydrocarbon reserves.

13. CORRUPTION

Thailand has several laws to combat corruption. The independent National Anti- Corruption Commission (NACC), together with the Office of the Public Sector Anti-Corruption Commission (PACC), coordinates official efforts against corruption and hold broad investigatory authority. In addition to these two agencies, the Office of the Ombudsman, the Constitutional Court, the Election Commission, the Office of the Auditor General, and the National Human Rights Commission have anti-corruption responsibilities. In December 2003, Thailand became a signatory to the UN Convention Against Corruption ratifying the convention in March 2011. In April 2005, Thailand endorsed the ADB-OECD Anticorruption Action Plan for Asia and the Pacific and assigned the Ministry of Justice to implement the Action Plan. The Office of Public Sector Anti-Corruption Commission, under the Ministry of Justice, was established to assist the NACC by investigating cases of lower ranking government officials.

According to some studies, a cultural propensity to forgive bribes as a normal part of doing business and to equate cash payments with finders' fees or consultants' charges, coupled with the low salaries of civil servants, encourages officials to accept illegal inducements. U.S. executives with experience in Thailand often advise new-to market companies that it is far easier to avoid corrupt transactions from the beginning than to stop such practices once a company has been identified as willing to operate in this fashion. American firms that comply with the strict guidelines of the Foreign Corrupt Practices Act (FCPA) are able to compete successfully in Thailand. U.S. businessmen say that publicly affirming the need to comply with the FCPA helps to shield their companies from pressure to pay bribes.

Recent Thai administrations have publicly stated their intention to improve transparency in the evaluation of bids and the awarding of contracts. In 2013, the Public-Private Partnership (PPP) Act passed, replacing the Public Participation in State Undertaking Act of 1992. Effective April 4, 2003, the PPP Act requires public projects over USD 1 billion to be awarded through a multi-agency committee instead of a single administrating agency, a practice which may help reduce corrupt practices. Despite recent improvements, both foreign and Thai companies continue to complain about irregularities in the Thai Customs Department. Increasing media scrutiny of public figures has raised political pressure to curtail favoritism and corruption. However, convictions against public officials on corruption-related charges are rare, and the legal system offers inadequate deterrence against corruption. According to the most recent Transparency International's annual Corruption Perceptions Index, Thailand ranked 85th out of 175 countries in 2014.

The press features frequent allegations of irregularities in public contracts, most notably over the use of public lands, procurement favoritism (e.g., revising requirements so that a preferred company wins over its competitors), and police complicity in a variety of illegal activities. In January 2010, the Thai press widely reported news of the U.S. Department of Justice indictment of a former Thai tourism minister accused of taking bribes from an American couple seeking to do business in Bangkok. In November 2011, the Permanent Secretary in the Ministry of Transportation resigned over allegations of corruption and bribery after large sums of cash were discovered in his home, allegedly from transportation contract kickbacks. In 2012, the Deputy Prime Minister and Interior Minister resigned after it was determined that he was involved in an improper land deal.

In recent years, the private sector has attempted to take the lead in fighting corruption through education and advocacy. Since 2010, the Thai Institute of Directors (IOD) has built an anti-corruption coalition of Thailand's largest businesses. Coalition members sign the Collective Action Against Corruption Declaration and pledge to take tangible, measurable steps to proactively reduce corruption-related risks that are verified by third party certification. CIPE equipped IOD and its coalition partners with an array of tools for training and collective action, based on examples from CIPE's programs around the world. Member companies now represent over 15 percent of the Thai economy and more than 1 million employees.

Founded in 2011, the Anti-Corruption Organization of Thailand (ACT) was established with the intent to pressure the government to create laws that can reduce levels of corruption. ACT has 47 member organizations drawn from the private, public and academic sectors. Their signature program is the 'integrity pact.' Drafted by ACT and the Finance Ministry and based on a tool promoted by Transparency International, the pact forbids bribes from signatory members in bidding for government contacts. Member agencies and companies must adhere to strict transparency rules by disclosing bidding information--such as the terms of reference and the cost of the project--easily available to the public.

Corruption, including bribery, raises the costs and risks of doing business. Corruption has a corrosive impact on both market opportunities overseas for U.S. companies and the broader business climate. It also deters international investment, stifles economic growth and development, distorts prices, and undermines the rule of law. It is important for U.S. companies, irrespective of their size, to assess the business climate in the relevant market in which they will be operating or investing, and to have an effective compliance program or measures to prevent and detect corruption, including foreign bribery. U.S. individuals and firms operating or investing in foreign markets should take the time to become familiar with the relevant anticorruption laws of both the foreign country and the United States in order to properly comply with them, and where appropriate, they should seek the advice of legal counsel.

The U.S. Government seeks to level the global playing field for U.S. businesses by encouraging other countries to take steps to criminalize their own companies' acts of corruption, including bribery of foreign public officials, by requiring them to uphold their obligations under relevant international conventions. A U.S. firm that believes a competitor is seeking to use bribery of a foreign public official to secure a contract should bring this to the attention of appropriate U.S. agencies, as noted below.

U.S. Foreign Corrupt Practices Act: In 1977, the United States enacted the Foreign Corrupt Practices Act (FCPA), which makes it unlawful for a U.S. person, and certain foreign issuers of securities, to make a corrupt payment to foreign public officials for the purpose of obtaining or retaining business for or with, or directing business to, any person. The FCPA also applies to foreign firms and persons who take any act in furtherance of such a corrupt payment while in the United States.

The U.S. Department of Justice (DOJ) and the Securities and Exchange Commission released a Resource Guide to the U.S. Foreign Corrupt Practices Act. The Guide is an excellent resource on the FCPA for U.S. companies with questions about the statute and its enforcement. The Guide explains the statute in detail and contains hypothetical examples of actual enforcement actions, and summaries of FCPA case law and DOJ opinion releases. For this and other useful resources, visit the DOJ Webpage: **http://www.justice.gov/criminal/fraud/fcpa/guidance/**.

Guidance on the U.S. FCPA: The Department of Justice's (DOJ) FCPA Opinion Procedure enables U.S. firms and individuals to request a statement of the Justice Department's present enforcement intentions under the anti-bribery provisions of the FCPA regarding any proposed business conduct. The details of the opinion procedure are available on DOJ's Fraud Section Website at www.justice.gov/criminal/fraud/fcpa. Although the Department of Commerce has no enforcement role with respect to the FCPA, it supplies general guidance to U.S. exporters who have questions about the FCPA and about international developments concerning the FCPA. For further information on the FCPA, transparency, and anti-bribery initiatives, see the Office of the Chief Counsel for International Counsel, U.S. Department of Commerce website, at **http://www.commerce.gov/os/ogc/transparency-and-anti-bribery-initiatives**. More general information on the FCPA is available on the websites listed below. Exporters and investors should be aware that generally all countries prohibit the bribery of their public officials, and prohibit their officials from soliciting bribes under domestic laws. Most countries are required to criminalize such bribery and other acts of corruption by virtue of being parties to various international conventions discussed above.

Other Instruments: It is U.S. Government policy to promote good governance, including host country implementation and enforcement of anti-corruption laws and policies pursuant to their obligations under international agreements. Since enactment of the FCPA, the United States has been instrumental to the expansion of the international framework to fight corruption. Several significant components of this framework are the OECD Convention on Combating Bribery of Foreign Public Officials in International Business Transactions (OECD Anti-bribery Convention), the United Nations Convention against Corruption (UN Convention), the Inter-American Convention against Corruption (OAS Convention), the Council of Europe Criminal and Civil Law Conventions, and a growing list of U.S. free trade agreements. Thailand is party to the UN Anticorruption Convention; Thailand is also a member of the Asia/Pacific Group against Money Laundering (APG).

OECD Anti-bribery Convention: Thailand is not a party to the OECD Convention (see**http://www.oecd.org/dataoecd/59/13/40272933.pdf**).

UN Convention: Thailand is a party to the UN Convention (see**http://www.unodc.org/unodc/en/treaties/CAC/signatories.html**).

OAS Convention: Thailand is not a party to the OAS Convention (see **http://www.oas.org/juridico/english/Sigs/b-58.html**).

Council of Europe Criminal Law and Civil Law Conventions: Thailand is not a member of the Council of Europe Conventions (see **www.coe.int/greco**).

Free Trade Agreements: The United States does not have an FTA with Thailand.

Local Laws: U.S. firms should familiarize themselves with local anticorruption laws, and, where appropriate, seek legal counsel. While the U.S. Department of Commerce cannot provide legal advice on local laws, the Department's U.S. and Foreign Commercial Service can provide assistance with navigating the host country's legal system and obtaining a list of local legal counsel.

Assistance for U.S. Businesses: The U.S. Department of Commerce offers several services to aid U.S. businesses seeking to address business-related corruption issues. For example, the U.S. and Foreign Commercial Service can provide services that may assist U.S. companies in conducting their due diligence as part of the company's overarching compliance program when choosing business partners or agents overseas. The U.S. Foreign and Commercial Service can be reached directly through its offices in every major U.S. and foreign city, or through its Website at www.trade.gov/cs. The Departments of Commerce and State provide worldwide support for qualified U.S. companies bidding on foreign government contracts through the Commerce Department's Advocacy Center and State's Office of Commercial and Business Affairs. Problems, including alleged corruption by foreign governments or competitors, encountered by U.S. companies in seeking such foreign business opportunities, can be brought to the attention of appropriate U.S. government officials, including local embassy personnel and through the Department of Commerce Trade Compliance Center "Report a Trade Barrier" website at **http://www.tcc.export.gov/Report_a_Barrier/index.asp**.

Anti-Corruption Resources: Some useful resources for individuals and companies on combating corruption in global markets include the following:

Information about the U.S. Foreign Corrupt Practices Act (FCPA), including a "Lay- Person's Guide to the FCPA" is available at the U.S. Department of Justice's Website at: **http://www.justice.gov/criminal/fraud/fcpa/guidance/**.

Information about the OECD Anti-bribery Convention, including links to national implementation legislation and country monitoring reports, is available at: **http://www.oecd.org/department/0,3355,en_2649_34859_1_1_1_1_1,00.html**.

See also new Anti-bribery Recommendation and Good Practice Guidance Annex for companies: **http://www.oecd.org/dataoecd/11/40/44176910.pdf**

General information about anticorruption initiatives, such as the OECD Convention and the FCPA, including translations of the statute into several languages, is available at the Department of Commerce Office of the Chief Counsel for International Commerce Website: **http://www.ogc.doc.gov/trans_anti_bribery.html**.

Transparency International (TI) publishes an annual Corruption Perceptions Index (CPI). The CPI measures the perceived level of public-sector corruption in 180 countries and territories around the world. The CPI is available at:**http://cpi.transparency.org/cpi2012**. TI also publishes an annual Global Corruption Report which provides a systematic evaluation of the state of corruption around the world. It includes an in-depth analysis of a focal theme, a series of country reports that documents major corruption-related events and developments from all continents, and an overview of the latest research findings on anti-corruption diagnostics and tools.
See **http://www.transparency.org/publications/gcr**.

The World Bank Institute publishes Worldwide Governance Indicators (WGI). These indicators assess six dimensions of governance in 212 countries, including Voice and Accountability, Political Stability and Absence of Violence, Government Effectiveness, Regulatory Quality, Rule of Law, and Control of Corruption.
See**http://info.worldbank.org/governance/wgi/sc_country.asp**.

The World Bank Business Environment and Enterprise Performance Surveys may also be of interest and are available at:**http://go.worldbank.org/RQQXYJ6210**.

The World Economic Forum publishes the Global Enabling Trade Report, which presents the rankings of the Enabling Trade Index, and includes an assessment of the transparency of border administration (focused on bribe payments and corruption) and a separate segment on corruption and the regulatory environment.
See**http://www.weforum.org/en/initiatives/gcp/GlobalEnablingTradeReport/index.htm**.

Additional country information related to corruption can be found in the U.S. State Department's annual Human Rights Report, available at **http://www.state.gov/g/drl/rls/hrrpt/**.

Global Integrity, a nonprofit organization, publishes its annual Global Integrity Report, which provides indicators for 92 countries with respect to governance and anti-corruption. The report highlights the strengths and weaknesses of national level anti-corruption systems. The report is available at: **http://report.globalintegrity.org/**.

UN Anticorruption Convention, OECD Convention on Combatting Bribery

Thailand is a party to the UN Convention, but not the OECD Convention.

Resources to Report Corruption

Government Contact for combating corruption:

International Affairs Strategy Specialist
Office of the National Anti-Corruption Commission
361 Nonthaburi Road, Thasaai District, Amphur Muang Nonthaburi 11000, Thailand
+662-528-4930
Email: **TACC@nacc.go.th**

Civil Society Contact on corruption:

Dr. Juree Vadakan
Secretary General
Transparency Thailand
Center for Philanthropy and Civil Society, NIDA, 118 SeriThai Road, Klong Jan, Ket Bang Kapi 10240, Thailand
+662-377-7206
Email: **juree@cpcnida.com**

14. BILATERAL INVESTMENT AGREEMENTS

The 1966 iteration of the U.S.-Thai Treaty of Amity and Economic Relations (AER), discussed above, allows U.S. citizens and businesses incorporated in the United States or in Thailand that are majority-owned by U.S. citizens, to engage in business on the same basis as Thai nationals. Under the AER, Thailand is permitted to apply restrictions to American investment only in the fields of communications, transport, banking, the exploitation of land or other natural resources, and domestic trade in agricultural products.

In October 2002, the United States and Thailand signed a bilateral Trade and Investment Framework Agreement (TIFA). The TIFA establishes a Trade and Investment Joint Council (TIJC), which serves as a forum for discussion of bilateral trade and investment issues such as intellectual property rights, customs, investment, biotechnology, and other areas of mutual concern.

Thailand also has bilateral investment agreements with 39 countries, including China, India, Taiwan, South Korea, United Kingdom, and members of the Association of Southeast Asian Nations (ASEAN). These agreements establish guidelines for expropriation compensation and the repatriation of capital, but do not include national treatment provisions.

Bilateral Taxation Treaties

Thailand has had a bilateral tax treaty with the United States since 1996.

15. OPIC AND OTHER INVESTMENT INSURANCE PROGRAMS

The Overseas Private Investment Corporation (OPIC) provides political risk insurance, debt financing, and private equity capital to support U.S. investors and their investments. OPIC can provide political risk insurance for currency inconvertibility, expropriation, and political violence for U.S. investments including equity, loans and loan guarantees, technical assistance, leases, and consigned inventory or equipment. OPIC debt financing in the form of direct loans and loan guarantees of up to USD 250 million per project are also available for business investments in Thailand, covering sectors as diverse as tourism, transportation, manufacturing, franchising, power, infrastructure, and others. In addition, OPIC supports eight private equity funds that are eligible to invest in projects in Thailand. OPIC is currently providing political risk insurance two U.S. organizations involved in humanitarian services and economic development in Thailand. In case of an incontrovertibility claim, the estimated annual U.S. dollar value of Thai baht likely to be used by the Mission in Thailand is approximately USD 112 million.

16. LABOR

According to the National Statistical Office (NSO), in 2014, Thailand's labor force stood at 38.4 million. Official unemployment rates remained very low at 0.8%. Despite being a middle income country, 57% of the labor force worked in the informal sector, including agriculture, forestry, and fishing, with limited protection under labor laws and the social security system. Thailand's fertility rate has been very low in recent years, averaging 1.4 in the years 2010 - 2015, the second lowest among ASEAN countries after Singapore. Thailand could experience negative population growth by 2025 and it has faced labor shortages in many sectors, especially those requiring low-skilled labor. The 2013 NSO labor demand survey reported that employers used various means to cope with labor shortages, including: increased working hours and overtime (26%), increased wages and benefits (24.5%), increased use of outsourcing or subcontracting (11.7%), increased use of migrant workers (10.7%), and increased use of machinery (8.7%). Thailand has had inflows of irregular migrant workers from neighboring countries such as Burma, Laos, and Cambodia since the 1980s, primarily for unskilled work. The United Nations (UN) estimated that as of 2013, approximately 3.7 million international migrants resided in Thailand, the highest in Southeast Asia, followed by Malaysia (2.4 million) and Singapore (2.3 million). International migrants account for 5.6% of the total population, a significant increase from 2% in 2000. In Southeast Asia, Thailand has the fourth highest share of international migrants in its total population, following Brunei (49.3%), Singapore (42.9%), and Malaysia (8.3%). Most migrant workers came to Thailand through unauthorized channels without any documentation. Some were granted temporary legal status to stay and work in Thailand through regularization programs, with collaboration from neighboring country governments to verify nationalities and issue passports.

A survey done by the World Bank found that firms report acute shortages for technical skills, especially at the vocational school level, as well as language and IT skills and soft skills such as leadership and creativity. This technical skill shortage is attributed in large part to a mismatch between market demands and educational preparation. Many multinational firms continue to bring in expatriate professionals because qualified local personnel are not available, even at high salaries. Finding, training, and retaining qualified employees to work in the manufacturing facilities being developed in industrial estates, such as those along the Eastern Seaboard, will continue to be a challenging government priority.

The 2008 Alien Employment Act requires all foreigners to obtain a work permit from the Ministry of Labor prior to starting work in Thailand. The term "work" is defined very broadly as "working by exerting one's physical energy or employing one's knowledge, whether or not for wages or other benefits". Therefore, volunteer or charity work also requires a work permit. A Royal Decree under the Act also restricted some occupations and professions which are closed to foreigners, such as laborer, agriculture, accounting auditing, goldsmith, engineering, architecture, etc.

Employers may dismiss workers for any reason, provided the employer pays severance.

Workers in Thailand are protected under the Labor Protection Act. The laws allow private sector workers to form and join trade unions of their choosing without prior authorization, bargain collectively, and conduct legal strikes with a number of restrictions. The law prohibits antiunion discrimination. Though the law does not require reinstatement of workers fired for involvement in trade union activity, a court decision may grant employee reinstatement and compensation of salary for losses while absent from work for various types of unfair termination, including antiunion discrimination. Noncitizen migrant workers do not have the right to form unions or serve as union officials. Registered migrants may be members of unions organized and led by Thai citizens.

Separate laws allow state-owned enterprise workers to form unions. The law does not allow civil servants, including public and private schoolteachers and university professors, soldiers, and police, to form or register a union. Civil servants may form and register associations, but these associations do not have the right to bargain collectively

The law restricts affiliations between state-owned enterprise unions and private sector unions as they are governed under two separate laws. The law allows only employees "working for the same employer" or "in the same description of work" to form a union, which limits the ability of contract workers to join unions formed by regular employees. In addition, the law allows employees in private enterprise with more than 50 workers to establish "employee committees" to represent workers' collective requests and to negotiate with employers and "welfare committees" to represent workers' collective request on welfare issues.

The law requires employers to begin negotiating within three days from the time a union submits its demands. If an agreement cannot be reached, the government considers it a labor dispute and begins reconciliation. The law permits workers to strike after an employee has submitted a demand resulting in a deadlock between the employer and employee. Workers must submit a letter of notification at least 24 hours in advance of strike action. The government has the authority to restrict private sector strikes that would affect national security or cause severe negative repercussions for the population at large, but it did not invoke this provision during the year. Employers can charge union leaders with libel for statements made during collective bargaining and strike action if they harm the employer's reputation.

During 2013, the latest year for which such data were available, the Department of Labor Protection and Welfare reported 146 informal conflicts between employers and employees involving 68,715 employees, a decline from 2012 (177 informal conflicts involving 94,124 employees). Of these, 124 conflicts were resolved without walkouts, 10 were referred to a labor court, and nine continued under the Department's process. Most cases referred to a labor court fell under the categories of violations of labor protection laws, breaches of working-condition agreements, and wrongful acts by employers and employees.

The Ministry of Labor is responsible for ensuring that employers adhere to minimum wage requirements in the formal sector, as well as inspecting for working hours, rest time, holiday and sick leave, overtime payment, etc. The ministry also enforces laws related to occupational safety and health. In 2013, the latest year for which such data are available, the ministry employed approximately 600 inspectors for an estimated 356,919 workplaces. It inspected 48,749 workplaces employing 2.1 million workers during 2013, according to ministry statistics, and found 465 workplaces that failed to comply with labor protection laws. By law, employers are subject to fines up to 100,000 baht (USD 3,100) and/or imprisonment up to six months for minimum wage noncompliance, but effective enforcement has varied. The maximum sentence for violations of occupational safety and health regulations is one year's imprisonment and fines not exceeding 400,000 baht (USD 12,000). Labor inspectors' limited resources, practice of interviewing employees at workplace locations that lacked privacy, reliance on document-based inspection, and lack of interpreters to accompany inspection teams resulted in ineffective inspections. There are also reports of significant abuses of the rights of migrant workers in seafood and agricultural supply chains which are difficult to inspect.

On occupational health and safety, the ministry in 2013 inspected 17,672 workplaces employing 1.5 million workers and found 974 workplaces (6 percent) that failed to comply with health and safety regulations. Most of these involved machines; cranes and boilers; health checkups; fire accidents; failure to establish safety committees; and inappropriate levels of heat, light, and noise. According to the Department of Labor Protection and Welfare, the incidence of violations regarding workers' safety was highest in manufacturing, wholesale and retail trade, construction, mining, electricity gas and water supply, and agriculture. While the majority of violations were resolved after the department issued orders to companies to make amends, there were at least 220 legal actions filed by labor inspectors after the employer failed to make amends or pay the required fines.

17. FOREIGN TRADE ZONES/FREE PORTS/TRADE FACILITATION

The Industrial Estate Authority of Thailand (IEAT), a state-enterprise under the Ministry of Industry, established the first industrial estates in Thailand, including Laem Chabang Industrial Estate in Chonburi Province (eastern) and Map Ta Phut Industrial Estate in Rayong Province (eastern). The IEAT was established under the IEAT Act B.E. 2522 (1979). Foreign owned firms have the same investment opportunities as Thai entities, but the IEAT Act requires the IEAT Committee to consider and approve the amount of space/land a foreign owned firm plans to buy or lease in industrial estates. In practice, there is no record of disapproval for the requested amount of land. More recently, private developers have become heavily involved in the development of these estates. The IEAT currently operates 9 estates, plus 39 more in conjunction with the private sector in 15 provinces nationwide. Private sector developers operate over 50 industrial estates, most of which have received promotion privileges from the Board of Investment.

In addition, the IEAT established 12 special IEAT Free Zones (renamed from export processing zones or free trade zones), reserved for the location of industries manufacturing for export only, to which businesses may import raw materials and export finished products free of duty (including value added tax). These zones are located within industrial estates, and many have customs facilities to speed processing. The free trade zones are located in Chonburi, Lampun, Pichit, Songkhla, Samut Prakarn, Bangkok (at Lad Krabang), Ayuddhya, and Chachoengsao. In addition to these zones, factories may apply for permission to establish a bonded warehouse within their premises to which raw materials, used exclusively in the production of products for export, may be imported duty free.

18. FOREIGN DIRECT INVESTMENT AND FOREIGN PORTFOLIO INVESTMENT STATISTICS

Table 2: Key Macroeconomic Data, U.S. FDI in Host Country/Economy

	Host Country Statistical source*		USG or international statistical source		USG or International Source of Data: BEA; IMF; Eurostat; UNCTAD, Other
Economic Data	Year	Amount	Year	Amount	
Host Country Gross Domestic Product (GDP) ($M USD)	2014	373,755	2013	387,300	www.worldbank.org/en/country
Foreign Direct Investment	Host Country Statistical source*		USG or international statistical source		USG or international Source of data:

					BEA; IMF; Eurostat; UNCTAD, Other
U.S. FDI in partner country ($M USD, stock positions)	2014	17,125	2013	14,428	BEA data available 3/19/14 athttp://bea.gov/international/direct_investment_ multinational_companies_comprehensive_data.htm
Host country's FDI in the United States ($M USD, stock positions)	2014	3,812	Not available		BEA data available 3/19/14 athttp://bea.gov/international/direct_investment_ multinational_companies_comprehensive_data.htm
Total inbound stock of FDI as % host GDP	2014	207,318	N/A		55.5%

* The National Economic and Social Development Board for GDP, and the Bank of Thailand for investment data

Table 3: Sources and Destination of FDI

Direct Investment from/in Counterpart Economy Data					
From Top Five Sources/To Top Five Destinations (US Dollars, Millions)					
Inward Direct Investment			Outward Direct Investment		
Total Inward	178,221	100%	Total Outward	56,602	100%
Japan	63,028	35%	Cayman Islands	6,741	12%
Singapore	26,629	15%	Mauritius	5,153	9%
United States	13,847	8%	China, Hong Kong	4,480	8%
Netherlands	11,412	6%	Singapore	4,332	8%
China, Hong Kong	7,861	4%	China, Mainland	4,073	7%
"0" reflects amounts rounded to +/- USD 500,000.					

Source: IMF Coordinated Direct investment Survey

Table 4: Sources of Portfolio Investment

Portfolio Investment Assets								
Top Five Partners (Millions, US Dollars)								
Total			Equity Securities			Total Debt Securities		
All Countries	35,137	100%	All Countries	9,982	100%	All Countries	25,155	100%
China, Hong Kong	5,460	16%	United States	4,125	41%	China, Hong Kong	4,985	20%
United States	5,012	14%	Luxembourg	2,243	22%	China, Mainland	2,848	11%
China, Mainland	3,118	9%	Australia	506	5%	Turkey	2,592	10%
Korea, Republic of	2,633	7%	China, Hong Kong	475	5%	Korea, Republic of	2,577	10%
Turkey	2,593	7%	Cayman Islands	459	5%	Brazil	2,498	10%

Source: IMF Coordinated Portfolio Investment Survey

IMPORTANT BUSINESS CONTACTS

CONTACT FOR MORE INFORMATION

Dean Matlack
Commercial Attaché

U.S. Embassy Bangkok
+662 205-5263
Dean.Matlack@trade.gov

LIST OF ATTORNEYS

Bangkok
1. A1 Litigation/Mackenzie Smith Law
Offices in Bangkok and Pattaya.
6/8 Somkid Place, Soi Somkid
Ploenchit Road, Lumpini, Pratumwan
Bangkok 10330
Contact:
Phone: (66) (2) 255-6496/98
Fax: (66) (2) 225-5185/3
Email: info@a1litigation.com or
info@macsmlaw.com
Website: www.macsmlaw.com
Fields of Specialization

* Civil and Criminal litigation
* Business consulting
* Commercial dispute resolution
* Commercial property law
* Banking/financial consulting
* Residential property law
* Arbitration/mediation
* Employment labor disputes
* Immigration
* Marriages and Divorces

Notes: Provides translation services.
Handles cases outside of Bangkok

American Embassy
Bangkok, Thailand
American Citizen Services Unit
95 Wireless Road, Bangkok 10330
Telephone: (66) (2) 205-4049, Fax: (66) (2) 205-4103
Website: http://bangkok.usembassy.gov Email: acsbkk@state.gov

2. Advance Adjusting Associates Co. Ltd.
100/119, 122 1st Fl. Liberty Plaza Building
Sukhumvit Soi 55 (Tong-Law), Klongton Nua
Wattana, Bangkok 10110
Contact: John Sobell
Phone: (66) (2) 381-9090-1
Fax: (66) (2) 715-9499
Email: sobell@aaacoth.com
Website: http://www.aaacoth.com

Fields of Specialization

* Aeronautical/ Maritime
* Auto Accidents
* Child Custody
* Collections
* Contracts
* Civil Damages
* Corporations
* Estates
* Foreign Claims
* Foreign Investments
* Government Relations
* Immigration
* Insurance
* Marketing Agreements
* Marriages and Divorces
* Mining and Petroleum
* Capital Cases
* Private Investigation
* Patents, Trademarks, Copyrights
* Raw Material Investments

Notes: Provides translation services
Handles cases outside of Bangkok
Does not handle narcotics trafficking cases
3. Baker & McKenzie
Unit 2601, 5th, 22nd-25th Floor
990 Abdulrahim Place

Rama IV, Silom, Bangrak
Bangkok 10500
Contact: John W. Hancock
Phone: (66) (2) 636-2000
Fax: (66) (2) 636-2111
Email: bangkok.info@bakernet.com
Website: http://www.bakermckenzie.com

Fields of Specialization

* Aeronautical / Maritime
* Banking / Finance
* Commercial
* Corporate
* Foreign Claims & Investment
* Government Relations
* Immigration
* Insurance
* Marketing Agreements
* Mining and Petroleum
* Patents, Trademarks, Copyrights
* Raw Material Investments
* Taxation
* Trade Disputes

Notes: Does not provide translation services
Does not handle cases outside of Bangkok
An international firm with 65 offices in cities around the world

4. Bamrung, Suvicha, Apisakdi Law Associates
155/19 Soi Mahadlekluang 1
Rajdamri Road, Lumpini, Patumwan
Bangkok 10330
Contact: Bamrung Tavehittiwatana
Phone: (66) (2) 252-1566, 652-2815-9
Fax: (66) (2) 253-9575
Email: bsalaw@access.inet.co.th

Fields of Specialization

* Aeronautical / Maritime
* Auto Accidents
* Banking & Finance
* Collections
* Contracts
* Civil Damages
* Corporations
* Estates
* Foreign Claims & Investments
* Government Relations
* Immigration
* Insurance
* Marriages and Divorces
* Narcotics & Capital Cases
* Private Investigation
* Patents, Trademarks, Copyrights
* Raw Material Investments
* Marketing Agreements
* Mining and Petroleum
* Taxation & Trade Disputes

Notes: Provides services of a translator
Handles cases outside of Bangkok
Does not handle child custody or adoption cases
Has legal relationship with U.S. firms of Gelles & Lawrence in Los Angeles, California and Radon & Ishizumi of New York, New York.

5. Bangkok Lawyer Limited Partnership
No. 1 Zuellig House, Level 8 & 9
Silom Road, Bangrak
Bangkok 10500
Contact: Noppamart Thammateeradaycho
Phone: (66) (2) 231-8390, 152-3195
Mobile: (66) 84-160-0985
Fax: (66) (2) 231-8391
Email: expatlawyer@gmail.com notarybkk@gmail.com
Website www.thailand-english-speaking-lawyer.com

Fields of Specialization

* Criminal
* Narcotics
* Divorce
* Extradition
* Personal injury
* Child Custody & Adoption

6. Bangkok Legal Associates, Ltd.
140/40 Suite A, ITF Tower, 19th Floor
140/38 Silom Road, Bangrak
Bangkok 10500
Contact: Puttri Kuvanonda
Phone: (66) (2) 231-6096
Fax: (66) (2) 231-6099
Email: blalaw@hotmail.com
Website:

Fields of Specialization

* Aeronautical / Maritime
* Auto Accidents
* Banking & Finance
* Child Custody
* Civil Damages
* Collections
* Contracts
* Corporations
* Estates
* Foreign Claims & Investments
* Government Relations
* Immigration & Labor Relations
* Insurance
* Marketing Agreements
* Marriages and Divorces
* Mining and Petroleum
* Narcotics
* Patents, Trademarks, Copyrights
* Raw Material Investments
* Theft / Fraud / Embezzlement

7. Chandler & Thong-Ek
Bubhajit Building, 7th Floor
20 North Sathorn Road, Silom
Bangrak, Bangkok 10500
Contact: Albert T. Chandler
Phone: (66) (2) 266-6485
Fax: (66) (2) 266-6483-4
Email: atchandler@ctlo.com
Website: http://ctlo.com

Fields of Specialization

* Banking & Finance
* Construction
* Corporate Restructuring
* Dispute Resolution
* International Banking
* Internat'l Business Transactions
* Investment Promotion
* Joint Ventures
* Mergers & Acquisitions
* Mining and Petroleum
* Real Estate
* Securities
* Taxation

8. Chaninat & Leeds Co.,Ltd.
Suite 10/154 Trendy Office Bldg.
18th Fl. Sukhumvit Rd. Soi 13
Klontoey Nua Vadhana
Bangkok 10110 Joe Leeds
Phone: (66) (2) 168-7001
Fax: (66) (2) 168-7004
E-Mail: info@chaninatandleeds.com
Website: www.chaninatandleeds.com
Fields of Specialization

* Civil Damages, Accidents & Lawsuits
* Collection
* Commercial Trade Disputes
* Company Formation and Licenses
* Contracts
* Criminal Defense and Prosecution
* Family
* Inheritance, Probate and Estate Law
* Investigation and Surveillance
* Labor Law and Employment Disputes
* Litigation/Arbitration
* Patents, Trademark, Copyrights
* Record Searches and Administrative
* US Immigration Law

Notes: The firm, comprised of American and Thai lawyers, handles cases in Bangkok and surrounding areas. The firm's staff includes attorneys, accountants, investigators, paralegals and translators.
9. Clifford Chance (Thailand) Limited
Floor 21
Sindhorn Building, Tower 3
130-132 Wireless Road
Pathumwan
Bangkok 10330
Contact: Fergus Evans
Phone: (66)(2) 401-8810
Fax: (66)(2) 401-8801
Email: Fergus.evans@cliffordchance.com
Website: www.cliffordchance.com

Fields of Specialization

* Banking & Finance
* Commercial and corporate
* Property
* Internat'l Business Transactions
* Investment
* Maritime and aviation
* Trade
* Securities

Notes: Provides Translation
Offices in Singapore, Hong Kong, Beijing, Shanghai, Tokyo, England and Wales (UK), New York and Washington D.C.
Does not handle narcotics issues, child custody or adoption

10. Dej-Udom & Associates, Ltd.
Charn Isara Tower, 9th Floor
942/ 142-3 Rama Road IV
Bangkok 10500
Contact: Jane Purananandа
Phone: (66) (2) 233-0055
Fax: (66) (2) 236-6681
Email: dej-udom@dejudom.com

Fields of Specialization

* Arbitration & Litigation
* Banking & Finance
* Foreign Investment in Thailand
* General Practice
* Government Relations
* Internat'l Commercial Contracts
* Internat'l Securities Transactions
* Immigration
* Intellectual Property Rights
* Joint Venture Projects
* Labor Issues
* Patents, Trademarks, Copyrights
* Property Development
* Taxation
* Work Permits
*

Notes: Provides translation services
Provides court translation services
Handles cases outside of Bangkok

11. DFDL Mekong Bangkok
9th Floor the Dusit Thani Building
946 Rama IV, Silom
Bangkok 10500
Contact: David Doran
Phone: (66) (2) 636 3282
Fax: (66) (2) 636 3290
Website: www.dfdlmekong.com
12. The Dharmniti International Co., Ltd
2/4 Nai Lert Tower, 4th Floor
Wireless Road, Lumpini, Pratumwan
Bangkok 10330
Contact Pichai Puchmongkol
Phone: (66) (2) 680-9777
Fax: (66) (2) 655-0429
Website: http://www.dlo.co.th

Fields of Specialization

* Adoption
* Auto Accidents
* Child Custody
* Civil Damages
* Contracts
* Collections
* Corporations
* Estates
* Foreign Claims
* Foreign Investment
* Government Relations
* Immigration
* Insurance
* Maritime / Aviation
* Narcotics & Capital Cases
* Private Investigation
* Patents, Trademarks, Copyrights
* Taxation
* Theft / Fraud / Embezzlement
* Visas / Work Permits

Notes: Provides translation services. Handles cases outside of Bangkok.
13. Marut Bunnag International Law Office
Forum Tower, 22nd Floor
184/130-136 Ratchadaphisek Road
Huaykwang, Bangkok 10320
Contact: Rujira Bunnag
Phone: (66) (2) 645-2556-67
Fax: (66) (2) 645-2568
Email: marut@loxinfo.co.th
Website: http://www.marut.th.com
Fields of Specialization

* Arbitration & Litigation
* Criminal
* Commercial Issues
* Factory Licensing
* Immigration & Labor
* Insurance
* Internat'l Business Transactions
* Joint Ventures
* Maritime Law
* Patent / Copyright / Trademarks

14. Natee International Law Office, Ltd.
Alma Link Building, 16th Floor
25 Soi Chidlom, Ploenchit Road
Bangkok 10330
Contact: Natee Thongdee
Phone: (66) (2) 655-5425
Fax: (66) (2) 253-6994
Email: nilo@ksc.th.com
Website: http://www.nateelaw.com
Fields of Specialization

* Administrative Law
* Banking & Securities
* Construction & Real Estate
* Contracts / Joint Ventures
* Corporate Law & Finance
* Taxation
* Immigration
* Intellectual Property
* International Law
* Investment Promotion
* Labor Law

15. Siam Firm Inter Laws Limited
120/7 Sukhumvit Soi 23, Sukhumvit Road
Klongtoey Nua District
Wattana District, Bangkok 10110
Contact : Mr. Somsak Chopaka
Phone : (+66) 02 260 3025 to 27
Fax : (+66) 02 260 3028
Mobile : (+66) 081 808 9175
Email : somsak@siamfirm.co.th
info@siamfirm.co.th
Website : www.siamfirm.co.th

Fields of Specialization

* Litigation
* Criminal Law
* Civil Law
* Family Law
* General Practice
* Work Permit
* Notary Republic
*

16. Tilleke & Gibbins
Supalai Grand Tower 26th Floor
1011 Rama 3 Road, Chongnonsi
Yannawa, Bangkok 10120
Contact: David Lyman
Phone: (66) (2) 653-5555
Fax: (66) (2) 653-5678
Email: chitchai.p@tillekeandgibbins.com
Website: http://www.tillekeandgibbins.com

Fields of Specialization

* Aviation / Insurance
* Banking & Finance
* Capital Cases
* Commercial Trade Disputes
* Communications
* Corporate Services
* Criminal
* Dispute Resolution
* General Litigation
* Human Resources
* Intellectual Property
* International Trade
* Maritime
* Minerals Resources / Energy
* Private Client Services
* Real Property / Construction

Notes: Provides services of a translator.
Handles cases outside Bangkok.
Clients: USAID, US Peace Corps, American Family Life Assurance Company, Ltd., Export-Import, Bank of the United States, United Parcel Service of America, Inc., Syntex (USA) Inc., American Home Products Corporation, AT&T (Thailand), Unocal Corporation, The Coca-Cola Company, Coca-Cola Export Corporation, Universal Foods Corporation, Ltd., Kimberly Clark Corporation, Eastman Kodak Company, Samsonite Corporation, Stanhome Inc., The Textile Museum (Washington, DC).
17. Vickery & Worachai, Ltd.
16th Floor, GPF Witthayu
93/1 Wireless Road
Bangkok 10300
Contact: Worchai Bhicharnchitr
Phone: (66) (2) 256-6311
Fax: (66) (2) 256-6317
Email: vwlaw@loxinfo.co.th

Fields of Specialization

* Aeronautical / Maritime
* Auto Accidents
* Civil Damages
* Contracts
* Corporations
* Estates
* Foreign Investments
* Government Relations
* Immigration
* Insurance
* Labor Relations
* Marketing Agreements
* Mining and Petroleum
* Patents/ Trademarks/ Copyrights
* Taxation
* Trade Disputes

Notes: Does not provide translation services.
Does not handle cases outside of Bangkok.
Clients: American Brands, Inc., Brown & Root, Inc., The Chubb Corp., Connell Bros, Co. (Thailand) Ltd., DigitalEquipment Corp., The Firestone Tire and Rubber Co., Flour-Daniel, Inc., General Electric Co., Foot-Joy, Inc., Johnson & Johnson, Kodak Far East Purchasing Co. Inc., Korn/Perry International, Unocal Corp., Esso Standard (Thailand) Ltd.
Investigative & Security Services
First Services
P.O. Box 42
Ban Krut Post Office

Prachuap Kirikhan 77190
Contact: Byron Bales / Kasama Buppaves Bales
Phone: (032) 695 555
Fax: (032) 695 456
E-mail: Kasama@firstpi.com / ByronBales@firstpi.com
Website: www.firstpi.com

Fields of Specialization	
* Trial Preparation	* Assets Investigations
* Due Diligence	* Competitive Intelligence Analysis
* Directors & Officers Liability	* Technical Surveillance Counter Measures (TSCM)
* Insurance Claims; Life & Health, Property & Casualty, Travel Insurance	* Private Investigations; Backgrounds, Locates, Document Retrieval, Surveillances, Service of Process

Notes: Legal services provided.
Handles cases in Thailand and worldwide.
International scope
U.S. Offices: First Services / New York, 216 9th Street, Suite 300, Brooklyn, NY 11215
Tel: (718)369-6300, Fax: (718) 369-7443
International Offices: Cancun / San Diego-Tijuana / Guadalajara / Bogota / London / Accra / Cairo / Damascus / Cochin / Manila / Qingdao.
Clients: Most U.S. L & H Companies; Swedish, British, Hong Kong, Australia L & H, Travel, and P & C Insurers, bankers and manufacturers.

Law Firms Outside Bangkok

Huahin	Siam Inter Law 13/59 Soi Huahin 47/1 Petkasem Rd., Huahin Prackjuabkirikhan 77110 Contact: Mr. Somsak Chopaka Phone: (+66) 02 260 3025 to 27 Mobile: (+66) 081 808 9175 Fax: (+66) 032 531 509 Website: www.siamfirm.co.th somsak@siamfirm.co.th Email: info@siamfirm.co.th
Pattaya/Chonburi	K-T International Law Office 183/14 Moo.1 Soi Post Office Nongprue, Banglamung Chonburi 20260 Contact: Sathaporn Sriyoha Phone: (66) (38) 710-612, 710-252 Mobile: (66) (1) 914-2282 Fax: (66) (38) 710-611 Email: sriyoha55@hotmail.com
Pattaya/Chonburi	Siam Inter Law 448/10 Moo 12 Theprasit, Nongprue Banglamung, Chonburi 20150 Contact: Mr. Somsak Chopaka Phone: (+66) 032 531 508 Mobile: (+66) 081 808 9175 Fax: (+66) 038 906 724 Email: somsak@siamfirm.co.th info@siamfirm.co.th Website: www.siamfirm.co.th
Pattaya/Chonburi	Thai Lawuit & Int'l Consulting Co. Ltd. 65/2 Therapasit Road, Moo 12 Nongprue, Banglamung, Chonburi 20150 Contact: Paisan Thunnok Phone: 038-301-015 Mobile: 086-867-8017 Fax: Email:

Pattaya/Chonburi	Thai Inter Law Consultants 20/26-27, Village No. 10 Day-Night Hotel Street South Pattaya Road Nongprue Sub District Banglamang District Chonburi 20150 Contact: Katrena Wonnasakda Phone: (66) (38) 425-269, 421-725 Fax: (66) (38) 723-624 Email: Thai_int_law@yahoo.co.th
Phuket	DFDL Mekong Phuket 100/208-210 Moo 3 Kamala, Kathu Phuket 83150 Phone: (66) (76) 279 921-4 Fax: (66) (76) 279 926 E-mail: Phuket@dfdlmekong.com Website: www.dfdlmekong.com
Phuket	Suporn, Surat & Associates 25/55 Chaofa Road Muang District Phuket 83000 Contact: Eric Snyder Phone: (66) (76) 222-424 , 223-498 Fax: (66) (76) 224-648 E-mail: jairak@phuket.ksc.co.th
Phuket	Vithaya Isaramalai 67/19 Ras U-Thit 200 Years Rd. Patong, Katoo Phuket 83150 Contact: Vithaya Isaramalai Phone: (66) (76) 340-999 Fax: (66) (76) 342-220 E-mail: ivithaya@hotmail.com
Krabi	Sanya Kiowkhong 387/4 Uttarakit Road Pak Nam, Muang District Krabi 81000 Contact: Sanya Kiowkhong Phone: (66) (75) 611-317 Fax: (66) (75) 611-451
Nakorn Ratchasima	Korat Lawyers 358 Po-Krang, Tambon Nai-maung Ampur Muang Nakorn Ratchasima 30000 Contact: Sebastian Brousseau Mobile Phone: (66) (87) 225-1340 Fax: (66) (44) 245-265

VIETNAM INVESTMENT AND BUSINESS CLIMATE - STRATEGIC INFORMATION AND CONTACTS FOR STARTING BUSINESS

Vietnam continues to improve its business climate to attract foreign direct investment (FDI), and has sustained registered FDI of roughly USD 17 billion per year over the last five years. In 2014 Vietnam successfully attracted new investment from world class IT companies including Samsung, Nokia, and LG. Investors commonly cite Vietnam's geographic proximity to global supply chains, relative political and economic stability, expected benefits from completion of the Trans-Pacific Partnership (TPP) trade agreement, and an increasing desire to diversify their manufacturing base in Asia away from China as reasons for investing in Vietnam.

In 2014, Vietnam continued to take concrete steps to improve the investment climate and further integrate into the global economy. It revised several key related laws including the Enterprise Law, the Investment Law, the Bankruptcy Law, in addition to the new Housing Law, and Real Estate Business Law. The State Bank of Vietnam (SBV) worked hard to stabilize the banking sector and maintain the stability of the Vietnamese Dong (VND). The Government of Vietnam (GVN) moved forward with its ambitious plan to equitize over 500 state-owned enterprises (SOEs) by the end of 2015. On the trade front, Vietnam continued to advance negotiations on six separate trade agreements, among which include the TPP and the European Union FTA, which it hopes to conclude in 2015.

While many international companies consider Vietnam an increasingly attractive destination, significant challenges remain. Problems include corruption, a weak legal infrastructure, a shortage of skilled workers to meet the needs of the IT and other sectors, continued land use limitations, the slow pace of SOE reform, and the need for better infrastructure and more reliable access to power. While businesses applaud the economic reforms made to date, more is needed to significantly increase FDI inflows.

1. OPENNESS TO, AND RESTRICTIONS UPON, FOREIGN INVESTMENT

Attitude toward Foreign Direct Investment

Vietnam is serious about attracting foreign investment, especially in sectors that will bring advanced technology and improve Vietnam's labor productivity. Vietnam's attractiveness as an FDI destination has grown as the country has made key legal reforms related to the business climate. Other draws are Vietnam's stable political system, strategic location near global supply chains, and an abundant labor force that is significantly less expensive than that of China.

Foreign invested companies continue to play an important role in the economy. The FDI sector contributed 62 percent of total exports in 2014, up from 47 percent in 2000, and foreign invested enterprises' contribution to GDP increased to 18 percent from 13 percent over the same period. Vietnam has maintained registered FDI levels of around USD 17 billion per year over the last five years. Conclusion of any or all of Vietnam's six active trade agreement negotiations -- the TPP, the Regional Comprehensive Economic Partnership (RCEP), the Vietnam-EU FTA, the Vietnam-Eurasian Customs Union FTA, the Vietnam-Republic of Korea FTA, and the Vietnam-European Free Trade Area FTA -- would open the door for a considerable increase in FDI. Additionally, by the end of 2015 Vietnam aims to fully integrate into the ASEAN Economic Community (AEC), which likely will increase foreign investment from their ASEAN neighbors. While Vietnam has made great effort to connect to the global supply chain and is committed to improving the business environment, it remains a developing economy with many areas for improvement. Key challenges include corruption and weak legal infrastructure, a shortage of skilled labor that can meet the demands of an increasingly sophisticated global market, low labor productivity, and a cumbersome bureaucracy that still focuses on monitoring and control rather than business facilitation.

In 2014, the United States was the 11th largest source country for FDI with a total investment of USD 259 million, up from 15th in 2013. South Korea, Japan, and Singapore, are consistently the top three foreign investors in Vietnam. FDI from China excluding Hong Kong decreased from USD 2.2 billion in registered capital in 2013 to USD 427 million in 2014.

Other Investment Policy Reviews

The first official WTO review of Vietnam's trade policies and practices took place September 17, 2013:**http://www.wto.org/english/tratop_e/tpr_e/tp387_e.htm**.

The government of Vietnam holds regular meetings with the private sector to discuss issues that will affect the private sector. One such forum, the Vietnam Business Forum, published an annual report in 2014:**http://www.vbf.org.vn/en/documentation-center/doc_download/1548-annual-vbf-2014-full-report-eng-reprint.html**

UNCTAD's Investment Policy Review was done in 2008. **http://unctad.org/en/Docs/iteipc200710_en.pdf**

OECD's Investment Policy Review was published in 2010. **http://www.oecd.org/countries/vietnam/vietnam-investmentpolicyreview-oecd.htm**

World Bank Fiscal Transparency Report: **http://www-wds.worldbank.org/external/default/WDSContentServer/WDSP/IB/2014/05/23/000333037_20140523121829/Rendered/PDF/882730WP0P12870iew0Final0May0210ENG.pdf**

Laws/Regulations of Foreign Direct Investment

In December 2014 Vietnam passed a new Investment Law with breakthrough changes aimed at improving the investment environment. Previously, Vietnam used a "positive list" approach, meaning that foreign businesses were only allowed to operate in a list of specific sectors outlined by law. Starting in July 2015, Vietnam will use a "negative list" approach, meaning that foreign businesses will be allowed to operate in all areas except for six prohibited sectors. Additionally, there are 267 conditional sectors that are now technically open to foreign investment but will require an investment license.

Under the new Investment Law, companies must apply for an investment license when establishing a new company, and update their business license when they: 1) make significant changes to an ongoing enterprise, such as increasing investment capital; 2) restructure the form of investment or investment ratios between foreign and domestic partners, 3) change the foreign management structure, or 4) add new business activities. The new law also says that foreign and domestic investors are treated the same in cases of nationalization and confiscation. However, foreign investors are subject to different business licensing processes and restrictions, and Vietnamese companies that have a majority foreign investment are subject to foreign investor business license procedures.

Conformity with Economic Master Plans

As restated in the new Investment Law, most FDI projects must conform to one or more sectorial master plans. Master plans are economic development policies that set five- to ten-year targets for an industry. The requirement for projects to conform to relevant master plans is potentially problematic for foreign investors, as the grounds for assessing compliance with a particular plan are unclear, and master plans may overlap as they are issued by both ministries at the national and provincial level.

Industrial Promotion

Vietnam promotes foreign investment in certain priority sectors and geographical regions, such as mountainous and remote areas of the country with difficult economic and social conditions. The government encourages investment in production of new materials, new energy sources, metallurgy and chemical industries, manufacturing of high-tech products, biotechnology, information technology, mechanical engineering, agricultural, fishery and forestry production, salt production, generation of new plant varieties and animal species, ecology and environmental protection, research and development, knowledge-based services, processing and manufacturing, labor-intensive projects (using 5,000 or more full-time laborers), infrastructure projects, education, training, and health and sports development.

Limits on Foreign Control

The ratio of total foreign ownership permitted in a project depends on a number of factors, including Vietnam's international commitments and the economic sector in question. There are also strict foreign ownership limitations for certain listed companies and service sectors. Foreign investors must negotiate on a case by case basis with the government on market access in sectors that are not explicitly open through a trade or investment agreement.

In addition, the lack of substantive regulations on M&A activities makes such transactions risky. For example, when a foreign investor buys into a local company through an M&A transaction, it is difficult to predict which business lines the acquired company is allowed to maintain as the government does not explicitly announce which sectors are not subject to the restrictions on foreign investment outside of WTO requirements.

Privatization Program

The GVN has a publicly stated goal of equitizing (i.e. convert SOEs to joint stock companies) more than 500 SOEs by the end of 2015. Foreign investors are allowed to buy shares in SOEs in accordance with WTO commitments. Investors can buy shares through a public auction, or invest as a strategic shareholder. The government has certain requirements to become a strategic shareholder, and prioritizes companies that can transfer technology or expertise to the SOE.

The low percentage of shares sold of many equitized firms has led many to question whether equitization will result in real changes in the operation of SOEs. For example, in their recent Initial Public Offering, Vietnam Airlines (VNA) equitized just 3.5 percent of its overall market capital. To date many foreign investors have been hesitant to invest in SOEs due to small percentages of equity being sold, lack of transparency, and unclear management structure.

Screening of FDI

Vietnamese authorities evaluate investment license applications using a number of criteria, including: 1) the legal status and financial capabilities of the investors; 2) the project's compatibility with Vietnam's "Master Plan" for economic and social development; projected revenue; 3) technology and expertise; 4) environmental protection; 5) plans for land use and land clearance compensation; 6) project incentives including tax rates, and 7) land, water, and sea surface rental fees.

Decentralization of licensing authority to provincial authorities has in some cases streamlined the licensing process and reduced processing times. It has also, however, given rise to considerable regional differences in procedures and interpretations of investment laws and regulations. Insufficient guidelines and unclear regulations sometimes cause local authorities to consult national authorities, creating delays. In addition, the approval process is often much longer than the time frame established by law. Many U.S. firms have invested successfully, though a lack of transparency in the procedure for obtaining a business license at times makes participation in investment opportunities too risky for companies that comply with the U.S. Foreign Corrupt Practices Act.

Investment projects that must be approved by the National Assembly include:

Projects with a large environmental impact,

Projects that change the land usage purpose in national parks

Projects located in protective forests larger than 50 hectares

Projects that require relocating 20,000 people in remote areas such as mountainous regions.

Investment projects that require Prime Ministerial approval include:

Projects to build airports and seaports; casinos; explore, produce and process oil and gas; produce tobacco;

Projects having investment capital more than 5,000 billion VND (USD 233 million);

Projects invested by foreign investors in sea transportation, telecommunication with network infrastructure, forest plantation, publishing, press and;

100 percent foreign-owned scientific and technology companies or organizations.

Projects which are not approved by the National Assembly or the Prime Minister will be approved by the provincial People's Committee.

Competition Law

The Vietnam Competition Administration (VCA) of the Ministry of Industry and Trade (MOIT) reviews transactions for competition-related concerns. In 2013, the VCA launched 12 investigations related to competition restriction, and data for 2014 is not yet available. The VCA continues to receive and process M&A cases in crucial sectors of the economy such as food processing and trading; production, trading and transmission of electricity; and import, export and distribution of steel, and in all cases the VCA did not allow the mergers to go through.

Investment Trends

Manufacturing dominates FDI inflows as investors continue to move large scale operations from other developing countries. In 2014 major investments were increasingly high in technological content, as seen in assembly facility investments by Intel, Samsung, Nokia and LG. This result is in line with Vietnam's strategic efforts to shift FDI from low-end manufacturing to the high tech sector. In 2014 the textiles and apparel industries also witnessed a significant wave of investment in anticipation of the conclusion of the Trans-Pacific Partnership. Investment in infrastructure, such as power generation, roads, railways and water treatment, is on the rise. Vietnam needs an estimated USD 170 billion in additional infrastructure development in order to meet growing economic demand.

Table 1

Measure	Year	Index or Rank	Website Address
TI Corruption Perceptions index	2014	119 of 175	transparency.org/cpi2014/results
World Bank's Doing Business Report "Ease of Doing Business"	2014	78 of 189	doingbusiness.org/rankings

Global Innovation Index	2014	71 of 143	globalinnovationindex.org/content.aspx?page=data-analysis
World Bank GNI per capita	2013	USD 1,740	data.worldbank.org/indicator/NY.GNP.PCAP.CD

Millennium Challenge Corporation Country Scorecard

The Millennium Challenge Corporation, a U.S. Government entity charged with delivering development grants to countries that have demonstrated a commitment to reform, produced scorecards for countries with a per capita gross national income (GNI) or USD 4,125 or less. A list of countries/economies with MCC scorecards and links to those scorecards is available here: **http://www.mcc.gov/pages/selection/scorecards**. Details on each of the MCC's indicators and a guide to reading the scorecards are available here: **http://www.mcc.gov/pages/docs/doc/report-guide-to-the-indicators-and-the-selection-process-fy-2015**.

2. CONVERSION AND TRANSFER POLICIES

Foreign Exchange

The Vietnamese Dong (VND) has been stable over the last two years as the State Bank of Vietnam (SBV) has prioritized stability in order to reduce dollarization and the use of gold. There is some concern headed into 2015 regarding what effect an appreciating U.S. dollar might have on the VND. The GVN generally does not provide foreign currency conversion guarantees to foreign investors.

The SBV publishes daily average interbank exchange rates, and allows USD/VND transactions within a trading band, maintaining a trading band of +/-1 percent since February 2011. The SBV does not typically publish foreign reserves, but the SBV Governor announced in late 2014 that in September 2014 foreign reserves exceeded USD 35 billion.

As part of its efforts to de-dollarize the economy, the GVN issued Decree 70 in 2014 to prohibit foreigners, residents and non-residents, from holding foreign currency in foreign currency denominated savings accounts. Foreigners are, however, still allowed to have checking accounts and investment accounts in any foreign currency and VND (previously foreigners were only allowed to have USD investment accounts).

According to the 2005 Ordinance on Foreign Exchange Control, currency transactions between residents must be conducted in VND. Exporters must remit all foreign currency earnings into a foreign currency account with an authorized credit institution in Vietnam. Retaining foreign currency earnings overseas requires SBV approval. Any resident or institution permitted to conduct offshore investment must open a foreign currency account at an authorized credit institution and register the account with the SBV.

Transfers of currency are protected by Article VII of the International Monetary Fund (IMF) Articles of Agreement (**http://www.imf.org/External/Pubs/FT/AA/index.htm#art7**)

Remittance Policies

The GVN allows foreign businesses to remit profits, capital contributions, and other legal revenues derived from their investment activities in Vietnam in hard currency. Outward foreign currency transactions require certain supporting documents (such as import/foreign service procurement contracts and proof of tax obligation fulfillment, etc.).

Bureau of International Narcotics and Law Enforcement's 2014 International Narcotics Control Strategy Report (INCSR) at**http://www.state.gov/j/inl/rls/nrcrpt/2014/database/index.htm**.

3. EXPROPRIATION AND COMPENSATION

Under the U.S.-Vietnam Bilateral Trade Agreement (BTA), Vietnam must apply international standards of treatment in any case of expropriation or nationalization of U.S. investor assets, which includes acting in a non-discriminatory manner with due process of law and with prompt, adequate and effective compensation. The U.S. Mission is monitoring four foreign investment expropriation cases without just compensation. Several foreign investors have reported that provincial or the national government pressured them to increase the pace of project development or to raise additional project capital or risk losing their investment license.

4. DISPUTE SETTLEMENT

Legal System, Specialized Courts, Judicial Independence, Judgments of Foreign Courts

The hierarchy of Vietnamese People's Courts includes: (1) the Supreme People's Court; (2) Provincial People's Courts; and (3) District People's Courts. The People's Courts operate in five divisions: criminal, civil, administrative, economic, and labor. Parallel to the court systems is the People's Procuracy, which is responsible for supervising judicial operations. The People's Procuracy can protest a judgment or ask for a review of a case. In addition, Vietnam has a system of independent arbitration centers established under the Commercial Arbitration Ordinance of 2003 that can grant enforceable arbitral awards.

Vietnam's legal system remains underdeveloped and ineffective in settling disputes. Negotiation between concerned parties is the most common means of dispute resolution. The Law on Arbitration does not allow a foreign investor to refer an investment dispute to a court in a foreign jurisdiction, and Vietnamese judges cannot apply foreign laws to a case before them, and foreign lawyers cannot represent plaintiffs in a court of law.

Vietnamese courts will only consider recognition of civil judgments issued by courts in countries that have entered into agreements on recognition of judgments with Vietnam or on a reciprocal basis. However, with the exception of France, these treaties only cover non-commercial judgments.

Under the 2005 Civil Code, all contracts are "civil contracts" subject to uniform rules. In foreign civil contracts, parties may choose foreign laws as a reference for their agreement, provided that the application of the law does not violate the basic principles of Vietnamese law. In addition, commercial contracts between businesses are regulated by the 2005 Commercial Law.

Bankruptcy

In 2014 Vietnam revised its Bankruptcy Law to make it easier for companies to declare bankruptcy. The new law clarifies the definition of insolvency as an enterprise that is more than 3 months overdue in meeting its payment obligations. The new law also provides provisions for when creditors can commence bankruptcy proceedings against an enterprise, and created for the first time procedures for credit institutions to file for bankruptcy. The new bankruptcy law is important as 58,322 companies suspended operations in Vietnam in 2014, up 14.5 percent over last year. However, in the past very few businesses formally declared bankruptcy as there were few benefits to doing so, and most companies either ceased operations or sold their businesses. According to the World Bank's 2015 Ease of Doing Business report, it takes five years on average to conclude a bankruptcy case in Vietnam, and the recovery rate is only 18 percent, which is half that of many other East Asia Pacific countries.

Investment Disputes

In January 2014, the Prime Minister named the Ministry of Justice (MOJ) as the government's legal representative in dealing with international investment disputes, while the Ministry of Finance (MOF) resolves disputes related to government loans, debts, and guarantees. The Vietnam International Arbitration Center (VIAC) handled 99 cases in 2013, up from 16 cases in 2003.

Under the investment chapter of the U.S.-Vietnam Bilateral Trade Agreement, U.S. investors have the right to choose a variety of third-party dispute settlement mechanisms in the event of an investment dispute with the government. Vietnam has not yet acceded to the Convention on the Settlement of Investment Disputes between States and Nationals of other States (ICSID), but has asked the United States to provide technical assistance in this area. The Ministry of Planning and Investment (MPI) has submitted a proposal to the government to join the ICSID, but this is still under consideration.

International Arbitration

The arbitration regime in Vietnam is still developing and awaits the issuance of implementation guidelines and regulations for the Arbitration Law. In 2014, the Ho Chi Minh City Economic Court recognized and enforced an arbitral award in Vietnam against an SOE. This is considered a healthy precedent, though the ruling is under appeal.

The Law on Commercial Arbitration took effect in 2011. At present, there are no foreign arbitration centers in Vietnam, though the Arbitration Law permits foreign arbitration centers to establish branches or representative offices. Foreign and domestic arbitral awards are legally enforceable in Vietnam, although in practice it can be very difficult.

ICSID Convention and New York Convention

Vietnam is a party to the New York Convention on the Recognition and Enforcement of Foreign Arbitral Awards, meaning that foreign arbitral awards rendered by a recognized international arbitration institution should be respected by Vietnamese courts without a review of cases' merits. Only a limited number of foreign awards have been submitted to the Ministry of Justice (MOJ) and local courts for enforcement so far, and almost none have successfully made it through the appeals process to full enforcement.

Duration of Dispute Resolution

The court system in Vietnam works slowly. International arbitration awards, when enforced, may take years from original judgment to payment.

5. PERFORMANCE REQUIREMENTS AND INVESTMENT INCENTIVES

WTO/TRIMS

When Vietnam joined the World Trade Organization in 2007, it established minimum commitments on market access for U.S. goods and services, as well as treatment for Vietnamese and foreign companies. Vietnam undertook commitments on goods (tariffs, quotas, and ceilings on agricultural subsidies) and services (provisions of access to foreign service providers and related conditions). It has also committed to implement agreements on intellectual property (TRIPS), customs valuation, technical barriers to trade, sanitary and phytosanitary measures, import licensing provisions, anti-dumping and countervailing measures, rules of origin.

As part of its WTO accession, Vietnam also committed to remove performance requirements that are inconsistent with the TRIMS agreement. The new Investment Law specifically prohibits the following requirements: giving priority to the purchase or use of domestic goods or services; compulsory purchase of goods or services from a specific domestic firm; export of goods or services at a fixed percentage; restricting the quantity, value or type of goods or services that may be exported or that may be sourced domestically; fixing import goods at the same quantity and value as goods exported; requirements to achieve certain local content ratios in manufacturing goods; stipulated levels or values on research and development activities; supplying goods or services in a particular location; or mandating the establishment of head offices in a particular location.

In addition, Vietnam has excluded certain products from its WTO distribution services commitments, including rice, sugar, tobacco, crude and processed oil, pharmaceuticals, explosives, news and magazines, precious metals, and gemstones.

Investment Incentives

Foreign investors are exempt from import duties on goods imported for their own use and which cannot be procured locally, including: machinery, vehicles, components and spare parts for machinery and equipment, raw materials, inputs for manufacturing and construction materials that cannot be produced domestically. Remote and mountainous provinces are allowed to provide additional tax breaks and other incentives to prospective investors.

In addition, projects in high tech, research and development, new materials, energy, clean energy, renewable energy, energy saving products, automobile, software, waste treatment and management, primary or vocational education; or locating in difficult areas or economic and projects in industrial zones are entitled to investment incentives such as lower corporate income tax, exemption of import tariffs, land rental.

Vietnam has instituted policies to attract investment by its diaspora community. Vietnam recognizes dual citizenship for Vietnamese expatriates, who are allowed to choose their status as either domestic or foreign investors. A 2008 law required that Vietnamese citizens who emigrated overseas before 2009 register their intent to retain Vietnamese citizenship with the Vietnamese Embassy in their country of residence by July 1, 2014. In April 2014, the Prime Minister agreed to postpone the deadline for registration for an additional five years, until July 1, 2019. U.S. citizens of Vietnamese descent may be treated as Vietnamese nationals unless they have formally renounced their Vietnamese citizenship.

The Law on High Technology came into force in 2009 to encourage investment in areas such as informatics, biotechnology, new materials and automation, and a number of companies now receive these incentives.

Research and Development

The list of high tech products that are given investment priority is updated on an ad hoc basis, and companies investing in research and development for items on the list are entitled to the highest tax incentives and may be eligible for funding from the National High Tech Development Program. Companies that develop infrastructure for high tech parks will also receive land incentives.

Performance Requirements

In 2013 Vietnam tightened enforcement of foreign worker permit requirements through Decree 102, which introduced significant changes to regulations and procedures on the use of foreign labor. The overarching goal of the decree is to encourage the use of domestic labor over foreign labor. It reduced the validity of a work permits from three years to two, and eliminated the work permit exemption for foreign workers on contracts.

The decree also requires employers to evaluate their needs for foreign employees on an annual basis and submit a justification report to the People's Committee of each province where the company's head office is located. Exceptions are granted to certain categories of foreign workers, including teachers at institutions under the management of diplomatic missions or international organizations; holders of a Master's degree or equivalent assigned to work in Vietnam for consultation, teaching, research at universities for less than 30 days; or foreigners working within the framework of an international agreement involving central authorities and political/social organizations at the central level.

In July 2014, the GVN issued a resolution to address some issues the foreign business community raised regarding Decree 102. The most welcome change was the reversion to the prior rule, which required foreign workers to have five years of related professional experience or a four year university degree, as opposed to the recent, controversial rule requiring both five years of experience and a four year degree.

Data Storage

The Ministry of Information and Communications (MIC) is the lead agency for administrative enforcement of cyber-related regulations, including data storage requirements. The Ministry of Public Security's cyber division may also get involved if there is a suspected criminal violation of data storage rules. MIC's Decree 72/2013 on Management, Provision, and Use of Internet Services and Information Content Online, which came into effect on September 1, 2013, is the primary legal document establishing data storage requirements.

The Decree requires all organizations establishing "general websites," or social networks and companies providing online gaming services or services across mobile networks to maintain at least one server inside Vietnam. It also establishes requirements on the type of data that these companies must store (personally identifiable information of users, user activity logs, etc.) but it is unclear if that information must be stored on a local server.

According to Decree 72, companies are required to comply with requests from authorities for access to their servers. To date this requirement only applies to companies established in Vietnam. MIC is expected to release an implementing circular in 2015 that will clarify if the local server requirement applies also to cross-border service providers.

6. RIGHT TO PRIVATE OWNERSHIP AND ESTABLISHMENT

The right to non-land private property was restated in Vietnam's revised Constitution in 2013, recognizing "the right of ownership with regard to lawful income, savings, housing, chattel, means of production funds and other possessions in enterprises or other economic organizations."

7. PROTECTION OF PROPERTY RIGHTS

Real Property

State protection of property rights is still evolving, as the state can expropriate land for socio-economic development. Under the new Housing Law and Real Estate Business Law passed by the National Assembly in November 2014, land can only be taken if it is deemed necessary for social-economic development in the public or national interest, and approved by the Prime Minister or the National Assembly, as well as the Provincial People's Council. However, 'socio-economic' development is loosely defined, and there are many outstanding legal disputes between land owners and local authorities. Foreign investors also may be exposed to land disputes through M&A activities when they buy into a local company.

Real estate rights in Vietnam are divided into collective land ownership by the government, and land-use and building rights, which can be held privately. All land in Vietnam is collectively owned and managed by the state, and as such neither foreigners nor Vietnamese nationals can own land. The majority of land in Vietnam (94.5 percent) has been issued a land use rights certificate. The GVN is also building a national land registration database, and some localities have already digitized their land records.

In addition to land, collective property includes "forests, rivers and lakes, water supplies, wealth lying underground or coming from the sea, the continental shelf and the air, the funds and property invested by the government in enterprises and works in all branches and fields - the economy, culture, society, science, technology, external relations, national defense, security - and all other property determined by law as belonging to the State."

The new Housing Law and Real Estate Business Law extended "land-use rights" to foreign investors, allowing title holders to conduct real estate transactions, including mortgages. Foreign investors can lease land for renewable periods of 50 years, and up to 70 years in some poor areas of the country. Certain foreigners can own apartments, durable construction, durable trees and planted forests for production purposes in Vietnam.

Some investors have encountered difficulties amending investment licenses to expand operations onto land adjoining existing facilities. Investors also note that local authorities may intend to increase requirements for land-use rights when current rights must be renewed, particularly in instances when the investment in question competes with Vietnamese companies.

Intellectual Property Rights

The legal basis for property rights includes the 2005 Civil Code, the 2005 Intellectual Property Law as amended in 2009, and implementing regulations and decrees. Vietnam has joined the Paris Convention on Industrial Property and the Berne Convention on Copyright and has worked to meet its commitments under these international treaties. In 2009, Vietnam revised the Intellectual Property (IP) Law and IP-related provisions in the Criminal Code with respect to criminal penalties for certain acts of IPR infringement or piracy. However, enforcement agencies still lack clarity in how to impose criminal penalties on IPR violators and continue to wait for further implementing guidelines.

Although Vietnam has made progress in establishing a legal framework for IPR protection, very significant problems remain and new challenges are emerging. The country remains on the Special 301 Watch List. Infringement and piracy remained widespread and complaints of "fakes" still abound. Companies continue to voice serious concerns about widespread Internet-based piracy and the increasing prevalence of counterfeit goods sold online. 2014 also saw the emergence of limited, but increasingly high quality, domestic counterfeit manufacturing operations in Vietnam.

Customs officers have authority to seize and destroy counterfeit goods and incur expenses from these activities. Vietnam's IPR agencies track and report seizures of counterfeit goods, although trend data may be difficult to discern due to varying data collection methods, cross-over from joint actions, and differing contributions from Vietnam's 63 provinces. Individual agencies have made efforts to improve their enforcement tracking in recent years, but coordination among them to aggregate data is very weak.

Ministry of Science and Technology (MOST) inspectors carried out 64 inspections in 2014, 17 less than the previous year. However, the inspectors discovered almost the same number of violations (42, compared to 39 the previous year) and issued 37 fines, 10 more than in 2013. Most importantly, MOST collected approximately USD 75,000, an increase of 115 percent from the previous year. MOST's average fine increased from approximately USD 1,300 in 2013 to over USD 2,000 in 2014, an increase of approximately 57 percent. A MOST official attributed the higher fines in 2014 to the fact that the inspectorate encountered more serious violations this year, which warranted higher fines. MOST inspectors also reported destroying hundreds of articles of counterfeit clothing and fashion accessories and removed the infringing aspects of thousands of infringing items, primarily food and beverage and pharmaceutical and supplemental products.

In 2014, the Ministry of Culture, Sports, and Tourism (MOCST) Inspectorate cooperated with the Ministry of Public Security (MPS) to carry out inspections for software licensing compliance on 86 individuals and companies throughout the country, a decrease of around 20% from 2013. Despite the lower number of cases, the inspectorate discovered 78 violations, resulting in fines totaling USD 88,500, which is on par with last year. MOCST officials reported that the copyright compliance rate of inspected companies was higher than in previous years. The inspectors also carried out 19 inspections of individuals and companies selling art and photography and found no infringements. The HCMC Department of Culture, Sports and Tourism was particularly active this year, collecting around USD 42,500 worth of fines for copyright infringement, and destroyed 21,268 pirated CDs and VCDs. Nationwide, MOCST confiscated 126,521 CDs and DVDs that lacked the required proof of copyright and destroyed 34,038 pirated CDs and DVDs.

In 2014, Vietnam's Customs captured 24 cases of counterfeit and IP infringing products with a total value of USD 1.8 million. In 2014 Custom's imposed fines worth USD 98,000. This was a significant increase from the previous year, when Customs reported 17 cases with an infringing value of less than USD 130,000.

The Ministry of Industry and Trade's Market Management Bureau (MMB) reported that it processed 17,396 cases of counterfeit, sub-par and IP infringing products in 2014, an increase of approximately 3,000 cases compared to 2013. MMB collected USD 2.4 million worth of fines in 2014, a slight decrease from the USD 2.8 million collected in 2013. The Ho Chi Minh City (HCMC) MMB reported that it uncovered 442 counterfeit cases, nearly twice as many as in 2013. The HCMC bureau seized over 430,000 counterfeit products with a total value of USD 138,000 and assessed fines of approximately USD 300,000 in 2014.

Despite continued serious shortcomings, the GVN has taken positive steps to improve IPR over the last two years. In 2014 the government formed a new National Steering Committee, known as Committee 389, to combat smuggling, counterfeit goods and commercial fraud. Despite the fact that it has only been operating since March 2014, Committee 389's proactive leadership has been credited as one of the factors driving the increased effort by law enforcement agencies to uncover and combat IP violations. In 2013, the government began implementing two new decrees on administrative sanctions (MOST's Decree 99 and the Ministry of Culture, Sports & Tourism's Decree 131), which contributed to the significant increase in fines for IP violations imposed in 2014. Average fines imposed by provincial Departments of Science and Technology (DOST) for violations of trademarks, geographic indicators and industrial designs increased in 2014 by 64, 350 and 368 percent respectively compared to 2013. The MOST Inspectorate's average fines increased by almost 60 percent from 2013 to 2014.

Most often, authorities use administrative actions such as warnings and fines to enforce IPR protection because they are less demanding on enforcement time and resources. The United States and other countries have conducted training for enforcement agencies, prosecutors and judges. Some businesses and rights holders have started to assert their rights under the law more forcefully. One positive sign is the growth of Collective Management Organizations (CMO), particularly for the music and publishing industries. Vietnam's most successful CMO, the Vietnam Center for the Protection of Musical Copyrights (VCPMC), boasts a membership of over 90 percent of Vietnam's music composers and collected nearly USD 3.3 million in royalties on behalf of its members in 2014. However, the ability of other CMOs to protect their members IP and collect royalties on their behalf remains weak. In recent years, the government pledged and but only partially implemented a plan to rid government offices of pirated software.

Vietnamese enforcement bodies have investigated, and in some cases raided and fined, businesses suspected of using pirated software. According to statistics from the Business Software Alliance, Vietnam reduced its online piracy rate by almost 20 percent over the last decade, one of the largest reductions for any country during that time period. However, Vietnam still has one of the highest rates of online piracy in the world (over 80 percent in 2013). Rights holders continue to seek additional enforcement actions against websites containing infringing digital content. To date, however, very little enforcement action has been taken to punish or prevent digital and internet piracy.

Substantial compensation for IPR violations is only available under the civil remedies section of the IP Law. Vietnam has yet to establish specialized IP courts, and knowledge on IP issues within the judiciary remains low. However, in 2014 the courts effectively resolved a number of significant IP dispute cases, particularly the HCMC People's Court. Significant improvements are still needed, but legal experts are optimistic that the court system is slowly improving its ability to handle civil IP cases. Criminal offenses are prosecuted under the Criminal Code, and criminal proceedings are regulated under the Criminal Procedure Code. In practice, however, criminal prosecutions are rarely used to prosecute IPR violations.

For additional information about treaty obligations and points of contact at local IP offices, please see WIPO's country profiles at **http://www.wipo.int/directory/en/**.

Resources for Rights Holders

NAME of IP Economic Officer: Jack Lambert
TITLE: Economic Officer
TELEPHONE NUMBER: (84 4) 850 5063
EMAIL ADDRESS: LambertJC@state.gov

Local lawyers list: **http://vietnam.usembassy.gov/list-of-attorneys---hanoi-consular-district.html**

8. TRANSPARENCY OF THE REGULATORY SYSTEM

The Law on the Promulgation of Legal Normative Documents requires all legal documents and agreements to be published online for comments for 60 days, and published in the Official Gazette before implementation. The strong presence of business associations and chambers of commerce, the availability for online commentary on draft laws and regulations, and the biannual Vietnam Business Forum all open up opportunities for direct dialogue between the foreign business community and Vietnamese government officials. However, when issuing more detailed implementing guidelines, government entities regularly issue circulars without public notification or with little advance warning or opportunity for comment by affected parties, arguing that these binding decisions are not legal documents.

Vietnam is a member of the U.N. Conference on Trade and Development's (UNCTAD) international network of transparent investment procedures: http://vietnam.eregulations.org/. Foreign and national investors may be able to find information on administrative procedures applicable to investment and income generating operations including the number of steps, name and contact details of the entities and persons in charge of procedures, required documents and conditions, costs, processing time, and legal bases justifying the procedures for the following provinces:

Danang - **http://danang.eregulations.org**
Ho Chi Minh City - **http://hochiminhcity.eregulations.org**
Binh Dinh - **http://binhdinh.eregulations.org**
Hai Duong - **http://haiduong.eregulations.org**
Phu Yen - **http://phuyen.eregulations.org**
Vinh Phuc - **http://vinhphuc.eregulations.org**

9. EFFICIENT CAPITAL MARKETS AND PORTFOLIO INVESTMENT

There are many challenges to raising capital domestically, including Vietnam's weak and poorly regulated financial system, low transparency, and non-compliance with internationally accepted accounting standards. While the government has acknowledged the need to strengthen both the capital and debt markets, there has been no substantial progress, leaving the banking sector as the primary channel of capital for Vietnamese companies.

Vietnam has two stock exchanges: the Ho Chi Minh City Stock Exchange (HOSE) and the Hanoi Stock Exchange (HNX). As of March 2015, 346 stocks were listed on the HOSE with total market capitalization of approximately USD 15.9 billion, and 369 companies were listed on the HNX with total market capitalization of approximately USD 6.6 billion. A trading floor for unlisted public companies (UPCOM) was launched at the Hanoi Securities Center in 2009. As of March 2015, 177 companies were listed on UPCOM, with total market capitalization of approximately USD 1.8 billion. Government bonds are traded on the HNX. UPCOM is important because equitized SOEs will first list on the UPCOM (due to lower transparency requirements) before moving to an exchange.

Money and Banking System, Hostile Takeovers

Vietnam's banking sector is concentrated at the top and fragmented at the bottom. The state-owned or majority state-owned banks accounted for 44 percent of the total assets and 34 percent of equity capital in the banking sector as of March 2015. Vietnam's 33 joint stock commercial banks are all smaller than the state-owned commercial banks, but gradually gaining market share, and the government has plans to reduce the number of private banks to 15-17 by the end of 2017.

The SBV has taken positive steps to stabilize the banking sector, through the establishment of the Vietnam Asset Management Company (VAMC), merging weak banks with stronger banks, taking over failing banks, and stepping in and ensuring deposits when private bank officials are arrested. In 2015, SBV took over Vietnam Construction Bank, which is the first time SBV has taken over a bank. Additionally, this year the SBV for this first time will allow a joint venture bank (VID Bank) to be transformed to a 100 percent foreign owned company.

Despite progress, most domestic banks remain under-capitalized and have high non-performing loan (NPL) levels. By law, banks must maintain a minimum chartered capital of VND 3 trillion (about USD 140 million). As of November 2014, under Vietnamese accounting standards and loan classification criteria, the SBV reported the NPL ratio at over 3.8 percent. The true level of NPLs is unknown, and many international credit rating agencies believe it is much higher. In addition, state-directed lending by state-owned commercial banks, cross-ownership and related-party lending under non-commercial criteria continue to be a source of concern.

In 2008, the SBV for the first time granted licenses to wholly foreign-owned banks. In January 2014, the ownership limit for a single foreign investor was raised from 15 percent to 20 percent. Currently, the ceiling for total foreign ownership in a Vietnamese bank remains at 30 percent, but can be raised by approval of the Prime Minister.

10. COMPETITION FROM STATE-OWNED ENTERPRISES

In 2014, 167 out of 532 SOEs were restructured, of which 143 were equitized, three were sold, three were dissolved, three filed for bankruptcy, and 14 were merged with other enterprises. Decision 37 /2014/QD-TTg, dated June 18, 2014, spells out the targeted sectors and percentages of SOE equitization. Recently, the GVN signaled that is plans to accelerate the equitization process of the transportation infrastructure - roads, seaports and airports. This includes plans to equitize the four biggest seaports in the country, reducing the percentage of state ownership in the four ports from 75 percent to 51 percent. The GVN is also looking to fully divest in smaller less strategic ports throughout the country, and to partially privatize components of various airports and newly-constructed highways currently held by the state.

According to Vietnam's General Statistics Office, state sector investment accounted for 11 percent of total economic investment in 2014. However, labor productivity in the state sector is low, and the state makes a disproportionately low contribution to the economy in comparison to its share of production resources. Vietnam's Central Economic Commission reported that through 2014, the state sector used 70 percent of total land, 70 percent of total ODA, and 60 percent of total credit, while contributing just 32 percent of GDP, and SOEs account for fifteen out of the 20 largest Vietnamese enterprises.

OECD Guidelines on Corporate Governance of SOEs

The appointment of senior managers and board members in SOEs is often not transparent, and not in clear adherence to the OECD Guidelines on Corporate Governance for SOEs. According to the World Bank, the Vietnamese state owned sector would benefit from a "modern corporate governance system that separates state ownership rights from regulatory functions and implements an objective and transparent mechanism for the selection of Chief Executive Officers (CEOs) and board members." While TPP negotiations are ongoing, developing a robust and transparent dispute settlement mechanism is one of the key principles under discussion, and would apply to SOEs. Currently, court processes involving SOEs are opaque.

Sovereign Wealth Funds

Vietnam does not have a sovereign wealth fund.

11. CORPORATE SOCIAL RESPONSIBILITY

Most multinational companies implement Corporate Social Responsibility (CSR) programs that contribute to improving the business environment in Vietnam, and awareness of CSR programs is increasing among domestic companies. However, only the largest Vietnamese companies have CSR programs. The Vietnam Business Forum (VCCI), which is the Vietnam Chamber of Commerce, conducts CSR training and has a web page dedicated to CSR: http://www.csr-vietnam.eu/.

OECD Guidelines for Multinational Enterprises

Vietnam is not an adherent to the OECD Guideline for Multinational Enterprises.

12. POLITICAL VIOLENCE

Incidences of violence against foreign investors in Vietnam were unheard of until anti-China protests on May 13-14, 2014. These protests were primarily motivated by a spike in tensions with China following their movement of an oil rig into disputed waters in the South China Sea in May 2014. The GVN successfully maintained public order and worked with investors to offer mutually negotiated compensation packages.

13. CORRUPTION

Vietnam's 2005 Anti-Corruption Law requires government officials to declare their assets and sets strict penalties for corrupt practices. However, enforcement remains problematic. Vietnam ratified the UN Convention on Anti-Corruption in 2009, but has not signed the OECD Convention on Combating Bribery of Foreign Public Officials in International Business Transactions.

The Government has tasked various agencies to deal with corruption, including the Central Steering Committee for Anti-Corruption (led by the Prime Minister), the Government Inspectorate, and line ministries and agencies. The Central Steering Committee for Anti-Corruption was formed in 2007 and initially was under the Office of the Prime Minister. In 2012 responsibility for oversight was shifted to the Communist Party of Vietnam (CPV) Politburo, and eventually transferred to the CPV Central Commission of Internal Affairs in February 2013.

Corruption is due in large part to a low level of transparency, accountability, and media freedom, as well as low pay for government officials and inadequate systems for holding officials accountable for their actions. Competition among agencies for control over business and investments has created overlapping jurisdictions and bureaucratic procedures that in turn create opportunities for corruption.

UN Anticorruption Convention, OECD Convention on Combatting Bribery

Vietnam signed the UN Anticorruption Convention in December 2003 and ratified it in August 2009.

Resources to Report Corruption

Contact at government agency or agencies are responsible for combating corruption:

NAME: Mr. Phan Dinh Trac
TITLE: Deputy Standing Chairman
ORGANIZATION: Communist Party Central Committee Internal Affairs
ADDRESS: 6 Ba Huyen Thanh Quan, Ba Dinh District, Hanoi
TELEPHONE NUMBER: (84) 0804-3557

Contact at NGO:

NAME: Ms. Dao Thi Nga
TITLE: Executive Director
ORGANIZATION: Towards Transparency
ADDRESS: 12B Floor, Machinco Building, 444 Hoang Hoa Tham, Tay Ho, Hanoi
TELEPHONE NUMBER: 84 (04) 3715-3532
EMAIL ADDRESS: **DaoNga@towardstransparency.vn**

14. BILATERAL INVESTMENT AGREEMENTS

Vietnam does not have a bilateral investment treaty with the United States. Vietnam has 58 bilateral investment agreements with the following countries and territories: Algeria, Argentina, Armenia, Australia, Austria, Belarus, Belgium and Luxembourg, Bulgaria, Burma, Chile, China, Cuba, Czech Republic, Cambodia, Denmark, Egypt, Finland, France, Germany, Hungary, Iceland, India, Indonesia, Italy, Iran, Japan, Kazakhstan, Korea, Kuwait, Laos, Latvia, Lithuania, Malaysia, Mongolia, Mozambique, Netherlands, North Korea, Oman, Philippines, Poland, Qatar, Romania, Russia, Singapore, Spain, Sri Lanka, Sweden, Switzerland, Taiwan, Tajikistan, Thailand, Ukraine, United Kingdom, Uruguay, Uzbekistan, United Arab Emirates, and Venezuela.

Bilateral Taxation Treaties

Vietnam does not have a bilateral taxation treaty with the United States.

15. OPIC AND OTHER INVESTMENT INSURANCE PROGRAMS

The Overseas Private Investment Corporation (OPIC) has a bilateral agreement with Vietnam. Vietnam joined the Multilateral Investment Guarantee Agency (MIGA) in 1995.

16. LABOR

Vietnam's labor force is large (over 54.5 million people), literate (94 percent literacy rate), inexpensive, and young (nearly 66 percent of the population is under 40). The labor pool is expected to increase by 1.5 percent annually through 2015.

Minimum wage varies geographically. In 2015, the minimum wage for workers in private businesses ranges from VND 3.1 million (USD 160) to VND 2.15 million (USD 110) monthly. Businesses in urban districts of Hanoi, Ho Chi Minh City, and neighboring areas are subject to higher minimum wage.

Vietnam witnessed 303 strikes in 2014, according to data from the Vietnam General Confederation of Labor (VGCL), much less than the number of the strikes in 2013, when 351 strikes occurred. However, all strikes are unofficial (due to the impracticality of a legal strike under Vietnamese labor law), making data reliability questionable. Approximately 68 percent of strikes took place in foreign invested enterprises (FIEs) and the remaining 32 percent in domestic private companies. The majority of strikes (80 percent) took place in Ho Chi Minh City and surrounding provinces where most FIEs are located, particularly in the garment, footwear, and furniture sectors. The government rarely takes action against "illegal" strikers.

Labor Code

The 2012 revised Labor Code introduced a process of mediation and arbitration for labor disputes, and stipulates that strikes can only be held if they relate to collective labor disputes about benefits. The code still requires that at least 50 percent of workers in the workplace must vote for strikes. The new labor code introduced several other revisions, including increasing maternity leave from four months to six months, restricting labor outsourcing services, and reducing the validity of foreign worker permits from three to two years.

Trade Union code

The Trade Union code was also revised in 2012. In principle employers are not obliged to establish trade unions at their workplace, but if a trade union is established the employer must provide a workspace and amenities to conduct trade union activities. In order to be legally recognized, all labor unions must register with the VGCL, a state-run organization under the Communist Party-affiliated Vietnam Fatherland Front that labor experts note has weak capacity at the provincial and enterprise level. Employers have to contribute two percent of their payroll to support trade union budgets regardless of whether trade unions exist at their workplace. Employees who are members of the trade union must also contribute one percent of their payroll.

ILO

Vietnam has been a member of the International Labor Organization (ILO) since 1992, and has ratified five of the core ILO labor conventions (Conventions 100 and 111 on discrimination, Conventions 138 and 182 on child labor, and Convention 29 on forced labor). Vietnam has not ratified Convention 105 dealing with forced labor as a means of political coercion and discrimination or Conventions 87 and 98 on freedom of association and collective bargaining, although the GVN is currently taking steps toward ratification. Under the 1998 Declaration on Fundamental Principles and Rights at Work, however, all ILO members, including Vietnam, have pledged to respect and promote core ILO labor standards, including those regarding association, the right to organize and collective bargaining. A number of technical assistance projects in the field of labor sponsored by foreign donors, including the United States, are currently underway in Vietnam.

17. FOREIGN TRADE ZONES/FREE PORTS/TRADE FACILITATION

In recent years Vietnam has worked hard to establish free trade zones (FTZs). Vietnam currently has approximately 270 industrial zones (IZs) and export processing zones (EPZs). Many foreign investors note that it is easier to implement projects in industrial zones because they do not have to be involved in site clearance and infrastructure construction, and enterprises pay no duties when importing raw materials if the end products are exported.

Customs warehouse keepers in FTZs can provide transportation services and act as distributors for the goods deposited. Additional services relating to customs declaration, appraisal, insurance, reprocessing, or packaging require the approval of the provincial customs office. In practice the time involved for clearance and delivery can be lengthy and unpredictable.

Most import or export pending goods can be deposited in bonded warehouses under the supervision of the provincial customs office. Exceptions include goods prohibited from import or export, Vietnamese-made goods with fraudulent trademarks or labels, goods of unknown origin, and goods dangerous or harmful to the public or environment. The inbound warehouse leasing contract must be registered with the customs bond unit at least 24 hours prior to the arrival of goods at the port. Documents required are a notarized copy of authorization of the holder to receive the goods, a notarized copy of the warehouse lease contract, the bill of lading, a certificate of origin, a packing list, and customs declaration forms. Owners of the goods pay import or export tax when the goods are removed from the bonded warehouse.

18. FOREIGN DIRECT INVESTMENT AND FOREIGN PORTFOLIO INVESTMENT STATISTICS

Table 2: Key Macroeconomic Data, U.S. FDI in Host Country/Economy

	Host Country Statistical source*		USG or international statistical source		USG or International Source of Data: BEA; IMF; Eurostat; UNCTAD, Other
Economic Data	Year	Amount	Year	Amount	
Host Country Gross Domestic Product (GDP) ($M USD)	2013	171,400	2013	171,400	www.worldbank.org/en/country
Foreign Direct	Host Country		USG or international		USG or international Source of data:

Investment	Statistical source*		statistical source		BEA; IMF; Eurostat; UNCTAD, Other
U.S. FDI in partner country ($M USD, stock positions)	2014	10,619	2013	1,398	http://bea.gov/international/factsheet/factsheet.cfm?Area=653
Host country's FDI in the United States ($M USD, stock positions)	2014	N/A	2013	N/A	http://bea.gov/international/factsheet/factsheet.cfm?Area=653
Total inbound stock of FDI as % host GDP	2014	7.3%	2014	N/A	

* General Statistic Office of Vietnam – Pledged FDI, not disbursed.

Table 3: Sources and Destination of FDI

Direct Investment from/in Counterpart Economy Data					
From Top Five Sources/To Top Five Destinations (US Dollars, Millions)					
Inward Direct Investment			Outward Direct Investment		
Total Inward	15.6	100%	Total Outward	N/A	100%
South Korea	7.3	47%			
Hong Kong	3.0	19%			
Singapore	2.8	18%			
Japan	2.1	13%			
Taiwan	1.2	7.5%			
"0" reflects amounts rounded to +/- USD 500,000.					

Source: IMF Coordinated Direct Investment Survey

IMPORTANT BUSINESS CONTACTS

CONTACT FOR MORE INFORMATION

NAME: Brett Rose
TITLE: Economic Officer
TELEPHONE NUMBER: (84-4) 3831-5151
EMAIL ADDRESS: **InvestmentClimateVN@state.gov**

ATTORNEYS IN VIETNAM

Allens Arthur Robinson

This law firm was the first licensed foreign law firm in Vietnam (1992). It has seven foreign lawyers permanently based in Vietnam. This law firm advises on all aspects of investing and doing business in Vietnam, including: banking, construction, contracts, distribution, foreign currency controls, foreign investment (joint ventures, 100% foreign-owned enterprises, and business cooperation contracts), franchising, import /export, intellectual property, labor, litigation, maritime and transport, property and leasing.

Allens Arthur Robinson website

Hanoi:
Unit 401, Hanoi Tower
49 Hai Ba Trung, Hanoi
Tel: (84-4) 3936-0990
Fax: (84-4) 3936-0984
Mobile: (84) 903-404-440
Email: Bill.Magennis@allens.com.au

Ho Chi Minh City:
Suite 605, Saigon Tower
29 Le Duan Boulevard, District 1
Tel: (84-8) 3822-1717
Fax: (84-8) 3822-1818
Mobile: (84) 903-404-443
Email: Robert.Fish@allens.com.au

An Phat Pham Law Firm

An Phat Pham was established in 2009 and bases in Hanoi with an office in Ha Long City. The firm is managed by a team of experienced professionals (02 partners and 04 associates) who speak fluent English and have extensive Vietnamese litigation experience. Our strengths lie in our uncompromised high level of professional quality, strong relationship with the local authorities, and deep understanding of local litigation and administrative practices.

Our practice covers a wide range of legal services including: Employment and Corporate; Real Estate; Litigation; Traffic Accident and Personal Injury; Criminal Law.

An Phat Pham website

Hanoi:
134 La Thanh Street
Dong Da District
Tel: (84-4) 3991-8279
Fax: (84-4) 3856-9383
Mobile: 0903 405 006
Email: phat@anphatpham.com

Ha Long Office
No. 4 Hai Van Street, Cot 3
Ha Long City, Quang Ninh Province
Tel: (84-33) 362-6216
Fax: (84-33) 362-6216
Email: contact@anphatpham.com

ANT Lawyers

ANT Lawyers is a Vietnamese law firm with English speaking lawyers. They pride themselves on international standard, local expertise and strong network with Vietnamese authorities and local experts. Their business strategy is driven by customers' needs and our focus to provide clients with a high quality legal advice within business context. They help clients to overcome cultural barriers and achieve their strategic and financial results, and in the meantime ensure best interest protection, risk minimization, and regulatory compliance.

They represent multinational and domestic clients, from industrial, commercial companies and individuals on a variety of business, investment, intellectual properties and civil matters

Hanoi:
5th Floor, Sentinel Place Building
41A Ly Thai To Street, Hoan Kiem District
Tel: (84-4) 6270-1106
Fax: (84-4) 6270-1104

Ho Chi Minh City:
7th Floor, Me Linh Point Tower
2 Ngo Duc Ke Street, District 1
Tel: (84-8) 3520-2779
Fax: (84-8) 3821-7843

ANT Lawyers website
Email: ant@antlawyers.vn
Hotline: (84) 912-817-823

ATES - American Tax & Expatriates Services

8/1-8/3 Nguyen Huy Tuong Street
Ward 6, Binh Thanh District
Ho Chi Minh City
Tel: (84-8) 3510-3226
Fax: (84-8) 3510-3225
Email: ates.info@hcm.fpt.vn, ates.massiasm@hcm.fpt.vn

Contact: Mrs. Mai Massias
MBA, Enrolled Agent since 1998, former Internal Revenue Service tax specialist.

Baker & McKenzie

This law firm provides services in following areas: contracts, major projects, foreign trade and investment, WTO and customs, dispute resolution, construction, representative offices, foreign investment, mining, agency, and labor law.

Hanoi:
Unit 1001, 10th Floor, Indochina Plaza
241 Xuan Thuy Street
Cau Giay District
Tel: (84-4) 3825-1428
Fax: (84-4) 3825-1432
E-mail: fred.burke@bakermckenzie.com

Ho Chi Minh City:
12th Floor, Sai Gon Tower
29 Le Duan Boulevard, District 1
Tel: (84-8) 3829-5585
Fax: (84-8) 3829-5618
Email: fred.burke@bakermckenzie.com
Partner: Frederick (Fred) R. Burke
Website: http://www.bakernet.com
Capital Tax & Accounting Services Ltd.
Capital Tax & Accounting Services website
#711 - 402 West Pender St.
Vancouver, BC, Canada V6B 1T6

Community Law Vietnam

Community Law Vietnam is a Vietnamese law firm and business consulting organization. This law firm has a 120 square meter office in the center of Hanoi, close to many company headquarters and government offices. Community Law is built up by a 12 experienced, English speaking staff members.

They have a proven track record of successfully introducing foreign companies to the business environment in Vietnam, and providing them with quality legal services once they have been established.

Their goal is to service clients from all parts of the world. They are especially interested in helping businesses that are not yet established in Vietnam.

Their practice areas include: Intellectual property, foreign direct investment, enterprise and representative office establishment, mergers and acquisitions, labor disputes, business consultancy

Community Law Vietnam website

Hanoi:
Unit 705, 7th Floor
DMC Tower, 535 Kim Ma Street
Ba Dinh District
Tel: (84-4) 2220-9868/9869
Fax: (84-4) 2220 9539

Email: Hanoi@cmwlaw.vn

Ho Chi Minh City:
9th Floor, Thanh Dung Building,
179 Nguyen Cu Trinh Street, Dist. 1, Ho Chi Minh City
Tel: (84-8) 6269 4166
Fax: (84-8) 2220 2201
Email: hcm@cmwlaw.vn

D.S. Avocats

This office assists foreign investors on all international and domestic legal fields related to foreign investments. Its services are provided in English, French, Spanish, German, and Vietnamese. Its domestic and international services consist of: legal and economic studies in all matters, setting up legal entities such as representative offices, branch offices and business cooperation contracts, establishment of joint ventures and enterprises with 100% foreign owned capital, turnkey projects, legal support through monthly subscription, tender and bidding, banking, financing operations and securities, agency and distribution agreements, patents, copyrights and trademarks, taxation and tax planning, corporate law, labor law, drafting all kinds of contracts, administrative formalities, and litigation arising before domestic courts or arbitrate bodies.

D.S. Avocats website

Hanoi Office
Opera Business Center
60 Ly Thai To, Suite 801
Hoan Kiem District, Hanoi
Tel: (844) 3826 9975
Fax: (844) 3824 4809
E-mail: dshanoi@dsavocats.com.vn
Website: http://www.dsavocats.com/

Ho Chi Minh City:
Suite 601, Saigon Trade Center
37 Ton Duc Thang Street, District 1
Tel: (84-8) 3910-0917
Fax: (84-8) 3910-1096
E-mail: dshochiminh@dsvocats.com.vn

Duane Morris LLP

A full-service law firm of more than 650 attorneys, offers innovative solutions across diverse industries in the United States and internationally to address the legal and business challenges of today's evolving global markets. The firm's locations in Hanoi and Ho Chi Minh City, together with its office in Singapore, give clients access to legal services in markets throughout the Asia Pacific region and the rest of the world. The firm's attorneys in Hanoi and Ho Chi Minh City represent a range of clients, including multinational corporations with operations in Asia, as well as businesses seeking to establish investments in Asia.

Range of Services: Corporate, Securities, Mergers and Acquisitions, Banking and Financial Services, Complex Financial Transactions, Energy, Environment and Resources, Information Technology and Telecommunications.

Duane Morris website

Hanoi Office
Duane Morris Vietnam LLC
Pacific Place-
Unit V1307/1308, 13th Floor
83B Ly Thuong Kiet Street
Hoan Kiem District, Hanoi
Tel: (844) 3946 2200
Fax: (844) 3946 1311
E-mail: dtqtrang@duanemorris.com

Ho Chi Minh City Office
Duane Morris Vietnam LLC
Suite 1503/04, Sai Gon Tower
29 Le Duan Street
District 1, Ho Chi Minh City
Viet Nam
Tel: (848) 3824 0240
Fax: (848) 3824 0241

Freshfields Bruckhaus Deringer

Freshfields Bruckhaus Deringer is one of the world's largest international law firms. We have been assisting clients in Vietnam since 1987 and have one of the largest practices with nine lawyers working out of Hanoi and Ho Chi Minh City. In Vietnam we regularly advise international and Vietnamese clients on foreign investment, infrastructure development, corporate and commercial, acquisitions, banking and finance, restructuring and dispute resolution.

Freshfields Bruckhaus Deringer now has over 2,000 lawyers working in 29 offices in 19 countries to provide our corporate, financial and governmental clients with business legal services and a wealth of experience in the world's major economics. We have a powerful platform for delivering the highest standards of service and achieving strength in depth across all areas. Our international approach has strong local capabilities, and we can link with home offices across Europe, Asia and the U.S. to put together a multi-disciplinary team from a number of jurisdictions to meet client needs.

Freshfields Bruckhaus Deringer website

Hanoi:
#05-01 International Center
17 Ngo Quyen
Tel: (84-4) 3824-7422
Fax: (84-4) 3826-8300
E-mail Hanoi: van.tran@freshfields.com

Ho Chi Minh City:
R. 1108 Saigon Tower
29 Le Duan, District 1
Tel: (84-8) 3822-6680
Fax: (84-8) 3822-6690
E-mail: milton.lawson@freshfields.com

Gide Loyrette Nouel

Gide Loyrette Nouel provides legal assistance in following areas: banking contract, labor, customs, intellectual property, joint ventures, real property transactions, construction, taxation, company law, project finance and dispute resolution.

Gide Loyrette Nouel website

Hanoi:

ConerStone Building
14th Floor, Unit 08
16 Phan Chu Trinh
Hanoi
Tel: (844) 3946 2350
Fax: (844) 3946 2351
E-mail: vietnam@gide.com
Website: http://www.gide.com/

Ho Chi Minh City:
4th Floor, 18 Hai Ba Trung
Tel: (84-8) 3823-8599
Fax: (84-8) 3823-8598
Email: gln.hcmc@gide.com

Hanoi Bar Association

This office is located at:

9Fl. Cung Tri Thuc Building
Lo D25 Tran Thai Tong Road
Dich Vong, Cau Giay, Hanoi
Tel: (844) 3762-4706/7
Fax: (844) 3762-4708
Email: doanluatsuhn@gmail.com

http://www.luatsuhanoi.vn/

Hoang Long

Chief of Office: Lawyer Phan Thi Huong Thuy
No. 768 Minh Khai Street
Hai Ba Trung, Hanoi
Tel: (844) 3987-1778/3971-2632
Fax: (844) 3987-1778
Email: lstshuongthuy@gmail.com
Hoang Long website

Hoang Minh Law Office

Chief of Office: Lawyer Hoang Huy Duoc
Address: 71 Mai Hac De Street
Hai Ba Trung, Hanoi
Tel: (84-4) 3974-3442
Fax: (84-4) 3974-3449
Email: info@luathoangminh.com
Hoang Minh Law website

Hung Vuong Law Firm

Managing lawyer: Tran Quang My
37 Le Hong Phong
Ba Dinh, Hanoi
Tel: (84-4) 3823-1949/ (84) 912-753-936
in USA: 01.91790.72963
Fax: (84-4) 3734-3327
Email: luathungvuong@vnn.vn

Hung Vuong Law Firm website

Kevin Chia Partnership

Areas of practice and services provided: arbitration, banking and finance, civil claims and collections, contracts and other commercial relations, corporations, government relations, infrastructure projects, insurance, intellectual property (patents, trademarks, copyrights, designs, and licensing), inward foreign investments, labor relations, litigation, marketing agreements, and mining.

Kevin Chia Partnership website

Hanoi Office
Unit F1609A, 16th Floor
CharmVit Tower, 117 Tran Duy Hung.
Cau Giay District
Tel: (844) 3822 8787/3822 8788

Fax: (844) 3943 9875
Website: http://www.kcpartnership.com/
E-mail: kelvin.chia@kcpartnership.com

Ho Chi Minh City Office
1404-1405, Saigon Riverside
2A-4A Ton Duc Thang
District 1
Tel: (848) 3822 4986/3823 6291
Fax (848) 3822 5441
E-mail: kelvin.chia@kcpartnership.com

Lawyers Association of the City of Hanoi, Vietnam

The Association comprises experienced Vietnamese Attorneys in many specialized areas. The Attorneys are fluent in foreign languages and provide a wide range of legal and representation services.

Following are local law firms claiming that beside providing legal consultancy and services to enterprises in respect of investment, commerce, business management, they also provide services relating to civil areas as family issues (marriage, divorce), dispute property issues (house, land...), criminal laws (detention...), labor laws, administrative procedures and civil transactions.

Hanoi Office - Branch No. 1
35 Nguyen Chi Thanh Street
Tel: (84-4) 3835-3548
Fax: (84-4) 3831-7473
Email: hoiluatgia.hanoi@yahoo.com

Luat Hanoi

Managing lawyer: Tran Vu Hai
No. 81 Chua Lang Street
Dong Da District, Hanoi
Tel: (84-4) 3775-4788
Fax: (84-4) 3835-2455

Mayer Brown JSM (Vietnam)

Mayer Brown JSM has developed a broad range of experience to provide our clients with high quality, commercially focused Vietnamese and international legal services. We are one of the largest law firms in Vietnam with 43 lawyers based in our full service offices in Ho Chi Minh City and Hanoi. We have a proven track record in advising on all forms of inward investment and related issues, including complex mergers & acquisitions, joint ventures, wholly foreign-owned enterprises, business co-operation contracts and BOT projects.

Mayer Brown JSM website

Hanoi:
12th Floor, 83B Ly Thuong Kiet
Hoan Kiem District
Tel: (84-4) 3825-9775
Fax: (84-4) 3825-9776
E-mail: hoanganh.nguyen@mayerbrownjsm.com

Ho Chi Minh City:
17th Floor, Saigon Tower
29 Le Duan Street, District 1
Tel: (84-8) 3822-8860
Fax: (84-8) 3822-8864
E-mail: dao.nguyen@mayerbrownjsm.com

Ngo, Cohen Amia-Asleneni & Associes

Established in Vietnam in 1992, Ngo, Cohen Amia-Aslaneni & Associes was the first European Law Firm authorized to establish offices in Vietnam, under the name Mandel, Ngo & Partners.

Ngo, Cohen Amia-Aslaneni & Associes provides legal advice to foreign investors on establishment and commercial activities in Vietnam in such varied fields as company and corporate law, tax and customs law, labor law, intellectual and industrial property law, banking law and foreign exchange, construction law and adjudication law, settlement of disputes, telecommunication law, pharmaceutical law and insurance law.

The Firm's clientele includes international groups operating in the fields of agribusiness, banking, cosmetics, distribution, electronics, energy and environment, health, insurance, luxury goods, media, pharmaceuticals, software and telecommunications.

Ngo, Cohen Amia-Aslaneni & Associes website

R.302, Opera Business Center
60 Ly Thai To Street, Hanoi
Tel: (84-4) 3826-9975
Fax: (84-4) 3824-4809
E-mail: huyent.guiborat@ncaa.com.vn

Nguyen Chien

Chief of Office: Lawyer Nguyen Van Chien
No. 52 Quan Su, Hoan Kiem, Hanoi
Tel: (84-4) 3826-1605
Fax: (84-4) 3928-6230
Email: lawoffice@fpt.vn

Pham & Associates

Chief of Office: Lawyer Vu Khanh Toan
No. 8 Tran Hung Dao Street, Hanoi
Tel: (84-4) 3824-4852
Fax: (84-4) 3824-4853
Email: Hanoi@pham.com.vn
Pham & Associates website

Pham Hong Hai

Chief of Office: Lawyer Pham Hong Hai
17 Trung Yen 10, Lot 11B
Trung Yen, Cau Giay, Hanoi
Tel: (84-4) 3783-0737
Fax: (84-4) 3783-1404
Hotline: 098-221-6183; 090-465-8299
Email: luatsuphamhonghai@yahoo.com
Official website

Russin & Vecchi

This law firm provides assistance in all corporate and commercial matters for foreign investors. In some cases, this law firm can assist with civil issues involving U.S. or Vietnamese individuals.

Russin & Vecchi website

Hanoi:
11th Fl., Hanoi Central Office Building
Suite 1104, 44B Ly Thuong Kiet St.
Tel: (84-4) 3825-1700

Fax: (84-4) 3825-1742
E-mail: lawyers@russinvecchi.com.vn

Ho Chi Minh City:
15th Fl., OSIC Building
8 Nguyen Hue Blvd, District 1
Tel: (84-8) 3824-3026
Fax: (84-8) 3824-3113
E-mail: lawyers@russinvecchi.com.vn

S&B Law

S&B Law is one of the business law firms which have been recognized and highly appreciated by both international and local clients. With more than 30 lawyers and legal experts in both Hanoi and Ho Chi Minh City, S&B Law owns a large and strong team of local lawyers in Vietnam.

S&B LAW provides administrative assistance in relation to investment in Vietnam, including legal and commercial translation, working with relevant governmental agencies and preparing routine applications to obtain licenses, registrations, notarization and approvals in all spheres including project development, financing, intellectual property and tax.

S&B Law website

Hanoi Office
18th Floor, Central Building
Hapulico Complex,85 Vu Trong Phung Street
Thanh Xuan Dist., Hanoi,
Tel: (844) 6262 0246
Fax: (844) 6664 0246
Hotline: (84) 904 304 664
Email: info@sblaw.vn

Ho Chi Minh City Office
5th Fl, VTP Building
8 Nguyen Hue
Ben Thanh, District 1.
Tel: (848) 3520 8101
Fax: (848) 3520 8102
Hotline: (84) 983 336 069
Email: info@sblaw.vn

Taxes for Expats

I.J. Zemelman, EA
Taxes for Expats
050 E34th Street #161
New York, NY 10036, USA
Tel: +1 646-397-2887
Email: questions@taxesforexpats.com
Taxes for Expats website

Miklos Ringbauer, CPA, PMP

Accounting Services, US Tax Strategy & preparation

1613 Chelsea Road #228

San Marino, CA 91108

TEL - US: +1.866.397.6184

E-mail: info@mikloscpa.com

Website: www.mikloscpa.com

YKVN

YKVN website

Hanoi:
Apt. 401 and 301, International Center
17 Ngo Quyen, Hoan Kiem, Hanoi
Tel: (844) 3934-5410/5411
Fax: (844) 3934-5412
Email: Hanoi.office@ykvn-law.com

Ho Chi Minh City:
Suite 1502 The Metropolitan
235 Dong Khoi Street
Tel: (848) 3822-3155
Fax: (848) 3823-6908

INTERNATIONS ORGANIZATIONS PROVIDING INVESTMENT AND DEVELOPMENT RESOURCES IN SOUTH-EAST ASIA

ASIAN DEVELOPMENT BANK: STRATEGIC INFORMATION

Formation	22 August 1966
Type	Regional organization
Legal status	Treaty
Purpose/focus	Crediting
Headquarters	Mandaluyong City, Metro Manila, Philippines
Region served	Asia-Pacific
Membership	67 countries
President	Haruhiko Kuroda
Main organ	Board of Directors
Staff	2,500+
Website	http://www.adb.org

The **Asian Development Bank (ADB)** is a regional development bank established on 22 August 1966 to facilitate economic development of countries in Asia. The bank admits the members of the UN Economic Commission for Asia and the Far East (now UNESCAP) and nonregional developed nations. From 31 members at its establishment, ADB now has 67 members - of which 48 are from within Asia and the Pacific and 19 outside. ADB was modeled closely on the World Bank, and has a similar weighted voting system where votes are distributed in proportion with member's capital subscriptions. At present, both USA and Japan hold 552,210 shares - the largest proportion of shares at 12.756 percent each

HEADQUARTERS

6 ADB Avenue
Mandaluyong
0401 Metro Manila
Philippines

Postal Add: P.O. Box 789
0980 Manila
Telephone: [63](2)632-4444
Facsimile: [63](2)636-2444
E-Mail: information@mail.asiandevbank.org
Internet: www.adb.org

LANGUAGE: ENGLISH

FUNCTIONS

The Asian Development Bank (AsDB) was established pursuant to a resolution on Asian economic cooperation adopted at the First Ministerial Conference on Asian Economic Cooperation held in December 1963 and to Resolution 62 (XXI) on the Asian Development Bank adopted by the United Nations Economic and Social Commission for Asia and the Pacific (ESCAP), formerly the United Nations Economic Commission for Asia and the Far East (ECAFE), in 1965. The Second Ministerial Conference on Asian Economic Development held in Manila, November 29-December 2, 1965, adopted and opened for signature the Agreement Establishing the Asian Development Bank. The Agreement entered into force on August 22, 1966. The inaugural meeting of the Board of Governors was held in Tokyo, November 24-26, 1966. The Bank opened for business on December 19, 1966 and commenced lending operations in 1968.

The Bank makes loans and equity investment for the economic and social advancement of its developing members; provides technical assistance to prepare and carry out development projects and programs and regional and advisory services; promotes investments of public and private capital for development; and responds to requests for assistance in coordinating development policies and plans of its members. In addition to providing loans, equity investments and technical assistance, the Bank has identified five strategic objectives in its Medium-Term Strategic Framework; to promote economic growth, reduce poverty, improve the status of women, develop human resources (including population planning) and help bring about sound management of natural resources and the environment.

Financial Data

As of December 31, 1998, the total authorized capital stock of the Bank, as valued in terms of the SDR for the purposes of the Bank's financial statements on the basis that each share had the value of SDR 10,000 and that the SDR was valued at US$1.40803 as of that date, was US$49.2 billion, of which US$48.5 billion had been subscribed by the Bank's 57 members. With the entry of Tajikistan in April 1998, the Bank has 57 members. To augment its ordinary capital resources, the Bank has borrowed funds in the capital markets of Australia, Austria, Belgium, Germany, Hong Kong SAR, Italy, Japan, the Republic of Korea, Kuwait, Luxembourg, the Netherlands, Saudi Arabia, Switzerland, Taiwan Province of China, the United Arab Emirates, the United Kingdom, and the United States, as well as in international capital markets. Until 1983, it also sold two-year dollar-denominated bonds to central banks or monetary authorities of member countries. The Bank has a policy not to enter into any new borrowings or guarantees chargeable to its ordinary capital resources if such borrowings or guarantees, when added to the outstanding borrowings and guarantees, would exceed 95 percent of the amount of the callable capital stock subscribed by the members whose currencies are convertible. As of December 31, 1998, the aggregate subscriptions of these members to the callable capital amounted to US$40,288 million, while the aggregate outstanding borrowings and guarantees of the Bank amounted to US$24,231 million, representing 60.1 percent of such callable capital.

On October 15, 1982 the Bank was prescribed by the IMF as a holder of SDRs, and thus authorized to acquire and use SDRs in operations and transactions with participants in the IMF's SDR Department and other holders under the same terms and conditions as participants.

Special Funds

The resources of the Bank available for financing concessional loan commitments are administered in the *Asian Development Fund* (ADF), which was established in June 1974. For new ADF loans approved from January 1, 1999, the service charge is redesignated as interest charge and will be 1 percent per annum during the grace period and 1.5 percent per annum during the amortization period. Project loans will have a maturity of 32 years including a grace period of 8 years while quick disbursing program loans will have a maturity of 24 years including a grace period of 8 years. Total resources under administration in ADF at the end of 1998 amounted to the equivalent of US$20,535 million.

The Bank also administers the *Technical Assistance Special Fund* (TASF), which is the principal vehicle for mobilization of resources for financing the Bank's technical assistance activities. So far, 31 members (including all of the developed members) have made contributions to the Fund. The total contributed resources under administration in the Fund at the end of 1998 amounted to US$721.7 million, of which US$624.5 million had been utilized.

The Bank administers the *Japan Special Fund* (JSF), which was established in March 1988 and consists of funds entirely contributed by the Japanese Government. The proceeds of the JSF are primarily utilized: (i) to finance, on a grant basis, technical assistance projects; and (ii) to finance private sector development projects through equity investments. During the period 1988 to 1998 the Japanese Government contributed a total of ¥66.5 billion to the JSF. The Japanese Government has also contributed a total of ¥14.2 billion for seminars or symposium-type projects on monetary and fiscal issues and environment-related activities.

On October 15, 1996, the Bank approved the establishment of the Asian Development Bank Institute (ADBI) and ADBISF. The ADBI, located in Tokyo, Japan, is to complement the Bank's activities in development research and training. It is to be funded by the ADBISF which has been established for such purpose. As of December 31, 1998, the total contributions to the ADBISF amounted to $28.1 million.

In addition, the Bank administers a scholarship program funded by the Government of Japan, on a grant basis. to provide opportunities for advanced training in development-related fields to persons selected primarily from developing members. As of December 1998, the cumulative total grants received from the Government of Japan for such program was $29 million.

In accordance with the Charter, the Bank's Special Funds resources must at all times be held, used, and committed separately from its ordinary capital resources.

COMPOSITION

41 regional members: Islamic State of Afghanistan, Australia, Bangladesh, Bhutan, Cambodia, China, Cook Islands, Fiji, Hong Kong SAR, India, Indonesia, Japan, Kazakhstan, Kiribati, Korea, Kyrgyz Republic, Lao People's Democratic Republic, Malaysia, Maldives, Marshall Islands, Federated States of Micronesia, Mongolia, Myanmar, Nauru, Nepal, New Zealand, Pakistan, Papua New Guinea, Philippines, Samoa, Singapore, Solomon Islands, Sri Lanka, Taiwan Province of China, Tajikistan, Thailand, Tonga, Tuvalu, Uzbekistan, Vanuatu, Vietnam

16 non-regional members: Austria, Belgium, Canada, Denmark, Finland, France, Germany, Italy, Netherlands, Norway, Spain, Sweden, Switzerland, Turkey, United Kingdom, United States

STRUCTURE

Board of Governors. Each member is represented on the Board of Governors by a Governor and an Alternate Governor.

The *Board of Directors* is composed of twelve Directors, of whom eight are elected by the Governors representing the regional members and four by the Governors representing the non-regional members. Directors serve for a two-year term and are eligible for re-election. Each Director appoints an Alternate. The President is the Chairman of the Board of Directors.

Management. The President, who is required to be a national of a regional member country, is elected by a majority of the total number of Governors, representing not less than a majority of the total voting power of the members. He serves for a five-year term and may be re-elected. The Vice-Presidents are appointed by the Board of Directors on the recommendation of the President.

GENERAL PUBLICATIONS

The Publications Index of the Asian Development Bank may be accessed via the Internet (address is *www.adb.org*).

The Publications Unit of the AsDB Office of External Relations is the central unit for handling requests for priced and non-priced Bank publications, including procurement and consultants' handbooks and sample bidding documents which, however, can also be procured directly from the Central Operations Services Office. For more information, contact the Publications Unit of the AsDB Office of External Relations at the Bank's headquarters (postal address listed above; fax no. (632)636-2648; and E:mail: *adbpub@mail.asiandevbank.org*).

ORGANIZATION

The highest policy-making body of the bank is the *Board of Governors* composed of one representative from each member state. The Board of Governors, in turn, elect among themselves the 12 members of the *Board of Directors* and their deputy. Eight of the 12 members come from regional (Asia-Pacific) members while the others come from non-regional members.

The Board of Governors also elect the bank's *President* who is the chairperson of the Board of Directors and manages ADB. The president has a term of office lasting five years, and may be reelected. Traditionally, and because Japan is one of the largest shareholders of the bank, the President has always been Japanese. The current President is Haruhiko Kuroda, who succeeded Tadao Chino in 2005.

The headquarters of the bank is at 6 ADB Avenue, Mandaluyong City, Metro Manila, Philippines, and it has representative offices around the world. The bank employs approximately 2,400 people, coming from 55 of its 67 member countries, and with more than half of the staff being Filipino.

ADB LENDING

The ADB offers "hard" loans from ordinary capital resources (OCR) on commercial terms, and the Asian Development Fund (ADF) affiliated with the ADB extends "soft" loans from special fund resources with concessional conditions. For OCR, members subscribe capital, including paid-in and callable elements, a 50 percent paid-in ratio for the initial subscription, 5 percent for the Third General Capital Increase (GCI) in 1983 and 2 percent for the Fourth General Capital Increase in 1994. The ADB borrows from international capital markets with its capital as guarantee.

In 2009, ADB obtained member-contributions for its Fifth General Capital Increase of 200%, in response to a call by G20 leaders to increase resources of multilateral development banks so as to support growth in developing countries amid the global financial crisis. For 2010 and 2011, a 200% GCI allows lending of $12.5-13.0 billion in 2010 and about $11.0 billion in 2011. With this increase, the bank's capital base has tripled from $55 billion to $165 billion.

NOTABLE ADB PROJECTS AND TECHNICAL ASSISTANCE

- Afghan Diaspora Project

- Funding Utah State University led projects to bring labor skills in Thailand
- Earthquake and Tsunami Emergency Support Project in Indonesia
- Greater Mekong Subregional Program
- ROC Ping Hu Offshore Oil and Gas Development
- Strategic Private Sector Partnerships for Urban Poverty Reduction in the Philippines
- Trans-Afghanistan Gas Pipeline Feasibility Assessment
- Loan of $1.2 billion to bail it out of an impending economic crisis in Pakistan and on going funding for the countries growing energy needs, specifically Hydro-power projects
- Micro finance support for private enterprises, in conjunction with governments, including Pakistan and India.
- The Yichang-Wanzhou Railway project in the mountainous area of western Hubei Province and north-eastern Chongqing Municipality, China. (A US $500,000 loan, approved in 2003.)

EFFECTIVENESS

Given ADB's annual lending volume, the return on investment in lesson learning for operational and developmental impact is likely to be high and maximizing it is a legitimate concern. All projects funded by ADB are evaluated to find out what results are being achieved, what improvements should be considered, and what is being learned.

There are two types of evaluation: independent and self-evaluation. Self-evaluation is conducted by the units responsible for designing and implementing country strategies, programs, projects, or technical assistance activities. It comprises several instruments, including project/program performance reports, midterm review reports, technical assistance or project/program completion reports, and country portfolio reviews. All projects are self-evaluated by the relevant units in a project completion report. ADB's project completion reports are publicly disclosed on ADB's Internet site. Client governments are also required to prepare their own project completion reports.

Independent evaluation is a foundation block of organizational learning: it is essential to transfer increased amounts of relevant and high-quality knowledge from experience into the hands of policy makers, designers, and implementers. ADB's Operations Evaluation Department (OED) conducts systematic and impartial assessment of policies, strategies, country programs, and projects, including their design, implementation, results, and associated business processes to determine their relevance, effectiveness, efficiency, and sustainability following prescribed methods and guidelines,. It also validates self-evaluations. By this process of evaluation, ADB demonstrates three elements of good governance: (i) accountability, by assessing the effectiveness of ADB's operations; (ii) transparency, by independently reviewing operations and publicly reporting findings and recommendations; and (iii) improved performance, by helping ADB and its clients learn from past experience to enhance ongoing and future operations.

Operations evaluation has changed from the beginnings of evaluation in ADB in 1978. Initially, the focus was on assessing after completion the extent to which projects had achieved their expected economic and social benefits. Operations evaluation now shapes decision making throughout the project cycle and in ADB as a whole. Since the establishment of its independence in 2004, OED reports directly to ADB's Board of Directors through the Board's Development Effectiveness Committee. Behavioral autonomy, avoidance of conflicts of interest, insulation from external influence, and organizational independence have made evaluation a dedicated tool—governed by the principles of usefulness, credibility, transparency, and independence—for greater accountability and making development assistance work better. *Independent Evaluation at the Asian Development Bank* presents a perspective of evaluation in ADB from the beginnings and looks to a future in which knowledge management plays an increasingly important role.

In recent years, there has been a major shift in the nature of OED's work program from a dominance of evaluations of individual projects to one focusing on broader and more strategic studies. To select priority topics for evaluation studies, OED seeks input from the Development Effectiveness Committee, ADB Management, and the heads of ADB departments and offices. The current thrusts are to: (i) improve the quality of evaluations by using more robust methodologies; (iii) give priority to country/sector assistance program evaluations; (iv) increase the number of joint evaluations; (v) validate self-evaluations to shorten the learning cycle; (vi) conduct more rigorous impact evaluations; (vii) develop evaluation capacity, both in ADB and in DMCs; (viii) promote portfolio performance; (ix) evaluate business processes; and (x) disseminate findings and recommendations and ensure their use. OED's work program has also been reinterpreted to emphasize organizational learning in a more clearly defined results architecture and results framework. It entails (i) conducting and disseminating strategic evaluations (in consultation with stakeholders), (ii) harmonizing performance indicators and evaluation methodologies, and (iii) developing capacity in evaluation and evaluative thinking. All evaluation studies are publicly disclosed on OED's website (some evaluations of private sector operations are redacted to protect commercially confidential information). OED's evaluation resources are displayed by resource type, topic, region and country, and date. Learnings are also gathered in an online *Evaluation Information System* offering a database of lessons, recommendations, and ADB Management responses to these. Details of ongoing evaluations and updates on their progress are made public too.

Beginning 2006, acting within the knowledge management framework of ADB, OED has applied knowledge management to lesson learning, using knowledge performance metrics. *Learning Lessons in ADB* sets the strategic framework for knowledge management in operations evaluation. Improvements have been made that hold promise not only in OED but, more importantly, vis-à-vis its interfaces with other departments and offices in ADB, developing member countries, and the international evaluation community. In the medium term, OED will continue to improve the organizational culture, management system, business processes, information technology solutions, community of practice, and external relations and networking for lesson learning. Among the new knowledge products and services developed, *Learning Curves* are handy, two-paged quick references designed to feed findings and recommendations from evaluation to a broader range of clients *Evaluation News* report on events in monitoring and evaluation. *Evaluation Presentations* offer short photographic or Powerpoint displays on evaluation topics. *Auditing the Lessons Architecture* highlights the contribution that knowledge audits can make to organizational learning and organizational health.

Of the 1,106 ADB-funded projects evaluated and rated so far (as of December 2007), 65% were assessed as being successful, 27% partly successful and 8% as unsuccessful.

Since the ADB's early days, critics have charged that the two major donors, Japan and the United States, have had extensive influence over lending, policy and staffing decisions.

Oxfam Australia has criticized the Asian Development Bank of insensitivity to local communities. "Operating at a global and international level, these banks can undermine people's human rights through projects that have detrimental outcomes for poor and marginalized communities." The bank also received criticism from the United Nations Environmental Program, stating in a report that "much of the growth has bypassed more than 70 percent of its rural population, many of whom are directly dependent on natural resources for livelihoods and incomes."

There had been criticism that ADB's large scale projects cause social and environmental damage due to lack of oversight. One of the most controversial ADB-related projects is Thailand's Mae Moh coal-fired power station. Environmental and human rights activists say ADB's environmental safeguards policy as well as policies for indigenous peoples and involuntary resettlement, while usually up to international standards on paper, are often ignored in practice, are too vague or weak to be affective, or are simply not enforced by bank officials.

The bank has been criticized over its role and relevance in the food crisis.The ADB has been accused by civil society of ignoring warnings leading up the crisis and also contributing to it by pushing loan conditions that many say unfairly pressure governments to deregulate and privatize agriculture—leading to problems such as the rice supply shortage in Southeast Asia.

The bank has also been criticized by Vietnam War veterans for funding projects in Laos, because of the United States' 15% stake in the bank, underwritten by taxes. Laos became a communist country after the U.S. withdrew from Vietnam and the Laotian Civil War was won by the Pathet Lao, which is widely understood to have been supported by the North Vietnamese Army.

In 2009, the bank endorsed a 2.9-billion-dollar funding strategy for proposed projects in India. The projects in this strategy were only indicative and still needed to be further approved by the bank's Board of Directors; however, PRC Foreign Ministry spokesman Qin Gang claimed, "The Asian Development Bank, regardless of the major concerns of China, approved the India Country Partnership strategy which involves the territorial dispute between China and India. China expresses its strong dissatisfaction over this... The bank's move not only seriously tarnishes its own name, but also undermines the interests of its members."

MEMBERS

ADB has 67 members (as of 2 February 2007). *Names are as recognized by ADB.*
The year after a member's name indicates the year of membership. The largest share holders of the ADB are Japan and USA, each holding 15.57% of the shares. At the time a country ceases to be a member, the Bank shall arrange for the repurchase of such country's shares by the Bank as a part of the settlement of accounts with such country in accordance with the provisions of paragraphs 3 and 4 of this Article.

Republic of China (Taiwan) initially joined as "China" as a founding member representing the whole of China. However, its share of Bank capital was based on the size of Taiwan's capital, unlike the World Bank and IMF where the government in Taiwan had had a share representing the whole of China prior to the People's Republic of China joining and taking the Republic of China's seat. In 1986, a compromise was effected when the People's Republic of China joined the institution. The ROC was allowed to retain its membership, but under the name of Taipei, China — a name it protests. Uniquely, this allows both sides of the Taiwan Straits to be represented at the institution.

Asian and Pacific region: 48 members

Afghanistan (1966)
Australia (1966)
Cambodia (1966)
India (1966)
Indonesia (1966)
Japan (1966)
Korea, Republic of (1966)
Lao People's Democratic Republic (1966)
Malaysia (1966)
Nepal (1966)
New Zealand (1966)
Pakistan (1966)
Philippines (1966)
Samoa (1966)
Singapore (1966)
Sri Lanka (1966)
Taipei, Republic of China[36] (1966)
Thailand (1966)
Viet Nam, Socialist Republic of (1966)
Hong Kong, China[37] (1969)
Fiji (1970)
Papua New Guinea (1971)
Tonga (1972)
Bangladesh (1973)
Myanmar (1973)
Solomon Islands (1973)
Kiribati (1974)
Cook Islands (1976)
Maldives (1978)
Vanuatu (1981)
Bhutan (1982)
China, People's Republic of (1986)
Marshall Islands (1990)
Micronesia, Federated States of (1990)
Mongolia (1991)
Nauru (1991)
Tuvalu (1993)
Kazakhstan (1994)
Kyrgyz Republic (1994)
Uzbekistan (1995)
Tajikistan (1998)
Azerbaijan (1999)
Turkmenistan (2000)
Timor-Leste (2002)
Palau (2003)
Armenia (2005)
Brunei Darussalam (2006)
Georgia (2007)

Other regions: 19 members

Austria (1966)
Belgium (1966)
Canada (1966)
Denmark (1966)
Finland (1966)
Germany[38] (1966)
Italy (1966)
Netherlands (1966)
Norway (1966)
Sweden (1966)
United Kingdom (1966)
United States (1966)
Switzerland (1967)
France (1970)
Spain (1986)
Turkey (1991)
Portugal (2002)
Luxembourg (2003)
Ireland (2006)

MEMBERSHIP

From 31 members at its establishment in 1966, ADB has grown to encompass 67 members - of which 48 are from within Asia and the Pacific and 19 outside. Some member countries enter a new phase in their relationship with ADB as defined under the Classification and Graduation Policy.

Figures are as of 31 December 2008, before the fifth general capital increase process began. The process is ongoing, and the final figures are expected to be available by 31 December 2010. Current subscription levels are available from the Office of the Secretary.

Georgia is the 67th and newest member, having joined ADB effective 2 February 2007.

ADB members, capital stock, and voting power are as follows (as of 31 December 2009):

		Subscribed Capital		Voting Power		
Members	Year of Membership	Number of Shares	Percent of Total[a]	Number of Votes	Percent of Total[b]	Percent of Regional/ Nonregional
Regional Members						
Afghanistan	1966	1,195	0.034	14,427	0.325	0.5

Armenia	2005	10,557	0.298	23,789	0.537	0.825
Australia	1966	204,740	5.773	217,972	4.917	7.56
Azerbaijan	1999	15,736	0.444	28,968	0.653	1.005
Bangladesh	1973	36,128	1.019	49,360	1.114	1.712
Bhutan	1982	220	0.006	13,452	0.303	0.467
Brunei Darussalam	2006	12,462	0.351	25,694	0.580	0.891
Cambodia	1966	1,750	0.049	14,982	0.338	0.52
China, People's Republic of	1986	228,000	6.429	241,232	5.442	8.367
Cook Islands	1976	94	0.003	13,326	0.301	0.462
Fiji Islands	1970	2,406	0.068	15,638	0.353	0.542
Georgia	2007	12,081	0.341	25,313	0.571	0.878
Hong Kong, China	1969	19,270	0.543	32,502	0.733	1.127
India	1966	224,010	6.317	237,242	5.352	8.229
Indonesia	1966	192,700	5.434	205,932	4.646	7.143
Japan	1966	552,210	15.571	565,442	12.756	19.612
Kazakhstan	1994	28,536	0.805	41,768	0.942	1.449
Kiribati	1974	142	0.004	13,374	0.302	0.464
Korea, Republic of	1966	178,246	5.026	191,478	4.320	6.641
Kyrgyz Republic	1994	10,582	0.298	23,814	0.537	0.826
Lao PDR	1966	492	0.014	13,724	0.310	0.476
Malaysia	1966	96,350	2.717	109,582	2.472	3.801
Maldives	1978	142	0.004	13,374	0.302	0.464
Marshall Islands	1990	94	0.003	13,326	0.301	0.462
Micronesia, Federated States of	1990	142	0.004	13,374	0.302	0.464
Mongolia	1991	532	0.015	13,764	0.310	0.477
Myanmar	1973	19,270	0.543	32,502	0.733	1.127
Nauru	1991	142	0.004	13,374	0.302	0.464
Nepal	1966	5,202	0.147	18,434	0.416	0.639
New Zealand	1966	54,340	1.532	67,572	1.524	2.344
Pakistan	1966	77,080	2.174	90,312	2.037	3.132
Palau	2003	114	0.003	13,346	0.301	0.463
Papua New Guinea	1971	3,320	0.094	16,552	0.373	0.574
Philippines	1966	84,304	2.377	97,536	2.200	3.383
Samoa	1966	116	0.003	13,348	0.301	0.463
Singapore	1966	12,040	0.34	25,272	0.570	0.877
Solomon Islands	1973	236	0.007	13,468	0.304	0.467
Sri Lanka	1966	20,520	0.579	33,752	0.761	1.171
Taipei,China	1966	38,540	1.087	51,772	1.168	1.796
Tajikistan	1998	10,134	0.286	23,366	0.527	0.81
Thailand	1966	48,174	1.358	61,406	1.385	2.13
Timor-Leste	2002	350	0.01	13,582	0.306	0.471
Tonga	1972	142	0.004	13,374	0.302	0.464
Turkmenistan	2000	8,958	0.253	22,190	0.501	0.77
Tuvalu	1993	50	0.001	13,282	0.300	0.461
Uzbekistan	1995	23,834	0.672	37,066	0.836	1.286
Vanuatu	1981	236	0.007	13,468	0.304	0.467
Viet Nam	1966	12,076	0.341	25,308	0.571	0.878
Total Regional		2,247,995	63.390	2,883,131	65.040	100.000
Nonregional Members						
Austria	1966	12,040	0.340	25,272	0.570	1.631
Belgium	1966	12,040	0.340	25,272	0.570	1.631

Canada	1966	185,086	5.219	198,318	4.474	12.797
Denmark	1966	12,040	0.340	25,272	0.570	1.631
Finland	1966	12,040	0.340	25,272	0.570	1.631
France	1970	82,356	2.322	95,588	2.156	6.168
Germany	1966	153,068	4.316	166,300	3.752	10.731
Ireland	2006	12,040	0.340	25,272	0.570	1.631
Italy	1966	63,950	1.803	77,182	1.741	4.98
Luxembourg	2003	12,040	0.340	25,272	0.570	1.631
The Netherlands	1966	36,294	1.023	49,526	1.117	3.196
Norway	1966	12,040	0.340	25,272	0.570	1.631
Portugal	2002	12,040	0.340	25,272	0.570	1.631
Spain	1986	12,040	0.340	25,272	0.570	1.631
Sweden	1966	12,040	0.340	25,272	0.570	1.631
Switzerland	1967	20,650	0.582	33,882	0.764	2.186
Turkey	1991	12,040	0.340	25,272	0.570	1.631
United Kingdom	1966	72,262	2.038	85,494	1.929	5.517
United States	1966	552,210	15.571	565,442	12.756	36.487
Total Nonregional		1,298,316	36.610	1,549,724	34.960	100.000
TOTAL		3,546,311	100.000	4,432,855	100.000	

ADB OPERATIONAL STRATEGY

Under the strategy, ADB will utilize the capabilities of both its public and private sector operations to deliver synergistic solutions to problems that impede private sector growth in the DMCs and the contribution of the private sector to poverty reduction. In public sector operations, the strategy has two thrusts: (i) to support DMC governments in creating enabling conditions for business, and (ii) to generate business opportunities in ADB-financed public sector projects. The third thrust is in PSO: to catalyze private investments through direct financing, credit enhancements, and risk mitigation instruments. All of ADB's instruments for advice and financing will be used to pursue PSD outcomes targeted by the three strategic thrusts (Table 1).

The three thrusts of the strategy are mutually reinforcing when brought to bear on a development challenge. Such has been the experience of ADB. In Bangladesh, for example, there was a need to develop fresh power supply without relying on government funding. ADB responded by providing TA, first, to create the right environment for the entry of private investment (sector restructuring, regulatory framework, tariff reform), and then, to prepare a build-operate-transfer (BOT) power-generating project for international competitive bidding. The winning bidder was to be supported by ADB with direct loan, cofinancing, and guarantee facilities to catalyze the project.

ADB□s experience has shown that creating the enabling conditions to open a sector to private investment may not be sufficient to attract entrants. Sometimes, a model project is needed to provide demonstration effects, and funds have to be catalyzed to actually make the project happen. By the same token, a single private sector project, made possible with ADB support, may achieve little if it cannot be replicated without ADB support because the enabling conditions are not in place. ADB recognizes the two sides of this equation and will have to tackle the twin challenges in tandem.

ADB uses public sector operations to help DMC governments establish the right conditions for business and a policy environment conducive to pro-poor growth. Reforms that spur entrepreneurial development and stimulate foreign and domestic private investment are designed to enlarge the private sector□s role in the economy. As the transition occurs, the government must reduce its presence as owner-producer and concentrate more on facilitating and regulating private sector activities to ensure markets work and to protect public interest. This shift in the government□s role will make government a neutral and objective regulator, and free public resources (such as those used to support loss-making state enterprises) that can then be redirected to basic education, health services, and social safety nets. In many DMCs, growth and, ultimately, poverty reduction depend on such a shift.

One of ADB□s strengths lies in conducting policy dialogue with government on needed reforms. Under the PSD strategy, the reform agenda will seek to achieve the following: stable macroeconomic management; investment, trade, and price liberalization; reduced barriers to competition; well-functioning financial and capital markets; flexible labor and land markets; good physical, social, and technological infrastructure; equitable tax systems; and legal and judicial systems that protect property rights, enforce contracts, and provide for dispute resolution. Improving the business environment for SMEs will be part of the reform agenda. In addition, the policy agenda will include measures to enable DMCs to maximize the benefits of globalization (e.g., increased trade and capital flow) and minimize the risks associated with it (e.g., sudden and disruptive movements of short-term capital). This will require, for instance, the introduction of regulatory frameworks to strengthen market institutions and establish social protection programs, including social safety nets and labor laws that protect workers. Measures may also be considered to regulate short-term speculative capital flows and encourage more stable, long-term investment.

Specific policy advice on these areas of reform will be based on economic and sector work. In addition, TA will be provided to governments to formulate the regulatory and institutional frameworks needed to make markets work better and to build the capacity of market regulatory authorities. ADB will also support policy and institutional changes to encourage private sector participation in key sectors through program and sector development loans as well as by linking project investments to progress in needed reforms.

An adequate physical environment is also important for the private sector. ADB will help governments build infrastructure facilities such as ports, roads, telecommunications, and power plants needed to enable the private sector to undertake business efficiently. Where found desirable based on benefit-cost analysis, the location of such facilities can deliberately be chosen to influence the flow of private investment to less-developed (and poverty-stricken) areas of a country.

Recent events in the region underscore the need for greater attention to labor market issues. The Asian financial crisis bared the vulnerability of people living close to the poverty line. Indeed, a stable macroeconomic environment is important for the welfare and protection of the poor. This justifies ADB□s involvement in financial sector reform issues from a poverty perspective. Experience in some DMCs indicates that distorted and fragmented labor markets generate inequality of labor incomes. To address this problem, ADB and the DMCs must be committed to effective labor market policies to generate private sector-led employment. Improved labor market policies can be achieved through policy dialogue and project interventions in active and passive labor programs. Dialogue on labor market policies may include the elimination of labor distortions, and the reform of discriminatory codes and practices. Active labor market programs include employment services (e.g., job brokerage and counseling) and redeployment and training programs. Passive labor market programs cover unemployment, injury and disability insurance, income support, and labor standards. Through these labor market interventions, ADB can enhance the role of the private sector in promoting employment and contributing to poverty reduction in the region. However, some labor protection policies (e.g., occupational safety legislation) may, in the short run, lead employers to substitute capital for labor on the margin, or to move production facilities to countries with less stringent labor laws. The situation should improve as corporate responsibility becomes more widely accepted and the playing field for labor becomes more even across countries.

Generating Business Opportunities

ADB□s public sector projects can be formulated in such a way that they provide specific opportunities in which the private sector can participate. Such opportunities may include model private sector projects that are designed to include poverty reduction impacts. Indeed, ADB has long been involving the private sector as suppliers and contractors in the implementation of its public sector investment projects. Under the PSD strategy, ADB will take deliberate steps to ensure that, in its public sector projects, where appropriate, business opportunities are generated for the private sector, particularly for the domestic private sector. This will be done in various ways. When preparing a public sector project, ADB will explicitly consider the scope for private sector participation, and include the nature and timing of this participation in the project design. For example, a state-owned sewerage treatment plant being processed for ADB financing can be required to subcontract its operation and maintenance to a qualified private sector entity to be selected on a competitive basis. Investment opportunities may also be created by considering the private sector alternative to a government-proposed investment project, as was the case with the Colombo port project approved in 1999.[5] In support of government efforts to encourage private sector participation in key sectors in more DMCs, ADB will continue to support privatization programs and prepare model BOT-type infrastructure projects that can be competitively bid to the private sector. As a rule, ADB must ensure that its public sector investments do not crowd out the private sector, and that ADB and DMC governments explore all possible opportunities to ensure private sector participation where this can be done effectively and efficiently.

Catalyzing Private Investments

ADB provides direct financial assistance to private sector projects through PSO. While ADB□s participation is usually limited, it leverages a large amount of funds from commercial sources to finance these projects.[6] ADB is viewed as a neutral long-term investor committed to the highest standards of corporate conduct; its presence is seen as a source of comfort by other lenders and investors. To facilitate mobilization of commercial debt finance for cofinancing, ADB will intensify the use of two instruments to mitigate perceived sovereign risks: the complementary financing scheme and the partial risk guarantee (PRG).[7] ADB□s role in sovereign risk mitigation is now much more critical as the crisis-affected DMCs try to regain the confidence of foreign investors and lenders. Where appropriate, ADB□s partial credit guarantee, which provides comprehensive protection to lenders, will also be used to mitigate credit risks and stretch the maturity of commercial loans in local currency for long-gestating private sector projects. Aside from contributing finance that is not available on reasonable terms elsewhere and catalyzing funding from other financiers, ADB□s involvement can, more importantly, exert influence on project design and implementation so that environmental and social concerns are addressed more effectively. ADB can also selectively attempt to encourage sponsors to incorporate project components that, for instance, extend essential services to the poor with government support.

ADB will seek to catalyze private sector projects that deliver specific development impacts and related demonstration effects in line with ADB□s strategic priorities and country-specific operational strategies. While ADB□s participation helps ensure successful project launches, ADB also benefits from the insights it gains into the workings of the private sector and the constraints the sector faces. The resulting institutional learning at the project level provides an important complement to ADB's macroeconomic and sector policy work to create enabling conditions. The individual ADB-assisted private sector projects themselves are also a potentially important influence on and input to policy. They can (i) pilot test the sufficiency of the enabling environment in a sector and open the sector to private sector involvement by providing demonstration effects, (ii) provide a template for other investors to replicate, and (iii) pioneer experimental projects that could provide the basis for a policy framework for private investment in a new sector.

As a multilateral development institution, ADB does not finance private sector projects based solely on their financial viability. Projects must have clear development impacts and/or demonstration effects that go beyond the benefits captured in the financial rate of return. ADB assistance to the project, whether in the form of offshore or local currency financing, must be (i) catalytic (leveraging ADB□s financial resources by attracting other investors and lenders), or (ii) additional (complementing, not substituting for commercial sources of finance), or (iii) adding value (influencing project design or structure to make it more environmentally or socially friendly, create more jobs, impart better skills or technology, or raise the standards of corporate governance).

OPERATIONAL PRIORITIES

The pursuit of the three strategic thrusts (creating enabling conditions, generating business opportunities, and catalyzing private investments) will be focused primarily on four priority areas of operation:

i. governance in the public and private sectors;
ii. financial intermediation;
iii. public-private partnerships; and
iv. regional and subregional cooperation.

These four areas of operational focus represent the key vehicles for promoting private sector development and pro-poor growth in the Asian context. They involve activities in which ADB has the underlying strength based on its track record and for which the three strategic thrusts can achieve significant PSD outcomes

GOVERNANCE IN THE PUBLIC AND PRIVATE SECTORS

Public sector governance. Effective governance is essential for the encouragement of private sector investment. There is no greater disincentive to business than the added cost and feeling of uncertainty and vulnerability brought about by corruption, abuse of discretion, and bureaucratic interference. Improving the efficiency of public administration and the accountability and transparency of government actions is essential to improve the climate for business and sustain development in the region. Improving public sector governance has been a major development objective of ADB since 1995. Depending on the need of specific DMCs, the areas that ADB can consider for assistance include:

i. strengthening the rule of law through legal and judicial reforms;
ii. establishing and maintaining effective and equitable taxation systems;
iii. formulating sound and transparent sectoral regulations;
iv. strengthening public administration;
v. fighting corruption;
vi. removing impediments and reducing transaction costs; and
vii. establishing efficient and competitive markets supported by appropriate fiscal, monetary, and trade policies.

ADB TA will also be needed for capacity building to educate and modernize the bureaucracy and agencies that regulate and supervise the private sector in the DMCs. A lesson learned in law and judicial reform is that a holistic, comprehensive approach is crucial as piecemeal interventions do not work. Overall, ADB will help ensure that economic management in the DMCs maximizes and fairly distributes the benefits of economic growth.

Commercialization and privatization. A key dimension of effective public governance relates to the efficient deployment of public funds. Reform of public resource management requires actions to improve efficiency of state-owned enterprises and relieve budgetary pressures from their subsidy and investment needs. This typically involves commercialization (restructuring to achieve cost-recovering operations) as a first step, followed by restructuring the entity into a corporation (giving full financial autonomy under government ownership), and finally privatization (involving private sector participation). Privatization does not always mean divestment of government ownership to the private sector; it can also be done by contracting out enterprise operations, partly or wholly, to the private sector through management contract, asset leasing, or concession.

Privatization in its various forms is currently not pursued with equal vigor and conviction in all DMCs, and there remain divergent political views on the extent to which it should be promoted. ADB will thus need to carefully consider how and in what form and time frame to promote the privatization alternatives in the context of specific DMCs. ADB can also help governments analyze options available, and formulate general principles for the appropriate mix of public and private sector activities. In the transitional economies, large parts of the economy are still in public hands, including most heavy industries and utilities. In South Asia and the Pacific DMCs, there are also many poorly performing state-owned enterprises in a wide range of sectors. Even Southeast Asia still has many state-owned or controlled enterprises and financial institutions. It is clear over the next few years that privatization (through management contract, asset leasing, concession, or divestment) will continue to be an important part of overall economic reform programs in many DMCs. The success of privatization efforts will depend heavily on the government's political will and on whether or not domestic investors are in a position to become owners of the privatized assets.

Many DMCs that are inclined to privatize, face severe capacity constraints to meet the challenges of privatization. ADB can help by providing technical advice, particularly in defining sound privatization strategies, establishing and implementing effective privatization programs, designing and operating sound postprivatization regulatory frameworks, and undertaking individual transactions transparently and professionally. But ADB assistance must explicitly require transparency in implementing privatization transactions, establishment of an appropriate tariff policy, protection of workers□ legitimate interests in the transition of ownership, as well as financial market regulations that adequately protect the interests of small investors (including those investing under employee stock ownership plans). As experience has shown, successful privatization requires effective consideration of the interests of all stakeholders. Labor retrenchment, in particular, presents significant social costs, and ADB will help establish social safety nets to address this issue. At the enterprise level, ADB will consider direct financial assistance to the projects resulting from privatization programs supported by ADB and/or other multilateral development banks. Equity investments may also be considered in state-owned enterprises to facilitate or initiate privatization through divestment of government-owned shares or issuance of new shares to broaden ownership.

Corporate governance. Just as good governance is essential in the public sector, so is quality corporate governance essential in the private sector. A systemic failure of corporate governance, as seen in the recent Asian crisis, can have pervasive consequences that place an undue burden on the shoulders of the poor. For individual enterprises, sound corporate governance provides confidence to lenders and investors, and facilitates access to lower cost capital. The development of the domestic capital market often hinges on the existence of a corporate governance culture that ensures voluntary compliance through effective regulatory enforcement. In most of the DMCs, the root causes of poor corporate governance have to be addressed to sustain recovery and growth. Through TA, ADB can help to review commercial laws and regulations and establish:

i. credible accounting and auditing standards;
ii. timely and accurate disclosure rules;
iii. sound environmental, labor, and social standards;
iv. provisions for adequate protection of minority shareholder rights; and
v. effective bankruptcy and foreclosure regimes.

ADB can also help train corporate directors on their duties and responsibilities, and on how they can be effective in balancing the interests of shareholders with those of other stakeholders□employees, customers, suppliers, investors, communities□while maximizing value. In PSO, ADB must invest only in companies that can demonstrate the capacity to establish and maintain sound corporate governance structures and practices. More proactively, ADB must diagnose the quality of corporate governance in its investee companies, benchmark this against best practice, and develop a time-bound action plan to remove deficiencies and introduce enhancements. ADB□s initiatives on corporate governance should extend to promoting corporate responsibility to maximize the opportunity for companies to integrate social and environmental awareness into core business practices and make private investment more sustainable.

FINANCIAL INTERMEDIATION

Well-functioning financial systems are critically needed to promote the private sector. Many DMCs need to strengthen their financial institutions and create diversified financial markets to develop the domestic capacity to finance private sector-led growth. Properly functioning capital markets are needed for effective privatization programs□to facilitate sale of government-divested shares, ensure fair and transparent share pricing, enable wide ownership of privatized shares (thereby enhancing political acceptability), and provide resources for modernization and expansion of privatized enterprises. In a financially integrated world, robust and well-regulated banking systems and financial markets, coupled with sound macroeconomic management, are necessary to reduce the risk of instability associated with sudden outflows of short-term capital. One advantage of the region is that many of the DMCs have substantial domestic savings that, if channeled through well-functioning capital markets, could help the private sector avoid excessive reliance on external finance and the concomitant exposure to exchange risks. ADB has the capability to address intermediation challenges, having undertaken financial sector reform programs through public sector operations and/or direct investments in financial intermediaries through PSO in several DMCs.

Financial institutions and markets. Under the strategy, ADB will continue its support for policy reform and institutional capacity building to strengthen the DMC's financial systems. Using TA and program loans, ADB will focus its assistance on government efforts to enhance regulation and supervision, develop sound banking systems, deepen and broaden securities markets, and create bond markets. Support will also be given for the development of mortgage markets to facilitate housing finance, and the reform of pension and insurance systems to develop sources of long-term capital. In PSO, ADB will complement funding with capacity building and governance strengthening for institutions such as banks, insurance companies, leasing companies, securities firms, and pension fund management companies, incorporating best practices and sound management. ADB can also arrange for the participation of a strategic partner in an institution to facilitate capacity building. The availability of credit information on borrowers and securities issuers is crucial to the functioning of credit markets; this will require establishing rating agencies and credit bureaus, which ADB can promote and catalyze as it has done in India, Malaysia, and Thailand. Preference will be given to supporting institutions that can serve as role models in the process of rehabilitating the financial sector, as in the crisis-hit countries, or in commercializing and privatizing the state-owned banking system, as in the transitional economies.

Progress thus far in bank restructuring in the crisis-hit and other DMCs is encouraging. But corporate sector reforms are lagging. If the banking system is to achieve full recovery, the performance of corporate borrowers must be improved. Progress to date has been achieved mainly in strengthening of insolvency laws, including bankruptcy and foreclosure procedures, which ADB has addressed and will continue to support through its public sector operations. ADB will also support the work of government restructuring agencies using TA. Actual corporate restructuring (through mergers and acquisitions, for example) and corporate debt restructuring have been limited. ADB will selectively catalyze such efforts through PSO in partnership with institutions that have the necessary expertise.

Restructuring the banking system provides an excellent opportunity to transform banks into instruments of effective intermediation in support of labor-absorbing growth. One difficult issue that will need to be addressed in the process is the extent to which targeted or policy lending should be used to channel funds to special needs, especially those of the poor. Most countries have found that it is best to strictly limit such guided credit, to provide it primarily for social purposes, and then at unsubsidized rates. The evidence is strong from many countries that the poor benefit most when they have access to unsubsidized credit. With subsidies, the coverage of credit programs is necessarily quite limited, and the affluent tend to squeeze out the poor for the subsidized funds.

Local currency financing. Foreign borrowings by domestic private firms result in a currency mismatch that cannot be easily hedged if the borrowers earn revenues in local rather than foreign currency. Failure to mitigate the risks associated with such an imbalance was one of the underlying causes of the Asian financial crisis. ADB will continue to address these risks by helping DMCs to develop diversified domestic capital markets, as well as markets for currency swaps and other hedging instruments. But this is a long process. To be more proactive in the interim, ADB will investigate the possibility of raising local currency debt in selected DMCs for its general operational requirements as well as for relending to domestic borrowers (e.g., infrastructure projects and financial institutions supporting SMEs). In addition, ADB will try to provide partial credit guarantees to enable domestic companies and institutions to directly source local currency financing through loans or bond issues and, in some cases, stretch the maturity and reduce the cost of such financing. Local currency bonds issued by ADB and those issued by domestic entities with ADB guarantee will be designed to transfer technology and add value to the domestic bond markets by supplying high-quality debt instruments that conform to global standards for, among others, syndication, pricing transparency, and secondary market liquidity. Similarly, ADB guarantees on local currency loans will help develop a corporate credit pricing curve and foster long-term lending operations among domestic financial institutions.

Investment funds. The potential size of long-term resources that can be mobilized by ADB through funds could be quite large considering its coinvestment experience to date with major pension funds and insurance companies. Investment funds enable ADB to leverage its own scarce capital much more than in other operations. In addition, the accumulated experience from ADB's sizable portfolio of investment funds (29 funds since 1983) represents an important resource base. ADB will tap the firsthand knowledge of its fund managers to identify pressing constraints to private sector development in DMCs where they operate.

Catalyzing funds is a core competence of PSO. To ensure that future funds seeking support are strategically aligned with ADB's development objectives, ADB will take more active involvement in designing investment funds, formulating the funds□ investment objectives in terms of country and sector focus, and working more closely with like-minded, governance-conscious institutional investors. Building on past experience, ADB will explore the possibility of new types of specialized funds to help finance the region□s investment needs, e.g., debt funds, microequity funds, SME funds, environment funds, governance funds, corporate restructuring and recovery funds, agribusiness funds, and internet and technology funds. To be effective in launching new funds, ADB must continue to build contacts with institutional investors from the capital-surplus countries.

Small and medium-sized enterprises. At the user end of financial intermediation, ADB□s focus will be on, among others, SMEs, which are a major generator of employment and income needed to achieve poverty reduction. Assistance to SMEs under credit lines has not been totally satisfactory, and lessons learned will need to be incorporated in the use of financial intermediaries in future SME assistance programs. Direct SME assistance may also be required, for example, in the Pacific and Central Asian DMCs. However, this is a very difficult and time-consuming task. It requires specialized teams that ADB does not have, and is not expected to have. So ADB financing for SMEs will continue to be handled through investment funds and specialized financial institutions that are competent and properly equipped. ADB will also seek to cooperate with existing regional organizations, such as the South Pacific Project Facility, to stimulate private sector investment in the Pacific DMCs. While SMEs require capital, they are also in need of advice and training for various aspects of their operations, e.g., business planning, accounting and finance, management capacity, and environmentally clean production. Hence, ADB will also consider technical and business advisory assistance to SMEs and/or continue to collaborate with organizations that are in a position to provide such support. Entrepreneurial education and business incubators will also be supported to help start up new SMEs. TA to governments will be provided to help develop a sound SME environment.

Due to difficulty assessing risks associated with SME credit, SME financing programs often face a dilemma between commercial viability, requiring collateral that most SMEs are unable to accommodate, and social development considerations, such as poverty reduction, that dictate liberal provision of credit to SMEs. One way to resolve the dilemna is to create state-sponsored credit enhancement schemes, such as small loan guarantee facilities for SMEs. ADB can support the establishment of such credit guarantee facilities, which may be partially funded by government and ADB. To ensure that due consideration is given to financial viability and that credit is not extended imprudently, lending institutions availing of guarantees must retain a share of the credit risk.

PUBLIC-PRIVATE PARTNERSHIPS

The public and private sectors should complement each other in the overall development effort. Government efforts to form partnerships with the private sector will lower the risks and costs associated with investments, particularly for infrastructure projects. ADB can help identify the risks and costs associated with the present business environment, and support the development of workable public-private partnerships. The role of government in risk mitigation is crucial for early projects in a sector newly opened to private investment. Care must be exercised, however, in judging where the government□s development function should cease and market mechanisms and institutions can take on the usual project risks, and when continued support to encourage project financing is still warranted.

An effective consultative mechanism can help promote and sustain public-private partnerships in the DMCs to balance social and development goals with commercial interests. ADB will embark on a much more proactive set of initiatives aimed at promoting and brokering such partnerships, particularly in infrastructure development, and advising governments on ways to develop substantive partnerships with the private sector. ADB will also tap into the extensive pool of private sector resources available regionally and globally, and develop networks and relationships with key PSD stakeholders. Respected business leaders from DMCs and countries providing bilateral aid will be invited periodically to a forum to provide ADB with feedback on trends and developments in the private sector and exchange ideas on promoting pro-poor growth.

A big challenge, and opportunity as well, for both the public and private sectors is the effective use of information technology to facilitate development efforts and enhance private sector competitiveness. New computing technologies in telecommunications and multimedia applications, including the Internet, can and do change the competitive advantage of industries and provide new ways to reach out to a broader market. DMC governments can establish partnerships with the private sector to widen the use of information technology in delivering basic social services (e.g., distance education and telemedicine) and to help local enterprises increase their technological development. ADB should help DMCs to develop national policies and programs to accelerate the dissemination of information technology.

Physical infrastructure development. The DMCs□ public sectors will continue to play a major role in the provision of infrastructure. However, private sector participation in partnership with the public sector can facilitate financing, construction, and operation of infrastructure facilities; improve efficiency; deliver much-needed services cost effectively; and release resources from public budgets at all levels. Through public sector operations, ADB will intensify assistance to DMC governments to create enabling conditions for private sector participation in areas such as energy, transport, and telecommunications. ADB will help establish an effective regulatory framework for private participation in infrastructure, build capacity of concerned regulatory agencies, strengthen state utilities dealing with the private sector as output offtaker or input supplier, and train and develop skills of public officials responsible for infrastructure development. In addition, ADB will develop sectoral templates for appropriate risk-sharing arrangements that would allow the private sector to earn reasonable rates of return, ensure equitable access to quality services, and save on the transaction costs of the lengthy processes involved. These approaches will be designed to help rationalize each sector and identify an effective role for the private sector in the provision of infrastructure services. ADB will ensure that the process of transferring infrastructure responsibilities to the private sector is transparent and competitive, and produces greater efficiencies and better service to consumers.

Public-private partnerships in physical infrastructure can take the form of BOT projects where there is a sharing of risks between the public and private sectors, with each risk being allocated to the party that can best manage it. The private parties involved in these projects normally assume the commercial risks that are under their control. ADB has achieved some success in using TA facilities to create and develop such BOT-type public-private partnerships in collaboration with DMC governments.[8]

Public-private partnerships can be enhanced when the private sector undertakes a BOT project and the government provides complementary support infrastructure (which may have too long a payback period to be commercially attractive), e.g., a breakwater to protect a BOT container port terminal, or transmission lines to evacuate power from a BOT generating plant. In such cases, ADB can also have a public-private partnership internally, with PSO providing direct assistance to the BOT project and public sector operations funding the related public investment. Other examples of such partnerships, with both the public and private sectors involved in financing, implementation, and operation, would be (i) an airport project with air-side works undertaken by the public sector and land-side works by the private sector; (ii) a railway project with the public sector taking care of squatter relocation and grade separation, and the private sector undertaking the railway rehabilitation and operation; and (iii) a toll expressway undertaken by the private sector, with connecting provincial and rural roads provided by the public sector. Another form of public-private partnership is the export-oriented Theun-Hinboun hydropower project in Lao People□s Democratic Republic (Lao PDR), which was implemented as a joint venture between private sponsors and the Government. The Government□s equity contribution to the project was financed through an ADB public sector loan.[9] The foregoing approaches to public-private partnership will be an increasingly prevalent way of doing business for ADB and call for close cooperation between public sector operations and PSO.

Catalyzing private infrastructure projects, a core competence of PSO, will be pursued under the strategy. ADB assistance for such projects will be provided through direct financing and risk mitigation, and through investments in specialized financial institutions and investment funds aiming to support private provision of infrastructure services. Priority will be given to those projects that have clear benefits to all segments of the community, including the poor.

Social infrastructure development. ADB will selectively assist DMCs to identify and develop opportunities by which the private sector can help deliver more effective social services such as education, health, nutrition, water supply, wastewater treatment, and solid waste management. An example of public-private partnership in social infrastructure development is where private operators supply in bulk treated water to public waterworks distribution networks. The use of information technology, as in distance learning and telemedicine, presents opportunities to extend the reach of these services, especially to the poor. There are also opportunities to involve the private sector to achieve more effective and efficient delivery of essential services, for example, by contracting out to the private sector the provision of publicly funded social goods and services. ADB must recognize, however, that private investors will be attracted to provide social services only if the expected financial returns meet or exceed their cost of capital, regardless of who pays for the services. Aside from education and health, ADB will assist in addressing shelter problems through transparent, efficient, and sustainable private sector-implemented housing and home ownership programs, involving government support where needed.

Agriculture and rural sector development. The DMCs□ agriculture sectors contain the single greatest concentration of private sector production. At the same time, the overwhelming majority of Asia's poor obtain their livelihood from agricultural production. Thus, ADB assistance in promoting public-private partnerships in agriculture can have a tremendous impact on poverty reduction in rural areas. For instance, a project in Papua New Guinea[10] provides support for performance-based agricultural services on a contract basis and shifts the role of government agriculture agencies from directly providing extension services to managing service providers. To stimulate small rural nonfarm enterprises that can help raise incomes and improve the welfare of the poor, particularly for poor women, ADB can support the establishment of viable and sustainable microfinance institutions. ADB will continue to assist DMCs in establishing mechanisms to facilitate market determination of input and output prices; in developing public-private partnerships in the supply of agricultural inputs, particularly in fertilizer distribution and agro-processing industries; and in transferring the management of on-field irrigation systems to farmer groups. ADB can also help strengthen public capacity to deliver rural credit, extension, and research, and manage irrigation and natural resources. Measures to clarify land title and ownership will advance private sector development in rural, as well as urban, areas.

REGIONAL AND SUBREGIONAL COOPERATION

Regional and subregional cooperation has emerged as an increasingly important development strategy in Asia. Such cooperation offers larger markets that allow production economies of scale and efficient division of labor. Whereas in North America and Europe economic integration has involved formal regional cooperation arrangements (i.e., the North American Free Trade Agreement and the European Union), in Asia, economic integration has been driven largely by private sector initiatives, with governments playing an active, if largely informal, facilitating role. One recent example is the Private Sector Forum on Economic Cooperation in the Eastern South Asia Subregion (Bangladesh, Bhutan, Nepal, and 11 eastern states of India), which is being organized by the chambers of commerce and other representatives of the private sector from the concerned countries.[11] Indeed, the private sector has been both a prime mover and a prime beneficiary of regional cooperation in a widening network of intraregional investment and trade that is likely to outlive the Asian crisis.

Subregional cooperation, a key area of involvement for ADB, involves encouraging specific, limited linkages of complementary activities across borders to create a region or subregion of economic growth. Economic cooperation can make a subregion, as a whole, relatively more attractive to private investors by extending access to factors of production, production processes, products, and markets beyond national boundaries: it provides wider business opportunities that accelerate development. Since subregional cooperation programs often involve lagging parts of participating countries, they can also contribute to poverty reduction.

In this context, ADB will concentrate on facilitating investment in subregional infrastructure projects that provide essential means for trade and investment linkages. For investors, such projects represent new types of business opportunities and new types of risks: their transborder nature requires appropriate mechanisms to support project preparation and financing. ADB will thus assist in preparing, financing, and providing risk management for subregional projects that involve private sector participation.[12]

Complementing this, ADB will continue to play a significant role by helping to address nonphysical barriers to the movement of goods, services, and people. Examples include initiatives related to trade and investment facilitation, and cross-border training and standards certification and accreditation. This focus will allow the realization of economic benefits from investment in subregional infrastructure and, more broadly, will facilitate subregional economic linkages, integration, and development. In addition, ADB will serve as a center of excellence and clearinghouse for information and ideas on subregional cooperation at the policy, program, and project levels.

The experience of ADB in promoting regional and subregional cooperation is building up. A program of economic cooperation in the Greater Mekong Subregion, for example, was initiated in 1992 and the effort and resources devoted to the program appear to be paying off. A framework of cooperation in seven priority sectors in the subregion has been established and about 100 subregional projects have been identified and prioritized. ADB is also encouraging cooperation among the governments of People's Republic of China, Kazakhstan, Kyrgyz Republic, and Uzbekistan. Projects are being designed to lay the foundation for economic growth through cross-border cooperation among these four countries. For the Pacific DMCs, ADB has provided assistance in examining the feasibility of a subregional securities market.

COUNTRY-SPECIFIC STRATEGIES

The stage and status of private sector development differs widely among the DMCs. Thus, while the strategic actions proposed in the strategy are designed to be applicable across the region, they have to be tailor-made at the country level to meet the diverse conditions and changing needs of individual DMCs and to maximize the contribution to growth and poverty reduction. Country-specific PSD strategies will be formulated within the framework of the PSD strategy and as an integral part of ADB's operational strategy for individual DMCs. Depending on the country setting, the country strategy for PSD may require:

i. a primary focus on facilitating the emergence of domestic entrepreneurs by supporting related microenterprises and SMEs; or
ii. support for rural nonfarm enterprises or agri-business; or
iii. formulation and implementation of programs to support privatization and financial sector reform; or
iv. assistance with broad-based reform of enterprise ownership and private property laws, particularly in the transitional economies.

Special consideration will need to be given to the small size of the Pacific DMCs and the great distances between them. A theme that is likely to run through all country strategies for PSD is improving the legal environment and the governance regime.

OPERATIONAL ORIENTATION

In support of its primary objective, ADB must place poverty reduction as the centerpiece of all its operations. ADB as a whole must recognize the essential contribution of the private sector to pro-poor growth, which is needed to achieve sustained poverty reduction. With this recognition, ADB will need to institute a systematic process to ensure that public sector projects are designed to incorporate, to the extent possible, elements that promote a better business environment and/or provide appropriate scope for private sector participation in projects. In PSO, on the other hand, there will be a need to ensure that ADB pursues private sector projects with specific development impacts and/or demonstration effects.

STAFF SKILLS

The strategy will require new staff skills from PSD specialists (as distinguished from PSO investment officers). Such skills will constitute a core of intellectual capacity in ADB to address public policy issues related to private sector participation in development (similar to the approach used for social development and environment issues). These PSD staff will prepare working guidelines to implement the strategy and sensitize other staff to PSD issues through training and consultation. PSD specialists will help identify areas for public-private partnerships, lead dialogue with governments on PSD issues, review ADB projects for private sector potential, and review government policies vis-a-vis the private sector. Skills relating to legal aspects of PSD, e.g., regulation of privatized utilities, will also be required.

PROCESSES AND PROCEDURES

A country-specific PSD strategy should be made an integral part of the country operational strategy (COS) to ensure that development of the private sector is explicitly targeted in ADB□s programs for any given DMC. This operational integration should not be difficult as ADB's public and private operations are under the same charter, management, and institution. PSO should support the development goals of the COS. In this context, catalyzing private investments under PSO may be needed even in sectors that are not prioritized for public sector operations.[13] The country assistance plan[14] should, at the earliest stages, proactively consider private sector alternatives to, and/or commercial cofinancing of, prospective public sector projects or parts of these projects. Such private sector alternatives need not involve ADB support through PSO, but may be considered for direct ADB assistance only if they can contribute to pro-poor growth. The Inter-American Development Bank systematically asks why the private sector is not taking up some of the burden in a public sector project when designing, selecting, and processing projects.

PSD specialists, as well as PSO investment officers, will need to work as part of the now largely public sector country teams that are responsible for country-level strategies and programs. PSD specialists will provide advice on PSD from a public policy perspective, while PSO investment officers will represent the private sector view based on their hands-on experience with private sector projects. Additionally, PSO investment officers will be included on project teams on a case-by-case basis where their skills are required in processing infrastructure and other projects involving public-private partnerships and public sector projects that have potential for private sector participation. Country and sector specialists in the programs and projects departments may support the processing of private sector projects, but because of the nature of risks involved and potential conflict of interest (Box 4), the lead responsibility will be with PSO investment officers.

ADB-assisted private sector projects will be screened for their development impact and poverty reduction contribution. The success or failure of any given private sector project will, from ADB□s point of view, be evaluated on how well it meets the development impact areas identified at appraisal, in addition to its financial performance. The impact of ADB□s public sector operations on PSD should likewise be benchmarked and tracked in terms, for example, of a public sector loan's contribution to creating a policy and/or physical environment conducive to private investment or to generating investment opportunities for the private sector. Scorecards will be developed, based on the rudimentary illustrations in Appendix 3, with each impact area in the scorecards to have specifically defined criteria.

ADB will need to enhance and institutionalize partnerships between public sector operations staff and PSO staff to achieve synergy across the organization, while keeping in mind the possibility of conflict of interest (Box 4). Networking and sharing of professional expertise will be encouraged. Disincentives to close collaboration will be removed.

OPERATING PRINCIPLES

To implement these fundamental changes required by the PSD strategy, two important operating principles are proposed to guide the delivery of assistance and concentrate ADB□s efforts on where it can contribute best.

□Think PSD□ in public sector operations. This entails deliberate efforts by public sector operations to improve the enabling environment for the private sector and to use the experiences of PSO as inputs to these efforts. The new operational orientation calls for disciplined, sequenced examination of private sector alternatives at key stages of ADB projects: (i) at project preparation, asking whether the private sector can undertake the project without government assistance or, if not, whether a public-private partnership is feasible, or whether parts of the project can be undertaken by the private sector; or (ii) after project completion when construction and implementation risks no longer exist, asking whether the private sector can step in by taking over management and/or ownership, partially or wholly, or by refinancing government debt. The deliberate pursuit of private sector approaches to ADB□s public sector operations does not necessarily mean less public sector lending. It will, however, mean that public sector operations should focus more on projects (i) that involve direct poverty interventions and/or (ii) that private investors are not prepared to undertake.

□Think development impact□ in private sector operations. PSO□s orientation will be to achieve greater development impact and/or demonstration effects, and work with governments to take deliberate steps to reduce poverty. At concept clearance and due diligence stages of any private sector project, due consideration should be given to ensuring development impact through, for example, employment opportunities, cleaner environment, access to public services, effective competition, and better corporate governance. At the same time, clarity and transparency should be observed in dealing with private sector partners to retain their confidence. Demonstration and catalytic effects are also important in PSO, and these will be pursued by seeking private sector projects that can be replicated if successful. To broaden the impact of PSO in the region, there may be a need to extend the reach of PSO to smaller DMCs or to sectors other than finance and infrastructure, which constitute PSO□s present core competence.

INSTRUMENTS

ADB will use all instruments at its disposal for PSD, including policy dialogue, public sector project and program lending, TA, equity investments, loans without government guarantees, cofinancing, and guarantee schemes. The existing instruments of public sector operations are considered adequate to meet the requirements of the strategy. There is, however, a need to consider enhancements in the PSO instruments (Box 5). These instruments will be examined in separate Board papers. Furthermore, as the headroom for PSO becomes exhausted within the next couple of years, a decision will have to be made on the need to increase PSO□s resource allocation, which currently stands at $1.5 billion.

SELECTED ASIAN TRADE, INVESTMENT AND DEVELOPMENT ORGANIZATIONS

ASIA-PACIFIC ECONOMIC COOPERATION (APEC)

HEADQUARTERS

14-00 Floor, Alexandra Point
438 Alexandra Road
Singapore 119958
Singapore

Telephone: [65]276-1880
Facsimile: [65]276-1775
E-Mail: info@mail.apecsec.org.sg
Internet: www.apecsec.org.sg

LANGUAGE: ENGLISH

ESTABLISHMENT AND FUNCTIONS

The Asia-Pacific Economic Cooperation (APEC) was established in 1989 in response to the growing interdependence among Asia-Pacific economies. Begun as an informal dialogue group, APEC has since become the primary regional vehicle for promoting open trade and practical economic cooperation. Its goal is to advance Asia-Pacific economic dynamism and sense of community. Despite the financial instability of 1997-98, the Asia-Pacific remains one of the fastest growing regions in the world. Today, APEC includes all the major economies of the region and the most dynamic, fastest growing economies in the world. APEC's 21 member economies had a combined Gross Domestic Product (GNP) of over US$16 trillion and 43 percent of global trade in 1997.

The initial years of APEC were focused largely on exchanges of views and project-based initiatives. The concerns were simply to advance the process of economic cooperation in the Asia-Pacific and promote a positive conclusion to the Uruguay Round of GATT negotiations. But as the need for greater economic cooperation steadily grew, APEC has evolved into a forum of greater substance and higher purpose, which is to build the Asia-Pacific community through achieving economic growth and equitable development through trade and economic cooperation.

In November 1995, APEC economic leaders established a permanent senior business advisory council, composed of up to three business people from each of APEC 18 members, to provide advice on the implementation of the Osaka Action Agenda and on other specific business sector priorities.

In 1994, APEC translated its vision of an open trading system into the very ambitious goal of free and open trade and investment in the Asia-Pacific by 2010 for developed member economies and 2020 for developing ones.

APEC's goal is being attained through the three pillars of APEC activities, namely: trade and investment liberalization, business facilitation, and economic and technical cooperation.

COMPOSITION

21 member economies: Australia, Brunei Darussalam, Canada, Chile, China, Hong Kong SAR, Indonesia, Japan, Korea, Malaysia, Mexico, New Zealand, Papua New Guinea, Peru, Philippines, Russia, Singapore, Taiwan Province of China, Thailand, United States, Vietnam.

STRUCTURE

The APEC *Secretariat* located in Singapore provides the central link and core support mechanism for all APEC activities among the various APEC fora. The Chair, which rotates annual among member economies, is responsible for hosting the annual ministerial meeting of foreign and economic ministers. New Zealand is the APEC Chair for 1999. The *Executive Director*, who is seconded from the member economy chairing APEC, serves for one year. The *Deputy Executive Director* is appointed by the member economy designated to assume the chair the following year.

APEC Senior Officials, who hold their meetings (called Senior Officials Meetings or SOMs) regularly prior to every ministerial meeting, make recommendations to the Ministers and carry out their decisions. With the approval of Ministers, they oversee and coordinate the budgets and work programs of the APEC fora.

Other ministerial meetings also being held are meetings for ministers of education, energy, environment and sustainable development, finance, human resources development, regional science and technology cooperation, small and medium enterprises, telecommunications and information industry, trade, and transportation.

APEC has three committees, a SOM sub-committee, nine working groups, an ad hoc policy-level group, and a technical experts group.

The *Committee on Trade and Investment* aims to create an APEC perspective on trade and investment issues and to pursue liberalization and facilitation initiatives. The *Economic Committee* analyzes economic trends and issues in support of APEC's trade and investment liberalization and facilitation and economic and technical cooperation agendas. The *Budget and Management Committee* advises APEC senior officials on budgetary, administrative, and managerial issues. The SOM Sub-committee on Economic and Technical Cooperation assists the SOM in coordinating and managing APEC's economic and technical cooperation (ECOTECH) agenda.

The working groups deal with the following areas: energy, fisheries, human resources development, industrial science and technology, marine resources conservation, telecommunications, trade promotion, transportation, and tourism.
The *ad hoc Policy Level Group on Small and Medium Enterprises* oversees activities for SMEs across all APEC fora. The *Agricultural Technical Cooperation Experts Group* seeks to enhance the capability of agriculture and its related industries to contribute to economic growth.
In 1995, APEC economic leaders established the APEC *Business Advisory Council*, a permanent council composed of up to three senior business people from each member economy that advises leaders and ministers on the implementation of APEC action plans and on other specific business sector priorities.

ASSOCIATION OF NATURAL RUBBER PRODUCING COUNTRIES (ANRPC)

HEADQUARTERS

7th Floor, Bangunan Getah Asli (Menara)
148 Jalan Ampang
50450 Kuala Lumpur
Malaysia

Telephone: [60](3)261-1900
Facsimile: [60](3)261-3014

Secretary-General: ***Gnoh Chong HOCK***

Secretariat Staff

Senior Research Officer: ***Arumugam RASIAH***
Publication/Documentation Officer: *(vacant)*

LANGUAGES: ENGLISH, FRENCH

ESTABLISHMENT AND FUNCTIONS

The Association of Natural Rubber Producing Countries (ANRPC) is an inter-governmental organization, formed by natural rubber producing countries to promote the overall interests of the commodity. It was founded by Indonesia, Malaysia, Singapore, Sri Lanka, Thailand and Vietnam in October 1970. Its membership is open to the governments of countries producing natural rubber.
The objectives of the Association are: to bring about co-ordination in the production and marketing of natural rubber; to promote technical co-operation among members; and to bring about remunerative and stable prices for natural rubber.
In furtherance of the above objectives, the Association's functions are as follows: make studies of the world rubber position and examine the short- and long-term problems facing the natural rubber industry; promote research and development in production, marketing and consumption of natural rubber; set up such institutional arrangements as may be considered necessary; cooperate with appropriate international organizations; make recommendations to members whenever necessary.
The Association engages in a number of activities which are of importance to the natural rubber industry in all member countries. The major ones include the following: (a) programs/projects/studies on natural rubber in the areas of statistics, South American Leaf Blight (SALB), rubber smallholder development, marketing, quality, packaging, pricing, cost of production of natural rubber in member countries, development of rubber-based manufacturing industries in member countries, etc.; (b) natural rubber information collection, documentation, and dissemination; (c) organization of seminars and workshops on any one of the areas cited; and (d) maintaining information linkages with other international organizations.

COMPOSITION

8 member countries: India, Indonesia, Malaysia, Papua New Guinea, Singapore, Sri Lanka, Thailand, Vietnam

STRUCTURE

The *Assembly*, which is the supreme body of the Association, is made up of all members of the ANRPC; its regular session is held once a year.
The *Executive Committee* of the Association exercises the functions of the Association between sessions of the Assembly. It consists of all members of the Association and it is empowered to determine procedural matters and to make such rules as may be necessary for the proper functioning of the Secretariat.
The Executive Committee appoints and determines the membership and functions of other committees as may be necessary. Each of these committees elects its own chairman. At present, there are four committees: Committee on NR Statistics; Coordinating Committee on Production and Marketing Strategies; Standing Committee on INRO Matters; and ANRPC Technical Committee on Pests and Diseases of *Hevea*. Working Groups and expert groups for specific purposes are established as and when necessary.
The *Secretariat* of the Association functions: to provide the necessary link between members; to make preparations for all meetings of the Assembly and the Executive Committee and to service such meetings; to maintain liaison with

international organizations whose work is of interest to the Association; to make such studies as specified from time to time by the various committees of the Association; and to carry out the directives of the Association.

GENERAL PUBLICATIONS

ANRPC News; ANRPC Quarterly Natural Rubber Statistical Bulletin; ANRPC Economic and Statistical Review; Reports of studies and meetings of the Association (some of the publications are of a confidential nature and are available only to members of the Association).

ASSOCIATION OF SOUTH EAST ASIAN NATIONS (ASEAN)

HEADQUARTERS

ASEAN Secretariat
70-A, Jalan Sisingamangaraja
Jakarta 12110
Indonesia

Postal Add: P.O. Box 2072
Telephone: [62](21)724-3372
[62](21)726-2991
Facsimile: [62](21)739-8234
[62](21)724-3504
Telex: 47213/4 ASEAN
Cable: ASEANSEC JAKARTA

LANGUAGE: ENGLISH

ESTABLISHMENT AND FUNCTIONS

The Association of South East Asian Nations (ASEAN) was established August 8, 1967 in Bangkok, Thailand with the signing of the Bangkok declaration by the five original member nations (Indonesia, Malaysia, Philippines, Singapore, and Thailand). On January 8, 1984, Brunei Darussalam was admitted as the sixth member. In July 1995, Vietnam joined ASEAN as the seventh member; Lao People's Democratic Republic and Myanmar joined in July 1997 as the eighth and ninth member, respectively.

The Bangkok Declaration sets out the objectives of the Association as follows: (1) To accelerate the economic growth, social progress and cultural development in the region through joint endeavors in the spirit of equality and partnership in order to strengthen the foundation for a prosperous and peaceful community of South-East Asian Nations; (2) To promote regional peace and stability through abiding respect for justice and the rule of law on the relationship among countries of the region and adherence to the principles of the United Nations Charter; (3) To promote active collaboration and mutual assistance on matters of common interest in the economic, social, cultural, technical, scientific and administrative field; (4) To provide assistance to each other in the form of training and research facilities in the educational, professional, technical and administrative spheres; (5) To collaborate more effectively for the greater utilization of their agriculture and industries, the expansion of their trade, including the study of the problems of international commodity trade, the improvement of their transportation and communications facilities and the raising of the living standards of their peoples; (6) To promote South-East Asian studies; and (7) To maintain close and beneficial cooperation with existing international and regional organizations with similar aims and purposes, and explore all avenues for even closer cooperation among themselves.

During the Ministerial Meeting in Jakarta, May 7-9, 1974, it was decided that Jakarta would be the site of the ASEAN Secretariat. The Agreement on the Establishment of the ASEAN Secretariat, adopted at the Heads of Government (Summit) Meeting in Bali, Indonesia, February 23-25, 1976, provides that the office of the Secretary-General shall be held in turn by nationals of the member countries for a two-year period. However, at the 18th ASEAN Ministerial Meeting in Kuala Lumpur on July 8-9, 1985, it was agreed that the term of office of the Secretary-General would be for a three-year period beginning July 1986.

An Agreement on ASEAN Preferential Trading Arrangements was signed in Manila on February 24, 1977. The Agreement states that member countries shall cooperate through mutual assistance in respect of basic commodities, particularly food and energy, provision of market support for products of ASEAN industrial projects, expansion of intra-ASEAN trade and increase in the utilization of raw materials available in the contracting states. The arrangements were improved by the Protocol on Improvements on Extension of Tariff Preferences under the ASEAN Preferential Trading Arrangements, Manila, December 15, 1987.

An Agreement on ASEAN Industrial Projects (AIP) and an Agreement on ASEAN Industrial Complementation (AIC) were signed in Kuala Lumpur on March 6, 1980 and in Manila on June 18, 1981, respectively. A new program for ASEAN industrial cooperation was launched with the signing of the Basic Agreement on ASEAN Industrial Joint Venture (BAAIJV) in Jakarta on November 7, 1983. The agreement on AIPs provides the framework for cooperation in the establishment of large-scale industrial projects that meet regional requirements for essential products. Projects currently in operation under the scheme are the Urea Fertilizer Projects in Indonesia and Malaysia. The Agreement on AICs provides for a system of schemes for the manufacture of different products within an industry or industries in the ASEAN countries and their subsequent exchange. A complementation program is currently being implemented in the automotive industry on a brand-to-brand basis. The AIJV Program, on the other hand, seeks to promote industrial joint ventures in the region through the effective consolidation of markets by granting AIJV products preferred access to the markets of participating countries and other privileges.

To further enhance industrial cooperation, the ASEAN Economic Ministers signed the ASEAN Industrial Cooperation (AICO) Scheme Agreement on April 27, 1996 in Singapore. The Scheme is the latest industrial cooperation program of ASEAN to promote the sharing of industrial activities between ASEAN-based companies. It is based on the principles and concepts of the CEPT Scheme for AFTA (as mentioned in later paragraphs). The Scheme minimizes tariff dissimilarities and offers qualified participating companies the immediate benefit of the CEPT tariff rates in the range of zero to five percent.

On March 7, 1980, ASEAN signed an economic cooperation agreement with the European Economic Community, to increase trade and economic links between the two regional groups. An agreement on economic cooperation was also signed with Canada on September 25, 1981. The Agreement provides for industrial, commercial and development cooperation, and transfer of technology.

The Fourth ASEAN Summit, held in Singapore on January 27-28, 1992, agreed to establish the ASEAN Free Trade Area (AFTA) within 15 years. At this Summit, the Framework Agreement on Enhancing ASEAN Economic Cooperation and the Agreement on the Common Effective Preferential Tariff (CEPT) Scheme for the ASEAN Free Trade Area were signed. The CEPT Scheme for AFTA was launched in January 1993. This was preceded by a simultaneous announcement by ASEAN Member Countries of their indicative lists of products for inclusion and exclusion in the CEPT in December 1992. The 26th ASEAN Economic Ministers Meeting held in Chiang Mai, Thailand, endorsed the Fifth AFTA Council's decision to accelerate the realization of AFTA from 15 to 10 years. The Fifth ASEAN Summit held in Bangkok on December 14-15, 1995 adopted an Agenda for Greater ASEAN Economic Integration. The Summit decided to accelerate and deepen tariff reductions under AFTA, made greater commitments in trade facilitation and launched new initiatives in services, intellectual property, industrial cooperation and investment. The ASEAN Leaders also decided to meet every year, with formal Summits to be held every three years and informal Summits in between. At the Bangkok Summit, the ASEAN Leaders met for the first time with their counterparts from Laos, Cambodia, and Myanmar, taking ASEAN one step closer to the realization of an ASEAN comprising all the ten Southeast Asian countries. The first informal meeting of the Heads of Government of ASEAN took place in Jakarta on November 30, 1996.

At the Singapore Summit earlier, a decision was also made to use established fora to promote external dialogues on enhancing security in the region. To this end, ASEAN would intensify its external dialogues on political and security matters using ASEAN Post-Ministerial Conferences (ASEAN-PMC). As a first step in implementing the Summit decision, political and security issues were put on the agenda of the 25th AMM/PMC in Manila. As a further step in strengthening the PMC process, Senior Officials from ASEAN, Australia, Canada, the EC, Japan, Korea, New Zealand, and United States held a Meeting on May 20-21, 1993 in Singapore. The Meeting agreed to hold consultations at least once a year and adopted a work program to guide their future activities.

As part of confidence-binding measures, ASEAN continued to reaffirm its commitment to the peaceful settlement of disputes and conflicts among nations. ASEAN initiated the resolution on the Treaty of Amity and Cooperation in South-East Asia which was adopted by consensus at the 47th session on the UNGA. The Treaty is expected to complement the role of the United Nations as it provides the only regional diplomatic instrument so far for dispute resolution in South-East Asia. Laos and Vietnam acceded to the Treaty at the 25th AMM in July 1992.

ASEAN's initiatives in confidence-building measures took a step forward in 1994 when the ASEAN Regional Forum (ARF) was inaugurated. ARF is a consultative forum for discussing regional and political security cooperation issues. Participants in the inaugural ARF were the Foreign Ministers of ASEAN, the seven Dialogue Partners, three Observers (Vietnam, Laos and Papua New Guinea) and two guests, China and Russia.

COMPOSITION

10 member countries: Brunei Darussalam, Cambodia, Indonesia, Lao People's Democratic Republic, Malaysia, Myanmar, Philippines, Singapore, Thailand, Vietnam. Cambodia joined ASEAN on April 30, 1999.

Dialogue Partners: Australia, Canada, China, the European Union, India, Japan, Korea, New Zealand, Russia, and the United States.

STRUCTURE

The Meeting of the ASEAN Heads of Government is the highest authority of the Association. The overall coordination is carried out by the ASEAN Ministerial Meeting (AMM) consisting of the Foreign Ministers of Member Countries.

The ASEAN *Standing Committee* carries on the work of the Association between Meetings of Foreign Ministers. All ASEAN economic cooperation activities are directed by the ASEAN Economic Ministers (AEM) through the ASEAN Senior Economic Officials (SEOM). Ministerial Meetings of other fields of ASEAN cooperation are held when necessary to draw up programs of cooperation in their respective ministerial areas.

The Secretary-General of ASEAN is appointed on merit by the ASEAN Heads of Government upon recommendation of the AMM. He is accorded ministerial status with an enlarged mandate to initiate, advise, coordinate and implement ASEAN activities. The Secretary-General chairs all ASEAN Standing Committee Meetings, except the first and last. Political consultation are carried out by Senior Political Officials (SOM) who report to the ASEAN Ministerial Meeting (AMM). Economic cooperation is directed by Economic Ministers of Member Countries through the Senior Economic Officials Meeting (SEOM). There are also six non-economic Committees or equivalent bodies: (1) Committee on Culture and Information (COC); (2) Committee on Social Development (COSD); (3) Committee on Science and Technology; (4) ASEAN Senior Officials on Drug Matters (ASOD); (5) ASEAN Senior Officials on Environment (ASOEN); and (6) ASEAN Conference on Civil Service Matters (ACCSM).

Since 1978, ASEAN Committees in Third Countries were established in order to safeguard and advance ASEAN interests through joint consultation with the host governments. To date, ASEAN Committees/Groups (composed of heads of diplomatic missions) have been established in: Australia (Canberra), Belgium (Brussels), Canada (Ottawa), France

(Paris), Germany (Bonn), India (New Delhi), Japan (Tokyo), Korea (Seoul), New Zealand (Wellington), Switzerland (Geneva), the United Kingdom (London), and the United States (Washington, DC). There are 41 Non-Governmental Organizations (NGOs) which are formally affiliated with ASEAN.

GENERAL PUBLICATIONS

Annual Report of the ASEAN Standing Committee; The ASEAN Selected Statistics; The ASEAN Ministerial Meeting and Post Ministerial Conferences with the Dialogue Partners; ASEAN Update; ASEAN Document Series; ASEAN Functional Cooperation: From Strength to Strength; Investing in ASEAN; ASEAN: An Overview; AFTA Reader (available by subscription)

ECONOMIC COOPERATION ORGANIZATION (ECO)

HEADQUARTERS

1, Golbou St.
Kamranieh, Tehran
Islamic Republic of Iran

Postal Add: P.O. Box 14155-6176
Telephone: [98](21)283-1731/3/4
[98](21)229-1305
[98](21)229-2066
Facsimile: [98](21)283-1732
Cable: ARCIDEVELOP
E-mail: eco.org@neda.net

Secretary General: ... ***Onder OZAR***

LANGUAGE: ENGLISH

ESTABLISHMENT AND FUNCTIONS

The Economic Cooperation Organization (ECO), is an inter-governmental regional organization established in 1985 by the Islamic Republic of Iran, Pakistan, and Turkey for the purpose of promoting regional economic cooperation among the member states.

ECO is the successor organization of Regional Cooperation for Development (RCD) which remained in existence from 1964 to 1979. Subsequently, the organization was restructured and revived under its present name, ECO. Accordingly, the basic charter of the organization, the Treaty of Izmir of 1977, was amended in 1990 providing a legal basis for the new organization. In 1992, the organization was expanded to include seven new members, namely, Islamic State of Afghanistan, Azerbaijan, Kazakhstan, Kyrgyz Republic, Tajikistan, Turkmenistan, and Uzbekistan. In this respect, November 28 is commenorated annually as the ECO Day.

The main objectives of ECO are: sustainable economic development of Member States; progressive removal of trade barriers and promotion of intra-regional trade; greater role of ECO region in the growth of world trade; gradual integration of the economies of the Member States with the world economy; development of transport and communications infrastructure linking the Member States with each other and with the outside world; economic liberalization and privatization; mobilization and utilization of ECO region's material resources; effective utilization of the agricultural and industrial potentials of ECO region; regional cooperation for drug abuse control, ecological and environmental protection and strengthening of historical and cultural ties among the peoples of the ECO region; and mutually beneficial cooperation with regional and international organizations.

The ECO's major areas of cooperation are: (a) transport and communications, (b) trade and investment, (c) energy, minerals, and environment, and (d) industry and agriculture. It has six regional institutions (ECO Trade and Development Bank, ECO Reinsurance Company, ECO Shipping Company, ECO Air, ECO Chamber of Commerce, and ECO College of Insurance) and two specialized agencies (ECO Cultural Institute and ECO Science Foundation).

Since the ECO's expansion in November 1992, its long-term perspectives and sectoral priorities have been defined in the form of action plans: the Quetta Plan of Action, the Istanbul Declaration, the Almaty Outline Plan, and the Economic Cooperation Strategy for the ECO region. Transport and communications, trade and investment, and energy figure as the priority areas of this Strategy. The project-oriented Almaty Outline Plan adopted in November 1993 underscores the importance that ECO Member States attach to the development of a modern transport and communication infrastructure linking the ECO Member States with each other and with the outside world. Necessary steps are also being taken to concretize regional cooperation in the field of energy by planning a network of gas and oil pipelines and interconnection of power grids within the region.

COMPOSITION

10 member states: Islamic State of Afghanistan, Azerbaijan, Islamic Republic of Iran, Kazakhstan, Kyrgyz Republic, Pakistan, Tajikistan, Turkey, Turkmenistan, Uzbekistan

STRUCTURE

The *Council of Ministers* is the highest policy and decision-making body of the ECO, and is composed of the Ministers of Foreign Affairs of the Member States or such other representatives of Ministerial rank as may be designated by their governments. The Council of Ministers meets at least once a year by rotation among the Member States.

The *Council of Permanent Representatives* is a permanent body based in Tehran. It is comprised of the Permanent Representatives/Ambassadors of Member States accredited to ECO. It meets regularly to formulate issues requiring decision by the Member States and to implement the decisions taken by the Council of Ministers.

The *Regional Planning Council* is composed of the Heads of the Planning Organizations of the Member States and/or such other representatives of corresponding authorities as may be nominated by their governments. It meets once a year in one of the Member States to review past programs, evaluate results achieved, and consider and evolve programs of action for realizing the objectives of the organization and for submission to the Council of Ministers for approval.

ECO Summits

Every two years, a Summit of Heads of States is organized in a member country's capital. The Summit meetings review the overall performance and progress in implementation of ECO programs and projects. So far, five such meetings have been held beginning with the First ECO Summit held in Tehran in February 1992 followed by the Second in Istanbul in July 1993.

The Third ECO Summit Meeting held in Islamabad, Pakistan, in March 1995 witnessed the signing of documents pertaining to six ECO Institutions (ECO Trade and Development Bank, ECO Reinsurance Company, ECO Shipping Company, ECO Air, ECO Cultural Institute, and ECO Science Foundation) and two regional agreements (ECO Transit Trade Agreement and Agreement on Simplification of Visa Procedures for the Businessmen of ECO Countries).

The Fourth ECO Summit Meeting held in Ashgabat, Turkmenistan, in May 1996 marked, inter-alia, the completion of groundwork for the reorganization of ECO and restructuring of its organs. Following this, an extraordinary meeting of the ECO Council of Ministers was held in Ismir, Turkey, on September 14, 1996 where the member countries signed the revised Treaty of Izmir, the Organization's Fundamental Charter.

An Extra-ordinary Summit Meeting was held in Ashgabat in May 1997 highlighting the importance of the development of transport and communication infrastructure and network of trans-national pipelines in the ECO region.

During the Fifth ECO Summit held in Almaty, Kazakhstan, in May 1998, ECO Member States signed a Transit Transport Framework Agreement (TTFA), an MOU against Smuggling and Customs Fraud and agreed to establish an ECO Educational Institute in Ankara, Turkey.

External Relations

Since its expansion, ECO has consolidated its international image and stature through cooperative relationships with various regional and international organizations, including UN-ESCAP, UNICEF, UNDP, UNDCP, UNESCO, UNFPA, UNIDO, FAO, and IsDB. ECO has also acquired observer status with the UN General Assembly and the Organization of Islamic Conference (OIC). Mutually beneficial cooperative relations were also established

FOOD AND AGRICULTURE ORGANIZATION OF THE UNITED NATIONS (FAO)

Organisation des Nations Unies pour l'alimentation et l'agriculture
Organización de las Naciones Unidas para la Agricultura y la Alimentación

HEADQUARTERS

Viale delle Terme di Caracalla
00100 Rome
Italy

Telephone: [39](06)5-7051
Facsimile: [39](06)5705-3152
Telex: 610181 FAO I
625853 FAO I
Cable: FOODAGRI ROME
E-Mail: telex-room@fao.org
Internet: www.fao.org

Director-General: ... ***Jacques DIOUF***
Deputy Director-General: ... ***David HARCHARIK***

Departments

Administration and Finance Dept *K. MEHBOOB, Asst. Director-General*
Agriculture Department *A. SAWADOGO, Asst. Director-General*
Sustainable Development Dept *H. CARSALADE, Asst. Director-General*
Economic and Social Policy Dept *H. DE HAEN, Asst. Director-General*
Fisheries Department: . *David HARCHARIK, Officer-in-Charge*
Forestry Department: .. *M. Hosny EL-LAKANY, Asst. Director-General*
General Affairs and
Information Dept.: .. *F. ZENNY, Asst. Director-General*

Office of Programme, Budget and Evaluation: ... P.A. WADE, Director
Technical Co-operation Dept.: A. REGNIER, Asst. Director-General

Regional Offices

Assistant Director-General and Regional Representative for Africa: ... *B.F. DADA*
Assistant Director-General and Regional Representative for Asia and the Pacific: ... *P. NATH*
Assistant Director-General and Regional Representative for Latin America and the Caribbean: ... *G. GORDILLO de Anda*
Assistant Director-General and Regional Representative for the Near East: ... *Atif Yehya BUKHARI*
Regional Representative for Europe: ... *M. LINDAU*

Commodities and Trade Division

Director: ... *J.N. GREENFIELD*
Chief, Raw Materials, Tropical and Horticultural Products Service: ... *Paola FORTUCCI*
Chief, Commodity Policy and Projections Service: ... *M. DE NIGRIS (Officer-in-Charge)*
Chief, Basic Foodstuffs Service: ... *W. LAMADE*
Chief, Global Information and Early Warning Service: ... *A. RASHID*

LANGUAGES: ARABIC, CHINESE, ENGLISH, FRENCH, SPANISH

ESTABLISHMENT AND FUNCTIONS

The Food and Agriculture Organization (FAO), an autonomous agency within the UN system, is the leading international body for food and agriculture. It has a membership of 175 countries - plus the European Community (member organization) - who have pledged themselves: to raise levels of nutrition and standards of living of their peoples; to improve the production and distribution of all food and agricultural products; and to improve the condition of rural people.

The Organization has four major tasks: it carries out a major program of technical assistance on behalf of governments and development funding agencies; it collects, analyzes, and disseminates information; it advises governments on policy and planning; and it provides opportunities for governments to meet and discuss food and agricultural problems. One of FAO's top priorities is food security, that is ensuring the availability of adequate food supplies, maximizing stability in the flow of supplies and securing access to food by the poor.

FAO was founded at a conference in Quebec, Canada, on October 16, 1945, following the United Nations Conference on Food and Agriculture at Hot Springs, Virginia, in 1943, which established a commission to plan the Organization.

In 1949, FAO became the first organization in the UN system to set up a specific commodities section, which developed into the Commodities and Trade Division, a part of the Economic and Social Policy Department of FAO. Through the Division, FAO maintains a watch on the world market situation and outlook for some 80 major agricultural commodities, identifies specific commodity problems and proposes international action to deal with them, and issues specialized reports on agricultural commodity developments and prospects. The Organization also provides advice and assistance to its member countries on national commodity and trade policy problems, particularly as follow-up to the Uruguay Round.

Specific services provided by FAO include the Global Information and Early Warning System on Food and Agriculture, which monitors global supply and demand for basic foodstuffs (in particular, cereals) and fertilizers. The System issues Food Outlook reports monthly, and special alerts whenever the food supply situation threatens to deteriorate in a country or region which may need assistance.

The Commodities and Trade Division services one of the standing committees of the FAO Council: the Committee on World Food Security and the Committee on Commodity Problems (CCP). The CCP coordinates 11 intergovernmental commodity groups: on rice (established in 1955), grains (1957), citrus fruit (1959), jute, kenaf, and allied fibers (1963), bananas (1965) with a sub-group on tropical fruits (1997), oilseeds, oils and fats (1965), hard fibers (1966), wine and vine products (1968), tea (1969), and meat (1970), together with sub-group on Hides and Skins. It also oversees the

Subcommittee on Surplus Disposal, which regularly monitors concessional transactions to ensure that they do not disrupt normal commercial trade.

COMPOSITION

175 member countries plus the European Community (member organization): Islamic State of Afghanistan, Albania, Algeria, Angola, Antigua and Barbuda, Argentina, Armenia, Australia, Austria, Azerbaijan, The Bahamas, Bahrain, Bangladesh, Barbados, Belgium, Belize, Benin, Bhutan, Bolivia, Bosnia and Herzegovina, Botswana, Brazil, Bulgaria, Burkina Faso, Burundi, Cambodia, Cameroon, Canada, Cape Verde, Central African Republic, Chad, Chile, China, Colombia, Comoros, Democratic Republic of the Congo, Republic of the Congo, Cook Islands, Costa Rica, Côte d'Ivoire, Croatia, Cuba, Cyprus, Czech Republic, Denmark, Djibouti, Dominica, Dominican Republic, Ecuador, Egypt, El Salvador, Equatorial Guinea, Eritrea, Estonia, Ethiopia, European Community (member organization), Fiji, Finland, France, Gabon, The Gambia, Georgia, Germany, Ghana, Greece, Grenada, Guatemala, Guinea, Guinea-Bissau, Guyana, Haiti, Honduras, Hungary, Iceland, India, Indonesia, Islamic Republic of Iran, Iraq, Ireland, Israel, Italy, Jamaica, Japan, Jordan, Kazakhstan, Kenya, Democratic People's Republic of Korea, Republic of Korea, Kuwait, Kyrgyz Republic, Lao People's Democratic Republic, Latvia, Lebanon, Lesotho, Liberia, Libya, Lithuania, Luxembourg, former Yugoslav Republic of Macedonia, Madagascar, Malawi, Malaysia, Maldives, Mali, Malta, Mauritania, Mauritius, Mexico, Moldova, Mongolia, Morocco, Mozambique, Myanmar, Namibia, Nepal, Netherlands, New Zealand, Nicaragua, Niger, Nigeria, Norway, Oman, Pakistan, Panama, Papua New Guinea, Paraguay, Peru, Philippines, Poland, Portugal, Qatar, Romania, Rwanda, St. Kitts and Nevis, St. Lucia, St. Vincent and the Grenadines, Samoa, São Tomé and Príncipe, Saudi Arabia, Senegal, Seychelles, Sierra Leone, Slovak Republic, Slovenia, Solomon Islands, Somalia, South Africa, Spain, Sri Lanka, Sudan, Suriname, Swaziland, Sweden, Switzerland, Syrian Arab Republic, Tajikistan, Tanzania, Thailand, Togo, Tonga, Trinidad and Tobago, Tunisia, Turkey, Turkmenistan, Uganda, United Arab Emirates, United Kingdom, United States, Uruguay, Vanuatu, Venezuela, Vietnam, Republic of Yemen, Yugoslavia, Zambia, Zimbabwe

STRUCTURE

The supreme governing body of the Organization is the *Conference*, composed of all member nations, which meets every two years to review the state of food and agriculture and FAO's work, and to approve the Regular Program of Work and Budget for the next two years. The Conference elects, as an interim governing body, a *Council* of 49 member nations, who serve three-year rotating terms. The Conference also elects an Independent Chairman of the Council: the 27th Session of the FAO Conference, in November 1997, elected Sjarifudin BAHARSJAH of Indonesia to this position for a two-year period.

The Conference also elects the *Director-General*, who is head of the *Secretariat*. The present Director-General, Jacques DIOUF of Senegal, was elected in November 1993, taking office for a six-year term in January 1994.

The Secretariat is staffed by over 2,288 personnel located at FAO's Rome headquarters and some 1,942 employed on field projects and at regional, sub-regional, liaison and country offices.

GENERAL PUBLICATIONS

The State of Food and Agriculture (annual); *FAO Production Yearbook* (also available in electronic form); *FAO Trade Yearbook* (also available in electronic form); *FAO Fertilizer Yearbook;*
Yearbook of Forest Products; Yearbook of Fishery Statistics (two volumes: "Catches and Landings" and "Fishery Commodities"); *Commodity Review and Outlook* (annual); *FAO Plant Protection Bulletin* (quarterly); *Food Aid Bulletin* (quarterly); *Food Outlook* (monthly); *FAO Periodic Bulletins of Statistics* (also available in electronic form); *Unasylva - forestry review* (quarterly); *Rural Development* (annual)

Major data bases and systems: *AGRIS* (International Information System for the Agricultural Sciences and Technology); *CARIS* (Current Agricultural Research Information System); *GIS* (Geographic Information System); *ASFIS* (Aquatic Sciences and Fisheries Information System); *FISHDAB* (Fisheries Data Base); *GLOBEFISH* (International Fish Market Indicators); *FORIS* (Forest Resources Information System); *Land Resources Data Base; FAO Fertilizer/Plant Nutrition Data Bank; Seed Information System; WAICENT* (World Agricultural Information Centre), composed of FAOSTAT and FAOINFO (textual database) at *www.fao.org.*

INTERNATIONAL COCOA ORGANIZATION (ICCO)

Organisation internationale du cacao
Organización International del Cacao

HEADQUARTERS

22 Berners Street	Telephone: [44](171)637-3211
London W1P 3DB	Facsimile: [44](171)631-0114
England	Telex: 28173 ICOCOA G
LONDON W1	Cable: WORLDCOCOA

LANGUAGES: English, French, Russian, Spanish

ESTABLISHMENT AND FUNCTIONS

The International Cocoa Organization (ICCO) was established to administer the provisions of the International Cocoa Agreement, 1972, and its successor Agreements of 1975, 1980, 1986, and 1993.
The main objectives of the successive Agreements have been to ensure the production of adequate supplies of cocoa at prices remunerative to producers and fair to consumers, to prevent excessive price fluctuations, and to secure a balance between supply and demand.
The present Agreement, that of 1993, came into force on February 22, 1994. Whereas the mechanisms embodied in previous Agreements tended to focus on the correction of temporary or short-term market imbalances, essentially through buffer stock intervention, the 1993 Agreement focuses on a longer term view of the market and emphasizes the need to avoid structural imbalances by promoting the necessary adjustments of production and consumption. In order to restore a balanced market at acceptable price levels, the Agreement contains provisions for the establishment of production-management plans and programs, and measures to increase consumption in the medium to long-term.
In order to ensure the competitiveness of cocoa, there will also be more emphasis on support for cocoa research and the improvement of cocoa quality. The implementation of the 1993 Agreement will also see attention focused on the following key areas:

- The development and strengthening of international co-operation in all sectors of the world cocoa economy and the provision of an appropriate forum for the discussion of all related matters;
- The promotion of transparency in the working of the world cocoa economy through the collection and dissemination of relevant statistical and other data;
- The promotion of scientific research and development in the field of cocoa; and
- The development of the role of ICCO as an International Commodity Body in relation to the preparation, submission and supervision of projects to be financed through the Second Account of the Common Fund for Commodities.

As the 1993 Agreement has no buffer stock provision, all buffer stock cocoa accumulated under previous Agreements has now been liquidated in accordance with the provisions of Article 38 of the 1986 Agreement.

COMPOSITION

18 exporting members: Benin, Brazil, Cameroon, Côte d'Ivoire, Dominican Republic, Ecuador, Gabon, Ghana, Grenada, Jamaica, Malaysia, Nigeria, Papua New Guinea, São Tomé and Príncipe, Sierra Leone, Togo, Trinidad and Tobago, Venezuela
22 importing members: Austria, Belgium, Czech Republic, Denmark, Finland, France, Germany, Greece, Hungary, Ireland, Italy, Japan, Luxembourg, Netherlands, Norway, Portugal, Russian Federation, Slovak Republic, Spain, Sweden, Switzerland, United Kingdom
1 intergovernmental organization: European Community

STRUCTURE

The highest authority is the *International Cocoa Council*, which consists of all members of the Organization. The Council holds one regular session in each half of the cocoa year which runs from October 1 to September 30. Voting powers in the Council are evenly divided between exporting and importing members.

Exporting members: Brazil, Cameroon, Côte d'Ivoire, Ecuador, Gabon, Ghana, Jamaica, Malaysia, Nigeria, Papua New Guinea
Importing members: Belgium/Luxembourg, France, Germany, Italy, Japan, Netherlands, Russian Federation, Sweden, Switzerland, United Kingdom

GENERAL PUBLICATIONS

Annual Report; Quarterly Bulletin of Cocoa Statistics; Cocoa Newsletter; World Cocoa Directory; Cocoa Consumption in the Russian Federation

INTERNATIONAL COFFEE ORGANIZATION (ICO)

Organización Internacional del Café
Organizaçao Internacional do Café
Organisation internationale du café

HEADQUARTERS

22 Berners Street
London W1P 4DD

Telephone: [44](171)580-8591
Facsimile: [44](171)580-6129

England E-Mail: info@ico.org

Executive Director: ... **Celsius A. LODDER**

INTERNATIONAL COFFEE COUNCIL (1998/99)

Chairman: ... *Walter A. Bastiaanse (Netherlands)*
First Vice-Chairman: ... *Takuma Yamaguchi (Japan)*
Second Vice-Chairman: ... *Fernando Andrade Diaz-Durán (Guatemala)*
Third Vice-Chairman: ... *(no nomination)*

Executive Board (1998/99)

Chairman: ... *Eugène Avi ADROH (Côte d'Ivoire)*
Vice-Chairman: ... *Hope Sona Ebai (Cameroon)*

Members of the Executive Board (1999/99)

Exporting Members: ... *Brazil, Colombia, El Salvador, India, Indonesia, Kenya, Mexico, OAMCAF,*

Importing Members: *France, Germany, Italy, Japan, Netherlands, Spain, Sweden, United Kingdom*

LANGUAGES: ENGLISH, FRENCH, PORTUGUESE, SPANISH

ESTABLISHMENT AND FUNCTIONS

The International Coffee Organization (ICO) was established September 28, 1962, when representatives of coffee producing and coffee consuming countries reached an agreement in principle. The Agreement entered into force provisionally in July 1963 and definitively on December 27, 1963.

A revision of the 1962 Agreement became effective on October 1, 1968. Under the provisions of the 1962 and 1968 Agreements the Organization attempted to secure cooperation between coffee producing and coffee consuming countries in order to achieve a balance between supply and demand, keep prices at fair levels, and encourage increased consumption so as to enhance the purchasing power of coffee exporting countries.

On October 1, 1973, the Agreement was extended in modified form for two years ending September 30, 1975. Under the provisions of the Extended Agreement the Organization was preserved as a forum for the negotiation of a new Agreement and as a center for the collection and dissemination of statistical information on the international trade in coffee. The Council decided on September 26, 1974 to extend the Agreement for another year to September 30, 1976.
On October 1, 1976, a six-year Agreement entered into force, which was extended on September 16, 1982 for another year to September 30, 1983. The International Coffee Agreement 1976 contained provisions for the regulation of exports and imports under certain price conditions, and for generic promotion of coffee. Coffee export quotas were introduced on October 1, 1980.
The International Coffee Agreement 1983 entered into force on October 1, 1983. It continued and developed the provisions of the International Coffee Agreement 1976, and remained in force until September 30, 1989. It was extended without quota/price provisions to September 30, 1994. The International Coffee Agreement 1994 entered into force provisionally for a period of 5 years on October 1, 1994 (definitively on May 17, 1995).

COMPOSITION

44 exporting members: Angola, Bolivia, Brazil, Burundi, *Cameroon, Central African Republic,* Colombia, Democratic Republic of the Congo, *Republic of the Congo*, Costa Rica, *Côte d'Ivoire*, Cuba, Dominican Republic, Ecuador, El Salvador, *Equatorial Guinea*, Ethiopia, *Gabon*, Ghana, Guatemala, Guinea, Haiti, Honduras, India, Indonesia, Jamaica, Kenya, *Madagascar**, Malawi, Mexico, Nicaragua, Nigeria, Papua New Guinea, Paraguay*, Philippines, Rwanda, Tanzania, Thailand, *Togo*, Uganda, Venezuela, Vietnam, Zambia, Zimbabwe
NOTE: OAMCAF Members are in italics.
18 importing members: Austria, Belgium/Luxembourg*, Cyprus, Denmark, Finland, France, Germany, Greece, Ireland, Italy, Japan, Netherlands, Norway, Portugal, Spain, Sweden, Switzerland, United Kingdom, European Community
* Notification of provisional application under the provisions of paragraph (2) of Article 40 of the 1994 Agreement.

STRUCTURE

The highest authority of the Organization is the International Coffee Council composed of a representative and one or more alternates for each member. As a rule, the Council meets twice a year; it elects an Executive Board of 8 exporting members and 8 importing members for each coffee year. The Chairmen of the Council and of the Board are appointed by the Council for each coffee year.

GENERAL PUBLICATIONS

Coffee Statistics (quarterly); *Trade Statistics* (annual); *Coffee Newsletter, Library Monthly Entries; Country Coffee Profiles.*

INTERNATIONAL CONFEDERATION OF FREE TRADE UNIONS (ICFTU)

Confederation Internationale des Syndicats Libres (CISL)
Internationaler bund Freier Gewerkschaften (IBFG)
Confederación Internacional de Organizaciones Sindicales Libres (CIOSL)

HEADQUARTERS

Bd. Emile Jacqmain 155
B-1210 Brussels
Belgium

Telephone: [32](2)224-0211
Facsimile: [32](2)201-5815
[32](2)203-0756
E-Mail: internetpo@icftu.org
Internet: www.icftu.org

President: ... ***C. LeRoy TROTMAN***
General Secretary: ... ***Bill JORDAN***
Assistant General Secretary: ... ***Eddy LAURIJSSEN***

LANGUAGES: ENGLISH, FRENCH, GERMAN, SPANISH

ESTABLISHMENT AND FUNCTIONS

The International Confederation of Free Trade Unions (ICFTU) was established at its inaugural Congress held in London in 1949, and attended by delegates from 53 countries. It is a confederation of national trade union centres, each of which groups together the trade unions of that particular country. Today, ICFTU consists of 213 affiliated organizations in 143 countries and territories, and counts a membership of 124 million workers.

The ICFTU exists to promote the interests of the working people throughout the world, to work for constantly rising living standards, full employment and social security, and the eradication of poverty. It is engaged in the fight against oppression, dictatorship, and all forms of exclusion, inequality and discrimination, and in efforts to defend fundamental human and trade union rights. By virtue of its Category I consultative status with ECOSOC, the ICFTU represents the international free trade union movement at the United Nations.

It also has consultative status with various specialized agencies of the UN, and provides representation in inter-governmental bodies such as the IMF, the World Bank, and the WTO. In these forums, the ICFTU puts forward the proposals it has worked out with and on behalf of affiliated organizations of workers world-wide, for the promotion of growth with equity, and the alleviation of unemployment and poverty. The unique tripartite structure of the ILO gives the ICFTU and affiliated organizations the opportunity to play an active role in standard-setting, and the harmonization of industrial relations policy on the international level, through the Workers' Group of the ILO Governing Body.

STRUCTURE

The *Congress*, the supreme authority of the ICFTU, convenes at least every four years; the next Congress will take place on April 2000 in Durban, South Africa. It is composed of delegates from the affiliated trade union organizations. The Congress elects the General Secretary and an Executive Board of 53 members including five members nominated by the Women's Committee and one member representing young workers.
The *Executive Board* meets at least once a year, and directs the activities of the Confederation between Congresses. It elects the President and Vice-Presidents of the ICFTU. The General Secretary runs the secretariat headquartered in Brussels. The ICFTU has established regional organizations as follows: (i) The Asian and Pacific Regional Organization (APRO) based in Singapore; (ii) The African Regional Organization (AFRO) based in Nairobi; and (iii) The Inter-American Regional Organization (ORIT) based in Caracas.
The ICFTU maintains close relations with the *International Trade Secretariat* (ITS), which groups together national unions from a particular trade or industry, and often speaks on their behalf in inter-governmental bodies. The ICFTU has two permanent offices in Geneva and in New York, and together with the ITS, also runs an office in Washington, DC.

Special committees established by the Executive Board are: (1) Steering Committee; (2) Economic and Social Committee; (3) Human and Trade Union Rights Committee; (4) Peace, Security and Disarmament Committee; (5) Women's Committee; and (6) Youth Committee. In addition, the ICFTU organizes a number of working groups in cooperation with the ITS. These are: (a) The Working Party on Multi-National Companies; (b) The Occupational Health, Safety, and the Environment Working Party; and (c) The Working Party on Trade Union Education. A number of informal Task Forces (e.g., on child labor and on trade, investment and labor standards) involving ICFTU and ITS affiliates have also been established.

GENERAL PUBLICATIONS

Trade Union World (monthly magazine); *Annual Survey of Violations of Trade Union Rights* (annual report); *ICFTU On-Line* (daily electronic news bulletin). The ICFTU also publishes various occasional papers (e.g., Annual Statements to the IMF/World Bank Board of Governors, reports on respect for internationally-recognized core labor standards in countries around the world) and books, such as *Fighting for Workers' Human Rights in the Global Economy* (1998) and *No Time to Play* (Child Labour). A list of all ICFTU publications may be obtained from the Department of Press and Publications.

INTERNATIONAL COTTON ADVISORY COMMITTEE (ICAC)

Comité consultatif international du cotton
Comité Consultivo Internacional del Algodón

HEADQUARTERS

Suite 702	Telephone: (202)463-6660
1629 K Street, NW	Facsimile: (202)463-6950
Washington, DC 20006	Telex: 408272789
USA	E-Mail: secretariat@icac.org
	Internet: www.icac.org

Standing Committee

Chairman: ...	***Paul MORRIS (Australia)***
First Vice Chairman: ...	***Alfonso PINO (Spain)***
Second Vice Chairman: ...	***(vacant)***

Secretariat

Executive Director: ...	*Terry P. TOWNSEND*
Statistician: ...	*Ioannis KALTSAS*
Technical Information Section: ...	*M. Rafiq CHAUDRY*
Economists: ...	*Andrei GUITCHOUNTS*
...	*Carlos VALDERRAMA*
Administrative Officer: ...	*Federico ARRIOLA*

LANGUAGES: ARABIC, ENGLISH, FRENCH, RUSSIAN, SPANISH

ESTABLISHMENT AND FUNCTIONS

The International Cotton Advisory Committee (ICAC) was established in September 1939 in Washington, DC, in accordance with a resolution of the International Cotton Meeting of 12 principal cotton exporting countries. The first meeting was held in Washington, DC in October 1940. The Committee is an association of governments having an interest in the production, export, import, and consumption of cotton, designated to promote cooperation in the solution of cotton problems, particularly those of international scope and significance. Its functions are to observe and keep in close touch with developments affecting the world cotton situation; collect and disseminate complete, authentic, and timely statistics on world cotton production, trade, consumption, stocks and prices; suggest, as and when advisable, to member governments any measures considered suitable and practicable for the achievement of ultimate international collaboration. ICAC is a Designated International Commodity Body (ICB) under the terms of the Common Fund for Commodities. Membership is open to all members of the United Nations or the Food and Agriculture Organization and to other governments having a substantial interest in cotton.

COMPOSITION

43 member countries: Argentina, Australia, Azerbaijan, Belgium, Bolivia, Brazil, Burkina Faso, Cameroon, Chad, Colombia, Côte d'Ivoire, Egypt, Finland, France, Germany, Greece, India, Islamic Republic of Iran, Israel, Italy, Japan, Korea, Mali, Netherlands, Nigeria, Pakistan, Paraguay, Philippines, Poland, Russian Federation, South Africa, Spain, Sudan, Switzerland, Syrian Arab Republic, Taiwan Province of China, Tanzania, Turkey, Uganda, United Kingdom, United States, Uzbekistan, Zimbabwe

STRUCTURE

Annual plenary meetings are attended by representatives of member countries and observers from other governments, international organizations and private sector. There is a Standing Committee which meets in Washington, DC in the interim between plenary meetings.

GENERAL PUBLICATIONS

COTTON--World Statistics (bi-annual bulletin); COTTON: Review of the World Situation (bi-monthly and monthly update by fax); Proceedings of Plenary Meetings; Surveys of Cotton Production Research and Textile Activity; ICAC Recorder (update on cotton production research) (quarterly); yearly CD-ROM with main publications; Cotton This Month (monthly publication). Most publications are available by e-mail or on the ICAC web page (*www.icac.org*).

INTERNATIONAL FUND FOR AGRICULTURAL DEVELOPMENT (IFAD)

Fonds International de Développement Agricole (FIDA)

HEADQUARTERS

Via del Serafico, 107
00142 Rome
Italy

Telephone: [39](06)5-4591
Facsimile: [39](06)504-3463
Telex: 620330 IFAD I
Cable: IFAD ROME
E-Mail: ifad@ifad.org

President: ... ***Fawzi H. AL-SULTAN***

LANGUAGES: ARABIC, ENGLISH, FRENCH, SPANISH

ESTABLISHMENT AND FUNCTIONS

Based on the recommendation of the UN World Food Conference held in Rome, Italy, in 1974, and created at the initiative of the UN Conference on the Establishment of an International Fund for Agricultural Development, convened in Rome, Italy, June 10-13, 1976, pursuant to paragraph 2 of General Assembly Resolution 3503(XXX) of December 15, 1975. The Agreement Establishing the International Fund for Agricultural Development (IFAD) was opened for signature on December 20, 1976, after pledges of initial contributions exceeding US$1 billion had been received.

The Agreement entered into force on November 30, 1977, and the Fund began operations in December 1977. The organization is a specialized agency in the United Nations system and possesses an international juridical personality. The objective of the Fund is to mobilize additional resources for agricultural and rural development in developing Member States. The Fund provides financing primarily for projects specifically designed to introduce, expand or improve food production systems, and to strengthen related policies and institutions within the framework of national priorities and strategies.

Consideration is given to: (1) the need to increase food production in the poorest food-deficit countries; (2) the potential for expanded food production in other developing countries, and (3) the importance of improving the nutritional level and conditions of life of the poorest populations in developing countries.

IFAD started its operations with initial contributions of approximately US$l,000 million. Category I countries (industrialized countries) contributed US$573 million, Category II countries (oil producing developing countries) contributed US$435.5 million, and Category III countries (other developing countries) contributed US$l9 million, of which US$10 million was in convertible currencies. The initial resources covered IFAD's operations over the 1978-1980 period.

In response to the persisting emergency situation in the mid-1980s in a number of Sub-Saharan countries due to drought and desertification, IFAD's Governing Council and Executive Board called for intensified efforts to design activities especially geared to meet this situation, and to mobilize increased funds from the international community. To that end, it was decided to complement IFAD's regular program in the African region by launching a Special Programme for Sub-Saharan African Countries Affected by Drought and Desertification, which became effective in 1986. The fund-raising campaign mobilized about US$323 million in additional resources over a three year period. The First Phase of the Special Programme was declared completed, including the mobilization of the target resources set for it and the effective utilization of these resources in projects in Sub-Saharan Africa.

Twenty-five countries, of which nineteen are members of the OECD donor group, and five Sub-Saharan countries contributed to the Special Resources for Sub-Saharan Africa. In addition, the Commission of the European Communities has made a contribution of US$20.1 million.

At the 13th Session of the Governing Council, held in January 1990, a resolution was approved requesting the President to consult donors about the possibilities of mobilizing additional voluntary contributions to the Special Resources for Africa for a further three years, without prejudicing deliberations on core-funding for IFAD's resources.

The Special Programme for Africa was launched in 1986 in response to the devastating droughts of 1984-85 and ran in two phases from 1986 to the end of 1995. A major goal of the SPA was to develop smallholder agricultural systems having high resilience to environmental stress in order to enhance household and community food security in drought-prone areas. Its emphasis was on the development of drought-tolerant traditional staples, small-scale water management schemes, agroforestry, the rehabilitation of productive assets, marketing, and off-farm income-generating activities. Under the SPA, 48 loans for 47 projects were financed in 25 sub-Saharan African countries, with funds totaling US$359.4 million (net of cancellations). Twelve of these projects were partly financed under the Regular Programme. In the same period, the SPA also funded 87 grants for a grant total of US$24.1 million.

On April 18, 1980, IFAD was prescribed by the IMF as a holder of SDRs, and thus authorized to acquire and use SDRs in operations and transactions with participants in the IMF's SDR Department and other holders under the same terms and conditions as participants.

Funding

While IFAD receives some income from loan repayments and investments, it is primarily funded through donor contributions. Its initial capital was nearly US$1 billion. Until 1992, those resources were replenished every three years at levels negotiated by its member countries. The First Replenishment which funded activities from 1981 through 1983 brought pledges of US$1.1 billion. Member countries pledged US$488 million in the Second Replenishment and the Third Replenishment brought pledges of US$566.6 million.

Of IFAD's 160 member nations, 139 are donors to the Fund. Prior to the finalization of the Fourth Replenishment, these members were divided into categories. Each member's contribution level and voting rights were linked to their category. Once a category established its collective contribution level, its individual members were locked into contributing a previously negotiated, fixed proportion of that amount. While contributions were not divided equally between the categories, each category received the same number of votes to distribute among its members.

In 1995, IFAD's Governing Council approved a resolution providing for the elimination of the category system upon the finalization of the Fourth Replenishment. Now that the replenishment is complete, all individual members receive an equal number of membership votes based on their contributions. Further, member nations' contributions are no longer limited by an overall commitment negotiated for their category. These reforms will make future replenishments more predictable while enabling IFAD's unique partnership between developed and developing country members to continue through the 21st Century.

COMPOSITION

161 Member States: Islamic State of Afghanistan, Albania, Algeria, Angola, Antigua and Barbuda, Argentina, Armenia, Australia, Austria, Azerbaijan, Bangladesh, Barbados, Belgium, Belize, Benin, Bhutan, Bolivia, Bosnia and Herzegovina, Botswana, Brazil, Burkina Faso, Burundi, Cambodia, Cameroon, Canada, Cape Verde, Central African Republic, Chad, Chile, China, Colombia, Comoros, Democratic Republic of the Congo, Republic of the Congo, Cook Islands, Costa Rica, Côte d'Ivoire, Croatia, Cuba, Cyprus, Denmark, Djibouti, Dominica, Dominican Republic, Ecuador, Egypt, El Salvador, Equatorial Guinea, Eritrea, Ethiopia, Fiji, Finland, France, Gabon, The Gambia, Georgia, Germany, Ghana, Greece, Grenada, Guatemala, Guinea, Guinea-Bissau, Guyana, Haiti, Honduras, India, Indonesia, Islamic Republic of Iran, Iraq, Ireland, Israel, Italy, Jamaica, Japan, Jordan, Kazakhstan, Kenya, Democratic People's Republic of Korea, Republic of Korea, Kuwait, Kyrgyz Republic, Lao People's Democratic Republic, Lebanon, Lesotho, Liberia, Libya, Luxembourg, former Yugoslav Republic of Macedonia, Madagascar, Malawi, Malaysia, Maldives, Mali, Malta, Mauritania, Mauritius, Mexico, Moldova, Mongolia, Morocco, Mozambique, Myanmar, Namibia, Nepal, Netherlands, New Zealand, Nicaragua, Niger, Nigeria, Norway, Oman, Pakistan, Panama, Papua New Guinea, Paraguay, Peru, Philippines, Portugal, Qatar, Romania, Rwanda, St. Kitts and Nevis, St. Lucia, St. Vincent and the Grenadines, Samoa, São Tomé and Príncipe, Saudi Arabia, Senegal, Seychelles, Sierra Leone, Solomon Islands, Somalia, South Africa, Spain, Sri Lanka, Sudan, Suriname, Swaziland, Sweden, Switzerland, Syrian Arab Republic, Tajikistan, Tanzania, Thailand, Togo, Tonga, Trinidad and Tobago, Tunisia, Turkey, Uganda, United Arab Emirates, United Kingdom, United States, Uruguay, Venezuela, Vietnam, Republic of Yemen, Yugoslavia, Zambia, Zimbabwe

STRUCTURE

IFAD membership is open to any state that is a member of the United Nations or any of its specialized agencies, or of the International Atomic Energy Agency. The 161 member states are classified as: List A (OECD members), List B (OPEC members), and List C (developing countries). List C is further divided into C1 (countries in Africa), C2 (countries in Europe, Asia and the Pacific), and C3 (countries in Latin America and the Caribbean).

The *Governing Council* is IFAD's highest decision-making authority, wherein each member state is represented by a Governor and an Alternate.

The *Executive Board* oversees the general operations of IFAD and approves loans and grants. Membership distribution on the Executive Board is determined by the Governing Council. The Executive Board is currently distributed as follows: List A, 8 seats and 8 alternates; List B, 4 seats and 4 alternates; and List C, 6 seats and 6 alternates.

The *President* of IFAD is elected by the Governing Council and chairs the Executive Board. *Mr. Fawzi H. AL-SULTAN* of Kuwait currently serves as the President and chief executive officer and is responsible for the day-to-day operations of IFAD.

With less than 300 employees, IFAD operates with a small yet well-motivated staff of the highest quality. The staff has implemented a program of re-engineering and reform, which has fine-tuned efficient, team-oriented work processes without sacrificing commitment and creativity.

GENERAL PUBLICATIONS

IFAD Annual Report from 1978; Partners in Success; Near East and North Africa Management Training in Agriculture; Meeting Challenges in a Changing World: IFAD's Strategic Framework for 1998-2000; Microfinance for the Rural Poor; Down to Earth: IFAD/CCD Forum Report; Symposium on Land Degradation and Poverty; Land Degradation and Poverty in Africa; Rural Women in IFAD's Projects: The Key to Poverty Alleviation; IFAD Partnership with Non-Governmental Organizations; Drylands: A Major Focus for IFAD; Common Property Resources and Rural Poor in sub-Saharan Africa; The State of World Rural Poverty: Profile for Africa; Soil and Water Conservation; The State of World Rural Poverty: Profile for Near East and North Africa; The State of World Rural Poverty: Profile for Latin America and the Caribbean; Monitoring and Evaluation in Irrigation Projects; Monitoring and Evaluation: Guiding Principles; Drylands: Sustainable Use of Rangeland into twenty-first century; The Status of Rural Women in China; Un Programma contra la fame; Combating Hunger and Rural Poverty; A Working Partner in the Islamic Countries; Rural Women: IFAD Experience in East and Southern Africa; Rural Women: Entry Point for Development; Unifying the Fight against Environmental Degradation and Poverty; IFAD Update from Issue 1; The Popular Coalition to Combat Hunger and Poverty; Regional Workshop on Financial Administration

INTERNATIONAL GRAINS COUNCIL

Conseil international du Céréales
Consejo Internacional del Cereales

HEADQUARTERS

One Canada Square
Canary Wharf
London E14 5AE
England

Telephone: [44](171)513-1122
Facsimile: [44](171)513-0630
E-Mail: denis@igc.org.uk
Internet: www.igc.org.uk

LANGUAGES: INTERNATIONAL GRAINS COUNCIL: ENGLISH, FRENCH, RUSSIAN, SPANISH; FOOD AID COMMITTEE: ENGLISH, FRENCH, SPANISH

ESTABLISHMENT AND FUNCTIONS

The International Grains Agreement, 1995 (IGA) comprises the Grains Trade Convention and the Food Aid Convention, which are separate legal instruments although linked by a common Preamble. The 1995 Conventions came into force on July 1, 1995, replacing the Wheat Trade and Food Aid Conventions of 1986 originally for a three-year period. They could be extended by decision of their respective member governments for successive periods of up to two years on each occasion. Both Conventions have been extended for one year to June 30, 1999.

The Grains Trade Convention, 1995 (GTC) applies to trade in wheat, coarse grains, and their products. It seeks to further international cooperation in all aspects of grains trade; to promote expansion, openness and fairness in the grains sector; to contribute to grain market stability; and to enhance world food security. These objectives are to be sought by improving market transparency through information-sharing, analysis and consultation on grain market and policy developments.

The GTC is administered by the International Grains Council (IGC), the intergovernmental forum for cooperation on wheat and coarse grain matters. Until 1995, it was known as the International Wheat Council (IWC), which had administered an unbroken succession of International Wheat Agreements starting with that of 1949. The IGC normally meets twice a year, in June and December; some of its administrative functions are delegated to a 14-member Executive Committee, which meets between the regular Council Sessions as required.

The IGC's Market Conditions Committee keeps the global grain market situation and outlook under close review. On the basis of independent information and analysis prepared by the IGC Secretariat, in particular the monthly Grain Market Reports, IGC members discuss and consult on market and policy developments and consider the short-term grains outlook. The Committee also reviews trends in ocean freight rates.

The Council organizes an annual self-financing IGC Grains Conference each June. Since 1992 these Conferences have provided a high-level forum where senior private-sector representatives and government policy-makers discuss topical issues facing the global grains industry.

The activities of the Council and the operations of the IGC Secretariat are financed by GTC members' annual contributions, which are proportionate to their votes and thus relate to their share of world grains trade. The total budget in fiscal 1998/99 was £1.37 million.

Under the Food Aid Convention 1995, donors pledged to provide annually a minimum of some 5.4 million tons of food aid to developing countries, with specific amounts being specified for each donor government. This mostly consists of gifts of grains suitable for human consumption, but donors may provide cash, with which grain is bought for the recipients, mainly from developing countries. Donors are encouraged to cover also the associated shipping and transportation costs, particularly for emergency shipments or those to low-income countries. Members are entirely free to decide on the distribution of their aid, although priority is to be given to least-developed and other low-income developing countries. They are also urged to channel their grain multilaterally, in particular through the World Food Programme.

The first Food Aid Convention came into force in 1968, having been negotiated in the context of the 1967 GATT Kennedy Round Agreement. It reflected the growing recognition of the food needs of low-income food deficit countries, and the wish of traditional food aid donors to share their efforts with other countries able to provide grains or finance for food aid. The Convention was, and remains, a legally separate multilateral cooperation instrument among food aid donors, but its existence depends on that of the IGC, and the IGC Secretariat provides its administrative services.

The Food Aid Committee (FAC) reviews the implementation of the Convention, and exchanges information on the functioning of members' food aid arrangements, on the basis of detailed records maintained by the IGC Secretariat. The FAC also shares information on policy developments affecting food aid, discusses the general world food situation and prospects, and considers ways in which donors' aid efforts may more effectively achieve their objectives.

In December 1997 the Committee agreed to open negotiations on a new Food Aid Convention, which would seek to increase the effectiveness of food aid provided by donor governments, and take account of the WTO Singapore Ministerial Conference and of the declarations of the World Food Summit in 1996, with respect to the least-developed and net-food-importing developing countries.

Negotiations were successfully completed in April 1999 and, subject to the necessary actions by Governments, the Food Aid Convention 1999 will enter into force on July 1, 1999 replacing the 1995 FAC. Under the new Convention, members will be able to express their commitments in tonnage, in value, or in a combination of tonnage and value. On the basis of the expected membership, minimum annual tonnage and value commitments will amount in total to 4,895,000 tons (wheat equivalent) and £130 million, respectively. The list of eligible products which may be supplied has been broadened significantly beyond cereals.

There are stronger provisions to cover transportation and other operational costs associated with food aid transactions, especially when food aid is directed to least developed countries and in emergencies. When allocating their food aid, donors will give priority to Least Developed Countries and other Low Income Countries. All food aid to LDCs covered by a member's commitments will be in the form of grants; overall, food aid in the form of grants will represent not less than 80 percent of a member's contributions. In general, the new FAC will seek to improve the effectiveness and impact of food aid.

COMPOSITION

Grains Trade Convention:

Exporting members: Argentina, Australia, Canada, *European Community*, Hungary, Kazakhstan, Saudi Arabia, Turkey, Ukraine, United States

Importing members: Algeria, Bolivia, Côte d'Ivoire, Cuba, Ecuador, Egypt, India, Iraq, Japan, Jordan, Kenya, Korea, Malta, Mauritius, Morocco, Norway, Pakistan, Panama, Russian Federation, South Africa, Switzerland, Tunisia, Vatican City, Republic of Yemen

Food Aid Convention: Argentina, Australia, Canada, *European Community* and its 15-Member States, Japan, Norway, Switzerland, United States.

GENERAL PUBLICATIONS

Grain Market Reports (monthly; subscribers from member countries can arrange for electronic access) containing comprehensive information and analysis of global market policy developments: trade, prices, production, consumption, stocks and ocean freight rates; they include the latest detailed estimates and forecasts, and special notes on major topical issues; *Grain Market Indicators* (weekly; available only to IGC members) containing the latest market information for the major grains; *World Grain Statistics* (annual) providing a compendium of time series of data for wheat and coarse grains; *Record of Shipments* (annual) detailing commercial and non-commercial trade in major grains; *Food Aid Shipments* (annual) based on reports submitted by members of the Food Aid Committee; *Fiscal Year Reports* (covering IGC and FAC activities from July 1 to June 30); an extensive historical database.

INTERNATIONAL JUTE ORGANISATION (IJO)

HEADQUARTERS

145 Monipuripara
Old Airport Road
Dhaka-1215
Bangladesh

Telephone: [880](2)912-5581/5
Facsimile: [880](2)912-5248
[880](2)912-5249
E-mail: ijoed@bdmail.net
ijodir@bdmail.net

Executive Director: ... ***Henri L. JASON (France)***

ESTABLISHMENT AND FUNCTIONS

The International Jute Organisation (IJO) was set up in 1984 in Dhaka, Bangladesh, to implement the provisions of the *International Agreement on Jute and Jute Products, 1982.* The Agreement was concluded within the framework of the *Integrated Programme for Commodities*, under the auspices of the United Nations Conference on Trade and Development (UNCTAD) in Geneva. The original Agreement was replaced by the *International Agreement on Jute and Jute Products, 1989*, the duration of which was extended recently until April 11, 2000.

The main objectives of the organization are to: (a) provide an effective framework for cooperation and consultation between the jute exporting and importing countries for the development of the jute economy; (b) improve structural conditions in the jute market; and (c) increase the competitiveness and quality of jute and jute products, upholding jute's positive environmental aspects.

The activities of IJO include: (a) formulating, supervising and implementing Research and Development (R&D) projects through relevant institutes (located in IJO member countries) in the areas of agriculture and industry, aimed at improving the competitiveness and quality of jute and jute products; (b) undertaking market promotion activities to promote existing and new products; and (c) organizing non-project activities such as studies, seminars, workshops, etc. Out of a total of 42 approved projects, 21 have so far been completed with 8 currently under implementation and 2 fully funded pipeline projects are due to commence shortly. In the meantime, funding is awaited for the remaining 11 approved projects.

COMPOSITION

3 exporting countries: Bangladesh, China, Nepal

21 importing countries: *European Union* (in its own right), Austria, Belgium, Denmark, Finland, France, Germany, Greece, Ireland, Italy, Luxembourg, Netherlands, Portugal, Spain, Sweden, United Kingdom, Egypt, Indonesia, Japan, Norway, Switzerland

STRUCTURE

The *International Jute Council* (IJC), comprising all IJO member countries, is the organization's highest authority. All policy decisions regarding the implementation of the Agreement rest with the Council.

The *Committee on Projects* (COP), which also comprises all IJO members, is a subsidiary body of the Council. It is vested with the responsibility to technically appraise and evaluate project and non-project proposals, to review their implementation status, and to make recommendations to the Council.

The Council elects a *Chairman* and a *Vice-Chairman* every year, one from among the representatives of exporting members and the other from among the representatives of importing members. There are several observers--26 countries, 9 UN specialized agencies, 5 inter-governmental organizations and 17 non-governmental organizations and jute-related associations. The Secretariat in Dhaka administers the provisions of the Agreement and functions as the implementing agency of decisions taken by the IJC and/or the COP.

The *Executive Director* is the chief administrative officer of the Secretariat. He is assisted by a *Director* (Projects and Administration), who also serves as *Secretary* to the IJC. In addition, the approved staffing structure provides for three Senior Professional Officers who are in charge of the three technical sections dealing respectively with Agriculture, Industry, and Market Promotion; an Agriculture Officer and 20 general service staff.

INTERNATIONAL LABOUR ORGANIZATION (ILO)

Organisation internationale du travail (OIT)
Organización Internacional del Trabajo (OIT)

HEADQUARTERS

4 route des Morillons
CH-1211 Geneva 22
Switzerland

Telephone: [41](22)799-6111
Facsimile: [41](22)798-8685
Telex: 415647 ILO CH
Cable: INTERLAB GENEVE
Internet: www.ilo.org

LANGUAGES: ENGLISH, FRENCH, SPANISH

ESTABLISHMENT AND FUNCTIONS

Concerned with both economic and social aspects of development, the International Labour Organization (ILO)is one of the specialized agencies that predates the United Nations, established in 1919 by the Treaty of Versailles. Its long and diverse work in the setting and monitoring of labor standards in the workplace has provided the framework of international labor standards and guidelines that have been adopted in national legislation in virtually all countries as well.

The ILO is guided by the principle that social stability and integration can be sustained only if they are based on social justice, particularly the right to employment with fair compensation in a healthy workplace. Over the decades, the ILO has helped to create such hallmarks of industrial society as the eight-hour day, maternity protection, child-labor laws, and a whole range of policies that promote peaceful industrial relations and safety in the workplace.
Specifically, the ILO engages in: (1) the formulation of international policies and programs to promote basic human rights, improve working and living conditions, and enhance employment opportunities; (2) the creation of international labor standards--backed by a unique system to supervise their application--to serve as guidelines for national authorities in putting sound labor policies into practice; (3) an extensive program of technical cooperation, formulated and carried out in partnership with beneficiaries, to help countries make these policies effective; and (4) training, education, research, and information activities to help advance all these efforts.
One of ILO's most important functions is the adoption by the tripartite International Labour Conference--made up of Government, employer, and worker representatives--of Conventions and Recommendations that set international standards. Through ratification by member states, Conventions create binging obligations to put their provisions into effect. Recommendations provide guidance on policy, legislation and practice. Over the years, the Governments of member states and their employers' and workers' organizations have built up a system of international standards in all work-related matters. Some 181 Conventions and 188 Recommendations have been adopted on work-related matters. They cover basic human rights, labor administration, industrial relations, employment policy, working conditions social security, occupational safety and health, employment of women, children and special categories.
ILO assistance to efforts at job creation has been made more urgent by the steady rise in poverty linked to unemployment and underemployment during the last decade. ILO provides research, analysis and advice to assist policy-makers and tripartite constituents to make the right choices and formulate optimal strategies in the effort to create more and better jobs.
ILO's technical cooperation focuses on support for democratization, poverty alleviation through employment creation, and the protection of workers. In particular, ILO helps countries to develop their legislation and take practical steps towards implementing ILO standards, for instance, by developing occupational health and safety departments, social security systems and worker education programs.
Opportunities for study and training are offered at the International Training Centre in Turin, Italy. The means of action of ILO's International Institute for Labour Studies include research networks; social policy forums; courses and seminars; visiting scholar and internship programs; and publications. On its 50th anniversary in 1969, ILO was awarded the Nobel Peace Prize.
ILO's budget for 1998-1999 is approximately US$481 million.

COMPOSITION

174 member countries: Islamic State of Afghanistan, Albania, Algeria, Angola, Antigua and Barbuda, Argentina, Armenia, Australia, Austria, Azerbaijan, The Bahamas, Bahrain, Bangladesh, Barbados, Belarus, Belgium, Belize, Benin, Bolivia, Bosnia and Herzegovina, Botswana, Brazil, Bulgaria, Burkina Faso, Burundi, Cambodia, Cameroon, Canada, Cape Verde, Central African Republic, Chad, Chile, China, Colombia, Comoros, Democratic Republic of the Congo, Republic of the Congo, Costa Rica, Côte d'Ivoire, Croatia, Cuba, Cyprus, Czech Republic, Denmark, Djibouti, Dominica, Dominican Republic, Ecuador, Egypt, El Salvador, Equatorial Guinea, Eritrea, Estonia, Ethiopia, Fiji, Finland, France, Gabon, The Gambia, Georgia, Germany, Ghana, Greece, Grenada, Guatemala, Guinea, Guinea-Bissau, Guyana, Haiti, Honduras, Hungary, Iceland, India, Indonesia, Islamic Republic of Iran, Iraq, Ireland, Israel, Italy, Jamaica, Japan, Jordan, Kazakhstan, Kenya, Korea, Kuwait, Kyrgyz Republic, Lao People's Democratic Republic, Latvia, Lebanon, Lesotho,

Liberia, Libya, Lithuania, Luxembourg, former Yugoslav Republic of Macedonia, Madagascar, Malawi, Malaysia, Mali, Malta, Mauritania, Mauritius, Mexico, Moldova, Mongolia, Morocco, Mozambique, Myanmar, Namibia, Nepal, Netherlands, New Zealand, Nicaragua, Niger, Nigeria, Norway, Oman, Pakistan, Panama, Papua New Guinea, Paraguay, Peru, Philippines, Poland, Portugal, Qatar, Romania, Russian Federation, Rwanda, St. Kitts and Nevis, St. Lucia, St. Vincent and the Grenadines, San Marino, São Tomé and Príncipe, Saudi Arabia, Senegal, Seychelles, Sierra Leone, Singapore, Slovak Republic, Slovenia, Solomon Islands, Somalia, South Africa, Spain, Sri Lanka, Sudan, Suriname, Swaziland, Sweden, Switzerland, Syrian Arab Republic, Tajikistan, Tanzania, Thailand, Togo, Trinidad and Tobago, Tunisia, Turkey, Turkmenistan, Uganda, Ukraine, United Arab Emirates, United Kingdom, United States, Uruguay, Uzbekistan, Venezuela, Vietnam, Republic of Yemen, Yugoslavia, Zambia, Zimbabwe

STRUCTURE

The *International Labour Conference* is the supreme body of the ILO, responsible for the formulation of international standards of working and living conditions, which are embodied in international labor conventions and recommendations which it has adopted. It normally meets once a year. The Conference is composed of national delegations, each comprising two government delegates, one employers' delegate, and one workers' delegate. The Conference elects the Governing Body and adopts the budget.

The *Governing Body* is the organization's executive council, normally meeting three or four times a year to decide policy and programs. It is composed of 56 members, of which 28 are government members, 14 are employers' members, and 14 are workers' members.

Ten of the government seats are reserved for the "states of chief industrial importance," i.e., Brazil, China, France, Germany, India, Italy, Japan, Russian Federation, the United Kingdom, and the United States. The remaining 18 government seats are elected from among the other member countries every three years. Among its functions are the general supervision of the International Labour Office; the formulation of policies and programs; the guidance of the various committees and other bodies; and the appointment of the *Director-General.*

The *International Labour Office* functions as the Secretariat of the organization. It is headed by the Director-General, who is also the Secretary General of the Conference.

Other ILO bodies include regional conferences and industrial committees.

GENERAL PUBLICATIONS

World of Work (5 times per year); *Official Bulletin* (quarterly); *Labour Law Documents* (3 times per year); *Bulletin of Labour Statistics* (quarterly); *Yearbook of Labour Statistics; International Labour Review* (6 times per year), *World Employment, World Labour Report Series.* Information on new and forthcoming titles is available vis the Internet (www.ilo.org) or by writing to the ILO Publications Bureau, International Labour Office, CH-1211 Geneva 22; facsimile [41](22)798-6358.

INTERNATIONAL LEAD AND ZINC STUDY GROUP

Groupe d'étude international du plomb et du zinc

HEADQUARTERS

2 King Street
London SW1Y 6QP
England

Telephone: [44](171)839-8550
Facsimile: [44](171)930-4635
E-Mail: root@ilzsg.org
Internet: www.ilzsg.org

Secretary-General: ... ***Francis LABRO***

Chairman of Committees

Study Group: ... *A. IGNATOW (Canada)*
Vice Chairmen: ... *J. Sebastian DE ERICE (Spain)*
... *V. BAKHTIN (Russia)*
Standing Committee: ... *G. MILES (United Kingdom)*
Vice Chairmen: ... *M. FARROW (Australia)*
... *R. KELLY (Ireland)*
Finance Member: ... *L. LEFERE (Belgium)*
Int'l. Economics Committee: ... *G. GOLIASCH (Germany)*
Statistical & Forecasting Committee: ... *D. LARRABEE (United States)*
Mining & Smelter Projects Committee: ... *M. COOK (Finland)*
Recycling Committee: ... *P.K. MOHANTY (Canada)*

Environment Committee: ... *D. WILSON (United Kingdom)*

LANGUAGES: CHINESE, ENGLISH, FRENCH, RUSSIAN, SPANISH

ESTABLISHMENT AND FUNCTIONS

Preparatory meetings on the establishment of an intergovernmental study group on lead and zinc were held under the auspices of the United Nations Economic and Social Council in London in September 1958, in Geneva in November 1958, and in New York in May 1959. The first meeting of the Group took place at the United Nations in Geneva in January 1960.

The Group provides opportunities for intergovernmental consultations on international trade in lead and zinc and for studies on the world situation in those commodities, having regard especially to providing continuous accurate information on the supply and demand position and its probable development. Financing is by annual assessment, half of which is divided equally among all members and half shared on the basis of trade interest.

COMPOSITION

27 member countries: Australia, Belgium, Brazil, Bulgaria, Canada, China, Finland, France, Germany, India, Ireland, Italy, Japan, Korea, Morocco, Netherlands, Norway, Peru, Poland, Russian Federation, South Africa, Spain, Sweden, Thailand, United Kingdom, United States, Yugoslavia

STRUCTURE

The Study Group is composed of representatives of all members and meets every year. It has a Standing Committee, composed of representatives of the members of the Study Group, to act for the Group between sessions. The other principal subsidiary bodies are the International Economics Committee, the Statistical and Forecasting Committee, the Mine and Smelter Projects, the Recycling Committee, and the Environment Committee. An Industry Advisory Panel, consisting of about ten senior experts from the lead and zinc industry, provides the Study Group with a body for advice and consultation.

GENERAL PUBLICATIONS

Lead and Zinc Statistics (monthly bulletin); *Lead and Zinc New Mines and Smelter Projects; Principal Uses of Lead and Zinc: 1992-1997; Zinc Usage by the Automotive Industry 1999; World Lead Sheet Supply and Demand 1999; Study on the Image of Lead; The Market Situation for Lead; The Market Situation for Zinc; Lead in Batteries; Trends in Production of Lead and Zinc; Zinc Die Casting and Hot Dip Galvanizing in Selected Developing Countries; Principal Uses of Lead and Zinc: 1960-1990; Lead and Zinc Statistics: 1960-1988* (database); *World Directory of Continuous Galvanizing Lines 1997; World Directory: Primary and Secondary Lead Plants; World Directory: Primary and Secondary Zinc Plans; World Directory: Lead and Zinc Mines and Primary Metallurgical Works (5th Edition); Environmental and Health Controls on Lead; Environmental and Health Controls on Zinc; Environmentally Friendly Lead and Zinc - The Challenge of the Recycling Millennium* (2 volumes); *The Future of Lead and Zince - Asia and the World* (2 volumes); *Recycling Lead and Zinc into the 21st Century* (2 volumes).

INTERNATIONAL MONETARY FUND (IMF)

Fonds Moneacutetaire International (FMI)
Fondo Monetario Internacional (FMI)

HEADQUARTERS

700 - 19th Street, NW
Washington, DC 20431
USA

Telephone: (202)623-7000
Facsimile: (202)623-4661
Telex: 64111 IMF UW
248331 IMF UR
Cable: INTERFUND WASHINGTON DC
E-Mail: communications@imf.org
Internet: www.imf.org

OFFICE IN GENEVA

58 rue de Moillebeau
1209 Geneva
Switzerland

Telephone: [41](22)918-0300
Facsimile: [41](22)918-0303

Special Representative to the World Trade Organization and Assistant Director: ... *G.B. TAPLIN*

REGIONAL OFFICE FOR ASIA AND THE PACIFIC

21/F Fukoku Seimei Bldg.
2-2-2 Uchisaiwai-cho
Chiyoda-ku, Tokyo 100
Japan

Telephone: [81](3)3597-6700
Facsimile: [81](3)3597-6705

Director: ... *Kunio SAITO*

FUND OFFICE UNITED NATIONS

Fourth Floor
828 Second Avenue
New York, NY 10017
USA

Telephone: (212)557-0894
(Headquarters) (202)623-8560
Facsimile: (212)687-9123
(Headquarters) (202)623-4006

Special Representative of the Fund to the UN:
Reinhard MUNZBERG
(also supervising Geneva office in his personal capacity)

LANGUAGES: THE WORKING LANGUAGE OF THE FUND IS ENGLISH; SELECTED DOCUMENTS AND PUBLICATIONS ARE TRANSLATED INTO CHINESE, FRENCH, PORTUGUESE, RUSSIAN, AND SPANISH.

ESTABLISHMENT AND FUNCTIONS

The International Monetary Fund (IMF) was established at a conference held in Bretton Woods, New Hampshire, USA, from July 1-22, 1944, and came into official existence on December 27, 1945, when 29 countries signed the Articles of Agreement of the IMF. Financial operations commenced on March 1, 1947.

The purposes of the IMF are to promote international monetary cooperation; to facilitate the expansion and balanced growth of international trade; to promote exchange stability; to assist in the establishment of a multilateral system of payments; to make the general resources of the Fund temporarily available to the members under adequate safeguards; and to shorten the duration and lessen the degree of disequilibrium in the international balances of payments of members.

COMPOSITION

182 member countries: Islamic State of Afghanistan, Albania, Algeria, Angola, Antigua and Barbuda, Argentina, Armenia, Australia, Austria, Azerbaijan, The Bahamas, Bahrain, Bangladesh, Barbados, Belarus, Belgium, Belize, Benin, Bhutan, Bolivia, Bosnia and Herzegovina, Botswana, Brazil, Brunei Darussalam, Bulgaria, Burkina Faso, Burundi, Cambodia, Cameroon, Canada, Cape Verde, Central African Republic, Chad, Chile, China, Colombia, Comoros, Democratic Republic of the Congo, Republic of the Congo, Costa Rica, Côte d'Ivoire, Croatia, Cyprus, Czech Republic, Denmark, Djibouti, Dominica, Dominican Republic, Ecuador, Egypt, El Salvador, Equatorial Guinea, Eritrea, Estonia, Ethiopia, Fiji, Finland, France, Gabon, The Gambia, Georgia, Germany, Ghana, Greece, Grenada, Guatemala, Guinea, Guinea-Bissau, Guyana, Haiti, Honduras, Hungary, Iceland, India, Indonesia, Islamic Republic of Iran, Iraq, Ireland, Israel, Italy, Jamaica, Japan, Jordan, Kazakhstan, Kenya, Kiribati, Korea, Kuwait, Kyrgyz Republic, Lao People's Democratic Republic, Latvia, Lebanon, Lesotho, Liberia, Libya, Lithuania, Luxembourg, former Yugoslav Republic of Macedonia, Madagascar, Malawi, Malaysia, Maldives, Mali, Malta, Marshall Islands, Mauritania, Mauritius, Mexico, Federated States of Micronesia, Moldova, Mongolia, Morocco, Mozambique, Myanmar, Namibia, Nepal, Netherlands, New Zealand, Nicaragua, Niger, Nigeria, Norway, Oman, Pakistan, Palau, Panama, Papua New Guinea, Paraguay, Peru, Philippines, Poland, Portugal, Qatar, Romania, Russian Federation, Rwanda, St. Kitts and Nevis, St. Lucia, St. Vincent and the Grenadines, Samoa, San Marino, São Tomé and Príncipe, Saudi Arabia, Senegal, Seychelles, Sierra Leone, Singapore, Slovak Republic, Slovenia, Solomon Islands, Somalia, South Africa, Spain, Sri Lanka, Sudan, Suriname, Swaziland, Sweden, Switzerland, Syrian Arab Republic, Tajikistan, Tanzania, Thailand, Togo, Tonga, Trinidad and Tobago, Tunisia, Turkey, Turkmenistan, Uganda, Ukraine, United Arab Emirates, United Kingdom, United States, Uruguay, Uzbekistan, Vanuatu, Venezuela, Vietnam, Republic of Yemen, Zambia, Zimbabwe

STRUCTURE

The *Board of Governors* is the supreme body of the Fund. It consists of one Governor and one Alternate Governor appointed by each member who each serve until a new appointment is made. The Board usually meets annually. The Annual Meeting is held jointly with that of the World Bank Group's Board of Governors.
The *Interim Committee*, which meets twice a year (in the spring and also at the time of the Annual Meeting of the Board of Governors), was established on October 2, 1974. Originally, the Committee was expected to serve as a high-level advisory board pending establishment of a Council of Governors. The latter has yet to be established. The members of the Committee are governors of the Fund, ministers, or others of comparable rank.
The *Executive Board* is responsible for conducting the day-to-day business of the Fund, and for this purpose exercises all the powers delegated to it by the Board of Governors. The Managing Director of the Fund is also Chairman of the Executive Board. Nineteen of the Directors are elected and five appointed by the five members having the largest quotas. Elections of Executive Directors are conducted at intervals of two years. Each Executive Director appoints an Alternate with full power to act for him or her in his or her absence.

GENERAL PUBLICATIONS

The Publications Index of the Fund may now be accessed through the Internet (address is *www.imf.org*).
The publications are available at a number of outlets around the world. For details of these addresses, information on how to order, method of payment, credit card information, special delivery arrangements, titles not listed, etc., contact:

International Monetary Fund
Publication Services, Catalog Orders
700 - 19th Street, NW
Washington, DC 20431
USA

Telephone: (202)623-7430
Facsimile: (202)623-7201
Telex:(RCA) 248331 IMF UR
Cable: INTERFUND
E-Mail publications@imf.org

INTERNATIONAL NATURAL RUBBER ORGANIZATION (INRO)

HEADQUARTERS

4th Floor, Wisma SPK
Jalan Sultan Ismail
50250 Kuala Lumpur
Malaysia

Postal Add: P.O. Box 10374
50712 Kuala Lumpur
Telephone: [60](3)248-6466
Facsimile: [60](3)248-6485
E-Mail: inro@po.jaring.my
Internet: www.inro.com.my/inro

Executive Director: ... ***(to be appointed)***
Deputy Executive Director: ... ***Gérard LOYEN***

LANGUAGES: CHINESE, ENGLISH, FRENCH, RUSSIAN

ESTABLISHMENT AND FUNCTIONS

The International Natural Rubber Organization (INRO) was established on October 23, 1980 pursuant to the International Natural Rubber Agreement, 1979 (INRA 1979), which recognizes the importance of UNCTAD Resolutions 93(IV) and 124(V) on the Integrated Programme for Commodities. INRA 1979 was replaced by INRA 1987 and subsequently by INRA 1995.
The new Agreement (INRA 1995), the text of which was established in 1995, came into force provisionally on February 6, 1997 and definitively on February 14, 1997. The current membership of the Organization comprises 6 exporting members and 17 importing members (plus the *European Community)*. The Agreement shall remain in force for a period of four years after its entry into force, with the possibility of extension for a maximum period of two years.
The objectives of the Organization are: (a) to achieve balanced growth in supply of and demand for natural rubber; (b) to achieve stable conditions in natural rubber trade through the avoidance of excessive fluctuations in prices; (c) to help stabilize the export earnings of natural rubber exporting members; (d) to ensure adequate supplies of natural rubber to meet importing members' requirements; (e) to take feasible steps in the event of a surplus or shortfall in supplies of natural rubber; (f) to seek to expand international trade in and improve market access for natural rubber and its products; (g) to improve competitiveness of natural rubber through research on its problems; (h) to encourage economies in natural rubber production through improvements in its processing, marketing and distribution; and (i) to further international cooperation on natural rubber through research, assistance and other programs.
To achieve its price stabilization objectives, the Agreement provides for an international Buffer Stock of natural rubber, with a total capacity of 550,000 metric tons. This Buffer Stock is the sole instrument of market intervention in the Agreement.
INRO is also a forum for meetings and discussions. It initiates, promotes and helps to source for financing for economic studies, research and development projects, with the objectives of improving the quality and marketing, increase the production and productivity and expansion in the usage of natural rubber.

COMPOSITION

6 exporting members: Côte d'Ivoire, Indonesia, Malaysia, Nigeria, Sri Lanka, Thailand
17 importing members (plus the European Community): Austria, Belgium, China, Denmark, Finland, France, Germany, Greece, Ireland, Italy, Japan, Luxembourg, Netherlands, Spain, Sweden, United Kingdom, United States

STRUCTURE

The highest authority of the Organization is the *International Natural Rubber Council*, which consists of all members, each represented by one Delegate. The Council exercises all powers necessary for carrying out the provisions of the Agreement, adopts the rules and regulations of the Organization including those with respect to the staff and governing the operation of the Buffer Stock, and publishes the Annual Report. It elects each year a Chairman and a Vice-Chairman, one from among the representatives of natural rubber exporting members and the other from among representatives of natural rubber importing members. These offices alternate each year between the two categories of members.
Under the Council are four committees, i.e., Administration; Buffer Stock Operations; Statistics; and Other Measures. The Council appoints an *Executive Director*, a *Deputy Executive Director*, and a *Buffer Stock Manager* by special vote in accordance with the Agreement. As the chief administrative officer of the Organization, the Executive Director is responsible for general operations of the Agreement. The Deputy Executive Director assists the Executive Director in the overall general operations of the Agreement and deputizes for the Executive Director in his absence. The Buffer Stock Manager, who is responsible to the Council and the Executive Director, is charged with conducting the day-to-day operations of the Buffer Stock.

GENERAL PUBLICATIONS

Annual Report; The INRO Newsletter (quarterly); studies and texts of conferences.

INTERNATIONAL RUBBER STUDY GROUP

Groupe international d'etudes du caoutchouc

HEADQUARTERS

Heron House
109/115 Wembley Hill Road
Wembley, Middx. HA9 8DA
England

Telephone: [44](181)903-7727
Facsimile: [44](181)903-2848
E-Mail: irsg@compuserve.com
Internet: www.rubberstudy.com

Secretary-General: ... ***M.E. CAIN***

LANGUAGES: ENGLISH (FRENCH AT ANNUAL MEETINGS)

ESTABLISHMENT AND FUNCTIONS

Established in London in l944 to provide a forum for the discussion matters affecting the production, consumption, and trade in natural and synthetic rubber, and publication of statistics of the world rubber industry. Subsequently, activities were extended to include economic, techno-economic and statistical studies of aspects of the industry.

COMPOSITION

19 member countries: Belgium, Cameroon, Côte d'Ivoire, France, Germany, India, Indonesia, Italy, Japan, Malaysia, Netherlands, Nigeria, Russian Federation, Singapore, Spain, Sri Lanka, Thailand, United Kingdom, United States

STRUCTURE

The Group meets annually, normally in an Assembly at the invitation of a Member Government, otherwise in a Group Meeting. An international conference, the International Rubber Forum, is held as part of each annual meeting. A Chairman and Vice-Chairman of the Group are elected to serve two years, and they are ex officio members of the Executive Committee. This consists of members elected annually, and exercises functions delegated by the Group. Two standing committees of all members, the Statistical and Economic Committees, also meet annually. They are advised by the Committee of Expert Rubber Statisticians and the Industry Advisory Panel, each consisting of invited industry experts. Commercial companies and other organizations may subscribe to the Panel of Associates which provides free access to the Group's publications and information databases.

GENERAL PUBLICATIONS

Rubber Statistical Bulletin (monthly); *International Rubber Digest* (monthly); *Outlook for Elastomers* (annual); *Rubber Statistics Yearbook* (annual); *Directory of Rubber Organizations* (1998); *Proceedings of the International Rubber Forum* (annual); *The Future of Natural Rubber in Africa* (1986); *Key Rubber Indicators* (1996); *The World Rubber Economy: Changes and Challenges* (1988); *World Rubber Statistics Handbook, Vol.1* (1946-70); *Vol.2* (1965-80); *Vol.3* (1960-85); *Vol.4* (1965-90); *Vol.5* (1975-1995); *World Rubber Statistics Historic Handbook* (1900-1960); *Secretariat Papers* (6-10 annually).

INTERNATIONAL SUGAR ORGANIZATION (ISO)

Organisation internationale du sucre
Organización Internacional del Azúcar

HEADQUARTERS

One Canada Square
Canary Wharf
London E14 5AA
England

Telephone: [44](171)513-1144
Facsimile: [44](171)513-1146
Cable: INTERSUGAR
E-Mail: isolondon@compuserve.com

Executive Director ... ***P. BARON***
Head, Economics and Statistics Division ... ***A.C. HANNAH***

Council (1999)

Chairman: ... *Ejner STENDERVAD (EU)*
Vice-Chairman: *Juan GALLARDO THURLOW (Mexico)*

LANGUAGES: ENGLISH, FRENCH, RUSSIAN, SPANISH

ESTABLISHMENT AND FUNCTIONS

The International Sugar Organization (ISO) was established to administer the International Sugar Agreement, 1968, as successor to the International Sugar Council which had operated under the International Sugar Agreement (ISA), 1953. Successor International Sugar Agreements of 1973 and 1977 were in force from 1974 through 1977, and from 1978 through 1984, respectively.

The Agreement of 1977 was designed to stabilize the price of sugar within a range originally of 11 to 21 US cents per pound, later 13 to 23 cents, through a system of export quotas and nationally held, but internationally controlled, stocks. A United Nations Sugar Conference held under the auspices of UNCTAD in 1983-1984 failed to negotiate a new agreement with economic provisions. A two-year administrative agreement was finally concluded and entered into force in 1985. Another three-year administrative Agreement, renewable on a year to year basis for a maximum of two years, was in force from 1988 until 1992.

A new International Sugar Agreement was negotiated in March 1992 which entered into force in January 1993.

The objectives set by the new Agreement open up wide scope for cooperation with, assistance to, and services for members. Therefore, the 1992 ISA represents a modern commodity agreement of the new generation which is perfectly suited to the requirements of its members in the 1990s and beyond.

The objectives of the International Sugar Agreement, 1992, in the light of the terms of resolution 93(iv) adopted by the United Nations Conference on Trade and Development(UNCTAD), are: (a) to ensure enhanced international cooperation in connection with world sugar matters related issues; (b) to provide a forum for inter-governmental consultations on sugar and on ways to improve the world sugar economy; (c) to facilitate trade by collecting and providing information on the world sugar market and other sweeteners; and (d) to encourage increased demand for sugar, particularly for non-traditional uses.

The Organization usually holds two Council sessions, three Administrative Committee meetings, and two Market Evaluation, Consumption and Statistics Committee (MECAS) meetings every year to achieve objectives (a) and (b) above.

With the entry into force of the Common Fund for Commodities, the ISO has been designated an International Commodity Body (ICB), which adds a new function for the ISO to process loan applications for sugar related projects prepared by the ISO Members.

The objectives (c) and (d) are developed in Articles 32 and 33 which state that the ISO will act as "a centre for the collection and publication of statistical information and studies on world production, prices, export and imports, consumption and stocks of sugar ... and other sweeteners" and includes an undertaking by members to supply information, backed up by appropriate statistical rules.

Further requirements are spelled out in Article 33 establishing the Market Evaluation, Consumption and Statistics Committee which is charged with studying, *inter alia*, the following: (a) preparation of sugar statistics and statistical analysis of sugar production, consumption, stocks,international trade and prices; (b) analysis of market behavior and factors which affect it, with special reference to participation of developing countries in world trade; and (c) analysis of demandfor sugar, including the effects of the use of any form of natural and artificial substitutes for sugar onworld trade in, and consumption of, sugar.

Hence a number of studies have been published by the Secretariat to meet a very comprehensive work program approved by the Council, covering all aspects of production, consumption, trade, prices, alternative sweeteners, taxes and duties, alternative uses of sugar and derivatives, sugar and environment, sugar and health, as well as fortification of sugar with Vitamin A.

Meetings of the Council and MECAS Committee also act as a conduit for national policy presentations by Members and their discussions. Numerous papers on this aspect have been discussed since 1990.

General Statistical Collection and Dissemination

(i) Prices are monitored by the calculation of an ISO daily price and the publication of daily, weekly and monthly price tables.

(ii) Production, consumption, trade and stock developments are monitored through the compilation and publication of a Monthly Bulletin of Statistics and the Annual Sugar Year Book.

(iii) Short term (one crop cycle ahead) estimations on a country by country basis are made for all elements of the sugar economy (production, consumption trade and stocks) and updated and published four times a year in the Quarterly Market Review.

More recently, the ISO has been holding yearly seminars and workshops. In 1992, they conducted a seminar on "Prospects for the Sugar Industry and Sugar Market in Eastern Europe"; 1993"Far East Sugar Market"; 1994 "The North African and Middle East Sugar Market"; 1995 "Latin American and Caribbean Sugar Economy"; 1996 "The Sugar Economies of the Indian Ocean Rim";1997 "Sugar in Europe: Challenges and Changes"; 1998 "Conflictual Issues in World Sugar; 1999 "Asia's Future Role in the World Sugar and Other Sweeteners Market". Workshops held in 1994, 1995, 1996, 1997, and 1998 respectively were: "Implications of the GATT Agreement for Sugar", "Sugar, Alcohol and the Environment", "Alternative Uses of Sugar and By-products", "Alternative Uses of Bagasse", "Developments, Opportunities in Sugar Technology, and Diversification Beyond 2000."

COMPOSITION

54 members (including the *European Union*): Argentina, Australia, Belarus, Belize, Brazil, Colombia, Costa Rica, Côte d'Ivoire, Cuba, Dominican Republic, Ecuador, Egypt, El Salvador, the *European Union* and its member States (Austria, Belgium, Denmark, Finland, France, Germany,Greece, Ireland, Italy, Luxembourg, Netherlands, Portugal, Spain, Sweden, United Kingdom), Fiji, Guatemala, Guyana, Honduras, Hungary, India, Jamaica, Japan, Kenya, Korea, Latvia, Malawi, Mauritius, Mexico, Moldova, Panama, Philippines, South Africa, Sudan, Swaziland, Switzerland, Thailand, Trinidad and Tobago, Turkey, Ukraine, Zimbabwe--representing 75% of world sugar production, 55% of world sugar consumption, 90% of world net exports and 21% of net imports.

STRUCTURE

The International Sugar Council, consisting of all members of the Organization, is the highest authority. The Council functions through an Administrative Committee composed of annually appointed and elected representatives of its members. The Council elects a Chairman and Vice-Chairman for each year and holds one regular session each half of the year. Additional meetings may be held as may be necessary.

Committees (1999)

Administrative Committee - Members: Australia, Brazil, Cuba, Egypt, *European Union*, Fiji, Guatemala, Guyana, India, Japan, Korea, Mauritius, Mexico, Philippines, South Africa, Swaziland, Thailand

Credentials Committee - Members: Cuba, Guyana, Hungary, Kenya, Thailand

Market Evaluation, Consumption and Statistics Committee (MECAS): Membership is open to all members of the Council.

GENERAL PUBLICATIONS

Statistical Bulletin (monthly); *Sugar Year Book* (annual); *Market Report and Press Summary*(monthly); *Quarterly Market Review* (quarterly); *Seminar Proceedings* (annual); *Workshop*(annual)

INTERNATIONAL TELECOMMUNICATIONS UNION (ITU)

HEADQUARTERS

Place des Nations	Telephone:	[41](22)730-5111
1211 Geneva 20	Facsimile:	[41](22)733-7256
Switzerland	Telex:	421000 UIT CH
GENEVA	Cable:	BURINTERNA

Internet: www.itu.int

Secretary-General: ... ***Pekka J. TARJANNE***

LANGUAGES: ENGLISH, FRENCH, SPANISH. SOME DOCUMENTS ARE ALSO TRANSLATED INTO ARABIC, CHINESE, AND RUSSIAN.

ESTABLISHMENT AND FUNCTIONS

Founded in Paris in 1865 as the International Telegraph Union, the International Telecommunications Union (ITU) took its present name in 1934 and became a specialized agency of the United Nations in 1947.
The ITU is an intergovernmental organization, within which the public and private sectors cooperate for the development of telecommunications. The ITU adopts international regulations and treaties governing all terrestrial and space uses of the frequency spectrum as well as the use of the geostationary-satellite orbit, within which countries adopt their national legislation. It also develops standards to facilitate the interconnection of telecommunication systems on a worldwide scale regardless of the type of technology used.
Spearheading telecommunications development on a world scale, the ITU fosters the development of telecommunications in developing countries, by establishing medium-term development policies and strategies in consultation with other partners in the sector and by providing specialized technical assistance in the areas of telecommunication policies, the choice and transfer of technologies, financing of investment projects and mobilization of resources, the installation and maintenance of networks, the management of human resources as well as research and development.

COMPOSITION

188 Member States: Islamic State of Afghanistan, Albania, Algeria, Andorra, Angola, Antigua and Barbuda, Argentina, Armenia, Australia, Austria, Azerbaijan, The Bahamas, Bahrain, Bangladesh, Barbados, Belarus, Belgium, Belize, Benin, Bhutan, Bolivia, Bosnia and Herzegovina, Botswana, Brazil, Brunei Darussalem, Bulgaria, Burkina Faso, Burundi, Cambodia, Cameroon, Canada, Cape Verde, Central African Republic, Chad, Chile, China, Colombia, Comoros, Democratic Republic of the Congo, Republic of the Congo, Costa Rica, Côte d'Ivoire, Croatia, Cuba, Cyprus, Czech Republic, Denmark, Djibouti, Dominica, Dominican Republic, Ecuador, Egypt, El Salvador, Equatorial Guinea, Eritrea, Estonia, Ethiopia, Fiji, Finland, France, Gabon, The Gambia, Georgia, Germany, Ghana, Greece, Grenada, Guatemala, Guinea, Guinea-Bissau, Guyana, Haiti, Holy See, Honduras, Hungary, Iceland, India, Indonesia, Islamic Republic of Iran, Iraq, Ireland, Israel, Italy, Jamaica, Japan, Jordan, Kazakhstan, Kenya, Kiribati, Democratic People's Republic of Korea, Republic of Korea, Kuwait, Kyrgyz Republic, Lao People's Democratic Republic, Latvia, Lebanon, Lesotho, Liberia, Socialist People's Libyan Arab Jamahiriya, Liechtenstein, Lithuania, Luxembourg, former Yugoslav Republic of Macedonia, Madagascar, Malawi, Malaysia, Maldives, Mali, Malta, Marshall Islands, Mauritania, Mauritius, Mexico, Federated States of Micronesia, Moldova, Monaco, Mongolia, Morocco, Mozambique, Myanmar, Namibia, Nauru, Nepal, Netherlands, New Zealand, Nicaragua, Niger, Nigeria, Norway, Oman, Pakistan, Panama, Papua New Guinea, Paraguay, Peru, Philippines, Poland, Portugal, Qatar, Romania, Russian Federation, Rwanda, St. Lucia, St.Vincent and the Grenadines, Samoa, San Marino, São Tomé and Príncipe, Saudi Arabia, Senegal, Sierra Leone, Singapore, Slovak Republic, Slovenia, Solomon Islands, Somalia, South Africa, Spain, Sri Lanka, Sudan, Suriname, Swaziland, Sweden, Switzerland, Syrian Arab Republic, Tajikistan, Tanzania, Thailand, Togo, Tonga, Trinidad and Tobago, Tunisia, Turkey, Turkmenistan, Tuvalu, Uganda, Ukraine, United Arab Emirates, United Kingdom, United States, Uruguay, Uzbekistan, Vanuatu, Venezuela, Vietnam, Republic of Yemen, Yugoslavia, Zambia, Zimbabwe
Around 400 members: composed of scientific and industrial companies, public and private operators, broadcasters, and regional/international organizations.

STRUCTURE

The supreme organ of the ITU is the *Plenipotentiary Conference*, composed of representatives of all the members, which meets once every four years. It sets out general policy. The Conference reviews the International Telecommunications Convention and elects the *ITU Council*. The Conference also elects the Secretary-General, who heads the *General Secretariat*, the Deputy Secretary-General and the Directors of the Radiocommunication, Standardization and Development Bureaux.
The *ITU Council* is composed of 46 members of the Union. Its role is to consider, in the interval between two plenitpotentiary conferences, broad telecommunication policy issues in order to ensure that the Union's policies and strategy fully respond to the constantly changing telecommunication environment. In addition, the Council is responsible for ensuring the efficient coordination of the Union's work and for exercising an effective financial control over the General Secretariat and the three Sectors that comprise the ITU structure, namely: (1) The Radio-communication Sector, including world and regional radio-communication conferences, radio-communication assemblies and the Radio Regulations Board; (2) The Telecommunication Standardization Sector, including world telecommunication standardization conferences; and (3) The Telecommunication Development Sector, including world and regional telecommunication development conferences.

ISLAMIC DEVELOPMENT BANK (ISDB)

Banque islamique de développement

HEADQUARTERS

P.O. Box 5925
Jeddah 21432
Saudi Arabia

Telephone: [966](2)636-1400
Facsimile: [966](2)636-6871
Telex: 601137 ISDB SJ
601407 ISDB SJ
601945 ISDB SJ
Cable: BANKISLAMI
E-mail: archives@isdb.org.sj
Internet: www.isdb.org

President and Chairman of the Board of Directors: ... ***Ahmad Mohamed ALI***
Vice President (Finance & Administration): ... ***Fuad Abdullah AL-OMAR***
Vice President (Operations): ... ***Ousmane SECK***
Vice President (Trade & Policy): ***Syed Jaafar AZNAN***

REGIONAL OFFICES:

Kazakhstan
65-69 Nauryzbay Batyr St.
Almaty
Telephone: [7](327)262-3555 8000 [7](327)262-3620
Facsimile: [7](327)262-3411
Director: ... Zeinal ABIDIN

Malaysia
Level 11, Front Wing, Bank Industri
Postal Add: P.O. Box 13671
Jalan Sultan Ismail
Kuala Lumpur 50818
Telephone: [60](3)294-6627
Facsimile: [60](3)294-6626

Director: ... Muhammad SIDDIK

Morocco
177, Ave. John Kennedy
Postal Add: P.O. Box 5003 Souissi, 10105
Rabat
Telephone: [212](7)75-7191
Facsimile: [212](7)75-7260
Director: ... Hani Salim

SUNBUL AFFILIATES Islamic Research and Training Institute (IRTI)
P.O. Box 9201
Telephone: [966](2)636-1400
Facsimile: [966](2)637-8927
Jeddah 21413

Saudi Arabia *Director: ... Ma'abed Ali AL-JARHI*
IDB Unit Investment Fund (UIF)
Telephone: [966](2)636-1400
P.O. Box 5925
Facsimile: [966](2)636-2968 Jeddah 21413
Saudi Arabia

Manager: ... Mohamed M. AWWAD
Islamic Corporation for the Insurance
Telephone: [966](2)636-
1400 Investment and Export Credit (ICIEC)
Facsimile: [966](2)644-3447
P.O. Box 15722 Jeddah 21454 Saudi Arabia

Manager: ... Abdul Rahman Ali TAHA

IDB Bio-saline Agriculture Centre
Telephone: [971](4)295-8136/8740
c/o Ministry of Agriculture & Fisheries
[971](4)295-8738-8739 P.O. Box 1509 Dubai
United Arab Emirates
Facsimile: [971](4)295-7110
[971](4)295-7204
Manager: ... Ahmad HARIRI

LANGUAGES: ARABIC (OFFICIAL LANGUAGE); ENGLISH, FRENCH (WORKING LANGUAGES)

ESTABLISHMENT AND FUNCTIONS

The Second Islamic Finance Ministers' Conference, held in Jeddah, Saudi Arabia, on August 10, 1974, adopted and opened for signature the Agreement establishing an Islamic Development Bank (IsDB). The Agreement entered into force on April 23, 1975. The inaugural meeting of the Board of Governors was held in Riyadh, Saudi Arabia, in July 1975, and the Bank commenced operations on October 20, 1975. Membership in the Bank is open to all countries that are members of the Organization of the Islamic Conference (OIC).

The main objective of the Bank is to foster economic development and social progress of member countries and Muslim communities individually as well as jointly in accordance with the principles of the Shariah. The Bank finances projects in its member countries through a number of modes of financing, which are compatible with the Islamic Shariah. These modes of financing are interest-free loans, equity participation, leasing, installment sale, and profit sharing. In addition, the Bank also supports the development efforts of its member countries by providing technical assistance and promoting technical cooperation among them.

The Bank has been active in the promotion of trade and the flow of investments among its member countries. This is being done through various schemes such as the Import Trade Financing Operations (ITFO), the Islamic Banks' Portfolio (IBP), and the Export Financing Scheme (EFS), formerly known as the Longer-Term Trade Financing Scheme (LTTFS).

To supplement these efforts, and to promote trade and the flow of investments among members countries of the OIC, the Bank established the Islamic Corporation for the Insurance of Investment and Export Credit (ICIEC) in 1994. The objective of the Corporation is to provide export credit insurance or insurance or reinsurance against commercial and political risks.

In order to supplement its capital resources, the Bank introduced schemes such as the Investment Deposit Scheme, the Islamic Banks' Portfolio (IBP), and the Unit Investment Fund (UIF) to mobilize resources from the private sector.

The Bank maintains a Special Assistance Fund, which is utilized to assist member countries afflicted by natural calamities and to finance health and educational projects aimed at improving the socio-economic conditions of Muslim communities in non-member countries.

With a view to undertaking research for enabling the economic, financial, and banking activities in Muslim countries to conform to Shariah and to extend training facilities to personnel engaged in economic development activities in member countries, the Bank established the Islamic Research and Training Institute (IRTI), which became operational in 1983. The IRTI undertakes research, conducts training, publishes studies, and organizes conferences on Islamic economics and Islamic banking, and other related areas. In order to encourage research in Islamic economics and Islamic banking, the Institute also undertakes the awarding of the Bank's prizes for Islamic Economics and Islamic Banking.

In 1998 the Bank also launched a US$1.5 billion IDB Infrastructure Fund to invest in infrastructure projects, mainly power, telecommunications, transportation, energy, natural resources, petro-chemical and other infrastructure-related sectors in member countries. The Fund is expected to provide a platform to structure long-term financial products to meet the needs of investors seeking Shariah-compatible instruments as well as the financing needs of infrastructure projects.

The Bank maintains close relations with the Organization of the Islamic Conference and its various organs and affiliated bodies, especially the OIC Standing Committee for Economic and Commercial Cooperation (COMCEC), in order to strengthen economic cooperation among the OIC member countries.

Since July 1992, the authorized capital of the Bank became 6 billion Islamic dinars, divided into 600,000 shares having a par value of 10,000 Islamic Dinars each. Its subscribed capital also became 4 billion Islamic Dinars payable according to specific schedules and in freely convertible currency acceptable to the Bank. The Islamic Dinar, which is the unit of account of the Bank, is equivalent in value to one SDR of the International Monetary Fund. On April 5, 1982, the Bank was prescribed by the IMF as a holder of SDRs, and thus authorized to acquire and use SDRs in operations and transactions with participants in the IMF's SDR Department and other holders under the same terms and conditions as participants.

COMPOSITION

53 members: Islamic State of Afghanistan, Albania, Algeria, Azerbaijan, Bahrain, Bangladesh, Benin, Brunei Darussalam, Burkina Faso, Cameroon, Chad, Comoros, Djibouti, Egypt, Gabon, The Gambia, Guinea, Guinea-Bissau, Indonesia, Islamic Republic of Iran, Iraq, Jordan, Kazakhstan, Kuwait, Kyrgyz Republic, Lebanon, Libya, Malaysia, Maldives, Mali, Mauritania, Morocco, Mozambique, Niger, Oman, Pakistan, Palestine, Qatar, Saudi Arabia, Senegal, Sierra Leone, Somalia, Sudan, Suriname, Syrian Arab Republic, Tajikistan, Togo, Tunisia, Turkey, Turkmenistan, Uganda, United Arab Emirates, Republic of Yemen

STRUCTURE

Each member country is represented on the *Board of Governors* by a Governor and an Alternate Governor.

The *Board of Executive Directors* is composed of 13 members, of whom seven are appointed by each of the seven member countries having the largest number of shares, and the remaining six are elected by all other Governors. The term of the Executive Directors is three years, which can be renewed. The President of the Bank acts as Chairman of the Board.

The *President*, who is responsible for day-to-day operations, is elected by the Board of Governors for a term of five years, which can be renewed. He is assisted by three Vice Presidents appointed by the Board of Executive Directors on his recommendation.

GENERAL PUBLICATIONS

Annual Report of the Bank; Annual Report of IRTI; Annual Report of UIF; Annual Report of ICIEC.

IMPORTANT TRADE AND INVESTMENT ORGANIZATIONS IN ASIA

AFGHANISTAN

AFGHAN CARPET EXPORTERS' GUILD*

Office/postal address:
Ministry of Commerce
P.O. Box 3159 Darulaman Road Kabul

Phone: (93 70) 224575 Year established: 1967 Principal functions:
- x To provide guidance in export of carpets and rugs;
- x To publicize Afghan carpets and rugs;
- x To identify markets for Afghan carpets and rugs;
- x To encourage Afghan carpet and rug producers and provide technical support;
- x To control quality of Afghan rugs at time of exportation so that unsatisfactory goods are not exported;
- x To control the imported dyestuffs and woolen yarns so that unfit materials are not used in Afghan carpet and rug industry.

Services/activities:
- x Encourages the carpet producers to use Afghan karakul wool in weaving carpets and kilims;
- x Establishes carpet-weaving, dusting and washing centres in important trade centres/cities of Afghanistan;
- x Conducts competition between producers of carpet for improving the quality of Afghan carpets;
- x Encourages producers to use attractive and historical carpet designs;
- x Promotes the Carpet Exporters' Guild and attracts new producers and exporters as new members;
- x Participates in exhibitions of carpets and other floor coverings within and outside Afghanistan;
- x Provides information on Afghan carpet traders and floor, covering companies of different countries of the world.

Training:
Each year the Guild, through the channel of its members, most of which are carpet and rug producers, trains a number of apprentices in the craft.
Category:
Carpet manufacturer and exporter.

AFGHAN CHAMBER OF COMMERCE AND INDUSTRY*

Office/postal address:
General Administration of International Economic Relations 119 Darulaman Watt Kabul
Phone: (93 2) 290196, 290090 Fax: (93 2) 290196, (93 1) 287458
Principal functions:
- x To facilitate importing: locating competitive suppliers throughout the world, collecting their catalogues, price list, samples and other promotional materials, disseminating the information to the relevant members of importers association, issuing proformas on behalf of the best competitive supplier and following the matter;
- x To facilitate exports and to process export goods;
- x To attract foreign assistance in the field of industries;
- x To participate in the establishment of industrial projects and to provide other facilities.

Services/activities:
As detailed under Principal functions.
Areas/industries where investment is encouraged:
Primary products.
Category:
Chamber of commerce.

AFGHAN NATIONAL INSURANCE COMPANY

Office/postal address:
Karte Parwan (near British Embassy) Kabul
P.O. Box: 329, Kabul Phone: (93 20) 2200189
Mobile: (93 70) 275511, 234528 Fax: (93 20) 2200189 E-mail: insurancenationalafghanco@yahoo.com Year established: 1964 Principal function:
- x To issue marine, aviation, fire, motor and accident insurance.

Services/activities:
x As detailed under Principal function.

Local branch:
Mazar Branch North of Rawza Mazar-e-sharif Balkh
Membership structure: Afghan National Insurance Company is a member of Asian Reinsurance Corporation in Bangkok.
Training:
Undertakes training courses in English and local languages, which are open to participation from other countries.
Category:
Insurance.

ANIMAL PRODUCTS TRADING AND INDUSTRIAL ASSOCIATION (APTIA)

Ministry of Commerce
Office/postal address:
Ayubkhan Mina South of Hibibia High School
2nd
ST, Darulaman Road Kabul
P.O. Box: 7005
Phone: (0093) 752023490 Fax: (0093) 752023490 E-mail: qaimiwasi@yahoo.com Year established: 1979 Principal function:
x To promote and export animal products (wool, cashmere wool, animal skins).
Local branches:
Herat, Kandahar, Balkh, Khost and Nangarhar. Membership structure: Association. Products/commodity responsible for: Wool; cashmere wool; animals pickle; wet blow; hide skin of domestic animals.
Areas/industries where investment is encouraged:
Herat; Nangarhar; and Kabul.
Category:
Trade association; and trade promotion organization.

EXPORT PROMOTION DEPARTMENT*

Office/postal address:
Ministry of Commerce Darulaman Watt Kabul
Phone: (92 02) 500328 Year established: 1969 (under Ministry of Commerce). Principal function:
To undertake export promotion of Afghan exportable products.
Services/activities:
- x Undertakes marketing of export products and market analysis;
- x Participates in international trade fairs;
- x Upgrades qualities of Afghan exportable products;
- x Collects and analyses statistics regarding markets;
- x Disseminates up-to-date prices by newspaper, radio and telex;
- x Undertakes training of personnel;
- x Establishes new organizations;
- x Undertakes studies on supply and demand for Afghan products;
- x Publicizes Afghan products;
- x Undertakes registration of importers and exporters.

Publications issued:
x *Foreign Trade Bulletin* (monthly). x Catalogues and pamphlets of Afghan products. x Demand and supply studies of importable products.
Offices abroad:
Afghan Trade Representative
R.B. Dunichand Road Amritsar, India
Afghan Trade Agency Maidan Sewom-e-Esfand Mashad, Islamic Republic of Iran
Afghan Trade Agency No. 10, The Mall Peshawar Catt, Pakistan
Afghan Trade Agency Makseem Gorki Street Termiz, Russian Federation
Commercial Attaché 2 Brestakaya Street 18/19 Moscow, Russian Federation
Category:
Trade promotion organization.

HANDICRAFT PROMOTION AND EXPORT CENTRE*

Office/postal address:
P.O. Box 389 In front of the Embassy of India Kabul
Phone: (92 02) 201329
Year established: 1975 (formerly: Afghan Handicraft Promotion Joint Corporation).
Principal function:
To export all kinds of Afghan handicraft products including:
x Leather products (bags, purses, travel bags, belts, footwear (sandals and shoes), etc.),
x Gift items,
x Garments,

x Stone products,
x Carpets and rugs,
x Hand-knotted woollen products,
x Embroidered garments and tablecloths,
x Genuine and imitation jewellery,
x Wooden statues.
Services/activities:
As detailed under principal function.
Category:
Trade promotion organization.

BANGLADESH

BANGLADESH CHEMICAL INDUSTRIES CORPORATION (BCIC)

Office/postal address:
BCIC Bhaban 30-31 Dilkusha C/A Dhaka 1000
Phone: (880 2) 9564153, 9556148 Fax: (880 2) 9564120
Year established: 1976
Principal functions:
x To develop chemical industries;
x To manufacture, market and distribute chemical products produced by enterprises under its management.

Services/activities:
x Supervises, coordinates and controls the enterprises placed under its management; x Sets up new industries in the chemical sector; x Undertakes joint ventures in collabouration with local and foreign entrepreneurs.

Publications issued:
x *Annual Report.* x *BI Monthly News Bulletin.*
Local branches:
The BCIC has the following enterprises under its management:
Bangladesh Insulator and Sanitaryware Factory Mirpur Dhaka Phone: (880 2) 8014145 Fax: (880 2) 8011326
Chhatak Cement Company Ltd. Chhatak Sunamganj Phone: (880 82) 8651 Fax: (880 82) 715216 E-mail: cement@bts.net
Chittagong Urea Fertilizer Factory Rangadia Chittagong Phone: (880 31) 622301-4 Fax: (880 31) 610564
Jamuna Fertilizer Co. Ltd. Tarakandi Jamalpur Phone: (880 2) 933288 Fax: (880 2) 933288 Karnaphuli Paper Mills Ltd. Chandraghona Rangamati Phone: (880 31) 624337 Fax: (880 31) 612833 E-mail: kpm@global.etg.net
Natural Gas Fertilizer Factory Ltd. Fenchuganj Sylhet Phone: (880 822) 688043 Fax: (880 821) 718425
Potash Urea Fertilizer Factory Ghorasal Narsingdi Phone: (880 2) 9351216 Fax: (880 2) 9351223
Triple Super Phosphate Complex North Patenga Chittagong Phone: (880 31) 741355 Fax: (880 31) 741357
Uamania Glass Sheet Factory Kalurghat Chittagong Phone: (880 31) 670430 Fax: (880 31) 670308 E-mail: ugsf@spet.net.com
Urea Fertilizer Factory Ghorasal Narsingdi Phone: (880 2) 9353076 Fax: (880 2) 9352550
Zia Fertilizer Company Ltd. Ashuganj
B. Baria Phone: (880 2) 9352015 Fax: (880 2) 9351847
Products/commodity responsible for:
Urea fertilizer; ammonium sulphate; TSP fertilizer; paper; cement; liquid chlorine; glass sheet; sanitary ware; insulators; ceramic floor and wall tiles; packaging materials.
Category:
Industrial promotion organization.

BANGLADESH EXPORT PROCESSING ZONES AUTHORITY (BEPZA)

Office/postal address:
BEPZA Complex House No 19/D, Road No. 6 Dhanmondi R/A Dhaka 1205
Phone: (880 2) 9670530, 8650058, 8650061 Fax: (880 2) 8650060, 9661849
E-mail: info@bepza.org, chairman@bepza.org, member-ip@bepza.org, gm-ip@bepza.org URL: www.epzbangladesh.org.bd
Year established: 1980

Principal functions: Services/activities:
x To plan, develop, operate and manage export processing zones in Bangladesh;
x To take possession of land to be acquired or requisitioned by the Government for creation and development of a zone;
x To allot land and building space in a zone to investors on lease or on rent and to allow them to mortgage the allotted lands for

raising loans from financial institutions or commercial banks;

- To provide infrastructure facilities, including buildings, utilities and warehouse;
- To process applications for setting up industries within a zone and accord sanction in accordance with the guidelines given by the Government from time to time;
- To provide customs bonded facilities in accordance with customs regulations for importation into a zone of building materials for construction purpose and packaging materials, raw materials and intermediate goods for the purpose of processing for export;
- To allow import of raw materials or semi-processed or other goods required for use in the zone and export of semi-processed, processed or other goods to be specified by the board in such manner as may be prescribed;
- To assist in the transportation of imported raw materials and intermediate goods in bonded condition and export of finished products;
- To provide necessary banking facilities within the zone in consultation with the Bangladesh Bank;
- To establish liaison with the port, municipal and other authorities to make arrangement for transportation of imported raw materials and intermediate goods on bonded condition and for export of finished products;
- To sanction the employment of foreign nationals, in accordance with the guidelines given by the Government from time to time, to posts for which local experts is not available for efficient running of the industries in zone;
- To enter into any contract or agreement for the purpose of the ordinance, subject to the approval of the Government;
- To set up, maintain and manage public warehouses at any place in Bangladesh to provide customs bonded facilities in accordance with customs regulations for importation into Bangladesh of raw materials, packaging materials, semi-processed goods and accessories required for export oriented industries, if directed to do so by the Government.
- Provides one window service in EPZs which includes provision of infrastructural facilities such as utilities (gas, water, electricity, telephone, telex and fax), issue of import/export permits, work permits and security.

Publications issued:

- Information brochures (published periodically).
- *A New Horizon for Investors* (English/Japanese/Korean/Chinese/French/Italian/German/Arabic).

Local branches:

Adamji Export Processing Zone Adamji Nagar, Narayangonj Phone: 7607037, 7607028 Fax: 7607039

Chittagong Export Processing Zone (CEPZ) South Halishahar, 4223 Chittagong Phone: (880 31) 741446, 740919, 740939 Fax: (880 31) 740031 E-mail: cezp@ctg-bd.net

Comilla Export Processing Zone (Comilla EPZ) Old Airport Area, Comilla Phone: (880 81) 77055, 71001, 71000 Fax: (880 81) 77056 E-mail: epzcom@bttb.net.bd

Dhaka Export Processing Zone (DEPZ) Ganakbari, Savar, Dhaka Phone: (880 2) 7701005, 7701002 Fax: (880 2) 7701003

Ishwardi Export Processing Zone (IEPZ) Pakshi, Pabna Phone: (880 7) 32663962, 32663861 Fax: (880 7) 32663961

Karnaphuli Export Processing Zone North Patenga, Chittagong 4204 Phone: (88 03) 1801069, 1741100 Fax: (88 03) 1740860

Mongla Export Processing Zone (MEPZ) Mongla Port Area Mongla, Bagerhat Phone: (880 4) 66275199, 66275195 Fax: (880 4) 66275198

Uttara Export Processing Zone (UEPZ) Shongalshi, Nilphamari Phone: (880 5) 5161586, 55161677, 55161119 Fax: (880 5) 5161468

Products/commodity responsible for:

In the industrial units of EPZs products such as garments and garments accessories, textile, terry towel, knitting and knit products, caps, electronics, fishing reel, golf equipment, metal products, plastic products, shoes and leather goods, tent, and ropes are being produced and exported.

Locations of EPZs:

- CEPZ established at the port city of Chittagong, is 2.41 km from the main seaport, 7.24 km from the international airport and 5.63 km from the main business centre of Chittagong. There are currently 106 enterprises operating in the Zone;
- Dhaka EPZ, established near the capital city, Dhaka, is 25 km from Zia International Airport and 35 km from the city centre. There are currently 56 enterprises operating in the Zone;
- Mongla EPZ established near the Mongla Port sea is 105 km

from Jessore Airport. There is currently one enterprise operating in the Zone;

- x Comilla EPZ established near the Comilla old airport area is 97 km from the capital city and 170 km from Chittagong Port. There are currently three enterprises sanctioned in the Comilla EPZ;
- x Ishurdi EPZ established near the Ishurdi Airport is 186 km from the capital city, 150 km from Bangabandhu Bridge and 450 km from Chittagong Port. There is currently one enterprise sanctioned in the Zone;
- x Uttara EPZ established near the Syedpur Airport is 360 km from the capital city and 640 km from Chittagong Port. There is currently one enterprise sanctioned in the Zone.

Areas/industries where investment is encouraged:
All sectors are encouraged with particular emphasis on hi-tech electronics and electrical equipment, hi-tech engineering, leather and leather-related industries, specialized textiles, jewellery, garments, automobile spares, light-medium engineering. (Industrial Policy 1991 encourages foreign investment through the introduction of deregulatory provisions.)
Titles of laws and regulations on foreign investment:
Foreign Private Investment (Promotion and Protection) Act, 1980.
Category:
Investment promotion authority; and export processing zone.

BANGLADESH STANDARDS AND TESTING INSTITUTION (BSTI)

Office/postal address:
116-A Tejgaon Industrial Area Dhaka 1208
Phone: (880 2) 8821462 Fax: (880 2) 9131581
E-mail: bsti@bangla.net
Year established: 1985 (through merger of Bangladesh Standards Institution and Central Testing Labouratories).

Principal functions:

- x To formulate and publish Bangladesh Standard Specification of commodities codes of practices;
- x To promote metrology science and render metrology services throughout the country;
- x To administer quality control activities through Testing and Certification Marking.

Services/activities:
x Formulates standards of commodities, processes/systems, codes of practice, etc., on national and international bases;
x Controls the quality of products through testing of locally produced consumer products, produce for the local market and for export through the issuance of Certification Marks Licences;
x Implements the systems of international units of weights and measures in the country;
x Renders scientific/industrial/legal metrology services.
Publications issued:
x *Standard specifications*. x *Yearbook*.

Local branches:
Dhaka Divisional Metrology Inspectorate BSTI Annex Building 116-A Tejgaon industrial area Dhaka 1208 Phone: (880 2) 9899631
BSTI Regional Office Jumbory Maat Agrabad, Chittagong Phone: (880 31) 710695, 721137
BSTI Regional Office 62 Old Jessore Road Khalispur, Khulna Phone: (880 41) 762152, 761542
BSTI Regional Office H-573 Ramchandrapur Nator Road Ghoramara, Rajshahi Phone: (880 721) 773181, 775897 BSTI Regional Office Thakurstate (Launch ghat) Fazlul Haq Avenue Barisal Phone: (880 431) 55796
BSTI Regional Office Mirza Villa, Pallobi-9/B West Pathan Tola, Sylhet Phone: (880 821) 719547
Membership structure: BSTI Council: 39 members.

Other Committees: Variable

- x BSTI Council (sets policy and oversees activities);
- x Executive Committee (for administration and technical guidance);
- x Divisional Committee (adoption of National Standards - members from different sectors and industries associations): 12 members;
- x Technical Committees (finalization of Draft Standards): 12 members.

Products/commodity responsible for:
Agricultural and food products; chemicals; jute and textiles; electrotechnical; and engineering products.
Category:
Commodity standard institute.

Office/postal address:
Prime Minister's Office Jiban Bima Tower, 19th floor, 10 Dilkusha Commercial Area Dhaka 1000
Phone: (880 2) 9559378, 9561430-1 Fax: (880 2) 9562312
E-mail: ecboi@bdmail.net, bdboi@bdmail.net URL: www.boi.gov.bd
Year established: 1989

Principal functions:
x To provide all kinds of facilities in the matter of investment of local and foreign capital for the purpose of rapid industrialization in the private sector;
x To implement government policy relating to the investment of capital in industries in the private sector; x To prepare the investment schedule in relation to industries in the private sector and its implementation;
x To prepare area-schedules for establishment of industries in the private sector and determination of special facilities for such areas;
x To approve and register industrial projects in the private sector involving local and foreign capital;
x To identify investment sectors and facilities for investment in industries in the private sector and provide wide publicity thereof abroad;
x To invent specific devices for the purpose of promotion of investment in industries in the private sector and their implementation;
x To create infrastructural facilities for industries in the private sector;
x To determine terms and conditions for employment of foreign officers, experts and other employees necessary for industries in the private sector;
x To prepare policies relating to the transfer of technology and phase-wise local production in the private sector and their implementation;
x To provide necessary assistance for the rehabilitation of industries in the private sector;
x To finance and provide assistance in the financing of important new industries in the private sector;
x To adopt necessary measures for the creation of capital for investment in industries in the private sector;
x To collect, compile, analyse and disseminate all kinds of industrial data and to establish a databank for that purpose;
x To do such other acts and things as may be necessary for the performance of the above functions.

Services/activities:
The services provided by BOI are categorized as follows:
x Investment promotion
-Country promotions,
-Sector/industry promotions,
-Publications on business processes.
x Investment facilitation
-Pre-investment information and counselling service,
-Investor welcome service (faster immigration),
-Registration/approval of foreign, joint-venture and local projects,
-Approving work permits for the foreign nationals,
-Approving foreign loan suppliers' credit, PAYE scheme, etc.,
-Facilitating utility connections (electricity, gas),
-Assistance in obtaining industrial plots,
-Approving remittance of royalty, technical know-how and technical assistance fees,
-Facilitating the import of capital machinery/raw materials.
x Policy sdvocacy
-Advocating policy suggestions to the Government, -Assisting Government in framing new policies for private sector development.

Publications issued:
x *FDI in Bangladesh during 2004*, June 2005.
x *Foreign Direct Investment in Bangladesh during 2002*, March 2003 (English).
x *Bangladesh Investment Handbook*, November 2002 (English).
x *GCC Countries and Bangladesh: Investment and Trade Cooperation*, May 2002 (English).
x *Utility Services and Environmental Clearance*, January 2001 (English).
Local branches:
Divisional Office Barishal Suraiya Bhaban 87/84 Jordon Road Barishal 8200 Phone: (880 431) 54797, 54399
Divisional Office Chittagong CGO Building No.1 Agrabad Commercial Area Chittagong 4100 Fax: (880 31) 722382
Divisional Office Khulna Shilpa Bank Bhaban 25-26 KDA C/A Khulna 9100 Phone: (880 41) 720017, 724716
Divisional Office Rajshahi Heea Bitan CandB Moor, Kazihata Rajshahi 6000 Phone: (880 721) 772047
Divisional Office Sylhet Prabaho -18, Taltala Sylhet 3100 Phone: (880 821) 724 306
Areas/industries where investment is encouraged:

All sectors, excluding: arms and ammunition and other defence equipment and machinery; forest plantation and mechanized extraction within the bounds of reserved forests; production of nuclear energy; and security printing (currency notes) and minting.

Titles of laws and regulations on foreign investment:

- x Foreign Private Investment (Promotion and Protection Act), 1980.
- x Investment Board Act, 1989.
- x Industrial Policy 2005.

Category:

Investment promotion and facilitation authority.

DHAKA CHAMBER OF COMMERCE AND INDUSTRY (DCCI)

Office/postal address:
65-66 Motijheel Commercial Area
Dhaka 1000 Phone: (880 2) 9552562, 9554383 Fax: (880 2) 9560830
E-mail: dcci@bangla.net, dcci@gononet.com URL: www.dhakachamber.com Year established: 1958 Principal functions:

- x To give suggestions for the formulation of government policies in import, export, industry, investment, banking, insurance, fiscal measures, annual budget, etc. and to provide inputs for meetings related to World Trade Organization (WTO), United Nations Conference on Trade and Development (UNCTAD), etc.;
- x To represent trade, commerce and industry on various advisory or consultative committees at different ministries and departments of the Government;
- x To comment on legislative measures affecting trade, commerce and industry;
- x To function as a forum for exchanging views on trade and economy among different chamber members, government agencies, DCCI members and local/foreign delegations;
- x To settle trade disputes by arbitration;
- x To issue Certificate of Origin and authenticate documents for promotion of exports;
- x To disseminate business information to members by electronic communication, fortnightly Trade Bulletin, DCCI Monthly Review, Current Awareness Service Bulletin, SDI: selective dissemination of information, newsletter, circulars, notifications, statistical data, etc.;
- x To organize training courses, seminars, workshops, symposia, meetings, delegations, fairs and participation thereof at home and abroad and to receive delegations;
- x To undertake activities such as survey and research to suggest for favourable business-related policies;
- x To prepare Economic Policy Papers (EPPs) for conducting policy advocacy for the benefit of the business sectors;
- x To sign Memorandums of Understanding (MOUs) with overseas chambers of commerce and industries and other business organization for promotion of trade and investment;
- x To prepare, implement and evaluate projects for entrepreneurship development and other trade related matters;
- x To develop business through Internet, web page, short link/cross link with DCCI, etc.

Services/activities:

- x Provides facsimile, e-mail, Internet, Web page browsing, commercial library; international tender documents, computer services, CD-ROM services; photocopy facilities, meeting and conference facilities;
- x Provides computerized trade information service;
- x Offers trade intelligence services such as export, import, investment inquiries, trade fairs/exhibitions, news, trade regulations, public notices, statutory regulatory orders (SROs) and foreign exchange circulars;
- x Issues Certificates of Origin (CO) and Letters of Recommendation/Introduction;
- x Provides advisory and consultancy services;
- x Provides institutional supports to small-scale enterprises (SSEs).

Publications issued:

x *DCCI Annual Report* (English/Bengali). x *DCCI Monthly Review* (English/Bengali). x *DCCI Members Directory: 2000* (English). x *Tax Guide 2002-2003*. x *Trade Secrets: the Export Answer Book for SME: 2001*

(Published jointly by DCCI and International Trade Centre (ITC), German Technical Cooperation Agency (GTZ)).

x *Arbitration and alternative dispute resolution: How to settle International business disputes: 2002* (Published jointly by DCCI and ITC, GTZ).
x *Introducing DCCI* (annually).
x *DCCI Trade Information Bulletin* (fortnightly). x *DCCI General Circulars and Special Circulars.* x *Economic Indicators.*
x *Trade Delegation Brochure* (occasional publications).
x Economic Policy Papers on different business issues. x Research reports.

x Seminar reports.
Membership structure: About 4,000 members classified under four categories: General Members, Associate Members, Town Association Members and Trade Group Members.
Membership composition: export 30 per cent, import 30 per cent, sales and services 20 per cent and manufacturing 20 per cent.
Training:
DCCI Business Institute (DBI) provides training programmes and counseling services to its members by year-wise scheduling.
DCCI has some projects through which the Chamber has been imparting specialized training namely training for women entrepreneurs, training on leather and leather goods, etc.
Category:
Chamber of commerce; industrial promotion; and trade promotion organization.

EXPORT PROMOTION BUREAU (EPB)*

Office/postal address:
1st
floor, 1/2 TCB Bhaban Kawranbazar Dhaka 1215
Phone: (880 2) 9144894, 9144886, 9144897 Fax: (880 2) 9119531
E-mail: epb.tic@pradeshta.net URL: www.epbbd.com
Year established: 1972
Principal functions:
Product development:
x To provide technical support to local manufacturers/exporters;
x To provide training on product development and adaptation;
x To provide advisory support in quality control, packaging, supply improvement, post-harvest handling, etc.

Market promotion:
x To participate and/or organize international trade fairs;
x To organize single country exhibitions, buyer-seller meets, contact promotion programmes, field business missions abroad;
x To organize product group international trade fairs.

Trade information:
x To disseminate trade enquiries to local exporting companies;
x To provide information on target markets including international prices and other information;
x To print/distribute *Bangladesh Export Directory*, product brochures, export statistics and other publications of interest.

Export policy:
x To formulate dynamic policy and programmes for the active promotion of exports and to assist in policy formulation;
x To coordinate export development efforts programme and export promotion efforts of the public and private sectors;
x To develop linkages with chambers and trade associations;
x To monitor export performance on a monthly basis.
Coordination and cooperation:
x To coordinate with Bangladesh embassies abroad for attaining the export target;
x To cooperate with foreign trade promotion organizations;
x To maintain working relationship with international/regional organizations such as WTO, UNCTAD, ITC, WIPO, ESCAP, OIC, World Bank, ADB and IDB and other trade promotion organization.

Textile products:
x To issue Generalized System of Preferences (GSP) Certificates and Certificates of Origin;
x To issue textile visa and licence.
Training: x Implements National Export Training Programmes of EPB; x Organizes seminars/workshops on export-related subjects; x Orientation programmes for trade officials posted abroad.

Services/activities:
To issue GSP, GSTP, SAPTA and Bangkok Agreement certificates of Origin for export abroad.

Publications issued:

- x *Bangladesh Export Directory.*
- x *Bangladesh Export Statistics* (annually).
- x *DITF-2003* (souvenir).
- x *EPB Annual Report.*
- x *Monthly Export Statistics.*
- x *Handbook for Exporters* (manual).
- x *Manuals of NETP programme.*
- x *Handicrafts from Bangladesh* (brochure).
- x *Trade Information* (quarterly).

Local branches:
Agrani Bank Building Ranir Bazar Comilla Phone: (880 81) 65019
Agrabad Commercial Area Chittagong Phone: (880 31) 720907 Fax: (880 31) 710540
5, K.D.A. Commercial Area Khulna Phone: (880 41) 720449
House No. 1/B, Block C Road #33/A Shahjalal Up Shahore Sylhet Phone: (880 821) 716144
Shaheb Bazar Samabay Bhaban
P.O. Ghoramara Rajshahi Phone: (880 721) 774420 Fax: (880 721) 774420
Training:

Funding from international organizations such as WTO, UNCTAD, ITC, ESCAP and EU, regional seminar/workshop.
Areas/industries where investment is encouraged:
IT sector, agro-process and light engineering products/services.
Titles of laws and regulations on foreign investment:
x Foreign Private Investment (Promotion and Protection) Act, 1980 secures all foreign investment in Bangladesh.
x OPIC's (Overseas Private Investment Corporation, United States of America) insurance and finance programmes applicable.
x Security and safeguards available under Multilateral Investment Guarantee Agency (MIGA) of which Bangladesh is a member.
x Arbitration facility of the International Centre for the Settlement of Investment Dispute (ICSID) available.
Category:
Trade facilitation body; trade fair and exhibition authority; and trade promotion organization.

FEDERATION OF BANGLADESH CHAMBERS OF COMMERCE AND INDUSTRY (FBCCI)

Office/postal address:
Federation Bhaban 60 Motijheel Commercial Area Dhaka
P.O. Box: 2079, Dhaka
Phone: (880 2) 9560102-3, 9560482 Fax: (880 2) 8613213 E-mail: fbcci@bol-online.com
URL: www.fbcci-bd.org Year established: 1973 Principal functions:

- x To promote the interests of its federating units;
- x To bring about a better cohesion, understanding and harmony at the national level among the trade organizations;
- x To aid and stimulate the development of trade, commerce, industry, agriculture and transport;
- x To protect, encourage and safeguard the cause of the private sector through consultation and interaction with the Government, Ministerial Consultative Committees and other related bodies or agencies;
- x To assist in the organization of chambers of commerce and industry and associations of trade and industry in different centres of Bangladesh;
- x To initiate and adopt appropriate measures for the protection of trade and persons engaged therein, especially members of the FBCCI;
- x To maintain relations and communicate with trade and industrial associations and other mercantile and public bodies abroad;
- x To liaise as a member of the International Chamber of Commerce, Islamic Chamber of Commerce, Industry and Commodity Exchange and Confederation of Asia-Pacific Chambers of Commerce and Industry.

Services/activities:
x Provides trade information services to members of FBCCI, foreign chambers, Bangladesh missions abroad and foreign missions in Bangladesh and related national and international organizations;
x Collects, maintains, analyses and disseminates statistical and other information on matters related to trade, commerce and industry of national and international importance and compiles a databank;
x Conducts research on policies and programmes relating to the development of trade, commerce and industry in the country;
x Plans to develop an information network, with international collabourators such as the ICC;

x Plans to develop a computerized database on members of the FBCCI in order to monitor their progress and performance;
x Coordinates and disseminates matters referred by the trade representatives of the different embassies in order to assist local industrialists and traders;
x Collects information and publications from the Trade Representatives and circulates them among all chambers and associations in the country;
x Prints and circulates project profiles on new industrial projects formulated by development finance institutes and the Board of Investment;
x Collects information through field studies and market surveys on priority sectors of the country and prepares study reports for the FBCCI member bodies and the relevant government ministries;
x Arranges occasional seminars on economic and commercial issues.

Publications issued:
x *Annual Report* (English). x *FBCCI Journal* (English). x *Yearly Recommendations of FBCCI*

Standing Committees
(English). x *Souvenirs of different important events* (English/Bengali).
Membership structure: 268 members, comprising 196 Trade and Industrial Associations and 72 Chambers of Commerce and Industry.

Areas/industries where investment is encouraged:
Non-profit promotional organization. Does not make investment itself, but works for promoting private sector investment.

Titles of laws and regulations on foreign investment:
Relevant for BOI and other concerned governmental organizations.
Category:

Chamber of commerce; industrial promotion; and trade promotion organization.

METROPOLITAN CHAMBER OF COMMERCE AND INDUSTRY, DHAKA

Office/postal address:
Chamber Building 122-124 Motijheel Commercial Area Dhaka 1000
Phone: (880 2) 9565208-10, 7161028-30 Fax: (880 2) 9565211-2
E-mail: sg@citechco.net URL: www.mccibd.org
Year established: 1904
Principal function:
x To deal with international trade and tariff, trade practices, taxation, commercial arbitration, training and human resources development, etc.
Services/activities:
x Provides advisory services to the member organizations on the aforementioned areas;
x Prepares updates on national macroeconomic trends;
x Is represented on the various policy-level bodies of the Government;
x Acts as Secretary to the Bangladesh Employers' Federation, the only organization in the country representing the employers.
Publications issued:
x *The Chamber News* (monthly, English). x *The Tax News* (monthly, English). x *Economic Indicators of Bangladesh* (annually, English). x *Annual Report of the Chamber* (English).

Local branch:
137 Bangabandhu Avenue Narayanganj

Membership structure: 277 members, representing the large enterprises in trading, manufacturing, banks, insurance companies and public sector corporations.
Products/commodity responsible for:
Manufacturing sectors such as jute, textiles, tea, chemicals and pharmaceuticals, garments, food products, and construction, and service sectors such as banks and insurance, hotels.

Training:

The Chamber has been giving an increased focus on training and human resources development in recent periods. It conducts regular training programmes on different disciplines of management functions. The courses are conducted by both local and foreign resource persons and the English language is used as the medium.

Areas/industries where investment is encouraged:
Agro-based industries, artificial flower-making, computer software and IT, electronics, frozen foods, jute goods, jewellery and diamond-cutting, leather, oil and gas, electricity, telecommunications, textiles, tourism, entertainment, hospitals and clinics, hotels and guest houses, etc.

Titles of laws and regulations on foreign investment:
The Government's policy framework for foreign investment is based on Foreign Private Investment (Promotion and Protection) Act, 1980, which provides for non-discriminatory treatment between foreign and local investments; protection of foreign investment from expropriation by the State; and ensured repatriation of proceeds from sale of shares and profit. Excepting a list of four reserve industries, foreign investments are encouraged in all sectors. To assist private investment, the Government, through the Investment Board Act, 1989, set up the Board of Investment.
Category:
Chamber of commerce; industrial promotion; and trade promotion organization.

SHIPPERS' COUNCIL OF BANGLADESH

Office/postal address:
3rd
Floor, Moon Mansion 12 Dilkusha Commercial Area Dhaka 1000
Phone: (880 2) 9556494, 9568520 Fax: (880 2) 9568520 E-mail: scb@bangla.net Year established: 1980

Principal functions:
x To act as representative body of shippers to protect their common interest on shipping lines and conferences;
x To monitor shipping services and maintain close contact with the shipping lines on a continuous basis;
x To bring together all shippers in various parts of Bangladesh on a common platform for discussion of various problems affecting the shippers with particular reference to exports;
x To protect the common interests of shippers vis-à-vis railway, inland waterways, port authorities, etc., on any major policy issues;
x To collect information and statistics, as required by the shippers and shipping lines, from different agencies and circulate such information and statistical data for the use and benefit of shippers;
x To provide for mutual consultations between shippers and shipowners/shipping conferences, port and other concerned authorities as well as government on matters of common interest;
x To negotiate and enter into agreements with shipowners/ shipping conferences and other concerned authorities on matters affecting shippers in the country;
x To convene, independently or jointly with other organizations, conferences, seminars or meetings on matters relating to transport and shipping for achieving the main objectives of the Council.

Services/activities:
x Represents the views of shippers to the concerned authorities and organizations in regard to ocean freight rates and surcharges and other terms and conditions of shipping services, port charges, port facilities, internal transport by rail, etc.;
x Collects and circulates shipping intelligence and information regarding developments in the shipping world;
x Safeguards and promotes the interest of shippers of member countries of the Association of Shippers' Councils of Bangladesh, India, Pakistan and Sri Lanka;
x Publishes a quarterly bulletin in which information such as advance export cargo forecasts and ships' schedules are published for the benefit of Bangladesh exporters and importers;
x Monitors ships' schedules and resolves problems arising out of any changes in the declared schedules through mutual discussions;
x Organizes joint meetings as and when necessary between the representatives of shipowners and shippers with a view to find out how the national flag carriers can serve the shippers better and how the shippers can provide cargo support to national carriers in the overall national interest;
x Resolves specific day-to-day problems faced by individual shippers in making shipment of their export cargoes in time;
x Deals with matters relating to container shipment and container handling problems in close contact with port authorities and shipping lines, railways and shippers;
x Attends to enquiries from shippers, importers and exporters regarding ship's programmes and space availability for their cargo, etc.

Publication issued:
x *Shipping News* (quarterly).

Membership structure: 46 ordinary members and 79 associate members.
Training:
Organizes workshops/seminars on different aspects of shipping, independently or in collabouration with ESCAP, to acquaint shippers and others concerned with shipping in matters relating to shipping techniques, etc.
Category:

Trade association.

BHUTAN

BHUTAN CHAMBER OF COMMERCE AND INDUSTRY (BCCI)

Office/postal address:
Daebum Lam Thimphu
P.O. Box: 147, Thimphu
Phone: (975 2) 323140, 322742 Fax: (975 2) 323936 E-mail: bsdbcci@druknet.bt
URL: www.bcci.com.bt Year established: 1980 Principal functions:
x To be responsible for advocacy with the Government;
x To protect interest of the private sector;
x To be involved in the evolvement of new policies, reformation process, trade promotion, sourcing markets, identification of products;
x To organize joint venture matchmaking;
x To encourage selective foreign direct investment (FDI).
Services/activities:
x Identifies market sourcing; x Disseminates information; x Prepares project reports; x Provides business support and advisory services.
Local branches:
Twenty one branches spread out all over the country. All business and trade associations are its registered members.
Membership structure: There are over 200 individual and corporate registered members. In addition, there are over 9,000 mandatory members.
Products/commodity responsible for:
Export of Bhutanese products and import of consumer goods.
Training:
For Bhutanese nationals only.
Areas/industries where investment is encouraged:
Agriculture; hydropower; tourism; wood-based industries; infrastructure development; IT industries, etc.
Titles of laws and regulations on foreign investment:
Almost all the requisite Acts are in place.
Category:
Chamber of commerce; trade association; trade facilitation body; trade fair and exhibition authority; trade promotion organization; and training/research institute.

BHUTAN EXPORT PROMOTION CENTRE

Office/postal address:
Department of Trade Ministry of Trade and Industry ThimphuG
P.O. Box: 141, Thimphu
Phone: (975 2) 321337, 322407, 325588 Fax: (975 2) 321338 E-mail: sonam.rinchen@druknet.bt
URL: www.mti.gov.bt Year established: 1998 Principal functions:
x To act as focal point for export promotion in Bhutan;
x To support and interact with related organizations;
x To enhance export promotion activities.
Services/activities:
x Collects and disseminates foreign market information; x Establishes links with international organizations; x Identifies market opportunities; x Coordinates and conducts market research; x Provides marketing assistance to exporters; x Organizes trade-related workshops; x Assists exporters in problem solving; x Provides technical assistance; x Organizes and promotes trade fairs and missions.
Publications issued:
x *Export News* (biannually, English). x *Exporters Directory* (biannually, English). Membership structure: 60 members.
Products/commodity responsible for:
Horticultural and agro-based products; handicraft products; mineral products; timber products; processed food products; handmade paper products; traditional medicines; and essential oils.
Training:
x ITC - Trade point seminars; x In-country training/workshop on trade promotion activities; x ITC - WTO/cost benefit workshop.
Titles of laws and regulations on foreign investment:
Based on the FDI policy (2002).
Category:
Export marketing board; ministry of trade; trade facilitation body; trade fair and exhibition authority; and trade promotion organization.

FOOD CORPORATION OF BHUTAN*

Office/postal address:

P.O. Box 80
Phuentsholing Phone: (975 5) 252241, 252429 Fax: (975 5) 252289
E-mail: drukfood@druknet.bt Year established: 1974 Principal functions:
Social functions:
x To provide support prices and necessary infrastructure to market cash crops through auctioning yards to farmers;
x To maintain the national food security reserves at strategic locations;
x To initiate market development activities through marketing and initiating product standardization;
x To look after the logistics of the World Food Programme;
x To provide services as an export house to the suppliers of fruits for export.
Commercial functions:
x To increase product lines and area coverage to meet the demands of consumers;
x To source quality products and marketing at a reasonable price;
x To consolidate market services and ensure timely delivery of goods;
x To ensure quality products for the export of horticultural products.
Services/activities:
x Provides storage facilities at the terminal markets in five locations;
x Caters to the World Food Programme (WFP) aid storage requirement;
x Distributes WFP commodities at various project sites;
x Over 100 Fair Price Shop agents are appointed all over the country;
x Monitors the retailing of foodstuff by Fair Price Shop agents;
x Conducts regular pest control treatment to maintain the quality of foodstuff;
x Conducts regular auction for horticultural products in the regulated markets;
x Provides market information to the growers;
x Maintains South Asian Association for Regional Cooperation (SAARC) Food Security Reserve Stock;
x Markets essential commodities and convenient consumer packed goods;
x Provides timely delivery of goods.
Local branches:
Thimphu Phone: (975 2) 322877 Fax: (975 2) 323957
Gelephu Phone: (975 6) 365131 Fax: (975 6) 251093
Samdrup Jongkhar Phone: (975 7) 251073 Fax: (975 7) 251123
Products/commodity responsible for:
Essential food items and manufactured consumer products.
Category:
Trading company in agricultural-related products.

BRUNEI

BRUNEI INDUSTRIAL DEVELOPMENT AUTHORITY (BINA)

Office/postal address:
Ministry of Industry and Primary Resources Km 8, Jalan Gadong Negara BE1118
Phone: (673 2) 444100, 444200 Fax: (673 2) 423300
E-mail: bruneibina@brunet.bn URL: www.bina.gov.bn
Year established: 1996
Principal functions:
x To develop and manage industrial sites and complexes to encourage the formation of new industry and cooperatives;
x To process the application of industrial activities to be allocated at the industrial sites and complexes;
x To register new cooperatives;
x To provide support services for the development of manufacturing and cooperative activities.
Services/activities:
x Licensing for industrial and cooperatives; x Industrial and cooperative development.
Publication issued:
x *Information on infrastructure and facilities.*
Local branches:
c/o Blok 2 A6 Pekan Belait Industrial Compleks Jalan Setia Diraja, Kuala Belait, KA3131, Negara Phone: (67 3) 3335052
Temburong Office Cawangan Daerah Temburong PA 1351, Temburong, Negara Phone: (67 3) 5221321
Tutong Office c/o A6 Block 2 Tutong Industrial Complex TA 2541, Tutong, Negara Phone: (67 3) 4261490
Products/commodity responsible for:

x Gas-related industries; x Manufacturing of chemicals, chemical products and plastic products; x Manufacturing of paper and paper products, printing and publishing; x Manufacturing of textiles, apparel and leather industries; x Manufacturing/assembling/servicing of electronics and electrical goods; x Manufacturing/processing of fabricated metal products, machinery and equipment; x Manufacturing/processing of food and beverages including packaging warehouse/cold storage; x Manufacturing/processing of non-metallic and mineral products; x Manufacturing/processing of wood and wood product.
Training:
All aspects of management and business development for cooperatives.
Areas/industries where investment is encouraged:
x Manufacture of food products, creameries and beverages; x Manufacture of silica products; x Manufacture of clay products; x Manufacture of non-metal products; x Manufacture of apparel products; x Manufacture of textile mill products; x Manufacture of leather products.
Titles of laws and regulations on foreign investment:
x Industrial Coordination Order 2001. x Cooperatives Act 1984.
Category:
Government agency.

PROMOTION AND ENTREPRENEURIAL DEVELOPMENT DIVISION

Office/postal address:
Ministry of Industry and Primary Resources Jalan Menteri Besar Bandar Seri Begawan BB3910
Phone: (673 2) 380026, 382822 ext. 2315 Fax: (673 2) 382838
E-mail: miprs3@brunet.bn URL: www.industry.gov.bn, www.bsmenet.org.bn
Year established: 2003
Principal functions:
The mission of the Division is to create self-reliant and competitive entrepreneurs and facilitate the development of high-quality marketable products that can contribute to the nation's goal of economic diversification.
The Division has set two main objectives:
x To identify potential entrepreneurs and support their development to become enterprising and socially responsible business owners and managers of enterprises engaged in the primary resources and industry sectors;
x To identify locally produced goods and services in the primary resources and industry sectors that have commercial potential and support their development as a competitive and marketable product in the local and international markets.
Services/activities:
The Division has four units to implement the above objectives:

- x Resource Centre: in charge of ascertaining that capacity-building programmes and services strengthen the business and management capabilities of small and medium business owners as well as their ability to produce competitive and marketable products;
- x Industry and Trade Promotion Unit: responsible for creating development strategies that will lead to the successful penetration of locally produced goods and services into the domestic and international markets;
- x National Standards and Accreditation Centre: has the responsibility of ensuring that local products have the appropriate standards and quality control recognition that contributes to their acceptance and competitiveness in the domestic and international markets;
- x Regulatory and Facilitation Services Unit: responsible for providing trade-related regulatory and facilitation services that can assist in fast-tracking the establishment, growth and expansion of local businesses in the primary resources and industry sectors.

Publications issued:
x *Setting up of a Company, a practical guide*, April 2000 (English). x *Brunei Darussalam Investment Guide*, 2001 (English). x *The Directory of Brunei Darussalam Products, Ministry of Industry and Primary Resources*, 2003. x *Investment Opportunities in 2004.*
Membership structure: The Promotion and Entrepreneurial Development Division is under the Ministry of Industry and Primary Resources.
Products/commodity responsible for:
All products/services under primary resources, and those enterprises under the category of small and medium enterprises
Training:
Training courses pertinent to the development of entrepreneurs in the small and medium enterprises category.
Areas/industries where investment is encouraged:
Primary resources, high-tech industries, manufacturing and processing and service industry.
Titles of laws and regulations on foreign investment:
x Industrial Coordination Order 2001. x Economic Development Board (Amendment) Order 2001. x Investment Incentive Order 2001.
Category:

Industrial promotion; Ministry of Trade; standard, testing and inspection body; trade fair and exhibition authority; trade promotion organization; and training/research institute.

SEMAUN HOLDINGS SDN BHD

Office/postal address:
Unit 10, Block B Warisan Mata-Mata Complex Kampong Mata-Mata Gadong BE1716 Negara
Phone: (67 3) 2456064/5 Fax: (67 3) 2456070
E-mail: semaun@brunet.bn URL: www.semaun.gov.bn
Year established: 8 December 1994
Principal functions:
- x An investment and trading arm of the Government of Brunei Darussalam in enhancing economic diversification programmes;
- x To spearhead industrial and commercial development through direct investment in key industrial sectors;
- x To accelerate industrial and commercial development through creating new industries and introducing new technology;
- x To generate business opportunities for active participation of local entrepreneurs.

Services/activities:
x Direct investment in high technology, value added industrial and commercial ventures;
x Investment into research and development leading to commercialization;
x Consideration to overseas investment in activities that will reinforce the position of local companies;
x Provides strategic partnership to foreign and local investors in strategic sectors in the economy.
Areas/industries where investment is encouraged:
x Development and management of industrial areas: development of infrastructure and facilities in industrial sites and/or land owned by the company;
x Enterprises and commercial activities: resource-based industries, both upstream and downstream activities and manufacturing industry;
x Involvement in the services sector: not related to the banking and financial industries;
x Investment promotion: operate and act as agent for investment promotion, industrial development and marketing of products in the local and foreign markets.
Titles of laws and regulations on foreign investment:
x Association of Sotheast Asian Nations (ASEAN) Agreement for the Promotion and Protection of Investments, 1987. x The Framework Agreement on the ASEAN Investment
Area, 1998.
x Convention on the Recognition and Enforcement of Foreign Arbitral Awards, 1958, and the Convention on the Settlement of Investment Disputes between States and Nationals of Other States, International Centre for Settlement of Investment Disputes (ICSID).
- x Avoidance of Double Taxation Agreements (DTAs) with United Kingdom and Indonesia Bilateral Agreement on Investment Promotion with Oman and Germany, and with the Republic of Korea and China in November 2000.
- x Convention Establishing the World Intellectual Property Organization (WIPO) in May 2000.
- x Companies Act (Chapter 39).
- x Income Tax (Chapter 35).
- x Investment Incentive Order 2001.
- x Industrial Coordination Order 2001.

Category:
Investment promotion authority.

TRADE DEPARTMENT

Office/postal address:
Ministry of Foreign Affairs and Trade International Convention Centre Second Floor Berakas BB3910
Phone: (673) 2383389 Fax: (673) 2384099
E-mail: vincent.kong@mfa.gov.bn URL: www.mfa.gov.bn
Year established: 2005
Principal functions:
- x To coordinate and facilitate regional and international cooperation;
- x To monitor regional and international trade, investment and development matters;
- x To formulate and prepare long-term and short-term domestic international trade policies;
- x To establish market linkage and facilitate exports;
- x To provide a focal point for trade information.

Services/activities:
As detailed under Principal functions.

Offices abroad:
Brunei Darussalam Trade and Tourism Office in Taipei
6th
Floor, No. 8 Jianguo North Road, Section 1 Taiwan Province of China
Areas/industries where investment is encouraged:
Business services; financial services; hospitality and tourism; transportation and logistics; agriculture; fisheries; forestry; manufacture of food products, creameries and beverages; manufacture of silica products; manufacture of clay products; manufacture of metal products; manufacture of non-metal products; manufacture of apparel products; manufacture of textile mill products; manufacture of leather products; manufacture of electrical and electronic machineries/equipment/apparatus; printing industry; manufacture of chemical products; shipyards.
Titles of laws and regulations on foreign investment:
Investment Incentives Order, 2001.
Category:
Trade facilitation body.

CAMBODIA

CAMBODIA CHAMBER OF COMMERCE

Office/postal address:
Office Vila No. 78 Corner of St. No. 81 and 109 Sangkat Boeung Raing Khan Daun Penh Phnom Penh
Phone: (855 23) 212265 Fax: (855 23) 212270
E-mail: ppcc@camnet.com.kh, ppcc@online.com.kh URL: www.ppcc.org.kh
Year established: 1995
Principal functions:
x Represents the commercial, industrial, agricultural and service communities;
x Develops the commercial environment through supporting, coordinating and advocating for entrepreneurs;
x Promotes trade management capacity-building.
Services/activities:
x To communicate with local and international information sources in order to exploit data for developing enterprises;
x To publish and disseminate economic and commercial data, to research and analyse economic and business issues, and to promote the tourism industry;
x To provide the Government and authorities in provinces and cities information related to commercial, industrial, agricultural and service issues;
x To act as the representative of commercial, industrial, agricultural and service sectors for coordinating encountered problems with the authorities;
x To be an arbitrator in business dispute settlements.
Publications issued:
x *Business Directory* (annually, English).
x *PPCC's Bulletin* (biannually), First to Seventh Circulations from 1998 to 2002 (Khmer/English).
x The *PPCC's Bulletin* was changed to the *PPCC's Newsletter* (quarterly) in 2003.
x *PPCC's Brochure,* Third issue, 2003 (English).
Membership structure: More than 500 company members.
Products/commodity responsible for:
Service for promoting private sector's activities.
Areas/industries where investment is encouraged:
Agricultural sector; tourist industries; and garment industries.
Category:
Chamber of commerce; trade association; trade facilitation body; trade fair and exhibition authority; and trade promotion organization.

COUNCIL FOR THE DEVELOPMENT OF CAMBODIA (CDC)

Office/postal address:
Government Palace Sisowath Quay Wat Phnom Phnom Penh
Phone: (855 23) 981154 Fax: (855 23) 428426, 428953-4
E-mail: cdc.cib@online.com.kh URL: www.cambodiainvestment.gov.kh
Year established: 1994
Principal functions:
x To act as a one-stop service organization;
x To be responsible for the rehabilitation, development and oversight of investment activities;
x To be responsible for the evaluation and decision-making on rehabilitation, development and investment project activities;
x To be responsible for approving investment activities;
x To grant exemption from customs duties and taxes;
x To be responsible for investment promotion.
Services/activities:

x Provides investment information and application procedure; x Evaluates and processes investment application; x Facilitates visa and work permit; x Facilitates company registration; x Grants customs duties and taxes exemption; x Facilitates downstream administrative procedure; x Pre- and post-monitoring of investment activities.
Publications issued:
x *An investment guide to Cambodia* (English, Chinese and Japanese).
x *Prime investment information in Cambodia (Province and city)* (English, Chinese, Khmer and Japanese).
x Compact Disc (CD) for promotion.
Areas/industries where investment is encouraged:
x Development of agriculture and agro-industry;
x Development of transport and telecommunication;
x Development of energy and electricity;
x Labour intensive industries and export oriented processing and manufacturing;
x Tourism-related industries.
Titles of laws and regulations on foreign investment:
x Law on Investment of the Kingdom of Cambodia; x Law on the Commercial Code and Commercial Registration; x Law on Chamber of Commerce; x Law on amendment of the Law on Taxation; x Law on currency exchange control; x Law on amendment of the law on commercial code; x Law on banking and financial institution;
x Law on corporate accounts, their audit and accounting profession;
x Labour law;
x Law on immigration;
x Nationality law;
x Law on environmental protection and natural resource management;
x Law on urbanization and construction;
x Land law;
x Forestry law;
x Law on trademarks and acts of unfair competition;
x Prakas No. 2895/99 CDC, on the provision of duty exempt incentive for supporting industry in subsequent year and authorization for share transfer;
x Notice No. 1538/99 CDC on the obligation to provide information with regard to import-export activity of investment companies;
x Notice on the required documents to apply for the change of location of investment companies;
x Notice No 49BSTH SSR on guidelines for the preparation of the environmental impact report;
x Declaration on management and elimination of forest anarchy.
Category:
Investment promotion organization.

GARMENT MANUFACTURERS' ASSOCIATION IN CAMBODIA

Office/postal address:
175 Jawaharlal Nehru (St. 215)
Phnom Penh Phone: (855 23) 301180 Fax: (855 23) 311181/369398
E-mail: gmac@online.com.kh URL: www.gmac-cambodia.org Year established: 1996 Principal functions:
x To represent the Cambodian textile and garment industry in both national and international forums;
x To liaise with the other stakeholders and all interested parties at the international and local levels.
Services/activities:
x Informs and advises members on government impediment and trades-related developments. x Assists members to resolve industrial issues.
Products/commodity responsible for:
All kinds of garment products and textiles.
Training:
x Conducts a garment factory supervisor course administered by Cambodian trainers.
Areas/industries where investment is encouraged:
x Garments and textiles related.
Category:
Trade association.

MINISTRY OF COMMERCE (MOC)

Office/postal address:
Building No. 20A-B Norodom Boulevard Phnom Penh
Phone: (855 23) 427358 Fax: (855 23) 426396
E-mail: info@moc.gov.kh URL: www.moc.gov.kh

Year established: 1979

Principal functions:

x To administer and regulate both the conduct of international and domestic trade;
x To foster the integration of the Cambodian economy into the region and international economies;
x To establish and develop sound legal commercial framework;
x To promote the rapid growth of Cambodian exports.

Services/activities:

The Ministry of Commerce (MOC) is structured into nine functional departments/divisions and a State-owned enterprise. A short description of each is given as follows:

x *Intellectual Property Division (IPD)* is mandated with the task of registering and granting certificates of trademarks and service marks to domestic and foreign applicants and resolving all disputes arising therefrom;
x *Foreign Trade Division* is responsible for (1) setting foreign trade policies and strategies, (2) conducting market research for domestic product demand and also issuing import licenses, (3) negotiating and drafting bilateral trade agreements and bilateral cooperation between the Royal Government and foreign countries, and acting as the contact point for Cambodian commercial counselors working abroad, and (4) conducting and publishing market research and studies on price and demand on goods in the international market;
x *Internal Trade Division* is acting as an important catalyst to stimulate the economic development of Cambodia. This division is responsible for facilitating the process of local trade and services development;
x *Export Promotion Division* plays a central role in the export promotion of Cambodian products in the framework of the transformation of Cambodia's economy into a market-oriented economy;
x *ASEAN and International Organizations Division* is composed of four offices (ASEAN Office, WTO Office, Coordination and International Organizations Office, and Greater Mekong Subregion (GMS) Office) and two enquiry points (WTO Legal Compliance Enquiry Point and Services Enquiry Point);
x *Trade Preferences Division* involves the dissemination of information on the GSP to investors and manufacturers who are interested in the export business, and the inspection and issuance of Certificate of Origin to exporters;
x *Legal Affairs Division* is responsible for maintaining the commercial register and for governing the conduct of commercial activities;
x *Cambodia Import Export Inspection and Fraud Repression Division (CAMCONTROL)* is responsible for controlling and suppressing the circulation of fraudulent goods;
x *Statistic Division* is responsible for the processing and compilation of trade statistics;
x *Green Trade Company (GTC)* is empowered to conduct businesses as a private autonomous company with the power to bind contracts, to borrow and lend money after the approbation of the Ministry of Economy and Finance (MEF), and engage in commercial activities in the field of domestic and foreign trade. Its main activities are related to trade in agricultural products, especially rice.

Publications issued:

x *Trade Research Newsletter, 2003* (monthly, English and Khmer).
x *Official Gazette for Trademark Registration* (quarterly, English).

Areas/industries where investment is encouraged:

Agriculture; food processing; export-oriented production; textile and garments; construction materials and tourism.

Category:

Ministry of Trade.

CHINA

BANK OF CHINA

Office/postal address:
1 Fuxingmen Nei Dajie Beijing 100818
Phone: (86 10) 66596688 Fax: (86 10) 66014024
E-mail: npa@bank-of-china.com URL: www.bank-of-china.com
Year established: 1912

Principal function:

x To be responsible for the unified operation of China's foreign exchange and for the centralized handling of international receipts and payments of the State.

Services/activities:

x Engages in foreign exchange business and related yuan renminbi transactions including trade and non-trade settlements, loans to foreign trade corporations, foreign currency loans with necessary matching yuan renminbi loans, loans to Sino-foreign joint ventures, export credits, international syndicated loans, commercial credits, international trust, investment and leasing, dealings in foreign exchange and bullion, issue of foreign currency bonds and other marketable securities, foreign currency and yuan renminbi deposits;

x Signs agreements with foreign Governments and central banks, and participates in international financial activities pursuant to authorization from the State and as entrusted by the People's Bank of China;

x Provides loans for students studying overseas, issues notes in Hong Kong, China and Macao, China.

Publication issued:

x *Annual Report*.

Local branches:

Branches of the Bank are located in Anhui, Beihai, Beijing, Changchun, Changzhou, Chengdu, Chongqing, Dalian, Fujian, Fuzhou, Gansu, Guangdong, Guangzhou, Guangxi, Guizhou, Hainan, Hangzhou, Harbin, Hebei, Heilongjiang, Henan, Hubei, Hunan, Inner Mongolia, Jiangsu, Jiangxi, Jilin, Jinan, Lianyungang, Liaoning, Nanjing, Ningbo, Ningxia, Pudong, Qingdao, Qinghai, Qinhuangdao, Shaanxi, Shandong, Shanghai, Shantou, Shanxi, Shenyang, Shenzhen, Shijiazhuang, Sichuan, Suzhou, Taiyuan, Tianjin, Tibet, Wuhan, Wuxi, Xiamen, Xinjiang, Yunnan, Zhanjiang, Zhejiang and Zhuhai.

Offices abroad:

The Bank has overseas branches or subsidies in Alma-Ata; Bangkok; Budapest; Frankfurt; Grand Cayman; Ho Chi Minh City, Hong Kong, China; Johannesburg; Kuala Lumpur; London; Lusaka; Luxembourg; Macao, China; Manila; Milan; Moscow; New York; Panama; Paris; São Paulo; Seoul; Singapore; Sydney; Tokyo and Toronto. It also has representative offices in Moscow and Rome.

Overseas branches and offices and all banks in the Bank of China Group in the Hong Kong, Chian; Macao, China; China region engage in all kinds of banking business permitted by local laws and regulations.

Category:

Banks.

CHINA COUNCIL FOR THE PROMOTION OF INTERNATIONAL TRADE (CCPIT)

Office/postal address:

1, Fuxingmenwai Street Beijing 100860

Phone: (86 10) 68013344, 68018718, 68034830 Fax: (86 10) 68030747, 68011370

E-mail: info@ccpit.org, ccpit@ccpit.org URL: www.ccpit.org

Year established: 1952 [since 1988, the separate name: China Chamber of International Commerce (CCOIC) is simultaneously used]

Principal functions:

x To promote China's foreign trade, attract and utilize foreign capital, introduce advanced foreign technology, and foster various forms of economic and technical cooperation with foreign countries;

x To sponsor and arrange Chinese exhibitions abroad and foreign exhibitions in China;

x To help foreigners to apply for patent rights and trademark registration in China;

x To promote foreign investment and organize technology exchanges with other countries;

x To provide legal services;

x To publish trade periodicals.

Services/activities:

x Conducts investigation and research work;

x Provides information and consultancy services concerning trade, economic and technological cooperation;

x Introduces potential cooperative partners;

x Promotes foreign trade and attracts and utilizes foreign funds;

x Introduces advanced foreign technology and helps revamp existing enterprises;

x Handles liaison work with foreign economic and trade circles, hosts foreign economic and trade delegations and professionals, and organizes and sends Chinese economic, trade and technology delegations abroad;

x Strengthens ties with foreign chambers of commerce, economic and trade associations and other organizations; x Participates in international economic and trade organizations or the activities sponsored by them;

x Handles liaison work with the Beijing Offices of overseas industrial and commercial organizations;

x Sends permanent representatives or establishes commercial representative offices in foreign countries if needed;

x Organizes and participates in international conferences;

x Assists in organizing exhibitions abroad, or participates in international fairs, and coordinates the activities of Chinese departments, or localities, which wish to hold exhibitions in China or abroad, or attend international fairs and administers the China International Exhibition Centre;

x Arranges and hosts foreign economic, trade and technical exhibitions in China, sponsors multinational exhibitions and international fairs in China;

x Organizes and holds technical exchanges between China and other countries and acts as national focal point for information exchange relating to trade and economy.

x Collects, distributes, displays and exhibits literature and new product samples, as well as various overseas publications on science and technology;

x Handles legal affairs pertaining to foreign commerce and trade, as well as maritime matters;

x Issues and legalizes documents, including Certificates of Origin, Certificates of Force Majeure, documents on foreign trade and shipping certificates;

x Acts as agent for patent applications and trademark registrations, provides consultancy services for industrial properties, and helps settle disputes and other issues regarding technological exchanges or trade;

x Compiles and publishes periodicals and other publications reporting on China's economic and trade relations as well as China's import needs or new export commodities;

x Cooperates with overseas advertising and publishing organizations in implementing mutual exchanges.

Publications issued:

x *China Trade Review* (daily, Chinese). x *China's Exports* (4-6 / year, Chinese/English). x *China's Foreign Trade* (monthly, Chinese/English). x *The Directory of CCPIT Membership Enterprises* (Chinese/ English). x *Information on Overseas Trade and Economy* (weekly, Chinese). x *Products and Technology Abroad* (bimonthly, Chinese). x *Survey of China's Economic Development* (annual, Chinese/English). x *Trade Promotion Newsletter* (semi-monthly, English).

Local branches:

Subcouncils in Anhui, Beijing, Changchun, Chengdu, Chongqing, Dalian, Fujian, Gansu, Guangdong, Guangxi, Guangzhou, Guizhou, Hainan, Harbin, Hebei, Heilongjiang, Henan, Hubei, Hunan, Inner Mongolia, Jiangsu, Jiangxi, Jilin, Liaoning, Nanjing, Ningbo, Ningxia, Qingdao, Shangdong, Shanghai, Shanxi, Shenyang, Shenzhen, Sichuan, Tianjin, Wuhan, Xi'an, Xiamen and Xinjiang.

Offices abroad:

Sydney; Brussels; Ontario; Santo Domingo; Paris la Defense; Frankfurt/Main; Hong Kong, China; Milan; Tokyo; Lomes de Tecamachalco; Seoul; Moscow; Abu Dhabi; London; and Washington, DC.

Category:

Trade promotion organization.

CHINESE ACADEMY OF INTERNATIONAL TRADE AND ECONOMIC COOPERATION (CAITEC)

Office/postal address:

No. 28 Dong Hou Xiang An Ding Men Wai Beijing 100710
Phone: (86 10) 64245742 Fax: (86 10) 64212175
E-mail: kyb@caitec.org.cn URL: www.caitec.org.cn

Year established: 1948

Principal functions:

x To advise government agencies and policymakers by submitting analytical reports on world development issues and China's international trade and economic relations and making recommendations on economic and trade policies with a view to improving China's economic and trade performance and realizing sustainable development over the medium and long terms;

x To keep the business community informed of economic and trade information and business opportunities.

Services/activities:

x Conducts academic and applied research on world economy, international trade, international economic cooperation, currencies and finance, commodity market, foreign direct investment, international organizations, multilateral trading system and development issues;

x Conducts collabourative research with other agencies including international organizations and domestic institutions;

x Collects, analyses and disseminates economic and trade data; x Conducts market investigation for domestic and foreign companies and institutions, on contract basis; x Edits and publishes books and periodicals relating to foreign trade and economic cooperation; x Translates books and documents on trade and economy; x Sponsors/organizes academic exchange activities including seminars, conferences, workshops, discussion meetings and lectures; x Conducts enterprise credit investigation and organizing trainings on credit management; x Provides expertise on receivables collection and management, etc.

Publications issued:

x *Inter-trade* magazine (monthly, Chinese). x *International Economic Cooperation* magazine (monthly, Chinese). x *Foreign Investment in China* magazine (monthly, Chinese). x *BusinessWeek/China* magazine (monthly, Chinese version). x *China Commerce* Yearbook (annually, Chinese). x *Study Report on China Commerce Development* (annually, Chinese and English).

x *China's White Paper on Foreign Economic Relations and Trade* (annually, Chinese).

x *Report on the Foreign Trade Situation of China* (semi annually, English/Chinese).

x *Country Report on Trade* (bimonthly, Chinese).

x *Transnational Corporation in China* (annually, Chinese).

Local branches:

Beijing International Trade Advertising Company 28 Donghou Xiang Andingmen Wai Beijing 100710 Fax: (86 10) 64222661 E-mail: gmmg@public3.bta.net.cn

Beijing Intertrade Business Promotion Co. Ltd. 28, Donghou Xiang Andingmen Wai Beijing 100710 Phone: (86 10) 86451067 Fax: (86 10) 64211322 E-mail: info@intertrade.com.cn

Merchants Alliance International Ltd. 28, Donghou Xiang Andingmen Wai Beijing 100710 Phone: (86 10) 64268551, 64235259 Fax: (86 10) 64217789

Leading Development and Trade Co. Rm. 805, Jiahui Centre Building 6. Jiqingli Chaoyang Dist., Beijing 100020 Phone: (86 10) 65529404 Fax: (86 10) 65529399
Huaxin International Economic and Trade Co. Ltd. Phone: (86 10) 65211431
Beijing Smart Economic and Trade Development Co. 28, Donghou Xiang Andingmen Wai Beijing 100710 Phone: (86 10) 64248941
Kompass Company 28, Donghou Xiang Andingmen Wai Beijing 100710 Phone: (86 10) 64248801 Fax: (86 10) 64229352
E-mail: haochen@compass.com.cn
Membership structure: 300 plus members.
Products/commodity responsible for:
Research on import/export of energy, textile, agricultural products, machinery and electronic products, and high-tech technology products, etc.
Training:
x Master's degree in international trade; x Master's degree in finance; x Business credit management training; x Computer skill training; x Overseas training service.
Areas/industries where investment is encouraged:
x Areas: central and western region of China.
x Industries: electronic information, software, aviation and space technology, opto-mechatronics, biomedicine and medical apparatus and instruments, new materials, new energy and high-efficiency energy saving, environmental protection, transportation, nuclear utilization technology and modern agriculture, etc.
Titles of laws and regulations on foreign investment:
x Provisions on the Establishment of Investment Companies by Foreign Investors (2004).
x Provisions on the Administration of Foreign-funded Advertising Enterprises (2004).
x Regulations on Foreign-invested Sourcing Centres for Exports (2003).
x Measures for the Administration of Foreign Insurance Institutions' Representative offices in China (2004).
x Supplementary Provisions on the Interim Measures for the Establishment of Chinese–Foreign Joint Venture Foreign Trade Companies (2003).
x Supplementary Provisions on the Measures for the Administration of Foreign-funded International Freight Agency Enterprises (2003).
x Supplementary Provisions of the Provisions on the Administration of Foreign-funded Construction Enterprises (2003).
x Supplementary Provisions of the Provisions on the Administration of Foreign-funded Construction and Engineering Design Enterprises (2003).
x Supplementary Provisions to the Provisions on the Administration of Foreign-funded Municipal Planning Enterprises (2003).
Category:
Trade promotion organization; training/research institute; and consultant institution.

CITIC GROUP

Office/postal address:
Capital Mansion 6 Xianyuan Nanlu Chaoyang Dist. Beijing 100004
Phone: (86 10) 64660088, 64661710 Fax: (86 10) 64662078, 64661186
E-mail: g-office@citic.com URL: www.citic.com
Year established: 1979
Principal functions:
x To bring in foreign capital for domestic construction; x To introduce advanced technologies and managerial expertise; x To develop domestic and foreign economic and technological cooperation; x To engage in domestic and international financial and banking business; x To invest at home and abroad; x To undertake domestic and foreign trade.
Services/activities:
x Organizes outbound and inbound investment and various forms of economic cooperation; x Undertakes new technology development and promotion, venture capital investment;
x Undertakes international and domestic financing and banking business, guarantee service for foreign and domestic clients, establishment and management of solely- or jointly-owned banks and finance companies inside and outside China;
x Floats various kinds of securities at home and abroad on CITIC's own or on commission; x Handles leasing business inside and outside China;
x Provides insurance for foreign investors in China, international insurance or reinsurance;
x Undertakes international and domestic trade;
x Undertakes international contracting, subcontracting and labour service;
x Handles real estate business and tourist service;
x Provides trust and consulting service, other services as an agent for domestic and foreign clients;
x Handles any other undertaking authorized by the Board of Directors of CITIC.
Publication issued:
Annual Report.

Offices abroad:
3rd
Floor, The LANDIC Third Akasaka Building 2-3-2 Akasaka, Minato-ku, Tokyo, Japan Phone: (81 3) 35842635-6 Fax: (81 3) 35056235 E-mail: citic.tyo@nifty.com
410 Park Avenue, 18/7 New York, NY 10022, United States of America Phone: (1 212) 9450273 Fax: (1 212) 9457749
There are also CITIC-wholly owned subsidiaries in China; Hong Kong, China; Macao, China; and overseas.
Category:
Investment promotion authorities.

SHANGHAI SMALL ENTERPRISES TRADE DEVELOPMENT SERVICE CENTER*

Office/postal address:
International Cooperation Division Room 502 No. 108, Damuqiao Road Shanghai 200032
Phone: (86 21) 64220814 Fax: (86 21) 64220827
E-mail: sbtdsc@online.sh.cn URL: www.tdsc.org
Year established: 1999
Principal function:
x To promote the development of Shanghai small enterprises.
Services/activities:
x To serve small and medium-sized enterprises (SMEs) in the field of finance, training, consulting, information, internal and external communication, etc.
Publications issued:
x *Shanghai Small Enterprises Communicator* (monthly). x *Shanghai Small Enterprises Biz-info Newsletter* (every 10 days).
Training:
x Short MBA courses; x International trade seminar; x Business English training.
Category:
Trade promotion organization.

KOREA

KOREA TRADE AND ECONOMY INSTITUTE (KOTEI)

Office/postal address:
Sungri Street Jungsong Dong Central District Pyongyang
P.O. Box: 504, Pyongyang
Phone: (850 2) 3815926 Fax: (850 2) 3815827
E-mail: koteitis@co.chesin.com
Year established: 1967
Principal functions:
x To conduct research on the world economy, international trade trends and international market movements;
x To provide world economy and trade information to the State economy organizations and domestic trade bodies.
Services/activities:
x Collects, analyses and disseminates information on the world economy trends, international financial and commodity market movement and major import/export prices through Intranet, which connects companies throughout the country;
x Conducts the introduction of domestic and overseas buyers/sellers, introducing of foreign traders/investors to local people, propaganda of imports/exports, opening trade fairs and other trade promotion activities;
x Runs training courses in cooperation with international/internal organizations.
Publications issued:
x *International Market Bulletin* (daily). x *Economy and Trade News.*
Membership structure: One president, one vice-president, 100 researchers and staff members.
Titles of laws and regulations on foreign investment:
x The law on foreign investment.
x The law on equity joint venture.
x The law on contractual joint venture regulations for the implementation of the law on foreign exchange control.
x The law on foreign-invested business and foreign individual tax.
x Regulations for the implementation of the law on foreign-invested business and foreign individual tax.
x The customs law.
x The law on the protection of the environment.
x The insurance law.
x The law on external economic arbitration.
x The notary public law on the registration of foreign-invested enterprises.
x Labour regulations for foreign-invested enterprises.
Category:
Training/research institute.

PYONGYANG CHAMBER OF COMMERCE (PCC)

Office/postal address:
Jungsong-dong Central District Pyongyang

P.O. Box: 504, Pyongyang
Phone: (850 2) 3815926 Fax: (850 2) 3815827 E-mail: micom@co.chesin.com Year established: 1 March 2000 Principal functions:
x Trade and investment promotion; x Trade information service; x Trade exhibition; x Arbitration and training.
Services/activities:
x Trade information service; x Arbitration; x Export and import promotion; x Matchmaking.
Publications issued:
x *Market Information* (daily, Korean). x *Understanding of INCOTERMS 2000* (Korean). x *Foreign Investment Related Laws and Regulations* (Chinese/ English/Korean).
Offices abroad:
PCC Representative in Beijing Phone: (86 10) 65324308, 65325518 Fax: (86 10) 65321145
Membership structure: 25 members (3 banks and 22 companies).
Training:
x Monthly workshop on trade practice; x Ad hoc training with ICC, other international organizations.
Areas/industries where investment is encouraged:
Energy industry; agriculture; light industry; trade; food industry; processing industry; mining industry.
Titles of laws and regulations on foreign investment:
x 14 laws on foreign investment.
Category:
Chamber of commerce; export marketing board; industrial promotion; investment promotion authority; trade fair and exhibition authority; and trade promotion organization.

HONG KONG

CHINESE GENERAL CHAMBER OF COMMERCE

Office/postal address:
4th Floor, Secretariat Department 24-25 Connaught Road Central
Phone: (852) 25256385 Fax: (852) 28452610
E-mail: cgcc@cgcc.org.hk URL: www.cgcc.org.hk
Year established: 1900
Principal functions:
- x To promote trade and industry and enhance the prosperity of Hong Kong, China;
- x To protect the rights and interests of the business and industrial community in Hong Kong, China;
- x To participate in public affairs and reflect the views of the business and industrial community;
- x To develop international and regional communication with a view to promoting economic cooperation.

Services/activities:
x Organizes/sponsors conferences, seminars, exhibitions and delegations;
x Issues Certificates of Origin recognized worldwide;
x Issues Certificates of Origin according to Hong Kong Closer Economic Partnership Arrangement (CEPA);
x Provides Electronic Trading Access Services including trade declarations;
x Handles trade enquiries;
x Handles enquiries on registration information of Hong Kong, China limited company;
x Provides business information on the Chamber's website;
x Provides trade enquiries services and maintains a comprehensive range of economic reference materials in the Chamber's library;
x Publishes monthly the *Chamber's Bulletin*;
x Handles trade disputes;
x Provides insertion services of promotion materials.
Publications issued:
x *Annual Report* (English/Chinese). x *Business Info* (monthly, English/Chinese). x *Chamber's Bulletin* (monthly, Chinese). x *Chinese General Chamber of Commerce Members' Business Directory*, available on Internet website.
Membership structure: Over 6,000 members.
Category:
Chamber of commerce.

HONG KONG COALITION OF SERVICE INDUSTRIES (HKCSI)

Office/postal address:
c/o Hong Kong General Chamber of Commerce 22nd

Floor, United Centre
95 Queensway Phone: (852) 25299229 Fax: (852) 25279843
E-mail: csi@hkcsi.org.hk URL: www.hkcsi.org.hk Year established: 1990 Principal functions:

- x To promote the continuing development and competitiveness of Hong Kong, China's service industries;
- x To promote the development of a "service friendly environment" in Hong Kong, China;
- x To provide a focal point for liaison with Government;
- x To establish and maintain cooperation between members of Hong Kong's service industries for the purpose of achieving common goals;
- x To represent the interests of service industries in Hong Kong, China and to formulate policies and make submissions on behalf of members of the Hong Kong Coalition of Service Industries;
- x To promote fair, effective and comprehensive international and multilateral rules for trade in services;
- x To contribute to the opening of the services sector of the mainland;
- x To establish and develop links with counterpart organizations elsewhere.

Services/activities:
As detailed under Principal functions.
Publications issued:
x *Servicing Economy Newsletter* (3-4 issues per year, English). x *Service Sector Statistical Card in Hong Kong* (annually, English).
Membership structure: Members of the Hong Kong General Chamber of Commerce in the service industries; and service sector trade associations.
Category:
Services promotion organization.

HONG KONG EXPORTERS' ASSOCIATION

Office/postal address:
825 Star House 3 Salisbury Road Tsimshatsui Kowloon
Phone: (852) 27309851 Fax: (852) 27301869
Year established: 1955
Principal function:
x To promote the export and re-export business in Hong Kong, China.
Services/activities:
x Undertakes library services; x Conducts regular seminars, meetings, luncheons, exhibitions.
Publications issued:

- x *Exporters' Bulletin* (quarterly).
- x *The Hong Kong Exporters' Association Members' Directory* (annual booklet and CD-ROM).
- x *Annual Report.*

Membership structure: One honorary member, 606 full members and 31 associate members as of 1 August 2005.
Category:
Trade association.

HONG KONG FRANCHISE ASSOCIATION (HKFA)

Office/postal address:
c/o Hong Kong General Chamber of Commerce 22nd
Floor, United Centre
95 Queensway Phone: (852) 25299229 Fax: (852) 25279843
E-mail: hkfa@franchise.org.hk URL: www.franchise.org.hk Year established: 1992 Principal functions:

- x To monitor and promote the development of franchising activities in Hong Kong, China;
- x To act as a focal point for liaison with the Government on matters concerning franchising and its applications;
- x To promote franchising and to strengthen standards of practice.

Services/activities:
As detailed under Principal functions.
Publications issued:
x *Franchise Training Kit* (English/Chinese, also available on CD-ROM). x *Essential Questions on Franchising in Hong Kong* (English).
Membership structure: Franchising companies in Hong Kong, China.
Category:
Franchise association.

THE HONG KONG GENERAL CHAMBER OF COMMERCE (HKGCC)

Office/postal address:
22/F United Centre 95 Queensway
Phone: (852) 2529 9229 Fax: (852) 2527 9843
Email: chamber@chamber.org.hk URL: www.chamber.org.hk
Year established: 1861
Principal function:
x To promote, represent and safeguard the interests of the Hong Kong, China business community.
Services/activities:
x Networking - Opportunities for fellowship with influential business leaders and government officials from both locally and abroad. To help identify business opportunities and exchange ideas;
x Chamber website - Contains an up-to-date database listing information on more than 10,000 potential buyers and sellers and attracting frequent users from more than 140 countries. It also contains business news, economic analyses and government tenders;
x Website design and hosting -Member company profiles are listed on the Chamber website;
x Business opportunities - Trade inquiries are published daily. Overseas delegation and visitors meet with Chamber members to discuss business opportunities;
x Hotline - Dedicated business information inquiry service with business matching services for members; x Representation -The Chamber is represented on over 30 key government advisory bodies and the Legislative Council;
x Trade documentation - Six offices around Hong Kong, China offering quality and prompt services. The Chamber is the only official authority in Hong Kong, China to issue the internationally recognized Admission Temporaire/Temporary Admission (ATA) carnets;
x Business services - Provide meeting venues, translation and mailings to members at special rates;
x Member benefits programme -Formed partnership with members to offer discounts and special privileges to fellow members.
Publication issued:
x *Bulletin* (monthly business magazine).
Membership structure: Corporate members who are Hong Kong, China registered companies.
Category:
Trade and industrial promotion organization.

HONG KONG PRODUCTIVITY COUNCIL (HKPC)

Office/postal address:
HKPC Building 78 Tat Chee Avenue Kowloon
P.O. Box: 99027 TST
Phone: (852) 27885678 Fax: (852) 27885900 E-mail: hkpcenq@hkpc.org
URL: www.hkpc.org Year established: 1967 Principal functions:

- x To promote productivity excellence through the provision of integrated support across the value chain of Hong Kong, China firms;
- x To achieve a more effective utilization of resources;
- x To enhance the value added content of products and services;
- x To increase international competitiveness.

Services/activities:
Provides a wide range of consultancy, professional training, manufacturing support programmes, publications, exhibitions, conferences and study missions in the core service areas of manufacturing technologies, management systems, information technologies and environmental technologies.
Publications issued:
x *Directory of Industries* (annually). x *Directory of Linkage Industry* (annually). x *Directory of Plastics Industry* (annually). x *Directory of Industrial Suppliers* (annually). x Specialized technical bulletins:
-*Electronics Bulleting* (bimonthly). -*Metals Bulletin* (bimonthly). -*Plastic Bulletin* (bimonthly). -*Textiles and Clothing Bulletin* (bimonthly). -*Toys Bulletin* (bimonthly). -*Logistics Bulleting* (quarterly). -*Automotive Parts and Components Bulletin* (quarterly).
Membership structure: 23 Council Members appointed by the Chief Executive of Hong Kong, China.
Training:
Manufacturing technologies, management systems, information technologies and environmental technologies.
Category:
Industrial promotion and productivity centre; and training/research institute.

HONG KONG TRADE DEVELOPMENT COUNCIL (HKTDC)

Office/postal address:
38th
Floor, Office Tower Convention Plaza 1 Harbour Road Wanchai
Phone: (852) 25844333 Fax: (852) 28240249
E-mail: hktdc@tdc.org.hk URL: www.tdctrade.com
Year established: 1966
Principal functions:

The Trade Development Council (TDC) is the statutory organization for promoting Hong Kong, China's external trade in goods and services:

x To create and facilitate opportunities in international trade for Hong Kong, China-based companies, most of which are SMEs, and to strengthen Hong Kong, China as the global trade platform of Asia with an ever-increasing critical mass of "players";
x To help Hong Kong, China manufacturers, traders and service providers succeed through marketing opportunities, trade contacts, market knowledge and competitive skills;
x To promote Hong Kong, China's trade in goods and services;
x To match overseas companies with Hong Kong, China service providers, manufacturers and traders in various business sectors;
x To provide information on 100,000 Hong Kong, China product suppliers and service providers.

Services/activities:
x Participates in major overseas trade fairs, product exhibitions in overseas markets, and consumer promotions with leading international retailers;
x Provides business matching service which helps companies from around the world find the right supplier, buyer or agent;
x Maintains TDC's databank of 380,000 international traders and 140,000 mainland firms;
x Publishes and disseminates a series of Hong Kong, China product magazines with a global circulation providing easy sourcing for overseas importers and buyers;
x Organizes 21 international trade fairs in Hong Kong, China attracting 500,000 international buyers per annum;
x Organizes high-level missions, both inward and outward, to strengthen Hong Kong, China's economic ties with key trading partners;
x Reinforces its promotional thrust through a multipronged international public relations effort -maintaining contacts with business leaders, economic policymakers and media around the world, keeping them informed of latest business developments in Hong Kong, China;
x Organizes and participates in business seminars and conferences at the international, regional and local levels.

Publications issued:
x *HK Enterprise* (monthly).
x *HK Toys* (biannually).
x *HK Electronics* (bimonthly).
x *HK Watches and Clocks* (quarterly).
x *HK Leather Goods and Bags* (quarterly).
x *HK Gifts, Premium and Stationery* (quarterly).
x *HK Electronic Components and Parts* (quarterly).
x *HK Household* (biannually).
x *HK Jewellery Collection* (biannually).
x *HK Apparel* (biannually).
x *HK Fabrics and Accessories* (biannually).
x *HK Optical* (annually).
x *HK Packaging* (biannually).
x *HK Footwear* (biannually).

Offices abroad:

China and Taiwan, Province of China: Beijing, Chengdu, Dalian, Fuzhou, Guangzhou, Kunming, Qingdao, Shanghai, Shenzhen, Wuhan, Taipei and Xian;
Asia: Bangkok, Ho Chi Minh City, Kuala Lumpur, Osaka, Seoul, Singapore, Tokyo and Mumbai;
Australia: Sydney; Europe: Amsterdam, Barcelona, Budapest, Frankfurt, London, Milan, Moscow, Paris, Stockholm, Vienna, Warsaw and Prague;
Latin America: Mexico City, Santiago and São Paulo; Middle East and Africa: Dubai and Johannesburg; North America: Chicago, Los Angeles, New York and Toronto.
Category:
Trade promotion organization.

INVEST HONG KONG

Office/postal address:
Suites 1501-9, Level 15 One Pacific Place 88 Queensway
Phone: (852) 31071000 Fax: (852) 31079007
E-mail: enq@InvestHK.gov.hk URL: www.InvestHK.gov.hk
Year established: 2000
Principal function:
Invest Hong Kong is an investment promotion agency established to spearhead Hong Kong, China's efforts to attract inward investment. Invest Hong Kong offers solution-oriented investment promotion and support services in a straightforward one-stop shop.
Services/activities:

x Provides solution-oriented investment promotion, facilitation and aftercare services for foreign companies to establish or expand operations in the dynamic Hong Kong, China economy;
x Provides ancillary services to foreign companies that have arrived in Hong Kong, China such as obtaining work visas, trademark registrations, business incorporation, and other administrative, legal and financial matters;
x Provides consultation, regulatory advice and logistics support guidance by sector-specific experts in financial services, information technology, electronics, biotechnology, telecommunications, tourism and entertainment, and transportation.
Publications issued:
x *Invest HK – It all adds up* (English/Chinese/Japanese/ Korean).
x *Invest in Hong Kong for success in Mainland China – The CEPA benefits* (English/Chinese). x *Investment Update* (quarterly newsletter, English/Chinese). x *The Greater Pearl River Delta* (English).
Offices abroad:
Rue d'Arlon 118 1040 Brussels, Belgium Phone: (32 2) 7750088 Fax: (32 2) 7700980 E-mail: general@hongkong-eu.org
Flat 7101, Citic Plaza 233 Tian He North Road Guangzhou 510613, China Phone: (86 20) 38911220 Fax: (86 20) 38911221 E-mail: general@gdeto.gov.hk
6 Grafton Street London W1S 4EQ, United Kingdom Phone: (44 207) 4999821 Fax: (44 207) 4090647 E-mail: general@hketolondon.gov.hk
115 East 54th Street, 5th Floor New York, NY 10022, United States of America Phone: (1 212) 7523320 Fax: (1 212) 7523395 E-mail: hketony@hketony.gov.hk
130 Montgomery Street San Francisco, CA 94104, United States of America Phone: (1 415) 8359300 Fax: (1 415) 3922963 E-mail: hketosf@ hketosf.gov.hk
Level 2, Hong Kong House 80 Druitt Street Sydney NSW 2000, Australia Phone: (61 2) 92833222 Fax: (61 2) 92833818 E-mail: enquiry@hketosydney.gov.hk
30-1 Sanban-Cho, Chiyoda-ku Tokyo 102-0075, Japan Phone: (81 3) 35568961 Fax: (81 3) 35568960 E-mail: Invest@hketotyo.gov.hk
174 St. George Street Toronto, Ontario M5R 2M7, Canada Phone: (1 416) 9245544 Fax: (1 416) 9243599 E-mail: etotor@hketotoronto.gov.hk
Category:
Investment promotion agency.

TRADE AND INDUSTRY DEPARTMENT

Office/postal address:
Trade and Industry Department Tower 700 Nathan Road Kowloon
Phone: (852) 23985333 Fax: (852) 27892491
E-mail: enquiry@tid.gov.hk URL: www.tid.gov.hk
Year established: 2000 (following the reorganization of the Trade Department and Industry Department in July 2000).

Principal functions:

- x To secure and preserve maximum access and fair treatment for exports from Hong Kong, China to international markets;
- x To provide certification and licensing services in order to facilitate trade and supplement controls imposed for reasons other than trade, such as to protect public health, safety or environment;
- x To support and facilitate the development of Hong Kong, China's SMEs and industries.

Services/activities:
x To conduct the commercial relations of Hong Kong, China internationally;
x To provide licensing facilities to traders on import and export of textiles and clothing, strategic commodities, rough diamonds, reserved commodities, radioactive substances and irradiating apparatus, as well as ozone depleting substances;
x To provide certification services for different commodities to establish the origin of the goods which Hong Kong, China exports and to meet the requirements of the importing authorities;
x To provide trade information to traders through the issue of trade information circulars, pamphlets, publications and the department's web portal;
x To provide information and advisory services for SMEs through its Support and Consultation Centre for SMEs (SUCCESS);
x To administer four SME funding schemes.

Publications issued:
Wide range of publications issued, including:
x *A Guide to Pollution Control Legislation Affecting Manufacturing Industries.*
x *Guidance Notes on How to Complete a Combined Form for Export and Import of Goods under Outward Processing Arrangement.*
x *Hong Kong: The Facts – Trade and Industry Fact Sheets.*
x *Notes on Application for Outward Processing Arrangement Registration.*
For full list of publications, please consult website: www.tid.gov.hk.

Offices abroad:

Hong Kong House 80 Druitt Street, Level 1 Sydney NSW 2000, Australia Phone: (61 2) 92833222 Fax: (61 2) 92833818 E-mail: enquiry@hketosydney.gov.hk

Rue d'Arlon 118 1040 Brussels, Belgium Phone: (32 2) 7750088 Fax: (32 2) 7700980 E-mail: general@hongkong-eu.org
174 St. George Street Toronto, Ontario M5R 2M7, Canada Phone: (1 416) 9245544 Fax: (1 416) 9243599 E-mail: info@hketotoronto.gov.hk
21st
Floor, Office Tower 1 Henderson Centre 18 Jianguomen Nei Avenue Dongcheng District Beijing, China Phone: (86 10) 65186318 Fax: (86 10) 65186321 E-mail: bjohksar@bjo-hksarg.org.cn
Flat 7101, Citic Plaza 233 Tian He North Road Guangzhou 510613, China Phone: (86 20) 38911220 Fax: (86 20) 38911221 E-mail: general@gdeto.gov.hk
6 Grafton Street London W1S 4EQ, United Kingdom Phone: (44 207) 4999821 Fax: (44 207) 4955033 E-mail: general@hketolondon.gov.hk
Hong Kong Economic and Trade Office Building, 30-1 Sanban-Cho, Chiyoda-ku Tokyo 102-0075, Japan Phone: (81 3) 35568980 Fax: (81 3) 35568968 E-mail: mailbox@hketotyo.gov.hk
#34-01, Suntec Tower Two 9 Temasek Boulevard Singapore 038989 Phone: (65) 63381771 Fax: (65) 63392112 E-mail: hketo_sin@hketosin.gov.hk
5 Allée David-Morse 1211 Geneva 20, Switzerland Phone: (41 22) 7301300 Fax: (41 22) 7301304 115 East 54th Street New York, NY 10022, United States of America Phone: (1 212) 7523320 Fax: (1 212) 7523395 E-mail: hketony@hketony.gov.hk
130 Montgomery Street San Francisco, CA 94104, United States of America Phone: (1 415) 8359300 Fax: (1 415) 4210646 E-mail: hketosf@hketosf.gov.hk
1520, 18th Street N.W. Washington DC 20036, United States of America Phone: (1 202) 3318947 Fax: (1 202) 3318958 E-mail: hketo@hketowashington.gov.hk
Category:
Industrial promotion; and trade promotion organiztion.

INDIA

AGRICULTURAL AND PROCESSED FOOD PRODUCTS EXPORT DEVELOPMENT AUTHORITY (APEDA)

Office/postal address:
3rd
Floor, NCUI Building 3, Siri Institutional Area Opp. Asaid Village August Kranti Marg New Delhi 110 016
Phone: (91 11) 26513219, 26513204, 26514572 Fax: (91 11) 26534870
E-mail: headQ@apeda.com, trade@apeda.com, dir@apeda.com URL: www.apeda.com
Year established: 1986
Principal function:
x To promote agricultural commodities and processed foods; x To promote their exports.
Services/activities:
x Identifies new markets;
x Provides better support systems to exporters and manufacturers;
x Introduces new products to the international markets;
x Undertakes development programmes: development of databases on products, markets and services; publicity and information dissemination; invites official and business delegations from abroad; organization of product promotion and trade missions abroad; participation in international trade fairs in India and abroad; organization of buyer-seller meets and other business interactions; dissemination of information; provides library services; distribution of Annual APEDA Awards; provides advisory and supporting services to trade and industry; problem solving;
x Provides financial assistance to exporters, growers, trade associations, governmental agencies, etc., for activities related to export promotion and market development through supply of samples to potential importers, brand publicity, etc.; strengthening of market intelligence and databases through studies, surveys, etc.; quality upgrading; development of infrastructure facilities; research and development; packaging; staffing development; and development of meat processing facilities.
Publications issued:
x *Export Statistics of Agro and Processed Food Products, 1990-2000.*
x *Guidelines for the exports of fresh fruits to the EU Market.*
x *Quality assurance manual for export of mangoes.*
x *Quality assurance manual for export of kinnow.*
x *Quality assurance manual for export of nagpur mandarian.*
x *Pre harvest manual for export of nagpur mandarian.*
x *Pre harvest manual for cultivation of kinnow for exports.*
x *Manual for production under protected environment – carnation.*
x *Manual for production of Anthrium Andreanuis.*
x *Manual for production of Perennial Statice.*
x *Manual for production of Eustoma Russaellianum.*
x *Manual for production of orchids.*
x *Manual for production of gladolius.*
x *Report on Guar gum.*

x *Report on honey.*
x *Report on Indian ethnic snack food market study.*
x *A study on status and prospects of frozen food industry (Vols. I and II).*
x *Newsletter* (quarterly).
Local branches:
12/1/1, Palace Cross Road Bangalore 560 020 Phone: (91 80) 3343425 Fax: (91 80) 3364560 E-mail: root@apedablr.kar.nic.in
Mayukh Bhawan Bidhan Nagar Calcutta 700 091 Phone: (91 33) 3376363 Fax: (91 33) 3378680 E-mail: apedacal@vsnl.net
c/o Assam Industrial Development Corporation
3rd
Floor, Jain Complex Opp. Dispur Old Post Office
G.S. Road, Dispur Guwahati 781 005 Phone: (91 361) 599010 Fax: (91 361) 452600 E-mail: apeda@gw1.dot.net.in
8th
Floor, Chandra Vihar Building Mukkaramjahi Road Hyderabad 500 001 Phone: (91 40) 4745940 Fax: (91 40) 4745947 E-mail: hyd@hyd.ap.nic.in
4th
Floor, Banking Complex Building Unit No. 3-4, Sector 19 A, Vashi New Bombay 400 705 Phone: (91 22) 7658949, 7882094 (D) Fax: (91 22) 7882273 E-mail: apedamum@bom.nic.in
Membership structure: 17,000 members.
Products/commodity responsible for:
Fruits, vegetables and their products; meat and meat products; poultry and poultry products; dairy products; confectionery, biscuits and bakery products; honey, joggery and sugar products; cocoa products; alcoholic and non-alcoholic beverages; cereal products; groundnuts, peanuts and walnuts; pickles, papads and chutneys; guar gum; horticulture and floriculture products; herbal and medicinal plants; rice (non-basmati).
Areas/industries where investment is encouraged:
AEZ (Agricultural Export Zone)/Agriculture and food processing sector.
Category:
Trade promotion organization.

ALL INDIA COTTONSEED CRUSHERS' ASSOCIATION

Office/postal address:
6th
Floor, Khetan Bhavan 198, J. Tata Road Churchgate Mumbai 400 020
Phone: (91 22) 22821935, 22821962 Fax: (91 22) 22872151
Year established: 1959
Principal function:
To promote optimum utilization of cottonseed through delinting, decorticating, crushing and solvent extraction.
Services/activities:
x Undertakes national seminars on standardization and upgrading of linters, workshops on use of cottonseed extraction in poultry feed, statistics on the market from members, government and other sources;
x Carries out research;
x Collects and disseminates information about the production and prices of the raw materials and products of the industry;
x Promotes export marketing of the products;
x Analyses problems of the industry and works for their solution with concerned authorities or in other appropriate ways.
Publications issued:
x *Annual Report of the All India Cottonseed Crushers' Association.* x *Newsletter of the All India Cottonseed Crushers' Association*
(monthly).
Membership structure: 44 members.
Mostly companies, cottonseed processors, cottonseed oil refiners, exporters of cottonseed extracting and other cottonseed products. (Managing committee of about 16 members elected by the general body every year.)
Products/commodity responsible for:
Cotton linters, hulls, cottonseed oil and cottonseed extraction.
Category:
Industrial promotion organization.

APPAREL EXPORT PROMOTION COUNCIL (AEPC)*

Office/postal address:
15, NBCC Tower Bhikaji Cama Place New Delhi 110 066
Phone: (91 11) 26183351, 26169393-4 Fax: (91 11) 26188584, 26188300
E-mail: hoadepd@nda.vsnl.net.in URL: www.aepcindia.com
Year established: 1978
Principal function:

x To promote Indian garment exports.

Services/activities:

x Quota distribution, monitoring;
x Marketing in foreign markets;
x Sends trade delegations to survey export potential;
x Publicity;
x General facilitation to exporters by way of assistance in understanding rules and procedures (for example duty drawback delays), import related helps;
x Conducts fashion forecast seminars;
x Provides training for garment manufacturing in Apparel Training and Design Centre (ATDC);
x Operates a trade information centre;
x Provides technical advice and market briefs;
x Publishes promotional material and other information;
x Organizes buyer-seller meets and participates in international fairs/exhibitions;
x Gives annual export awards to outstanding exporter of ready-made garments.

Publications issued:

x *Apparel Fortnightly.* x *Exporters' Directory.* x *Guidelines on Registration and Membership.* x *Handbook of Export Statistics.* x *PP/NQ Allotment Book.* x *Quota Policy Book.* x *Buying Agents Directory.* x Reports on various activities, technical and statistical publications.

Local branches:

Local branches in Bangalore, Chennai, Jaipur, Kolkata, Ludhiana, Mumbai, New Delhi, Tirpur.

Membership structure: Approximately 30,000 members.

Category:

Trade promotion organization.

BASIC CHEMICALS, PHARMACEUTICALS AND COSMETICS EXPORT PROMOTION COUNCIL (CHEMEXCIL)*

Office/postal address:

4th Floor, Jhansi Castle 7, Cooperage Road Mumbai 400 039
Phone: (91 22) 22021288, 22021330 Fax: (91 22) 22026684
E-mail: chemexcil@vsnl.com URL: www.chemexcil.gov.in

Year established: 1963

Principal functions:

x To promote and develop exports;
x To undertake liaison activities;
x To provide market information.

Services/activities:

x Compiles export data, trade plan, commodity profiles, etc.; x Conducts panel meetings; x Undertakes market surveys; x Sponsors individual and group delegations abroad; x Provides guidance to exporters regarding licensing, customs, banking, etc.; x Organizes seminars, workshops, etc., for exporters; x Disseminates overseas enquiries, tenders; x Undertakes investigation of quality/delivery complaints, arbitration, etc.; x Participates in trade fairs and exhibitions; x Publishes bulletins, reports, directories; x Liaises with various organizations.

Publications issued:

x *CHEMEXCIL Sales Bulletin.* x Directories. x Market Survey Reports. x Exhibition Reports. x Promotional literature on products under Council's purview. x Reports of study-cum-sales teams.

Local branches:

901, Karma Near Mahalaxmi Cross Road Paldi, Ahmedabad 380 007 Phone: (91 79) 6640224 Fax: (91 79) 6630061
No. 18/4,, 1st Floor - C, N.S. Bhavan 4th Cross, 4th Main Road Gandhinagar Bangalore 560 009 Phone: (91 80) 2269037 Fax: (91 80) 2260446 507, 5th Floor, Aditya Enclave Ameer Pet Hyderabad 500 038 Phone: (91 40) 26622311 Fax: (91 40) 26622411
9th Floor, Kankaria Estate 6, Little Russell Street Kolkata 700 071 Phone: (91 33) 22805791 Fax: (91 33) 22475562
424, 4th Floor, Ansal Chamber - II 6, Bikaji Cama Place New Delhi 110 066 Phone: (91 11) 26160937 Fax: (91 11) 26169891

Products/commodity responsible for:

Drugs, pharmaceuticals and fine chemicals; dyes, intermediates, coaltar chemicals and alcohol dyes; basic inorganic and organic chemicals and agro chemicals; cosmetics and toiletries; essential oils, detergents, soaps, perfume, agarbattis, medicinal plants, castor oils, etc.

Membership structure: 6,178 members.

Membership consists of large and small-scale manufacturers and large and small merchant exporters of drugs and pharmaceuticals, dyes, chemicals, cosmetics and toiletries and agarbattis.

Category:

Export promotion council.

BENGAL NATIONAL CHAMBER OF COMMERCE AND INDUSTRY (BNCCI)

Office/postal address:
Foreign Trade Section BNCCI House 23, R.N. Mukherjee Road Kolkata 700 001
Phone: (91 33) 22482951 (3 lines) Fax: (91 33) 22487058 / 0387
E-mail: bncci@bncci.com URL: www.bncci.com
Year established: 1887
Principal function:
x To perform function of a Chamber of Commerce.
Services/activities:
x Promotes industry, trade and commerce, particularly in the eastern region of India as well as in West Bengal;
x Promotes entrepreneurship, integrated development of rural areas, protection of environment and improvement of the socio-economic condition of the people;
x Organizes trade fairs, promotion of international trade and business, and business delegations abroad.
Publications issued:
x *BNCCI Newsletter* (quarterly). x *Committee Roster* (annually). x *Annual Report* (annually). x *Guidebook on Industrial India Trade Fair* (annually). x *Membership Directory in floppy* (annually). x *Trade Bulletin* (monthly). x *Tender Circular* (monthly).
Membership structure: 500 industries/firms, about 35 industrial trade associations.
Training:
x Entrepreneurship development training; x Training on trade promotion; x Training courses on business promotion and management,
etc.
Areas/industries where investment is encouraged:
Whole of West Bengal in general and rural areas in particular.
Category:
Chamber of commerce.

BOMBAY CHAMBER OF COMMERCE AND INDUSTRY

Office/postal address:
3rd
Floor, Mackinnon Mackenzie Building 4, Shoorji Vallabhdas Marg, Ballard Estate Mumbai 400 001
Phone: (91 22) 22614681-84 Fax: (91 22) 22621213
E-mail: edoffice@bombaychamber.com, bcci@bombaychamber.com URL: www.bombaychamber.com
Year established: 1836
Principal functions:
x To conduct investment promotion;
x To promote interests of trade and industry;
x To establish business contacts.
Services/activities:
Trade services: x Trade information and library services; x International Trade Division to promote trade, investment, technology transfer; x Certification of export documentation and visa recommendations; x Declares weather working days and charter party holidays for Mumbai ports.
Advisory services: x Labour advisory services; x Safety, health and environment protection advisory services; x Arbitration services; x Executive training and development programmes.
Publications issued:
x *International Trade News* (monthly, English). x *Bombay Chamber Monthly Bulletin* (monthly, English). x *Labour Digest - Labour Law and Industrial Relations*
(monthly, English). x *Safety, Health and Environment (SHE) Bulletin* (quarterly, English). x *AnalytiQue Economics* (quarterly, English).
Membership structure: Almost 1,600 members.
Represents large and medium-sized companies from the manufacturing and service sectors, leading banks and financial institutions and multinationals having their corporate headquarters in Mumbai, including Foreign Consulates/Trade Commissions in Mumbai. Membership of Bombay Chamber accounts for around one third of India's GDP in the manufacturing and service sectors.
Products/commodity responsible for:
Electrical, electronics, telecom, computer, software and hardware, textiles and garments, chemicals and pharmaceuticals, agri and food processing, automobiles, power and energy, shipping and transportation, basic products, consumer goods, building and construction, consultancy services, banking and financial services.
Training:
The Bombay Chamber's Executive Training Development Programmes caters to the knowledge upgrading of its constituent members and their employees.
Areas/industries where investment is encouraged:
For products and services represented by the Chamber's membership.
Category:
Chamber of commerce; trade facilitation body; and trade
promotion organization.

BUREAU OF INDIAN STANDARDS (BIS)*

Office/postal address:
Manak Bhavan 9, Bahadur Shah Zafar Marg New Delhi 110 002
Phone: (91 11) 23233375 Fax: (91 11) 23234062, 23239399, 23239382
E-mail: bis@vsnl.com URL: www.bis.org.in
Year established: 1987 (formerly Indian Institution).
Principal functions:
To formulate and publish national standards; Standards
x To grant certification marks licensees to manufacturers;
x To grant license for Management Systems such as ISO 9001, ISO 14001, OSHAS, HACCP;
x To test and evaluate the quality of products for the formulation of standards and operation of Certification Marking Scheme;
x To provide training in the areas of standardization, management systems, statistical quality control and certification marking.
Services/activities:
x Publishes national standards;
x Grants licenses under BIS Certification Marking Scheme;
x Provides training facilities in standardization, management systems, statistical quality control, certification marking and labouratory testing;
x Undertakes consultancy services in company standardization and Statistical Quality Control (SQC);
x Undertakes promotion and publicity of standardization activities;
x Provides technical information on standards, regulations, etc.;
x Handles sale of national standards, standards of other countries and international standards;
x Grants certificate against various Management Systems such as ISO 9001, ISO 14001, OSHAS, HACCP, etc.
Publications issued:
x *Buyer's Guide* (list of manufacturers holding licenses under BIS Certification Marking Scheme) (on computer floppy).
x *Catalogue of Indian Standards.* x *Indian Standards.* x *Manakdoot* (quarterly). x *Standards India* (monthly). x *Standards Monthly Additions.* x *Standards Worldover - Monthly Additions.* x Handbooks of standards on various subjects. x Miscellaneous publications such as brochures, pamphlets posters, etc.
Local branches:
National Institute of Training for Standardization, Quality and Management (NITSQM) A-20, 21, Institutional Area Sector - 62, Noida 201 307 (UP) Phone: (91 120) 2402201-7 Fax: (91 120) 2402202-3
Regional offices in Chandigarh, Chennai, Kolkata, Mumbai.
Branch offices in Ahmedabad, Bangalore, Bhopal, Bhubaneshwar, Coimbatore, Faridabad, Ghaziabad, Guwahati, Hyderabad, Jaipur, Kanpur, Lucknow, Nagpur, Nalagarh, Patna, Pune, Rajkot, Thiruvananathapuram, Vishakhapatnam.
Category:
Standard, testing and inspection body.

CHEMICAL AND ALLIED PRODUCTS EXPORT PROMOTION COUNCIL (CAPEXIL)

Office/postal address:
"Vanijya Bhavan", International Trade Facilitation Centre, 3rd Floor, 1/1 Wood Street Kolkata 700 016
Phone: (91 33) 22890524/0525 Fax: (91 33) 22891724
E-mail: info@capexil.com URL: www.capexil.com B2B Portal: www.capexiltrade.com
Year established: 1958 (formerly: Chemicals and Allied Products Export Promotion Council).
Principal function:
x To facilitate export by way of promotion, organizing trade shows, embracing the latest technology to help exporters, matching the needs of buyers and sellers.
Services/activities:
x Services to overseas importers: -Locates a reliable supplier of made-in-India products; -Organizes buyer-seller meets; -Provides up-to-date information on supply sourcing; -Publishes trade directory, brochure on individual products; -Caters information through website www.capexil.com; -B2B Portal www.capexiltrade.com - online directory of Indian exporters with their products and services; highly effective platform to generate business opportunities.
x Service to exporters: -Assists in identifying potential markets; -Assists in overcoming export constraints and operational bottlenecks; -Provides publicity and marketing backup; -Organizes overseas trade delegations and participation in trade fairs and buyer-seller meets; -Organizes training, seminars on export; -Caters information through website www.capexil.com; -B2B Portal www.capexiltrade.com - online directory of Indian exporters with their products and services; highly effective business platform to generate business opportunities; -Education through programme: Certificate Course in International Marketing.
Publications issued:
x *CAPEXIL Trade News* (monthly, English). x *A Statistical Profile* (yearly, English). x *Trade Directory* (biannually, English).
Local branches:
Eastern Region: Tobacco House 1-2, Old Court House Corner Kolkata 700 001 Phone: (91 33) 22207620 Fax: (91 33) 22435945 E-mail: capexler@vsnl.net
Northern Region: Flat No. 4 C
4th

Floor, Vandana Building 11 Tolstoy Marg New Delhi 110 001 Phone: (91 11) 23356703, 23711479, 23752282 Fax: (91 11) 23314486 E-mail: capexiln@bol.net.in

Southern Region: Rasheed Mansion 408 (Old No. 622), Anna Salai Chennai 600 006 Phone: (91 44) 28292310, 28294713 Fax: (91 44) 28295386 E-mail: capexils@vsnl.com
Western Region: Commerce Centre Block No. D-17, Tardeo Road Mumbai 400 034 Phone: (91 22) 24943410, 24960084 Fax: (91-22) 24937665 E-mail: capexilm@vsnl.com
Membership structure: 3,542 members, as of 4 July 2003.
Products/commodity responsible for:
Rubber manufactured products (including automobile tyres and tubes); paints, enamels, varnishes, pigments and paint raw materials; glass and glassware; ceramics and allied products; wood products; refractory bricks; cement, clinkers and asbestos cement products; paper, paper boards and paper conversion items including stationery; ossein and gelatine; crushed bones, bone grist, animal glue, horn and hoof meal; safety matches, pyrotechnical articles, dyeing and tanning extracts; graphite electrodes, detonators and explosives; granite, marble, stones; mineral and ores; books, publications and job printing.
Training:
x Course offered in English: Certificate Course in International Marketing
Category:
Trade facilitation body; and trade promotion organization.

CASHEW EXPORT PROMOTION COUNCIL OF INDIA

Office/postal address:
Chittoor Road Ernakulam South Kochi 682 016 Kerala
P.O.Box: 1709
Phone: (91 484) 2376459, 2376080 Fax: (91 484) 2377973
E-mail: cashew@vsnl.com, cepc@cashewindia.org URL: www.cashewindia.org
Year established: 1955
Principal function:
x To promote the export of cashew kernels, cashew nut shell liquid and allied products from India. Services/activities: x Conducts trade promotion activities.
Publications issued:
x *Cashew Bulletin* (monthly, English).
x *Indian Cashew Journal* (quarterly, English).
x *Directory of Indian Cashew Exporters* (English).
x *A Survey of CNSL Patents* (English).
x *Indian Cashew Grades Folder* (English).
x *Cashew - The Millennium Nut - Cashew Recipes* (English).
x *Cashew Statistics* (English).
Membership structure: 137 members (varying from year to year).
Products/commodity responsible for:
Cashew kernels, cashew nut shell liquid and allied products.
Category:
Trade promotion organization.

CENTRAL SILK BOARD

Office/postal address:
Dr. H. Basker, I.A.S, CEO and Member Secretary Ministry of Textiles CSB Complex, Hosur Road BTM Layout, Madivala Bangalore 560 068
Phone: (91 80) 26688831, 26680190 Fax: (91 80) 26681511
E-mail: csb@silkboard.org URL: www.indiansilk.kar.nic.in
Year established: 1948
Principal function:
x To promote the development of the silk industry.
Services/activities:
x Advises the Government of India on development of the silk industry;
x Assists various provinces of the Indian Union in development planning for sericulture through jointly funded schemes, or centrally sponsored schemes;
x Undertakes, assists and encourages scientific, technological and economic research in the silk sector and production of basic and commercial silkworm seed for supplementary assistance to various provinces;
x Initiates measures for the standardization and quality control of silk and silk products;
x Rationalizes the marketing and stabilization of prices of silk cocoons and silk products;
x Voluntary inspection of silk goods meant for exports, and certification for quality and content.
Publications issued:

Periodicals: x *Indian Silk* (monthly, English). x *Indian Journal of Sericulture* (English). x *SERIDOC* (English).

Books:

x *Handbook Of Sericulture Technologies.* x *Seri Business Manual – A User's Guide.* x *Sericulture & Silk Industry Statistics* – 2003 (with CD-ROM version).

x *Directory Of Exporters And Manufacturers Of Silk Goods In India.*

x *Disinfection In Sericulture: A Ready Reckoner.*

x *Handbook Of Practical Sericulture.*

x *Handbook Of Muga Culture.*

x *Ericulture In India.*

x *Tips To Successful Silkworm Cocoon Crops.*

x *CSR&TI (Mysore) Bulletins On Improved Practices Of Sericulture.*

CDs/video cassettes:

x *Sericulture in India.* x *Package for Prosperity.* x *A Stitch in Time.*

x *Bivoltine for Higher yield; more income.*

x *Reeling for Quality Silk.*

x *Capsule films on Post Cocoon Technology.*

x *Strong Ties; Loose Threads: Women in Silk.*

x *Prevention is better than cure.*

x *Sericulture deserves credit.*

x *Mulberry cultivation and Farm Management.*

x *Silkworm rearing Technology.*

x *The Story of Tasar.*

x *Eri silk in the North East.*

x *Golden Muga: The Cultural Heritage of Assam.*

x *Life Story of a Moth: The Silkworm..*

x *Mulberry cultivation and maintenance of garden.*

x *Nutrient management for healthy growth of mulberry garden.*

x *Sericulture extension.*

x *Sericulture training.*

x *Hygiene and chawki rearing.*

x *Late age silkworm rearing and quality cocoon production.*

Others:

x Translations of various project reports, popular publications, manual reprints.

Local branches:

Regional Offices:

MEGHDOOT 95-B
Marine Drive, Ph.:203468
Mumbai 400 002
Phone: (91 22) 2811826, 2815532
Fax: (91 22) 2812842

342-347 (2nd Floor) A-Wing
August Kranti Bhavan
Bhikaji Cama Place
New Dehli 110 066
Phone: (91 11) 26108316
Fax: (91 11) 26176177

House No.16-B (Extension)
Gandhi Nagar
Jammu 180 007
Phone: (91 191) 2433677
Fax: (91 191) 2542917

MEGHDOOT 95-B
Marine Drive
Mumbai 400 002
Phone: (91 22) 2811826, 2815532
Fax: (91 22) 2812842

Regional Development Offices:

Road No 72 Prasashan Nagar

D.S. Mansion II Floor
Near State Zoo
Central Silk Board
P.O. Dispur,
Guwahati 781 005
Phone: (91 361) 203468, 200168
Fax: (91 361) 200 168

Mahesh mati
P.O. & Dist
Malda 732 101.

18 Satyanagar
Bhubaneswar 751 007
Phone: (91 674) 505153

63 A 12th Avenue
Ashok Nagar
Chennai 83
Phone: (91 44) 4892044, 4894189
Fax: (91 44) 4892044

Vikas Deep Building
5th Floor
22 Station Road
Lucknow 226 019.(U.P)
Phone: (91 522) 635123

Majra
Dehradun 248171
Phone: (91 135) 3261239

Certification Centres:

CSB Complex
B.T.M. Layout Madivala
Hosur Road
Bangalore 560 068, Karnataka
Phone: (91 80) 26688831
Fax: (91 80) 26681511
E-mail: eps@silkboard.org

32, Radha Rani Sinha Road,
Bhagalpur 812001; Bihar

Plot No.13
Vivekananda Nagar Colony
Maldahiya
Varanasi 221002, Uttar Pradesh

Main Research Institutes:

Srirampura Manandavadi Road
Mysore 570 008, Karnataka
Phone: (91 821) 2362406, 2362585

Adjacent Hills
Jubilee Hills
Hyderabad 500 033
Grams: SILK BOARD
Phone: (91 40) 3541293

Fax: (91 821) 2362845
URL: www.csrtimys.res.in

Berhampore 742 101, West Bengal
Phone: (91 3482) 253962-4
Fax: (91 3482) 251046
E-mail: director@csrtiber.res.in
URL: www.csrtiber.res.in

Post Bag # 88, GPO, Srinagar 190 001, Jammu and Kashmir Phone: (91 1933) 222839, 223176 Fax: (91 1933) 223215 E-Mail: csrtippr@sancharnet.

P.O. Ladoigarh Charali, Jorhat 785 700, Assam Phone: (91 3763) 385513, 395528

Carmelram Post, Kodathi Bangalore 560 035, Karnataka
Phone: (91 80) 28439598
Fax: (91 80) 28439596
E-mail: seedtech@vsnl.com

Post Box No. 44, Thally Road, Hosur 635 019, Tamilnadu Phone: (91 4344) 221148, 221149, 222013 Fax: (91 4344) 220520 E-mail: director@silkgermplasm.com URL: www.silkgermplasm.com

Carmelram Post, Kodathi Bangalore 560 035, Karnataka Phone: (91 80) 28439598 Fax: (91 80) 28439597 E-mail: sbrl93@vsnl.com

Piska Nagri Ranchi 835 303, Jharkand Phone: (91 651) 2775815, 2775630 Fax: (91 651) 2775629 E-mail: rch_silkmc@sancharnet.in

B.T. M. Layout, Madiwala Bangalore 560 068, Karnataka Phone: (91 80) 26688831 Fax: (91 80) 26680435 E-mail: cstri@silkboard.org

CSB Complex B.T. M. Layout Madivala Bangalore 560 068, Karnataka Phone: (91 80) 26688831 Fax: (91 80) 26680387 E-mail: nsso@silkboard.org

Training:

Provides training on sericulture to local and international students in its research institutes in the following three categories: x Structured courses: courses of long-term duration ranging from 3 to 24 months; x Capsule courses: courses of short-term duration ranging from 3 to 45 days; x Ad hoc courses: short duration courses conducted upon request from different agencies.

Products/commodity responsible for:

Silk and silk products.

Category:

Commodity board.

COCHIN CHAMBER OF COMMERCE AND INDUSTRY

Office/postal address:

Bristow Road Willingdon Island Cochin 682 003
P.O. Box: 503, Cochin
Phone: (91 484) 2668349, 2668650 Fax: (91 484) 2668651 E-mail: chamber@md2.vsnl.net.in Year established: 1857

Principal functions:

- x To provide an accepted focal point for the region's commerce, industry and trade;
- x To protect the individual businessperson's right to self-determination in the conduct of his or her business affairs, without undue interference from any quarter;
- x To promote the genuine interests of its members, acting as the focus for the views and reactions of the organized trade sector in South-West India;
- x To act as a liaison body between industry and government, to ensure that the voice of industry is heard in the corridors of power and that its views are given due consideration in the formulation of the State's policies with regard to trade and industry as also other matters that relate to the all-round socio-economic development of the State;
- x To emphasize the need for long-term policy planning in the interest of industry in the State.

Services/activities:

x Serves as an intermediary between commerce/industry and the Government;
x Ensures that its members are kept informed of the various legislations, notifications, resolutions, etc. on a regular basis;
x Offers its comments/suggestions and consults with the members, on draft resolutions placed before it for consideration;
x Advises the Government on trade and industry;
x Represents on all the different expert committees of the Associated Chambers of Commerce and Industry of India (ASSOCHAM) which helps in presenting the State's problems at the national level;
x Maintains information on the import/export trade carried on through Cochin Port;
x Processes trade enquiries received from different trade organizations both from within and outside the country;
x Disseminates information to all its members;
x Undertakes weighment/measurement of cargo;
x Issues quality certificates and certificates of origin;

x Is also the sole authorized representative for the "Southern Region" for all export documentation/legalization requirements vis-à-vis the Arab/African countries.
Publications issued:
x *Statistical Report* (monthly and annually, English).
x *Newsletter* (monthly, English).
x *Information Bulletin* (monthly, English).
x *Annual Report* (English).
Membership structure: 168 members.
Areas/industries where investment is encouraged:
Information technology and tourism.
Category:
Chamber of commerce.

COCONUT DEVELOPMENT BOARD

Office/postal address:
(Ministry of Agriculture Government of India) Kera Bhavan Kochi - 682 011 Kerala State
Phone: (91 484) 2376265, 2377266, 2377267 Fax: (91 484) 2377902
E-mail: enk_cdrkochi@sancharnet.in URL: www.coconutboard.nic.in
Year established: 1981
Principal functions:
x To adopt measures for the development of the coconut industry;
x To recommend measures for improving the marketing of coconut and its products;
x To advice those engaged in coconut cultivation and industry;
x To provide financial and other assistance for expansion of area under coconut;
x To encourage the adoption of modern technologies for processing of coconut and its products;
x To recommend measures for regulating imports and exports of coconut and its products;
x To fix grades, specifications and standards for coconut and its products;
x To finance suitable schemes to increase the production of coconut and to improve the quality and yield of coconut;
x To assist, encourage, promote and finance agricultural, technological, industrial or economic research on coconut and its products;
x To collect statistics on coconut and its products and publish them;
x To undertake publicity activities and publish books and periodicals on coconut and its products.
Services/activities:
x Increases production of quality planting materials;
x Creates future production potential by bringing more area under coconut;
x Improves the productivity of existing coconut holdings;
x Product diversification and by-product utilization;
x Promotes coconut and coconut base products.
Publications issued:
x *Bharatiya Nariyal Patrika* (quarterly, Hindi). x *Bharatiya Thengu Patrika* (quarterly, Kannada). x *Indian Thennai Idhazh* (quarterly, Tamil). x *Indian Coconut Journal* (monthly). x *Indian Nalikera Journal* (monthly, Malayalam). x Other ad hoc publications on various aspects of coconut culture and industry.
Local branches:
Regional Offices:
Karnataka: Hulimavu, Bannerghatta Road (Beside Horticulture Farm, Govt. of Karnataka) Bangalore South Taluk, Bangalore - 560 076, Karnataka Phone: (080) 26593750 Fax: (080) 26594768 E-mail: cdbroblr@vsnl.net
Bihar: M-2/40, S.K. Puri, Patna 800 001, Bihar Phone: (0612) 2221367 Fax: (0612) 2221608 E-mail: cdbrop@sify.com
Tamil Nadu: AF-6/2204, 7th Street, 11th Main Road Anna Nagar, Chennai - 600 040, Tamil Nadu Phone: (044) 26286640 Fax: (044) 26286732 E-mail: cdbtn@vsnl.net
State Centres:
Andaman and Nicobar Islands: VIP Road, Junglighat P.O. Port Blair - 744 103, South Andaman Phone: (03192) 233918 E-mail: cdban@sancharnet.in
Andhra Pradesh: A-23 (269), IIIrd Street, 1st Line Indian Airlines Colony, Begumpet Secundrabad - 500 003 Phone: (040) 27902978 Fax: (040) 27902978 E-mail: cdbhyd@satyam.net.in
Demonstration-Cum-Seed Production (Dsp) Farms Vegivada (Village) P.O. House No. 688, Tadikalapudi (Via) W. Godavari (Dist.) Andhra Pradesh - 534 452 Phone: (08812) 228401 E-mail: elr_coconut@sancharnet.in

Aluva :
Technology Development Centre
Keenpuram, South Vazhakkulam
Aluva, Ernakulam Dist. Pin. 683 105
Phone: (0484) 2679680

Assam:
Housefed Complex (Sixth Floor), Beltola Road, Last Gate,
Dispur

Kerchowmohani, Ramnagar P.O.
Agartala - 799 002, Tripura
Phone: (0381) 2222205
E-mail: cdb_agt@sancharnet.in

West Bengal:
BJ-108 - Sector - II, Salt Lake
Kolkata - 700 091
Phone: (033) 23599674

Guwahati - 781 006, Assam
Phone: (0361) 2220632
Fax: (0361) 2220632
E-mail: cdbassam1@sancharnet.in
Abhayapuri, Bongaigoan
Assam - 783 384
Phone: (03664) 281473
Bihar:
P.O. Singheswar - 852 128,
Madhepura District, Bihar
Phone: (06476) 283015
E-mail: cdb_singheswar@sify.com
Chattisgarh:
Kondagaon - 494 226, Bastar District
Chattisgarh
Phone: (07786) 242443
Fax: (07786) 242443
E-mail: cdb_kgn@rediffmail.com
Karnataka:
Pura Village, Loksara P.O.
Mandya District, Karnataka - 571 403
Phone: (08232) 234059
E-mail: dspfmand@sancharnet.in
Kerala:
Neriamangalam, Kerala
Pin-686 693
Phone: (0485) 2554240
E-mail: dspfarmnrlm@sancharnet.in
New Delhi:
Market Development cum Information Centre
120, Hargobind Enclave
New Delhi – 110 092
Phone: (011) 22377805
Fax: (011) 22377806
E-mail: cdbmdic@sify.com
Orissa:
N-1/297 Nayapally IRC Village P.O.
Bhubaneswar - 751 015, Orissa
Phone: (0674) 2550439
Fax: (0674) 2550439
E-mail: cdbbbs@ori.nic.in
At Pitapally, Post Kumarbasta
District Khurda - 752 055, Orissa
Phone: (0674) 2330053
E-mail: dspor@rediffmail.com
Tripura:
Belbari, Champaknagar P.O.,
West Tripura
Phone: (0381) 262413

Fax: (033) 23599674
E-mail: cdbkol@sify.com

Membership structure: 23 board members.
Products/commodity responsible for:

Coconut and coconut products.
Training:

Courses arranged as per requirements.

Areas/industries where investment is encouraged:
Coconut and allied industries.

Category:

Commodity board.

CONFEDERATION OF INDIAN INDUSTRY (CII)*

Office/Postal address:
CII Mantosh Sondhi Centre 23 Institutional Area, Lodhi Road City New Delhi, 110 003
Phone: (91 11) 24629994 Fax: (91 11) 24621649, 24633168, 2460198
E-mail: ciico@ciionline.org URL: www.ciionline.org
Year established: 1895 (formerly Confederation of Engineering Industry (CEI)).
Principal functions:
x To create and sustain an environment conducive to the growth of industry in India, partnering industry and Government through advisory and consultative processes;
x To provide information to industry and government; x To promote cooperation with counterpart organizations.
Services/activities:
x Catalyses change by working closely with Government on policy issues, enhancing efficiency, competitiveness and expanding business opportunities for industry through a range of specialized services and global linkages;
x Provides a platform for sectoral consensus building and networking by projecting a positive image of business, assisting industry identify and execute corporate citizenship programmes;
x Provides information, advisory and consultative services to the industry and the Government;
x With 35 offices in India, 12 overseas offices and institutional partnerships with 216 counterpart organizations in 94 countries, serves as a reference point for Indian industry and the international business community.
Publications issued:

Various publications, periodicals and directories in the areas of defence; economics/finance; energy; environment; food and agriculture; healthcare; international business; industry; information technology; infrastructure; small and medium enterprises; social development; technology; and quality.
Regional offices:
Offices in New Delhi, Gurgaon, Kolkata, Mumbai, Bangalore, Hyderabad, Chandigarh, Chennai, Bhubaneswar, Guwahati, Jamshedpur, Kohima, Patna, Dehradun, Jaipur, Lucknow, Noida, Coimbatore, Kochi, Madurai, Mysore, Trichy, Ahmedabad, Bhachhau, Bhopal, Goa, Gwalior, Indore, Pune.
Offices abroad:
Offices in Kabul, Vienna, Brussels, Paris, Jerusalem, Milan, Kuala Lumpur, Singapore, Johannesburg, London, Rosslyn.
Category:
Industrial promotion organization.

COUNCIL FOR LEATHER EXPORTS

Office/postal address:
3rd
Floor, CMDA Tower II Gandhi Irwin Bridge Road Egmore, Chennai 600 008
Phone: (91 44) 28594367-71 Fax: (91 44) 28594363-4
E-mail: cle@vsnl.com, cle@cleindia.com URL: leatherindia.org
Year established: 1984
Principal functions:
x To undertake export promotion activities relating to leather and leather products;
x To promote the development of the Indian leather industry.
Services/activities:
x Collects market intelligence and conducts market studies;
x Maintains constant touch with the world market, business environment, market conditions and economic issues;
x Keeps close watch on technology, buyers' needs, product design and fashion;
x Formulates appropriate strategy to make the Indian products globally competitive;
x Disseminates vital information through magazines/ periodicals, newsletters, brochures and study team reports;
x Assists the Indian Government in formulating policies and procedures to develop the leather industry;
x Promotes foreign direct investment and joint ventures; foreign direct investment;
x Promotes Indian leather products abroad through publicity campaigns;
x Sponsors overseas trade missions;
x Arranges training of Indian technicians in foreign institutes;
x Invites foreign experts to help upgrade the quality of Indian products;
x Assists exporters by keeping effective liaison with various authorities in Customs, Central Excise, RBI and banks, etc.;
x Organizes exhibitions in India.
Publications issued:
x *Leathers* (monthly).
x *Directory of Members of Council for Leather Exports*, 2005.
x *Facts & Figures on Export of Leather & Leather Products.*
x *Manual on "Occupational Safety & Health Aspects of Leather Manufacture".*
Local branches:
Western Regional Office 11/4, World Trade Centre I Cuffe Parade Mumbai 400 005 Phone: (91 22) 22184060 Fax: (91 22) 56335503 E-mail: cleb@vsnl.com
Northern Regional Office Flat No. 6 G and F, Gopala Towers Rajendra Place New Delhi 110 008
Phone: (91 11) 25718516, 25715517
Fax: (91 11) 25752760
E-mail: cle@ndf.vsnl.net.in, cle@dishnetdsl.net
Central Regional Office
H.B.T.I Campus (Adjacent to Central Bank of India), Nawab Ganj, Kanpur-208 002. Phone: (91 512) 2534198 Fax: (91 512) 2534197 E-mail: knpcle@sancharnet.in
Eastern Regional Office 1B, First Floor, Duckback House 41, Shakespeare Sarani Kolkata 700 017 Phone: (91 33) 22835479/80 Fax: (91 33) 22877270 E-mail: cle_er@vsnl.com
Southern Regional Office CMDA Tower II, 3rd Floor, Gandhi Irwin Bridge Road Egmore, Chennai 600 008 Phone: (91 44) 28594367-71 Fax: (91 44) 28594363-4 E-mail: cle@vsnl.com, cle@cleindia.com
Agra Extension Office S-6, 2nd Floor, Friends Tower, Block no. 41 –B, Sanjay Place, Agra-282 002. Phone: (91 562) 2852619 Fax: (91 562) 2854053 E-mail: cle@datainfosys.net
Membership structure: 2,300 members.
There are three categories of members:
x Ordinary Members: Those persons, Hindu Undivided Family (HUF), firms, joint stock companies, cooperative societies or corporations who have exported leather for a minimum value of Rs.3 lakhs in the previous year as evidenced by their Bankers or Chartered Accountants Certificates.
x Nominated Members: Individuals nominated by the Government on the Council or the Committees.
x Associate Members: Those persons, Hindu Undivided Family (HUF), firms, joint stock companies, cooperative societies or corporations who are engaged in the manufacture, processing or conversion of leather for export or exporters of leather who are not qualified to be enrolled as ordinary members.
Products/commodity responsible for:

Semi-finished and finished leather all sorts, handbags, purses, wallets, belts, watch straps, leather garments, industrial leather manufactures such as gloves, leather aprons, fancy leather gloves, sport gloves, leather footwear and non-leather footwear and their components, saddlery and harness articles, and other leather goods and accessories.
Category:
Commodity board; export marketing board; and trade promotion organization.

DELHI CHAMBER OF COMMERCE

Office/postal address:
49, Rani Jhansi Road
New Delhi 110 055 Phone: (91 11) 23616421, 23610397, 23515828, 23518994 Fax: (91 11) 23628847, 23622815
E-mail: dccnd@nda.vsnl.net.in URL: www.delhichamber.com Year established: 1950 Principal functions:

- x To promote and protect the trade, commerce and manufacture of the Union Territory of Delhi and other states;
- x To protect the general interests of persons engaged in trade or industry in the Union Territory of Delhi and in the adjoining areas/states;
- x To handle all questions relating to trade, commerce and manufacture;
- x To collect and circulate statistics and other information relating to trade, commerce and industry;
- x To establish a commercial economic and statistical library and to help developing commercial education;
- x To consider legislation and other governmental measures affecting trade, commerce or industry;
- x To adjudicate controversies between members of the Chamber;
- x To arbitrate in the settlement of disputes arising out of commercial transactions;
- x To formulate codes of practice, to simplify and facilitate transaction of business and to maintain uniformity in rules, reputations and usages of trade.

Services/activities:
x Issues Certificate of Origin;
x Assists local members obtaining their export documents;
x Issues recommendations to its members in obtaining visa from various foreign embassies in India;
x Handles trade enquiries received from all over the world, and circulates to its members;
x Publishes *DCC Trade Directory* and disseminates to all the members, and other agencies in India and abroad;
x Encourages its members to participate in exhibitions in India and abroad, and organizes trade delegations for the members;
x Provides secretariat and management services to smaller associations and members;
x Provides financial assistance to the members and members of Foreign Chambers of Commerce;
x Issues status and performance certificate to the members for securing business/contract abroad;
x Arranges for assessment of loss or damage to goods in transit or at destination.
Publications issued:
x *DCC Trade Directory* (annually, English). x *DCC Trade Bulletin* (fortnightly, English).
Membership structure: 1,200 members.
Products/commodity responsible for:
Engineering goods; chemical products including plastics; handicrafts and leather goods; sport goods; cotton, woollen and silk textiles including garments; gem and jewellery; agricultural and processed food; pharmaceuticals and cosmetics; meat and meat products; hospital equipment and other miscellaneous items; marine products; electronic and computer software; spices, tea, coffee and tobacco; and other commodities.
Areas/industries where investment is encouraged:
All sectors.
Category:
Chamber of commerce.

EXPORT CREDIT GUARANTEE CORPORATION OF INDIA LIMITED (ECGC)

Office/postal address:
10th
Floor, Express Towers Nariman Point Mumbai 400 021
P.O. Box: 11677, Mumbai
Phone: (91 22) 56590500 Fax: (91 22) 56590517
E-mail: ecgcedp@bom2.vsnl.net.in URL: www.ecgcindia.com, www.indianexporterregister.com
Year established: 1957
Principal functions:
x Export credit insurance: to provide insurance covers to exporters against loss in export of goods and services, supplier and buyer credit facilities for medium- and long-term exports and lines of credit cover;
x Export credit guarantees: to provide guarantees to banks and financial institutions to enable exporters to obtain better facilities from them;

x Overseas investment insurance: to provide overseas investment insurance to exporters - Indian entrepreneurs in overseas ventures (equity/loans);

x Bonds and guarantees: to provide cover for bid bonds, performance bonds, advance payment/local finance bonds, retention of money;

x Maturity factoring: undertaking to pay the amount due for a shipment on the maturity of the credit period.

Services/activities:

As detailed under Principal functions.

Publications issued:

x *ECGC newsletter* (quarterly; English/Hindi). x *ECGC Services* (English/Hindi). x *Brochures* of Various Schemes (English/Hindi). x *Annual Report* (annually; English/Hindi).

Local branches:

Western Regional Office The Metropolitan, 7th Floor Plot No. C-26/27, E Block Bandra-Kurla Complex Bandra (E), Mumbai - 400 051 Phone: (91 22) 26571600/2353, 26572775-77 Fax: (91 22) 26572779/26572046

Northern Regional Office NBCC Place, South Tower

4th

Floor, Pragati Vihar Bishma Pitamah Marg, New Delhi - 110 003 Phone: (91 11) 24365645/53/93/95 Fax: (91 11) 51506400

Southern Regional Office (I) Spencer Towers, 7th floor 770-A, Anna Salai, Chennai - 600 002 Phone: (91 44) 28491026-33 Fax: (91 44) 28514550/28515715

Southern Regional Office (II) Raheja Towers, 11th floor West Wing, 26, M G Road Bangalore - 560 001 Phone: (91 80) 25589775/25591729/25585375 Fax: (91 80) 25589779

Eastern Regional Office AC Market Complex, 9th floor 1, Shakespeare Sarani Kolkata - 700 001 Phone: (91 33) 22820963-66 Fax: (91 33) 22820939, 22820967

Membership structure: ECGC is an autonomous company with 100 per cent shareholding by the Government of India. It is headed by a Chairman and Managing Director appointed by the Government of India.

Products/commodity responsible for:

Export credit insurance.

Training:

ECGC conducts training programmes for other export credit agencies.

Category:

Export credit insurance.

EXPORT-IMPORT BANK OF INDIA

Office/postal address:
21st Floor, Centre One Building
World Trade Centre Complex
Cuffe Parade
Mumbai 400 005
Phone: (91 22) 22185272 Fax: (91 22) 22182572
E-mail: eximcord@vsnl.com URL: www.eximbankindia.com

Year established: 1982

Principal functions:

x To finance, facilitate and promote India's international trade;

x To coordinate the working of institutions engaged in financing exports and imports.

Services/activities:

x Extends finance to exporters of capital and manufactured goods, and extends funded and non-funded facilities;

x Extends lines of credit to overseas financial institutions, foreign Governments, enabling them to finance the import of goods and associated services from India;

x Provides buyers' credit to import Indian goods on deferred payment terms;

x Provides financial support for the promotion of service exports including software and IT;

x Extends term loans and working capital finance for projects located within India;

x Operates a programme on equity finance, loans, guarantees and advisory services to support Indian outward investment;

x Provides financial support for product development and for research and development;

x Promotes and supports agri-business and agri-exports;

x Promotes and supports SMEs to achieve and sustain international competitiveness;

x Provides guarantee support and multicurrency financing facility;

x Facilitates transfer of technology, trade and investment;

x Provides advisory services, including information access, knowledge building, financial counselling, commercial consulting and internationalization support;

x Provides export marketing services for Indian companies; advises Indian companies on overseas investments including subsidiaries, joint ventures and acquisitions;

x Provides consultancy services in areas related to countries, products, markets, capacity creation and institution strengthening.

Publications issued:

x *Annual Report* (English/Hindi). x *Performance Highlights* (annually, English/Hindi). x *Corporate Brochure* (periodically, English/Hindi). x *Exim Bank's Annual Lecture Series* (English/ Hindi). x *Tax Benefits for Indian Exporters* (annually, English). x *Eximius: Export Advantage* (quarterly, English/Hindi). x *Agri Export Advantage* (bimonthly, English/Hindi/several Indian regional languages).

x *Directory of Useful Addresses* (annually, English).
x *Exporting Indian Healthcare*, 2002/2003 (English/Hindi).
x *Thoughts on the New Global Economy*, 2001 (English).
x *Business Practices of Successful Indian Exporters,* 2001.
x *India: Joining the World Economy* (English).
x *Achieving Excellence* (English).
x *Exporting Indian Healthcare* (English).
x *Road beyond Boundaries -The Case of Select Indian Healthcare Systems* (English).
x *Project Exports - Connecting Continents with Indian Expertise,* 2004 (English).
x *Market Maker-Technology Aided Business Solutions - Food Processing* (English).
x *Indo-LAC Business* (quarterly).
x *Indo-CIS Business* (quarterly).
x *Indo-Africa Business* (quarterly).

Local branches:
1st
Floor, Sakar II Next to Ellisbridge Shopping Centre Ellisbridge P.O., Ahmedabad 380 006 Phone: (91 79) 26576852, 26576843 Fax: (91 79) 26578271 E-mail: eximindadl@sancharnet.in
4th
Floor, Ramanashree Arcade 18, M.G. Road Bangalore 560 001 Phone: (91 80) 25585755, 25589101-4 Fax: (91 80) 25589107 E-mail: eximbro@blr.vsnl.net.in
1st
Floor, UTI House 29, Rajaji Salai Chennai 600 001 Phone: (91 44) 25224714, 25224749 Fax: (91 44) 25224082 E-mail: chenexim@vsnl.com
4th
Floor, Sanmati Plaza Near Sentinel Building
G.S Road, Guwahati 781 005 Phone: (91 361) 2599135 Fax: (91 361) 2462925
2nd
Floor, Golden Edifice 6-3-639/640, Raj Bhavan Road Khairatabad, Hyderabad 500 004 Phone: (91 40) 23307816-21 Fax: (91 40) 23317843 E-mail: eximhyd@vsnl.com
4th
floor Vanijya Bhavan (International Trade Facilitation Centre) 1/1 Wood Street Kolkata 700016 Phone: (91 33) 22833419-20 Fax: (91 33) 22891727 E-mail: eximca@vsnl.com
8th
Floor, Maker Chambers IV 222, Nariman Point Mumbai 400 021 Phone: (91 22) 22830761, 22823320 Fax: (91 22) 22022132 E-mail: eximwrro@vsnl.com
Ground Floor, Statesman House 148, Barakhamba Road New Delhi 110 001 Phone: (91 11) 23326254, 23326625 Fax: (91 11) 23322758, 23321719 E-mail: eximnd@vsnl.com
44, Shankarseth Road Pune 411 037 Phone: (91 20) 26458599 Fax: (91 20) 26458846 E-mail: eximpune@vsnl.com
Offices abroad:
3rd
Floor, Unit 308 ECE City Centre Bajcsy-Zsilinszky UT.12 1051 Budapest, Hungary Phone: (36 1) 3382833, 3176699 Fax: (36 1) 3178354 E-mail: eximindia@axelero.hu
Via Disciplini, 7 20123 Milan, Italy Phone: (39 02) 58430546 Fax: (39 02) 58302124 E-mail: exim.india@tin.it
20, Collyer Quay No. 10-02 Tung Centre Singapore 049319 Phone: (65) 65326464 Fax: (65) 65352131 E-mail: eximbank@singnet.com.sg
158, Ground Floor, Jan Smuts 9, Walters Avenue, Rosebank Johannesburg 2196, South Africa
P.O. Box 2018, Saxonwold 2132 Johannesburg, South Africa Phone: (27 11) 4428010, 4422053 Fax: (27 11) 4428022 E-mail: eximindia@icon.co.za
Suite 1202, 12th Floor 1750, Pennsylvania Avenue NW Suite 1202, Washington DC 20006 United States of America Phone: (1 202) 2233238-9 Fax: (1 202) 7858487 E-mail: indexim@worldnet.att.net
Training:
The Bank conducts short-term, focused seminars/workshops on international trade and related activities.
Category:
Export financing organization; investment financing organization; trade facilitation body; and trade promotion organization.

FEDERATION OF INDIAN CHAMBERS OF COMMERCE AND INDUSTRY (FICCI)*

Office/postal address:
Federation House Tansen Marg New Delhi 110 001
Phone: (91 11) 23738760-70 Fax: (91 11) 23320714, 3721504
E-mail: ficci@ficci.com URL: www.ficci.com
Year established: 1927
Services/activities:
x Promotes trade and technology cooperation between India and the rest of the world; x Takes up various business issues with the government and semi-government authorities; x Liases and interacts with foreign governments, international, multilateral organizations; x Provides information on export and import; x Provides information for technology collabouration and
investment; x Undertakes research studies; x Provides information to the public through appropriate

media; x Organizes seminars and conference.
Publications issued:
x *Business Digest.* x *India Economic Profile* (annually).
Local branches:
Local branches in Raipur, Secunderabad, Baroda, Chennai, Mumbai.
Offices abroad:
Offices abroad in Beijing, Tamirtau, Selangor, Singapore, London, Washington DC.
Membership structure: 433 Ordinary Members, 1,286 Associate Members and 50 Corporate Members.
Category:
Chamber of commerce.

FEDERATION OF INDIAN MICRO AND SMALL AND MEDIUM ENTERPRISES (FISME)

Office/postal address:
B-4/161, Safdarjung Enclave
New Delhi 110 029 Phone: (91 11) 26187948, 26712064 Fax: (91 11) 26109470
E-mail: info@fisme.org.in URL: www.fisme.org.in Year established: 1995 Principal functions:
- x To advocate micro-, small- and medium-sized enterprises' (MSMEs) interests;
- x To conduct studies and research and to disseminate trade intelligence through www.smenetwork.net;
- x To provide international marketing support;
- x To help create enabling environment for MSMEs.

Services/activities:
x Trade fairs and trade delegations; x Support in international trade/matchmaking; x Authentication of documents and issuing Certificate of
Origin.
Publications issued:
x *Business Bulletin.* x *Annual Report.* x *Guides on WTO, IT,* etc. x *Smenetwork Update* (electronic).
Membership structure: About 100,000 members.
Products/commodity responsible for:
Electricals; electronics; plastics and plastic products; leather and leather products; paper and paper products; micronutrients/fertilizers; food processing; information technology; textiles; rubber and rubber products; handicrafts; chemicals and pharmaceuticals; plants and machines.
Training:
Export marketing and documentation (in collabouration with Indian Institute of Foreign Trade).
Areas/industries where investment is encouraged:
Focus on agro and food processing.
Titles of laws and regulations on foreign investment:
Please see the Economy Section at www.smenetwork.net
Category:
Chamber of commerce; trade association; and trade promotion organization.

FEDERATION OF SMALL AND MEDIUM INDUSTRIES (FOSMI)

Office / postal address:
23, R.N. Mukherjee Road
Kolkata 700 001 Phone: (91 33) 22485114 Fax: (91 33) 22104075
E-mail: fosmi@cal3.vsnl.net.in URL: www.fosmi.org.in Year established: 1959 Principle functions:
x To facilitate the promotion and development of SMEs; x To alleviate problems of existing units; x To represents FOSMI members.
Services/activities:
x Participates in various policy matters; x Trains and promotes medium, small/tiny enterprises; x Develops self-employment projects; x Confers awards of excellence to successful entrepreneurs; x Organizes seminars, lectures, discussions concerning SMEs.
Publications issued:
- x *FOSMI SSI News* (monthly).
- x *FOSMI Members Directory.*
- x Publication of annual souvenir.

Membership structure: Over 1,200 members and 25 affiliated associations.
Products/commodity responsible for:
Services-oriented organization for the development of small-scale and tiny units.
Training:
x Post Graduate Programme in Entrepreneurship Development (PGEM), long term (12 months); x Certificate in Small Industrial Management (CSIM), short term (3 months);
x Management Bridge Courses, short term (one month), on marketing and sales management; international marketing and export management; taxation practice and procedures; information entrepreneurship; financial management; production management and inventory control;
x Entrepreneurship Development and Industrial Studies (EDIS), short term (two weeks).
Areas/industries where investment is encouraged:
Engineering; chemicals; food processing; plastics; software; pharmaceuticals; ready-made garments; leather; jute.

Category:
Chamber of commerce.

FOREIGN TRADE DEVELOPMENT CENTRE

Office/postal address:
N-5, South Extension Part-1
New Delhi 110 049 Phone: (91 11) 24647505, 24616839 Fax: (91 11) 24646361
E-mail: info@ftdcindia.org URL: www.ftdcindia.org Year established: 1992 Principal functions:
x Export/import training and promotion organization; x Trade advisory organization and trade information centre.
Services/activities:
x Trade information dissemination;
x Organizes and participates in fairs/seminars/conferences on trade promotion, marketing, e-governance in international trade and import management.
Publications issued:
x *How to Enter Export Trade* (annually, English). x *Export Development Through Internet* (monthly, English). x *Export Management* (annually, English).
Local branches:
37, Bungalow Road Kamla Nagar, Delhi 110 007 Phone: (91 11) 27662268, 27662275
C-115, Savitri Path, Bapu Nagar, Jaipur, India. Phone: (91 11) 2703952
Membership structure: 8,685 members, as of 1 August 2005.
Products/commodity responsible for:
Artisanal handicrafts, furniture, gems and jewellery, ready-made garments, leather products, silk products, and software.
Training:
x Export management: regular and through distance learning; x E-business in export development;
x Entrepreneurial development programmes on export promotion;
x Import management.
Areas/industries where investment is encouraged:
SMEs in various sections with exporting potential.
Category:
Trade facilitation body; trade promotion organization; and training/research institute.

HANDICRAFTS AND HANDLOOMS EXPORTS CORPORATION OF INDIA LTD. (HHEC)

Office/postal address:
Jawahar Vyapar Bhavan Annexe 1, Tolstoy Marg New Delhi 110 001
Phone: (91 11) 3701086 Fax: (91 11) 3701051
E-mail: hhecnd@eth.net, mcpaid@indiamart.com URL: www.hhecworld.com
Year established: 1958 (under the Ministry of Textiles)
Principal function:
x To promote exports and trade development.
Services/activities:
x Undertakes activities in the export of handicrafts, handlooms goods, ready-to-wear clothes, carpets and precious jewellery.
Local branches:
11th
Floor, Nirmal Building Nariman Point, Mumbai 400 021 Phone: (91 22) 2027273, 2882098 Fax: (91 22) 2024312
15 N, Neli Sengupta Sarani, 6th Floor, Lindsay Street New Market Complex, Phase I Kolkata 700 087 Phone: (91 33) 2456863 Fax: (91 33) 2456864
Ramanshree Business Centre, 1st - 2nd Floor 143, Greams Road, Thousand Lights Chennai 600 006 Phone: (91 44) 8295609, 8294614 Fax: (91 44) 8294610
Offices abroad:
3rd
Floor, Union Roppongi, 2-3-9 Roppongi Minato Ku Tokyo 106-0032 Tokyo, Japan Phone: (81 3) 35890771 Fax: (81 3) 35890772
Sona of India, Apt. # 3B, The Stanton 41-40, Union Street Flushing, New York, NY 11355 United States of America Phone: (1 718) 8889806 Fax: (1 718) 8889803
Products/commodity responsible for:
Handicrafts, handlooms, ready-to-wear, gold jewellery and carpets.
Category:
Trade promotion organization.

HANDLOOM EXPORT PROMOTION COUNCIL

Office/postal address:
34 Cathedral Garden Road Nungambakkam Chennai 600 034
Phone: (91 44) 28278879, 28276043 Fax: (91 44) 28271761
E-mail: hepc@hepcindia.com URL: www.hepcindia.com
Year established: 1965
Principal function:

x To promote exports of handloom cotton textile goods from India.

Services/activities:

x Promotes participation in domestic and overseas exhibitions; x Organizes buyer-seller meets abroad; x Attends to complaints received from both importers and exporters; x Assists traders in the development of their products; x Undertakes publicity activities for handloom industry both within the country and abroad; x Publishes newsletters; x Acts as liaison between export trade and various government authorities;

x Invites foreign buyers/delegations, etc.;

x Disseminates feedback information from various organizations abroad amongst the members;

x Facilitates product diversification and adaptation to meet modern market requirements;

x Provides impetus to the modernization of handlooms for the export market;

x Provides design inputs to promote the export of handloom products;

x Provides consultancy and guidance services to handloom exporters.

Publications issued:

x *Indian Color Catalogue (Color Catalogue Vol. II (Revised), Color Catalogue Vol. III, New Colors.*

x *Importers Directory* (CD-ROM).

x *Color trends (Color trend Catalogue (2003-04)).*

x *Source Book.*

x *Exporters Directory* (CD-ROM and print form).

x *Directory of Buying Houses/ Buying Agents* (CD-ROM).

x *Directory of Handloom Manufacturers of Andhra Pradesh.*

x *Dyeing Manual.*

x *Handbook on Handloom Export Statistics.*

x *Indian Handloom Map.*

x Monthly newsletter *Handloom Export.*

Local branches:

10th Floor, Padma Towers No.5, Rajendra Place New Delhi 110 008
Phone: (91 11) 25826965
Fax: (91 11) 25826966
E-mail: hepcrond@vsnl.com

15-A, Mama Paramananda Marg Opera House Mumbai 400 004 Phone: (91 22) 3672921 Fax: (91 22) 3610923 E-mail: hepcromu@vsnl.com

Membership structure: 2,000 members.

Products/commodity responsible for:

Cotton handloom fabrics/made-ups.

Category:

Trade production organization.

INDIA INTERNATIONAL TRADE CENTRE

(Export Import Promotion Organization)

Office/postal address:

Murlidhar Baldev Estate, Off. Aarey Road, Goregaon (East), Mumbai - 400 063
Phone: (91) 5677 0218, 2871 1396, 2877 1918, 2876 8031 Fax: (91 22) 2874 3543
Email: info@iitcindia.com, iitcindia@vsnl.net URL: www.iitcindia.com

Principal function:

x To provide assistance and support to Indian and foreign companies specially SMEs, to promote export-import and to establish and enhance business contacts by organizing various trade promotional activities in India and abroad.

Services/activities:

Exports: x Locates prospective marketplace for products; x Sources out potential buyers/agents for products; x Negotiates deals with clients; x Advertises and propagates products in the desired market region.

Imports: x Identifies product, market and exporter; x Sourcing out capital goods as per requirement; x Sourcing of products/services.

Trade/business enhancement: x Provides support for contract manufacturing in India and abroad; x Assists in business matchmaking, joint venture formations; x Joint advertising, group marketing, etc.; x Assists in turnkey projects, industrial plants, business set up.

Trade information: x Enhances export-import; x Develops business contacts; x Trade promotion events; x Support services.

Local branches:

Trade Promotion and Relations 37, World Trade Centre Cuffe Parade, Mumbai - 400 005

30-A, Prestige Point, 1st Floor CTS No. 283, Shukrawar Peth Bajirao Road, Pune - 411 002 Fax: (91 20) 56012344

Gajanan V. Gongane c/o Siddhi International Bhaskar Plaza, S4, Shahupuri, Kolhapur 416001
Phone: (91 231) 2663302, 2652495 Fax: (91 231) 2663302

Membership structure: Four membership categories:
x Small (SSI units) and medium entrepreneurs, buying agents, traders and agri-based small industries;
x Private and public Ltd. companies, government agencies, banks and financial institutes, sugar-textile-dairy-agro industries, multinational companies and international organizations;
x Consultants, commercial agents-distributors, chambers, associations, organizations and other any professional;
x Overseas: exporters-importers, industry, buying agents, chambers of commerce, trade promotion organizations, associations, government agencies, companies and individuals.
Category:
Trade promotion organization.

INDIA TRADE PROMOTION ORGANISATION (ITPO)

Office/postal address:
Trade Information Department Pragati Bhawan Pragati Maidan Lal Bahadur Shastri Marg New Delhi 110 001
Phone: (91 11) 23315277, 23371540, 23371582 Fax: (91 11) 23317896, 23318142
E-mail: info@itpo-online.com, itpo@vsnl.com URL: www.indiatradepromotion.org
Year established: 1992 (formed by a merger of the Trade Development Authority with the Trade Fair Authority).
Principal functions:

- x To develop and promote exports, imports and upgrade technology through fairs in India and abroad;
- x To undertake publicity through print and electronic media;
- x To assist Indian companies in product development;
- x To organize export development programmes, buyer-seller meets, contact promotion programmes and integrated marketing programmes for specific products in specific markets;
- x To provide information and market intelligence;
- x To organize visits of buyers and trade delegations to industry and trade establishments in India to promote contacts.

Services/activities:
x Organizes participation in international trade fairs and exclusive Indian trade-related exhibitions abroad;
x Organizes international and national trade fairs in India;
x Organizes specialized programmes for trade development and promotion such as buyer-seller meets, contact promotion programmes, department store promotions, exchange of business delegations, etc.;
x Assists technically competent units in product development and adaptation;
x Coordinates programmes of trade delegations;
x Encourages and involves medium- and small-scale industrial units in export promotion efforts;
x Provides trade promotion and trade fair related information;
x Conducts in-house and needs-based research on trade and export promotion;
x Enlists the involvement and support of state governments in the promotion of India's foreign trade;
x Promotes the establishment of trade fair facilities in state capitals or other suitable locations in consultation with concerned state governments;
x Operates a Business Information Centre which provides trade information services with electronic accessibility to the business community in general and ITPO members in particular;
x Maintains a collection of national production and foreign trade statistics;
x Provides information on national and foreign trade regulations;
x Produces lists of manufacturers/exporters and importers;
x Organizes Foreign Product Catalogue Shows in India;
x Organizes Indian Product Catalogue Shows overseas.
Publications issued:

- x *Annual Report* (annually, English).
- x *Data Kits on India's Trade* (English).
- x *Indian Export Bulletin* (weekly, English).
- x *Pragati India* (bimonthly, English/Spanish).
- x *Product Studies* (English).
- x *Udyog Vyapar Patrika* (monthly, Hindi).
- x *Darpan* (quarterly, Hindi).
- x *Log On* (quarterly, English).

Local branches:
24-A, Imperial Court 33/1, Cunningham Road Bangalore 560 052 Phone: (9180) 2268867, 2268969 Fax: (9180) 2258662
E-mail: itpo@blr.vsnl.net.in

Flat No. 9, 4th Floor, Shantineketan 8 Camac Street Calcutta 700 017 Phone: (91 33) 22825820 Fax: (91 33) 22828269 E-mail: itpocal@cal3.vsnl.net.in

Raja Annamalai Building
2nd
Floor, 18-A Rukhmanai Lakshmipathi Road Egmore, Chennai 600 008 Phone: (91 44) 28554655, 28587294 Fax: (91 44) 28554740 E-mail: itpochn@md4.vsnl.net.in
7 Cooperage Jhansis Castle Mumbai 400 039 Phone: (91 22) 22021730, 22021788, 22026629 Fax: (91 22) 22044922 E-Mail: itpomum1@mantraonline.com
World Trade Centre - I 11th
Floor, Cuffe Parade Mumbai 400 005 Phone: (91 22) 22184135, 22183734 Fax: (91 22) 22184125 E-mail: itpomum@vsnl.net
Offices abroad:
India House Friedrich-Ebert-Anlage 26 D-60325 Frankfurt Main, Germany Phone: (49 69) 553773, 7434760 Fax: (49 69) 554230 E-mail: info@itpofrankfurt.com
33, Mori Building, 8/F 3-8-21, Toranomon, Minato-ku Tokyo 105-0001, Japan Phone: (81 3) 34365060, 34365063 Fax: (81 3) 34315659 E-mail: info@itpotyo.org URL: www.itpotyo.org
1st
Floor, 38, Lomonosovsky Prospect Moscow 119330, Russian Federation Phone: (70 95) 1476215, 9561390 Fax: (70 95) 1471403 E-mail: itpomos@caravan.ru URL: www.itpomos.ru
60-E. 42nd Street, Suite 863 Lincoln Building New York, NY 10165, United States of America Phone: (1 212) 3705262 to 63 Fax: (1 212) 3705250 E-mail: itpony@telcocom.com
C/o Consulate General of India (São Paulo)
7th
Floor, Avenida Paulista, 925oor CEP 01311-100-SP Brazil Phone: (55 11) 284 5966 Fax: (55 11) 31710342 E-mail: itpo@indiaconsulate.org.br
Membership structure: 883 Regular Members, 1,884 Associate Members (as of 14 August 2003). Regular membership for marketing services; associate membership for trade information services.
Category:
Trade promotion organization.

INDIAN CHAMBER OF COMMERCE AND INDUSTRY, COCHIN

Office/postal address:
Indian Chamber Road Mattancherry Cochin 682002 Kerala
P.O. Box: 236
Phone: (91 484) 2224335, 2225966, 2227230
Fax: (91 484) 2224203
E-mail: mail@iccicochin.com, iccicochin@eth.net
URL: www.iccicochin.com
Year established: 1897
Principal functions:
x To promote and protect trade, commerce and industry and to develop export, import and other activities;
x To watch over and protect the general commercial interests of India;
x To establish just and equitable principles in trade and commerce.
Services/activities:
x Issues Certificates of Origin, quality, weighment and measurement;
x Attests internationally accepted commercial documents;
x Disseminates information and data of concern and interest to the business community;
x Organizes periodical interactive meetings for the exchange of views between representatives of the Government and business community on matters connected with the promotion of industry and trade;
x Is actively involved in projects and programmes for the benefit of the society (for example construction of children's ward, donations to educational and service institutions).
Local branch:
Indian Chamber of Commerce and Industry Indian Chamber Building
G.V Iyyar Road Willingdon Island Cochin – 682 003 Kerala Phone: 2666901
Membership structure: Around 350 ordinary members and 10 affiliated members.
Training:
Conducting various seminars, conferences and meetings in the State of Kerala to promote and protect trade, industry and business. Also providing consultancy service to SMEs.
Category:

INDIAN COUNCIL OF ARBITRATION (ICA)

Office/postal address:
Federation House Tansen Marg New Delhi 110 001
Phone: (91 11) 23738760-70, 23719103, 3319760, 23319849 Fax: (91 11) 23320714, 23721504
E-mail: ica@nda.vsnl.net.in URL: www.binetworld.net/icanet
Year established: 1965
Principal functions:

x To advance the knowledge and use of arbitration as a means of amicable and quick settlement of domestic and international trade disputes and to promote amity, goodwill and confidence among the trade;

x To conduct research and provide training facilities in commercial arbitration.

Services/activities:

x Provides arbitration facilities in domestic and international commercial disputes;

x Provides facilities for international maritime arbitration disputes;

x Undertakes conciliation services;

x Provides training facilities in commercial arbitration for Indian and foreign participants;

x Handles enquiries and provides advisory services;

x Acts as Appointing Authority and Administering Agency under the United Nations Commission on International Trade Law (UNCITRAL) Arbitration Rules;

x Enters into arbitration cooperation agreements with central arbitral organizations in different countries; currently mutual cooperation agreements with 40 arbitral institutions round the world;

x Provides administrative and secretarial services for conducting arbitration proceedings.

Publications issued:

x *Arbitration and Conciliation Law of India.*

x *Arbitration and Alternative Dispute Resolution.*

x *Arbitration and Contract Law in South Asian Association for Regional Cooperation (SAARC) Countries.*

x *Arbitration Made Easy.*

x *Case Law on UNCITRAL Model Law on International Commercial Arbitration.*

x *Case Law on UNCITRAL Convention on Contracts for the International Sale of Goods.*

x *Construction Industry Arbitration.*

x *ICA Arbitration Quarterly.*

x *ICA Pamphlet.*

x *Rules of Arbitration of the Council.*

x *Rues of Conciliation of the Council.*

x *Maritime Rules of Law.*

Chamber of commerce.

Local branches:

Branch offices:

Indian Chamber of Commerce 4, India Exchange Place Kolkata 700 001 Phone: (91 33) 22203242-44 Fax: (91 33) 22213377

Indian Merchants' Chamber IMC Buildings, IMC Marg 76, Veer Nariman Road Churchgate, Mumbai 400 020 Phone: (91 22) 22046633 Fax: (91 22) 22048508

Southern India Chamber of Commerce and Industry Indian Chamber Buildings Esplanade Road, Opp. High Court Chennai 600 0018 Phone: (91 44) 25342228 Fax: (91 44) 25341876

State level offices:

Andhra Pradesh Federation of Andhra Pradesh Chamber of Commerce and Industry 11-6-841, Red Hills P.B. No. 14, Hyderabad 500 004

Phone: (91 40) 23393428, 23393658

Fax: (91 40) 23395083, 23393712

Gujarat

Gujarat Chamber of Commerce and Industry Shri Ambica Mills Gujarat Chamber Building Ashram Road Post Box No. 4045 Ahmedabad 380 009 Phone: (91 79) 26582301-02, 26587992 Fax: (91 79) 2407992

Maharashtra Maratha Chamber of Commerce and Industry Post Box No. 525 Tilak Road, Pune 411 002 Phone: (91 20) 24440371, 14440472 Fax: (91 20) 24447902

Karnataka Federation of Karnataka Chamber of Commerce and Industry Federation House Kempegowda Road Bangalore 560 009 Phone: (91 80) 22262157, 22262355/56 Fax: (91 80) 22251826

Orissa Utakal Chamber of Commerce and Industry 301, Vandana Apaertments, Vivekananda Marg Bhubaneswar 751 0022 Phone: (91 674) 2301211, 2344056 Fax: (91 674) 2302059 Rajasthan Rajasthan Chamber of Commerce and Industry Rajasthan Chamber Bhawan, MI Road Jaipur 302 003 Phone: (91 141) 2565163 Fax: (91 141) 2561419

Kerala Kerala Chamber of Commerce and Industry Chamber Corner, Shanmugham Road Cochin 682031 Phone: (91 484) 2354885, 2380950 Fax: (91 484) 2374253

North-East States North-East Chamber of Commerce and Industry Zoo Road Tiniali, Opp. Geeta Nagar Police Station Guwahati 781024 Phone: (91 361) 2417074 Fax: (91 361) 2410461

Membership structure: Over 4,700 members.

Foundation membership: organizations providing arbitration facilities.

Ordinary membership: chambers of commerce, trade associations, export promotion councils, commodity boards, etc.

Associate membership: companies, firms, import-export houses and individuals.

Individual membership: any individual experienced and/or interested in arbitration matters.

Training:

x Pprofessional development programme on commercial arbitration.

x National and international seminars, workshops and arbitration meetings on different aspects of the law and practice of arbitration and allied matters.

The training programmes are open to businesspersons, professionals and executives mainly from India. However, interested persons from other countries may attend on a sponsored basis.

Category:
Council of arbitration.

INDIAN INSTITUTE OF FOREIGN TRADE (IIFT) (DEEMED UNIVERSITY)

Office/postal address:
IIFT Bhawan Qutab Institutional Area New Delhi 110 016
Phone: (91 11) 26965124, 26965051, 26564409, 26966563, 26966360, 26966304, 26966613
Fax: (91 11) 26853956, 26859520, 26867851
E-mail: diroffice@iift.ac.in, dgoffice@iift.ac.in URL: www.iift.edu
Year established: 1964
Principal functions:
x To develop export management skills through training and research;
x To carry out supply and demand studies in India and abroad for products/commodities/countries and regions of interest to India;
x To carry out research on international trade focusing on World Trade Organization (WTO) issues.
Services/activities:
x Undertakes research on areas that relate to the efficacy of policy measures, strategies for multilateral trade negotiations, international commercial and financial operations, international business opportunities, supply base for exports and management of foreign trade operations;
x Conducts a full-time two-year MBA (International Business) at Delhi and Dar-es-Salaam; three-year part-time MBA (International Business) at Delhi; one-and-a-half-year Executive Masters in International Business at New Delhi and Dubai; and Post Graduate Diploma in International Trade at Dar-es-Salaam;
x Designs and conducts specialized training programmes for export management personnel of public and private sector organizations, officers of the Government of India as well as for other developing countries and international organizations;
x Designs and conducts training programmes for diplomats from India and other developing countries;
x Conducts management development programmes for participation by business executives and officials of trade facilitating agencies on such subjects as international marketing operations, export procedures and documentation, supply-chain management and international trade logistics, risk management, international financing, managing projects abroad, distribution strategy for overseas markets, product development including adaptation for exports, export office administration, setting up in-house trade information units, electronic commerce, implications of WTO provisions, etc.;
x Conducts part-time evening certificate course in export management and international business language;
x Conducts a full-time Ph. D programme.
Publications issued:
Wide range of journals, papers and reports issued, including:
x *Focus WTO* (bimonthly, English).
x *Foreign Trade Review* (quarterly, English).
x *Technology Exports* (quarterly, English).
x *Trade Environment Linkages: The Issue from Indian Standard.*
x *Non-Tariff Measures on India's Exports: An Assessment.*
x *China's Accession to Bangkok Agreement.*
For a full list of publications, please consult the website: www.iift.edu.
Training:
x Two-year MBA (International Business), New Delhi and Dar-es-Salaam;
x Three-year MBA (International Business, part-tme), New Delhi;
x One-and-a-half year Executive Masters in International Business, New Delhi, Dubai and Post Graduate Diploma in International Trade at Dar-es-Salaam;
x One-and-a-half year Executive Masters in International Business through Very Small Aperture Terminal Satellite Equipment and Services (VSAT) at various centres in India;
x Certificate Course in Export Marketing, New Delhi and Guwahati;
x Course on International Business Languages: five months, part-time for business executives;
x Short-term management development programmes of various duration on different facets of international marketing management, such as import management, export procedures and documentation, shipping orientation, management of international contracts, management of foreign exchange at corporate level;
x Ph. D programme.
Category:
Training/research institute.

INDIAN INVESTMENT CENTRE (IIC)*

(A Government of India Organization, Ministry of Finance)
Office/postal address:
Jeevan Vihar Building Sansad Marg New Delhi 110 001
Phone: (91 11) 23743673 Fax: (91 11) 23742245
E-mail: iic@giasdl01.vsnl.net.in URL: www.iic.nic.in
Year established: 1960

Principal functions:

x To promote foreign direct investment in India and in Indian joint ventures abroad;

x To be a nodal agency for investment in India by non-resident Indians and persons of Indian origin residing abroad;

x To be a member of the World Association of Investment Promotion Agencies.

Services/activities:

x Is a service organization for establishment of joint ventures, technical collabourations and third country ventures between Indian and foreign entrepreneurs;

x Provides guidance and information to Indian entrepreneurs and assists them in locating suitable foreign firms for collabouration;

x Provides authentic information on Government of India's foreign investment policies, procedures, availability of infrastructural facilities, incentive and investment opportunities;

x Advises overseas investors on setting up industrial projects by providing information regarding the investment environment, government policies, facilities and incentives, taxation laws and regulations; also assists them in identifying locations and collabourators.

Publications issued:

x *List of Foreign Collabourations during 2000* (annually, English).

x *Special Facilities Available to Non-resident Indians* (English).

x *Guidelines for Indian Joint Ventures and Wholly Owned Subsidiaries Abroad* (English).

x *Foreign Direct Investment Policy and Business Opportunities* (English). x *IIC Monthly Newsletter* (monthly, English).

Areas/industries where investment is encouraged:

All sectors of industrial activities.

Category:

Investment promotion authority.

INSTITUTE OF SMALL ENTERPRISES AND DEVELOPMENT (ISED)

Office/postal address:

ISED House ISED Road Vennala, P.O. Cochin 682 028

P.O. Box: 4425, Vennala, Cochin

Phone: (91 484) 2808171, 2809884, 2808727 Fax: (91 484) 2809884 E-mail: ised@md2.vsnl.net.in, insmall@eth.net, laghu@asianetindia.com URL: www.isedonline.org Year established: 29 May 1988 Principal functions:

x To undertake scientific studies at an international level, on development problems, with special emphasis on SMEs;

x To identify and popularize technologies suitable for the development of small SMEs through various measures;

x To develop and maintain an information base for the use of researchers, entrepreneurs, planners and policymakers;

x To organize both academic as well as action-oriented training programmes;

x To organize seminars, workshops and discussions;

x To offer consultancy services;

x To organize and maintain a specialized research and reference library;

x To undertake a scheme of publications in order to disseminate research findings and to extend topical information;

x To promote development activities through liaison, lobbying and direct intervention, if needed;

x To promote an international fraternity in the area of SME development.

Services/activities:

x Undertakes research on small enterprises;

x Organizes training for entrepreneurship development;

x Provides consultancy services for business, institutions and funding agencies;

x Provides networking services in the area of small enterprise development.

Publications issued:

x *ISED Book Series.* x *ISED Monograph Series.* x *ISED Occasional Papers.* x *ISED Research Reports.* x *SME Network.*

Membership structure: 100 members.

Category:

Training/research institute.

JUTE MANUFACTURES DEVELOPMENT COUNCIL (JMDC)

Office/postal address:

3A, Park Plaza 71 Park Street Kolkata 700 016

Phone: (91 33) 22172107, 22263438 Fax: (91 33) 22172456

E-mail: jmdcindia@vsnl.com, jmdc@jute.com URL: www.jmdcindia.com, www.jute.com

Year established: 1976

Principal function:

x The apex body of the Government of India, Ministry of Textiles, the Council is primarily responsible for market promotion of jute and jute products in India and abroad.

Services/activities:

x Organizes and participates in domestic and international fairs/exhibitions, buyer-seller meets, seminars and workshops; x Conducts visit of delegations; commissions product/market studies; x Disseminates trade intelligence information/data, etc.; x Facilitates buyers in sourcing products and vice versa.

Publications issued:

x *Indian Jute* (half-yearly statistical bulletin, English). x *Indian Jute* (quarterly newsletter, English). x *National Directory* (occasionally, English). x Product-specific brochures.

Local branches:

18, Cathedral Gardens Road
2nd
Floor, Nungambakkam, Chennai 600 034 Phone: (91 44) 28224967 Fax: (91 44) 28224462 E-mail: jmdc.chennai@vsnl.com
2nd
Floor, Chenetha Bhawan Shop No. 4, Nampally Hyderabad 500 001 Phone: (91 40) 24656733 Fax: (91 40) 24614918 E-mail: jmdchyd@hd2.dot.net.in
Flat Nos. 411-412, 4th Floor, "Prakash Deep" 7, Tolstoy Marg, New Delhi 110 001 Phone: (91 11) 23352652, 23310884 Fax: (91 11) 23353519 E-mail: jmdcndel@vsnl.net

Membership structure: 704 members as of 30 June 2005.

They are private/individual Indians registered with the Council under a particular scheme. Otherwise, a general or compulsory membership system is not in vogue with the Council until now.

Products/commodity responsible for:

Jute and jute diversified products.

Areas/industries where investment is encouraged:

Jute and jute-related industries, market research, product development, market promotion, design, market, technical consultancy.

Category:

Trade promotion organization.

M VISVESVARAYA INDUSTRIAL RESEARCH AND DEVELOPMENT CENTRE (MVIRDC)

Office/postal address:

World Trade Centre 31st
Floor, Centre 1 Building World Trade Centre Complex Cuffe Parade Mumbai 400 005
Phone: (91 22) 56387272 Fax: (91 22) 22180823, 22188385
E-mail: wtcbom@vsnl.com

Year Established: 1970

Principal function:

x To promote bilateral trade.

Services/Activities:

x Conducts research studies/projects in the areas of international trade, technology and marketing; x Organizes seminar/symposia/workshops; x Provides trade information, international trade library service, IMPEX - India's Import and Export Statistical Data; x Centre-Point: Offers business centre facilities and conference rooms; x Expo Centre: Offers exhibition facilities for trade shows and international exhibitions;
x World Trade Center Association (WTCA) Online: WTCA website provides access to bulletin board which facilitates trading online access to trade-related databases.

Publications issued:

x Current and Research and Development Briefs (monthly, English). x *Trade Promotion Bulletin* (monthly, English). x *World Trade Research and Information Report* (bimonthly, English). x *WTC Intercom* (quarterly, English).

Membership structure: 400 life members and 600 associate members.

Products/commodity responsible for:

Services to promote bilateral trade.

Training:

x Post-graduate diploma in foreign trade (PGDFT); x Diploma in FOREX management.

Areas/industries where investment is encouraged:

Exports in general.

Category:

Trade facilitation body; trade promotion organization; and training/research institute.

MADRAS CHAMBER OF COMMERCE AND INDUSTRY (MCCI)

Office/postal address:

1st
Floor, Karumuttu Centre 634 Anna Salai Chennai 600 035
Phone: (91 44) 24349452, 24349871 Fax: (91 44) 24349164
E-mail: mascham@md3.vsnl.net.in URL: www.mascham.com

Year established: 1836

Principal function:

x To act as the mediator between trade and industry and the Government.

Services/activities:

x Disseminates information;
x Provides advisory services;
x Represents members' problems before government bodies;
x Holds arbitration and issues certificate of origin;
x Arranges seminars/meetings on topical interest for the benefit of members.

Publications issued:

x *Monthly Bulletin.* x *Annual Report.* x *Directory of Members 2005.*

Membership structure: 375 members.

Products/commodity responsible for:

Engineering; manufacturing; textile; leather; plantations; chemicals; pharmaceuticals; cement; automobiles, etc.

Training:

Training courses organized on excise and customs, sales tax, etc. for the benefit of members only.

Areas/industries where investment is encouraged:

Automobile sector; IT sector.

Category:

Chamber of commerce.

NATIONAL CENTRE FOR TRADE INFORMATION (NCTI)

Office/postal address:

NCTI Complex Pragati Maidan New Delhi 110 001

Phone: (91 11) 23371948, 23371953 Fax: (91 11) 23371979

E-mail: ncti@nda.vsnl.net.in, ncti@ncti-india.com URL: www.ncti-india.com

Year established: March 1995

Principal functions:

x To collect, collate, process, analyse and disseminate information on trade and commerce;
x To keep constant communication with trade and commercial bodies throughout the world including Indian missions abroad and foreign missions in India;
x To establish and maintain library collection, and sell literature connected with trade and commerce;
x To disseminate information from databases of export/import promotion;
x To establish linkages with export promotional bodies, regulatory bodies, trade associations, chambers, commodity boards etc., for the collection and dissemination of information;
x To provide trade opportunities to the business community by providing trade leads;
x To organize training programmes and seminars.

Services/activities:

x Provides list of overseas importers on CD-ROM;

x Electronic Trading Opportunities (ETOs): uploading information about Indian trading community on Global Trade Point Network (GTPNet), downloading and disseminating enquiries to members;

x Undertakes selective dissemination of information: wherein NCTI disseminates enquiries to specific interest downloaded from GTPNet to its members;

x Provides trade information to government;

x Undertakes website development;

x Creates websites for members/non-members;

x Compiles trade statistics - Indian and global;

x Compiles country profiles;

x Undertakes consultancy assignments; x Market studies; x Various CD-ROMs as Electronic Book on *Latin American Countries* (LAC), CD-ROM on *Indian Exporters*, CD-ROM on *Global Trading Opportunities*, *Electronic Product Catalogue for LAC Market*, *Overseas Importers and Indian Exporters of Textiles, Leather and Leather Products*, etc;

x Highlights developments affecting Indian industry, economy and trade through its electronic journal, titled *Trade Connect*;

x Provides hyperlinks to Memorandum of Understanding (MOU) counterpart organization on its website;

x Sets up Trade Information Centres in India and abroad - Coir Trade Information Centre, Kochi;

x Undertakes other services as outlined under Principal functions above.

Publications issued:

x *Trade Bulletin: Trade Point India* (weekly, English).

x *Trade Connect* (online, English).

x *Trade Block Series: -SAARC and India - 2000. -Latin American Countries and India - 2002. -Indian Ocean Rim Countries - 2000. -Sub-Saharan Region African Countries and India 2003.*

Membership structure: Mostly SMEs; the cumulative membership including regular members, subscription and miscellaneous services exceeded over 3,000 members.

Products/commodity responsible for:
All categories: service industry providing trade-related information.
Training:
x Training programmes relevant to trade such as workshop on trade information and e-commerce, Internet technical training programme on Internet and other sources of business information for international trade, conducted in cooperation with ITC (UNCTAD/WTO), Geneva, involving foreign participants also;
x One-day seminars related to trade information and e-commerce.
Areas/industries where investment is encouraged:
All.
Category:
Trade information service.

NATIONAL INSTITUTE OF SMALL INDUSTRY EXTENSION TRAINING (NISIET)

(An organization of Ministry of SSI)
Office/postal address:
Yousufguda Hyderabad 500 045
Phone: (91 40) 23608544-6, 23608316-8 Fax: (91 40) 23608547, 23608956
E-mail: webmaster@nisiet.org URL: www.nisiet.com
Year established: 1960
Principal function:
x To assist in the promotion and modernization of small industries through training, research, consultancy and information services in the four related fields of small industry development, management, extension and information for development. It has enlarged its training activities to include special annual international programmes for officers from Africa and Asia.
Services/activities:
x Undertakes research projects and consultancy assignments on request from state and central government as well as from international organizations;
x Has a highly specialized library consisting of 60,000 books and reports, 500 journals, and a specialized collection of 3,600 product profiles and project reports;
x Disseminates information on all aspects of small industry development.
Publications issued:
x *SEDME* (quarterly, English). x *SME Policy* (bimonthly, English). x *SME Technology* (bimonthly, English). x *nisiet bulletin* (monthly, English). x *SSI Cluster News* (quarterly, English).
Membership structure: 15 faculties headed by a principal director.
Products/commodity responsible for:
All products reserved for small sector, products in the medium-scale industry, tiny sector and micro enterprises.
Training:
Organizes training programmes for personnel of a number of organizations of both national and international levels.
Category:
Industrial promotion; and training/research institute.

PHD CHAMBER OF COMMERCE AND INDUSTRY (PHDCCI)

Office/ postal address:
PHD House 4/2 Siri Institutional Area, August Kranti Marg New Delhi 110 016
Phone: (91 11) 26863801-4 Fax: (91 11) 26863135, 26568392, 26855450
E-mail: phdcci@phdccimail.com URL: www.phdccimail.com
Year established: 1905
Principal functions:
- x To serve trade and industry;
- x To promote international trade, technical and economic cooperation, promotion of cooperation in areas of research and development; transfer of technology and foreign investment;
- x To participate in national and international trade fairs and exhibitions.

Services/Activities:
x Provides advice and guidance on policies and procedures pertaining to exports, imports, foreign investment, foreign exchange, trade regulations, customs, direct and indirect taxes; identification and dissemination of commercial information on opportunities on trade and business, both within India and abroad;
x Services foreign business missions visiting India by coordinating their visits and organizing business meetings for the delegates with Indian businesspersons;
x Assists foreign companies in establishing joint ventures in India by matchmaking with Indian companies;
x Sponsors business delegations abroad for trade and investment promotion;
x Provides a common platform for meetings of the representatives of trade, business and industry with senior government officials.
Publications issued:
x *Directory of Members.*
x *Diplomatic Missions and Government Officials.*

x *Labour Judgements.*
x *Central and State Governments Incentives for Industrial Development.*
x *State Investment Guides.*
Local branches:
Punjab, Haryana and Chandigarh 107, Sector 18-A, Chandigarh 160 018 Phone: (91 172) 2781665 Fax: (91 172) 2548802 E-mail: phdcci@glide.net.in
Himachal Pradesh Room No. 205, Udyog Bhawan Shimla 170 004 (HP) Fax: (91 177) 2807855
Madhya Pradesh and Chhattisgarh 61, Betwa Apt., New Market Bhopal 462 003 (MP) Phone: (91 755) 2553728 Fax: (91 755) 2555280
Uttar Pradesh and Uttaranchal 1A, La Place, Shah Najaf Road Hazrat Ganj, Lucknow 226 001 (UP) Phone: (91 522) 2221052 Fax: (91 522) 2280871 E-mail: phdccilko@zyberwayavadh.com
Rajasthan Jai Niwas, S-53, Arvind Marg, C-Scheme Jaipur 302 001 (Rajasthan) Phone: (91 141) 2367131 Fax: (91 141) 2370757 E-mail: phdccijp@datainfosys.net
Membership structure: Over 1,600 direct members consisting of manufacturing units of large and medium enterprises, export houses and professionals. Indirectly, serving over 40,000 organizations. In addition to the direct membership, PHDCCI also serves 12 secretarial affiliates and 125 association members.
Products/commodity responsible for:
All products and services as PHDCCI serves the entire trade and industry.
Training:
Short-duration training programmes for entrepreneurial development and consultancy services for development of small and medium enterprises.
Category:
Chamber of commerce.

PLASTICS EXPORT PROMOTION COUNCIL

Office/postal address:
Ground Floor, Crystal Tower Gundivali RoaD, Off Sir M.V. Road Andheri (East) Mumbai 400 069
Phone: (91 22) 26833951-2, 26834352 Fax: (91 22) 26834057, 26833953
E-mail: plexconcil@vsnl.com, plexho@bom3.vsnl.net.in URL: www.plexconcil.org
Year established: 1955
Principal function:
x To promote the exports of goods made wholly or partly of plastics, finished or semi-finished, plastics raw materials and linoleum products of India.
Services/activities:
x Undertakes market studies in individual foreign markets;
x Sends trade missions to foreign countries;
x Participates in international exhibitions, trade fairs;
x Appoints representatives, agents or correspondents in foreign markets for collecting market data;
x Conducts propaganda regularly and continuously through
publications;
x Collects statistics and other information;
x Lays down standards of quality and packing;
x Issues certificates or gives certification marks relating to standards of quality;
x Acts as arbitrator in trade disputes.
Publications issued:
x *Exporters Directory.* x *Plexconcil Bulletin* (quarterly). x *Statistical Book.* x *Product catalogues/general catalogues.* x *Members' Directory* on CD-ROM.
Local branches:
World Trade Centre 14/1B, Ezra Street Kolkata 700 001 Phone: (91 33) 22354548 Fax: (91 33) 22358946 E-mail: plexcoer@giascl01.vsnl.net.in; plexer@cal.vsnl.net.in,
3rd
Floor, Rasheed Mansion
408, Anna Salai
Chennai 600 006
Phone: (91 44) 28292620
Fax: (91 44) 28291518
E-mail: plepcsr@md3.vsnl.net.in; plexsr@md3.vsnl.net.in
306, Dohil Chambers 46 Nehru Ploace New Delhi 110 019 Phone: (91 11) 26445610 Fax: (91 11) 26236070 E-mail: plexnr@del2.vsnl.net.in
Membership structure: More than 2,000 members.
Products/commodity responsible for:
Plastic items.
Areas/industries where investment is encouraged:
Export-oriented plastic industries.
Category:
Trade promotion organization.

RUBBER BOARD

Office/postal address:

Rubber Board - Head Office Jail Road, Keezhukunnu, Kottayam 686 002 Kerala State
P.O. Box: 1122, Kottayam
Phone: (91 481) 2571231 (4 Lines) Fax: (91 481) 2571380 E-mail: chairman@rubberboard.org.in
URL: www.rubberboard.org.in, www.indianrubberexport.com Year established: 1955 Principal functions:

x To promote by such measures as it thinks fit the development of the rubber industry;
x To undertake, assist or encourage scientific, technological or economic research;
x To train students in improved methods of planting, cultivation, manuring and spraying;
x To provide technical advice to rubber growers;
x To improve the marketing of rubber;
x To collect statistics from owners of estates, dealers and manufacturers;
x To secure better working conditions and the provision and improvement of amenities and incentives to workers;
x To carry out any other duties which may be vested with the Board as per rules made under the Rubber Act;
x To advise the central Government on all matters relating to the development of the rubber industry, including import and export of rubber;
x To advise the central Government with regard to participation in any international conference or scheme relating to rubber;
x To submit to the central Government and such other authorities as may be prescribed, half-yearly reports on its activities and the working of the Rubber Act;
x To prepare and furnish such other reports relating to the rubber industry as may be required by the central Government from time to time.

Services/activities:
The Rubber Board is designated by the Government of India as the Export Promotion Council for Natural Rubber (NR). The Board promotes the export of NR and rubber wood articles from India. Major services provided to facilitate the export of rubber:
x Helps international buyers to identify potential exporters of rubber in India;
x Provides assistance to source quality forms of rubber at international standards and packings;
x Provides services to exporters for quality improvement and helps them to export the rubber with inspection and quality certificates issued by the Board;
x Obtains feedback on exported rubber from overseas buyers. In the event of complaints, takes appropriate corrective measures for obtaining better acceptance of Indian rubber in foreign markets.

Publications issued:
Trade-related publications:
x *Booklet on Exporters of Natural Rubber.* x *Directory of Rubber Products Exporters in India.* x *Directory of Rubber Goods Manufacturers in India.* x *Directory of World Importers of Rubber Products.* x *Booklet on Natural Rubber Importers.* x *Market Survey Reports on Rubber Products.*
General publications: x *Indian Journal of Natural Rubber Research* (half-yearly, English). x *Rubber Board Bulletin* (quarterly, English). x *Rubber* (monthly, Malayalam). x *Rubber Statistical News* (monthly, English). x *Inside Rubber Statistics* (annually, English). x *Rubber Wood: Production and utilization* (annually, English). x *Rubber Grower's Companion cum Diary* (annually, English). x Advisory pamphlets (English) - Available for rubber growers on request.
x *Natural Rubber Agro management and Crop Processing* (English). x *Technical Bulletin* (English).

Local branch:
Export Promotion Section Department of Training and Technical Consultancy Rubber Board Rubber Training Centre Kottayam 696 009 Phone: (91 481) 2353127, 2353168, 2353201 Fax: (91 481) 2353187

Products/commodity responsible for:
Natural rubber; ribber smoked sheet (RSS); Indian standard natural rubber-ISNR (block rubber); 60 per cent centrifuged latex.

Training:
x Advanced training on the processing of natural rubber as tailor-made forms are internationally accepted standards; x Advanced training on rubber product manufacture and product development; x Advanced training on rubber cultivation and plantation management.

Areas/industries where investment is encouraged:
Replantation and new plantation of rubber; productivity enhancement through agro management; infrastructure development and management; rubber processing and quality improvement; road rubberization projects; research development activities; export promotion and marketing support activities; rubber wood processing and marketing; human resource management: training and development.

Category:
Commodity board.

SHELLAC EXPORT PROMOTION COUNCIL

Office/postal address:
"Vanijya Bhawan" International Trade Facilitation Centre 1/1 Wood Street, 2nd Floor Kolkata - 700 016
Phone: (91 33) 22834417, 22834697-8 Fax: (91 33) 22834699
E-mail: sepc@vsnl.net URL: www.shellacepc.com
Year established: 1957
Principal functions:
- To support, protect, maintain, increase and promote the export of shellac and other lac products;
- To collect statisticd and information on growing, import, manufacture, trade or use of lac in various countries and propagate information;
- To advise or represent Government, local authorities and public bodies regarding different policy aspects;
- To promote exports of minor forest produce products.

Services/activities:
x Issues Quality Certificates;
x Sends delegations abroad, participates in international trade fairs and maintains liaison with trade associations, government bodies, Indian missions abroad;
x Sponsors research on value added products of lac through various national research institutes for higher unit value realization and regularly organizes publicity campaigns.
Publications issued:
x *The Story of Shellac.* x *Industrial Uses of Lac.* x *Physical Properties and Chemical Constants of Lac.* x *Shellac in Coating Composition for Various Surfaces.* x *Shellac Varnishes.* x *Electrical Industry & Shellac.* x *Shellac for Food Confectionery & Pharmaceutical Products.* x *Leather & Shellac.* x *Lac Coated Urea.* x *Shellac in Printing Ink.* x *Plastic & Shellac.*
Membership structure: 72 members.
Products/commodity responsible for:
Shellac and other lac based products and minor forest products.
Areas/industries where investment is encouraged:
Shellac and lac based industries.
Category:
Export promotion council.

SOLVENT EXTRACTORS' ASSOCIATION OF INDIA (SEA)

(Premier Association of Vegetable Oil Industry and Trade)
Office/postal address:
142, 14th Floor Jolly Maker Chamber No.2 225, Nariman Point Mumbai 400 021
Phone: (91 22) 22021475, 22822979 Fax: (91 22) 22021692
E-mail: solvent@vsnl.com URL: www.seaofindia.com/
Year established: 1963
Principal functions:
- To promote the export and market development of de-oiled meals, vegetable fats, compound feeds for cattle and poultry feeds;
- To assess international trends in feed ingredients, and prices thereof, for guiding exporters;
- To assist trade in quality assurance;
- To collect and disseminate market information and statistics on trends of contracting, physical exports, status of crop situation and marketing strategies;
- To provide a strong organizational nucleus;
- To ensure timely and regular shipment performance;
- To inspire confidence in foreign buyers;
- To depute delegations to foreign countries to explore and study export markets;
- To organize and participate in trade fairs, exhibitions and buyer-seller meetings in India and abroad.

Services/activities:
As detailed under Principal functions.
Publications issued:
x *SEA News Circular* (monthly).
x *Handbook on Rice Bran Processing.*
x *National Seminar on Edible Rice Bran Oil.*
x *SEA Delegation Report 2001 - Rice Bran Oil Technical Delegation to Japan and Thailand.*
x *National Seminar on Oilmeals usage in Compound Feeds.*
x *SEA Millennium Handbook on Indian Vegetable Oil Industry and Trade.*
x *Annual Report 2001-2003* (includes list of members and

31st
statistics).

x *National Seminar on Technology Upgradation in Vegetable Oil Industry.*
x *2001 - SEA Delegation Report on Malaysian Palm Oil Complex Study Tour.*
x *2002 -SEA Delegation Report on Indnesian Palm Oil Complex Study Tour.*
Membership structure: 706 as of 30 April 2003.
Ordinary members (Those having solvent extraction plants): 255; Associate (any person/company interested): 451.
Products/commodity responsible for:
Vegetable oil, oilmeals, oilseeds and related products.
Training:
x Organizing seminars and inviting members and others to participate.
Areas/industries where investment is encouraged:
Technology upgrading in oilseed and oil processing; international trade.
Category:
Trade association.

SPORTS GOODS EXPORT PROMOTION COUNCIL (SGPEC)

Office/postal address:
Export Promotion Department 1E/6, Swami Ram Tirth Nagar New Delhi 110 055
Phone: (91 11) 23525695, 23516183 Fax: (91 11) 23632147
E-mail: sgepc@vsnl.com URL: www.sportsgoodsindia.org
Year established: 1958
Principal function:
x To support and promote the export of sports goods and toys.
Services/activities: Local branch:

- x Authentication of exporters: SGEPC is a platform for the projection of the sports goods and toys industry at a national level;
- x Enquiries from buyers: SGEPC assists foreign buyers in sourcing their requirement from India;
- x India Pavilion in leading international fairs: SGEPC organizes Indian participation in international fairs and forms an India Pavilion where exhibitors are provided with thematic stands as per their individual requirement at highly negotiated rates;
- x Buyer-seller meets: SGEPC organizes buyer-seller meets in potential countries with the help of Indian missions and/or local marketing consultants. A buyer mobilization strategy is undertaken before the event to ensure meetings with relevant buyers for individual participants;
- x Promotion of industry in overseas events: the Council promotes the industry in international markets through a newsletter, industry profiles, members' directory (print and digital format), advertisements, industry posters and website;
- x Link between industry and Government: SGEPC provides the feedback of the industry to the Government helping it to evolve the national export-import policy;
- x Market studies and dissemination of information: SGEPC provides information on market intelligence, trends, related international news, through newsletters, seminars and also through the website. SGEPC undertakes specific market studies and disseminates them to the industry though mails/newsletters;
- x Visa support to members;
- x Annual export awards: these provide recognition to top exporters and entrepreneurs.

9, Shakti Nagar Jalandhar 144 001 Phone: (91 181) 2403734
Publication issued:
x *Newsletter* (monthly).
Membership structure: Approximately 250 members.
Product/commodity responsible for:
Sports goods and toys.
Category:
Trade promotion organization.

TOBACCO BOARD

Office/postal address:
Srinivasarao Thota

G.T. Road, Guntur Andhra Pradesh 522004
P.O. Box: 322
Phone: (91 863) 2358399, 2358068 Fax: (91 863) 2354232
E-mail: info@indiantobacco.com, exports@indiantobacco.com URL: www.indiantobacco.com
Year established: 1976
Principal functions:
x To regulate the production of flue cured virginia (FCV) tobacco; x To assist growers in production of quality tobaccos;
Services/activities:
x Markets FCV tobacco through auction to ensure fair and remunerative prices to growers; x Promotes exports of tobacco and tobacco products.
Publications issued:
x *Tobacco Directory*. x *Tobacco News Letter* (quarterly).
Local branches:
Mission Road, 1/9 III Cross
4th
Floor, Unity Building Annexe
C.S.I. Compound Bangalore 560 027 Phone: (91 80) 22236599, 22233304
Tobacco Board Transit House Mega City No. 90 Avenue No. 1, (formerly Road No. 12) Banjara Hills, Hyderabad 500 034 Phone: (91 40) 23317503, 23319989
Tobacco Board Transit House B-11, 1st Floor, Green Park (Main) New Delhi 110 016 Phone: (91 11) 26568841
Tobacco Board Transit House Flat No. 2A, 2nd Floor Aravind Apartments 9, Visweswara Puram Mylepoor, Chennai 600 004 Phone: (91 44) 24661766
Membership structure: Growers, exporters, processors and manufacturers.
Products/commodity responsible for:
Unmanufactured tobacco and tobacco products.
Category:
Commodity board.

INDONESIA

IMPORTERS' ASSOCIATION OF INDONESIA (GINSI)

Office/postal address:
Wisma Kosgoro 8th Floor Jl. M.H. Thamrin 53 Jakarta 10350
Phone: (62 21) 39832510, 39832534 Fax: (62 21) 39832499, 39832504
Year established: 1956
Principal functions:
- x To promote international trade and cooperation;
- x To strengthen the role of private enterprises;
- x To improve the condition of international trade.

Services/activities:
x Provides advisory service to members, particularly for customs clearance, claims, etc.; x Conducts a staff training scheme on customs procedures, insurance, banking and shipping methods; x Conducts business luncheons, seminars for members as well as for foreign visiting businessmen;
x Accepts enquiries from foreign exporters, suppliers and manufacturers which are either forwarded to members or published in the Association's bulletin;
x Provides library service for members.
Publication issued:
x *Bulletin Ekonomi Indonesia* (Indonesian).
Local branches:
BPD GINSI DKI Jakarta Wisma Kosgoro 8th Fl Jl. MH. Thamrin No. 53 Jakarta 10350
BPD GINSI Jawa Barat Jl. Merdeka No. 54 Bandung 40115
BPD GINSI Jawa Tengah Jl. Letjen. Suprapto No. 22 Semarang 50175
BPD GINSI Jawa Timur Jl. Nginden Intan Selatan No. 49 F Surabaya 60118
BPD GINSI Kalimantan Barat Jl. Jambu Mente No. 8 Pontianak 78113
BPD GINSI Sumatera Barat Jl. Arau Blok A.II/III Padang
BPD GINSI Sumatera Utara Jl. Setia Budi No. 782 A Medan BPD GINSI Sulawesi Selatan Jl. Andi Tonro V Blok A2/3 Makassar
BPD GINSI Bali – Nusa Tenggara D/a. PT. MITRA SAHATA Jl. Hayam Wuruk No. 238 Denpasar 80235
Membership structure: 7,800 members.
Category:
Chamber of commerce.

INVESTMENT COORDINATING BOARD (BKPM)

Office/postal address:
Jalan Gatot Subroto No. 44 Jakarta
P.O. Box: 3186, Jakarta
Phone: (62 21) 5252008 Fax: (62 21) 5254945
E-mail: benny@bkpm.go.id, baktio@bkpm.go.id URL: www.bkpm.go.id

Year established: 1976

Principal function:

x To assist the Government in deciding upon a judicious policy on investment, issuing necessary approvals, permits and licences for both domestic and foreign investments and controlling its implementation.

Services/activities:

x Formulates investment policies; x Coordinates an integrated investment plan; x Prepares and issues the priority list of investment/list of sectors
that are closed for investment;

x Conducts effective communication and promotional activities and disseminates information to potential investors and business community;

x Evaluates investment proposals on both domestic and foreign
investments; x Approves domestic investment proposals; x Issues necessary licences and permits for the implementation of the approved projects on behalf of the Ministers concerned; x Provides necessary services to facilitate the implementation of the approved investment projects;

x Controls and supervises the implementation of the approved investment projects in close cooperation with Regional Investment Offices (BKPM) and Ministries concerned.

Publications issued:

x *A Guide for Investors.*
x *Investment Laws and Regulations.*
x *Indonesian Investment News.*
x *Indonesian Potential Business Partners.*
x *Investment Procedures in Indonesia.*
x *List of Sectors that Are Closed for Investment,* 2000.
x *Project Profiles.*
x *Regional Profiles.*

Local branches:

Regional investment institutions are located in the provinces as well as in its regencies of provinces as follows: Special Territories of Jakarta, Jogyakarta and Aceh, North Sumatra, Riau, Kepulauan Riau (Riau Islands), West Sumatra, South Sumatra, Jambi, Bengkulu, Bangka-Belitung, Lampung, West Java, Banten, Central Java, East Java, Bali, West Kalimantan, Central Kalimantan, South Kalimantan, East Kalimantan, West Nusa Tenggara, East Nusa Tenggara, North Sulawesi, Gorontalo, West Sulawesi, Central Sulawesi, South Sulawesi, South East Sulawesi, North Maluku, Maluku Irian Jaya Barat (West Irian Jaya) and Papua.

Offices abroad:

Indonesian Embassies/Consulates in the following countries/group of countries undertake foreign investment promotion programmes: Australia (Sydney), Canada (Toronto, Vancouver), Germany (Bonn), France (Paris), Japan (Tokyo), Netherlands (The Hague), United Kingdom (London), United States of America (Chicago, Los Angeles, New York, Washington, DC) and ASEAN countries [Brunei Darussalam (Bandar Seri Begawan), Malaysia (Kuala Lumpur), Philippines (Manila), Singapore (Singapore), Thailand (Bangkok), etc.]. In addition, BKPM has representative offices in Los Angeles, Nagoya, London, Amsterdam and Taipei.

Areas/industries where investment is encouraged:

Projects utilizing natural and human resources; export-oriented projects; labour-intensive projects; projects making use of Indonesia's comparative advantage; projects producing capital goods and raw materials; projects on infrastructure such as ports, generation and transmission as well as distribution of electricity for public use, telecommunications, shipping, airlines, potable water and public railways.

Titles of laws and regulations on foreign investment:

Foreign Investment Law No. 1 of 1967 and No. 11 of 1970.

Category:

Investment promotion authority.

LABORATORY FOR QUALITY TESTING OF EXPORT AND IMPORT GOODS

Directorate of Quality Control, Directorate General for Foreign Trade, Ministry of Industry and Trade

Office / postal address:

Jl. Raya Bogor, Km 26 Ciracas Jakarta 13740
P.O.Box: 4235, Jakarta
Phone: (62 21) 8710321-3 Fax: (62 21) 8710477-8 E-Mail: dirppmb-daglu@dprind.go.id
URL: www.dprind.go.id/ppmb Year establised: 1977 Principal functions:

x To implement testing and certification of export and import of product quality;
x To render services of testing and certification of product quality;
x To implement general affairs of institution.

Services/activities:

x Microbiology testing; x Sensory and organoleptics testing; x Pesticide residue testing; x Food testing; x Industrial chemical products testing; x Agricultural and forestry products testing; x Textiles and multifarious products testing; x Electronical products and household equipment testing; x Calibration.

Publications issued:

x Leaflets (Bahasa Indonesia; English). x Quality journal (Bahasa Indonesia).

Local branches:

The local branches are no longer under the organization structure. They have already been under the auspices of the respective regional administration since 2001. However, these former local branches are now functioning as the members of laboratory networking which are coordinated by the organization.

The members of Laboratory Networking: Jl. Panglima Batur Banjarbaru 70700 Phone: (62 511) 772237 Fax: (62 511) 772237 E-mail: tarigan@banjarmasin.wasantara.net.id

Jl. Mangga V Lingkar Timur Bengkulu 38229 Phone: (62 736) 20189 Fax: (62 736) 24002 E-mail: marsal@bengkulu.wasantara.net.id

Jl. Raya Puputan Renon Denpasar Denpasar Phone: (62 361) 223096 Fax: (62 361) 223097

Jl. Letjen Suprapto No. 29 Telanaipura Kotak Pos 115 Jambi 36112 Phone: (62 741) 60822 Fax: (62 741) 60740

Jl. Kalimantan No. 1 Tromol Pos 1 JR Jember 68121 Phone: (62 331) 88396 Fax: (62 331) 84825 E-mail: bpsmbjr@jember.telkom.net.id

Jl. Andi Petarani Makasar 90222 Phone: (62 411) 441239 Fax: (62 411) 457368

Jl. Pumorow Manado 95125 Phone: (62 431) 867447 Fax: (62 431) 857447 E-mail: bpamb@manado.wasantara.net.id

Jl. STM No. 17 Kotak Pos 407, Medan 20146 Phone: (62 61) 8764040 Fax: (62 61) 8764040 E-mail: soer@indo.net.id

Jl. Pocut Baren No. 9 Banda Aceh 23123 Phone: (62 651) 23098

Jl. Belibis Air Tawar No. 3A Kotak Pos 65 Padang 25131 Phone: (62 751) 54202, 53484 Fax: (62 751) 53484 E-mail: bpsmb@padang.wasantara.net.id

Jl. RTA Milono Km 5,5 Palangkaraya 73112 Phone: (62 536) 21551 Fax: (62 536) 21551

Jl. Demang Lebar Daun No. 90 Palembang 30139 Phone: (62 711) 41646 Fax: (62 711) 41646

Jl. Mentok Raya Km 3 Pangkalpinang 33134 Phone: (62 717) 422162 Fax: (62 717) 422162 E-mail: mulyadi@bpsmbpkp.wasantara.net.id

Jl. Dr. Sutomo No. 108 Pekanbaru 28133 Phone: (62 761) 21325 Fax: (62 761) 22173 E-mail: paulina@pbaru.wasantara.net.id

Jl. Abdulrahman Saleh No. 31

P.O.

Box 357 Pontianak 78124 Phone: (62 561) 762849 Fax: (62 561) 732972 E-mail: raswilmy@pontianak.wasantara.net.id

Jl. Letjen MT Haryono

P.O.

Box 1111 Samarinda 75126 Phone: (62 541) 733731 Fax: (62 541) 733731 E-mail: payaman@samarinda.wasantara.net.id

Jl. Gayung Kebonsari dalam 12 A Tromol Pos 8 SBWC Surabay 60235 Phone: (62 31) 8280762 – 8280753 Fax: (62 31) 8294291 E-mail: bpsmbsby@sby.rat.net.id

Jl. Pajang Kartosuro Km 8 Pabelan Surakarta 57162 Phone: (62 271) 743959 Fax: (62 271) 743959 E-mail: bpsmbslo@indo.net.id

Jl. Cut Meutia No. 36 Kotak Pos 100 Bandar Lampung 35214 Phone: (62 721) 480410 Fax: (62 721) 482712

Jl. Baru Ubo Ubo Ternate 97717 Phone: (62 921) 22193 Fax: (62 921) 22757 E-mail: bpsmbtnt@ternate.wasantara.net.id

Jl. R.A. Kartini No. 18 Palu Phone: (62 451) 424229 Fax: (62 451) 456885

BPSMB Kendari Jl. Drs. H. Abd. Silondae No. 116 Kendari 93111 Phone: (62 401) 329386 Fax: (62 401) 321783

BPMNPI Jayapura Jl. Raya Sentani Wamena Jayapura – Papua Phone: (62 967) 571265 Fax: (62 967) 571265

Membership structure: 23 members.

Products / commodity responsible for:

Agricultural export and import products, industrial products.

Category:

Standard, testing and inspection body.

NATIONAL AGENCY FOR EXPORT DEVELOPMENT (NAFED)*

Office/postal address:

5th

Floor, Dharma Niaga Building 6-8, Jl. Abdul Muis Jakarta 10160

P.O. Box: 1443, Jakarta

Phone: (62 21) 3448164 Fax: (62 21) 3858850, 3518669 E-mail: nafed@nafed.go.id

URL: www.nafed.go.id Year established: 1971 Principal functions:

- x To be responsible for promoting and developing export;
- x To act as a facilitator to link buyers and sellers, aimed at increasing sales of Indonesian products especially of non oil and gas products;
- x To provide a comprehensive range of services to both Indonesian exporters and overseas buyers including studies to identify potential market, advice on export procedures and the government regulations and help in organizing fairs, selling mission and exhibition.

Services/activities:

For overseas buyers:

- x Provides information on product availability, by sector and company;
- x Provides advice and information on current government trade regulations and procedures;
- x Assists foreign buyers to find the Indonesian products and exporters.

For Indonesian sellers:

- x Provides up-to-date information on trade trends and prospects, presented with specific data on the target markets;
- x Assists Indonesian manufacturers to find buyers for their products;
- x Provides information on overseas trade procedures, restrictions and incentives;

x Provides specific counselling on potential prospects and assistance in preparing meetings with overseas buyers;

x Assists and organizes Indonesian participation in international trade fairs and selling missions.
Publications issued:
x *Export Newsletter* (monthly, English). x *Price Info* (monthly, Indonesian). x *Source of Business Information* (monthly, Indonesian). x *Directory of Indonesian Exporters* (annually, English). x *Statistic of Indonesian Export Balance of Trade* (annually,
English).
x *Annual Report* (annually, English).
x *NAFED's Brochures* (annually, English).
x *Export Bulletin* (monthly, Indonesian).
Local branches:
Regional Export Training and Promotion Centre in Surabaya, Medan, Makassar.
Offices of industry and trade service in Banda Aceh, Medan, Pekanbaru, Telanapura, Padang, Bengkulu, Palembang, Bandar Lampung, Jakarta Utara, Bandung, Semarang, Yogyakarta, Surabaya, Pontianak, Palangkaraya, Banjarmasin, Samarinda, Manado, Palu, Makassar, Kendari, Renon, Mataram, Kupang, Ambon, Jayapura, Ternate, Serang, Bangka, Gorontalo.
Offices abroad:
Indonesian Trade Promotion Centre (ITPC) branches in Osaka, Los Angeles, Deira Bubai, Budapest, Hungary, Johanesburg, São Paulo.
Indonesian industry and trade representative offices overseas: Embassies or missions in Canberra; Vienna; Brussels; Beijing, China; Copenhagen, Cairo; Paris; Berli; Hong Kong, China; New Delhi; Rome; Tokyo; Kuala Lumpur; The Hague; Makati City; Seoul; Moscow; Riyadh; Singapore; Madri; Geneva; Taipei Province of China; Bangkok; London; Washington.
Products/commodity responsible for:
Non-oil and gas products.
Training:
NAFED's training programmes are aimed at initiating new exporters, both individually and through their enterprises, focusing especially on small and medium firms and cooperatives. Training and other forms of support are conducted through domestic promotional events, specific projects and the creation of regional marketing points such as the one on Batam island.
Seminars, tutorials and one-on-one meetings are held regularly at the Indonesian Export Training Centre (IETC) in Jakarta.
Since IETC was established with assistance from the Japan International Coopertion Agency (JICA) in 1990, more than 14,000 people have taken advantage of its programmes, which are more necessary then ever in an era of globalization, wider trade liberalization ad sharpening competition. By 2002, a Regional Export Training and Promotion Centre (RETPC) was established in Surabaya and regional export training and promotion centres in Medan and Makassar opened in 2003 and Banjarmasin in 2004.
Category:
Ministry of Industry and Trade; trade facilitation body; trade fair and exhibition authority; trade promotion organization; and training/research institute.

LAO PDR

BANK OF THE LAO PDR

Office/postal address:
Yonnet Road Vientiane
P.O. Box: 19, Vientiane
Phone: (856 21) 213109-10 Fax: (856 21) 213108
E-mail: bol@bol.gov.la URL: www.bol.gov.la
Year established: 1955
Principal function:
x To perform the task of state management within the framework of the Government, in the role of a Central Bank as an organization equivalent to a ministry.
Services/activities:
x Safeguards the stability of the national monetary and economic system; x Fosters conditions conducive to orderly balanced and sustained economic growth; x Promotes and facilitates control on the flows of money to
serve the socio-economic development plan; x Maintains and manages the foreign reserves; x Issues bank notes and withdraws notes from circulation or
redeems such notes; x Approves the application for establishing, auditing and supervising commercial banks and other financial institutions.
Publication issued:
x *Annual Report.*
Local branches:
Bank of Lao PDR's Southern Branch Pakse District Champasack Province Phone: (856 31) 214125 Fax: (856 31) 214120
Bank of Lao PDR's Northern Branch Oudomxay District Oudomxay Province Phone: (856 81) 211492 Fax: (856 81) 211494
Training:
x Twice for internal training, conducted in English, 45 times for outsiders.

Areas/industries where investment is encouraged:
Lending for the agricultural sector, such as rice planted, cattle, cultivation, coffee planted and growing trees planted.
Titles of laws and regulations on foreign investment:
x Law on the promotion and management of foreign investment in the Lao People's Democratic Republic issued by Presidential Decree No. 23 of 21 April 1994 and coming into force on 20 June 1994.
x Decree of the President of the Lao People's Democratic Republic governing the management of foreign exchange and precious metals, issued by Decree No. 01 of 9 August 2002 and coming into force instead of decree No. 53 of the council ministry.
Category:
Banks.

DEPARTMENT OF DOMESTIC AND FOREIGN INVESTMENT (DDFI)

Office/postal address:
Luang Prabang Road Vientiane 01001
Phone: (856 21) 222690, 222691, 217005 Fax: (856 21) 215491
E-mail: fimc@laotel.com URL: http://www.invest.laopdr.org
Principal functions:
x To administer the foreign investment system and to review investment applications;
x To offer a "one-stop" service to foreign investors by providing information and assistance during the investment process.
Services/activities:
x Is the first stop for information on the investment process in the Lao People's Democratic Republic; x Promotes the Lao People's Democratic Republic as an
investment destination; x Screens investment proposals; x Offers investment incentives; x Facilitates foreign investment.
Publications issued:
x *The Promising Investment Destination* (brochure). x Online Newsletter.
Titles of laws and regulations on foreign investment:
x The Law on the Promotion and Management of Foreign
Investment (1994). x The Law on Domestic Investment (1995). x The Business Law (1994). x The Customs Law (1994). x The Tax Law (1995).
Category:
Investment authority.

LAO NATIONAL CHAMBER OF COMMERCE AND INDUSTRY (LNCCI)

Office/postal address:
Sihom Road Ban Haisok Chanthabury District Vientiane
P.O. Box: 4596, Vientiane
Phone: (856 21) 21923-24 Fax: (856 21) 219223 E-mail: laocci@laotel.com
URL: www.incci.laotel.com Year established: 1989 Principal functions:
- x To promote and assist in trade, investment and other business matters in the Lao People's Democratic Republic and abroad;
- x To represent the Lao People's Democratic Republic business community for the promotion and protection of its interest in domestic and international relations;
- x To provide Lao People's Democratic Republic and foreign business enterprises and other organizations with information on trade, laws and regulation.

Services/activities:
x Organizes the participation of the Lao People's Democratic Republic and foreign business enterprises and other organizations in international fairs and exhibitions, displayssand similar events in the country and abroad;
x Organizes professional training in the interest of improving the knowledge and entrepreneurship of businesspersons; x Conducts any work as may be assigned by the Government
of the Lao People's Democratic Republic; x Issues Certificate of Origin.
Local branches:
Bokeo Phone: (856 84) 211057 Mobile: (856) 016027955
Champassk Phone: (856 31) 212337 Fax: (856 31) 212337
Khommouane Phone: (865 51) 212037 Fax: (856 51) 212395
Luang Prabang Phone: (856 71) 212379,212198 Fax: (856 71) 212728 E-mail: ibtravel@laotel.com
Savannakhet Phone: (856 41) 212046 Mobile: (856) 540293 Fax: (856 41) 213688
Membership structure: 510 members and 14 groups of trade associtions operate under LNCCI.
Areas/industries where investment is encouraged:
Agriculture production (food, fruit, vegetable); education; handicraft; hotel and restaurant; mining; service and commercial production; textile and garment; tourism; and wood processing.
Category:
Chamber of commerce.

MACAO

MACAO TRADE AND INVESTMENT PROMOTION INSTITUTE (IPIM)

Office/postal address:
1st
– 4th Floors, World Trade Centre Building 918, Av. da Amizade
Phone: (853) 710300 Hot line 24 hours: (853) 881212 Fax: (853) 590309
E-mail: ipim@ipim.gov.mo URL: www.ipim.gov.mo
Year established: 1994
Principal functions:

- x To introduce potential investors to the local investment environment and opportunities; also to provide "One-Stop Service": information enquiries, project assessment, company registration assistance provided by IPIM's notary, guidance on administrative procedures concerned with licence applications, project follow-up and assistance in the implementation of projects;
- x To provide trade, economic, statistical, general information and market analysis to assist clients in exploring the market and the development of their business;
- x To organize and co-organize exhibitions and other promotional events locally, to participate in such events held outside Macao, China and to sponsor the participation of local enterprises in such events, as a way to create trade opportunities;
- x To organize local economic delegations to search for business opportunities, welcome visits by delegations to Macao, China in order to create channels for exchange and cooperation;
- x To be responsible for the issuing of licences, technical assistance and supervision for non-financial offshore institutions; to promote local offshore development with various activities;
- x To evaluate applications for local residency by investors, company managers and professionals;
- x To edit and publish trade and economic magazines, to promote Macao, China's business environment.

Services/activities:
As detailed under Principal functions.
Publications issued:
x *Investing in Macao* (English/Chinese). x *Macao Image* (biannually, English/Chinese). x *Newsletter* (every two months, English/Chinese).
Areas/industries where investment is encouraged:
General services; professional services; and offshore services.
Category:
Government agency for promotion of trade and investment.

MACAO IMPORTERS AND EXPORTERS ASSOCIATION*

Office/postal address:
3rd
Floor, Centro Comercial Central
Av. do Infante D. Henrique No. 60-62 Phone: (853) 553187 Fax: (853) 512174
E-mail: aeim@macau.ctm.net URL: www.macauexport.com Year established: 1965 Principal function:
x To promote, develop and protect the interests of Macao, China's export and import trading.
Services/activities:
x To protect and secure legal rights for members.
Publication issued:
x Monthly newsletter in Chinese. Membership structure: Around 250 members. Category:
Chamber of commerce; industrial promotion; trade association; and trade promotion organization.

MALAYSIA

FEDERAL AGRICULTURAL MARKETING AUTHORITY (FAMA)

(Lembaga Pemasaran Pertanian Persekutuan)
Office/postal address:
Bangunan FAMA Point Lot 17304, Jalan Persiaran Satu Bandar Baru Selayang 68100 Batu Caves Selangor

Phone: (60 3) 61389622 Fax: (60 3) 61383650
E-mail: fama@fama.net.my URL: www.famaxchange.org/

Year established: 1965

Principal functions:

- x To coordinate the marketing of agricultural activities between private sectors and agencies/government departments;
- x To improve the marketing system and to expand as well as to develop new markets for Malaysian agricultural products;
- x To cooperate with the private sector and government departments/agencies to establish effective and efficient agricultural marketing;
- x To develop and enhance efficient management in the agriculture industry particularly in the marketing or agriculture output processed;
- x To participate directly in the agriculture industry especially in marketing or agriculture output processed.

Services/activities:

x Undertakes marketing research involving supply, demand and price monitoring, market potential studies, marketing costs and margin studies and consumption surveys;
x Undertakes analysis and dissemination of market information;
x Carries out adaptation and commercial trials of improved marketing practices;
x Develops and implements grades and standards;
x Engages in agricultural marketing to improve product quality and marketing practices, for producers and intermediaries;
x Encourages increased farmers' involvement in marketing;
x Undertakes market promotion, domestic and foreign, for fresh and processed products;
x Promotes agro-processing, including product identification and development, project feasibility studies and investment advisory services;
x Undertakes horticulture sectoral planning, policy analysis and programme/budget planning;
x Engages in commercial marketing of consumer products through various FAMA retail (FR) outlets.

Local branches:

Pejabat FAMA Negeri Perlis No. 22, 24 and 26, Tingkat Atas Jalan Simpang Tiga, Taman Sena Indah Persiaran Jubli Emas 01000 Kangar, Perlis Phone: (60 4) 9765615, 9761513 Fax: (60 4) 976 0564 Pejabat FAMA Negeri Kedah Lot 1276, Kawasan Perusahaan Mergong Jalan Perak 05150 Alor Setar, Kedah Phone: (60 4) 7319344, 7319103 Fax: (60 4) 7335154

Pejabat FAMA Negeri Pulau Pinang 2442, Tingkat Perusahaan Kawasan Perusahaan Prai 13600 Prai, Pulau Pinang Phone: (60 4) 3907886, 3907222 Fax: (60 4) 3908107

Pejabat FAMA Negeri Perak Tingkat 9, Bangunan KWSP Jalan Hospital 30450 Ipoh, Perak Phone: (60 5) 2546322, 2546684 Fax: (60 5) 2416545

Pejabat FAMA Negeri Selangor No. 12-01 Tingkat 12 Plaza Masalam Jalan Tengku Ampuan Zabedah 40100 Shah Alam, Selangor Phone: (60 3) 55118114-6 Fax: (60 3) 55118124

Pejabat FAMA Negeri Melaka Lot 73, Kawasan Perindustrian Air Keroh Jalan Usaha 12 75450 Air Keroh, Melaka Phone: (60 6) 2319650, 2312760 Fax: (60 6) 2317172

Pejabat FAMA Negeri Johor Km 8, Jalan Tun Abd. Razak Susur 6, Peti Surat 25 80700 Johor Bahru, Johor Phone: (60 7) 2341185-6 Fax: (80 7) 2370832

Pejabat FAMA Negri Sembilan Tingkat 5, Bangunan Yayasan Negeri Jalan Yam Tuan 70000 Seremban, Negri Sembilan Phone: (60 6) 7635797, 7638959 Fax: (60 6) 7637466

Pejabat FAMA Negeri Terengganu Tingkat U3, Menara Permint Jalan Sultan Ismail 20200 Kuala Terengganu, Terengganu Phone: (60 9) 6224144, 6224191 Fax: (60 9) 6221606

Pejabat FAMA Negeri Pahang Km 9, Jalan Gambang 25150 Kuantan, Pahang Phone: (60 9) 5366110, 5366113 Fax: (60 9) 5366106 Pejabat FAMA Negeri Kelantan Jalan Dato' Lundang, 15200 Kota Bharu, Kelantan Phone: (60 9) 7482431, 7482577 Fax: (60 9) 7443030

Pejabat FAMA Negeri Sabah Tingkat 12 Wisma Bandaraya Jalan Padang 88000 Kota Kinabalu, Sabah Phone: (60 88) 225741-2 Fax: (60 88) 223526

Pejabat FAMA Negeri Sarawak Lot 1003-1005, Seksyen 65 KTLD Jalan Jawa Kampung Pinang Jawa
P.O. Box 1929 93738 Kuching, Sarawak Phone: (60 82) 422578, 414744 Fax: (60 82) 244551

Products/commodity responsible for:

Marketing of agricultural products/commodity (fruits, vegetables, livestock, fisheries, flowers, etc.).

Training:

x Regular courses are only offered to staff and public, conducted in Bahasa Malaysia (national language).

Areas/industries where investment is encouraged:

Contract farming; small and medium industries projects.

Category:

Statutory body.

FEDERATION OF MALAYSIAN MANUFACTURERS (FMM)

Office/postal address:

Wisma FMM, No. 3 Persiaran Dagang, PJU 9 Bandar Sri Damansara 52200 Kuala Lumpur
P.O. Box: Jinjang, 52000 Kuala Lumpur

Phone: (60 3) 62761211 Fax: (60 3) 62741266, 62747288 E-mail: webmaster@fmm.org.my
URL: www.fmm.org.my Year established: 1968 Principal functions:

- x To work in concert with the Government to create and sustain a dynamic business environment;
- x To assist Malaysian industries to increase productivity and business efficiency;
- x To mobilize efforts to modernize and improve the range and quality of supporting industries;
- x To stimulate entrepreneurship and creativity in the Malaysian business community.

Services/activities:

x Maintains online value added information through the website on government policies and regulations, trade opportunities and other up-to-date economic and business information;

x Represents the industry's problems and concerns to the Government, as well as consultative representation in major public sector organizations on issues such as industrial development, technology, trade promotion, quality controls and standards;

x Provides members with up-to-date information on government policies, incentives, legislation and procedure;

x Offers guidance and advice on matters pertaining to trade and industry such as customs regulations, fiscal and monetary incentives, economic perspectives, investment incentives, labour laws, environmental issues, safety at work;

x Informs members of trade and business contacts through trade enquiries and incoming and outgoing missions;

x Produces the annual directory of members which is recognized as the authoritative handbook on manufacturing companies in Malaysia and overseas;

x Provides management and administrative services for a number of industry groups to promote their respective industries;

x Assists members to participate in Association of Southeast Asian Nations (ASEAN) industrial and trade cooperation activities;

x Issues and endorses Certificates of Origin;

x Maintains a business information centre for references on foreign trade, economic reports and other useful commercial and business news and statistics;

x Produces several recurrent and other publications;

x Organizes trade fairs and exhibitions in the country, trade missions overseas and participates in trade exhibitions in foreign countries;

x Manages and promotes the EAN.UCC system of article numbering and bar coding;

- x Assists members to apply for an exclusively designed insurance scheme on public and product liability plus product recall to all countries offered by a major insurance firm;
- x Operates a network of branches to attend to members' needs on local issues.

Publications issued:

x Circulars on government policies, customs orders, training programmes etc. (weekly). x *FMM Directory* (annually). x *FMM Industry Directories*. x *FMM Forum* (annually). x *Malaysian Manufacturers' Digest* (quarterly). x *Berita FMM* (quarterly). x *FMM Trade Bulletin* (quarterly). x *EAN Newsletter* (quarterly). x *SMI Handbook*.

Local branches:

Eastern Branch (Pahang, Kelantan, Terengganu) Suite 4 and 5, 10th Floor, Kompleks Teruntum Jalan Mahkota, 25000 Kuantan Pahang Darul Makmur Phone: (60 9) 5156857-8 Fax: (60 9) 5156855 E-mail: fmmktan@fmm.jaring.my

Johor Branch Nos. 1 and 3, Jalan Kencana Mas 1/1 Tebrau Business Park Kawasan Perindustrian Tebrau III 81100 Johor Bahru Johor Darul Takzim Phone: (60 7) 3577613 Fax: (60 7) 3577617-8 E-mail: fmmjhr@fmm.jaring.my

Malacca Branch D3-4 Plaza Jayamuda Jalan Pelanduk Putih, 75300 Melaka
P.O. Box 61, 75710 Melaka Phone: (60 6) 2831639 Fax: (60 6) 2838090 E-mail: fmm_mcca@streamyx.com

Negeri Sembilan Branch No. 83-1 and 84-1, Jalan Toman 5 Kemayan Square, 70200 Seremban Negeri Sembilan Darul Khusus Phone: (60 6) 7627564, 7627568 Fax: (60 6) 7627566 E-mail: fmmns@fmm.jaring.my

Northern Branch (Penang, Kedah and Perlis) 2767, Mukum Satu, Lebuh Tenggiri 2 Bandar Seberang Jaya 13700 Prai, Penang Phone: (60 4) 3992057, 3994091, 3997805 Fax: (60 4) 3994863 E-mail: fmmpng@fmm.jaring.my

Perak Branch No 1, Lorong Raja Di Hilir, Off Jalan Raja Di Hilir 30350 Ipoh, Perak Darul Ridzuan
Phone: (60 5) 5488660 (Hunting Line), 5488550, 5488770
Fax: (60 5 5488221, 5488331
E-mail: fmmprk@streamyx.com

Selangor Branch No. 34, Jalan U1/36, Hicom Glenmarie, Industrial Park, 40150 Shah Alam, Selangor Darul Ehsan P.O. Box 7510 40718 Selangor Darul Ehsan Phone: (60 3) 55692950, 55694171, 55694471 Fax: (60 3) 55694346, 55692576 E-mail: fmmsgor0@streamyx.com

Sabah Representative Office Room No. 1014-1016, 10th Floor The Gaya Centre, Jalan Tun Fuad Stephens 88000 Kota Kinabalu, Sabah Phone: (60 88) 230620 Fax: (60 88) 240620 E-mail: fmmsbah@fmm.jaring.my

Sarawak Representative Office Level 5 (South), Wisma STA 26, Jalan Datuk Abang Abdul Rahim 93450 Kuching, Sarawak Phone: 082 – 332784/7 Fax: 082-332785 E-mail: fmmsrwk@streamyx.com

Membership structure: 2,133 members.

Membership is drawn from all categories of manufacturers, and associations. Also, affiliate membership is open to companies in service industries, for example banks, accounting firms, transport companies.

Products/commodity responsible for:

Manufactured products.

Training:
The Federation organizes conferences and seminars from time to time to enable members to obtain a clear understanding of government policies and procedures, trade and investment opportunities, and provides a forum for a frank interchange of ideas between the public and private sectors.
As part of FMM's effort to assist in the creation of an adequate supply of industrial skills and management capabilities for the industry, a training centre known as the FMM Entrepreneur Skills and Development Centre (FMM ESDC) was established in October 1991. This centre was upgraded to the FMM Institute of Manufacturing (FMM IM) and was officially incorporated on 12 January 1999. As the training arm of the Federation of Malaysian Manufacturers, FMM IM provides a comprehensive range of training programmes and advanced learning opportunities with educational excellence in manufacturing practices and technology.
Category:
Chamber of commerce; trade association; and training/research institute.

MALAYSIA EXPORT CREDIT INSURANCE BERHAD (MECIB)

Office/postal address:
Level 17, Bangunan Bank Industri Bandar Wawasan No. 1016 Jalan Sultan Ismail 50734 Kuala Lumpur
P.O. Box: 11048, Kuala Lumpur
Phone: (60 3) 26910677 Fax: (60 3) 26910353 E-mail: mecib@mecib.com.my
URL: www.mecib.com.my Year established: 1977 Principal function:
x To provide insurance for exporters of locally manufactured products.
Services/activities:
x Conducts seminar/road shows for the policyholders and Malaysian exporters.
Publications issued:
x *Annual Financial and Directors' Report* (vernacular/English). x *Activities/facilities leaflets* (vernacular/English).
Local branches:
Regional Office North (RON)
2nd
Floor, No. 53, Jalan Selat Taman Selat 12000 Butterworth, Pulau Pinang
Phone: (60 4) 3321862
Fax: (60 4) 3322172
E-mail: ron@mecib.com.my
Regional Office South (ROS)
2nd
Floor, No. 95, Jalan Damai Taman Setia Off Jalan Stulang Darat 80300 Johor Bahru Johor Darul Takzim Phone: (607) 2231191 Fax: (607) 2240370 E-mail: ros@mecib.com.my
Membership structure: MECIB is a member of the International Union of Credit and Investment Insurers (Berne Union), and a partner in Coface's Credit Alliance and Info Alliance Group.
Category:
Export credit insurance.

MALAYSIA EXTERNAL TRADE DEVELOPMENT CORPORATION (MATRADE)

Office/postal address:
7th
Floor, Wisma Sime Darby
Jalan Raja Laut
50350 Kuala Lumpur
P.O. Box: 13509, 50812 Kuala Lumpur
Phone: (60 3) 26947259 Fax: (60 3) 26947362-3
E-mail: info@matrade.gov.my URL: www.matrade.gov.my
Year established: 1 March 1993
Principal functions:
x To promote, assist and develop Malaysia's external trade with particular emphasis on the export of manufactured and semi-manufactured products and services;
x To formulate and implement export marketing strategies and trade promotion activities to promote Malaysia's exports;
x To undertake commercial intelligence and market research and create a comprehensive database of information for the improvement and development of Malaysia's trade;
x To enhance and protect Malaysia's international trade interest abroad;
x To promote, facilitate and assist in the service area related to trade.
Services/activities:
x Maintains and updates a database of Malaysian exporters comprising manufacturers, traders and services providers;
x Maintains MATRADE Business Library that provides a wide range of business and trade information;
x Maintains MATRADE online, a computerized database which comprises "Stats Online" and "Biz Info";
x Produces publications for international and domestic circulation;
x Disseminates information on overseas markets and business opportunities to Malaysian companies;
x Organizes and manages Malaysia's participation in international trade fairs overseas;
x Organizes, together with the Ministry of International Trade and Industry and the Malaysian Industrial Development Authority, a number of trade and investment missions to major existing and emerging markets;
x Organizes specialized marketing missions overseas to explore and identify trade opportunities for selected products and services;

x Organizes Malaysian products exhibitions to showcase "Made-in-Malaysia" products and services;

x Organizes, in collaboration with major departmental stores, "Made-in-Malaysia" in-store promotion to introduce Malaysian products directly to consumers overseas;

x Sets up information booths in selected trade fairs to disseminate information on Malaysian products and services as well as to display product catalogues of Malaysian companies;

x Promotes, in collaboration with relevant government agencies, professional bodies and associations, the export of major services sectors such as construction and engineering, education, healthcare, information and communications technology.

x Manages the Malaysia Export Exhibition Centre, a permanent display centre located in Kuala Lumpur, where Malaysian companies can showcase their products to foreign buyers and incoming trade delegations;

x Manages Malaysia's first overseas trade exhibition centre in West Asia: Malaysia Trade Centre, Dubai;

x Responds to trade related enquiries from foreign buyers, trade associations, chambers of commerce, foreign missions in Malaysia as well as business visitors to Malaysia;

x Organizes inward buying missions;

x Receives visits of foreign trade delegations;

x Disseminates trade enquiries from foreign companies wishing to source for Malaysian products and services;

x Posts international tender notifications on website;

x Organizes seminars and workshops to nurture new exporters and update existing exporters on trade developments and business opportunities in international markets;

x Is involved in evaluating candidates for Export Excellence Awards.

Publications issued:

x *Malaysia ICT Products and Services Directory and CD ROM.*

x *Building Materials 2004/05.*

x *Malaysia Exports 2003/04 and CD-ROM.*

x *Electrical & Electronics Directory 2003/04.*

x *Malaysia Branding For The World and CD-ROM.*

x *Malaysia Automotive Component Parts and Accessories and CD-ROM.*

x *Malaysia Conventions Exhibitions 2005 -March 2005 Edition* (biennial).

x *Malaysia Heavy Vehicles & Machinery Directory and CDROM.*

x *Trade Mart* (bimonthly).

Local branches:

Lot C5.2A, 5th Floor, Block C Peti Mel No. 5 Bangunan KWSP Jalan Karamunsing 88100 Kota Kinabalu Sabah Phone: (60 88) 240881, 242881 Fax:: (60 88) 243881 E-mail: sabah@matrade.gov.my

1st
floor, FMM Building
2767, Mukim 1, Lebuh Tenggiri 2
Bandar Seberang Jaya
13700 Seberang Perai Tengah
Penang
Phone: (60 43) 982020
Fax: (60 43) 982288
E-mail: penang@matrade.gov.my

Offices abroad:

Africa:

Malaysian Trade Commission Ground Floor Building 5 Commerce Square Office Park 39, Rivonia Road Sandhurst, Sandton Johannesburg, South Africa Phone: (27 11) 2682380, 2682381 Fax: (27 11) 2682382 E-mail: johannesburg@matrade.gov.my

MalaysianTrade Commission
3rd
Floor, North Wing
Victoria Towers, Kilimanjaro Avenue
Upper Hill
P.O. Box 48916 00100 Nairobi GPO, Kenya Phone: (254 20) 2730070-1 Fax: (254 20) 2730069 E-mail: nairobi@matrade.gov.my

Australia: Malaysian Trade Commissioner Malaysia External Trade Development Corporation (MATRADE) Consulate of Malaysia Level 4, Malaysian Airlines Building 16, Spring Street Sydney, NSW 2000 Australia Phone: (61 2) 92522270 Fax: (61 2) 92522285 E-mail: sydney@matrade.gov.my

East Asia:

Embassy of Malaysia
Trade Section, C501 and C502

Office Building, Kempinski HoPhone:
Beijing Lufthansa Centre
50, Liangmaqiao Road
Chaoyang District
Beijing 100016, China
Phone: (86 10) 84515109, 84515113 (86 10) 84515110
Fax: (86 10) 84515112
E-mail: beijing@matrade.gov.my
Consulate General of Malaysia Trade Section (MATRADE) Tower A, 23/F Centre Plaza 161 Lin He Xi Lu, Tian He Guangzhou, 510620, China Phone: (86 20) 28858212-3, 28858215 Fax: (86 20) 28858393 E-mail: guangzhou@matrade.gov.my
Trade Consul Consulate General of Malaysia Trade Section Ground Floor, Malaysia Building 50, Gloucester Road, Wanchai Hong Kong, China Phone: (85 2) 25278273 Fax: (85 2) 28042866 E-mail: hongkong@matrade.gov.my
Malaysian Trade Commissioner Embassy of Malaysia Commercial Section
2nd
Floor, 4-1, Hannam-Dong Yongsan-Gu Seoul 140-210, Republic of Korea Phone: (82 2) 7953210, 79521503 Fax: (82 2) 7927746 E-mail: seoul@matrade.gov.my
Malaysian Trade Commissioner Consulate General of Malaysia Trade Section Units 807-809
8th
Floor, Shanghai Kerry Centre 1515, Nanjing Road (West) Shanghai 200040, China Phone: (86 21) 62894420, 62894467 Fax: (86 21) 62894381 E-mail: shanghai@matrade.gov.my
Malaysian Friendship and Trade Centre Trade Section 10-D, Hung Kuo Building 167, Tun Hwa North Road Taipei City 11151, Taiwan Province of China Phone: (88 62) 25452260, 27199830 Fax: (88 62) 27181877 E-mail: taipei@matrade.gov.my
Malaysia External Trade Development Corporation (MATRADE) Ginza Showadori Building, 6F. 8-14-14, Ginza, Chuo-ku Tokyo 104-0061, Japan Phone: (81 3) 3544 0712-3 Fax: (81 3) 3544 0714 E-mail: tokyo@matrade.gov.my
Consulate General of Malaysia Malaysian Trade Commissioner 2A, 2nd Floor 554 and 555, Anna Salai Teynampet Chennai – 600 018, India Phone: (91 44) 24313722-3 Fax: (91 44) 24313725 E-mail: chennai@matrade.gov.my
Embassy of Malaysia (Trade Office) 35, South Sathorn Road Tungmahamed, Sathorn Bangkok, 10120, Thailand Phone: (66 2) 6792190-9 ext: 2209, 679 2131 Fax: (66 2) 6792200 E-mail: bangkok.chun@matrade.gov.my Malaysian Trade Commissioner Consulate General of Malaysia Trade Commissioner's Office 1208, 12th Floor, Me Linh Point Tower 2, Ngo Duc Ke Street, District 1 Ho Chi Minh City, Viet Nam Phone: (84 8) 8299023, 8298256 Fax: (84 8) 8231882 E-mail: hcmc@matrade.gov.my
Malaysia External Trade Development Corporation (MATRADE) 12th
Floor Plaza Mutiara Jl. Lingkar Kuningan Kav E1.2 No. 1 and 2 Kawasan Mega Kuningan Jakarta 12950, Indonesia
Phone: (62 21) 5764297, 5764322
Fax: (62 21) 5764321
E-mail jakarta@matrade.gov.my
Embassy of Malaysia (Trade Office) 3/F, Malaysian Embassy Bldg 107, Tordesillas Street Salcedo Village Makati, Metro Manila, Philippines Phone: (63 2) 8174581, ext: 218, 8174551, 8174553 Fax: (63 2) 8163114 E-mail: manila.neil@matrade.gov.my
Malaysia External Trade Development Corporation (MATRADE) Singapore Office 100, Beach Road #33-01/03 Shaw Towers 189702, Singapore Phone: (02) 63922238 Fax: (02) 63922239 E-mail: singapore@matrade.gov.my
West Asia:
Malaysia External Trade Development Corporation (MATRADE) 17th
Floor, North Tower
Nile City Building
Cornish El Nil ST
Ramlet Beulac
Cairo, Egypt
Phone: (20 2) 5806632
Fax: (20 2) 5806601
E-mail cairo@matrade.gov.my
Consul General / Malaysian Trade Commissioner Consulate General of Malaysia Lot 1-3 Ground and 6 – 10 Mezzanine Floors Al-Shafeena Building, Near Lamcy Plaza Al Za'abeel Road, P.O. Box 4598 Dubai, United Arab Emirates Phone: (97 14) 3355528, 3355538 Fax: (97 14) 3352220 E-mail: dubai@matrade.gov.my
Malaysian Trade Commissioner Consulate General of Malaysia Commercial Section
14th
Floor, Saudi Business Centre Madina Road, P.O Box 20802 Jeddah 21465, Saudi Arabia Phone: (96 62) 6532143, 6532198 Fax: (96 62) 6530274 E-mail: jeddah@matrade.gov.my
Latin America:
Malaysian Trade Commissioner Malaysia External Trade Development Corporation (MATRADE) Oficina Comercial De Malasia Embajada De Malasia Avda. Tajamar 183 Oficina 302 – Las Condes Santiago, Chile Phone: (56 2) 2342647, 4310080 Fax: (56 2) 234 2652 E-mail: santiago@matrade.gov.my
Malaysian Trade Commissioner Embassy of Malaysia 771, Alameda Santos, Suite 72
7th
Floor, 01419-001, São Paulo, Brazil Phone: (55 11) 32852966 Fax: (55 11) 32891595 E-mail: saopaulo@matrade.gov.my
North America:
Trade Commissioner/ Consul Commercial Consulate General of Malaysia Commercial Section 550, South Hope Street, Suite 400 Los Angeles, CA 90071, United States of America Phone: (1 213) 8929034 Fax: (1 213) 9559142 E-mail: losangeles@matrade.gov.my

Trade Commissioner/ Consul Commercial Consulate General of Malaysia (Commercial Section)

3rd
Floor, 313 East, 43rd Street New York, NY 10017, United States of America Phone: (1 212) 6820232 Fax: (1 212) 983 1987 E-mail: newyork@matrade.gov.my
Europe:
Embassy of Malaysia (Malaysian Trade Office) Museum Atrium Budapest
VI. Dosza Gyorgy Ut 84/B Budapest, Hungary Phone: (36 1) 4880810 Fax: (36 1) 4880824 E-mail: budapest@matrade.gov.my
Malaysian Trade Commissioner Embassy of Malaysia Trade Section Malaysia Trade Commission Rolex Haus, 6th Etage Dompropst-Ketzer-Street 1-9 50667 Cologne, Germany Phone: (49 221) 124000, 124007 Fax: (49-221) 1390416 E-mail: cologne@matrade.gov.my
Malaysian Trade Commissioner Commercial Section
3rd
and 4th Floor 17 Curzon Street London W1J 5HR, United Kingdom Phone: (44 20) 74995255, 74994644 Fax: (44 20) 74994597 E-mail: london@matrade.gov.my
Malaysia Trade Commissioner Service Commercial de Malaisie Ambassade de Malaisie 90, Avenue des Champs Elysées 75008 Paris, France Phone: (33 1) 40760000, 40760034 Fax: (33 1) 40760001 E-mail: paris@matrade.gov.my
Consul and Trade Commissioner Consulate of Malaysia Commercial Service
5th
Floor, Via Vittor Pisani 31 20124 Milan, Italy Phone: (39 02) 66981839, 6690501 Fax: (39 02) 6702872 E-mail: milan@matrade.gov.my
Malaysian Trade Commissioner Trade Section Embassy of Malaysia Mosfilmovskaya Ulitsa 50 Moscow 117192 Russia Federation Phone: (70 95) 1471514, 1471523 Fax: (70 95) 1436043 E-mail: moscow@matrade.gov.my
Malaysia Trade and Distribution Centre Rotterdam Innsbrugweg 226 3047 AH Rotterdam, Netherlands Phone: (31 10) 4627759 Fax: (31 10) 4627349 E-mail: rotterdam@matrade.gov.my
Membership structure: 9,465 members (as of 30 June 2005).
Products/commodity responsible for:
Export of manufactured and semi-manufactured products and services.
Category:
Trade promotion organization.

MALAYSIAN INDUSTRIAL DEVELOPMENT AUTHORITY (MIDA)

Office/postal address:
Block 4, Plaza Sentral Jalan Stesen Sentral 5 Kuala Lumpur Sentral 50470 Kuala Lumpur
Phone: 60 (3) 2267 3633 Fax: 60 (3) 2274 7970
E-mail: promotion@mida.gov.my URL: www.mida.gov.my
Year established: 1967
Principal functions:
The Malaysian Industrial Development Authority (MIDA) is the Government's principal agency for the promotion and coordination industrial development. It is the first point of contact for investors who intend to set up projects in manufacturing and its related support services sectors in Malaysia. Overseas investors can contact MIDA for assistance in planning their fact-finding trip to Malaysia.
Functions of MIDA:

- To promote foreign and local investments in the manufacturing and services sectors;
- To undertake planning for industrial development in Malaysia;
- To recommend policies and strategies on industrial promotion and development to the Minister of International Trade and Industry;
- To evaluate applications for manufacturing licences and expatriate posts; tax incentives for manufacturing activities, tourism, R&D, training institutions and software development; and duty exemption on raw materials, components and machinery;
- To assist companies in the implementation and operation of their projects, and to offer assistance through direct consultation and cooperation with the relevant authorities at both the federal and state levels;
- To facilitate the exchange of information and coordination among institutions engaged in or connected with industrial development;
- To further enhance MIDA's role of assisting investors, senior representatives from key agencies are stationed at MIDA headquarters in Kuala Lumpur to advise investors on government policies and procedures. These representatives include officials from the Immigration Department, Royal Customs Malaysia, Department of Environment and Tenaga Nasional Berhad.

Services/activities:

As detailed under Principal functions.

Publications issued:

- *Malaysia: Investment in the Manufacturing Sector Policies, Incentives and Facilities* (English/Japanese/French/German/Italian/Mandarin/Taiwan Province of China Mandarin/ Korean).
- *Guidebook on Key Services Supporting the Manufacturing Sector* (English).
- *The Costs of Doing Business in Malaysia* (English/Bahasa Malaysia/Japanese/French/German/Italian/Mandarin/Taiwan Province of China Mandarin).
- *Business Opportunities in Malaysia's Electronics Industry* (English).
- *Business Opportunities in Malaysia's Medical Device Industry* (English).
- *Profit from Malaysia's Petrochemical Industry* (English).
- *Photonics: Opportunities for Growth in Malaysia* (English).
- *Electronics Manufacturing Services: Malaysia's EMS Advantage* (English).
- *Make Malaysia Your Biotechnology Hub* (English).
- *Food Industry in Malaysia* (English).
- *Malaysia's Machinery and Equipment Industry* (English).
- *Map of Malaysia* (English).
- *MIDA Annual Report, 2003* (English/Bahasa Malaysia).
- *Why Malaysia* (English).
- *MIDA Corporate Leaflet* (English/Japanese/French/German/ Italian/Mandarin/Taiwan Province of China Mandarin).

Local branches:

Room 15.03, Level 15 Wisma LKN 49, Jalan Wong Ah Fook 80000 Johor Bahru Johor Darul Ta'zim Phone: 60 (7) 224 2550/ 5500 Fax: 60 (7) 224 2360 E-mail: midajb@tm.net.my

5th

Floor, Menara Yayasan Islam Terengganu Jalan Sultan Omar 20300 Kuala Terengganu Terengganu Darul Iman Phone: 60 (9) 622 7200 Fax: 60 (9) 623 2260 E-mail: midakt@pd.jaring.my

8th

Floor, Wisma PKNK Jalan Sultan Badlishah 05000 Alor Setar Kedah Darul Aman Phone: 60 (4) 731 3978 Fax: 60 (4) 731 2439 E-mail: midaas@po.jaring.my

Suite 3, 11th Floor Kompleks Teruntum

P.O. Box 178 25720 Kuantan Pahang Darul Makmur Phone: 60 (9) 513 7334 Fax: 60 (9) 513 7333 E-mail: midaphg@po.jaring.my

5th

Floor, Bangunan PKINK Jalan Tengku Maharani Puteri 15000 Kota Bharu Kelantan Darul Naim Phone: 60 (9) 748 3151 Fax: 60 (9) 744 7294 E-mail: midakb@po.jaring.my

2nd

Floor, Wisma Wan Mohamed Jalan Panglima Bukit Gantang Wahab

P.O. Box 210, 30720 Ipoh Perak Darul Ridzuan

Phone: 60 (5) 253 9300

Fax: 60 (5) 255 2661

E-mail: midaprk@po.jaring.my

3rd

Floor, Menara MITC Kompleks MITC Jalan Konvensyen 75450 Ayer Keroh Melaka Phone: 60 (6) 232 2876/78 Fax: 60 (6) 232 2875 E-mail: midamel@po.jaring.my

Jalan Lapan Belas, Off Jalan Tun Razak, P.O.Box 11915 88821 Kota Kinabalu Sabah Phone: 60 (88) 211 411 Fax: 60 (88) 211 412 E-mail: midasbh@tm.net.my

4.03 Tingkat 4, Menara PSCI 39, Jalan Sultan Ahmad Shah 10050 Pulau Pinang Pulau Pinang Phone: 60 (4) 228 0575 Fax: 60 (4) 228 0327 E-mail: midapg@po.jaring.my

Room 404, 4th Floor Bangunan Bank Negara No. 147, Jalan Satok

P.O. Box 716 93714 Kuching Sarawak Phone: 60 (82) 254 251 / 237 484 Fax: 60 (82) 252 375 E-mail: mida_kch@tm.net.my

Offices abroad:

Level 3, MAS Building 16 Spring Street Sydney NSW 2000, Australia Phone: (61 2) 9251 1933 Fax: (61 2) 9251 4333 E-mail: midasyd@bigpond.net.au

4th

Floor, Aoyama 246 Building 5-6-26, Minami-Aoyama Minato-ku, Tokyo 107-0062, Japan Phone: (81 3) 3409 3680 / 3409 3681 Fax: (81 3) 3409 3460 E-mail: midatyo@blue.ocn.ne.jp URL: www.midajapan.or.jp

3rd

Floor, Takahashi Building 5-9-3, Nishi-tenma Kita-ku, Osaka 530-0047, Japan Phone: 81 (6) 6313 3121 / 313 3221 Fax: 81 (6) 6313 3321 E-mail: midaosaka@mida.or.jp

Embassy of Malaysia 4-1 Hannam-dong Yongsan-gu, Seoul 140-210, Republic of Korea Phone: (82 2) 798 0115 Fax: (82 2) 792 2427 E-mail: midasel@chollian.net

Malaysian Friendship and Trade Centre

8th

Floor, San Ho Plastics Building 102 Tun Hua North Road Taipei, 105 Taiwan Province of China
Phone: (88 62) 2713 2626 Fax: (88 62) 2514 7581 E-mail: midatpe@ms18.hinet.net

Consulate General of Malaysia Units 807-809, Level 8, Shanghai Kerry Centre No. 1515, Nanjing Road (West) Shanghai, 200040, China Phone: (86 21) 6289 4547 / 5298 6335 Fax: (86 21) 6279 4009 E-mail: midash@online.sh.cn
42 Avenue Kleber 75116 Paris, France Phone: (33 1) 4727 3689 / 4727 6696 Fax: (33 (1) 4755 6375 E-mail: mida.paris@wanadoo.fr
6th
Floor, Rolex Haus Dompropst-Ketzer-Str. 1-9 50667 Cologne, Germany Phone: (49 221) 124 008 / 9 Fax: (49 221) 136 198 E-mail: mida.cologne@t-online.de
Consulate of Malaysia
4th
Floor Via Vittor Pisani 31 20124 Milan, Italy Phone: (39 02) 6698 4614 / 6698 4647 Fax: (39 (02) 6698 4749 E-mail: midamln@tin.it
Embassy of Malaysia Karlavagen 37
P.O. Box 26053 S-10041 Stockholm, Sweden Phone: 46 (8) 791 7690 / 7942 Fax: 46 (8) 791 8761 E-mail: mida@malemb.se
17, Curzon Street London W1J 5HR, United Kingdom Phone: 44 (20) 7493 0616 Fax: 44 (20) 7493 8804 E-mail: midalon@btconnect.com
Consulate General of Malaysia Malaysian Industrial Development Authority 550, South Hope Street, Suite 400 Los Angeles, CA 90071, United States of America Phone: 1 (213) 955 9183 / 9877 Fax: 1 (213) 955 9878 E-mail: lacamida@aol.com
John Hancock Centre, Suite 1515 875, North Michigan Avenue Chicago, IL 60611, United States of America
Phone: 1 (312) 787 4532
Fax: 1 (312) 787 4769
E-mail: mida@midachicago.org
Consulate General of Malaysia 313 East, 43rd Street New York, NY 10017, United States of America Phone: 1 (212) 687 2491 Fax: 1 (212) 490 8450 E-mail: mida@midany.org
226 Airport Parkway, Suite 480 San Jose, CA 95110, United States of America Phone: 1 (408) 392 0617/8 Fax: 1 (408) 392 0619 E-mail: midasanjose@aol.com
2 Oliver Street, Suite 1107 Boston, MA 02109, United States of America Phone: 1 (617) 338 1128 / 338 1129 Fax: 1 (617) 338 6667 E-mail: midaboston@aol.com
Areas/industries where investment is encouraged:
x High technology, capital intensive and knowledge driven industries in areas such as: -Biotechnology; -Advanced electronics; -Optics and photonics; -Wireless technology; -Display technology (TFT, LCD, plasma and parts).
x Manufacture of intermediate goods in industries such as: -Machinery and equipment; -Components and parts; -Moulds and dies.
x Resourced-based sector, particularly in the following sectors: -Food; -Value added products from oil palm biomass (particle
board, MDF board and animal feed).
x Activities and products in the promoted list (Publication -
Malaysia: Investment in the Manufacturing Sector – Policies, Incentives and Facilities).
Titles of laws and regulations related with investment:
x Industrial Coordination Act (ICA), 1975. x Promotion of Investment Act (PIA), 1986. x Income Tax Act, 1967. x Customs Act, 1967. x Free Zones Act, 1990. x Sales Tax Act, 1967. x Excise Act, 1976.
Category:
Investment promotion agency.

MALAYSIAN INTERNATIONAL CHAMBER OF COMMERCE AND INDUSTRY (MICCI)*

Office/postal address:
8th
Floor, Block C Plaza Mont Kiara No. 2, Jalan Kiara 50480 Kuala Lumpur
Phone: (60 3) 62017708 Fax: (60 3) 62017705-6
E-mail: micci@micci.com URL: www.micci.com
Year established: 1837
Principal functions:
x To promote investment and protect free enterprise and the interest of the international investment community;
x To enhance trade, commerce, industry and investment.
Services/activities:
x Liaises with government ministries and departments; x Provides an information and consultation service; x Issues Certificate of Origin and ATA Carnets.
Publications issued:
x MICCI Members' Directory. x Investor's Guide. x MICCI Bulletin. x Annual Report.
Local branches:
MICCI Penang Branch Phone: (60 4) 2270589 Fax: (60 4) 2270124
MICCI Perak Branch Phone: (60 5) 2532233 Fax: (60 5) 2533206
MICCI Johor Branch Phone: (60 7) 2224448 Fax: (60 7) 2248088
MICCI Sabah Branch Phone: (60 88) 248332 Fax: (60 88) 268332
MICCI MNS Branch Phone: (60 6) 2816998 Fax: (60 6) 2844368
Membership structure: 1,050 members.

Category:
Chamber of commerce.

MALAYSIAN PALM OIL PROMOTION COUNCIL (MPOPC)*

Office/postal address:
2nd
Floor, Wisma Sawit Lot 6, SS6, Jalan Perbandaran 47301 Kelana Jaya Selangor Darul Ehsan
Phone: (60 3) 78064097 Fax: (60 3) 78062272
E-mail: kamal@mpopc.org.my, haron@mpopc.org.my URL: www.mpopc.org.my
Year established: 1990
Principal functions:
x To undertake promotional activities and to remove obstacles and create opportunities;
x To enhance the marketability and image of Malaysian palm oil in the world.
Services/activities:
x Promotes a positive image of Malaysian palm oil; x Packages and disseminates plausible technical information to influence the market; x Generates comprehensive market information; x Collates, analyses and disseminates market information to the
local industry.
Publications issued:
x *Annual Report* (annually, English). x *Palm Oil Link* (twice a month, English). x *Perspective* (quarterly, English). x Palm oil information series.
Offices abroad:
MPOPC Regional Office 62-63, Motijheel Commercial Area
7th
Floor, Amin Court Building Dhaka, Bangladesh Phone: (880 2) 9571216 Fax: (880 2) 9551836 E-mail: mpopc@bangla.net
MPOPC Regional Office Shanghai Westgate Mall Co. Ltd. Room 1610B, No. 10, Nanjing Road (W) Shanghai 200041, China Phone: (86 21) 62182085-6 Fax: (86 21) 62181125 E-mail: mpopc@mail.onloin.sh.cn
MPOPC Regional Office No. 54, Michel Bakhoum Street Dokki-Giza, Cairo, Egypt Phone: (20 2) 7618190 Fax: (20 2) 7618190 E-mail: mpopc@brainyl.ie-eg.com
MPOPC Regional Office C-10, Gulmohar Park New Delhi 110 049, India Phone: (91 11) 26520500 Fax: (91 11) 26535315 E-mail: mpopc@giasd101.vsnl.net.in
MPOPC Regional Office 11- 3rd Floor, Leeds Centre Main Boulevard Gulberg III Lahore, Pakistan Phone: (92 42) 5716600-1 Fax: (92 42) 5716602 E-mail: mpopc@brain.net.pk
MPOPC Regional Office 21515 Hawthorne Boulevard, Suite 690 Torrance, CA 90503, United States of America Phone: (1 310) 9443910 Fax: (1 310) 9443544 E-mail: mpocusa@aol.com URL: www.malaysianpalmusa.com
MPOPC Regional Office Rua Estella, 515-Bloco H - Conj. 192 Vila Mariana 0401-002-São Paulo-Sp-Brazil Phone: (55 11) 55722699 Fax: (55 11) 50846131 E-mail: mpopc@icn.com.br
MPOPC Regional Office
P.O. Box 1591, M.E.C.C. 4301 South Africa Phone: (27 31) 5666171-2 Fax: (27 31) 5666170 E-mail: mpopc@castcoast.co.za
Products/commodity responsible for:
Palm oil.
Category:
Market promotion for palm oil.

MALAYSIAN PINEAPPLE INDUSTRY BOARD (MPIB)

Office/postal address:
Wisma NANAS No. 5, Jalan Padi Mahsuri Bandar Baru UDA 81200 Johor Bahru
Phone: (60 7) 2361211, 2361012 Fax: (60 7) 2365694
E-mail: mpib@tm.net.my URL: www.mpib.gov.my
Year established: 1957
Principal functions:
x To provide financial assistance for research; x To negotiate agreement on prices and grades of pineapple; x To regulate production and marketing; x To administer a cess fund and make recommendations
regarding the rate of cess; x To administer quality control programmes; x To collect statistics of the industry; x To handle any other matters affecting the industry.
Services/activities:
x Undertakes registration of exporters; x Undertakes registration of canneries, transporter and vendor; x Endorses canned/fresh pineapple export's permit; x Promotes the programmes of marketing development
infrastructure to support the growth of the industry;
x Promotes the quality control programmes, which include the production of fresh pineapple, canned pineapple and pineapple base products to ensure that the quality of the products is within the specification and "Codex Alimentarius" Standard.
Publication issued:
x *The Malaysian Pineapple Directory.*
Products/commodity responsible for:

Processing of canned pineapple products; processing of related products such as cottage industries, pharmaceuticals and cosmetics; domestic market; export market; and research and development.

Areas/industries where investment is encouraged:
Canneries; plantations; cottage industries; and research and development.
Titles of laws and regulations on foreign investment:
x Pineapple Industry (Export Marketing) Regulation, 1957; x Pineapple Industry (Cess on Export) Regulation, 1959; x Pineapple Industry (Fruit Control) Regulation, 1957; x Pineapple Industry (Cannery Control) Regulation, 1959.
Category:

MALAYSIAN RUBBER BOARD (MRB)

Office/postal address:
Tingkat 17-18 Bangunan Getah Asli (Menara) 148, Jalan Ampang 50450 Kuala Lumpur
P.O. Box: 10150, 50908 Kuala Lumpur
Phone: (60 3) 92062000 Fax: (60 3) 21634492
E-mail: dg@lgm.gov.my URL: www.lgm.gov.my
Year established: 1998 (as a result of the merger of the Malaysian Rubber Research and Development Board (MRRDB), Rubber Research Institute of Malaysia (RRIM) and Malaysian Rubber Exchange and Licensing Board (MRELB)).
Principal function:
x To develop Malaysian natural rubber through research and development, and trade through market intelligence activities and services, management of rubber exchange, licensing and supervision of rubber producing and dealing activities including quality control.
Services/activities:
x To implement policies and developmental programmes to ensure the viability of the rubber industry in Malaysia;
x To promote and implement research and development activities in the production, use and consumption of rubber; x To plan, coordinate and monitor all rubber research and development activities;
x To regulate the rubber industry, in particular in relation to dealings in rubber, packing, grading, shipping and export of rubber;
x To control and monitor the quality of rubber, rubber planting materials and rubber products; x To develop, transfer, exploit and promote research findings; x To provide technical, advisory and consultancy services to the rubber industry; x To administer and manage the fund; x To regulate the Malaysian rubber market and manage the Malaysian rubber exchange; x To formulate and implement an international marketing strategy for the rubber industry of Malaysia; x To liaise and cooperate with rubber agencies within or outside Malaysia to further enhance the rubber industry of Malaysia; x To plan and implement human resources training in line with the needs of the rubber industry; x To be the resource and information centre for the rubber industry.
Publications issued:
x *Annual Report*. x *Malaysian Rubber Review*. x *Journal of Rubber Research*. x *Malaysian Rubber Digest*. x *Monographs*.
Commodity board.
Local branches:
Lot PT. 117753 Jalan Sultan Azian Shah Utara 31400 Ipoh, Perak DR Phone: (60 5) 5485048
No. 23F, Jalan Zaaba 70100 Seremban, Negeri Sembilan DK Phone: (60 6) 7655801
No. 58A, Jalab Buloh Kasap 85000 Segamat, Johor DT Phone: (60 7) 9311512
No. 4, Jalan IM 6/1, Bandar Indera Mahkota 25200 Kuantan, Pahang DM Phone: (60 9) 5721210
Lot 3322, Blok 14, Jalan Sultan Tengah Petra Jaya 93050 Kuching, Sarawak Phone: (60 82) 447977
No. 127, Taman Peringatan Petagas
P.O.
Box 14890 88859 Kota Kinabalu, Sabah Phone: (60 88) 212139
Rubber Research Institute of Malaysia (RRIM) 260, Jalan Ampang
P.O.
Box 10150 50908 Kuala Lumpur Phone: (60 3) 42567033
RRIM Research Station RRIM Research Station Sungai Buloh 47000 Sg. Buloh, Selangor DE Phone: (60 3) 61561121
RRIM Research Station Kota Tinggi Batu 3 ½, Jalan Mawai 81900 Kota Tinggi, Johor DT Phone: (60 7) 8831277
Tun Abdul Razak Research Centre Brickendonbury, Hertford SG13 8NL United Kingdom Phone: (44 1992) 584966
Membership structure: 225 members (as of 1994).
x Ordinary members: producers, manufacturers' buying agents, estates' selling agents, brokers, dealers (total 208 as of 1994);
x Associate members: overseas members (total 17 as of 1994).
Products/commodity responsible for:
Natural rubber.
Category:
Commodity board.

NATIONAL CHAMBER OF COMMERCE AND INDUSTRY OF MALAYSIA (NCCIM)

Office/postal address:
37, Jalan Kia Peng
50450 Kuala Lumpur Phone: (60 3) 21419600 Fax: (60 3) 21413775
E-mail: enquiry@nccim.org.my URL: www.nccim.org.my Year established: 1962 Principal functions:
x To act as an umbrella organization representing five Chambers

of Commerce in Malaysia, namely, the Malay Chamber of Commerce and Industry of Malaysia, Associated Chinese Chamber of Commerce and Industry of Malaysia, the Malaysia Associated Indian Chamber of Commerce and Industry, Malaysian International Chamber of Commerce and Industry, and the Federation of Malaysian Manufacturers;

x To hold consultative status in dealing with the Government effecting economic, trade, investment, human resources and infrastructure development.

Services/activities:

x Organizes seminars, workshops, symposia, conferences, exhibitions and trade missions abroad;

x Participates in annual dialogues with the Ministry of International Trade, Ministry of Finance, Ministry of Domestic Trade and Consumer Affairs, Ministry of Human Resources, Customs Department, Prime Minister's Department, Port Kalang, Authority Standards and Industrial Research Institute of Malaysia.

Publication issued:

x *Suara NCCIM* (quarterly, English).

Membership structure: The Chamber's membership consists of five constituent chambers and two associate members. The constituent Chambers represent the interest of the Malay, Chinese and Indian business communities, the international investors in Malaysia and Malaysian manufacturers.

Category:

Chamber of commerce.

NATIONAL TOBACCO BOARD (NTB)

Office/postal address:

P.O. Box 198 15720 Kota Bharu Kelantan

Phone: (60 9) 7652933 Fax: (60 9) 7655640

E-mail: ltnm@ltn.gov.my URL: www.ltn.gov.my

Year established: 1973

Principal functions:

x To restructure the production system in order to increase the efficiency, productivity and viability of the tobacco industry;

x To provide proper and adequate infrastructure and support services (such as extension, enforcement and marketing) for the production of quality tobacco and the orderly growth of the tobacco industry;

x To promote the development of the upstream and downstream activities of the tobacco sector; x To uplift the socio-economic status of the farmers; x To promote the development of crop integration as an additional source of income to tobacco farmers in achieving the objectives of the Tobacco Industry Restructuring Plan.

Services/activities:

x Provides comprehensive extension services, farm mechanization and transfer of technology (from seed preparation to marketing activities of cured leaves);

x Provides appropriate research and development (R&D) support;

x Provides adequate funding and proper financial management;

x Promotes other food crops to be integrated with tobacco as an additional income for the farmers and maximizing production resources;

x Stabilizes the industry through a quota system;

x Issues licences to curers, grower curers, cigarette manufacturers and also registers tobacco farmers;

x Provides enforcement services to ensure that all rules and regulations of NTB Acts are adhered to; x Produces and distributes quality tobacco seeds; x Undertakes enforcement activities to ascertain that all the rules and regulations and techniques are obeyed by all sectors, monitors and takes necessary actions in preventing tobacco smuggling activities;

x Provides effective human resources development and availability of trained and skilled personnel; x Coordinates between manufacturers, curers and growers.

Publications issued:

x *Annual Report* (Malay). x *Annual Statistics* (Malay/English). x *Quarterly Bulletin* (Malay).

Local branches:

Throughout Malaysia.

Products/commodity responsible for:

Tobacco.

Training:

Courses on tobacco management for curers, farmers and staff. Courses on integrated crop and livestock management fur curers, farmers and staff.

Areas/industries where investment is encouraged:

Food crops/livestock to be integrated with tobacco.

Category:

Commodity board.

PEPPER MARKETING BOARD

Office/postal address:
Lot 1115, Jalan Utama Tanah Putih 93450 Kuching, Sarawak
P.O. Box: 1653, 93450 Kuching, Sarawak
Phone: (60 82) 331811 Fax: (60 82) 336877 E-mail: pmb@pepper.po.my
URL: www.sarawakpepper.gov.my/ Year established: 1972 Principal function:
x To be responsible for the statutory grading of all Sarawak pepper for export, licensing of pepper dealers and exporters, market promotion, farmers' development, trading and the development and promotion of pepper storage, processing and sterilization facilities.
Services/activities:
x Undertakes market regulation through the licensing of dealers and exporters;
x Provides market extension through dialogues and visits to farming communities;
x Conducts domestic and overseas market promotion;
x Provides market information service;
x Undertakes statutory grading of pepper for export;
x Trades in pepper and pepper products;
x Undertakes product development on specialty pepper and new uses of pepper;
x Provides laboratory and industrial services including processing, steam treatment, storage and physical forward market.
Publications issued:
x *Pepper Market Bulletin* (quarterly). x *Pepper Industry Bulletin* (ad hoc). x *Sarawak Pepper Flavours the World* (international cookbook).
Local branches:
BDC Industrial Area
P.O.
Box 279, 96107 Sarikei, Sarawak Phone: (60 84) 654161 Fax: (60 84) 653510
Lot 1152 and 1154, SEDC Industrial Estate Jalan Teng Kung Sui
P.O.
Box 476, 96007 Sibu, Sarawak Phone: (60 84) 211059 Fax: (60 82) 212033
Sub Lot 2, Lot 160 Undup Land District, Km 189 Jalan Sri Aman/ Serian 95007 Bandar Sri Aman, Sarawak Phone: (60 83) 322139 Fax: (60 82) 324069
Batu 9, Jalan Kelupu
P.O.
Box 74, 96507 Bintangor, Sarawak Phone: (60 84) 691618 Fax: (60 84) 691544
Lot 659, Jalan Industri
P.O.
Box 87, 94707 Serian, Sarawak Phone: (60 82) 874234 Fax: (60 82) 874234
Lot 3510, Kemena Light Industrial Area No. 3, Jalan Nyigu, 97000 Bintulu, Sarawak Phone: (60 86) 336900 Fax: (60 86) 311651
Lot 1208, Midgulf Building Jalan Permaisuri
P.O. Box 1245, 98008 Miri, Sarawak Phone: (60 85) 420705 Fax: (60 85) 420745
Km 8, Jalan Tun Razak, Susur Enam 80200 Johor Bahru, Johor Darul Takzim Phone: (60 7) 2352071 Fax: (60 7) 2369872
Products/commodity responsible for:
Pepper and pepper products.
Category:
Commodity board; commodity standard institute; export marketing board; standard, testing, and inspection body; and government agency.

THE PALM OIL REFINERS ASSOCIATION OF MALAYSIA (PORAM)

Office/postal address
801C/802A, Block B Executive Suites Kelana Business Centre 97 Jalan SS7/2 47301 Kelana Jaya, Selangor
Phone: (60 3) 74920006 Fax: (60 3) 74920128
E-mail: poram@poram.org.my URL: www.poram.org.my
Year established: 1975
Principal functions:

- x To collectively support and enhance the status and interest of the palm oil refining industry;
- x To promote the processing, refining and fractionation of palm oil and the manufacture of all products and by-products therefrom;
- x To project an international image of sophistication and reliability;
- x To establish an identity with the public at large as an organization with an important role to play in Malaysia's economic development and as an organization responsibly acting in the interest of the community;

x To be both responsive to the Malaysian Government's overall socio-economic policies and responsible in this role.

Services/activities:

PORAM and the Government: Through PORAM, palm oil refiners in Malaysia can act collectively and in unison to better ensure that the Government understands and recognizes the needs and problems of the industry at all times. PORAM is represented in the relevant government bodies, among which are: x Malaysian Palm Oil Board (MPOB); x Malaysian Palm Oil Promotion Council (MPOPC).

Services to members:

x Provides a continuous flow of valuable information to members, including market reports, summaries of reports on trade missions and research reports;

x Keeps members informed of new or amended government regulations affecting members;

x Handles government contacts and the interpretation to members of the legislative and administrative actions of government regulations;

x Provides guidance to members on problems arising from government regulations and procedures;

x Provides facilities for members to meet and resolve common problems;

x Provides facilities for arbitration under the auspices of the Association;

x Publishes newsletters, guidebooks, brochures and other documents desirable for the promotion and enhancement of the palm oil refining industry;

x Organizes seminars, workshops and training courses for members.

PORAM and export promotion: PORAM assists members in establishing business contacts and promoting their exports, through a wide range of export promotion activities such as: x Receiving trade delegations, receiving trade enquiries and channelling them to members; x Organizing trade missions and arranging for members' participation in government-sponsored missions; x Making recommendations/proposals to Government aimed at increasing exports of processed palm oil products.

PORAM and related organizations: Since its inception, the Association has played significant roles in enhancing the position of the palm oil refining industry in this country as well as abroad. PORAM works closely with the Malaysian Palm Oil Association (MPOA), the Malayan Edible Oil Manufacturers' Association (MEOMA), the Malaysian Oleochemical Manufacturers Group (MOMG) and The Palm Oil Millers' Association (POMA).

PORAM is a member of the National Institute of Oilseed Products (NIOP) and the Federation of Oils, Seeds and Fats Associations Ltd (FOSFA International). Together with FOSFA International, PORAM has jointly issued a contract for Palm Oil Products in Bulk (CIF) or more widely known as the FOSFA 81 Contract.

PORAM is also a founder member of the ASEAN Vegetable Oils Club (AVOC) and is currently serving AVOC as its Secretariat.

Membership structure: 16 members, 57 associate members and supplementary members (subsidiary of full members). The House of PORAM comprises the Chairman of the Association and a ruling Management Board. Members of the Management Board lead the other principal committees which are responsible for specific areas of activity.

These committees are:

1. Commercial and Technical Committee;
2. Price Settlement Committee;
3. Arbitration Rules Execution Committee;
4. Associate Members Committee.

Products/commodity responsible for:

Palm oil products.

Category:

Trade association.

MALDIVES

MALDIVES ASSOCIATION OF TOURISM INDUSTRY (MATI)

Office/postal address:
3rd
Floor, Gadhamoo Building
Boduthakurufaanu Magu
Malé
P.O. Box: 2056
Phone: (960) 321701, 326640 Fax: (960) 326641
E-mail: mati@dhivehinet.net.mv
Year established: 1982

Principal functions:

x To enhance economic and tourism development;

x To seek membership of all important tourism-related bodies;

x To improve organizational capability in serving the members;

x To make the Association become nationally and internationally recognized;

x To actively participate in policy formulation and national development planning activities;

x To enhance MATI's role as liaison between the industry and government;

x To provide members with relevant information to improve their performance.

Services/activities:

Organizational development:

x Provides training;
x Conducts studies and research on tourism-related issues;
x Maintains a library and computerized database on tourism;
x Enhances in-house expertise on relevant areas;
x Disseminates information via newsletters, bulletins and magazines.

Sectoral development: x Attempts to obtain development finance; x Undertakes activities to promote tourism; x Attempts to improve the operation of air travel; x Increases management capabilities; x Makes bidding procedures for resort islands more favourable;

x Recommends new laws and regulations and suggests amendments to existing laws and regulations;
x Promotes environmentally sound solid waste disposal methods;
x Creates awareness of reef resources management;
x Encourages utilization of ozone friendly appliances;
x Promotes excursion, diving, marine sports, game fishing, souvenirs, arts and culture, entertainment.

Membership structure: 99 members. Areas/industries where investment is encouraged:
Tourism promotion: Asia/Pacific and Europe.
Category:
Industrial promotion organization.

MALDIVES INDUSTRIAL FISHERIES COMPANY LIMITED

Office/postal address:
Block No. 389 Hilaalee Magu Malé 20-04
Phone: (960) 3323932, ext. 123 Fax: (960) 3323955
E-mail: info@mifco.com.mv URL: www.mifco.com.mv
Year established: 1 November 1993
Principal functions:

x To export raw, frozen and canned fish;
x To establish branch offices, agencies and subsidiary companies for the purpose of overseas trading.

Services/activities:
As detailed under Principal functions.
Category:
Industrial promotion organization.

MALDIVES TOURISM PROMOTION BOARD

Office/postal address:
4th
Floor, Bank of Maldives Building Boduthakurufaanu Magu Malé 02-05
Phone: (960) 323228 Fax: (960) 323229
E-mail: mtpb@visitmaldives.com URL: www.visitmaldives.com
Year established: 1998
Principal functions:

x To promote quality and sustainable growth in the tourism industry;
x To foster a well utilized and financially healthy private sector industry, enabling the industry to deliver long-term economic, social and cultural benefits to Maldives;
x To contribute to enhancements in Maldives' unspoiled marine environment for the benefit of the people and visitors of Maldives.

Services/activities:
x Promotes Maldives using various forms of media and other promotional media.
Publications issued:
x *Resort and Hotel Guides.* x *Promotional leaflets.* x *Statistic reports.* x *Market reports.*
Office abroad:
Maldives Government Tourist Information Office Bethmann Strasse 58 60311 Frankfurt/Main, Germany Phone: (49 69) 27404420 Fax: (49 69) 27404422 E-mail: maldivesinfo.ffm@t-online.de URL: www.visitmaldives.com
Areas/industries where investment is encouraged:
Tourism and fisheries.
Category:
National tourism board; and tourism promotion board.

MINISTRY OF TRADE AND INDUSTRIES

Office/postal address:

Ghaazee Building Ameeru Ahmed Magu Malé 20-05
Phone: (960) 323668 Fax: (960) 323840
E-mail: contact@trademin.gov.mv URL: www.trademin.gov.mv
Year established: 1982
Principal functions:

- x To formulate and implement regulations governing imports and exports;
- x To issue import and export licences;
- x To issue licences for sale of imported goods;
- x To issue licences for foreign parties who wish to conduct trading activities in the country;
- x To inspect and maintain quality control for dried and salted fish exported from Maldives;
- x To maintain calibration standards;
- x To undertake registration of trade marks, shipping marks and logos;
- x To formulate industrial development policy;
- x To promote, regulate and facilitate private sector investment;
- x To issue licences for fishery activities in the EEZ;
- x To undertake registration of local and foreign investment;
- x To organize the national industrial exhibition.

Services/activities:
As detailed under Principal functions.
Category:
Ministry of Trade.

MARSHALL ISLANDS

TRADE AND INVESTMENT SERVICES DIVISION

Office/postal address:
Ministry of Resources and Development Majuro, MH 96960
P.O. Box: 1727, Majuro
Phone: (692) 6253206/4020 Fax: (692) 6257471
E-mail: rndsec@ntamar.net, rmitisd@ntamar.net
Year established: 1988 (re-established in 2000).
Principal functions:
x To promote sustainable economic advancement and development through support for small business development - including services, exports and import substitutes;
x To promote domestic and foreign investment, giving due concern to the needs, constraints and environmental vulnerabilities of the Marshall Islands.

Services/activities:
Small Business Support Unit:
x Acts as point of information and resources for business and market opportunity assessment;
x Organizes and conducts small business management workshops and seminars aimed at skills training, in collabouration with other agencies involved in business development;
x Assists in developing business plans, proposals, strategic workplans;
x Supports businesses in securing business capital, small business loans, etc.;
x Sets policies, guidelines and standards for the establishment of microenterprise financing services, in cooperation with communities, NGOs and the private sector;
x Identifies and assists in the removal of legal and regulatory barriers to the economic participation of disadvantaged people;
x Advises the Government on business policies conducive to private sector growth;
x Conducts regular surveys among the local business community to determine needs, and respond accordingly;
x Establishes and maintains contacts with other small business support agencies outside the Marshall Islands;
x Develops cooperative partnerships with the Chamber of Commerce and other local businesses not represented in the Chamber;
x Coordinates and cooperates with the local governments, Ministry of Internal Affairs, academic institutions and other relevant bodies on local business development;
x Encourages, supports and undertakes, where necessary, environmental reviews of business projects, in cooperation with the Environmental Protection Authority and relevant local governments, to ensure no undue harm is caused to the natural environment.
Trade Promotion Unit:

- x Encourages and assists the promotion of Marshallese produce and products, either in its own right or in cooperation with any organization involved in exporting;
- x Conducts and/or facilitates product and market research;
- x Facilitates and participates in trade fairs/missions, both regional and international, in order to promote ongoing

product development, awareness and support;
- Establishes and maintains a database of export products, including all trade statistics;
- Identifies new trade opportunities;
- Conducts ongoing product profiles;
- Provides assistance to exporters in the area of customs and quarantine requirements in overseas markets;
- Facilitates the obtaining of funds for the purposes of trade development and promotion, including discussion and negotiation with aid donors;
- Undertakes research into any aspect of domestic trade, commerce and industry, including the conducting of surveys, gathering statistics and publishing reports from time to time;
- Coordinates with the Ministry of Foreign Affairs in formulating advice for the Government on trade policy;
- Creates and maintains a library of trade-related resources for use by the general public;
- Coordinates and cooperates with the local governments, Ministry of Internal Affairs, Environmental Protection Agency, academic institutions and other relevant bodies on trade-related activities.

Investment Promotion Unit:
- Establishes an effective and efficient "one-stop shop" for foreign and domestic investment;
- Coordinates and facilitates investment and trade promotion with overseas representatives;
- Develops and maintains a Foreign Investment Guide;
- Coordinates with other agencies involved in investment promotional activities;
- Develops and maintains a national database and tracking system for foreign investment (Registry of Foreign Investment);
- Develops and maintains a national Reserve List for foreign investment;
- Facilitates current investors and visitors in an efficient and timely manner;
- Develops a list of private sector projects, land and partners available for foreign investment (industry and sector profiles);
- Researches and promotes new investment opportunities;
- Establishes a database of potential investors, for use by the general public;
- Facilitates the further development of an enabling investment environment through close cooperation with the Attorney General's Office on investment policies and legislation;
- Coordinates with the Ministry of Foreign Affairs in formulating advice for the Government on investment policy and legislation;
- Coordinates with the Marshall Islands Development Authority on the Government's privatization efforts of state-owned enterprises (SOEs).

Publications issued:
- *National Investment Policy Statement.*
- *General Guide for Foreign Investors.*
- *Foreign Investment Advisory Board Act, 1989.*
- *Foreign Investment Act, 2000.*

Category:

Trade promotion organization; and investment promotion authority.

Offices abroad:

Ambassador to Fiji
41 Borron Road
P.O. Box 2088
Suva, Fiji
Phone: (679) 387899
Fax: (679) 387115
E-mail: rmisuva@sopacsun.org.fj

Ambassador to the Republic of China
4th Floor, No. 9-1, Lane 62
Tienmou West Road
Shihlin Taipei
Taiwan Province of China
Phone: (886) 2-2873-4884
Fax: (886) 2-2873-4904
E-mail: rmiembtp@ms41.hinet.net

Ambassador to Japan
Rm. #101, Meiji Park Heights
9-9 Minamimoto-Machi
Shinjuku-ku, Tokyo, Japan
Phone: (81 3) 53791701-2
Fax: (81 3) 53791810
E-mail: rmito@din.or.jp

Ambassador to the United States of America
2433 Massachusetts Ave., NW

Washington, DC 20008, United States of America
Phone: (1 202) 2345414
Fax: (1 202) 2323236
E-mail: info@rmiembassyus.org
Consul General to the United States of America
Suite#103, 1888 Lusitania Street
Honolulu, HI 96813, United States of America
Phone: (1 808) 5457767
Fax: (1 808) 5457211
E-mail: rmiconsulate@aol.com
Permanent Mission to the United Nations
18th Floor, 800 2nd Avenue
New York, NY 10017, United States of America
Phone: (1 212) 9833040
Fax: (1 212) 9833202
E-mail: rmiun@aol.com
Membership structure: The Division currently has two employees in its small business support unit, and two in the trade promotion and investment promotion units. They are under the supervision of the Secretary and Deputy Secretary of the Ministry of Resources and Development.
Products/commodity responsible for:
All exportable products.
Training:
Small business development, product development, quality standards.
Areas/industries where investment is encouraged:
Fisheries, tourism, agro-forestry.
Titles of laws and regulations on foreign investment:

DEPARTMENT OF ECONOMIC AFFAIRS*

Office/postal address:
P.O. Box PS-12 Palikir Pohnpei 96941
Phone: (691) 3202646, 3205133 Fax: (691) 3205854
E-mail: fsmrd@mail.fm, fsminvest@mail.fm URL: www.fsminvest.fm
Year established: 1996 (successor of the Department of Resources and Development, 1979).
Principal functions:
x To coordinate and facilitate commerce, industry, trade, tourism, investment and banking matters at the national government level;
x To provide/facilitate technical assistance to the states.
Services/activities:
x Coordinates trade information to the state governments and chambers of commerce in the states;
x Provides and facilitates technical assistance in industry and tourism development;
x Promotes investment, tourism and trade opportunities.
Publications issued:
x *FSM Statistical Yearbook* (periodical, English). x *FSM International Visitor Arrivals;* 2002 (periodical, English).
x *The FSM Planning Framework,* 2000 (triennially, English).
x *FSM Consumer Price Index* (annually, English).
x *FSM 2000 Population and Housing Census Report* (triennially, English).
x *FSM Investment Guide* (English).
x Promotional brochures (English/Japanese).
Local branches:
Department of Commerce and Industry Chuuk State Government
P.O.
Box 280 Weno, Chuuk FM 96942 Phone: (691) 3302552, 3302761 Fax: (691) 3302233 E-mail: ignstephen@msn.com
Department of Commerce and Industry Kosrae State Government
P.O.
Box 600 Tofol, Kosrae FM 96944 Phone: (691) 3703044, 3703170 Fax: (691) 3702066 E-mail: kosraeci@mail.fm
Office of Economic Affairs Pohnpei State Government
P.O.
Box AD Kolonia, Pohnpei FM 96941
Pohnpei Foreign Investment Board
P.O.
Box 539 Kolonia, Pohnpei FM 96941 Phone: (691) 3206689 Fax: (691) 3205296
Department of Resources and Development Yap State Government
P.O.
Box 336 Colonia, Yap FM 96943 Phone: (691) 3502182 Fax: (691) 3502571 E-mail: jgrd@mail.fm
Phone: (691) 3202712, 3202820

Fax: (691) 3205167
E-mail: oea@mail.fm

Offices abroad:
Embassy of the Federated States of Micronesia 1725 N Street, NW Washington, DC, 20036 United States of America Phone: (1 202) 2234383 Fax: (1 202) 2234391 E-mail: fsm@fsmembassy.org
Embassy of the Federated States of Micronesia
2nd
Floor, Reinanzaka Building 1-14-2, Akasaka 1-Chome Minato-ku, Tokyo 107, Japan Phone: (81 3) 35855456 Fax: (81 3) 35855348 E-mail: fsmemb@fsmemb.or.jp
Embassy of the Federated States of Micronesia
P.O. Box 15493 Suva, Fiji Phone: (679) 304180 Fax: (679) 304081 E-mail: fsmsuva@sopacsun.sopac.org.fj
Office of the Federated States of Micronesia Consulate-General 3049 Ualena Street, Suite 908 Honolulu, Hawaii 96819 United States of America Phone: (1 808) 8364775 Fax: (1 808) 8366896 E-mail: fsmcgm@lava.net
Office of the Federated States of Micronesia Consulate-General
P.O. Box 10630 Tamuning, Guam 96931 Phone: (1 671) 6469154-6 Fax: (1 671) 6466320 E-mail: fsmcg@kuentos.guam.net
Products/commodity responsible for:
The Department, through the Trade and Investment Unit, promotes the development and export of agricultural and fisheries products and handicrafts, tourism and business development through foreign direct investment.
Training:
x The Department coordinates and facilitates training for personnel from both the private and public sectors.
Areas/industries where investment is encouraged:
Agriculture, fisheries and tourism.
Titles of laws and regulations on foreign investment:
x FSM Foreign Investment Act of 1997, PL. No. 10-49. x FSM Foreign Investment Regulations, 1998. x Chuuk State Foreign Investment Act of 1998,
CSL No. 4-99-03. x Chuuk State Foreign Investment Regulations. x Kosrae State Foreign Investment Act of 1998, S.L. No. 6-163. x Kosrae State Foreign Investment Regulations. x Pohnpei Foreign Investor Permit Act of 1986, as amended, S.L. No. 4L-98-99. x Pohnpei States's Foreign Investment Regulations, 1999. x Yap State Foreign Investment Act, 2002, Y.S.L. No. 5-72. x Yap State Foreign Investment Regulations.
Category:
Investment promotion authority; Ministry of Trade; trade facilitation body; trade fair and exhibition authority; and trade promotion organization.

MONGOLIA

FOREIGN INVESTMENT AND FOREIGN TRADE AGENCY (FIFTA)*

Office/postal address:
Government Building 11 Sambuu Street, 11 Ulaanbaatar 211238
Phone: (976 11) 326040, 310599 Fax: (976 11) 324076
E-mail: fifta@investmongolia.com URL: www.investmongolia.com
Year established: 1996
Principal functions:
x To promote and facilitate foreign direct investment and foreign trade in the country;
x To promote industrial development and export growth;
x To promote Mongolia as a destination for new investment and business.
Services/activities:
Investment Promotion and Cooperation Division:
x Carries out investment promotion activities in order to facilitate the adequate image of Mongolian investment and business environment, including organization of conferences and workshops on investment opportunities in Mongolia and bilateral business meetings, hosting business and trade missions;
x Provides investment matchmaking services to both foreign and Mongolian investors seeking investment and business cooperation; to introduce investment projects to foreign investors;
x Maintains close relations with various government and non-government institutions of Mongolia, as well as foreign embassies and international organizations;
x Prepares various promotional publications and materials on the investment and business climate of Mongolia;
x Handles information database on investment and business climates of countries and regions, as well as on activities of international organizations.
One-stop Service Centre which provides investors with the following three staged services:
x Its *pre-registration service* focuses on providing investors with first-hand information, advice and guidance on making investment and doing business in Mongolia, including professional assistance in compiling registration documents;
x Its *registration service* is directed to issue a certificate of incorporation with foreign investment or representative office based on investor's application;
x Its *post-registration service* concentrates on assistances to investors in facilitating initial stages of the investment process and running the business, including supporting import of capital and equipment, issuing official letter to a

responsible authority for investor's residency permission and multiple entry visa to Mongolia, and assisting with guidance on problems faced by investors at relevant authorities level.

Small and Medium-sized Enterprises Support Office:
x Provides entrepreneurs with business start-up related information including on business legal environment, banking and financing issues, main business costs, site development, licensing regulations;
x Assists entrepreneurs in developing investment project plans, better managing financial and human resources and finding out more about product market;
x Supports entrepreneurs in promoting their products, finding suitable partners for investment projects and bringing their requirements to the policymaking level.
Export Promotion Centre:
x Assists national export companies in increasing their ability to export to overseas markets by providing in-depth research and market information;
x Organizes overseas trade exhibitions of national export products;
x Maintains close relations with international trade promotion organizations;
x Makes a branding and marketing strategy;
x Manages international market and importers database.
Information and Planning Team:
x Maintains investment database structured by sectors and countries;
x Makes analysis on investment trend and process investment statistics;
x Provides information on investment statistics to governmental or non-governmental organizations, companies and investors upon request;
x Updates FIFTA website with the latest information on investment, business and trade environment of Mongolia;
x Does FIFTA Strategic Planning;
x Makes FIFTA quarter and annual reports.
Publications issued:
x *Business and Investment Guide for Mongolia, 2002.*
x *Investment Policy Statement.*
x *Sector Profiles (Compiled comprehensive information on mining, oil, infrastructure, agro-industry, ICT, tourism).*
x *Investment Seeking Project Profiles (compiled 176 investment seeking project profiles in mining, oil, infrastructure, agro-industry, ICT, tourism sector).*
x *Investors Forum Invitation.*
x *Investors Forum Introduction Brochure.*
x *Mongolian Investment Directory - Business Pages (compiled information on major companies and corporations operating in Mongolia).*
x *Business and Investment-related Laws and Regulations (over 50 laws and regulations translated into English and compiled).*
x *"MONGOLIA" brochure.*
x *"Envoy of the Year" (Best Foreign Investor/Person Certificates).*
x *FIFTA Brochure, 2003.*
x *FIFTA Weekly News.*
x *Multimedia CD-ROM (contained economic, business and investment environment of Mongolia, particularly, investment guide, investment opportunities, laws and regulations, priority sectors' information and video presentation).*
Offices abroad:
FIFTA does not have offices abroad, but has several FIFTA representatives in China, Germany; Taiwan Province of China, the United Kingdom and the United States of America.
Products/commodity responsible for:
Foreign direct investment; and export items.
Training:
x Occasionally conduct various investment, business and trade promotion seminars and courses.
Areas/industries where investment is encouraged:
The existing Foreign Investment Law of Mongolia imposes high potential for foreign investment in all sectors of the economy except in the production of narcotics, guns and explosives, pornography and running a casino.
Titles of laws and regulations on foreign investment:
x Law on Foreign Investment, 1991 and subsequently revised in 1993, 1998 and 2002.
Category:
Investment promotion authority.

MONGOLIAN BUSINESS DEVELOPMENT AGENCY (MBDA)

Office/postal address:
MBDA Prime Minister Amar's Street Ulaanbaatar 13
P.O. Box: P.O.-20A, Box-39, Ulaanbaatar
Phone: (976 11) 311150 Fax: (976 11) 311092 E-mail: mbda@mongol.net Year established: 1994 Principal functions:
x To coordinate and bridge between the private sector and government organizations;

x To provide advice, consultancy, information and training to private enterprises, foreign companies and international agencies.

Services/activities:

- x Delivers business consultancy on management, marketing and financing;
- x Conducts marketing research;
- x Prepares business plan, "Strengths, Weaknesses, Opportunities and Threats (SWOT) analysis";
- x Identifes foreign partners for Mongolian companies, establishes contacts;
- x Negotiates with banks, assists in the loan applications;
- x Provides business information;
- x Organizes business meetings and training workshops.

Local branches:

Arkhangai Rbac Phone/fax: (976 133) 221215
Baganuur Rbac Phone: (976 31) 20422 Fax: (976 121) 1239
Darkhan-Uul Rbac Phone/fax: (976 137) 224610
Dornod Rbac Phone: (976 158) 211802
Khovd Rbac Phone: (976 143) 22210 Fax: (976 143) 21212
Orkhon Rbac Phone/fax: (976 135) 222627
Selenge Rbac Phone/fax: (976 136) 223639 E-mail: selengerbac@mongol.net
Sukhbaatar Rbac Phone: (976 151) 2674 Fax: (976 151) 21209 Khubsgul Rbac Phone: (976 138) 221021 Fax: (976 138) 221037

Products/commodity responsible for:

Consultancy and business services.

Training:

- x Business English courses (basic, intermediate and advanced);
- x Managers' training programme (EU);

x MBA outreach programme in cooperation with Maastricht School of Management.

Areas/industries where investment is encouraged:

x Small and medium enterprises.

x Sectors: food, agriculture, wool and cashmere processing, leather processing

Category:

Industrial promotion; and training/research institute.

MONGOLIAN NATIONAL CHAMBER OF COMMERCE AND INDUSTRY (MNCCI)

Office/postal address:
J. Sambuu Street 11 Ulaanbaatar 38
Phone: (976 11) 312501, 327176 Fax: (976 11) 324620, 312501
E-mail: chamber@mongolchamber.mn, apmc@mongolchamber.mn
URL: www.mongolchamber.mn
Year established: 2 July 1960

Principal functions:

x To render overall business services to its members and nonmembers;
x To develop dialogue/partnership with the Government and its institutions on creating a sound business environment;
x To arbitrate foreign trade disputes;
x To certify foreign trade documentation;
x To register patents and trademarks;
x To organize domestic and international exhibitions and trade fairs.

Services/activities:

x Inspects export and import goods on a neutral basis; x Conducts export and SME promotional activities; x Handles trade inquiries; x Sends and hosts business missions; x Gathers, processes and disseminates business information; x Holds training, seminars and conferences; x Provides translation services.

Publications issued:

- x *Business Times Newspaper* (weekly, Mongolian).
- x *"White Book" on foreign trade* (annually, Mongolian).
- x *Overview of Mongolian Economy* (annually, Mongolian/English).
- x *Economic overview of Mongolia* (annually, English; monthly, Mongolian).
- x *Issues of development economy* (quarterly, Mongolian).
- x *Metal, Mineral and Raw Material* (twice a year, Mongolian).
- x *Foreign and domestic survey of agricultural products* (twice a year, Mongolian).
- x *Business education series* (overall 67 series).

Local branches:

Arkhangai Province Bayankhongor Province Bayan-Ulgii Province Darkhan city Erdenet city Govi-Altai Province Huvsgul Province Khenti Province Khovd Province Ovorkhangai Province Selenge Province Tuv Province Uvs Province Zavkhan

Offices abroad:

No. 2, Xiu Shui Beijie Jian Guo Men Wai, 100600 Beijing, China Phone: (86 10) 85751433 Fax: (86 10) 85751433 E-mail: baigal@163bj.com

Gotland Str. 12 10439 Berlin, Germany Phone: (49 30) 43734126 Fax: (49 30) 43734127 E-mail: binderva@aol.com

6th Floor, Yokohama, World Porters 2-1 Shinko 2 Chome, Naka-ku Yokohama Japan 231-0001

1434 E. 1st Drive # 2-305 Aurora, CO 80011 (3854) Denver, United States of America

Representative in Singapore E-mail: respect1@pacific.net.sg

Representative in Switzerland E-mail: enhbaatar.m@magicnet.mn

Representative in Belgium and the Netherlands E-mail: batulzii@magicnet.mn

Representative in the Czech Republic E-mail: monemb@bohemia-net.cz, natsagv@yahoo.com

Representative in Hungary E-mail: erdenesuvd@freemail.hu, pandaso@axelero.hu

Representative in Turkey E-mail: ulaanaat@yahoo.com

Representative in the Russian Federation E-mail: 734231altaiz@magicnet.mn, mongolconsul@tuva.ru

Representative in Sweden E-mail: Tuvshee7@yahoo.com

Representative in Africa E-mail: msraeb1@yahoo.com

Representative in Ukraine E-mail: tsogo@dlkiev.relc.com

Representative in the Republic of Korea E-mail: burentogtokh@yahoo.com

Representative in Poland E-mail: gangold@wp.pl

Membership structure: Over 600 members including private and public companies.

Products/commodity responsible for:

Trade and industry promotion service.

Training:

- Courses on management, marketing, finance and economy for domestic Mongolian businesspersons;
- Training of director's assistant;
- Training of professional secretary.

Areas/industries where investment is encouraged:

Agro and food industry sector, infrastructure sector, tourism sector, information and communication technology sector and other sectors.

Titles of laws and regulations on foreign investment:

x Foreign Investment Law, 1993 (amendments in 1998 and 2002). x Foreign Trade Arbitration Law, 2003. x The Law of Chamber of Commerce, 1995.

Category:

Chamber of commerce; industrial promotion; inspection institution; trade facilitation body; trade fair and exhibition authority; and training/research institute.

MYANMAR

DIRECTORATE OF INVESTMENT AND COMPANY ADMINISTRATION*

Office/postal address:

653/691, Merchant Street Pabedan Township Yangon

Phone: (95 1) 372855, 372052, 377053, 377104 Fax: (95 1) 254660 E-mail: DICA.NPED@mptmail.net.mm Year established: 1993 Principal functions:

- To coordinate foreign and local promotion to invest in Myanmar;
- To appraise the investment proposal and submit to the Myanmar Investment Commission (MIC) and higher authorities;
- To monitor and report the performance of the permitted enterprises to MIC;
- To register and administer limited companies, joint ventures, partnerships and business associations;
- To coordinate with international and regional organizations regarding trade and investment affairs.

Areas/industries where investment is encouraged:

Agriculture sector; agro-supportive industries, export-oriented industries; petrochemical industries; natural resource-based industries; and labour-intensive export-oriented industries.

Titles of laws and regulations on foreign investment:

x Union of Myanmar Foreign Investment Law, 1988. x Procedures relating to the Union of Myanmar Foreign Investment Law, 1988. x Myanmar Citizens Investment Law, 1994. x Procedures Relating to Myanmar Citizens Investment Law, 1994. x Myanmar Companies Act, 1914.

Category:

Investment promotion authority.

DIRECTORATE OF TRADE*

(Ministry of Commerce)
Office/postal address:
228-240, Strand Road
Yangon Phone: (95 1) 371217 Fax: (95 1) 253028
E-mail: com@mptmail.net.mm Year established: 1984 Principal functions:
- x To collect, process and disseminate trade information;
- x To establish contacts with foreign buyers;
- x To provide technical assistance to State economic and private enterprises.

Services/activities:
x Disseminates current information on trade development; x Organizes seminars and workshops; x Replies to queries received by telephone, correspondence and
personal visits; x Circulates a fortnightly trade information newsletter.
Publication issued:
Trade News (bimonthly, English).
Areas/industries where investment is encouraged:
Agro-based industries.
Titles of laws and regulations on foreign investment:
x Union of Myanmar Foreign Investment Law, 1988. x State-owned Economic Enterprises Law, 1989.
Category:
Ministry of Trade; trade facilitation body, trade fair and exhibition authority; and trade promotion organization.

UNION OF MYANMAR FEDERATION OF CHAMBERS OF COMMERCE AND INDUSTRY (UMFCCI)

Office/postal address:
504/506, Merchant Street Kyauktada Township Yangon
P.O. Box: 1557, Yangon
Phone: (95 1) 246495, 243151, 282208 Fax: (95 1) 248177
E-mail: umcci@mptmail.net.mm URL: www.umfcci.com.mm
Year established: 1 April 1999 (formerly Chamber of Commerce and Industry, since 1919).
Principal functions:
x To encourage the participation of the private sector in government committees; x To maintain continuous dialogue with private businesspersons; x To issue commercial documents and Certificate of Origin for goods to be exported; x To provide consultancy services on industrial, economic, legal and environmental issues.
Service/activity:
x Undertakes activities to promote trade, industry and investment.
Publication issued:
x *Business* (monthly, Myanmar/English).
Membership structure: 11,527 members (as of 3 April 2003).
Areas/industries where investment is encouraged:
Investment is encouraged for promotion and expansion of exports; exploitation of natural resources which require heavy investment; and acquisition of high technology.
Titles of laws and regulations on foreign investment:
x The Union of Myanmar Foreign Investment Law, 1988.
Category:
Chamber of commerce.

DEPARTMENT OF ISLAND DEVELOPMENT AND INDUSTRY*

Office/postal address:
Government Offices Aiwo District
Phone: (674) 4443191 Fax: (674) 4443791
Year established: 1968
Principal function:
To administer:
-telecommunications;
-lands and surveying;
-phosphate industry;
-trade and investment promotion;
-media and news production centre;
-fisheries and marine resources authority;
-agriculture and forestry development;
-government printery;
-environment;
-development projects;
-culture and tourism.
Publication issued:
Nauru Bulletin (weekly, English).

Areas/industries where investment is encouraged:
Transport, communications, real estate, trade, culture and tourism, fisheries, science and small-scale industries.
Titles of laws and regulations on foreign investment:
Foreign Trust, Estates and Wills Act, 1972. Nauru Corporation Act, 1972.
Categories:
Industrial promotion; investment promotion authority; Ministry of Trade; national productivity centre; state trading organization; trade association; and trade promotion organization.

PAKISTAN

ALL PAKISTAN COMMERCIAL EXPORTERS ASSOCIATION

(of rough and unpolished precious and semi-precious stones)
Office/postal address:
1, 2nd Floor, Al-Jalil Market Namak Mandi Peshawar
Phone: (92 91) 2213396, 2213396 Fax: (92 91) 2213520 E-mail: apceap@brain.net.pk Year established: 1988 Principal functions:

- x To aid and stimulate the production and development of rough and unpolished precious and semi-precious stones marketing and export of stones and to promote business in which Pakistan Commercial Exporters Association of rough and unpolished and semi-precious stones is engaged;
- x To promote the correct understanding and unanimity among its members in particular and the businesspersons and industrialists in Pakistan in general on all subjects involving their common goods, and to safeguard their interests generally;
- x To frame rules and regulations governing the export trade in rough and unpolished precious and semi-precious stones and make alterations therein from time to time;
- x To make representations to the local and provincial authorities on any matter concerned with trade, commerce and industry of its members;
- x To elect or nominate members to represent the Association on any local or public body.

Services/activities:
x Diffuses among its members information on all matters affecting trade and commerce, and collects, prints, publishes, issues and circulates papers, periodicals, books, circulars, statistics and such other publications as may seem conducive to any of these objects;
x Circulates, fosters and stimulates the spirit of mutual self-help on the principal of cooperation and coordination among the members of the Association;
x Diffuses among the members information affecting their trade, commerce and industry, and collects, prints, publishes, issues and circulates papers, periodicals, books statistics and such other publication as may be deemed to conducive to the objects of the Association;
x Renders technical, managerial, supervisory and advisory assistance to members;
x Frames and enforces rules and regulations with a view to regularizing the purchase and sale of the products and to changes therein from time to time in the interest of trade, commerce and industry and the public;
x Attempts to settle or compromise or arbitrate in disputes arising between non-members or between a member and a non-member willing or agreeing to submit to arbitration in accordance with the arbitration rules of the Association;
x Works actively for the eradication of unethical business practices from the field of trade, commerce and industry;

- x Appoints delegations to present the case of the members of the Association before the authorities concerned;
- x Raises funds to meet the expenses of the Association and sells, mortgages, disposes of or otherwise deals with all or any part of the property of the Association;
- x Subscribes, pays or donates money, out of the funds of or collected by the Association for charitable, benevolent, humanitarian or social purposes and raises and maintains funds with a view to providing help to dependents of persons in employment of the Association;
- x Buys or acquires, takes on lease or by way of transfer any property, moveable or immoveable, for the purpose of the Association;
- x Files, prosecutes, defends or concurs, joins in prosecuting or defending any action, suit, application appeals for or conducive to the objectives of the Association;
- x Subscribes to, and sources affiliation with, the Federation of Pakistan Chambers of Commerce and Industry and procures from and such information as may be likely to forward the objectives of the Association;

x Complies with all the requirements of the Trade Organizations Ordinance, 1961 (XLV of 1961) as amended from time to time and directive issued thereunder;
x Carries out all such other lawful functions as may be incidental or conducive to the attachment of the above aims and objectives.

Local branches:
208 Gems Jewellery Trade Bleanken Street Office Zebunisa Saddar Karachi Phone: (92 21) 5671985 Fax: (92 21) 5687014 E-mail: nauratan@cyber.net.pk
No. 4, AandB, Block F, Super Market, F-6 Islamabad Phone: (92 51) 2820453 Fax: (92 51) 2820727 E-mail: gems@comsats.net.pk
Camp Office Khawaz Khella, Swat, NWFP Phone: (92 936) 744184 Fax: (92 936) 7454556 E-mail: shuaibzs@hotmail.com
Membership structure: 400 members.
Products/commodity responsible for:
Precious and semi-precious stones.
Training:
In the process of the establishment of gemstones cutting and Gemological Institute at Peshawar, Pakistan in collabouration with the Export Promotion Bureau, Government of Pakistan.
Areas/industries where investment is encouraged:
Precious and semi-precious stones mining, cutting and polishing.
Category:
Trade facilitation body; and training/research institute.

BOARD OF INVESTMENT (BOI)*

Office/postal address:
Sector G-5/1 Ataturk Avenue Islamabad
Phone: (92-051) 9206161, 9207531 Fax: (92-051) 9215554, 9206160
E-mail: mail@pakboi.gov.pk URL: www.pakboi.gov.pk
Year established: 1989
Principal function:
To promote, encourage and facilitate both local and foreign investment in Pakistan.
Services/activities:

x Assists the Government in the formulation and review of national investment policy and laws;
x Identifies and promotes investment opportunities in different sectors of the economy;
x Acts as a national focal point of contact between the potential investors and all investment-related government agencies responsible for providing infrastructure facilities, etc. to the investors;
x Enhances Pakistan's international competitiveness and contributes to its economic and social development;
x Provides support services and assistance to the potential investors to set up or expand their business in Pakistan through One Desk Facilitation Service;
x Makes available all essential information, publicity material and data, etc. to the investors.

Publications issued:
Booklet (English):
x *Pakistan Investment Policies, Incentives and Facilities.*
Brochures (English):
x *Explore the Potential of Pakistan - The New Business Frontier.*
x *Investment Opportunities in Pakistan.*
x *An Open Door for Investors.*
x *A Compendium on Industrial Estates/Zones in Pakistan.*
Investors' information guides (English):
x *Agriculture Sector Profile.* x *Power Sector Profile.* x *Small and Medium Enterprise Sector Profile.* x *IT and Telecom Sector Profile.* x *Infrastructure Sector Profile.* x *Oil and Gas Sector Profile.* x *Tourism Sector.*
Local branch:
Board of Investment Kandawala Building
M.A. Jinnah Road Karachi Phone: (92 21) 9215967 Fax: (92 21) 9215078
Offices abroad:
At present, the Board of Investment does not have offices abroad. However, 31 Honorary Investment Counsellors (HICs) are working for the Board of Investment in 23 countries whose names, addresses (telephones, fax and e-mail) are available on BOI's website: www.pakboi.gov.pk.
Membership structure: 27 members.
Products/commodity responsible for:
Investment promotion and facilitation to boost socio-economic development in Pakistan.

Training:

BOI does not conduct any courses for outside participants.

Areas/industries where investment is encouraged:

Priority sectors for investment in Pakistan are (1) oil and gas; (2) manufacturing and industry; (3) infrastructure; (4) information technology; (5) agriculture; (6) tourism; (7) the social sector; and (8) the services sector.

Titles of laws and regulations on foreign investment:

Foreign investment is fully protected by:

- x Foreign Private Investment (Promotion and Protection) Act, 1976.
- x Protection of Economic Reforms Act, 1992.
- x Foreign Currency Accounts (Protection) Ordinance, 2001.
- x Board of Investment Ordinance, 2001.

Category:

Industrial promotion; and investment promotion authority.

EXPORT PROMOTION BUREAU (EPB)*

Government of Pakistan

Office/postal address:

5th

Floor, Block A Finance and Trade Centre Shahrah-e-Faisal Karachi 75400

P.O. Box: 1293, Karachi

Phone: (92 21) 9206487-90 Fax: (92 21) 9206497, 9202713 E-mail: epb@epb.gov.pk

URL: www.epb.gov.pk Year established: 1963 Principal function:

To promote and support sustained growth in export of goods and services both in terms of volume and value.

Services/activities: Local branches:

- x Assists in establishing contact with prospective buyers abroad;
- x Explores possibilities for export markets and identifies items possessing export potential;
- x Publishes regularly specialized publications featuring export opportunities, foreign trade information, training courses, directory, statistics, etc.;
- x Conducts product/market surveys abroad and provides up-to date intelligence;
- x Organizes seminars/conferences and training programmes for motivating people to export and apprises them of ways and means of going about the export business;
- x Assists in enhancing the skills and knowledge of established exporters in marketing and promotion for exports;
- x Provides inputs, based on its field experience, for the formulation of export policies;
- x Issues GSP Certificates;
- x Organizes/assists in organizing exhibitions at home and abroad, and assisting the participation of exporters in such trade displays;
- x Arranges and programmes the visits of overseas buyers and exploratory missions delegations to Pakistan;
- x Assists in resolving trade disputes and operational constraints;
- x Provides face-to-face counselling to resolve export problems;
- x Maintains a well-organized library;
- x Assists in facilitating the standardization and simplification of procedures;
- x Assists in overseas publicity to create brand/country/product awareness;
- x Enhances the awareness of environmental and social issues such as child labour;
- x Helps the industry to adopt standards such as ISO 9000 and 14000;
- x Promotes buyer-seller contacts;
- x Recommends the establishment of export-oriented industries.

Regional offices in Islamabad, Lahore, Peshawar, Quetta.

Subregional offices in Faisalabad, Hyderabad, Sukkur, Sialkot, Gujranwala, Multan, Abbotaad, Swat, Mirpur Azad Kashmir.

Publication issued:

x *Export Intelligence Bulletin* (weekly, English).

Category:

Trade promotion organization.

FEDERATION OF PAKISTAN CHAMBERS OF COMMERCE AND INDUSTRY (FPCCI)

Office/postal address:
Federation House Main Clifton Karachi 75600
P.O. Box: 13875, Karachi
Phone: (92 21) 5873691, 5873693-4 Fax: (92 21) 5874332
E-mail: fpcci@cyber.net.pk URL: www.fpcci.com.pk
Year established: 1950
Principal functions:
x To advocate the collective opinion, concern and aspiration of the private sector;
x To offer helpful advice and solid assistance to the Government in its efforts to promote exports, encourage foreign investment and stimulate economic activity;
x To bridge between the private sector and the Government;
x To play an active role in presenting problems of trade, industry and environment and safeguarding the interests of the private sector through constant dialogue with the Government.
Services/activities:
x Sponsors general and specialized business and investment delegations to foreign countries; x Organizes Pakistan's participation in international fairs and exhibitions; x Maintains constant liaison with Pakistan diplomatic and commercial missions abroad; x Exchanges information relating to trade, industry and the economy with the foreign chambers and institutions; x Encourages leading exporters of the country by giving them Export Trophy Awards every year; x Mediates in the resolution of commercial disputes between Pakistani and foreign businesspersons.
Publications issued:
x *Annual Report of FPCCI Activities.*
x *Compendium of G-77 CCI of Developing Countries.*
x *FPCCI Bulletin* (monthly).
x *Pakistan Trade Directory.*
x Souvenir of Annual Export Trophy Awards.
x Brochures of bilateral relations.
x Booklet on *Regional Economic Groupings.*
Local branches:
Zonal Office: 50-A, Tufail Road, Lahore Cantt-54810 Phone: (92 42) 6670970-71 Fax: (92 42) 6670972 E-mail: fpcci@brain.net.pk
Liaison Office: 99-W (B-Side), 1st Floor, Shalimar Plaza Jinnah Avenue, P.O. Box 2927, Islamabad Phone: (92 51) 2273178-80 Fax: (92 51) 2273177 E-mail: fpcci.isb@cyber.net.pk
Membership structure: 47 chambers of commerce and industry, and 166 all Pakistan associations of trade and industry.
Products/commodity responsible for:
Services; training; seminars, conferences, symposia and meetings; and all areas of business and industry.
Category:
Chamber of commerce.

INTERNATIONAL TRADE ORGANIZATION WING

Office/postal address:
Ministry of Commerce Government of Pakistan
6th
Floor Pakistan Secretariat Block A Islamabad
Phone: (92 51) 9201796, 9201851 Fax: (92 51) 9203024
E-mail: mocito@isb.paknet.com.pk URL: www.commerce.gov.pk
Principal functions:
x To undertake policy matters of the global system of trade preference; x To plan/monitor/evaluate development projects and schemes of the Ministry of Commerce and its attached departments; x To prepare and review the annual plans, mid-term plans and five-year plans and to prepare trade reviews; x To deal with donor agencies for technical/financial assistance for trade-related projects.
Services/activities:
As detailed under Principal functions.
Category:
Ministry of Trade.

JHELUM CHAMBER OF COMMERCE AND INDUSTRY

Office/postal address:
Rani Nagar
G.T. Road Jhelum
P.O. Box: Post Office: Chak Akka Via: Dina, Distt: Jhelum
Phone: (92 544) 646532 Fax: (92 544) 646533 Year established: 1994 Principal functions:
x To issue membership certificates as well as certificates of origin for the export cargoes and attestation of commercial documents;
x To issue recommendation letters for visa and passport;
x To circulate trade enquiries and exhibitions/fairs received from FPCCI and the export promotion bureau;
x To help in training exporters and importers;
x To organize a local exhibition once a year.

Publications:
Circular regarding trade and business interest (fortnightly). Membership structure: 500 members. Category
Chamber of commerce.

PAKISTAN READYMADE GARMENTS MANUFACTURERS AND EXPORTERS ASSOCIATION (PRGMEA)

Office/postal address:
18-A, Shaheen View Building Block - VI, P.E.C.H.S. Shahra-e-Faisal Karachi 75400
Phone: (92 21) 4549073, 4547912 Fax: (92 21) 4539669
E-mail: prgmea@cyber.net.pk URL: www.prgmea.org
Year established: 1980
Principal functions:

- x To advise, protect, safeguard and promote the rights, interests and privileges of its members;
- x To remove difficulties and shortcomings in the ready-made garment trade;
- x To create sympathy and unity among the manufacturers and exporters of ready-made garments;
- x To disseminate information of interest to the garment trade and to print literature conducive to the objectives of the Association;
- x To provide forms of contracts and other documents used in garment trade and commerce;
- x To encourage and facilitate the settlement of commercial disputes by arbitration or conciliation;
- x To consider, initiate and promote improvements in the commercial laws, rules and regulations for representation to the Government;
- x To enter into arrangements with the Government conducive to the objectives of the Association;
- x To issue certificates in accordance with the requirements of the trade to exercise the rights and objectives of the Association;
- x To cooperate and work with other recognized associations, chambers of commerce and industries;
- x To organize participation in trade fairs and exhibitions and to organize trade delegations to selected markets abroad;
- x To provide service to foreign trade delegations;
- x To provide advice and guidance to members on trade, industry and fiscal aspects of production and exports;
- x To advise the Government on textile negotiations with quota countries and other related export problems of the members as well as on budgetary, trade and fiscal policies;
- x To represent the Association in various government and trade bodies.

Services/activities:
x As detailed under Principal functions.
Publications issued:
x *PRGMEA Directory of Members* (annually, English). x *PRGMEA Newsletter* (monthly, Urdu/English). x *PRGMEA Circulars* (fortnightly, English). x *PRGMEA Members Directory CD* (annually, English). x *PRGMEA Export Excellence Awards Ceremony Brochure*
(annually, English).
Local branches:
Suit 114, Latif Centre 99 Ferozepur Road Ichhra, Lahore
Phone: (92 42) 7596296-7
Fax: (92 42) 7586101
E-mail: prgmea_north@yahoo.com
18-A, Shaheen View Building Block - VI, P.E.C.H.S. Shahra-e-Faisal, Karachi 75400 Phone: (92 21) 4382601-3, 4535394, 4313087 Fax: (92 21) 4539669 E-mail: prgmea@cyber.net.pk
Oberoy Sports Building Paris Road Sialkot Phone: (92 432) 592683 Fax: (92 432) 592683 E-mail: prgmea_skt@hotmail.com
Membership structure: 1,200 members.
Products/commodity responsible for:
All sorts of woven ready-made garments, made-ups and accessories.
Training:
Maintains two Technical Training Institutes (PRGTTI):
18-G, Block-VI, PECHS, Karachi Phone: (92 21) 4526918, 4546446-7 Fax: (92 21) 4546448 E-mail: prgtti@cyber.net.pk
71-L, Gulberg-III, Lahore Phone: (92 42) 9230756, 9230757 Fax: (92 42) 9230758 E-mail: prgtti@sol.net.pk
Training is being provided in the fields of special marketing in apparel; quality control and assurance; merchandising; pattern cutting and grading; inventory control and material management; garment machine mechanic courses for computerized pattern generation.

Areas/industries where investment is encouraged:
Ready-made garment manufacturing and exporting units including both woven and knitted.

Titles of laws and regulations on foreign investment:
x The Association is registered with the Ministry of Commerce, Government of Pakistan under the Trade Associations Act in Category-A.
Category:
Trade association.

RAWALPINDI CHAMBER OF COMMERCE AND INDUSTRY

Office/postal address:
39 Civil Lines Mayo Road Oawalpindi
P.O. Box: 323
Phone: (92 51) 5584397 Fax: (92 51) 5586849 E-mail: rcci@rcci.org.pk
URL: www.rcci.org.pk Year established: 1952 Principal functions:
- x To liaise the business community with the Government and counterparts abroad;
- x To collect and disseminate commercial and industrial information;
- x To organize functions as ISO, total quality management and semantic meta-databse cells;
- x To stimulate economic and investment activities.

Service/activity:
x Provides services to the business community.
Publication issued:
x News Bulletin Trade Directory. Membership structure: 2,500 members. Training:
Arranges different training courses.
Areas/industries where investment is encouraged:
National industrial zone.
Category:
Chamber of commerce.

TRADING CORPORATION OF PAKISTAN LIMITED (TCP)

Office/postal address:
4th
-5th
Floor, Block B, Finance and Trade Centre Sharea Faisal Karachi 74400
P.O. Box: 1244, Karachi 74200
Phone: (92 21) 9202947-9 Fax: (92 21) 9202722, 9202731, 9202592 E-mail: tcpkhi@pk.netsolir.com Year established: 1967 Principal functions:
- x To export selected items of public sector corporations, agencies, etc.;
- x To channel export through TCP to various markets under credit given by the Government to expand business in areas such as the Commonwealth of Independent States (CIS)/Central Asian Republics (CAR)/Malaysia, African countries, etc;
- x To export Pakistani products to new/non-traditional markets by way of giving concessions/incentives by the Government to prospective buyers for capturing new markets;
- x To perform the innovative role of undertaking the export of non-traditional items to non-traditional markets on an experimental basis;
- x To undertake and develop the export of fresh fruits/vegetables and minerals in collabouration and on a partnership basis with the private sector;
- x To import essential commodities in emergent conditions as in the past;
- x To import S.B. oil under future PL-480/416 Programme and CC Credit, etc;
- x To import palm oil from Malaysia under Malaysian credit;
- x To import industrial raw materials and other selected bulk items;
- x To utilize credit facilities;
- x To undertake countertrade to discover new markets and to promote exports, particularly to the countries facing cash constraints;
- x To purchase/sell cotton, sugar and other items, etc., as per the directive of the Federal Government;
- x To inspect the quality and quantity of brown rice and to issue

an authenticity certificate for the export of brown rice to European Union countries.

Local branch:
Trading Corporation of Pakistan (Pvt) Limited Regional Office
1st
Floor, LDA Plaza Egerton Road, Lahore 54000 Phone: (92 42) 6304349, 6309148, 6316558, 6310980 Fax: (92 42) 6301011
Category:
Public limited company handling international trade for and on behalf of the federal Government.

THE SIALKOT CHAMBER OF COMMERCE AND INDUSTRY

Office/postal address:
Shahrah-e-Awain-e-Sanat-o-Tijarat Sialkot
P.O. Box: 1870
Phone: (92 432) 261881-3 Fax: (92 432) 267919, 268835
E-mail: scci@brain.net.pk URL: www.scci.com.pk
Year established: 1984
Principal functions:
x To promote, aid, develop, stimulate and protect the economic interest of Pakistan in general and of those engaged in industry, agriculture, commerce, trade, banking an insurance in particular;
x To consider all questions connected with trade, industries, agriculture, manufacture and commerce and to initiate and/or support necessary actions connected therewith;
x To consider, support or oppose legislative or other government measures affecting the economic interest of businesspersons and industrialists and also to make representations to the Government or grievances, if any;
x To adjust controversies between members of the Chamber relating to the commercial, industrial, agricultural and financial interest of the businesspersons and industrialists;
x To arbitrate in settlements of disputes arising out of commercial transactions between parties willing and agreeing to abide by the judgment and decision of the Chamber;
x To communicate with the Chamber of Commerce and Industry of public bodies within or outside Pakistan and to concert and promote measures for the projection of trade, commerce and manufacturers and the labour engaged therein and to remove mutual hardships;
x To establish a commercial and statistical library.
Services/activities:
x As detailed in Principal functions.
Publication issued:
x *Commercial News Bulletin* (fortnightly, English/Urdu).
Membership structure: More than 5,000 members registered.
Products/commodity responsible for:
Surgical instruments, sports goods, leather garments, sportswear, musical instruments, military uniforms and badges, martial arts, saddlery, cutlery and kitchenware, etc.
Training:
Offers short-term, trade-related courses for members as well as non-members.
Areas/industries where investment is encouraged:
Manufacturing of surgical instruments, leather garments and sports goods.
Titles of laws and regulations on foreign investment:
x Companies Ordinance 1984 of Pakistan. x Securities Exchange Act, 2000.
Category:
Chamber of commerce.

COFFEE INDUSTRY CORPORATION LTD. (CIC)

Office/postal address:
P. O. Box 137 Goroka Eastern Highlands Province
Phone: (675) 7321266,7322466 Fax: (675) 7321431,7321351
E-mail: cicgka@daltron.com.pg URL: www.coffeecorp.org.pg
Year established: 1964
Principal function:
x To control and regulate the production, processing, marketing and export of coffee grown in Papua New Guinea.
Services/activities:
x Promotes Papua New Guinea coffee internally and overseas;
x Lobbies on behalf of the Papua New Guinea coffee industry;
x Operates pulper maintenance services for growers;
x Provides price and marketing information;
x Maintains a database for the industry and disseminates information;
x Imposes quality controls through inspection;
x Takes part in negotiations at the International Coffee Organization (ICO);
x Enforces ICO requirements;
x Undertakes research on coffee;

x Undertakes extension services for smallholder coffee growers;

x Administers a price stabilization scheme.

Publications issued:

x *ACIAR working papers project 8734*. x *Coffee Discussion Papers*. x *Coffee Report*. x *Papua New Guinea Coffee Export Statistics*. x CIC submission/papers.

Local branch:

Coffee Industry Corporation Ltd. Industry Operations Division Export Control Department
P. O. Box 3993 Lae, Morobe Province Phone: (675) 4725044, 4724979 Fax: (675) 4724934

Office abroad:

Corporation Representative-United Kingdom St. Lawrence, Kingsway, Hullbridge Essex SS5 6DR, United Kingdom Phone: (44 702) 231285 Fax: (44 702) 232373 E-mail: wheeler@globalnet.co.uk

Products/commodity responsible for:

Coffee: green bean, roast and ground.

Training:

x Coffee Factory Manager course.
x National Exporter Training Course.
x Coffee Quality Ratio Workshop.

Areas/industries where investment is encouraged:

Expansion of smallholder production; rehabilitation of the plantation sector; downstream processing; marketing; and quality improvement.

Titles of laws and regulations on foreign investment:

x Coffee Industry Act of 1991. x Coffee Industry Regulations.

Category:

Commodity board.

INVESTMENT PROMOTION AUTHORITY (IPA)*

Office/postal address:

P.O. Box 5053
Boroko NDC 111 Phone: (675) 3217311 Fax: (675) 3202237
E-mail: iepd@ipa.gov.pg URL: www.ipa.gov.pg Year established: 1992 Principal functions:

x To promote and facilitate investments in Papua New Guinea;
x To be first contact point for foreign investors for advice on project proposals and for approvals of applications for registration to conduct business in the country;
x To contribute to planning for investment and recommend priority areas for investment to the Government;
x To coordinate investment proposals.

Services/activities:

Investment and Export Promotion Division:

x Informs and educates the business community about investment opportunities in Papua New Guinea;
x Answers enquiries from the public and facilitates business introduction through its database of foreign and domestic investors.

Business and Investment Facilitation Division:

x Certifies foreign enterprises wishing to carry on business in Papua New Guinea; conducts research on investment-related issues and prepares country report on investment trends.

Business Registration Division:

x Administers the registration of companies, business names and trademarks under the key business laws; maintains a national registry of all companies and corporate bodies operating in the country;
x Administers "Reserved Activities" - small-scale operations or traditional business activities reserved for citizens and national enterprises.

Industrial Business Development Division:

x Facilitates investment through the development of industrial commerce and enforces quality control.

Publications issued:

x *Investment Papua New Guinea Magazine* (quarterly, English). x IPA brochures.

Priced publications:

x *Environment in PNG*. x *Foreign Exchange Controls in PNG*. x *Foreign Investment Guidelines*. x *Investment incentives*. x *Land in PNG*. x *Taxation and Customs in PNG*. x *Telecommunications in PNG*.
x *Wages in PNG*.
x *A Business Guide to Papua New Guinea* (CD-ROM).
x *Agricultural Manual* (CD-ROM\).
x *Fisheries Resource Manual* (CD-ROM).
x *Forestry Resource Profile* (CD-ROM).

Training:

Through a bilateral arrangement for assistance with Australia, and through other multilateral donor agreements, training courses are an important part of the arrangement.

Areas/industries where investment is encouraged:

Foreign investment, particularly through joint ventures, which involve upstream and downstream processing of natural resources is encouraged. Specific areas include agriculture and manufacturing.

Titles of laws and regulations on foreign investment:

x Associations Incorporation Act. x Business Groups Incorporation Act. x Business Names Act.
x Companies Act. x Investment Promotion Act. x Trademarks Act.

Category:
Investment promotion organization.

PHILIPPINES

BANGKO SENTRAL NG PILIPINAS (BSP)

Office/postal address:
International Department Bangko Sentral ng Pilipinas
A. Mabini corner Pablo Ocampo Sr. Sts. Malate, Manila 1004
Phone: (63 2) 536 6077 Fax: (63 2) 536 0053
E-mail: cgonzalez@bsp.gov.ph, bspmail@bsp.gov.ph URL: www.bsp.gov.ph
Year established: 1993 (formerly Central Bank of the Philippines, 1949-1993)
Principal functions:
On trade:
- x To review and formulate policies and rules governing international trade and disseminate these to the public;
- x To provide rediscounting of export financing granted by banks;
- x To compile/prepare reports on the country's balance of payments, showing information on trade and investments, among others;
- x To compile data on trade-related external debt and related transactions;
- x To organize and conduct meetings/dialogues with exporters to discuss the export outlook and issues affecting exporters.

On foreign investments:
x To review and formulate policies and rules governing foreign investments (inward and outward) and disseminate these to the public; x To register inward foreign investments and to monitor transactions pertaining to registered investments; x To evaluate applications of Philippine residents to purchase foreign exchange for outward investments that require prior BSP approval;
x To compile data on registered investments and inflows and outflows of foreign exchange pertaining to foreign investments.
Under existing rules, foreign investments are required to be registered with BSP (through the International Department) if the foreign exchange to service the repatriation of capital and the remittances of dividends, profits and earnings thereon shall be purchased from the Philippine banking system. Foreign direct investments in shares of stocks of corporations not listed on the Philippine Stock Exchange (PSE) are required to be registered directly with the BSP, together with investments in: (1) peso time deposits with maturity of at least 90 days; (2) government securities; and (3) money market instruments. Foreign investments in stocks listed in the PSE may be registered directly with the BSP or by commercial banks, which are required to report to the BSP such registration of investments as well as transactions on registered investments. BSP delegated to commercial banks the registration of foreign investments in PSE-listed stocks acquired through the PSE-trading floor.
Services/activities:
- x Renders advice and services to exporters and importers on banking procedures, and trade documentation;
- x Monitors compliance of banks/exporters/importers with the BSP export and import rules including reporting requirements;
- x Evaluates and acts on requests to purchase foreign exchange to service trade payments that do not squarely fall under existing rules;
- x Monitors credits granted by/outstanding credits of selected government financial institutions to small- and medium-scale export enterprises;
- x Assists in conducting of studies for further simplification of export/import procedures/documentation and export financing needs of exporters;
- x Publishes the annual "Directory of Philippine Exporters";
- x Actively participates in meetings of the Export Development Council.

Publication issued:
x *Directory of Philippine Exporters* (annually, English).
Titles of laws and regulations on foreign investment:
x BSP Circular No. 1389 (Consolidated Foreign Exchange Rules and Regulations) dated 13 April 1993, as amended.
Category:

Banking - statutory and public.

BOARD OF INVESTMENTS (BOI)*

Office/postal address:
385 Sen. Gil Puyat Avenue Makati City Metro Manila 1200
Phone: (63 2) 8958322, 8967342 Fax: (63 2) 8953521
E-mail: osac@boi.gov.ph URL: www.boi.gov.ph
Year established: 1967
Principal functions:

- x To promote domestic and foreign investments by identifying investment opportunities, providing investor assistance, encouraging regional dispersal of industries, and broadening the entrepreneurial base;
- x To build an environment conducive to the expansion of existing industries and investments, and what will attract new capital;
- x To enhance worldwide competitiveness of Philippine industries.

Service/activities:
x Information assistance to local and foreign investors;
x Timely investment advice and facilitation regarding investors' business transaction;
x Assistance in the selection of ideal investment location;
x Joint Venture Matching Services for international local and foreign entrepreneurs;
x Investment advice and facilitation for SMEs;
x Business linkages with the public and private sectors;
x Evaluation and supervision of investment applications;
x Training on Investment Promotion;
x Seminar on Investment Networking for Local Executives;
x Facilitation of Environmental Clearance Certificate and advocacy for environment-related projects;
x Investment briefings, inbound and outbound missions, seminars and conferences for local and foreign investors;
x After-sales service through the Investment Promotion Network (IPN), a system of hotlines connecting Investment Promotion Units (IPUs) across 24 related government agencies;
x Entrepreneurial assistance to Overseas Filipino Workers;
x Industry sectors planning and preparation of Industry sector profiles.
Local branches:
BOI-Cagayan de Oro Extension Office c/o DTI-Region X Corrales-Luna Streets, Cagayan de Oro City Phone: 722278, 723604 BOI-Cebu Extension Office Espina Building 135 Juana Osmena Extension Capitol Site, Cebu City Phone: 210017 Fax: 52660
BOI-Davao Extension Office c/o DTI-Davao Escalona Building, 3/F Ponciano Reyes Street, Davao City Phone: 76841, 75250, 78984
BOI-Iloilo Extension Office Cnr. J.M. Basa and Peralta Streets, Iloilo City Phone: 270060 Fax: 270083
BOI-Legaspi Extension Office Del Rosario Building Rizal Street, Legaspi City Phone: 23347, 23307 Fax: 23307
Publications issued:

- x *Annual Report, 2001.*
- x *BOI-Approved Projects under EO 226.*
- x *Briefing Folios with Basic Facts on the Philippines.*
- x *Checklist on Doing Business in the Philippines.*
- x *Foreign Investments Act of 1991 (R.A. 7042).*
- x *Investment Priorities Plan.*
- x *It's a Pleasure to Do Business in the Philippines* (English/ Japanese/Chinese/Korean).
- x *Omnibus Investments Code of 1987 (E.O. 226).*
- x *Philippines Handy Economic and Trade Indicators.*
- x *The Philippines: Your Competitive Edge.*
- x *Primer on Built-Operate-Transfer Scheme.*
- x *Primer on Built-Operate-Transfer (BOT) and Built Transfer (BT) Schemes.*
- x *Primer on Foreign Investment Policies in the Philippines.*
- x *Primer on Foreign Investments Act of 1991.*
- x *Primer on Special Investors Resident Visa (SIRV).*
- x *Rules and Regulations to Implement E.O. 226.*

Areas/industries where investment is encouraged:
Listed in annual Investment Priorities Plan.
Titles of laws and regulations on foreign investment:
x Omnibus Investments Code of 1987 (E.O. 226). x Rules and Regulations to Implement E.O. 226.
Category:
Investment promotion authority.

BUREAU OF PRODUCT STANDARDS (BPS)

Office/postal address:
3/F, Trade and Industry Building 361 Sen. Gil J. Puyat Avenue Makati City 1200
Phone: (63 2) 7513123, 7514736 Fax: (63 2) 7514706
E-mail: bps@dti.dti.gov.ph URL: www.bps.dti.gov.ph
Year established: 20 June 1964
Principal function:
x To develop, implement and coordinate standardization activities in the Philippines.
Services/activities:
x Standards development;
x Standards promotion and media relations;
x Enforcement of consumer assistance;
x Product testing services, and certification programme;
x Registration of assessors services;
x Standards information services;
x WTO/TBT (technical barriers to trade) enquiry print and services;
x International relations;
x Private emission testing centre (PETC) - accreditation services;
x Labouratory accreditation services;
x Accreditation of conformity assessment bodies scheme;
x Special projects;
x Financial, administrative, human resource development, and information technology services.
Publications issued:
x *BPS Information Kit* (English). x *List of Philippine National Standards (PNS) under Mandatory Product Certification.* x *Directory of Accredited Labouratories.* x *Product Guides.* x *List of Companies with PS/ICC* (monthly, English). x *Catalogue of Philippine National Standards.* x *BPS Directions* (through e-mail). x *List of Accredited Certifying Bodies.*
Products/commodity responsible for:
All industrial products.
Training:
Seminars on ISO 9000 - Quality Management, ISO 14000 Environmental Management System and PNS ISO IEC Guide 17025 - Labouratory Accreditation.
Category:
Standard, testing, certification inspection and accreditation body.

CEBU CHAMBER OF COMMERCE AND INDUSTRY

Office/postal address:
11th
and 13th Avenue North Reclamation Area Cebu City 6000
Phone: (63 32) 2321421, 2321423, 2323951, 2323957 Fax: (63 32) 2321422
E-mail: ccci@esprint.com URL: www.esprint.com/~ccci
Year established: 1913
Principal functions:
x To promote business and investment development; x To enhance SME development.
Services/activities:
x Organizes fairs and exhibits;
x Provides training services;
x Disseminates information and maintains databases;
x Encourages labour and management cooperation;
x Establishes industry-academic linkage.
Publication issued:
Chamber Updates (monthly, English).
Local branches:
32 affiliated industry and professional associations with CCCI.
Membership structure: 2,436 members [936 direct members and 1,500 indirect members (32 affiliated sectoral associations)].
Training:
x Sales and Marketing; x HR Development; x E-Commerce; x Global Competitiveness Training.
Areas/industries where investment is encouraged:
Information and communication technology; tourism; light engineering; electronics; semi-conductors; food and agriculture; and food processing.
Category:
Chamber of commerce; commodity board; industrial promotion; inspection institution; investment promotion authority; productivity centre; shipper's council, port authority, national shipping corporation; trade association; trade facilitation body; trade fair and exhibition authority; trade promotion organization; and training/research institute.

DEVELOPMENT ACADEMY OF THE PHILIPPINES (DAP)

Office/postal address:
DAP Building San Miguel Avenue Ortigas Centre Pasig City
P.O. Box: 12788, Ortigas Centre, Pasig City
Phone: (63 2) 6312124 or 6312153 (Office of the Executive Director) Fax: (63 2) 6312123
E-mail: academy@dap.edu.ph URL: www.dap.edu.ph
Year established: 1973
Principal functions:
x To build capacities and partnerships among the key sectors of Philippine society; x To generate innovative, value-adding and synergistic solutions to national and local concerns;
x To join hands with the international community in promoting sustainable human development and global competitiveness.
Service/activity:
x DAP offers training and education, technical assistance, consultancy, research, advocacy and publications in the areas of governance, productivity and quality, and management.
Publications issued:
x The Academy publishes books, manuals and monographs on a wide range of development topics. Featured on the website are a few of its recent publications which are available for sale or for free. Interested parties may e-mail decastrot@dap.edu.ph.
Local branches:
DAP Sa Mindanao (DSM) Rm. 202 Villa Abrille Building
C. M. Recto Avenue Davao City 8000 Phone: (63 82) 2212677 E-mail: dapdavao@mozcom.com
DAP Conference Centre (DAPCC) Barrio Sungay, Tagaytay City 2720 Phone: (63 46) 4131291, 4131292 E-mail: dapcc@dap.edu.ph
DAP Sa Visayas Office (DSV) Room 205, LDM Building
M.J. Cuenco cor. Legaspi Sts. Cebu City Phone: (63 32) 2541126
Offices abroad:
Since 1973, DAP has been the national productivity organization (NPO). As NPO, DAP fulfills the country's commitment to the Asian Productivity Organization (APO) in promoting productivity in the Philippines. It spearheads the development of productivity consciousness and promotes the principles, techniques and practice of productivity and quality in key sectors of the economy.
The APO, of which the Philippines is a founding member, is an intergovernmental agency dedicated to the promotion of productivity improvement to accelerate economic growth of member countries through mutual cooperation.
The APO Headquarters is in Tokyo with the following address:
Asian Productivity Organization Hirakawa-cho Dai-ichi Seimei Building 2F 1-2-10 Hirakawacho, Chiyoda-ku Tokyo 102-0093, Japan
Category:
National productivity organization (NPO)/productivity centre.

GARMENTS AND TEXTILE EXPORT BOARD (GTEB)

Office/postal address:
2nd
-4th
Floor, New Solid Building 357 Sen. Gil Puyat Avenue Makati City
Phone: (63 2) 8904651-2 Fax: (63 2) 8904653
E-mail: market@gteb.gov.ph, osac@gteb.gov.ph URL: www.gteb.gov.ph/about/aboutus.htm
Year established: 1979
Principal functions:
x To formulate negotiation strategies and bilateral trade agreements with major importing countries (United States of America, EU, Canada);
x To carry out the overall administration and allocation of export quotas;
x To process and issue garment textile export clearances/export licenses, licenses of bonded manufacturing warehouses and authorization to import raw materials;
x To conduct activities that aim to diversify and expand markets and optimize quota utilization.
Service/activities:
Export registration:
x Garment exporters are required to submit a company profile form designed for the purpose. This is the equivalent of being registered with the GTEB. Registered companies are included in the publication of the *GTEB Directory of Philippine Garments and Textile Exporters* distributed worldwide to foreign buying offices and overseas Philippine trade centres.
Re-accreditation/monitoring of social compliance:
x Re-accredits exporters that comply based on the standard criteria patterned after the Worldwide Responsible Apparel Production Program (WRAPP);
x Monitors compliance of exporters to global ethical sourcing

standards.

Export information services through website and publications:

x Provides updated statistics on garment and textile exports;
x Gives information on trends, trade opportunities, trade fairs, selling missions, seminars and training through publications and through the Internet;
x Maintains files of foreign buyers and listings according to country of destination and product line, for easy access of prospective exporters;
x Distributes *Directory of Philippine Garments and Textile Exporters*, supplemented by current listing of Export Quota Holders.

Export assistance and facilitation services:
x A frontline service counter is provided for speedy assistance to current and potential exporters and traders.

Trade facilitation:
x Export/import licensing – time-bound processing of export/import documents: -Evaluates applications and issues licences to import raw
materials and to operate a bonded manufacturing
warehouse,
-Evaluates and issues Export Licences, textile Visa, Textile Export Clearance, Certificate of Origin, Special export Licence, and certifications as required by the importing countries;
x Continuous enhancement of the quota system and its implementing rules, regulations and procedures: -Grant of quota as incentive to firms that engage in
productivity or growth enhancement programmes
(technology/skills upgrading, participation in trade
promotional activities, etc.).

Seminars and training:
x Conducts seminars/trainings on GTEB Rules and Regulations to facilitate transactions between the Board and garment exporters;
x Coordinates with other government agencies and private entities in the conduct of technical training programmes and seminars on specialized topics.

Buyer-supplier matching programme:
x Matching between buyers and sellers and with other potential partners;
x Provides valuable contacts and business information to both buyers and sellers.

Market research and product promotion:
x Conducts exploratory market research missions and studies in untapped markets such as non-quota countries;
x Prepares country and product specific marketing strategies.

International fairs/missions:
x Conducts/organizes participation of exporters to trade fairs and selling missions.

Product design and development:
x Assists exporters develop design-oriented and market adapted products through the hiring of foreign/local fashion designers;
x Extends product development assistance to exporters to upgrade the quality of Philippine products.

Development assistance programme for the industry:
x Promotion/implementation of GTEB Scholarship Programme for training courses chosen by garment firms;
x Provision for micro firms to avail of the General Sewing Data (GSD) system at the GTEB common service facility;
x Eliciration of cooperation between government, management, and labour groups through tripartite dialogue to get support for Networking for Gain-sharing Programme for the parties to agree on acceptable standards of outputs and incentives;
x Encouragement of firms to be compliant with international standards of quality by providing certain subsidy in the cost of undergoing the ISO 9001, 2000, WRAP/SA 8000 certifications;
x Partnership with financing institutions for the grant of loan facility to garment and textile manufacturer-exporters;
x Coordination with the Bureau of Customs to address speed-tomarket concerns;
x Development of Web-based Inquiry and Report System (WIReS) to provide the industry access to wider, accurate and timely information; and facilitate online transactions.

Publications issued:
x *Directory of Philippine Garments and Textile Exporters.* x *Export Quota Holders.* x *GTEB Annual Report.* x *GTEB Sales Kit How We Can Help You.*

Products/commodity responsible for:
Garments/apparel item; textile/textile made-ups (bed linens, table cloths, stuffed toys, etc.).

Training:
Coordinates with allied government agencies in conducting training programmes and seminars on specialized subjects;
Organizes dialogues in the provincial regions to promote garment exports and to disseminate market-related information

Areas/industries where investment is encouraged:
Garments/textile industry.

Category:
Commodity board; Ministry of Trade; and trade facilitation body.

INTERNATIONAL TRADE GROUP (ITG)

Office/postal address:
Department of Trade and Industry (DTI)
5th

Floor, Industry and Investments Building 385 Sen. Gil Puyat Avenue Makati City, Metro Manila 1200
Phone: (63 2) 8953318, 8976682 loc. 239 Fax: (63 2) 8953393
E-mail: tgaquino@boi.gov.ph URL: www.dti.gov.ph, tradelinephil.dti.gov.ph
Year established: The Executive Order 133, signed in 1987, reorganizes the International Trade Group (ITG) of DTI. However, several executive issuances were made since 1987 that authorizes the Secretary of DTI to conduct internal reorganization. Today, ITG is operating under a lean organizational set-up with focused agencies catering to specific client needs. ITG has emerged as the country's Trade Promotion Office (TPO).
Principal functions:

x To be the primary coordinative, promotive, facilitative and regulatory arm of the Government for the country's trade, industry and investment services;
x To act as catalyst for intensified private sector activity in order to accelerate and sustain economic growth through: (a) a comprehensive industrial growth strategy, (b) a progressive and socially responsible liberalization and deregulation programme, and (c) policies designed for the expansion of and diversification of trade, both domestic and international.

The International Trade Group is involved in standards and programme development, and policy formulation on international trade and commerce. It is also tasked to monitor the developmental, regulatory and service delivery programmes of DTI that are pertinent to international trade and commerce.
Services/activities:
The ITG agencies are organized by functions, according to the services required by exporters in their value chain:
Bureau of Export Trade Promotion:
x Formulates and monitors programmes, plans and projects pertinent to the development, promotion and expansion of the foreign trade of the Philippines;
x Formulates country and product export strategies;
x Conducts research on new product development and adaptation opportunities in the export markets, identifies the domestic supply base for such products;
x Prepares situation reports on all export production; prepares and updates country and regional market profiles; x Maintains an integrated information system on all aspects of the products relevant to export marketing.
Bureau of International Trade Relations:
x Responsible for all matters pertaining to foreign trade relations (bilateral, regional, multilateral) market access and market access-related matters;
x Formulates positions and strategies for trade negotiations, consultations and conferences; supervises trade negotiations, consultations and conferences.
Foreign Trade Service Corps:

x Assists Philippine businesspersons, producers and exporters with marketing information and project development support, and liaises with foreign government agencies;
x Develops market and commercial intelligence for dissemination to Philippine businesspersons, provides direct support to DTI's overseas promotional programmes;
x Assists businesspersons handle complaints against foreign firms and Governments;
x Supports DTI's units in import and export administration, monitoring of trade agreements and investments promotion;
x Is accountable for established foreign investment and export targets for their respective areas of responsibility.

Publications issued:
x *Export/Import Manuals: Handy Guide to Export.* x *Export/Import Manuals: Handy Guide to Import.* x *Philippine Exporter's Manual Vols. 1 and 2.* x *Philippine Export Development Plan.* x *Guidebook on Exports for Local Chief Executives.* x *Early Bird News* (available on the DTI website). x *Philippine Business Report.* x *Online Catalogue of CITEM.*
Local branches:
Bureau of Export Trade Promotion (BETP)
5th
-8th
Floor, New Solid Bldg. 357 Sen. Gil Puyat Ave. Makati City, Metro Manila Phone: (63 2) 8953654, 8990133, 7593381 Fax: (63 2) 8904707, 8904716 E-mail: infobetp@dti.gov.ph
Bureau of International Trade Relations (BITR)
3rd
Floor, Trade and Industry Bldg. 361 Sen. Gil Puyat Ave. Makati City, Metro Manila Phone: (63 2) 7510384 Fax: (63 2) 7513262 E-mail: bitr_mon@dti.gov.ph
Foreign Trade Service Corps Coordinating Office (FTSC)
5th
Floor, New Solid Bldg. 357 Sen. Gil Puyat Ave. Makati City, Metro Manila Phone: (63 2) 8979659, 8979661, 8979672 Fax: (63 2) 8904774 E-mail: ftscmnl@dti.gov.ph
Offices abroad:
The DTI offices abroad are managed by the Foreign Trade Service Corps, under the International Trade Group of DTI. The directory of DTI's Overseas Trade Offices is available on the *Business Guide of the DTI website:* www.dti.gov.ph/contentment.
Products/commodity responsible for:

Construction materials; electronics; food; giftware and holiday décor; home furnishings; IT and IT-enabled services; marine products; motor vehicle parts and components; organic and natural products; and wearables.

Training:
Trade Business Management Courses:
- Export Management Courses,
- Entrepreneurial Development Courses,
- E-commerce Programmes.

Testing and Inspection Courses: -Food (e.g. Hazard Analysis and Critical Control Point - HACCP, Current Good Manufacturing Practice (GMP),
- Garments (e.g. Quality Control for Garment Industry, Production Management of the Garment Industry),
- Furniture (e.g. Production Management for the Furniture Industry, Quality Management for the Furniture Industry),
- Quality and Productivity Courses (e.g. Supervisory Effectiveness for Improved Quality and Productivity, ISO 14000 Environment Management System).

Areas/industries where investment is encouraged:
The Board of Investments (BOI) is a government agency under the Industry and Investment Group (IIG) of DTI, which promotes investments in the Philippines. Investors, who are located outside of economic zones, register with the BOI. On the other hand, investors who wish to locate in economic zones must apply and register with the Philippine Economic Zone Authority (PEZA). PEZA manages and operates economic zones all over the country and collects application and registration fees. To facilitate the processing of export documentation, One-Stop-ExportDocumentation-Centres are located in economic zones. Also, to facilitate the processing of Permanent Resident Status of foreign nationals and their families, offices of the Bureau of Immigration and Deportation are located in economic zones.
The Investment Priorities Plan 2005 (IPP 2005) is a rolling annual plan of priority industries and service areas, which are being encouraged through the grant of fiscal and non-fiscal incentives. IPP 2005 contains a list of Priority Investment Areas under the following: Preferred Activities, Other Preferred Activities, Mandatory Inclusions and the Autonomous Region for Muslim Mindanao (ARMM) List. All activities under these lists shall be eligible to incentives prescribed under EO No. 226 or the Omnibus Investment Code, as amended, subject to the general policies and guidelines of the BOI.
The Preferred Activities covers the Medium-Term Philippine Development Plan (MTPDP) identified 11 investment areas: agribusiness, healthcare and wellness products and services, ICT, electronics, motor vehicle products, energy, infrastructure, tourism, shipbuilding/shipping, jewelry and fashion garments.
Other Preferred Activities covers other export industries, clustering and modernization activities.
Mandatory Inclusions cover all areas/activities where the inclusion in the IPP and/or the grant of incentives under E.O. 226 is mandated by law.
The ARMM List covers priority areas that have been independently determined by the Regional Board of Investments (RBOI) of the ARMM in accordance with E.O. 458. The BOIARMM can administer incentives granted to activities located in the ARMM subject to General and Specific Guidelines.

Titles of laws and regulations on foreign investment:
x Export Development Act (Republic Act No. 7844).
x Foreign Investment Act (Republic Act No. 8179).
x Foreign Investment List (Executive Order No. 286).
x Omnibus Investment Code (Executive Order No. 226).
x Retail Trade Liberalization Act (Republic Act No. 8762).

Category:
Design centre; Ministry of Trade; state trading organization; trade facilitation body; trade fair and exhibition authority; trade promotion organization; and training/research institute.

PHILIPPINE ECONOMIC ZONE AUTHORITY (PEZA)

Office/postal address:
Almeda Building Roxas Boulevard cornor San Luis Street Pasay City
P.O. Box: 3403, Makati CPO
Phone: (63 2) 5513438, 5513436 Fax: (63 2) 5113436
E-mail: info@peza.gov.ph URL: www.peza.gov.ph
Year established: 1995
Principal function:
x To promote investments to the Philippines, particularly in PEZA economic zones.
Services/activities:
x Provides investment information, guidelines and assistance to prospective PEZA investors and visitors; x Undertakes promotion and marketing of PEZA Ecozones, IT Parks and Buildings;
x Provides assistance in the application of investors for registration as an Ecozone Export Enterprise, Ecozone IT Enterprise, Ecozone Utilities Enterprise or Ecozone Facilities Enterprise;
x Facilitates the prompt issuance of investors' visa to expatriates working for PEZA locator enterprises; x Organizes inbound/outbound investment missions.
Publications issued:
x *The Special Economic Zone Act of 1995* (Republic Act No. 7916 as amended by Republic Act No. 8748).
x *Rules and Regulations to Implement Republic Act No. 7916.* x *The PEZA Economic Zones, Your Investment Destination in Asia.*
x *Awaiting Your Investments! Philippine Economic Zones: World-Class Environment-Friendly, Ideal Locations for World Industry Leaders.*
x *The PEZA Network* (official newsletter published quarterly in English).
Local branches:
Regular/Public PEZA Ecozones:

Baguio City Economic Zone Loakan Road, Baguio City
Bataan Economic Zone Nassco, Mariveles, Bataan
Cavite Economic Zone Rosario, Cavite
Mactan Economic Zone Lapu-Lapu City, Mactan, Cebu
Number of operating/proclaimed special economic zones over the country: 123 (as of 9 June 2005).
Areas/industries where investment is encouraged:

- x IT services (software development and applications in business, e-commerce, education, media and entertainment; engineering, architectural and other design services; multi media graphics, animation, printing and other services; call centres; data encoding, transcribing and related services; IT research and development);
- x Electronics;
- x Electrical machinery;
- x Transport and car parts;
- x Medical, precision and optical products;
- x Precision equipment;
- x Processed food;
- x Metal products;
- x High-value plastic products;
- x Refined chemicals;
- x Garments and textiles;
- x Other manufactures.

Titles of laws and regulations on foreign investment:
Special Economic Zone Act of 1995 or Republic Act (RA) 7916
as amended by RA 8748. Implementing Rules and Regulations of RA 7916 as Amended. Omnibus Investment Code (Executive Order No. 226).
Category:
Investment promotion agency.

PHILIPPINE EXPORTERS CONFEDERATION, INC. (PHILEXPORT)

Office/postal address:
International Trade Centre Complex Roxas Blvd. Cor. Sen Gil Puyat Avenue Pasay City 1300
Phone: (63 2) 8332531-4 Fax: (63 2) 8312132, 8310231, 8313707
E-mail: publications@philexport.net.ph URL: www.philexport.ph
Year established: 1991 (a merger of the Confederation of Philippine Exporters and the Philippine Exporters Foundation).
Principal functions:

- x To provide programmes and services that will promote the growth and development of the Philippine export industry;
- x To work with the Government in the development of policies that will support an export-led economic development.

Services/activities:
x Trade advisory and facilitation; x Specialized training programmes, seminars and workshops; x Special trade and investment promotions programme; x Information collection and dissemination; x Technical support to regional and provincial chapters and
sectoral associations; x One-stop export documentation centre (OSEDC); x Bonded warehousing operations; x Support for trade and investment policy analysis and
advocacy.
Publications issued:
x *PHILEXPORT News and Features* (weekly, English). x *Industry Update, Policy Advisories.* x *Early Bird News Service.*
Membership structure: 3,000 members, representing 16 product sectors and company sizes in the export industry. Exporters in the regions are reached though 18 regional chapters based in Baguio (Cordillera Administrative Region, Pangasinan, Cagayan Valley, Pampanga, Calabarzon, MIMAROPA, Bicol, Iloilo, Negros Occidental, Cebu, Leyte, Zamboanga, Cagayan de Oro, Iligan, Davao, SOCSARGEN, CARAGA, ARMM (Sulu, Maguindanao, Lanao del Sur, Tawi-Tawi).
Products/commodity responsible for:
Members produce and export automotive parts and accessories, chemicals, electronics, food, footware, leather goods, fashion accessories, furniture, garments, gifts, toys and housewares, information products, technology and services, metals and nonmetals, resource-based products and textiles. Also has service providers such as freight forwarders, brokers, trade associations, financial institutions in roster.
Category:
Trade promotion organization.

PHILIPPINE EXPORT-IMPORT CREDIT AGENCY (PHILEXIM)

(Trade and Investment Development Corporation of the Philippines)
Office/postal address:
17th Floor, Citibank Tower
Valero Street
1200 Makati City

and
3rd

and 4th Floors, Citibank Centre
Citibank Plaza
8741 Paseo de Roxas
1226 Makati City
Phone: (63 2) 8934809, 8934632 Trunkline: (63 2) 8481900, 8934204 Fax: (63 2) 8934480, 8934852
E-mail: info@philexim.gov.ph URL: www.philexim.gov.ph
Year established: 1977
Principal functions:
x To guarantee approved foreign loans for developmental purposes having special regard to the needs of export-oriented industries, BOI-registered industries, public utilities and industries, the promotion of which is encouraged by government policy;
x To guarantee Philippine banking and financial institutions against loss that may be incurred in connection with the grant of loans/credit accommodations to exporters, producers of export products or contractors with approved service contracts abroad, organized or licensed to engage in business in the Philippines;
x To guarantee letters of credit/guarantee issued by Philippine banks and financial institutions to secure the performance of approved service contracts abroad entered into by any entity or corporation organized or licensed to engage in business in the Philippines;
x To provide insurance cover, credits and appropriate services to facilitate the export of Philippine goods or services by any entity, enterprise or corporation organized or licensed to engage in business in the Philippines;
x To guarantee or provide insurance cover for investments of any entity, enterprises or corporation organized or licensed to engage in business in the Philippines;
x To enter into contract of re-insurance with any organized export credit agency or insurance organization;
x To extend direct loans or other credit facilities to any person or entity for the financing of export contracts and foreign trade transactions;
x To provide technical assistance preparation, financing, execution of development or expansion programmes, including the formulation of specific project proposals.
Services/activities:
PhilEXIM offers the following export financing programmes: Guarantee Programmes:

x Preshipment Export Finance Guarantee (PEFG) Program - guarantee coverage on preshipment working capital loans extended by participating financial institutions (PFI) to collateral-deficient small and medium exporters;
x Postshipment Export Risk Guarantee (PERG) Program - guarantee coverage on export bill purchases arising from export transactions under PEFG and other receivable financing extended by PFIs;
  Alternative Schemes of PEFG and PERG:
  -Export Trade Finance Guarantee (ETFG) -guarantee coverage on transaction-based loans;
  -Revolving Export Loan Guarantee (RELG) -guarantee coverage to revolving lines;
x Term Loan Guarantee Program (TLGP) -guarantee coverage on medium- and long-term loans of up to P50 million extended by PFIs to medium and large exporters, and to small exporters with PEFG and PERG accounts, for asset acquisition, expansion and production modernization and related expenditures;
x General Facility Program (GFP) -guarantee coverage on domestic and foreign loans of medium and large exporters and other domestic enterprises to finance any export promotion activities, import substitution industries and other government priority projects;
x Omnibus Line Guarantee under the General Facility Program (OLG-GFP) - guarantee coverage on short-term loans of up to P300 million granted by banks to large, direct and indirect exporters, with disbursement against letters of credit (L/Cs), confirmed purchase orders (CPOs) and confirmed sale contracts (CSCs);
x Programme for Large Projects in Priority Sectors of the Government - guarantee coverage on loans from foreign lending institutions to finance government projects in tourism, ICT, agri-modernization and infrastructure and other projects listed under the Investment Priority Plan of the National Government.

Leading Programmes:
x Short-Term Direct Lending Program -loans of up to P5 million to finance pre-shipment working capital requirements of SMEs;
x Medium- and Long-Term Direct Lending Program - loans of up to P40 million to finance capital asset acquisition, expansion and plant modernization and related expenditures of SMEs, as well as large exporters;

x Special Credit Facility for Export Development - short-term loans of up to P1.5 million to finance the pre-shipment working capital requirements of small exporters;

x SME Unified Lending Opportunities for National Growth (SULONG) – in support of the National SME Development Plan, the government financial institutions (GFIs) collabourated to design a uniform lending programme, tailor-made to meet the funding needs of SMEs. Under the unified lending program, the participating GFIs shall apply simplified and standardized lending procedures and guidelines, for example loan purpose, fee structures, interest rates, application forms, financial ratios and other lending parameters, for evaluating the loan application of SMEs.

Trade Credit Insurance Programmes:

- x Export Credit Insurance - insurance coverage to exporters against non-payment by foreign buyers of export shipments on credit arising from political and commercial risks;
- x Domestic Credit Insurance (Globalliance) -insurance coverage on receivables of a multinational's subsidiary companies against non-payment of buyers in the subsidiary's country;
- x @rating (Credit Rating Service) - a web-based global trade debt rating service system which certifies, rates and secures B2B trades online, and assesses the transaction risks involved as well as the creditworthiness and payment capacity of buyers across the globe.

Trade Information Exchange System (TRADEX) – an Internet-based information system designed to enable real-time and interactive matching and exchange of information on buyers and sellers in international trade to facilitate financing and other services (http://tradex.philexim.gov.ph).

Publications issued:

x *Annual Report.* x *Corporate Profile of PhilEXIM.* x *Newsletter.* x *News Bulletin.* x *PhilEXIM Law Digest.* x Brochures and primers of programmes.

Local branches:

Naga Field Unit Unit B-2, 2nd Floor, DMG Building Peñafrancia Avenue, Naga City Fax: (63 54) 4738588
Cebu Field Unit Room 406 Keppel Centre, Samar Loop corner Cardinal Rosales Ave., Cebu City Fax: (63 32) 4738588
Davao Field Unit Unit 43, 4th Floor, Landco Building PDCP Corporate Centre
J.P. Laurel Avenue, Davao City Fax: (63 82) 2222241

Areas/industries where investment is encouraged:

Export sector, priority projects of the Government, i.e. tourism, ICT, agri-modernization and infrastructure projects.

Category:

Export credit insurance; export financing organization; investment financing organization; export-import credit agency; and government owned and controlled corporation.

PHILIPPINE SHIPPERS' BUREAU

Office/postal address:
5th
Floor, Trade and Industry Building 361 Sen. Gil Puyat Avenue Makati City, Metro Manila
P.O. Box: 3828 Makati Central Post Office, Metro Manila
Phone: (63 2) 7510384, 7512512-7, 7513304, 89104892 Fax: (63 2) 7513305 E-mail: psb@dti.dti.gov.ph
URL: www.dti.gov.ph Year established: 1973 Principal functions:

- x To promote and protect the common interests of Philippine exporters, importers and other commercial users of water transport;
- x To consult/negotiate with cartelized, as well as individual lines, on proposed general and specific freight charges, the provision and maintenance of adequate, reliable and economic shipping services, and provision of equitable shipping contracts;
- x To serve as a clearing house of information on shipping services and other matters of interest to Philippine shippers;
- x To bring to the attention of the Government the laws, policies, rules and regulations that hamper the development of Philippine trade and commerce, especially those which may delay or obstruct the speedy, economical and efficient carriage of goods, and recommend and work for appropriate legislation and adoption of remedial measures;
- x To maintain and develop close relations with shippers' councils and relevant organizations in Asia and other countries for the attainment of the objectives of the Bureau;
- x To serve as the central implementing authority for the use of Philippine flag vessels in the country's foreign trade, as prescribed by PD 1466.

Services/activities:

x Organizes/strengthens shippers' associations;

x Undertakes research and analysis of projected increases in freight rates and various surcharges and other shipping terms and conditions;

x Computes freight costs of exporters' shipments to specific port destinations, as well as price quotations of their exports to prospective buyers;

x Educates shippers in the proper and economical stuffing, packing and packaging of export cargoes;

x Secures adequate shipping services for the carriage of Philippine exports/import through the use of the Philippine flag vessels, pursuant to PD 1466;

x Conducts seminars/workshops on how to save shipping costs in the transport of shippers' cargoes;

x Provides systematic vessel chartering services or charter vessels for the benefit of Philippine shippers;

x Accredits international and domestic sea freight forwarders.

Offices abroad:

Philippine consular offices, which may have been delegated authority by the Bureau to grant waivers pursuant to the implementation of PD 1466 (Philippine Cargo Reservation Law).

Services/activities:

x Conducts seminars/training programmes on:

Entrepreneurship development

Membership structure: 577 accredited freight forwarders (as of 1 August 2005) and 11 regional shipping association.

Products/commodity responsible for:

Provides assistance to shippers.

Training:

Conducts seminars/workshops on how to save on shipping costs in the transport of shippers' cargoes.

Areas/industries where investment is encouraged:

Accreditation/registration of freight forwarding companies.

Titles of laws and regulations on foreign investment:

x Executive Order No. 226 "Omnibus Investments Code of 1987".

x Foreign Investment Act of 1991 - Republic Act No. 7042.

Category:

Ministry of Trade; shipper's council, port authority, national shipping corporation; trade facilitation body; and trade support.

PHILIPPINE TRADE TRAINING CENTER (PTTC)

Office/postal address:
PTTC Building Sen. Gil J. Puyat Avenue corner Roxas Boulevard 1300 Pasay City
Phone: (63 2) 8341344 - 49 Fax: (63 2) 8341343
E-mail: info@pttc.gov.ph URL: www.business.gov.ph
Year established: 1987

Principal functions:

PTTC is an attached agency of the Department of Trade and Industry that serves as the Government's training arm for export trade. Its mandates are:

x To design and develop training curricula and corresponding instructional materials, and conduct training programmes for micro, small and medium enterprises (MSMEs), business support organizations, and the government sector;

x To provide post-training advisory and counselling services for MSMEs; x To provide customized in-company training programmes and services;

x To provide a venue for MSMEs as well as large enterprises to promote their products by marketing, renting out and maintaining exhibition facilities, and providing events management support.

-How to Start a Business; -Entrepreneurship Development Programme: new business creation; -Entrepreneurship Development Programme: business improvement and sustainability; -Franchising: how to select and buy a franchise/how to start and manage a franchise; -Business plan preparation for SMEs; -Preparing a feasibility study for SMEs; -Strategic marketing: how to win customers; -Basic business recording for SMEs; -How to improve selling skills; -Effective market research; -Effective customer service; -Effective business presentation; -Effective procurement/purchasing management; -Financial management for SMEs; -Retail management; -Brand management; -Sharpening staff writer skills for business.

Export management -Expanding business through export (basics of exporting); -Product costing and pricing; -Effective negotiation skills; -Market briefing and understanding market access measures; -Import procedures and documentation; -Understanding customs valuation; -How to Avoid and Resolve Trade Complaints; -International transportation and INCO terms; -Chinese-Mandarin/French/Japanese Business Language Courses; -Supply chain management/logistics management.

Trade exhibition management and participation -Creative and technical aspects of exhibition and visual merchandising; -How to participate in trade fairs.

E-commerce/ICT -Introduction to computers and MS Windows; -Basic MS Word/MS Excel/MS Powerpoint; -Adobe Pagemaker; -Adobe Photoshop; -Dreamweaver MX; -Macromedia Flash MX; -Macromedia Fireworks.

Business support and development -Basic business advisor's course; -Business management systems; -Training and development of business advisors and counsellors; -Capability build-up for MSME business counsellors. -General quality and productivity improvement; -Supervisory effectiveness for improved quality and productivity; -Effective leadership skills; -Problem-solving and decision-making techniques; -Management of change; -ISO 9000 quality management system; -ISO 9001: 2000 quality management system documentation; -ISO/IEC 17025:1999 the standards of a labouratory competence; -ISO/IEC 17025 internal quality audit; -ISO 14000 environmental management system; -Internal quality audit; -Total quality management; -Basic productivity tools and techniques; -5S of good housekeeping; -Values orientation; -Statistical process control; -Social responsibility; -Managing issues, problems and conflict in a family-owned enterprise; -Time and motion study; -Introduction to ergonomics; -Occupational health and safety; -Process optimization through design of experiments; -Materials management and inventory control; -Structural packaging.

x Provides training courses and advisory services for the food, garment and furniture sectors. Emphasis is given to operational efficiency of SMESs.

Quality and productivity improvement for the food sector -Current good manufacturing practices; -Hazard analysis and critical control points (HACCP); -Application of sensory evaluation in food testing and product development; -Packaging and labelling for processed food; -Cost management for the food industry; -Shelf life determination; -Food safety; -Quality inspection and testing of processed fruits and vegetables; -Post-harvest handling of fruits and vegetables.

Quality and productivity improvement for the garment sector -Production management for the garment industry; -Quality management for the garment industry; -Fabric sourcing; -Fabric and thread: selection and usage; -Fashion merchandising; -Colour merchandising; -Patternmaking; -Clothing machinery repair and maintenance.

Quality and productivity improvement for the furniture sector -Production management for the furniture industry; -Quality management for the furniture industry; -Materials management and inventory control for the furniture industry; -Basic furniture finishing techniques; -Advanced furniture finishing techniques.

x Rents out exhibition facilities and seminar rooms for domestic and international trade fairs, conventions, special events and other promotional activities;

x Conducts WTO capacity-building programmes and maintains a WTO Resource Centre.

Publications issued:

Books:

- x *Trade Secrets: The Export Answer Book for Small and Medium-sized Enterprises.* (March 2000, English; in cooperation with the International Trade Centre UNCTAD/WTO).
- x *Secrets of Electronic Commerce: A Guide for Exporters.* (June 2001, English; in cooperation with the International Trade Centre UNCTAD/WTO).

Courseware (CD-ROM):

x *eBiz Plan – A reference material for preparing a business plan.* x *Exporting made e-Z – A guide to prospective exporters.* x *Good Practices in Food Manufacturing – A guide intended for food handlers and supervisors of food manufacturing plants.*

Training:

As detailed under services/activities.

Category:

Training institute; trade fair and exhibition venue; and trade promotion organization.

PRODUCT DEVELOPMENT AND DESIGN CENTER OF THE PHILIPPINES (PDDCP)

Office/postal address:

Cultural Centre Complex Roxas Boulevard 1300 Pasay City

Phone: (63 2) 8321112-9 Fax: (63 2) 8323649 E-mail: pddcp@dti.gov.ph, pddcp@mozcom.com Year established: 1973

Principal functions:

- x To promote industrial design as a tool for improving the quality and competitiveness of Philippine products, and services the design needs of entrepreneurial groups and associations from every level of industry;
- x To design, develop or improve products and packages based on market requirements and manufacturer's production capability;
- x To gather and disseminate data on design and market directions and developments and cultural references, and to undertake applied research on materials and technologies related to product development;
- x To advance awareness and appreciation of the Industrial design profession through exhibitions, seminars, dialogue, and publications.

Services/activities:

x Design of new product, product adaptation, product diversification or expansion of existing product or line based on market needs and available technology;

x New design and redesign of packages of food and non-food products based on requirements of target market;

x Hands-on learning and application of skills such as finishing, knotting, bleaching and dyeing techniques related to product development;

x Seminars on product development and trends, and information on generic product and package design details and processes-related to product development;

x Access to design and industry publications for individuals interested in the study of design.

Publications issued:

x *PDDCP Design Digest Update.* x *PDDCP Design Digest.*

Local branches:

DTI Bldg., corner J.M. Basa - Peralta Streets Iloilo City

Jomil Bldg., Georgetown Park Rizal Street, Cabangan 4500 Legaspi City, Albay

Category:

Design centre.

TRADE AND INDUSTRY INFORMATION CENTER

Office/postal address:
Industry and Investments Building 385 Sen. Gil J. at Avenue Makati City
Phone: (63 2) 8953611
Fax: (63 2) 8956487
E-ail: tiic@boi.gov.ph
URL: www.dti.gov.ph
Year established: 1981
Principal functions:
x To design, operate and maintain a system for the collection, storage and retrieval of trade and industry information;
x To disseminate comprehensive and relevant information on trade, industry and investments;
x To coordinate and monitor the information campaigns on the Department of Trade and Industry's (DTI) services, programmes and projects;
x To develop communication programmes promoting Philippine trade and investment opportunities;
x To provide editorial and creative services in support of other DTI unit's information programmes.
Services/activities:
x Packages and disseminates publications (print/online) and periodic reports;
x Provides assistance to DTI agencies;
x Maintains database on trade and investments;
x Provides enquiry services;
x Provides library and reach-out services;
x Maintains/manages a Business Research Centre;
x Maintains a mailing list for publications and information dissemination.
Publications issued:
x *Directory of DTI Officials.* x *DTI Annual Report.* x *DTI Dataline* (biweekly). x *DTI Guide to Services* (biennium). x *Philippine Business Report* (monthly newsletter). x DTI papers (occasionally).
Areas/industries where investment is encouraged:
x Export activities;
x Industrial tree plantation;
x Iron and steel projects;*
x Exploration, mining, quarrying and processing of minerals;*
x Publication or printing of books or textbooks;*
x Refining, storage, marketing and distribution of petroleum products;
x Ecological Solid Waste Management Act;
x Agricultural/fishery production and processing;*
x Energy sources;
x Logistics;
x Drugs and medicines;* * with modernization projects.
x Engineered products;*
x Information and communication technology;*
x Infrastructure;
x Mass housing projects including development and manufacture of housing components;*
x Research and development activities, including biotechnolgy
x Social service;*
x Tourism-related projects endorsed by the Department of Tourism;*
x Motion picture limited to films with historical and socio cultural significance, and documentary films;
x New projects and bio-technology projects with a minimum project cost of US$ 2 million and which were not commercially undertaken in the Philippines as of 31 December 2001;
x Printing facilities.
Titles of laws and regulations on foreign investment:
x The Omnibus Investment Code of 1987 (Executive Order No. 226).
x The Foreign Investments Act of 1991 (Republic Act No. 704).
x The Special Economic Zone Act (Republic Act No. 7916).
x The Bases Conversion and Development Act of 1992.
x Republic Act No. 7721.
x The Build-Operate-Transfer Act (Republic Act No. 7718).
x Republic Act No. 7888.
x Electronic Commerce Act of 2000 (Republic Act No. 8792).
x Export Development Act (Republic Act No. 7844).
x Foreign Investment Act (Republic Act No. 8179).

x Foreign Investment List (Executive Order No. 286).
x Omnibus Investment Code (Executive Order No. 226).
x Retail Trade Liberalization Act (Republic Act No. 8762).
x Safeguards Measures Act (Republic Act No. 8800).
x Transaction Value Act (Republic Act No. 8181).
x Motor Vehicle Development Program (MVDP) (OE # 156).
Category:
Trade and industry development promotion organization.

WORLD TRADE CENTER METRO MANILA

Office/postal address:
WTCMM Building Financial Centre Area Roxas Boulevard cor. Gil Puyat Avenue Pasay City 1300
Phone: (63 2) 551-5151 Fax: (63 2) 551-5243
E-mail: wtcclub@wtcmanila.com.ph URL: www.wtcmanila.com.ph
Year established: 1989 Principal function:
x To provide a variety of services and facilities to members and clients, which include: access to and exchange of trade information, business opportunities and trade leads through WTCA OnLine (www.wtca.org), display and exhibit facilities, meeting facilities, trade missions, international trade show participation, training and educational services, lounge and dining services, and consumer and business services.
Services/activities:
x Reciprocity - provides members an access to the services and facilities being offered at all World Trade Centres worldwide;
x WTCA OnLine - provides access to World Trade Centres Association's Internet website which is a premier destination for businesses who want to succeed in the world of international trade;
x Trade information service - provides access to various information on business, trade and investment opportunities, world markets, trade statistics, e-commerce, government regulations and other business developments;
x International trade library - maintains a library which houses an extensive collection of trade journals, directories, magazines and other publications on world markets, laws and regulations in different countries, tariffs and other periodicals;
x Trade missions/trade show participation -organizes incoming/outgoing trade missions and international trade show participation in cooperation with other World Trade Centres abroad;
x Training and educational services - organizes training programmes and seminars conducted by local and foreign experts, with topics covering various facets of business and trade;
x Lounge and dining services - provides lounge and dining services at special discounted rates to members for their business meetings and private functions;
x Consumer and business services such as: computer rentals, Internet access, facsimile and photocopying services, answering service, translation services and other clerical and secretarial services;
x Meeting facilities - provides meeting room facilities for members and guests;
x Display and exhibit services -provides a venue for showcasing products and services and the newest technologies in the different industries.
Publication issued:
x *WTC News* (quarterly, English; it has a readership of around 750,000 worldwide).
Offices abroad:
World Trade Centre Metro Manila is a member of the World Trade Centres Association (WTCA). WTCA has a total of 288 member centres operating in 77 countries all over the world.
Membership Structure: 258 corporate and individual members as of June 2005.
Category:
Trade association; trade fair and exhibition authority; and trade promotion organization.

KOREA

EXPORT-IMPORT BANK OF KOREA

Publications issued:

Office/postal address:
16-1, Yeouido-dong Yeoungdeungpo-gu Seoul, 150-996
P.O. Box: 641, Yeouido, Seoul 150-606
Phone: (82 2) 37796114 Fax: (82 2) 7841030
E-mail: iro@koreaexim.go.kr URL: www.koreaexim.go.kr
Year established: 1976
Principal functions:
x To facilitate the sound development of the national economy and enhance economic cooperation with foreign countries;
x To engage in a variety of financial business activities to achieve its purpose;
x To extend financial support for export and import transactions, overseas investment projects, development of natural resources overseas and trade finance, to operate the Economic Development Cooperation Fund (EDCF) and the Inter-Korea Cooperation Fund.
Services/activities:

x Provides medium- and long-term export loans to domestic suppliers, including SMEs, and foreign buyers to support the export of Korean capital goods and technical services;

x Provides medium- and long-term credits to domestic importers for the import of raw materials and to domestic investors for overseas ventures;

x Provides guarantees for domestic and foreign financial institutions against losses incurred in financing either the domestic supplier or the foreign buyers;

x Provides economic development cooperation loans for industrial development and economic stabilization in developing countries;

x Operates the Economic Development Cooperation Fund (EDCF) that assists developing countries in implementing development projects by extending bilateral Official Development Assistance (ODA) loans;

x Operates Inter-Korea Cooperation Fund under the initiative and policy coordination of the National Unification Board to expand mutual exchange and cooperation with the Democratic People's Republic of Korea in the areas of home visits, cultural activities, sports, trade and economic cooperation;

x Operates Overseas Economic Research Institute to provide local firms seeking overseas investment opportunities with coordinated and comprehensive services for launching businesses overseas.

x *Annual Report* (English).

x *A Guide to the Export-Import Bank of Korea* (English/Korean).

x *A Guide to EDCF* (English/Korean).

x *The Project and Structured Finance Program* (English). x *Outline of Relending Facility* (English). x *Biannual Handbook of Foreign ECAs* (Korean). x *Biannual Handbook of Country Information* (Korean). x *Monthly Exim Report* (Korean).

Local branches:

3rd Floor, Shinhan Bank Building 71-1 Sangnam-dong, Changwon 641-831 Phone: (82 55) 2876830 Fax: (82 55) 2876831 E-mail: changwon@koreaexim.go.kr

13th Floor, Samsung Securities Trust Building 190-5, Beomeo-dong Suseong-gu, Daegu 706-742 Phone: (82 53) 7541021 Fax: (82 53) 7541020 E-mail: daegu@koreaexim.go.kr

16th Floor, Capital Tower Bldg. 931 Dunsan 2-dong Seo-gu, Daejeon 302-828 Phone: (82 42) 4899715 Fax: (82 42) 4899716 E-mail: daejeon@koreaexim.go.kr

7th Floor, Korea First Bank Building 9-2 Geumnam-ro 3-ga Dong-gu, Gwangju 501-023 Phone: (82 62) 2326944 Fax: (82 62) 2326946 E-mail: gwangju@koreaexim.go.kr

15th Floor, KORAM Bank Building 1127, Guwol-dong Namdong-gu, Incheon 405-220 Phone: (82 32) 2356114 Fax: (82 32) 2356121 E-mail: inchon@koreaexim.go.kr

14th Floor, Hongwoo Building, 945-1 Daechi 3-dong, Gangnam-gu, Seoul 135-846 Phone: (82 2) 62486114 Fax: (82 2) 62486119 E-mail: kangnam@koreaexim.go.kr

6th Floor, LG Bldg. 257-5, Bujeon 2-dong Busanjin-gu, Busan 614-737 Phone: (82 51) 8175050 Fax: (82 51) 8176060 E-mail: pusan@koreaexim.go.kr

9th Floor, Gyeonggi Small and Medium Business Centre, 906-5 Iui-dong, Yeongtong-gu, Suwon 443-766 Phone: (82 31) 2596600~7 Fax: (82 31) 2596609 E-mail: suwon@koreaexim.go.kr

5th Floor, Dongyang Investment Bank
1358-8 Dahl-dong
Nam-gu, Ulsan 680-727
Phone: (82 52) 2745272~6
Fax: (82 52) 2745278
E-mail: ulsan@koreaexim.go.kr

6th Floor Chungcheongbuk-do SandM Business Centre
1508-1, Gagyeong-dong
Heungduk-gu, Cheongju, 361-802
Phone: (82 43) 2370471
Fax: (82 43) 2370476
E-mail: cheongju@koreaexim.go.kr

10th Floor KTCU Jeonbuk Bldg., 769-1
Seoshin-dong, Wansan-gu, Jeonju, 560-720
Phone: (82 63) 2716134~8
Fax: (82 63) 2716139
E-mail: jeonju@koreaexim.go.kr

Offices abroad:

São Paulo Representative Office
Av. Paulista, 1439 cj. 142,
CEP 01311-200, C
Cesar, São Paulo, Brasil
Phone: (55 11) 32833021
Fax: (55 11) 32870548

Frankfurt Representative Office
Zeppelinallee 65-67, Ecke Blanchardstrasse
60487 Frankfurt am Main, Germany
Phone: (49 69) 9778320
Fax: (49 69) 9778316
E-mail: eximff@t-online.de

New Delhi Representative Office
B2 Qutab Hotel Shaheed Jeet Singh Marg,
New Delhi 110016 India
Phone: (91 11) 51688721
Fax: (91 11) 51688723
E-mail: bkkim@koreaexim.go.kr

P.T. Koexim Mandiri Finance
Menara Mulia Tower Suite 2007 JL
Jend Gatot Subroto Kav. 9-11
Jakarta 12930, Indonesia
Phone: (62 21) 5257261
Fax: (62 21) 5257260
E-mail: jakarta@koreaexim.go.kr

Iran Liaison Office
No. 18 West Daneshvar Street
Shaekhbahaei Avenue, Vanak Square
Tehran, Islamic Republic of Iran
Phone: (98 21) 8065301
Fax: (98 21) 8054899

E-mail: exspaulo@dialdata.com.br

Beijing Representative Office
Office C-716, Beijing Lufthansa Centre
50 Liangmaqiao Road, Chaoyang District
Beijing 100016, China
Phone: (86 10) 64653371
Fax: (86 10) 64637116
E-mail: exbjing@public3.bta.net.cn

Kexim Asia Ltd.
Suite 2511, 25th Floor, Jardine House
1 Connaught Place, Central
Hong Kong, China
Phone: (852) 28100182
Fax: (852) 28104460
E-mail: keximhk@netvigator.com

Qingdao Liaison Office
Rm. 1422, Hisense Tower No. 17
Donghai west Rd.
Qingdao, 266071, China
Phone: (86 532) 3095896
Fax: (86 532) 3095897
E-mail: sdabby@hanmail.net

Shanghai Representative Office
19E, PUFA Bldg., No. 588
Pudong Road(S), Shanghai, China
Phone: (86 21) 58768575
Fax: (86 21) 58761782
E-mail: aaron@koreaexim.go.kr

Paris Representative Office
36 Ave. Hoche, 75008 Paris, France
Phone: (33 1) 44218317
Fax: (33 1) 44218315
E-mail: keximparis@yahoo.fr

E-mail: last5ever@hanmail.net

Tokyo Representative Office
Rm. 1904, 19th Floor, Hibiya Daibiru,
1-2-2 Uchisaiwaicho, Chiyoda-ku
Tokyo 100-0011, Japan
Phone: (813) 35808702-3
Fax: (813) 35808705
E-mail: extokyo@hotmail.com

Mexico City Representative Office
Paseo de la Reforma #350 Edif.
Torre del Angel piso 8,
Col. Juarez del Cuauhtemoc Mexico DF
Mexico C.P. 06600
Phone: (52 55) 55118445
Fax: (52 55) 55118472
E-mail: mexchoi2003@yahoo.co.kr

Poland Liaison Office
Korea Trade Centre, 21th Floor, Warsaw
Financial Centre ul. Emilii Plater 53
00-113, Warszawa, Poland
Phone: (48 22)5206248
Fax: (48 22)5206249

Moscow Representative Office
Office Building 1704 A
World Trade Centre
12 Krasnopresnenskaya Nab.
123610 Moscow, Russian Federation
Phone: (7 095) 2582366
Fax: (7 095) 2582368
E-mail: keximmos@sovintel.ru

Dubai Representative Office Level 4, The Gate PO Box 74777 Dubai, United Arab Emirates Phone: (971 50) 2502937 Fax: (971 40) 2279686

Kexim Bank (UK) Limited Boston House 63-64 New Broad Street London EC2M 1JJ, United Kingdom Phone: (44 20) 75625500 Fax: (44 20) 75883642 E-mail: london@koreaexim.go.kr

New York Representative Office 460 Park Avenue, 8th Floor New York, NY 10022 United States of America Phone: (1 212) 3557280 Fax: (1 212) 3086106 E-mail: exim-ny@earthlink.net

Washington Representative Office 1300 L Street, N.W. Suite 825 Washington, DC 20005 United States of America Phone: (1 202) 4088838~9 Fax: (1 202) 4087858 E-mail: eximstn@hotmail.com

Uzbekistan Liaison Office 16th
Floor, Project Finance Centre National Bank for Foreign Activity of the Republic of Uzbekistan 101 Amir Temur Str. Tashkent 100084, Uzbekistan Phone: (998 71) 1375944 Fax: (998 71) 1355610 E-mail: exim@dostlink.net

Kexim Viet Nam Leasing Co., Ltd.
9th
Floor, Diamond Plaza Building 34 Le Duan Street, District 1 Ho Chi Minh City, Viet Nam Phone: (84 8) 8257000 Fax: (84 8) 8230854 E-mail: keximvt@hcm.vnn.vn

Category:
Export financing organization.

FEDERATION OF KOREAN INDUSTRIES (FKI)*

Office/postal address:
2nd
Floor, FKI Building
28-1, Yoido-dong
Yongdeungpo-ku
Seoul 150-756
Phone: (82 2) 37710114 Fax: (82 2) 37710110
E-mail: webmaster@fki.or.kr URL: www.fki.or.kr
Year established: 1961
Principal functions:

x To promote entrepreneurial spirit and the free enterprise system;
x To develop a sound national economy through fully mobilizing entrepreneurs' knowledge, experience and capital resources;
x To play a vital role in the private sector in promoting economic cooperation with foreign business communities;
x To conduct research and survey work on domestic and overseas economic conditions and trends;
x To advise the Government and other interested parties on economic matters;

x To exchange economic and trade missions with other countries;
x To sponsor business conferences.

Services/activities:
x Conducts studies on various domestic and international problems which affect the Korean economy including financial and fiscal developments, taxation, business trends, technological development, industrial structure, resources, urban problems, domestic and foreign trade conditions, international economy;
x Provides the Government and its agencies with the consolidated views and recommendations of the private business community on overall economic policies as well as specific areas including investment, taxation, financing, price structure, resources, foreign trade, export credit, technical cooperation and improvement of industrial structure;
x Promotes international economic cooperation. Bilateral economic cooperation committees and cooperative bodies established under the umbrella of FKI have been serving as principal channels for cooperation between the business sector of the Republic of Korea and its foreign counterparts.
Publications issued:
x *Annual Report, (*English). x *Chun Kyung Ryun* (monthly, Korean). x *Korean Economic Yearbook* (Korean). x *FKI Newsletter* (monthly, English, also online).
Membership structure: 342 corporate members and 61 business associations.
Category:
Industrial promotion organization.

KOREA CHAMBER OF COMMERCE AND INDUSTRY (KCCI)

Office/postal address:
45, 4-ga, Namdaemun-ro Chung-gu Seoul 100-743
Phone: (82 2) 3163546 Fax: (82 2) 7579475
E-mail: trade@korcham.net URL: www.korcham.net, www.korchambiz.net
Year established: 1884
Principal functions:
x To promote economic development, international cooperation; x To promote sound development of commerce and industry.
Services/activities:
x Provides counselling and training on business management;
x Organizes seminars, conferences and meetings both domestic and international;
x Reviews government economic policies and makes recommendations to improve any inadequacies in them;
x Undertakes economic research and surveys;
x Operates a library, publishes and disseminates economic information and handles business enquiries;
x Sends and receives trade missions;
x Certifies trade documents;
x Provides assistance and guidance to foreign investors;
x Provides information on industrial locations;
x Participates in international economic organizations including International Chamber of Commerce and the Confederation of Asian Pacific Chambers of Commerce and Industry.
Publications issued:
x *Doing Business with Korea* (English). x *Economic and Industrial Research Series* (Korean). x *Guide to Investment in Korea* (English). x *KCCI Quarterly Review* (English). x *Weekly Chamber Bulletin* (Korean). x Reports on conferences, seminars and workshops, etc.
(occasional, Korean or English/Korean combined). x Korean Business Directory (online at www.korchambiz.net).
Office abroad:
401/38 Xiondaiquiche dasha Shoo Yun Iv, Chao Yong Qv Beijing
Membership structure: 70 local chambers of commerce.
Training:
The Chamber's Vocational Training Centre provides a course in factory automation data processing, computer and graphic design, etc.
Category:
Chamber of commerce; and industrial promotion organization.

KOREA IMPORTERS ASSOCIATION (KOIMA)

Office/postal address:
KOIMA Building 218 Hankangro 2-ka Yongsan-ku Seoul 140-875
Phone: (82 2) 7921581-4 Fax: (82 2) 7854373
E-mail: cmlee@aftak.com URL: www.import.or.kr/
Year established: 1970
Principal functions:
x To approve thereby register membership;
x To confirm foreign-issued offers for sale (or quotations) being submitted by non-members which are required for import approval;

x To recommend items adequate for import approval to the authorities concerned which fall under import restriction;

x To liaise and coordinate affairs in question with the government authorities concerning the rights and interests of members;

x To provide a trade balance with international markets as well as promote mutual trade development, friendly ties and diversification of import markets;

x To run the office of market consulting for foreign business people as one part of government import diversification policy.

Services/activities:

x Provides intermediary services in linking foreign firms with local partners for trade promotion; x Dispatches buying missions overseas to promote and expand international trade; x Makes hotel reservations at special rates on behalf of member firms.

Publications issued:

x *KOIMA Magazine.* x *Monthly Bulletin.* x *Trading Agents Directory* (biennial). x Other brochures.

Local branch:

3F, Architecture Centre 847-18, Beomchon-1 Dong Jin-ku, Pusan Phone: (82 51) 6437142-3 Fax: (82 51) 6437144

Category:

Trade association.

KOREA INTERNATIONAL TRADE ASSOCIATION (KITA)*

Office/postal address:

Trade Tower Korea World Trade Centre 159-1, Samsung-dong Kangnam-gu Seoul 135-729

Phone: (82 2) 5515303-6 Fax: (82 2) 5515181, 5515300

E-mail: ckim@kotis.net; kwtcsl@kotis.net URL: www.kita.or.kr, www.kita.org

Year established: 1946 (formerly: Korea Foreign Trade Association, name changed in 1996).

Principal functions:

x To represent all licensed traders in the Republic of Korea;

x To provide foreign businesspersons with information, contacts and advice;

x To facilitate and promote international trade;

x To represent and enhance the interests of the entire international business community throughout the Republic of Korea;

x To function as a leading trade promotion organization in expanding the Republic of Korea's foreign trade and enlarging its role in the world market;

x To maintain and operate the Korean World Trade Centre (KWTC) providing a "one-stop service" to both domestic and overseas businesspersons;

x To provide supporting services in overseas marketing and to enhance economic cooperation through trade-related activities, information services and specialized training courses.

Services/activities:

x Organizes business matchmaking programmes for trade missions, hotel accommodation and tour arrangements;

x Undertakes activities to promote international cooperation: provides member firms with opportunities to interact fully with the international community, maintains cooperative relationships with major international organizations;

x Promotes trade facilitation through the business inquiry office with support of a computerized database, organizes and dispatches trade missions and market survey teams overseas, assists visiting trade delegations: provides members with information on investment and business opportunities overseas;

x Offers training courses to both international and Korean businesspersons on trade-related issues including information technology;

x Operates Korean Convention and Exhibition Centre (COEX): provides facilities and service for international exhibitions and permanent display of Sample Showcase and Trade Mart and foreign trade shows;

x Operates Korean Trade Information Service (KOTIS), a nationwide online network of databases on economic and trade statistics, trading systems and procedures, trade and industrial trends, tariffs and non-tariff barriers, importers/exporters, buyers/suppliers overseas: provides trade and business counselling services;

x Operates Korean Trade Information Centres, a clearing house for trade-related information, publishes a wide range of periodicals and reports including statistics, handbooks, directory and catalogues of export products;

x Conducts research and surveys on various subjects relating to international trade and economy, promotes Korea's international competitiveness.

Publications issued:

x KITA publishes over 100 trade-related materials, including 23 periodicals, some of which are: x *Korea Export* (annually). x *Korea Trading Post* (monthly).

Local branches:

Local branches in Chunbuk, Daegu, Daejun, Inchun, Kangwon, Kwangju, Kyungki, Kyungnam, Ulsan, Pusan.

Offices abroad:

Offices abroad in Brussels, Beijing, Shanghai, Tokyo, New York, Vienna.

Membership structure: 70,000 member companies.

Training:

KITA operates the International Trade Institute (ITI) whose 47 specialized programmes include numerous trade specialist courses. The ITI cultivates approximately 10,000 specialists every year by developing systematic curricula, pursuing new fields of academic management and identifying promising recruits through advanced database management.

Titles of laws and regulations on foreign investment:

x Foreign Investment Promotion Act. x The Enforcement Decrees of the Foreign Investment Promotion Act. x Regulations on Foreign Direct Investment. x Foreign Exchange Management Law.

Categories:
Trade association; trade promotion organization; training/research institute; and owner and operator of Korea World Trade Centre (Seoul).

KOREA TRADE-INVESTMENT PROMOTION AGENCY (KOTRA)

Office/postal address:
International Trade Organization Division 300-9, Yomgok-dong Seocho-gu Seoul 137-170
P.O. Box: 101, Seocho
Phone: (82 2) 34607114 Fax: (82 2) 34607777
E-mail: digitalkotra@kotra.or.kr URL: english.kotra.or.kr
Year established: 21 June 1962
Principal functions:
x To promote the Republic of Korea's foreign trade;
x To promote inbound and outbound investment;
x To explore measures to become truly globalized and a leading member of the new world economic order.
Services/activities:
x Undertakes trade promotion activities: identifying new marketing opportunities, arranging business meetings between domestic and overseas buyers and suppliers, organizing trade missions abroad;
x Undertakes overseas market studies, product development and industrial research programmes, namely, Strategic Marketing Initiative (SMI);
x Organizes and participates in international trade fairs and exhibitions;
x Provides "Globalization Service" to assist local SMEs in export marketing;
x Conducts research on international economic trends, international trade developments and current trade-related issues;
x Maintains close cooperative working ties with international and foreign trade organizations;
x Undertakes investment promotion activities through seminars/meetings, publications, missions, exhibitions and "Investment Information Centres" at Korea Trade Centres overseas;
x Provides trade information services through a Global Network which links KOTRA's Head Office with its Overseas Trade Office and through KOTRA-NET;
x Publishes and disseminates trade and product-related materials;
x Provides consultation, advisory and library services;
x Provides marketing support services to local SMEs through electronic commerce and home page;
x Maintains Korea Investment Service Centre (KISC), a joint bureau of KOTRA, government officials and specialists in law and economy which enables one-stop service on inbound/outbound FDIs.
Publications issued:
x *Managing the Road to Globalization: The Korean Experience* (English).
x *Introduction to Foreign Direct Investment* (English).
x *A Practical Labour Guide for Foreign Investors* (English).
x *Overseas Market News* (daily, Korean).
Local branches:
Korea Trade Centre, Kangwon Room 308, GongYoung B/D Jung Ang Ro 1-9 Chuncheon Kangwondo Phone: (82 33) 2564181 Fax: (82 33) 2564182 E-mail: ktckw@kotra.or.kr URL: www.kotra.or.kr/ktc/kw
Korea Trade Centre, Kwang Ju-Chonnam 5th Floor, Gwangju Small and Medium Business Support Centre 621-15, Dochen-dong, Gwangsan-gu, Gwangju Phone: (82 62) 9545500/2 Fax: (82 62) 9545505 E-mail: kjktc@kotra.or.kr URL: www.kotra.or.kr/ktc/kj
Korea Trade Centre, Kyonggi 12th Floor, KSBC Building, #-Mt.111-8 Iui-Dong, Paldal-Gu Suwon City, Kyonggi-Do, 442-270 Phone: (82 31) 2597820/27 Fax: (82 31) 2597848/49 E-mail: kgtc0621@kotra.or.kr URL: www.kotra.or.kr/ktc/kg
Korea Trade Centre, Kyongnam 4th Floor, Chamber of Commerce and Industry Building 97-6 Shinwol Dong, Changwon, Kyungsangnam-Do Phone: (82 55) 2871041/2 Fax: (82 55) 2871030 E-mail: ktckn@kotra.or.kr URL: www.kotra.or.kr/ktc/kn
Korea Trade Centre, Taegu-Kyongbuk 2nd Floor, Daegu Exhibition Convention Centre (Exco Daegu) 1676, Sangyeok-2dong Buk-Gu, Daegu 702-845 Phone: (82 53) 3838444 Fax: (82 53) 3838443 E-mail: kotratg@bora.dacom.co.kr URL: www.kotra.or.kr/ktc/tg
Korea Trade Centre, Taejon-Chungnam #504, TSSc B/D, 23-14, Jang-Dong Yusung-Gu, Daejeon Phone: (82 42) 8641717 Fax: (82 42) 8641716 E-mail: ktctj@kotra.or.kr URL: www.kotra.or.kr/ktc/tj
Korea Trade Centre, Pusan 3rd Floor, Office Building Busan Exhibition and Convention Centre 1291 Woo 2-Dong, Haeundae-Ku, Busan Phone: (82 51) 7407801 Fax: (82 51) 7407800 E-mail: pusan@kotra.or.kr URL: www.kotra.or.kr/ktc/ps
Korea Trade Centre, Incheon 16th Floor, Koram Bank Building 1127 Guwol-Dong, Namdong-Gu, Inchon Phone: (82 32) 4216456 Fax: (82 32) 4216459 E-mail: inchon@kotra.or.kr URL: www.kotra.or.kr/ktc/ic

Korea Trade Centre, Chonbuk
5th
Floor, Chonbuk Small and Medium Business Support Centre 337-2 Palbok-1dong, Duckjin-ku Chonju, Chonbuk Phone: (82 63) 2144611 Fax: (82 63) 2144811 E-mail: chonbuk@kotra.or.kr URL: www.kotra.or.kr/ktc/cb
Korea Trade Centre, Chungbuk 1508-1, Gakyung-dong, Hhungduk-ku 361-802 Cheongju, Chungbuk Phone: (82 43) 2364492/4 Fax: (82 43) 2364495 E-mail: kotracj@kotra.or.kr URL: www.kotra.or.kr/ktc/cj
Korea Trade Centre, Ulsan
4th
Floor, Tong Yang Investment Bank Co. B/D, 1358-8, Dal-Dong, Nam-Gu Ulsan, 680-030 Phone: (82 52) 2277744 Fax: (82 52) 2277745 E-mail: ktcus@kotra.or.kr URL: www.kotra.or.kr/ktc/us
Korea Trade Centre, Incheon International Office 2851 Unseo-dong, Joong-gu Incheon City, 400-340
Phone: (82 32) 7402601/3
Fax: (82 32) 7402600
URL: www.kotra.or.kr/ktc/ica
Taejon Exhibition Centre 3-8 Toryong-dong, Yusong-Gu, Taejon Phone: (82 42) 3653000, 3001, 3002 Fax: (82 42) 3653007, 3008
Offices abroad:
There are 99 overseas Korea Trade Centres in 73 countries located in:
Middle East and Africa (Amman; Baghdad; Beirut; Cairo; Casablanca; Dubai; Kuwait; Muscat; Riyadh; Tehran; Tel Aviv; Alger; Johannesburg; Lagos; Nairobi; Tripoli);
Asia and Oceania (Auckland; Bangkok; Chennai; Colombo; Dhaka; Hanoi; Ho Chi Minh City; Jakarta; Karachi; Kuala Lumpur; Manila; Melbourne; New Delhi; Phnom Penh; Singapore; Sydney; Yangon; Tokyo; Osaka; Nagoya; Fukuoka; Beijing; Chengdu; Dalian; Guangzhou; Qingdao; Shanghai; Taipei; Hong Kong, China; Wuhan);
Europe (Amsterdam; Athens; Berlin; Brussels; Budapest; Bucharest; Copenhagen; Dublin; Frankfurt; Hamburg; Helsinki; Istanbul; Lisbon; London; Madrid; Milano; Munich; Oslo; Paris; Prague; Sofia; Stockholm; Vienna; Warsaw; Zagreb; Zürich);
North America (Atlanta; Chicago; Dallas; Detroit; Los Angeles; Miami; New York; San Francisco; Washington; Toronto; Vancouver);
Latin America (Bogotá; Buenos Aires; Caracas; Guatemala; Lima; Mexico City; Montevideo; Panama; Santiago; Santo Domingo; São Paulo);
Russian Federation and Commonwealth of Independent States (Almaty; Kiev; Moscow; Tashkent; Vladivostok).
Membership structure: 653 members (domestic 355 and overseas 298).
Training:
English learning courses including conversation and writing.
Titles of laws and regulations on foreign investment:
x Foreign Investment Promotion Act. x Enforcement Decree of the Foreign. x Foreigner's Land Acquisition Act. x Act on Private Investment in Infrastructure. x Industrial Placement and Factory Construction Act.
Category:
Investment promotion authority.

KOREAN AGENCY FOR TECHNOLOGY AND STANDARDS (KATS)

Office/postal address:
2, Jungang-dong Gwacheon Gyeonggi-do, 427-716
Phone: (82 2) 5097399/7400, 5074376 Fax: (82 2) 5037977
E-mail: standard@ats.go.kr URL: www.ats.go.kr
Year established: 1973 (formerly: Korean National Institute of Technology and Quality (KNITQ), changed as of 24 May 1999).
Principal functions:
x To manage a national industrial standardization system;
x To operate a labouratory accreditation system;
x To manage the safety control of electrical appliances and consumer goods;
x To take responsibility for legal metrology system;
x To provide testing/analysis/evaluation functions to industry;
x To conduct R&D for standardization;
x To operate a national inquiry point for industrial products.
Services/activities:
x Develops and manages Korean Industrial Standards (KS); x Accredits testing and calibrations labouratories; x Operates safety certification system for electrical goods; x Conducts safety inspections for consumer goods; x Operates national calibration system; x Designates verification bodies for legal metrology devices; x Acts as a member of international and regional organizations
including the International Organization for Standardization, International Electrotechnical Commission, International Labouratory Accreditation Cooperation, International Organization of Legal Metrology, Pacific Area Standards Congress, Asia-Pacific Labouratory Accreditation Cooperation, and Asia-Pacific Legal Metrology Forum;
x Functions as World Tade Organization Inquiry Point; x Undertakes research and development of industrial technology for standardization; x Operates certification system for technologies; x Provides technical assistance to small and medium enterprises; x Provides technical assistance to developing countries.
Training:
Plans and conducts training programmes on standardization, legal metrology and labouratory accredition as follows: x "TIC-CAR Project through the APEC Cooperation Centre for

Conformity Assessment" (2000-2005); x "Training Program Standardization and Conformity Assessment" for Experts from ASEAN Countries (2002~).

Category:
Commodity standard institute; industrial promotion; Ministry of Trade; and standard, testing and inspection body.

KOREAN SHIPPERS COUNCIL (KSC)

Office/postal address:
Trade Tower #4806 World Trade Centre 159-1 Samsung 1-dong Kangnam-gu Seoul 135-729
Phone: (82 2) 60005382-8 Fax: (82 2) 60005200
E-mail: kscn@kotis.net, k5kim@kotis.net, annechoi@kotis.net URL: http://shippersgate.kita.net/
Year established: 1972
Principal functions:
x To represent the interests of the shippers of the Republic of Korea concerning transportation of cargoes and to promote cooperation among shippers, carriers and other organizations associated with shipping;
x To facilitate international trade by ensuring the smooth flow of export/import cargoes, reducing logistics expenses, protecting the rights of shippers, and improving cargo transportation conditions.
Services/activities:
x Conducts negotiations/consultations on freight rates and charges and other matters including documentation and cargo distribution with liner conferences, airlines, inland truckers, freight forwarders and other interested parties on behalf of all shippers in the country;
x Provides suggestions/recommendations on shipping matters to the Government and other transportation-related organizations to improve domestic cargo transportation conditions and reduce cargo distribution costs;
x Maintains close relations with international shippers and shipping organizations;
x Provides advisory services to its members including shipping schedules and freight rates, conducts research activities on ways to reduce transportation costs, and organizes seminars on shipping to enhance the knowledge and skills for shippers of the Republic of Korea;
x Conducts research on the current situations of logistics and logistics costs, the possible solutions to enhance logistic efficiency of infrastructure, the trends of freight rates and the bottlenecks of shippers;
x Facilitates the national project of making the Republic of Korea a North-East Asian economic and logistics hub;
x Provides logistics information such as market freight rates, shipping schedules, logistics news, transportation guidance and so on via KSC's website at www.shippersgate.net;
x Operates RADIS (Rate Discount Service) in order to reduce shippers' burden of freight costs;
x Operates and facilitates related committees such as the Logistics Working Committee.
Publications issued:
x *Practical Guidelines for Export and Import Transportation* (2000, Korean) – online publication.
x *Logistic Facilitation among Korea, Japan and Far Eastern Russia* (2001, Korean).
x *Practical Guidelines for Export and Import Transportation* (2001, Korean) – online publication.
x *Practical Guidelines for Export and Import Transportation* (2002, Korean) – online publication.
x *Cyber Korean Shippers* (quarterly, Korean).
Local branches:
7th Floor, Busan Trade Centre 87-7 Joongang-dong 4-ga Joong-gu Busan Metropolitan City Phone: (82 51) 9933300-5 Fax: (82 51) 4634402 E-mail: pusans@kotis.net
7th Floor, Kukje Officetel 299-2 Shinchon 4-dong Dong-gu Daegu Metropolitan City Phone: (82 53) 7537531-3 Fax: (82 53) 7537530 E-mail: taegu@kotis.net
5th Floor, Trade Centre 1589-1 Woosan-dong Kwangsan-gu Kwangju Metropolitan City Phone: (82 62) 9439400-3 Fax: (82 62) 9139404 E-mail: kwangjudv@kotis.net
1st Floor, Jeonbuk Small and Medium Business Support Centre 337-2 Palbok-dong 1-ga Duckjin-gu Jeonju Jeonbuk Phone: (82 63) 2146991-2 Fax: (82 63) 2136993 E-mail: cheonbuk@kotis.net
5th Floor, Chungbuk Small and Medium Business Support Centre 1508-1 Kagyung-dong Hungduck-gu Chongju Chungbuk Phone: (82 43) 2361171-3 Fax: (82 43) 2361174 E-mail: chungbuk@kotis.net
Daejon Small and Medium Business Support Centre #406 23-14 Jang-dong Yusong-gu Daejon Metropolitan City Phone: (82 42) 8644620-2 Fax: (82 42) 8644623 E-mail: taejeon@kotis.net
5th Floor, Kyungnam Trade Centre 7-4 Yongho-dong Changwon Kyungnam Phone: (82 55) 2824115-6 Fax: (82 55) 2822010 E-mail: kyongnamdv@kotis.net
11th

Floor, Renaissance Tower 989-1 Jooan-dong Nam-gu Incheon Metropolitan City Phone: (82 32) 4200011-3 Fax: (82 32) 4200016 E-mail: inchondv@kotis.net

3rd

Floor, Kongyoung Building 9 Joongangno 1-ga Chunchon Gangwon-do Phone: (82 33) 2563067-8 Fax: (82 33) 2563069 E-mail: gangwon@kotis.net

12th

Floor, Gyunggi Small and Medium Business Support Centre 111-8 Iui-dong San Paldal-gu Suwon Gyunggi-do Phone: (82 31) 2597850-3 Fax: (82 31) 2597854

3rd

Floor, Ulsan Small and Medium Business Support Centre 758-2 Yonamdong Buk-gu Ulsan Metropolitan City Phone: (82 52) 2873060-1 Fax: (82 52) 2873062 E-mail: ulsandv@kotis.net

Offices abroad:

Korea International Trade Association Room 1201, China World Trade Centre No. 1 Jian Guo Men Wai Da Jie Beijing 100004, China Phone: (86 10) 65052671-3 Fax: (86 10) 66052670 E-mail: beijing@kotis.net

Korea International Trade Association Room 3201, New Town Centre No. 83, Lou Shan Guan Road Shanghai, 200336, China Phone: (86 21) 62368287 Fax: (86 21) 62368292 E-mail: laojin@kotis.net

Korea International Trade Association Avenue Louise 165 1050 Brussels, Belgium Phone: (32 2) 6462180 Fax: (32 2) 6467006 E-mail: brussels@kotis.net

Korea International Trade Association 460 Park Avenue Suite 2200 New York, NY 10022, United States of America Phone: (1 212) 4218804/06 Fax: (1 212) 2233827 E-mail: newyork@kotis.net

Korea International Trade Association

2nd

Floor, Kamiyacho, Mori Building 4-3-20 Toranomon, Minato-ku Tokyo, Japan Phone: (81 3) 54722641 Fax: (81 3) 54722640 E-mail: tokyo@kotis.net

Korea International Trade Association 8192 Quinn Terrace Vienna, VA 22180, United States of America Phone: (1 703) 8760699 Fax: (1 703) 5735179 E-mail: kwto@kotis.net

Membership structure: Currently the Korea International Trade Association (KITA) has 86,633 members, which are also members of KSC. Trading companies join voluntarily. They pay entrance fee (about US$ 155) and annual membership fee (about US$ 115).

Training:

x KSC organizes many seminars and workshops such as: x A Seminar on Government's Policy on Logistics and Transportation; x A Seminar on How to Reduce Logistics Costs; x A Seminar on How to Conduct Global SCM More Effectively; x A Workshop on Developing E-Logistics; x A Seminar on How to Rationalize Korean Logistics System; x International Conference on Building a Northeast Asian

Logistics Hub in Korea.

Category:

Shipper's council; port authority; and national shipping corporation.

KOREAN STANDARDS ASSOCIATION (KSA)

Office/postal address:

Korean Technology Centre Bldg. 701-7, Yeoksam-Dong Gangnam-Gu Seoul 135-513

Phone: (82 2) 60094630-2 Fax: (82 2) 60094639

E-mail: marykim@ksa.or.kr URL: www.ksa.or.kr

Year established: 1962

Principal function:

x To contribute to innovations in business management by engaging in training, education for building company-wide quality management systems, and disseminating and promoting managerial skills such as certification according to industrial standards for the Republic of Korea and international standards.

Services/activities:

x Engages in research, training, education and certification for industrial standardization and quality management; x Publishes and disseminates industrial standards for the Republic of Korea.

Publications issued:

x *KS Catalogue* (annually, Korean). x *Quality and Originality* (monthly, Korean). x *Quality Management* (monthly, Korean). x *Global Standards* (quarterly, Korean).

Local branches: 14 regional offices.

Office abroad:

Office in China Room #115, Estoril House No. 2 Jiangtai Road Chaoyang District Beijing, China 100016 Phone: (86 10) 64331897 E-mail: jskim@ksa.or.kr

Membership structure: 4,400 firms.

Products/commodity responsible for:

Training and education; providing information for quality standards.

Training:

Regular courses in fields of QM, VE, IE, TPQ, ISO 9000/14000 and so on. Courses can be organized according to the requirement of customers.

Category:

Industrial promotion organization.

RUSSIA

NIZHNY NOVGOROD REGION CHAMBER OF COMMERCE AND INDUSTRY*

Office/postal address:
Business Information Centre Oktyabrskaya Sq. 1 Nizhny Novgorod 603005
Phone: (7 8312) 194210, 194469 Fax: (7 8312) 194009
E-mail: tpp@tpp.nnov.ru URL: www.tpp.nnov.ru/win/english/
Year established: 1989
Principal functions:
x To promote economic, trade and industrial development; x To undertake economic research studies.
Services/activities:
x Creates contacts with foreign and international organizations
for obtaining development assistance; x Provides certification and examination; x Undertakes marketing studies; x Organizes exhibition activities; x Provides legal and publicity services.
Category:
Chamber of commerce.

ST. PETERSBURG CHAMBER OF COMMERCE AND INDUSTRY

Office/postal address:
ul. Tchaikovskogo 46-48
191123 St. Petersburg Phone: (7 812) 2735908 Fax: (7 812) 2726406
E-mail: spbcci@spbcci.ru, irc@spbcci.ru URL: www.spbcci.ru Year established: 1921 Principal function:
x To support business.
Services/activities:
x Organizes business and cultural programmes for representatives of foreign enterprises, arranges meetings and negotiations for foreign and domestic firms and looks for Russian partners;
x Organizes exhibitions, seminars and other events to promote trade and disseminates information on exhibitions held abroad;
x Provides advisory services and consultation on trade- and investment-related issues and conducts marketing studies; x Provides information service on trade and investmentand local
enterprises; x Provides translation and interpreter services for conferences, symposia, seminars and business negotiations; x Prepares documents for the registration of foreign investment enterprises; x Publishes bulletins, proceedings and handbook in cooperation with foreign firms and institutions; x Undertakes the execution of orders for direct mail service over
Russian Federation; x Provides expertise in various trade-related issues; x Determines the code of nomenclature for customs declaration; x Executes quality controls of joint venture products.
Publications issued:
x *Exhibitions in St. Petersburg* (annually, English/Russian). x *St. Petersburg CCI Information Bulletin* (monthly, Russian).
Membership structure: 110 companies (voluntary). Training:
Business Education Centre which holds training seminars monthly and teaches English and training programme for foreign businesspersons and companies interested in conducting business in the northwest region of the Russian Federation.
Areas/industries where investment is encouraged:
Heavy and light industry, agriculture, information technologies.
Category:
Chamber of commerce.

SINGAPORE

INTERNATIONAL ENTERPRISE SINGAPORE

Office/postal address:
230 Victoria Street, #09-00 Bugis Junction Office Tower Singapore 188024
Phone: (65) 63376628 Fax: (65) 63375253
E-mail: enquiry@iesingapore.gov.sg URL: www.iesingapore.com
Year established: 1983 (formerly known as the Singapore Trade Development Board).
Principal functions:
x International Enterprise Singapore (IE Singapore) is an agency under the Ministry of Trade and Industry spearheading Singapore's effort to develop its external economic wing;
x The mission is to help Singapore-based companies grow and internationalize successfully; offers a wide range of services in 37 locations worldwide by using a "3C" framework of assistance – Competency, Connections and Capital; provides market information, and assist enterprises to develop their business capabilities and find overseas partners. At the same time, IE Singapore works to position Singapore as a base for foreign businesses to expand into the region in partnership with Singapore-based companies.
Services/activities:

x Resource Centre: the resource centre is a rich reserve of vital and up-to-date market and industry information. The Centre serves Singapore-based enterprises in their quest to globalize through its Business Library, In-house Publications, Information Services, and Trade Statistics and Business Matching services. For more information, please visit www.iesingapore.com/resourcecentre;
x i.e. journal: IE Singapore's flagship publication, i.e. journal is a publication for international enterprise. With its global reach, i.e. journal serves to herald the business moves and achievements of Singapore-based enterprises on the world stage. i.e.journal may be viewed online at www.iesingapore.com;
x IE Singapore Portal: the IE Singapore portal reflects its role in helping Singapore-based enterprises expand and venture abroad, and promoting Singapore as the global business destination for foreign companies looking for opportunities in Asia. A wide range of services and resources can be found here, including market reports and publications, updates on the latest events and the opportunity to sign up for IE Singapore's business matching services and activities;
x IE Singapore's Global Network: IE Singapore has a global network of Overseas Centres (OCs), Honorary Business Representatives and Business Advisors in 37 locations around the world. The global network provides market intelligence and business facilitation services to Singapore-based enterprises;
x Global Business Insights Pte Ltd: Global Business Insights Pte Ltd (GBI) offers a range of resources to equip Singapore-based companies for globalization. It is a subsidiary of IE Singapore Holdings which is wholly-owned by International Enterprise Singapore (IE Singapore). Through its two divisions – Market Strategy Services (MSS) and Business Support Office (BSO) – GBI offers companies a comprehensive array of services and facilities to assist them in their expansion into new markets.
Offices abroad:
Overseas centres in Bangkok; Beijing; Mumbai; Brussels; Budapest; Chengdu; Dubai; Frankfurt; Geneva; Guanzhou; Ho Chi Minh City; Hong Kong, China; Jakarta; Kuala Lumpur; Chennai; Manila; Mexico City; Moscow; New Delhi; New York; Pekanbaru; San Francisco; Seoul; Qingdao; Shanghai; Taipei City; Tokyo; Washington DC; Yangon.
Honorary business representative offices in Dhaka; Liaoning; Santiago; South Carolina; Sydney.
Business support offices in Beijing; Shanghai; Chengdu; Guangzhou.
Category:
Government statutory board.

MONETARY AUTHORITY OF SINGAPORE (MAS)

Office/postal address:
MAS Building 10 Shenton Way Singapore 079117
P.O. Box: 52, Robinson Road
Phone: (65) 62255577 Fax: (65) 62299491
URL: www.mas.gov.sg
Year established: 1970
Principal functions:
x To conduct monetary policy and issue currency, and to manage the official foreign reserves and the issuance of government securities;
x To supervise the banking, insurance, securities and futures industries, and develop strategies in partnership with the private sector to promote Singapore as an international financial centre;
x To build a cohesive and integrated organization of excellence.
Services/activities:
As detailed under Principal functions.
Publications issued:
x *MAS Annual Report.*
x *Monthly Statistical Bulletin.*
x *MAS Macroeconomic Review.*
x *Financial Stability Review.*
x *Consumer Guides.*
Offices abroad:
MAS New York Office 17 State Street, 25th floor New York, NY 10004, United States of America Phone: (1 212) 8094018 Fax: (1 212) 8096067
MAS London Office Representative Office
1st
floor Old Change House 128 Queen Victoria Street London EC4V 4BJ Phone: (44 20) 73326300 Fax: (44 20) 73326309
Category:
Integrated Central Bank.

PORT OF SINGAPORE AUTHORITY CORPORATION LTD. (PSA)

Office/postal address:
Corporate Communications Department PSA Building 460 Alexandra Road Singapore 119963
Phone: (65) 62794266, 62794010 Fax: (65) 62744261, 62794213
E-mail: ccd1@psa.com.sg URL: www.psa.com.sg
Year established: 1964
Year corporatized: 1997
Principal function:
x To operate port and logistics businesses around the world;
x To provide shippers an unrivalled choice of 250 shipping lines with connections to 600 ports in 123 countries. This includes daily sailings to every major port in the world.

Services/activities:
x Port Services: provides a comprehensive range of port-related services, including cargo-handling, warehousing and distribution. Its wholly-owned subsidiary, PSA Marine, also offers a comprehensive range of marine services including pilotage, ocean and harbour towage, international salvage and emergency response, heavy lift services, marine transportation and marine advisory.
x Container Terminals: operates four container terminals in Singapore at Tanjong Pagar, Keppel, Brani and Pasir Panjang. It has 37 berths, including 6 berths at its new mega-terminal at Pasir Panjang Terminal. Equipped with 15-metre deep berths and quay cranes with an outreach of 18 rows across, the new terminal can accommodate the world's largest container vessels available in the world today. Utilizing innovative Bridge Cranes that can stack containers nine-high, Pasir Panjang Terminal exemplifies the new generation of ports;
x International Business: participates in 14 port projects in 8 countries: the Port of Antwerp and Port of Zeebrugge in Belgium; Muara Container Terminal in Negara, Brunei Darussalam; Dalian, Fuzhou, Fuzhou Jiangyin International and Guangzhou Container Terminals in China; Tuticorin Container Terminal and Pipavav Port in India; Voltri Terminal Europa and Venice Container Terminal in Italy; Sines Container Terminal in Portugal; Inchon Container Terminal in the Republic of Korea; and Aden Container Terminal in Yemen;
x Portnet.com Pte Ltd.: through www.portnet.com, a wholly owned subsidiary, PSA also provides its customers with advanced IT systems to help them increase their productivity and reduce costs. The backbone of the Portnet.com suite of e-products is the PORTNET® system, which had 7,000 subscribers and around 69 million transactions in year 2000. PORTNET® is the world's first nation-wide e-commerce network that has the participation of the entire shipping and port community that operates through Singapore;
x Logistics Services: includes the management of airport ground-handling services, the operations of two multipurpose terminals, cruise and passenger terminals, exhibition services and supply chain management.
Publications issued:
x *PSA Port View* (monthly, English). x *Annual Report.*
Training:
x PSA Institute is the training arm of PSA Corp. In addition to the training of PSA employees, the Institute also provides training for personnel from the local and regional maritime industries. PSA Institute also provides training for participants from other ports, through a range of courses on port management, operations, engineering and ship-handling. Some of the courses offered are Port Management and Operations, Management of Container Operations and Effective Management of a Multi-purpose Terminal;
x Simulators are used where appropriate to provide realistic training scenarios for trainees, thus reducing the time required on actual equipment. It is an effective tool for corrective training and skill-upgrading. PSA Institute uses both Crane Simulators and Full Mission Ship handling simulator for training purposes.
Category:
Port authority.

SINGAPORE CHINESE CHAMBER OF COMMERCE AND INDUSTRY (SCCCI)

Office/postal address:
47 Hill Street #09-00 Singapore 179365
Phone: (65) 63378381 Fax: (65) 63390605
E-mail: corporate@sccci.org.sg URL: www.sccci.org.sg
Year established: 1906
Principal functions:
x To develop and promote industry and commerce in Singapore: -provide useful contacts and information on local and international business trends and developments,
-organize trade and investment missions to explore and create business opportunities as well as establish closer ties with trading partners,
-organize seminars and exhibitions based on advances and developments in the business, technology and economic arenas,
-publish business leads, business opportunities and features on economic and business trends, -compile and analyse economic data and statistics on new and existing markets, -identify and embark on projects with members that will enhance and bring benefits to their operations, -attend to trade enquiries from members and the public; x To promote culture, education and community activities: -conduct staff training programmes and language and computer courses, -organize talks, seminars and activities on cultural and educational issues, -provide scholarships and awards to recognize and promote academic excellence,
-organize public charities and welfare works to address the needs of the less fortunate and promote community cohesiveness;
x To develop closer ties between government and private sector: -maintain regular dialogues with ministries, statutory boards and relevant government departments, -keep members abreast of economic policies and provide their feedback to the Government,
-maintain constant interaction with and represent the interests of the Chinese business community in Singapore.
Services/activities:
As detailed under Principal functions.
Publications issued:
x *Annual Report* (English/Chinese). x *Chinese Enterprise* (monthly, English/Chinese). x *Council Members' Directory* (biennial, English/Chinese). x *The Price of Peace* (Chinese). x *Eternal Vigilance - The Price of Freedom* (Chinese).
Membership structure: Trade association member, life corporate member, ordinary corporate member, life individual member, ordinary corporate member.
Training:

The Singapore Chinese Chamber Institute of Business (SCCIOB) is a non-profit training and education body registered under the Registry of Societies and an affiliated member of the SCCCI.

The Institute's history as a training and education provider can be traced back to 1984 when it first started as a Training Centre with governmental aid and upgraded to its current status, the Institute of Business, in 1996.

The Institute aims to be a leading training institution, providing quality, up-to-date and practical training and education to the local and foreign communities, and to promote lifelong learning in the Asia-Pacific region.

The objective of the Institute is to promote the development of both local and overseas industries through the organization of quality educational and training activities. A wide range of training and development programmes are offered by the Institute for all levels of local and foreign working adults and overseas students. These programmes are structured into three main categories: Business Studies Programmes, Language and Culture Programmes and Training Promotion Programmes.

Category:

Chamber of commerce.

SINGAPORE COMMODITY EXCHANGE (SICOM)

Office/postal address:

#23-04/05, Peninsula Plaza 111 North Bridge Road Singapore 179098

Phone: (65) 63385600 Fax: (65) 63389116

E-mail: marketing@sicom.com.sg URL: www.sicom.com.sg

Year established: 1992 (formerly RAS Commodity Exchange (1992); name changed in February 1994 to better reflect its aim to become a broad-based commodity exchange).

Principal functions:

- x To regulate, promote and develop commodity futures trading in Singapore, including the establishment and dissemination of official prices for various grades and types of rubber;
- x To provide clearing facilities, endorse Certificates of Origin and licences for packers, shippers and manufacturers;
- x To provide a centralized and regulated marketplace for commodity futures trading in Singapore;
- x To maintain financial integrity of the marketplace through its membership criteria, trading rules, and audit and market surveillance activities;
- x To maintain a Clearing House to facilitate and clear all futures contracts transacted between buyers and sellers who are Clearing Members;
- x To develop into a premier commodity exchange within the Asian time zone.

Services/activities:

x Conducts market research, develops and launches suitable new futures contracts; x Educates the commodity trading community and the public on the economic benefits of futures trading;

x Endorses Certificates of Origin and processes licences for rubber dealers, packers, shippers and manufacturers of technically specified rubbers (TSRs) under the Rubber Industry Act (Cap. 280);

x Establishes and disseminates official prices for various grades and types of rubber; x Provides clearing facilities on all SICOM's futures contracts.

Publications issued:

x *Singapore Commodity Exchange Rules and Regulations.* x *The Singapore Rubber Market*, 2003 (English/Chinese).

Membership structure: 125 members comprising seven categories: Clearing Brokers, Clearing Market Makers, Clearing Dealers, Non-clearing Trade Members, Non-clearing Associate Members, Non-clearing Brokers and Non-clearing Individual Members (or "Locals").

Products/commodity responsible for:

RSS1, RSS3, TSR20(FOB), RSS3 index and robusta coffee futures contracts.

Training:

Commodity futures trading course organized by the International Trade Institute of Singapore.

Category:

Commodity futures exchange.

SINGAPORE MANUFACTURERS' FEDERATION (SMA)

Office/postal address:

No 1, Science Centre Road #02-02 The Enterprise Singapore 609077

Phone: (65) 6826 3000 Fax: (65) 6822 8828

E-mail: hq@smafederation.org.sg URL: www.smafederation.org.sg

Year established: 1932 (formerly Singapore Confederation of Industries (SCI), name changed in July 2003).

Principal functions:

- x To represent and promote the interests of manufacturers and manufacturing-related industries (defined as manufacturing community) in Singapore;
- x To encourage cooperation amongst the manufacturing community, as well as between the manufacturing community and the Government;

x To promote the sales of Singapore-made goods at home and abroad;

x To promote the productivity and technological upgrading of the manufacturing community, especially among the SMEs.

Services/activities:

x Makes representations to government bodies at home and abroad on matters affecting the manufacturing community;

x Liaises with local associate groups such as the various chambers of commerce, the Singapore Business Federation as well as with the numerous statutory boards on matters of common interest;

x Liaises with foreign economic associations and businesspersons;

x Organizes trade missions abroad and participates in international trade fairs;

x Provides accreditation of quality management system certification bodies and test labouratories;

x Produces an annual trade directory and guide for buyers to promote local goods and services as well as a bimonthly newsletter and a quarterly publication to keep members informed of developments in the manufacturing community, investments and Singapore trade;

x Operates an economics research section and a library which receives publications from all over the world;

x Endorses Certificates of Origin and other export documents;

x Acts as the national body to implement and administer the international articles number system (bar coding) in Singapore;

x Acts as the national body to implement the e- supply chain management programme in Singapore;

x Conducts skills upgrading courses.

Publications issued:

x *The Singapore Manufacturer* (annually). x *Tradelink* (annually). x *SMa Connect* (bimonthly). x *Other directories and handbooks* (ad hoc).

Membership structure: 2,800 members.

Ordinary member: any company that is directly engaged in any type of manufacturing and manufacturing-related activity in Singapore is eligible to join as an ordinary member.

General member: any company which is not directly involved in any manufacturing activity but provides a service to manufacturers may be admitted as a general member. General members have full voting rights too.

Any association with less than 50 per cent of its members who are ordinary members of SCI can also join as a general member.

Life member: any person or company who contributes a minimum of US$ 250,000 to SCI can join as a life member (subject to the approval of the Executive Committee).

Category:

Industrial promotion organization.

SINGAPORE NATIONAL SHIPPERS' COUNCIL (SNSC)

Office/postal address:

SCCCI Building 47 Hill Street, #07-05 Singapore 179365

Phone: (65) 3372441 Fax: (65) 3363851

E-mail: snsc@pacific.net.sg URL: www.snsc.org.sg

Year established: 1972

Principal functions:

x To represent the interest of Singapore exporters, importers, manufacturers, producers, trade associations, commodity associations and other organizations associated with trade in relation to the transport tof goods and/or commodities;

x To secure the greatest possible cooperation between exporters, importers, manufacturers, producers, trade associations, commodity associations and other organizations associated with trade;

x To secure efficient, economical and adequate shipping services and transport facilities;

x To present a united front in negotiations and consultations with transport operators, port authorities, Governments and other organizations engaged in transportation services;

x To arrange for and/or obtain the most suitable mode and terms of transportation; x To undertake all other things as the Council may deem fit to achieve the objectives set out herein.

Services/activities:

x Updates members on current major issues and developments in the shipping industry; x Organizes training courses, workshops, tea-cum-talks, forums, and seminars for its members and interested parties;

x Acts as a resource centre which carries out research on shipping developments periodically to look into the needs of shippers;

x Publishes an annual report and a bimonthly magazine.

Publications issued:

x *Annual Report.* x *Shippers' Times.*

Membership structure: Ordinary members: comprising individual companies, firms or businesses associated with the import and export trade, and trade or commodity associations, guilds and other organizations associated with trade.

Associated members: comprising mainly freight forwarders and agents who have no voting rights.

Category:

Shipper's council.

SINGAPORE QUALITY INSTITUTE (SQI)

Office/postal address:

Blk. 23 #01-01 (Inside Ngee Ann Polytechnic) 535 Clementi Road Singapore 599489
Phone: (65) 4674225 Fax: (65) 4674226
E-mail: enquiries@sqi.org.sg URL: www.sqi.org.sg
Year established: 1971 (formerly Singapore Quality Reliability Associations).
Principal functions:
x To promote an appreciation of the importance of quality in
Singapore; x To correlate quality activities of all members of the Institute; x To provide means for the interchange of information among
individuals and organizations; x To promote training and education in the field of quality.
Services/activities:
x Conducts certification and developmental courses for the
industry on quality; x Conducts evening talks; x Conducts educational visits for members; x Updates members with bimonthly publication *QC Focus*; x Organizes social functions such as the presentation
ceremony/annual dinner and dance.
Publications issued:
x *QC Focus*. x *Yearbook*.
Membership structure: 1,000 individual and 200 corporate members.
Products/commodity responsible for:
Posters on quality.
Training:
Organizes training courses for certified quality engineer, certified quality supervisor, certified quality inspector, certified reliability engineer, statistical process control, ISO 9000 standards and quality auditing, calibration system, measurement control system, geometric tolerancing fundamental applications, and design of experiments, certified quality manager.
Areas/industries where investment is encouraged:
ISO 14000 developments.
Category:
Training institute.

SRI LANKA

COMMODITIES EXPORT MARKETING AUTHORITY*

Office/postal address:
P.O. Box 54 Honiara
Phone: (677) 22528-9 Fax: (677) 21262
Year established: 1985 (formerly S.I. Copra Board established in 1953).
Principal function:
x To undertake commodity/product procurement, licensing, development, promotion, marketing and export.
Services/activities:
x Promotes and assists the development of commodity
industries; x Provides export marketing information; x Undertakes standards specifications, grading and marketing; x Buys and sells for export at predetermined prices; x Provides grants, loans and credit facilities for commodity
export promotion; x Undertakes studies, surveys, investigations and research; x Provides training, education and consultancy services; x Undertakes investment procurement and promotion and joint
ventures with local or foreign interests; x Provides sales agreement contracts to export commodities.
Local branches:
Buala Buying Centre Buala Post Office, Isabel Province
Kaonasughu Buying Centre Kira Kira Post Office, Makira Province
Auki Buying Centre Post Office Auki, Malaita Province
Lata Buying Centre Lata Post Office, Temotu Province
Choiseul Bay Buying Centre Taro Is Postal Agency Choiseul, Western Province
Noro Branch
P.O. 14 Munda, Western Province
Operates a network of 32 buying points throughout the country.
Products/commodity responsible for:
Copra, coconut and coconut products, copra, cocoa pods, unfermented cocoa beans, fermented cocoa beans and products, palm oil, palm kernel, palm-based products, spices, coffee and ngalinut.
Category:
Commodity board.

DEPARTMENT OF COMMERCE, INDUSTRIES AND EMPLOYMENT

Office/postal address:
P.O. Box G-26 Honiara
Phone: (677) 28614, 22856 Fax: (677) 25084
E-mail: pscommerce@pmc.gov.sb, ps@commerce.gov.sb URL: www.commerce.gov.sb
Principal functions:
x Investment; x Local entrepreneur; x Immigration; x Labour; x Trade and testing; x Industrial development; x Commerce; x Internal and external trade.
Services/activities:

x Designs an economic and financial package which aims to rehabilitate struggling businesses and encourage new investments;
x Repeals and replaces the Foreign Investment Act;
x Establishes infrastructure and land for various investments;
x Establishes a one-stop shop to receive and decide on investment proposals;
x Reserves areas of investment opportunities for indigenous Solomon Islanders;
x Sets up trade consulars in selected overseas countries;
x Researches into alternative sources of imports and encourages bulk purchase;
x Creates an investment climate which will yield more jobs through increased foreign investment and by providing more development opportunities in rural areas;
x Provides more financial assistance to local Solomon Islanders through the use of its fiscal and monetary policies; x Encourages more practical training to local business people; x Allocates available land for development purposes; x Supports and encourages trade delegations to other trading partner nations;
x Establishes an industrial commission to promote fair trading and arbitrates over unfair trading between businesses and corporations.
Areas/industries where investment is encouraged:
Coffee Processing Facility; cargo vessels; Bina Habour and Noro Development; duty free zones; Wairokai Industrial seaport; Suava Bay Fisheries Centre; Ranadi and Henderson Industrial Estates; and Pineapple Juice processing facility; Selwyn Bay Industrial Seaport; and Vanikoro Industrial seaport.
Category:
Ministry of Commerce.

BOARD OF INVESTMENT OF SRI LANKA (BOI)

Office/postal address:
Level 26, West Tower World Trade Centre Echelon Square Colombo 1
Phone: (94 1) 434403-5, 386953-4 Fax: (94 1) 447994-5, 422407
E-mail: info@boi.lk, webmaster@boi.lk URL: www.boi.lk
Year established: 1978 (formerly Greater Colombo Economic Commission, changed to BOI in 1992).
Principal functions:
x To promote, approve and facilitate foreign direct investment into Sri Lanka and to administer the eight Export Processing Zones at Katunayake, Biyagama, Koggala, Mirigama, Wathupitiwela, Polgahawela, Mawathagama and Horana.
x To administer the industrial parks at Kandy, Seethawaka and Mirijjawila, and the Export Processing Park at Malwatta.
Services/activities:
The BOI provides advice and assistance at each stage of the investment process and can help in the following ways:
x Provides information and guidance before submission of the application and coordinating approvals from other agencies, if required;
x Evaluates applications and provides concessions, where applicable to the project;
x Provides assistance during the start-up of the project: site selection and clearance, advice on factory building and other technical matters, arranges support services such as water, power, waste treatment and telecommunications;
x Makes recommendations to immigration authorities for issuing resident visas;
x Facilitate import/export clearance and customs procedure for the import of capital goods, raw materials and the export of the final product;
x Advises on environmental norms and facilitating environmental approvals;
x Assists, when necessary, in the maintenance of good industrial relations and in the formation and operation of Employee Councils;
x Provides post-approval services by a separate division within the BOI.
Publications issued:
Mini brochure: x *Make it in Sri Lanka*, June 2003 (English/Japanese/Korean/ French/Chinese).
Sectoral brochures: x *Textile & Apparel Sector - An overview*, May 2002 (English). x *The IT Industry*, June 2003.
Country profiles:
x *Direct Investment by Indian Companies in Sri Lanka*, 2003 (English).
x *Direct Investment by UK companies in Sri Lanka*, 2002 (English).
x *Direct Investments by German Companies in Sri Lanka - An Overview*, January 2003 (English).
x *Direct Investments by Japanese Companies in Sri Lanka*, April 2003 (English, Japanese).
x *Direct Investment by US Companies in Sri Lanka*, 2000 (English).
x *Direct Investment by Australian Companies in Sri Lanka*, 2003 (English).
Indo-Lanka Free Trade Agreement:
x *Indo-Lanka Free Trade Agreement - Investment Opportunities*, April 2003 (English).
x *Indo-Lanka Free Trade Agreement: A Sectoral Analysis*, June 2000 (English).
x *Impact of Indo-Lanka FTA on the Electronic Sector*, June 2000 (English).
x *Impact of Indo-Lanka FTA on the Agriculture Sector*, July 2000 (English).
x *The Complete Duty Structure of the Potential Sectors for Investment*, April 2002 (English).
x *Indo-Lanka FTA: Potential Products for Investment in Sri Lanka by Country of Origin*, February 2001 (English).
x *Duty Rates and Values of Major Indian Imported Products, Sector and Country of Origin*, March 2001 (English).
x *Selection of Potential Electronics Items for Investment in Sri Lanka by Country of Origin*, May 2001 (English).
x *Some Key Issues to be Addressed*, May 2001 (English).

x *The Major Issues and Proposals - After 12 Months of Trade*, July 2001 (English).

Other: x *Factor Cost*, June 2003 (English). x *Investor Magazine - Newsletter, 11th Edition*, April 2003. x *Investment Opportunities* (English/Sinhala/Tamil). x *BOI "Puwath" - Sinhala Newsletter.* x *BOI publication on infrastructure*, June 2003. x *Mini CDs - Invest in Sri Lanka* (English/French). x *BOI Corporate Video* (English/French/Japanese). x *Labour Standard and Employment Relations Manual.* x *General Guidelines for Factory Buildings.* x *Environmental Norms.*

Local branches:

BOI Office: EPZ, Katunayake Phone: (94 1) 2252364-5, 2252140, 2252038 Fax: (94 1) 2252030
BOI Office: BEPZ, Biyagama Phone: (94 1) 465206-9 Fax: (94 1) 465227
BOI Office: KEGPZ, Koggala Phone: (94 9) 83323 Fax: (94 9) 83370
BOI Office: Kandy Industrial Park, Kandy Phone: (94 8) 420019 Fax: (94 8) 420091 BOI Office: Seethawaka Industrial Park, Avissawella Phone: (94 36) 31082/3 Fax: (94 36) 31083
BOI Office: Horana EPZ Phone/Fax: (94 34) 69296, 69752
BOI Office: Hiriyala Dedicated Economic Centre Phone/Fax: (94 37) 28656
BOI Office: Malwatta Export Processing Park Phone/Fax: (94 33) 88826
BOI Office: Mawathagama EPZ Phone/Fax: (94 37) 98147
BOI Office: Mirigama EPZ Phone/Fax: (94 33) 74657
BOI Office: Polgahawela EPZ Phone/Fax: (94 37) 44657

Areas/industries where investment is encouraged:

x Manufacture of non-traditional goods for export including deemed exports; x Export-oriented services; x Manufacturing of industrial tools and/or machinery; x Small-scale infrastructure projects; x Information technology (IT), IT-enabled services and IT-related training institutes; x Regional operation headquarters; x Any industrial, agriculture, construction or services or any other business activities approved by the Board; x Research and development; x Agriculture and/or agro-processing other than processing of black tea; x Export trading house; x Large-scale infrastructure:

+ Power generation, transmission and distribution,
+ Development of highways, seaports, airports, railways and water services, establishment of industrial estates. Any other infrastructure.

x Large-scale (new/existing) projects;

x In addition to the above target sectors: + Existing enterprises undertaking an expansion, + Non-performing or under-performing enterprises.

Titles of laws and regulations on foreign investment:

x Greater Colombo Economic Commission Law No. 4 of 1978. x Greater Colombo Economic Commission (Amendment) Act No. 43 of 1980. x Greater Colombo Economic Commission (Amendment) Act No. 21 of 1983. x Greater Colombo Economic Commission (Amendment) Act No. 49 of 1992. x BOI (amendment) Act No. 10 of 2002.

CEYLON CHAMBER OF COMMERCE

Office/postal address:
50 Navam Mawatha
Colombo 02 Phone: (94 1) 2452183, 2421745, 2329143 Fax: (94 1) 2437477, 2449352
E-mail: info@chamber.lk URL: www.chamber.lk Year established: 1839 Principal functions:

- x To promote and protect the interest of the business sector in Sri Lanka and abroad;
- x To consider all questions connected with business in Sri Lanka;
- x To circulate statistical and other information relating to trade and industry, in particular with a view to promoting exports and investment;
- x To liaise with governmental authorities in matters relating to business;
- x To maintain contacts with chambers of commerce and industry in other countries.

Services/activities:

x Maintains close contacts with overseas chambers of commerce and organizations such as the International Trade Centre UNCTAD/WTO, ESCAP and United Nations Industrial Development Organization (UNIDO);
x Maintains close links with other chambers and trade associations in Sri Lanka;
x Serves as the representative of the business sector in liaison with the Government;
x Helps the Government to ascertain the views of the private sector on relevant matters;
x Operates 18 bilateral Business Councils with Australia; Benelux (Belgium, Luxembourg and Netherlands); Canada; Denmark; Finland; Hong Kong, China; India; Indonesia; Japan; Malaysia; Myanmar; Norway; Pakistan; Republic of Korea; Singapore; Sweden and Eastern Europe; United Kingdom;
x Represents and expresses the opinions of the business community in Sri Lanka on business matters;
x Provides an information service to its members with a view to promoting trade service associations;
x Organizes outward investment and trade promotion missions and receives inward trade and investment promotion missions;
x Provides a panel of expert quality surveyors who can certify the quality of export cargo;
x Registers export documents;
x Operates a Board of Arbitration with a view to a speedy

settlement of trade disputes;
x Operates a library;
x Conducts seminars/workshops of relevance to the business community;
x Issues business/trade publications and bulletins;
x Provides advisory service on export marketing/promotion;
x Provides secretarial services to 18 Bilateral Councils;
x Operates a Foreign Trade/Information Division.
Publications issued:
Bulletins:
x *Business Opportunities Bulletin.* x *Library Alert.* x *Library News.* x *Overseas Buyers Contacts.* x *Periodical Highlights.* x *Techno Info.* x *Trade Contacts.* x *Trade Reporter.*
Publications:
x *Annual Report.* x *Annual Review of Business and Trade.* x *Directory of Exporters.* x *Enterprise* (a tabloid). x *Register of Members.* x *Sri Lanka in Brief* (a booklet).
Membership structure: 515 members.
Encompasses virtually every sphere of economic activity in Sri Lanka - industry, import, export, agriculture, banking, hire-purchase, leasing, tourism, shipping, engineering, mining, consultancy services, wholesale, retail, financial services, legal, broking, construction and other services and includes every size of business ranging from the sole proprietorship to the multinational.
The Ceylon Chamber of Commerce is a member of the Confederation of Asia-Pacific Chambers of Commerce and Industry and the Sri Lanka National Council of the International Chamber of Commerce.
Members of the Ceylon Chamber of Commerce include organizations engaged in practically every type of economic activity in Sri Lanka. Membership is open to organizations of any nationality.
Training:
The Chamber nominates candidates from its membership for training courses and seminars offered under various aid programmes, through the Government.
Category:
Chamber of commerce.

NATIONAL CHAMBER OF COMMERCE OF SRI LANKA

Office/postal address:
450, D R Wijewardene Mawatha Colombo 10
P.O. Box: 1375, Colombo
Phone: (94 11) 2689600, 5 374801-3 Fax: (94 11) 2689596 E-mail: sg@nccsl.lk Year established: 1948 Principal functions:
x To promote trade activities;
x To assist the Government in the formation of trade policies and issuance of commercial documents.
Services/activities:
x Provides trade information; x Trade fairs and delegations; x Organizes trade-related seminars and workshops; x Makes representations to the government bodies; x Issues commercial documents; x Advises the Government on trade-related matters.
Publications issued:
x *NCCSL Newsletter.* x *Trade Information Bulletin.*
Membership structure: 400 members.
The Chamber is the focal point for member companies representing virtually the entire spectrum of industry, trade and commerce in Sri Lanka. Among them, the Chamber counts some of the most vibrant and progressive business houses in the country.
Training:
Short-term training course and seminars, workshops only for local members and non-member companies.
Areas/industries where investment is encouraged:
Joint ventures.
Category:
Chamber of commerce.

SRI LANKA BUSINESS DEVELOPMENT CENTRE (SLBDC)

Office/postal address:
32B, 5th Floor Huejay Court Sir Mohammed Macan Markar Mawatha Colombo 3
Phone: (94 11) 2434952, 2437684-5 Fax: (94 11) 2541170
E-mail: slbdc@sri.lanka.net URL: www.slbdc-lk.org
Year established: 1984
Principal functions:
x To develop, strengthen and stimulate business and industry in Sri Lanka;
x To provide a comprehensive package of services in the areas crucial to business and industrial development.
Services/activities:

x Assists in setting up new businesses as well as expanding and diversifying existing businesses, improving business performance/profitability and establishing link-ups for joint ventures and marketing;
x Assists in selecting business opportunities, developing enterprises and conducting market surveys/feasibility studies;
x Human resource and enterprise development:
x Surveys/studies and special assignments.
Category:
Industrial promotion organization.

SRI LANKA EXPORT CREDIT INSURANCE CORPORATION (SLECIC)

Office/postal address:
Level 4, Export Guarantee House 42 Nawam Mawatha Colombo 2
Phone: (94 74) 719410-3 Fax: (94 74) 719400
E-mail: info@slecic.lk URL: www.slecic.lk
Year established: 1979
Principal functions:

- x To issue policies to exporters of goods and services against non-receipt or delayed receipt of payments resulting from commercial and non-commercial risks;
- x To issue guarantees to banks and other financial institutions to facilitate the granting of pre- and post-shipment finance;
- x To issue guarantees to persons or institutions abroad in connection with goods exported from Sri Lanka or for the due performance of any services to be rendered to such persons or institutions within or outside Sri Lanka;
- x To provide financial assistance to exporters for the promotion and development of export from Sri Lanka;
- x To help exporters to diversify and expand exports, find new markets and sell their goods abroad on competitive terms of payment.

Services/activities:
x Issues insurance policies to exporters against non-payment by buyers abroad due to commercial and non-commercial (political) risks. Policies include standard, specific and small-scale insurance policies. Policies also cover export of services, shipments on consignment basis and entrepot trade;
x Issues Guarantees to commercial banks to facilitate the granting of finance to exporters. This facilitates granting of working capital at pre-and post-shipment;
x Issues direct export performance guarantees to the International Chamber of Commerce-Sri Lanka (ICC) for exporters to obtain the ATA Carnet Document to participate in trade fairs and exhibitions abroad;
x Type of Policies available:
-Export Payment Insurance Policy: designed to indemnify exporters against losses they may suffer due to nonpayment or delayed payment due to commercial/noncommercial (political) risks: is operated on the whole turnover principal which means the exporters should declare all their credit shipment to all their buyers;
-Specific Policy: issued to cover specific buyers, specific destinations or a specific transaction;
-Entrepot Trade Shipment Policy: designed to cover nonpayment risks of shipments effected to a third country from a second country by exporters operating in Sri Lanka;
-Comprehensive Services Policy: issued to exporters of services to cover non-payment or delayed payment by overseas buyers due to commercial or non-commercial risks;
x Type of Guarantees available: -Export Production Credit Guarantee: issued to commercial banks against domestic letters of credit/confirmed orders opened by exporters in favour of manufactures/producers/suppliers, enabling them to obtain finance for the procurement of goods to be supplied to exporters; -Pre-shipment Credit Guarantee: for exporters to obtain pre-shipment finance on more liberal terms for purchasing raw materials, manufacture, processing of goods and packing for export against Letters of Credit or Confirmed Orders; -Post-Shipment Credit Guarantee: issued to commercial banks to enable them to grant post-shipment finance to exporters on more liberal terms; -Export Performance Guarantee: issued to commercial banks as a counter guarantee (which is non-financial in nature) to enable them to issue bid bonds, performance bonds, etc., for export of services: it also helps banks to issue guarantees to the director general of customs for export of garments to clear raw materials and accessories used to make finished products for export: it helps postponement of import duty until realization of export proceeds; -Export Performance Guarantee Covering the ATA Carnet System: issued to ICC facilitating issue of ATA Carnets to participate in trade fairs and exhibitions abroad; -Whole-turnover Bank Guarantee Scheme covering cost of passage advances to Sri Lankans going abroad for employment. This guarantee scheme extends coverage to banks with respect to advances granted to migrant workers in respect of entire predeparture loan; -Whole-turnover Pre/Post Shipment Guarantee: issued to commercial banks to enable them to grant pre/post shipment finance to total exporter clientele of the bank on liberal terms; The above credit guarantees cover of non-payment by the exporter/non-fulfilment of obligations by the exporter due to this insolvency or protracted default.
x BiZinfo: providing financial information and credit status reports on overseas companies to the banking sector is branded as BiZinfo. SLECIC acts as a "Reseller" of credit and status reports from a network of principals worldwide.
x Export Finance: SLECIC-Export Finance caters to the post-shipment needs of medium- and small-scale exporters by encashing their export bills and thereby improving their cash flow.
Publications issued:
x *Annual Report.* x *SLECIC Newsline* (Quarterly Newsletter). x Product Brochures.
Membership structure: Secretary of the Treasury and the Central Bank of Sri Lanka.

Category:
Export credit insurance; export financing organization; trade facilitation body; and trade promotion organization.

SRI LANKA EXPORT DEVELOPMENT BOARD

Office/postal address:
42 Navam Mawatha Colombo 2
P.O. Box: 1872, Colombo
Phone: (94 1) 300723-4, 300705-11 Fax: (94 1) 300715, 300724 E-mail: serve@edb.tradenetsl.lk
URL: www.srilankabusiness.com Year established: 1979 Principal functions:

x To promote and develop products and services for export from Sri Lanka;
x To motivate exporters by providing assistance and removing disincentives for exports;
x To induce the expansion of production of export-related products and services;
x To provide specialized support services to producers and exporters.

Services/activities:
x Formulates export policies for the preparation of the National Export Development Plan;
x Assists research and development, product adaptation, supply/supplier and market development activities for exports from Sri Lanka;
x Organizes overseas market surveys and promotional programmes, which include support for exporters' participation in trade fairs, sales missions and other export promotion efforts;
x Provides services to exporters, simplification of trade procedures and training to export organizations;
x Provides trade information and advisory services to exporters, overseas importers, policymakers and government officials;
x Entrepreneurship development export marketing, export and import procedures, quality and productivity improvement, product specific programmes for export-oriented small and medium enterprises;
x Conducts "Exporters' Forum" to resolve problems of exporters related to infrastructure procedures;
x Development of entrepot trade;
x Programmes for supply development, product development, product adaptation and quality improvement;
x E-promotion (web hosing and designing, web advertising, web links, CD-ROM preparation);
x E-communication (e-mail, Internet and videoconferencing);
x Itineraries of business/travel meeting.
Publications issued:
x *Business Lanka* (quarterly, English). x *Expo News* (fortnightly, English/Sinhalese). x *Sri Lanka Directory of Exporters.*
Local branches:
Provincial Office (Central Province) 129, 1/1 D.S.Senanayake Mawatha Kandy Phone: (94 8) 2233592 Fax: (94 8) 2201147
North Western Province 30 Baudhaloka Mawatha Kurunegala Phone: (94 37) 2224256 Fax: (94 37) 2221972
Southern Province 45 Devamitta Mawatha Galle Phone: (94 9) 2223595 Fax: (94 9) 2223595
Office abroad:
Sri Lanka Trade Centre Girithereyege Hithafineeva Magu Male, Maldives Phone: (960) 315183 Fax: (960) 315184 E-mail: dirsltc@avasmail.com.mv
Products/commodity responsible for:
All non-traditional products and services.
Training:

x Certificate course on import and export procedures (7 days);
x Course on operational aspects of international trade (10 days).

Areas/industries where investment is encouraged:
Export-oriented projects.
Titles of laws and regulations on foreign investment:
Board of Investment Law No. 4 of 1978.
Category:
Trade promotion organization.

SRI LANKA HANDICRAFTS BOARD (LAKSALA)

Office/postal address:
Laksala 60 York Street Colombo 01
P.O. Box: 538, Colombo
Phone: (94 11) 2323635 Fax: (94 11) 2446582 E-mail: laksala@itim.net, chair@itim.net
URL: www.laksala.lk Year established: 1983 Principal functions:

x To undertake the promotion, marketing and export of Sri Lanka handicrafts;
x To maintain shops and showrooms, both in Sri Lanka and abroad, for the display and sale of handicrafts and to conduct displays, exhibitions and sales.

Services/activities:

x Establishes, maintains, operates and assists in the establishment, maintenance and operation of centres, workshops or other institutions for the purpose of creating, or adapting designs to be used in the production of handicrafts and the marketing of goods produced at such centres or other institutions;

x Expands the production of handicrafts and improves the quality of the raw material used for such production and of the finished products;

x Cooperates with scientific and technical institutions, organizations and agencies for the improvement of crafts materials and craft production techniques;

x Acts as the Certifying Authority of EEC Certificates of Origin for handicrafts.

Publications issued:

x Brochures, catalogues and Laksala web.

Local branches:

The commercial arm consists of the Laksala sales outlets. Within a period of 40 years, Laksala has established 17 branches in Colombo-Fort, Bambalapitiya, Bentota, Galle, Hotel Galadari, Kandy, Katubedda, Katunayake (Airport), Kurunegala, Matara, Moragalla, Negambo, Nuwara-Eliya, Polgolla, Thummulla, Tangalle and Sigiriya.

Offices abroad:

Franchise Agent for the United Kingdom ARP Enterprises 2 Pages Hill, Muswall Hill London N10 1QA, United Kingdom Phone: (44 208) 3654618 Fax: (44 208) 3654619 Franchise Agent for Australia and New Zealand Exotic Concepts Pty. Ltd. Shop 5/300, Beach Road Black Rock, Victoria 3193, Australia Fax: (61 3) 95890299

Franchise Agent for Japan Gesyla Japan Co. Ltd. Taito-ku, Tokyo, Japan Phone: (81 3) 38426871 Fax: (81 3) 38426859

Products/commodity responsible for:

Jewellery with stones; silver jewellery; silver items; silver-plated items; brass items; wood carvings; ebony items; wooden wall hangings; bamboo items; lacquered items; musical items; masks; coconut items; seashell items; handloom (Polgolla); handloom (other); voil; mosquito nets/pillows/pillowcases/embroidered pillowcases; batik wall hangings; cloth dolls; lace; flags; embroidered handkerchiefs; batik dresses/batik sarongs, cushion cover-bags (Myanmar); handloom sarongs/ready-made garments; handloom vetti; serviettes/dusters/carpets; reedware items (Wetakey); reedware (Iluck); reedware (Nava); reedware items (mats); palmyrah items; talipot items; leather items; coir items; clay items (unglazed); clay items (glazed); plaster of Paris items; soft toys/wintage cars; baby garments; oxidized items; artificial flowers; thread items; plywood items; tea/wax item/spices/macrams; cards; embroidered table cloths, etc.; bed covers and sheets; wool carpets; copper items; bracts (Matalu); B/S/C (brass, silver and copper mixed product); precious stones; semi-precious stones; paintings; granite items; silk; wooden furniture; glass items; natural stones (non gems); paintings/statues.

Training:

Trains local youths at present for the fields of woodcarving, lace, pottery, reed weaving, textiles, carpentry and flower making.

Areas/industries where investment is encouraged:

Pottery, terra cotta and handicrafts.

Category:

State trading organization.

SRI LANKA IMPORTERS', EXPORTERS' AND MANUFACTURERS' ASSOCIATION (SLIEMA)

Office/postal address:

28 Rajamalwatta Road Colombo 15

P.O. Box: 12, Colombo

Phone: (94 1) 696321 Fax: (94 1) 268480, 2522524 E-mail: worldtrd@slt.lk Year established: 1955 Principal functions:

- x To collect enquiries and the latest information on trade, investment, new markets and opportunities and disseminate essential information to its members and other interested companies;
- x To process and promptly answer both import-export enquiries from overseas, and disburse them among interested parties;
- x To act as a go-between to establish profitable contacts, meetings with exporters, importers, investors, entrepreneurs and other international business and financial institutions at home and abroad;
- x To undertake a "Business Start-up Scheme" which aims to make small businesspersons around the country aware of measures taken to support them and provide them with consultation, financial and legal services.

Services/activities:

As detailed under Principal functions. Membership structure: 200 members. Category:

Trade association; trade facilitation body; trade fair and exhibition authority; trade promotion organization; and training/research institution.

SRI LANKA SHIPPERS' COUNCIL

Office/postal address:

c/o Ceylon Chamber of Commerce 50 Nawam Mawatha Colombo 2

P.O. Box: 274, Colombo

Phone: (94 1) 421745-7 Fax: (94 1) 449352

E-mail: sushani@chamber.lk URL: www.slsc.ws

Year established: 1966
Principal functions:
x To represent and carry out consultations and negotiations with shipping lines on behalf of shippers with regard to freight rates, availability and adequacy of shipping services, port efficiency, port charges, port facilities and others;
x To make representations to the Government on matters and issues affecting ship users and port users; x To carry out training programmes to educate ship users and port users on shipping procedures and other related matters.
Services/activities:
x Acts on behalf of ship users and port users by making representations to the Government and other agencies on matters concerning the affairs of both importers and exporters, such as negotiating competitive freight rates, resolving of trade disputes/complaints and making representations to safeguard interests of importers/exporters;
x Provides advisory services on shipping, freight, ports, customs formalities and other related activities of ship users and port users;
x Provides expertise from within the Council to importers and exporters for training and development in selected areas.
Publication issued:
x *Annual Report* (English).
Membership structure: 16 members and 20 associate members.
Training:
No regular training courses, but conducts short-term seminars, training programmes to create awareness on export-related issues.
Category:
Shipper's council; port authority; and national shipping corporation.

SRI LANKA TEA BOARD

Office/postal address:
574 Galle Road Colombo 3
P.O. Box: 1750 Phone: (94 1) 582236, 583687, 587386 Fax: (94 1) 589132 E-mail: teaboard@pureceylontea.com, promotion@pureceylontea.com URL: www.pureceylontea.com Year established: 1976 Principal functions:
x To regulate the production and cultivation of tea;
x To regulate the establishment and operation of tea factories;
x To regulate the conduct of tea auctions;
x To regulate the sale of tea and the export of tea;
x To assist and encourage scientific and technological research;
x To conduct, assist and encourage research into the economic state of the tea industry;
x To facilitate securing of supplies of machinery and equipment for the development of the tea industry in Sri Lanka;
x To provide financial or advisory services on matters relating to the tea industry and to publish such statistics at its discretion;
x To safeguard the interests of the workers in the tea industry;
x To collect statistics from growers, manufacturers, dealers or other persons on any matter relating to the tea industry and to publish such statistics at its discretion;
x To regulate, control and direct all institutions and organizations engaged in the management of tea estates and in the production and marketing of tea;
x To provide the necessary liaison between the tea industry and the departments of Government or State Corporations;
x To develop the tea industry through research and promotion in Sri Lanka and in world markets.
Services/activities:
As detailed under Principal functions.
Publications issued:
x *Sri Lanka Tea Board Annual Report.* x *Sri Lanka Tea Board Monthly Statistical Summary.* x *Sri Lanka Tea Board Annual Statistical Bulletin.* x *Newsletter* (fortnightly).
Local branches:
Regional Office - Galle 20 Lower Dickson Road Galle Phone: (94 9) 2232052 Regional Office - Gampola 140 Ambagamuwa Road Gampola Phone: (94 81) 2352279
Regional Office - Matara 4 Wijetunga Mawatha Matara Phone: (94 41) 2222636
Regional Office - Ratnapura 9 Moragabayata Ratnapura Phone: (94 45) 2222136
Regional Office - Bandarawela 1 Ambatenna Gardens Bandarawela Phone: (94 57) 2222812
Offices abroad:
Tea Promotion Unit Sri Lanka Embassy 2-1-54, Takanawa Minato-ku Tokyo 108-0074, Japan
Phone: (81 3) 54489122, 34401611/6912
Fax: (81 3) 54489121
E-mail: ceylontea@vesta.ocn.ne.jp
Tea Promotion Unit Sri Lanka Embassy Al. Wilanowska 313A 02-665 Warsaw, Poland Phone: (48 22) 8538896/7 Fax: (48 22) 8538907
E-mail: srilankatea@neostrada.pl
Tea Promotion Unit Sri Lanka Embassy 24, Shchepkina Str., Moscow, Russian Federation Phone (70 95) 6881363, 6883511 Fax: (70 95) 6881363, 6883511 E-mail: ceyteabu@online.ru

Tea Promotion Unit Consulate General of Sri Lanka Villa No.2, Plot B-44 Street 322-B A Hudhaiba Dubai, United Arab Emirates Phone: (97 14) 3987871 Fax: (97 14) 3987872 E-mail: ctbureau@emirates.net.ae

Products/commodity responsible for:

Tea in bulk, packets, bags and other tea products (all originating from the plant *Camellia Sinensis*).

Category:

Standard, testing, aid inspection; and trade promotion organization.

THAILAND

BOARD OF TRADE OF THAILAND

Office/postal address:

150/2 Rajabopit Road

Pranahkon, Bangkok 10200 Phone: (66 2) 6221860-70 Fax: (66 2) 6221880, 6221882, 6221991

E-mail: inc@thaiechamber.com URL: www.thaiechamber.com Year established: 1955 Principal functions:

- x To act as the central business organization to promote and protect the trading interests of the country and the Thai business community;
- x To represent the business community to inform and advise the government sector on important policies and issues which affect trade, industry, commerce and investment;
- x To promote trade and business contacts between importers/exporters of Thailand and foreign importers/ exporters;
- x To promote cooperation among enterprises and to act as an intermediary between the Government and the private sector;
- x To undertake by arbitration the settlement of disputes arising out of trade and commerce.

Services/activities:

x Informs the Government and its agencies of the views and recommendations of the private business community on economic and trade policies which affect trade, industry and commerce;

x Participates in discussions of economic and trade policy formulation and plans for trade and market development;

x Provides statistical data and information on domestic and foreign markets and changes in economic and trade policies and legislation;

x Provides services to members by informing and channelling trade enquiries and business opportunities directly and/or through publications;

x Maintains a trade reference library for use of members;

x Publishes trade directories and publications for the interest of members;

x Organizes meetings, seminars and training on economic, trade and technical matters for members;

x Organizes trade missions abroad and encourages participation in international trade fairs and exhibitions;

x Arranges business meetings for foreign trade missions;

x Organizes and stimulates the organization of international trade fairs and exhibitions in the country;

x Undertakes market studies, research and surveys of domestic and export markets;

x Facilitates communication and the exchange of views on economic and trade issues among members, as well as among members and government departments and public bodies;

x Strengthens and expands economic and trade cooperation with foreign private business organizations and regional economic organizations in trade, investment, tourism and financing and expedites exchange of trade, technical, marketing, and managerial information and experience;

- x Issues Certificates of Commodity Standard and other commercial certificates;
- x Provides trade arbitration services;
- x Provides ATA Carnet services.

Publications issued:

x *Business Directory* (English). x *Economic Newsletters* (biweekly, Thai). x *Business Opportunities* (biweekly, English).

Membership structure:

Ordinary members: -The Thai chamber of commerce -Foreign chambers of commerce in Thailand (23) -Trade associations (71) -Public enterprises (7)

Associate members: -Individual companies and partnerships (500).

Titles of laws and regulations on foreign investment:

Please contact the Board of Investment.

Category:

Trade association.

BUREAU OF TRADE MEASURES

Office/postal address:

Department of Foreign Trade 44/100 Nonthaburi 1 Road Nonthaburi 11000

Phone: (66 2) 5474756 Fax: (66 2) 5474736

E-mail: dft_info@mocnet.moc.go.th URL: www.dft.moc.go.th

Year established: 1942

Principal functions:

- x To proceed in accordance with the Law on Export and Import of Goods, the Law on Anti-Dumping and Countervailing Duties, the Law on Export of Commodity Standard, the Law on Prevention of Export of Vessels and other related laws;
- x To encourage trade activities between state agencies or between state agencies and international trade organizations with an aim to boost the benefits of export;
- x To protect Thailand's trade interests by pursuing and solving problems involving trade barriers set by Thailand's trade partners;
- x To defend the interests of Thailand's producers and exporters when Thai exports are subject to foreign anti dumping, countervailing or safeguard investigations and subsequent measures;
- x To conduct anti-dumping, countervailing or safeguard investigations on imports and implement appropriate measures in compliance with Thailand's obligations to WTO Agreements;
- x To cooperate with the neighbouring countries to encourage and systemize the legal border trade in accordance with their laws and regulations;
- x To exercise its functions to gain trade preferences and encourage the private sector to pay more attention to trade preferences;
- x To regulate export and import of goods in order to ensure maximum benefit to the domestic producers and consumers in accordance with WTO Agreements;
- x To establish exporting commodity standards and regulations for the purpose of quality control;
- x To administer the government-to-government business transactions and agreements;
- x To promote trade relations with other countries in order to increase market shares and diversify foreign markets;
- x To study and follow up the trade situation so as to cope with Thailand's external trade problems;
- x To study and follow up the development of Thai trade partners' trade restrictions and regulations;
- x To study and follow up the foreign trade situation of Thai principal products for the benefit of Thailand's economy including ways and means to reduce barriers to Thailand's export and import;
- x To promote Thailand's external trade for the benefit of the Thai economy;
- x To study and analyse trade measure, trade barrier and non-tariff barrier of Thai partners;
- x To solve trade measures imposed by trading partners on Thai exporters who have not complied with WTO Agreements;
- x To study and evaluate trade competitiveness and the effect of Thailand's trade partner measures;

x To conduct and monitor the inspection of export commodity standards carried out by private inspectors and other related tasks concerning the Export Commodity Standards Act B.E. 2503 (1960);

x To study, monitor and analyse, investigate, prevent and take administrative action against circumvention practice.

Services/activities:

x Conducts anti-dumping and countervailing investigations under the anti-dumping and countervailing Act B.E. 2542 (1999);

x Operates as a representative of Thailand's trade sector; x Provides assistance in trade promotion and export expansion; x Harmonizes import-export regulations in accordance with provisions under the World Trade Organization; x Issues import, export licences especially for products under the Export and Import Act B.E.2522 (1979);

x Allocates export quotas on tapioca products, and issues Certificate of Origin for GSP, ASEAN's Preferential Trading Arrangements (PTA), Common Effective Preferential Tariff Scheme (CEPT), Global System of Trade Preference Among Developing Countries (GSTP), other Certificates of Origin and Kimberley Process Certificate Scheme (KPCS);

x Coordinates between state organizations for trade facilitation of private sectors.

Publications issued:

x *DFT statistical report.* x *Report on Thai Rice Situation.* x *Rice: Production and Export.*

Local branches:

Office of Foreign Trade Chiang Mai International Airport Chiangmai 50200 Phone: (66 53) 274671-2 Fax: (66 53) 277901 E-mail: oftcm@mocnet.moc.go.th

Office of Foreign Trade 5 Sripoowanart Nai Road Hatyai District, Songkhla 90110 Phone: (66 74) 252500-2 Fax: (66 74) 252501 E-mail: oftsl@cscoms.com

Office of Foreign Trade 334/1 Moo 10, Sukhumvit Road Bang Pra, Sriraja District Chonburi 20210 Phone: (66 38) 341174 Fax: (66 38) 341173 E-mail: oftcb@hotmail.com

Office of Foreign Trade 165/21 Prachasamorsorn Road Khon Kaen 40000 Phone: (66 43) 238115, 336674 Fax: (66 43) 238115 E-mail: oftkk21@cscoms.com

Office of Foreign Trade Srakaew Provincial Administration Office Suwannasorn Road Srakaew 27000
Phone: (66 37) 421013, 421267
Fax: (66 37) 421267
E-mail: oftsk@cscoms.com

Training:

x Seminar of GSP, GSTP, CEPT, WTO's Harmonized Non-Preferential Rules of Origin open to exporters, businesspersons and others (6-7 times a year);

x Seminar on Quota Administration System open to textile exporters (3 times a year, the courses will be conducted in Thai);

x Seminar on Border Trade open to exporters, businesspersons and others at regional provinces (4 times a year); x Seminar on AD, CVD and Safeguard open to exporters and producers (12 times a year).

Product/commodity responsible for:

Main goods: rice, tapioca, textile; import-export regulation Goods: more than 118 items; and standard commodities: 11 items.

Category:

Commodity standard institute; Ministry of Trade; and standard, testing and inspection body.

DEPARTMENT OF EXPORT PROMOTION (DEP)

Office/postal address:
22/77 Rachadapisek Road Chatuchak Bangkok 10900
Phone: (66 2) 5115066-77, 5120093-104 Fax: (66 2).5121079, 5131917
E-mail: tidep@depthai.go.th URL: www.depthai.go.th

Year established: 1952

Principal functions:

x To promote Thai products in foreign markets through various activities;
x To cooperate with public and private organizations concerned to develop and promote Thai exporting under the policy and procedure issued by the Export Development Committee;
x To conduct research and plan market strategies for export promotion;
x To suggest means and procedures to solve and eliminate the export problems and obstacles;
x To develop the knowledge, skill and quality of Thai exporters in an attempt to enable them to conduct their export business more successfully;
x To prepare trade information and provide services for Thai manufacturers/exporters and foreign importers;
x To cooperate with organizations concerned to improve and develop the quality and design of Thai products to serve foreign markets;
x To cooperate and coordinate with other institutions and organizations both domestic and overseas to develop and promote Thai exports.

Services/activities:

x Conducts marketing research, product research for planning policymaking;
x Provides advisory services for export marketing, information and research, and product adaptation and development;
x Undertakes buyers services;
x Conducts export training for the business community and public agencies;
x Directs, organizes and sponsors trade displays, fairs and exhibitions;
x Directs, organizes and sponsors selling and buying missions;
x Collects and disseminates market information through publications and issues publicity materials;
x Facilitates links between Thai exporters and overseas importers through trade advisory and information services; x Conducts studies of problems affecting exports in order to recommend possible solutions;
x Operates overseas trade centres and a National Exhibition Centre;
x Acts as focal point for technical cooperation in trade promotion;
x Acts as Secretariat of the Export Development Committee and executor of the International Trade Promotion Fund.

Publications issued:

x *Exporters' Review* (fortnightly, Thai).

x *Statistics Files* (monthly/annually, English).
x *Thailand: Practical Guide for Business Visitors.*
x *Thailand's Selected List of Exporters* (biennial, English).
x Product brochures, fair catalogues.

Local branches:

30/31-32 Trirat Road Muang District, Chanthaburi 22000 Phone: (66 39) 325962-3 Fax: (66 39) 325962 E-mail: epcchan@hotmail.com

29/19 Singharaj Road Muang District, Chiang Mai 50000 Phone: (66 53) 216350-1, 221376 Fax: (66 53) 215307 E-mail: depcm@chmai.loxinfo.co.th

269/74-75 Mithaphap Road Muang District, Khon Kaen 40000 Phone: (66 43) 325025-8 Fax: (66 43) 325029 E-mail: repckk@kknet.co.th

7-15 Jootee-Uthit 1 Road, Haadyai District, Songkhla 90110 Phone: (66 74) 234349, 231744 Fax: (66 74) 234329 E-mail: dephd@hadyai.loxinfo.co.th

148/59 Kanjanavitee Road Tambon Bang Kung, Muang District Suratthani 84000 Phone: (66 77) 287108, 289108, 286916, 287107 Fax: (66 77) 288632 Mobile: (66 1) 5697936 E-mail: depsurat@samart.co.th

Offices abroad:

DEP also cooperates with Office of Commercial Affairs, under Office of the Permanent Secretary, as follows:

Europe:

Office of Commercial Affairs Royal Thai Embassy Kopalgasse 47, 1110 Vienna, Austria Phone: (43 1) 7485020 Fax: (43 1) 748502012 E-mail: thaicommvienna@magnet.at
thaitcvienna@depthai.go.th

Office of Commercial Affairs Royal Thai Embassy Heleckova 29, 150 95 Praha 5-Smichov Prague, Czech Republic Phone: (420 2) 57323030, 57325867, 57325882 Fax: (420 2) 57327555 E-mail: thaicom@iol.cz
thaitcprague@depthai.go.th

Office of Commercial Affairs Royal Thai Embassy, Hellerupvej 76 2900 Hellerup, Denmark Phone: (45 39) 626999 Fax: (45 39) 626099 E-mail: dep@thaicom.dk
thaitccopenhagen@depthai.go.th

Bureau des Affaires Commerciales, Ambassade Royale de Thaïlande 8 Rue Greuze,75116 Paris, France Phone: (33 1) 56901212 Fax: (33 1) 56901213 E-mail: comparis@micronet.fr
thaitcparis@depthai.go.th

Office of Commercial Affairs, Royal Thai Embassy Petzower Str. 1 14109 Berlin, Germany Phone: (49 30) 8050040 Fax: (49 30) 80500451 E-mail: berlin@thaicom.b.uunet.de
thaitcberlin@depthai.go.th

Thai Trade Centre Bethmannstrasse 58 60311 Frankfurt/Main, Germany Phone: (49 69) 281091-2 Fax: (49 69) 292460 E-mail: thaitrade@t-online.de
thaitcfrankfurt@depthai.go.th

Office of Commercial Affairs Royal Thai Embassy Jozsefhegyi Ut.28-30, No A/1 1025 Budapest, Hungary Phone: (36 1) 2122738, 2125358 Fax: (36 1) 2122736 E-mail: thaicommbp@mail.datanet.hu
thaitcbudapest@depthai.go.th

Thai Trade Centre Milan Via a. Albricci, 8 20122 Milano, Italy Phone: (39 2) 89011467 Fax: (39 2) 89011478 E-mail: thailand@comm2000.it
thaitcmilan@depthai.go.th

Office of Commercial Affairs Royal Thai Embassy Viale Erminio Spalla 41 00142 Rome, Italy Phone: (39 6) 5030804-5 Fax: (39 6) 5035225 E-mail: thcomrm@flashnet.it
thaitcrome@depthai.go.th

Office of Commercial Affairs Royal Thai Embassy Laan Copes Van Cattenburch 123 2585 EZ The Hague, Netherlands Phone: (31 70) 3455444 Fax: (31 70) 3461005 E-mail: comhague@euronet.nl
thaitchague@depthai.go.th

Office of Commercial Affairs
Royal Thai Embassy
NATPOLL Business Centre
Ul. Migdalowa 4
Warsaw 02-796, Poland
Phone: (48 22) 6451210 / 6451230
Fax: (48 22) 6451250
E-mail: thaicom@perytnet.pl thaitcwarsaw@depthai.go.th

Office of Commercial Affairs
Royal Thai Embassy
9 Bolshaya Spasskaya Str.
Moscow 129090, Russian Federation
Phone: (7 095) 9741501
Fax: (7 095) 9741531
E-mail: thaico@dol.ru thaitcmoscow@depthai.go.th

Oficina de Asuntos Commerciales
Embajada Real de Thailandia
Segre, 29-2A
28002 Madrid, Spain
Phone: (34 91) 5630190/5630196
Fax: (34 91) 5638090
E-mail: thaicom@ntserver.codeinf.com thaitcmadrid@depthai.go.th

Office of Commercial Affairs

Royal Thai Embassy
Hertford Street
London W1Y 7 DX, United Kingdom
Phone: (44 207) 4935749
Fax: (44 207) 4937416
E-mail: thaicomuk@dial.pipex.com thaitclondon@depthai.go.th
North America:
Thai Trade Centre Suite 401, 80 Bloor Street West Toronto, Ontario M5S 2V1, Canada Phone: (1 416) 9215400 Fax: (1 416) 9217545 E-mail: thaitradetoronto@onaibn.com
Thai Trade Centre
Dunsmuir St., Vancouver
BC. V6C 3K4, Canada
Phone: (1 604) 6876400, 6877079
Fax: (1 604) 6836775
E-mail: ttcvan@telus.net thaitcvancouver@depthai.go.th
Commercial Section
Royal Thai Consulate General
North Michigan Ave.,Suite 544
Chicago, IL 60611, United States of America
Phone: (1 312) 4670044
Fax: (1 312) 4671690
E-mail: ttcc@wwa.com thaitcchicago@depthai.go.th
Commercial Section Royal Thai Consulate General
3rd
Floor, 611 North Larchmont Boulevard Los Angeles, CA 90004, United States of America Phone: (1 323) 4669645 Fax: (1 323) 4661559 E-mail: ttcla@earthlink.net
thaitclosangeles@depthai.go.th
Thai Trade Centre Suite 4420, S. Biscayne Boulevard Miami, Florida 33131, United States of America Phone: (1 305) 3795675 Fax: (1 305) 3795677 E-mail: ttcmiami@earthlink.net
thaitcmiami@depthai.go.th
Latin America:
Thai Commercial Office Royal Thai Embassy AV. Cidade Jardim, 400 Cj 51 Edificio Dacon- Jardim Europa São Paulo, SP-Brazil Phone: (55 11) 30316252 Fax: (55 11) 30316254 E-mail: thaicomsp@aduaneiras.com.br
thaitcsaopaulo@depthai.go.th
Officina Consejeria Commercial Embajada real de Thailandia E1 Arcangel 4916 Vitacura, Santiago, Chile Phone: (56 22) 634 186 Fax: (56 22) 634214 E-mail: thaicom@chilesat.net
thaitcsantiago@depthai.go.th
Middle East:
Office of Commercial Affairs, Royal Thai Embassy No. 27, 1st Floor East Armaghan St. Africa Express way, Tehran 19177, Islamic Republic of Iran Phone: (98 21) 2057378 / 7379 / 9776 Fax: (98 21) 2055136 E-mail:
thaicomaff@istn.irost.com
thaitctehran@depthai.go.th
Office of Commercial Affairs Royal Thai Embassy Hayarkon Street Tel Aviv 63451, Israel Phone: (972 3) 5244277 –8 Fax: (972 3) 5244270 E-mail: thaicomt@internet-zahav.net
thaitctelaviv@depthai.go.th
Commercial Section Royal Thai Consulate General Shacker Building Room 303 Al Hail Rd., P.O. Box 8014 Jeddah 21482, Saudi Arabia Phone: (966 2) 6445059 Fax: (966 2) 6442234 E-mail: thaicom@sbm.net.sa
thaitcjeddah@depthai.go.th
Office of Commercial Affairs Royal Thai Embssy Hill Street. Arcadia Pretoria South Africa Phone: (27 12) 3420835 / 0850 / 0856 / 0859 Fax: (27 12) 3420855 E-mail: royaltha@global.co.za
thaitcpretoria@depthai.go.th
Thai Trade Centre Mete CAD. No. 20/3, Ayannolglu Ishani Taksim 80090, Istanbul, Turkey Phone: (90 212) 2920910-11 Fax: (90 212) 2920912 E-mail: ttcist@turk.net
thaitcistanbul@depthai.go.th
Commercial Section Royal Thai Consulate General 407, Deira Tower, P.O. Box 1083 Dubai, United Arab Emirates Phone: (971 4) 2284553 Fax: (971 4) 2220934 E-mail: ttcdubai@emirates.net.ae
thaitcdubai@depthai.go.th
Asia and Pacific:
Commercial Section Royal Thai Consulate General 1 St. Floor, 75 Pitt Street Sydney, NSW 2000, Australia Phone: (61 2) 92411075-6 Fax: (61 2) 92515981 E-mail: thaitrade@netwizard.net.au
thaitcsydney@depthai.go.th
Office of Commercial Affairs, Royal Tai Embassy No. 10 SPG. 40-22, JLN. Subok
P.O. Box 3038 Bandar Seri Begawan 1930 Brunei Darussalam Phone: (673 2) 334715, 331932 Fax: (673 2) 334500 E-mail: thaicomm@brunet.bn
thaitcbandarseri@depthai.go.th
Office of Commercial Affairs, Royal Thai Embassy No.196 M.V. Norodom Boulevard Sangkat Tonle Bassac, Khan Chamcar Mon Phnom Penh, Cambodia Phone: (855 23) 363869 ext. 217 Fax: (855 23) 310150 E-mail:
thaicompnh@bigpond.com.kh
thaitcphnompenh@depthai.go.th

Commercial Section Royal Thai Consulate General Room No.304-306, White Swan Hotel Shamian Island Guangzhou, 510133, China Phone: (86 20) 81886968 ext. 3304, 3305 Fax: (86 20) 81904448 E-mail:
thaicom@public.guangzhou.gd.cn
thaitcguangzhou@depthai.go.th
Royal Thai Consulate General
1st
Floor, Commercial Building, Kunming Hotel 52 Dongfeng East Road, Kunming Yunnan 650051, China Phone: (86 871) 3165006, 3165001, 3165019,
3162063 ext. 62336 Fax: (86 871) 3165026 E-mail: csrtcg@ns.istiy.yn.cn
thaitckunming@depthai.go.th
Commercial Section Royal Thai Consulate General
8th
Floor, Fairmont House 8 Cotton Tree Drive, Central Hong Kong, China Phone: (852) 25259716 (2 lines) Fax: (852) 28684927 E-mail: thaicomm@netvigator.com
thaitchongkong@depthai.go.th
Office of Commercial Affairs Royal Thai Embassy 56-N, Nyaya marg, Chanakyapuir New Delhi 110021, India Phone: (91 11) 4105608, 4105610 Fax: (91 11) 4105609 E-mail: thaicom@del2.vsnl.net.in
thaitcnewdelhi@depthai.go.th
Office of Commercial Affairs Royal Thai Embassy Jl. Imam Bonjol, No. 74 Jakarta 10310, Indonesia Phone: (62 21) 31901363 (3 lines hunting) Fax: (62 21) 31901360 E-mail: mincomjk@cbn.net.id
thaitcjakarta@depthai.go.th
Thai Trade Centre 4f. Akasaka Wing, 1-13-8 Akasaka, Chuo-Ku, Fukuoka Japan Phone: (81 92) 7516311 Fax: (81 92) 7516522 E-mail: ttcfkk@po.iijnet.or.jp
thaitcfukuoka@depthai.go.th
Commercial Section Royal Thai Consulate General
2nd
Floor, Hommachibashi Nishi Building 1-1-3 Hommachi, Chuo-ku Osaka 5410053, Japan Phone: (81 6) 6262 4418 Fax: (81 6) 62711053 E-mail: ttcosaka@ab.inbox.ne.jp
thaitcosaka@depthai.go.th
Office of Commercial Affairs Royal Thai Embassy Shuwa Kioicho TBR Building Room No. 1115- 6, 11th Floor 5-7 Kojimachi, Chiyoda-ku Tokyo 102-0083, Japan Phone: (81 3) 32219482, 32219483, 32219463 Fax: (81 3) 32219484 E-mail: thaicommtk@ro.bekkoame.ne.jp
thaitctokyo@depthai.go.th

Office of Commercial Affairs
Royal Thai Embassy
738-20 Hannam-Dong, Yongsan-GU
Seoul 140-210, Republic of Korea
Phone: (82 2) 7952431, 7954446
Fax: (82 2) 7952998
E-mail: thaitrad@nuri.net
thaitcseoul@depthai.go.th
Office of Commercial Affairs
Royal Thai Embassy
Phonkeng Road, Xayasettha District
P.O. Box 128 Vientiane
Lao People's Democratic Republic
Phone: (856 21) 413706, 413704
Fax: (856 21) 412089

Office of Commercial Affairs
Royal Thai Embassy
Jalan Ampang
50450 Kuala Lumpur, Malaysia
Phone: (60 3) 21424601, 21458545
Fax: (60 3) 21489818
E-mail: commercial@ppp.nasionet.net
thaitckualalampur@depthai.go.th

Office of Commercial Affairs
Royal Thai Embassy
No. 97 Kaba Aye Pagoda Road
Bahan Township Yangoon, Myanmar
Phone: (95 1) 525518, 542654
Fax: (95 1) 532768
E-mail: thaitrade.ygn@mptmail.net.mm
thaitcyangoon@depthai.go.th
Office of Commercial Affairs
Royal Thai Embassy Director
Rada Street, legaspi Village
Makati, City, Philippines
Phone: (63 2) 8940403, 8940406

Office of Commercial Affairs
Royal Thai Embassy
6 Cao Ba Quat Street, Dien Bien Precinct
Ba Dinh Distict, Hanoi, Viet Nam
Phone: (84 4) 7330671, 7330670, 8455224
Fax: (84 4) 7330669
E-mail: thaicomm@fpt.vn
thaitchanoi@depthai.go.th
Commercial Section
Royal Thai Consulate General
143 Nguyen Dien Chieu Street
District 3, Ho Chi Minh City
Viet Nam
Phone: (84 8) 9303717, 9300001
Fax: (84 8) 9300001
E-mail: thaitradecentre@hcm.fpt.vn
thaitchochiminh@depthai.go.th

Training:

The Department organizes a number of Thai and English language training/seminar programmes annually in areas related to trade promotion including export marketing, product adaptation, and financing export documentation. Acceptance of trainees from other developing countries for programmes in the English language will be considered on a case-by-case basis.

Category:

Trade promotion organization.

Fax: (63 2) 8160698
E-mail: thaicommnl@pacific.net.ph
thaitcmanila@depthai.go.th
Office of Commercial Affairs
Royal Thai Embassy
370 Orchard Rd.
Singapore 238870, Singapore
Phone: (65) 7373060, 7327769
Fax: (65) 7322458
E-mail: thcommsg@mbox4.singnet.com.sg
thaitcsingapore@depthai.go.th
Thailand Trade and Economic Office (Commercial Division)
Taipei World Trade Centre
7E-10, 5 Hsin Yi Road, Section 5
P.O. Box 109-862 Taipei
Taiwan Province of China
Phone: (886 2) 27231800-2
Fax: (886 2) 27231821
E-mail: thaicomm@tpts4.seed.net.tw
thaitctaipei@depthai.go.th

DEPARTMENT OF TRADE NEGOTIATIONS (DTN)

Office/postal address:
44/100 Nontaburi 1 Road Bangkrasor Nonthaburi 11000
Fax: (66 2) 5475630-1
E-mail: dtnwebmaster@moc.go.th URL: www.dtn.moc.go.th, www.thaifta.com Year established: 1942 Principal functions:

- x To act as core coordinator in formulating and recommending international economic policy measures;
- x To provide recommendations on international trade policy and measures;
- x To formulate and recommend positions and strategies supporting multilateral/bilateral trade negotiations and Free Trade Area negotiations, and to participate therein;
- x To formulate and recommend positions and strategies supporting negotiations under regional, subregional and other international organization groupings, and to participate therein;
- x To research and analyse the impact of economic evolution both short and long term, in order to support the formulation of policy and trade negotiations' position;
- x To develop international trade and economic information system;
- x To perform other duties as stipulated by law, by the Ministry of Commerce or by assignment given by the Cabinet of Ministers.

Services/activities:
As detailed under Principal functions.
Publications issued:
x *ASEAN Economic Community: Thailand's Opportunities*
(Thai). x *ASEAN-China Free Trade Area: Effects to Thailand* (Thai). x *The Future of Doha Negotiation Round: Success Factors*
(Thai). x *Thailand and FTA: Opportunities or Threat* (Thai). x *China-Hong Kong Closer Economic Partnership Arrangement (CEPA)* (Thai). x *Singapore: Thailand's Economic Partnership in ASEAN*
(Thai). x *Bilateral Acccession Agreement: Thailand-Russia* (Thai). x *Thailand's International Trade Negotiations* (Thai) x *ASEAN Competitiveness* (Thai).
Category:
Trade negotiation organization.

EXPORT-IMPORT BANK OF THAILAND (EXIM THAILAND)

Office/postal address:
1193 EXIM Building Phaholyothin Road Phayathai Bangkok 10400
Phone: (66 2) 2713700, 2780047, 6172111 Fax: (66 2) 2713204
E-mail: info@exim.go.th URL: www.exim.go.th
Year established: 1993
Principal function:
x To provide financial facilities to strengthen competitiveness of Thai exporters and Thai investors investing overseas.
Services/activities:

- x Pre-shipment financing (baht, US dollar and yen);
- x Working capital:

-Pre-shipment financing (baht, US dollar and yen)
-Pre-shipment financing for small- and medium-sized enterprises (PSF SMEs)
-Express export credit (EEC)
-Exporter supplier's finance
-Packing credit plus
-Financing facilities for re-export
-Negotiation of export bills;

x Term loans:
-Term loan for business expansion
-Term loan for machinery upgrading
-Long-term credit for export of capital goods
-Merchant marine financing
-Trade fair financing;

x Financing for overseas project:
-Financing facilities for overseas construction contract
-Financial facilities for overseas investment
-Financing facility for Thai restaurants overseas;

x Export credit insurance:
-Export credit insurance L/C policy
-Export credit insurance D/P, D/A and O/A policy
-Small export bill insurance (SEBI)
-Buyer/bank risk assessment report (BRA);

x Medium- and long-term export insurance;

x International trade services.

Publications issued:

x *Annual report* (Thai/English). x Brochure on the Bank's services, 2005 (Thai, English). x *Company profile,* 2003 (Thai, English). x *EXIM News*, newsletter (monthly, Thai).

Local branches:

Branches in Bangkok:

Business Promotion Office at Department of Export Promotion

3rd

Floor, Thailand Export Mart Building 22/77 Ratchadapisek Road Lad Yao, Chatuchak Bangkok 10900 Phone: (66 2) 5115772-3 Fax: (66 2) 5115774

Bangna-Trad Km. 3 Branch Ground Floor, Thosapol Land Building 3 947 Moo 12, Bangna-Trad Road (Km. 3) Bangna, Bangkok 10260 Phone: (66 2) 7440551-3, 7440556-7, 7440573-4 Fax: (66 2) 7440571

Rama II Branch 111/917-919 Moo 6 Rama II Road, Samaedum Bang Khunthian, Bangkok 10150 Phone: (66 2) 8959080-6 Fax: (66 2) 8959087

Rama IV Branch Green Tower 3656/2 Rama IV Road Klongton, Klongtoey Bangkok 10110 Phone: (66 2) 3673300-6 Fax: (66 2) 3673307-8

Sathorn Branch Ground Floor, Empire Tower 195 South Sathorn Road Yannawa, Sathorn Bangkok 10120 Phone: (66 2) 6700300-8 Fax: (66 2) 6700309

Branches in provinces:

Chiang Mai Branch 158/5-6 Chiang Mai-Lampang Road Paton, Muang Chiang Mai 50300 Phone: (66 53) 220596-7, 220541 Fax: (66 53) 220585

Hat Yai Branch Sinbenjapol Building 24 Soi P. Nataphol 2 Sripuwanart Road Hat Yai, Songkhla 90110 Phone: (66 74) 428722-6, 221131-2 Fax: (66 74) 221133-4

Khon Kaen Branch: 381/44-45 Mittraphap Road Nai Muang, Muang Khon Kaen 40000 Phone: (66 43) 271535-7 Fax: (66 43) 271538 Laem Chabang Branch 53/71-74 Moo 9, Sukhumvit Road Thungsukhla Sriracha Chonburi 20230 Phone: (66 38) 330121-7 Fax: (66 38) 330128

Rangsit Branch: 44, 46, 48 Soi Phaholyothin 87 Phaholyothin Road Prachathipat, Thanyaburi Pathum Thani 12130 Phone: (66 2) 5364677-82 Fax: (66 2) 5364683-4

Areas/industries where investment is encouraged:

Export of all kinds of goods; construction in all countries, with particular interest in Cambodia, Lao People's Democratic Republic, Myanmar, Viet Nam, as well as Yunnan and Guangdong Provinces of China.

Category:

Export financing organization; export credit insurance; and investment financing organization.

FEDERATION OF THAI INDUSTRIES (FTI)

Office/postal address:

4th

Floor, Zone C Queen Sirikit National Convention Centre 60 New Rajadapisek Road Klongtoey Bangkok 10110

Phone: (66 2) 2294255
Fax: (66 2) 2294941-2
URL: www.fti.or.th

Year established: 29 December 1987 (formerly Association of Thai Industries (ATI), 1967-1987).

Principal functions:

x To act as the sole representative of all industrial enterprises in Thailand; x To promote industrial development; x To disseminate information on technology; x To conduct testing of products and issue Certificate of Origin and Certificate of Quality Assurance, Certification of Existence/Non-existence of producers/suppliers of raw materials in Thailand for claiming of investment promotion privileges under the Investment Promotion Act;

x To offer appropriate advice and recommendations to the Government for the overall benefits of the industrial sector; x To ensure that the FTI members comply with the laws governing industrial activities.

Services/activities:

- x Provides consultancy services, workshops, training, seminars, educational and observation tours within the country and aboard;
- x Encourages the study and upgrading of skills in various specific industries;
- x Operates the Human Capacity Building Institute, Institute of Industrial Energy and Industrial Environment Institute within the organizational structure of FTI to encourage all technical services and the coordination of technology transfer;
- x Provides registration of products under EAN-UCC Standard Barcode and EDI in Supply Chain;
- x Encourages members' Code of Ethics and Corporate Good Governance;
- x Produces and distributes a bimonthly magazine (*Industry Focus*) and education videos;
- x Disseminates information through the internet (www.fti.or.th);
- x Produces FTI Directory and CD-ROM;
- x Serves as the national secretariat of the ASEAN Chambers of Commerce and Industry or ASEAN-CCI;
- x Cooperates with Ministry of Foreign Affairs in issuing the APEC business travel card;
- x Serves as the secretariat of the Asia-Europe Business Forum (AEBF);
- x Participates in WTO joint committee, which comprises the Board of Trade of Thailand, the Thai Banker Association and FTI to study and follow up WTO rules, regulations and concerned issues.

Publications issued:

x *Annual Report* (Thai). x *FTI Directory* (English). x *Industry Club Directories* (English/Thai). x *Industry Focus* (bimonthly, Thai). x *Provincial Chapters Directories* (English/Thai). x Other newsletters.

Local branches:

FTI Provincial Chapters:

Pathum Thani Chapter Boonrawd Brewery Co. Ltd. 999 Samsen Road Dusit, Bangkok 10300 Phone: (66 2) 2411360-9, 2434731-40 Fax: (66 2) 2412539

97/7 Inchannarong Road Nai-Muang Muang, Bureeram 31000 Phone: (66 44) 617483 Fax: (66 44) 617483

2nd

Floor, Royal Commemorate Community Centre Yuthadamnoen Road Muang, Chachoengsao 24000 Phone: (66 38) 814409 Fax: (66 38) 814409 Chainat Industry Office Moo 7, Kao Ta Pha Muang, Chainat 17000 Phone: (66 56) 411923, 411983 Fax: (66 56) 412471

310/90 Nontanakorn Road Muang, Chaiyaphum 36000 Phone: (66 44) 812795 Fax: (66 44) 812795

200 Thanon Thaluang, Watmai Muang, Chantaburi 22000 Phone: (66 39) 312135 Fax: (66 39) 322125

1st

Floor, Northern Industrial Promotion Centre Building 158 Tung Hotel Road Muang, Chiang Mai 50000 Phone: (66 53) 304346-7 Fax: (66 53) 246353

4th

Floor, Macro Building 545/1 Ratanakhet Road Viang, Muang, Chiang Rai 57000 Phone: (66 53) 752415 Fax: (66 53) 752415

97/125 Sukhumvit Road, Moo 1 Samed Muang, Chonburi 20000 Phone: (66 38) 274124-5 Fax: (66 38) 276851

Chumphon Town Hall Poramintaramanka Road Thatapao, Muang, Chumphon 86000 Phone: (66 77) 503001 Fax: (66 77) 503975

Lert Kasikorn Group Co. Ltd. 639 Moo 5, Phaholyothin Road Tumbol Nakornchoom Muang, Kamphaeng Phet 62000 Phone: (66 55) 799587-9 Fax: (66 55) 799258

41 Moo 4, Wangsala Thamuang, Kanchanaburi 71110 Phone: (66 34) 647581-6 Fax: (66 34) 647581

4th

Floor, Kow Yoo Hah Motor Building 359/2 Mittaphab Road Muang, Khonkaen 40000 Phone: (66 43) 324886 Fax: (66 43) 324885

1/23-24 Watchara Road Krabi-Yai, Muang, Krabi 81000 Phone: (66 75) 620-084 or (66 1) 4775580 Fax: (66 75) 620-084

2nd

Floor, New Lampang Provincial Industrial Office Lampang-Denchai Road Phrabhat, Muang, Lampang 52000 Phone: (66 54) 265079 Fax: (66 54) 265080

2nd

Floor, Northern Region Industrial Estate 60 Moo 4 Ban-Klang, Muang, Lamphun 51000 Phone: (66 53) 552271 Fax: (66 53) 552272

Sahafam Co., Ltd. 99 Moo 8, Saraburi-Lomsuk Road Huayhin, Chaibadan, Lopburi 15130 Phone: (66 36) 643206 Fax: (66 36) 643207

87 Moo 1 Nakhien, Muang Nakhon Si Thammarat 80000 Phone: (66 75) 312040 Fax: (66 75) 346121, 312040

55 Moo 7, Petchakasem Road Klongmai, Sampran, Nakhonpathom 73110 Phone: (66 34) 223131 Fax: (66 34) 223132
Nakorn Swan Viriyalai Technology College Pahol Yothin Road, Nongkrod Muang, Nakorn Swan 60240 Phone: (66 56) 334565 Fax: (66 56) 229969
276/11 Phol Saen Road, Nai Muang Muang, Nakornratchasima 30000 Phone: (66 44) 267117-8 Fax: (66 44) 267118
Faikaew, Poopeang Nan 55000 Phone: (66 54) 771616, 751539 Fax: (66 54) 751359
Government Offices Centre 37 Moo 9, 1st Floor, Koakkien Muang, Narathiwat 96000 Phone: (66 73) 512205 Fax: (66 73) 512205 E-mail: ftinwt@hotmail.com
Government Offices Centre Udorn-Nongkhai Road Muang, Nongkhai 43000 Phone: (66 42) 421272 Fax: (66 42) 411999
9/2 Moo 5, Talingchan-Supanburi Road Saothonghin, Bang Yai, Nontaburi 11140 Phone: (66 2) 9032051 Fax: (66 2) 9032052
355 Moo 8 Naklua Road, Bana Muang, Pattani 94000 Phone: (66 73) 334611 Fax: (66 73) 334611
335 Phaholyothin Road Bhantom, Muang, Payao 56000 Phone: (66 54) 481266, 412877 Fax: (66 54) 481797, 431160 42 Moo 4, Phetchabun-Chaleanglub Muang, Phetchabun 67000 Phone: (66 56) 748650-1 Fax: (66 56) 748649
87/2 Phetchakasem Road Tonmamuang Muang, Phetchaburi 76000 Phone: (66 32) 414128 Fax: (66 32) 414128
4/91-92 Sara Lung Road Nai Muang, Muang, Phichit 66000 Phone: (66 56) 612450 Fax: (66 56) 612450
808/1-2 Pichaisongkram Road Nai Muang, Muang, Phitsanulok 65000 Phone: (66 55) 258497, 212101 Fax: (66 55) 241718
3rd
Floor, 123 Asia Road, Khlong Suanphlu Phra Nakhonsi Ayutthaya 13000 Phone: (66 35) 345966 Fax: (66 35) 345967
369 Moo 5 Sai Ban Namcham 1-Ban Rongkhem Road Mae Lai, Muang, Phrae 54000 Phone: (66 54) 649731/741 Fax: (66 54) 649731/741
2nd
Floor, Phuket Provincial Industrial Office 48/4 Dumrong Road, Talad Yai Muang, Phuket 83000 Phone: (66 76) 240362 Fax: (66 76) 240362
67 Moo 3, Bang Boriboon Muang, Prachinburi 25000 Phone: (66 37) 200678 Fax: (66 37) 200678
65 Sukjai Road Muang, Prachubkhirikhan 77000 Phone: (66 32) 611030, 611580 Fax: (66 32) 602344
41/125 Thamuang Road Kao Nivhet, Muang, Ranong 85000 Phone: (66 77) 824689 Fax: (66 77) 824689
33 Amphur Road, Namuang Muang, Ratchaburi 70000 Phone: (66 32) 337301/315048 Fax: (66 32) 323346
140/20 Moo 1 Sukhumvit Road Noenphra, Muang, Rayong 21080 Phone: (66 38) 808177 Fax: (66 38) 808178
Inter Concrete Industry Co., Ltd. 143 Moo 5, Jangsanit Road Nivetch, Tawatburi, Roi-et 45170 Phone: (66 34) 569010, 527123-6 37 Office Building Srisamut Road Paknam, Samutprakarn 10270 Phone: (66 2) 7028675-6 Fax: (66 2) 7028673
923-49 Ekachai Road, Mahachai Muang, Samuthsakorn 74000 Phone: (66 34) 836740, 833606 Fax: (66 34) 836740
13 Soi Pichaironnarongsongkram Pahol Yothin Road, Muang, Saraburi 18000 Phone: (66 36) 212940 Fax: (66 36) 212940
Singburi-Bangpan Road Muang, Singburi 16000 Phone: (66 36) 523149 Fax: (66 36) 523149
Muang, Sisaket 33000 Phone: (66 45) 631616 Fax: (66 45) 613497
3rd
Floor, Southern Industrial Promotion Centre 165 Karnjanavanich Road Namnoi, Hatyai, Songkla 90110 Phone: (66 74) 211902-3 Fax: (66 74) 211903
9 Moo 4, Ruayai Muang, Suphanburi 72000 Phone: (66 35) 555210, 555267 Fax: (66 35) 545601
99/44-46 Moo 2 Karnchana Vidhi Road Vat Pradu, Muang, Suratthani 84000 Phone: (66 77) 212520 Fax: (66 77) 273977
60 Jitbumroong Road Muang, Surin 32000 Phone: (66 44) 511348 Fax: (66 44) 514348
8/1-2 Soi Ruamraeng Intarakiri Road Mae-sod, Tak 63110 Phone: (66 55) 542381, 542927 Fax: (66 55) 542927
322/10 Moo 5, Nongsamed Muang, Trad 23000 Phone: (66 39) 511945, 512619 Fax: (66 39) 520228
85 Kokkan Road Tapthieng Muang, Trung 92000 Phone: (66 75) 218699 Fax: (66 75) 212841
2nd
Floor, Ubon Ratcha Thanee Provincial Industrial Office Surasakdi Road Muang, Ubon Ratchathanee 34000 Phone: (66 45) 262449 Fax: (66 45) 262449
83/21 Wattana Road Muang, Udorn Thani 41000 Phone: (66 42) 246498 Fax: (66 42) 246498
280/9 Baromaard Road Muang, Uttaradhit 53000 Phone: (66 55) 440389 Fax: (66 55) 414449
36 Sribumrung Road Sateng, Muang, Yala 95000 Phone: (66 73) 243316 or (66-1) 6781010 Fax: (66 73) 243615
New regional chapters:
1st
Floor, Industrial Development Centre Toonghotel, Chiang Mai 50000 Phone: (66 53) 304346-7 Fax: (66 53) 246353
44/4 Moo 11, Nawamidth Kannayao, Bangkok 10230 Phone: (66 2) 5100051-62 ext. 701 Fax: (66 2) 5105737
5/9-12 Moo 7, Bangna-Trad Road (Km.41) Bangsamak, Bangpakong Chachoengsao 24180 Phone: (66 38) 538155 Fax: (66 38) 538099
267/11 Polsann Road, Naimuang Muang, Nakhonrajasrima 30000 Phone: (66 44) 267117-8 Fax: (66 44) 267118
165 Kanchanawanid Road Namnoi, Hadyai Songkla 90110 Phone: (66 74) 211902 Fax: (66 74) 211903
Industry clubs:
Agricultural Machinery Manufacturers Club, Air Conditioning and Refrigeration Industry Club, Aluminium Industry Club, Auto Parts Industry Club, Automotive Industry Club, Ceramic Industry Club of Thailand, Chemical Industry Club, Electrical, Electronics and Allied Industry Club, Environmental Management Industry Club, Food Processing Industry Club, Footwear Industry Club, Garments Industry Club, Gems and Jewellery Industry Club, Glass Manufacturers Club, Granite and Marble Industry Club, Leather Based Industry Club, Machinery and Metal Work Industry Club, Petrochemical Industry Club, Petroleum Refining Industry Club, Pharmaceuticals Industry Club, Plastic Industry Club, Printing Industry Club, Pulp and Paper Industry Club, Roofing and Accessories Industry Club, Rubber Based Industry Club, Textile Industry Club, Thai Furniture Industry Club, Thai Gas Manufacturers Industry Club, Thai Panel Product Industry Club, Thailand Fellowship of Cement Manufacturer, Thailand Iron and Steel Industry Club.

Membership structure: 5,400 members.
Ordinary membership: any industrial enterprises in the country who must comply with the Factory Act or the trade association in the industrial sector.
Associate membership: those individuals and juristic persons not in the industrial sector or other trade associations. These members are grouped into industrial club and countrywide provincial chapters.
Category:
Industrial promotion organization.

FOOD AND DRUG ADMINISTRATION (FDA)

Office/postal address:
Ministry of Public Health Tiwanond Road, Muang District Nonthaburi 11000
Phone: (66 2) 5907001, 5907003, 5907063 Fax: (66 2) 5918636
E-mail: library@fda.moph.go.th, fda@fda.moph.go.th URL: www.fda.moph.go.th
Year established: 1974
Principal functions:
x To protect consumer's health, to ensure safety, quality and efficacy of health products under responsibilities of the Thai FDA, i.e. foods, drugs, psychotropic substances, narcotics, medical devices, volatile substances, cosmetics and hazardous substances available in the country. This has to be implemented in accordance with laws and international agreements.
Services/activities:
x Grants licences for manufacturing and importation of all products, including food commodities, pharmaceuticals, narcotic and psychotropic substances, medical devices and household hazardous substances;
x Strictly regulates the above-mentioned products to ensure and monitor safety quality and efficacy of both high-risk and low-risk products;
x Controls advertisement of food and drug products and provides guidance related to the above-mentioned products for entrepreneurs and organizations involved;
x Acts as an information service centre to disseminate relevant information and publications;
x Carries out post-marketing surveillance and monitoring job, including the direct sampling of the products for labouratory analysis and testing to find out whether or not the distributed products do conform to their regulatory standards;
x Supervises manufacturing plants to upgrade their production process to meet with the standard criteria, such as GMP and Hazardous Analyses Critical Criteria Point (HACCP);
x Monitors adverse reactions of health products in Thailand and disseminates summarized reports to network hospitals and World Health Organizaiton (WHO) ;
x Participates in various activities and cooperates with many international organizations, such as WHO, United Nations Developemtn Programme (UNDP);
x Acts as the national focal point for the International Programme on Chemical Safety (IPCS) and Adverse Drug Reaction Monitoring Centre of WHO (ADRM);
x Provides public education information through various types of media such as radio, television, newspaper, posters, electronic machines, audio-text system;
x Organizes training courses and seminars.
Publications issued:
x *FDA Journal.* x *Medical and Health Product Bulletin.*
Local branches:
Provincial Public Health Offices (located in all provinces throughout the country).
Products/commodities responsible for:
Foods; drugs; psychotropic substances; narcotics; medical devices; volatile substances; cosmetics; and hazardous substances.
Training:
Various training courses (both national and international) related to regulatory control of health product.
Titles of laws and regulations on foreign investment:
x Drug Act B.E. 2510 (1967).
x Psychotropic Substance Act B.E. 2518 (1975).
x Food Act B.E. 2522 (1979).
x Narcotic Act B.E. 2522 (1979).
x Medical Devices Act B.E. 2531 (1988).
x The Emergency Decree on Prevention against Abuse of Volatile Sustances B.E. 2535 (1990).
x Cosmetic Act B.E. 2535 (1992).
x Hazardous Substance Act B.E. 2535 (1992).
x The single Convention on Narcotic Drugs 1961.
x Commentary on the protocol amending at Geneva on 25 March 1972.
x The International Convention on Psychotropic Substances 1971.
x The International Code of Marketing of Breast Milk Substitute 1981.
x The United Nations Convention against Illicit Traffic in Narcotic Drugs and Psychotropic Substances 1988.
Category:

Standard, testing, and inspection body.

INDUSTRIAL ESTATE AUTHORITY OF THAILAND (IEAT)

Office/postal address:
618 Nikom Makkasan Road Rajthevee Bangkok 10400
Phone: (66 2) 2530561 Fax: (66 2) 2526582, 2534086
E-mail: ieat@ieat.go.th, investment.1@ieat.go.th URL: www.ieat.go.th
Year established: 1972 (as a State Enterprise attached to the Ministry of Industry).
Principal functions:

- x To provide a one-stop service for Thai and foreign industrial organizations from start to completion, including all types of permits, information and advice on investment and how to set up, incentive and privileged, promoted zones, loan services and design of factory;
- x To establish "industrial estates" which are fully equipped with standardized infrastructure and public utilities;
- x To provide strategic trade and manufacturing bases that are integrated concurrently with the social and cultural environment.

Services/activities:
x Undertakes surveying, planning, designing, construction and maintenance of facilities and provision of services to industrial operators and persons engaged in activities beneficial to or connected with industrial operations;
x Designates categories and sizes of industrial activities
permissible in an industrial estate; x Supervises living conditions of workers in an industrial estate; x Controls the operation of industrial enterprises, and the
utilization of land in an industrial estate in accordance with
rules, regulations and laws; x Handles investment; x Issues bonds or other instruments for investment.
Publications issued:
x Annual Reports x Corporate
-Supporting Industries and Factories in Industrial Estate. -Corporate Information 2001. -Information 2001. -Success Today Toward a Sustainable Future 2002.
x Brochure
-Industrial Estate Authority of Thailand (IEAT). -Paradise of Investment Success and Happiness. -Southern Region Industrial Estate (Songkhla). -Phichit Industrial Estate Rubber City. -Rubber City. -Halal Food Processing.
Local branches:

- x General Industrial Zone (GIZ): this area is reserved for the location of industrial manufacturing for export and or domestic consumption.
- x Export Processing Zone (EPZ): this area is reserved for the location of industrial manufacturing, trade and service with the minimum export of at least 40 per cent. Most of the industrial estates with EPZ will have a government custom house for fast clearing.
- x Commercial Zone: this area is reserved for commercial support such as bank, post office, regular supplies and other facilities to serve the industries in the industrial zone.
- x Residential Zone: this area is reserved for the residence purposes of both the employers and employees.

Zone 1 (6 central provinces surrounding Bangkok):
Bangchan Industrial Estate 60 Moo 14, Seiree Thai Road Minburi, Bangkok 10510 Phone: (66 2) 5170744, 5171895, 5179653, 9060399 Fax: (66 2) 5176965
Gemopolis Industrial Estate 47/31 Moo 4, Sukhapibal 2 Road Prawes, Bangkok 10260 Phone: (66 2) 3260221-3, 3260137 Fax: (66 2) 3260220 Company Office: Phone: (66 2) 7270022 Fax: (66 2) 7270099
Latkrabang Industrial Estate 94 Chalong Krung Road Lamplathiew, Latkrabang, Bangkok 10520 Phone: (66 2) 3260221-3, 3260234, 3260137 Fax: (66 2) 3260220
Bangplee Industrial Estate 136/2 Moo 17, Thepharuk Road Bangsaothong Subdistrict Samutprakarn 10540 Phone: (66 2) 3152200, 7050697-9 Fax: (66 2) 3151498
Bangpoo Industrial Estate 649 Sukhumvit Road, Bangpoo Mai Muang, Samutprakarn 10280 Phone: (66 2) 3240358, 7093450-3 Fax: (66 2) 3230730-1
Samut Sakhon Industrial Estate 39/5 Moo 2, Bangkrajao Maung, Samut Sakhon 74000 Phone: (66 34) 490066-8 Fax: (66 34) 490070
Zone 2 (12 provinces surrounding Zone 1):
Bangpa-In Industrial Estate 139 Moo 2, Udomsorayuth Road Klong Jik, Bangpa-In, Ayudhaya 13160 Phone: (66 35) 258409-10 Fax: (66 35) 258411
Ban Wa Industrial Estate (Hi-Tech) Saraburi Industrial Estate (Kaeng Khoi)
99 Moo 5, Asia-Nakhon Sawan Road, Km. 59-60 72 Banthad, Kaengkhoi, Saraburi 18100
Ban Wa, Bangpa-In Phone: (66 35) 258409-10
Ayudhaya 13160 Fax: (66 35) 258411
Phone: (66 35) 250141 Company Office:

Fax: (66 35) 244651

Phone: (66 36) 245131-2
Fax: (66 36) 245131

Saharattananakorn Industrial Estate
103 Moo 4, Bangprakru
Nakhon Luang, Ayudhaya 13220
Phone: (66 35) 350777, 350141, 3501/44
Fax: (66 35) 244651
Company Office:
Phone: (66 35) 359884-7
Fax: (66 35) 359889

Gateway City Industrial Estate
Highway 331, Km. 10
T. Hua Saem Rong, Plangyao
Chachoengsao 24190
Phone: (66 38) 575274-6
Fax: (66 38) 575274

Well Grow Industrial Estate
78 Moo 1, Bangna-Trad Road, Km. 36
Bangpakong, Chachoengsao 24180
Phone: (66 38) 570001
Fax: (66 38) 570002

Amatanakorn Industrial Estate
700 Moo 1, Klongtamru
Bangna-Trad Road, Km. 57
Muang, Chonburi 20000
Phone: (66 38) 213011-2
Fax: (66 38) 213013

Chonburi Industrial Estate (Bo-Win)
331/8-9 Moo 6, Highway 331, Km. 91-92
Bowin, Sriracha, Chonburi 20230
Phone: (66 38) 954543-4, 954546
Fax: (66 38) 954545
Company Office:
Phone: (66 38) 345234, 345251
Fax: (66 38) 38345233

Pinthong Industrial Estate
789 Moo 1, Nong Ko-Laem Chabang Road
Nong-Kham, Sriracha, Chonburi 20280
Phone: (66 38) 954543-4
Fax: (66 38) 954546
Company Office:
Phone: (66 38) 296334-7
Fax: (66 38) 296333

Nong Khae Industrial Estate (Saraburi)
Phaholyothin Road, Km. 92-93
Nong Khae, Saraburi 18140
Phone: (66 35) 258409-10
Fax: (66 35) 258411
Company Office:
Phone: (66 36) 371720-2
Fax: (66 36) 371721

Ratchaburi Industrial Estate
110 Moo 9, Don Sai
Photharam, Ratchaburi 70120
Phone: (66 32) 375718-9
Fax: (66 32) 356938

Zone 3 (60 provinces or remainder of Thailand including Laem Chabang Industrial Estate):

Laem Chabang Industrial Estate
49/19 Moo 5, Sukhumvit Road, Km. 125-128
Thungsukhla, Sriracha, Chonburi 20230
Phone: (66 38) 490942-5
Fax: (66 38) 490940-1

Khon Kaen Industrial Estate
86 Friendship Highway
Samran Sub-District
Muang, Khon Kaen 40000
Phone: (66 43) 379436, 241834
Fax: (66 43) 379436

Northern Region Industrial Estate
60 Moo 4, Super-Highway Road
Bangklang, Muang, Lamphun 51000
Phone: (66 53) 581050, 581061, 581 054, 581070-2
Fax: (66 53) 581060

Phichit Industrial Estate
71 Moo 1, Tambon Nhonglum
Amphur Wachira Baramee, Phichit 66220
Phone: (66 56) 692191-2
Fax: (66 56) 692193

Amata City Industrial Estate
7 Highway 331, Km. 95
Mapyangporn, Pluakdaeng
Rayong 20230
Phone: (66 38) 490942-5
Fax: (66 38) 490940
Company Office:
Phone: (66 38) 346007
Fax: (66 38) 345771

Eastern Industrial Estate
18 Pakorn Songkhrao-Rat Road
Huay Pong, Muang, Rayong 21150
Phone: (66 38) 683930-8, 681128-9
Fax: (66 38) 683941
Company Office:
Phone: (66 35) 258409-10
Fax: (66 38) 683963

Eastern Seaboard Industrial Estate (Rayong)
112 Moo 4, Highway 331, Km. 91.5
Pluakdaeng, Rayong 21140
Phone: (66 38) 954543-4
Fax: (66 38) 954546

Map Ta Phut Industrial Estate 1 Road I-1, Tambol Map Ta Phut Muang, Rayong 21150 Phone: (66 38) 683930-8, 681128-9 Fax: (66 38) 683941

Padaeng Industrial Estate 1 Padaeng Road, Padaeng Industrial Estate Map Ta Phut, Muang, Rayong 21150 Phone: (66 38) 683930-8, 681128-9 Fax: (66 38) 683941 Company Office: Phone: (66 38) 683318-20 Fax: (66 38) 683361

Thai-Singapore Industrial Estate Highway 3138, Km.29 Tasit, Pluakdaeng, Rayong 21150 Phone: (66 2) 2569798, 2569035-6 Fax: (66 2) 2569553

Southern Industrial Estate (Songkhla Province) 9/6 Moo 4, Chalung Hadyai, Songkhla 90110 Phone: (66 74) 472182-3 Fax: (66 74) 472182

Asia Industrial Estate 682 Moo 2, Banchang Sukhumvit Road, Km. 201 Rayong 21150 Bangkok Office: Phone: (66 2) 2315800, 2315900 Fax: (66 2) 2315933

Products/commodity responsible for:

- x Establishment of industrial estates;

---

x Management and services of utility systems and other facilities;
x Management of properly and commercial activities;
x Development and management of industrial ports;
x Provision of supplies and services in order to enhance quality of life and the environment, as well as the balanced synergy between businesses, communities and society;
x Management of the environmental and occupational safety;
x One-stop-services for permission, approval and special privileges.

Areas/industries where investment is encouraged:
Rubber industry; textile industry; agro-industry; Halal food industry; fishery industry; SMEs auto supporting industry; aviation industry; and waste recycling industry.
Titles of laws and regulations on foreign investment:
x Industrial Estate Authority of Thailand Act B.E. 2522 (1979).
x Announcement of the Board of Industrial Estate Authority of Thailand, No. 1/2525 (1982). Subject: criteria and conditions surcharge under the law on promotion of investment, import duty and business tax in the export processing zone.
x Announcement of the Board of Industrial Estate Authority of Thailand, No. 2/2535 (1992). Subject: Criteria and conditions of payment of surcharge under the law on promotion of investment, import duty, value added tax and excise tax in the export processing zone.
x Announcement of the Board of Industrial Estate Authority of Thailand, No. 5/2535 (1992). Subject: criteria, method and conditions of take the goods used for products into the export processing zone with tax exemption or refund of taxes.
x Announcement of the Industrial Estate Authority of Thailand, No. 107/2535 (1992). Subject: application for tax exemption for the industrial operator in the export processing zone.
x Announcement of the Industrial Estate Authority of Thailand, No. 109/2535 (1992). Subject: application for tax exemption for the industrial operator in the export processing zone.
x Announcement of the Industrial Estate Authority of Thailand, No. 194/2535 (1992). subject: Form of certificate, a written permission and report.
x Announcement of the Director-General of the Revenue Department Governing the Value-Added Tax. Subject: criteria, method and conditions for importing of products into the kingdom and transporting them to the export processing zone; and for selling of products of the bonded warehouse in the category of duty-free shop under the law governing customs as per section 77/1 (14) (a) of the code of revenue.
x Announcement of the Industrial Estate Authority of Thailand, No. 62/2537 (1994).
x Subject: list of goods to be transported into the export processing zone under section 48 of the Industrial Estate Authority of Thailand B.E. 2522 (1979).
x Announcement of the Industrial Estate Authority of Thailand, No. 2/2525 (1982). Subject: Criteria, method and conditions for permission to transport goods out of the export processing zone.
x Announcement of the Industrial Estate Authority of Thailand, No. 1/2531 (1988). Subject: requirements on criteria, method and conditions in an application and approval for operating in industrial estate.
x Announcement of the Board of Industrial Estate Authority of Thailand, No. 3/2525 (1982). Subject: criterion, methods and process for approval of person to access and stays in the export processing zone.
x Announcement of the Industrial Estate Authority of Thailand, No. 3/2535 (1992). Subject: criteria, procedures and conditions in granting approval to own land in industrial estates.
x Announcement of the Board of Industrial Estate Authority of Thailand, No. 6/2535 (1992). Subject: criterion, methods and condition for obtaining approval and giving approval to operate business in industrial estate (2nd revised edition).
x Announcement of the Board of Industrial Estate Authority of Thailand, No. 64/2536 (1993). Subject: general criterion on land development in industrial estate.
x Announcement of the Industrial Estate Authority of Thailand, No. 95/2538 (1995). Subject: general criteria on land development in industrial estate (revised).
x Announcement of the Board of Industrial Estate Authority of Thailand, No. 2/2540 (1997). Subject: to stipulate for category of industrial operation, trading and service to be received permit to operate in export processing zone.
Category:
Export processing zone; industrial promotion; and investment promotion authority.

OFFICE OF THE BOARD OF INVESTMENT (BOI)*

Office/postal address:
555 Vipavadee Rangsit Road Chatuchak Bangkok 10900
Phone: (66 2) 5378111-55 Fax: (66 2) 5378177
E-mail: head@boi.go.th URL: www.boi.go.th
Year established: 1958
Principal functions:
x To publicize investment potential and encourage economically and socially beneficial investments;
x To administer investment promotion incentives and to encourage investment in priority areas which are important and beneficial to the development of the country.
Services/activities:
x Grants tax and non-tax incentives and guarantees to projects;
x Offers business-related services to investors which include assistance in obtaining required licences and permits, finding prospective joint-venture partners, identification of potential investment opportunities, assistance in identifying subcontractors and sourcing opportunities.

Publications issued:

x *A Business Guide to Thailand.* x *A Guide to the Board of Investment.* x *Cost of Doing Business in Thailand.* x *BOI Investment Review* (quarterly newsletter).

Local branches:

46 Moo 5, Leam Chabang Industrial Estate Sukhumvit Road, Tambol Toongsukhla Amphur Sriracha, Chonburi 20230 Phone: (66 38) 491820 Fax: (66 38) 490479 E-mail: chonburi@boi.go.th

2112/22, Mittraphab Road Amphur Muang, Nakhon Ratchasima 3000 Phone: (66 44) 213184 to 86 Fax: (66 44) 213182 E-mail: korat@boi.go.th

213, Aubpalisan Road Amphur Muang, Ubon Ratchathani 34000 Phone: (66 45) 240127 to 29 Fax: (66 45) 240130 E-mail: Ubon@boi.go.th

Airport Business Park #112 90 Mahidol Road Amphur Muang, Chiang Mai 50100 Phone: (66 53) 203400 Fax: (66 53) 203404 E-mail: chmai@boi.go.th

7-15 Chaiyong Building Jootee-Unit 1 Road, Haad Yai Songkhla 90110 Phone: (66 74) 347161-6 Fax: (66 74) 347160 E-mail: songkhla@boi.go.th

49/21-22 Surat-Punpin Road Tambol Makamtia Amphur Muang, Suratthani 84000 Phone: (66 77) 284637, 284622 Fax: (66 77) 284638 E-mail: surat@boi.go.th

Offices abroad:

Bethmannstr 58, 5. OG 60311 Frankfurt am Main, Germany Phone: (49 69) 9291230 Fax: (49 69) 92912320 E-mail: fra@boi.go.th and boifrankfurt@nexgo.de

61 Broadway, Suite 2810 New York, NY 10008, United States of America Phone: (1 212) 4229009 Fax: (1 212) 4229119 E-mail: boiny@aol.com

8th

Floor, Fukuda Building West 2-11-3 Akasaka, Minato-ku Tokyo 107-0052, Japan Phone: (81 3) 35821806 Fax: (81 3) 35895176 E-mail: tyo@boi.go.th

8, Rue Greuze 75116 Paris, France Phone: (33 1) 56902600-1 Fax: (33 1) 56902602 E-mail: boiparis@mail.club-internet.fr, par@boi.go.th

2nd

Floor, Zhong Shan Dong Yi Lu Shanghai, China Phone: (86 21) 63219621 Fax: (86 21) 62319383 E-mail: shanghai@boi.go.th

Areas/industries where investment is encouraged:

Agriculture and agricultural products; mining, ceramics and basic metals; light industry; metal products, machinery and transport equipment; electronics industry and electrical appliances; chemicals, paper and plastics; and services and public utilities.

Titles of laws and regulations on foreign investment:

x Investment Promotion Act 1977, Investment Promotion Act (No. 2) 1991 and Investment Promotion Act (No. 3) 2001.

x Board of Investment Announcement No. 1/2000 and No. 2/2000.

Category:

Investment promotion authority.

PORT AUTHORITY OF THAILAND (PAT)

Office/postal address:

444 Tarua Road Klongtoey District Bangkok 10110

Phone: (66 2) 2490399 Fax: (66 2) 2490885

E-mail: central@port.co.th URL: www.port.co.th

Year established: 1951

Principal functions:

x To provide services and facilities to vessels and cargoes;

x To conduct dredging operations and maintenance of the bar channels and basins;

x To supervise stevedoring, handling, moving, storing and delivering of cargoes;

x To cooperate and coordinate with other government agencies concerned and international ports;

x To develop organization to cope with the economic growth.

Services/activities:

As detailed in Principal functions.

Publications issued:

x *Bimonthly PAT Magazine* (Nitayasan Karntarua) (Thai). x *PAT's Annual Report* (Thai/English). x *House Journal* (Sarnsampan), (Thai). x Brochures, leaflets, etc. (Thai/English).

Local branches:

Laem Chabang Port Toongsukhla Sub-district Sriracha District Chonburi 20230 Phone: (663) 8490000 Fax: (663) 8490149 E-mail: lcp@lcp.pat.or.th

Products/commodity responsible for:

Container and conventional cargo.

Training:

The Authority arranges training in the following areas: working development; basic management; port administration; management; cargo storage; warehousing; cargo handling equipment drivers; mechanical technician; security guard;

dangerous goods; cargo handling; improving port performance; containerization; basic computer; English for Meeting and Discussion; etc.

The courses conducted in English are Port Administration, Development in Container Shipping and Intermodalism, Training in Application of Information Technology, and Human Resource Development and Re-engineering in Port Industry.

Areas/industries where investment is encouraged:

Port Operations at Bangkok Port, Laem Chabang Port, Chiang Saen Port, Chiang Khong Port and Ranong Port for instance container terminal, cargo handling equipment, etc.

Titles of laws and regulations on foreign investment:

All contracts shall be governed by and constructed according to the law and regulations of the Government of Thailand.

Category:

Port authority.

THAI CHAMBER OF COMMERCE (TCC)

Office/postal address:

P.O. Box: 2-146, Bangkok 10200

Phone: (66 2) 6221860-70 Fax: (66 2) 6221882, 6221991 E-mail: inc@thaiechamber.com

URL: www.thaiechamber.com Year established: 1933 Principal functions:

x To enhance competitiveness of business;
x To lead private sectors in negotiating with the Government;
x To be highly recognized by members;
x To be highly recognized by the public;
x To network with all provincial Chambers of Commerce;
x To cooperate with the government sector on economic and trade development;
x To support the role of Chamber of Commerce and trade associations in promoting, developing and solving economic problems such as overseas goods exhibitions;
x To report on the FTA negotiations;
x To organize the Thailand business forum.

Services/activities:

x Organizes domestic and international trade fairs and exhibitions;
x Establishes business information centre;
x Builds business networking centre;
x Issues Certificates of Origin;
x Issues Certificate of Commodity Standards;
x Provides Certify ATA Carnet;
x Organizes and support seminar and training through Thai Entrepreneur Development Institution (TEDI);
x Provides service related to arbitration work.

Publications issued:

x *Thai Chamber of Commerce Membership Directory* (biennial, English).
x *Thailand Showcase: A Buyer's Guide* (annually, English).

Membership structure: 26,035 companies.

Category:

Chamber of commerce.

THAI PLASTIC AND PETROCHEMICAL BUSINESS DEVELOPMENT CENTER (TPDC)

Office/postal address:

TPI Tower 26/56 Chan Tat Mai Road Kwang Tungmahamek Khet Sathorn Bangkok 10120

Phone: (66 2) 6785050, 6785000 ext. 10080-1 Fax: (66 2) 6785159

E-mail: tpdc@tpigroup.co.th URL: www.plastictradepoint.org

Year established: 1996

Principal functions:

x To promote export opportunities for Thai manufacturers of plastics and the articles thereof; x To support export potential of Thai manufacturers of plastics and the articles thereof;

x To enhance business opportunities between Thai manufacturers of plastic and the articles thereof, and those in foreign countries.

Services/activities:

x Facilitates trade missions to visit the centre which is Thailand's only specialized one-stop-service plastic centre; x Arranges matchmakings between the members and interesting overseas businesspersons; x Participates in international and local exhibitions and trade fairs; x Provides data of plastic importers worldwide to the members; x Organizes training programmes aimed at enhancing members' readiness for more business opportunities; x Represents its members in seeking business opportunities in trade promotion forums.

Membership structure: 105 members.

Products/commodity responsible for:

Plastics and articles ranging from petrochemical products, molds and machinery for plastic industry, semi-finished plastic components, and finished plastic products.

Areas/industries where investment is encouraged:
Trading of plastic raw materials, plastic finished products, plastic semi-finished products, molds and machinery for plastic processing.
Categories:
Export marketing board; trade association; trade promotion organization; training/research institute; and permanent exhibition centre.

VIETNAM

DANANG TRADE AND SERVICE COMPANY

Office/postal address:
07 Tran Phu str Danang City
Phone: (84 511) 826831 Fax: (84 511) 873002
E-mail: tscdn@dng.vnn.vn, thangtsc@dng.vnn.vn
Year established: 29 March 1998 [Wholly owned by the Vietnam Chamber of Commerce and Industry (VCCI)].
Principle functions:

- x To support the Vietnam Chamber of Commerce and Industry (VCCI);
- x To facilitate cooperation between foreign business and VCCI.

Services/activities:
x Provides advisory services on investment and business; x Provides services concerning trade fairs and exhibitions; x Organizes overseas missions; x Organizes short-term professional training courses.
Membership structure: 17 members.
Products/commodity responsible for:
Seafood; pepper; tea; coffee; cinnamon; and spice.
Category:
Industrial promotion, investment promotion. and trade promotion organization.

DIRECTORATE FOR STANDARDS AND QUALITY (STAMEQ)

Ministry of Science and Technology
Office/postal address:
8 Hoang Quoc Viet Cau Giay Hanoi
Phone: (84 4) 7562608 Fax: (84 4) 8361556
E-mail: tttt@tcvn.gov.vn URL: www.tcvn.gov.vn
Year established: 1962
Principal functions:
The Directorate for Standards and Quality (STAMEQ) is the governmental body under the Ministry of Science and Technology having responsibility to advise the Government on issues in the fields of standardization, metrology and quality management in the country and representing Viet Nam in international and regional organizations in the fields concerned.
The main activities are:

- x To prepare the rules and regulations on standardization, metrology and quality management and submit them to the authorities for approving;
- x To organize the supervision and control on the implementation of the approved rules and regulations;
- x To establish the organization system on standardization, metrology and quality management and provide methodological guidance for all activities of the above system;
- x To organize the development of national standards and maintain the national metrology standards;
- x To provide the product quality and quality system certification, testing and calibration labouratory accreditation;
- x To implement the state supervision on quality of goods and measurement;
- x To conduct studies on standardization, metrology and quality management;
- x To carry out the activities of information, training and international cooperation on standardization, metrology and quality management.

Services/activities:
Standards and Quality Centre:

x To study disciplines on standardization and its related matters, to draft policies and legal documents on developing and applying Viet Nam national standards (TCVNs);
x To set up programmes and plans on developing and applying TCVN standards and participating in the preparation of international standards; to supervise and inspect on implementation of these programmes or plans;
x To establish and supervise branch commissions and technical committees and subcommittees on standardization;
x To publish, print and distribute TCVN standards and other documents relating to standardization;
x To carry out consultative, information and training activities in the standardization field;
x To provide consultative services on developing branch, company standards and conformity assessment activities;
x To be representatives of Viet Nam in regional and international organizations for standardization; to cooperate with these organizations and other countries in the standardization field.

Metrology Centre:
x To establish, maintain and custody national measurement standards;
x To ensure trace ability of measurement standards to SI system;
x To conduct scientific and technical research in metrology;
x To develop measurement and evaluation technology for industries;
x To carry out metrology activities of dissemination measurement, technology, calibration, testing, information, training and international cooperation;
x To organize scientific study on measurement, standards of measuring unit, verification methods and equipments;
x To take part in writing legal regulations on metrology, plans for national metrology development.

Training Centre:
x To set up basic and follow-up training programmes, to organize the compilation of textbooks and reference documents;
x To organize training courses on standardization, quality management, testing and measurement techniques for managers, officers and technicians of government bodies, provincial and city organizations and business;
x To cooperate with international organizations on training for standardization metrology and quality management (organizing seminars, workshops, training courses; organizing study tours and training courses overseas; organizing training for foreign trainees in Viet Nam.)

Information Centre:
x To serve as a national reference library which collects, maintains and updates international/regional/foreign and domestic information and documentation relating to standards-metrology-quality (SMQ) issues and the others concerned;
x To provide domestic research and development institutions and all economic sectors with information on standards, technical regulations, accreditation and certification and recognition procedures and others in various service forms;
x To play the role of a national member of ISONET, the Information Network of the International Organization for Standardization (ISO).

Viet Nam Productivity Centre (VPC):
x Formulating development strategy, objectives and methods in productivity improvement in Viet Nam;
x Disseminating, impacting and carrying out productivity promoting activities in Viet Nam and international organizations;
x Researching all productivity factors; training, consulting in productivity improvement for enterprises and socioeconomic organizations;
x Undertaking projects and other activities organized by APO; establishing a Membership Network, formulating the Productivity Movement throughout the country;
x Managing staff, equipment, asset and finance of the Centre in accordance with state policies.

Quality Certification Centre (Quacert):
x To take part in developing orientation policy, plan, regulations on quality certification in Viet Nam;
x To join in studying the elements' effect on quality, quality assurance, total quality management to enhance product and service quality for entrepreneurs and social organizations;
x To carry out product certification for quality mark in conformity with national or international standards;
x To participate in training and dissemination activities on quality and certification;
x To take part in bilateral and multilateral international cooperation in concerned sectors.

Viet Nam Accreditation Bureau: x To develop a plan and programme on quality accreditation;
x To carry out the auditing for recognizing the competence of certification bodies, inspection bodies, testing and calibration labouratories; play a role as Secretariat of the National Accreditation Committee;
x To take part in training auditing assessors and run registeration for auditing assessors;
x To take part in development of Viet Nam National Standards, training courses and related propaganda activities;
x To be Viet Nam's representative in the international and regional organizations on accreditation.

Viet Nam WTO/TBT Office
x To notify any technical regulations and conformity assessment procedures adopted or proposed in Viet Nam to the WTO Secretariat; to receive the notification from other WTO country members and to notify to relating document bodies in accordance with WTO;

x To answer reasonable questions which concern the technical regulations, standards (including proposal draft), conformity assessment procedures adopted or proposed in Viet Nam, and technical barriers to trade in accordance with WTO/TBT Agreement;
x To organize all professional activities and popular knowledge to relevant individual, organization bodies about the technical barriers to trade;
x To provide information and consultant services on technical barriers to trade for domestic and foreign individual, organization, in accordance with the current governmental regulations and laws;
x To carry out multilateral and bilateral international integration activities on the technical barriers to trade.
Viet Nam-German Technology Transfer and Training Centre: x To plan and organize training courses on welding technique, automation, automobile; x To provide technical assistance and consultancy to entrepreneurs to upgrade and renew technology;
x To organize compilation of training documents, quality handbooks for technical training and technology-applied consultancy;
x To transfer technology, provide entrepreneurs with information and services of technique and equipment; x To take part in international cooperation in related sectors.
Magazine of Standards, Metrology and Quality:
x To publish magazine, other special publications on standards, metrology, quality and customers' rights protection;
x To disseminate the magazine to state authorities, research institutes, entrepreneurs, universities;
x To play a roleas contact point with other relevant organizations to disseminate activities of SMQ on the mass media.
Small and Medium Enterprises Development Centre (SMEDEC):
x To study targets, orientation, policies, measures; establish technical-support projects to accelerate SME development, improve the effectiveness of production and product/service quality;
x To support technical assistance, consultancy SMEs on barcode, financial techniques to develop production and improve product/service quality;
x To carry out consultant activities on standards, metrology, quality for SMEs;
x To organize training courses for SMEs on product quality management, manufacturing management, financial management, business administration, marketing and technics;
x To provide SMEs with information as follows: standards, metrology, product quality, technology, equipments, innovation, business and other related to manufacturing development, business and services.
Main activities:
x Carries out state inspection, testing, calibration of goods quality, measuring equipment;
x Maintains, utilize measurement standards, verifies measuring equipment as authorized by STAMEQ;
x Takes part in developing Viet Nam national standards and international standards;
x Provides training and information activities as authorized by STAMEQ;
x Collabourates with domestic and foreign organizations in the field of inspection, testing, verification, calibration.
Local branches:
8 Hoang Quoc Viet Street Cau Giay, Hanoi Phone: (84 4) 7564188 Fax: (84 4) 8361199
97 Ly Thai To Street Da Nang City 2 Ngo Quyen Street Da Nang City Phone: (84 511) 820868, 831511, 848376 Fax: (84 511) 820868, 910064
49 Pasteur Street District1 Ho Chi Minh City Phone: (84 8) 8294274 Fax: (84 8) 8293012
Publications issued:
x *Magazine for SMQ,* (monthly, Vietnamese).
x *TCVN News* (bimonthly, English).
x *Library information* (bimonthly, Vietnamese).
x Subject publication.
Membership structure: 16 member centres and 60 provincial departments for standards, metrology and quality.

Products/commodity responsible for:

All industry sectors.
Training:
x Technical training for entrepreneurs and/or successors aiming at improving their technical capability;
x Technology and management training for SMEs aiming at improving technology and management competency;
x Extension training: to improve the capability of SMEs extension officers.
All the training courses are conducted by experienced, highly qualified resource persons, coming from reputed foreign institutions or well-known Vietnamese educational institutions. The content of training courses as well as the teaching method are specially studied to be most adaptable to SME entrepreneurs.
Titles of laws and regulations on foreign investment:
x 13/1999/PL-UBTVQH10, Order No. 04/L-CTN promulgating the Ordinance on the Protection of Consumers' Interests, 1999-04-27.
x 14/1999/Q§-TTg, Decision No. 14/1999/QD-TTg on the establishment of the Department for Management of Food quality, Hygiene and Safety under the Ministry of Health, 1999-02-04.
x 14-Q§/KHCN, Decision No. 14-QD/KHCN issuing the Regulation on Registration of Commodities Quality of the Specialized Aquatic Product Service, 1997-01-09.
x 17/2000/Q§-BXD, Decision No. 17/2000/QD-BXD of August 2, 2000 promulgating the Regulation on quality control of construction works, 2000-08-02.

x 20/2000/Q§-BTC, Decision No, 20/2000/QD-BTC dated 21/02/2000 issuing the Table of charge and fee rates for the aquatic resource protection, 2000-02-21.

x 22/2000/Q§-BTC, Decision No, 22/2000/QD-BTC dated 21/02/2000 issuing the charge and fee rates for plant protection and quarantine.

x 23/2000/Q§-BTC, Decision No, 23/2000/QD-BTC dated 21/02/2000 promulgating Tables of charges and fees for food quality hygiene and safety control.

x 27/2000/Q§-BTC, Decision No, 27/2000/QD-BTC dated 24/02/2000 on the issuance of fee levels for granting certificates of technical and quality evaluation of communications and transport equipment and means, 2000.

x 37/2001/TTLT/BKHCNMT-TCHQ, Joint Circular guiding the customs procedures for and quality inspection of export and import goods subject to the State quality inspection, 2001-06-28.

x 57/CP, Decree No.57-CP on sanctions against administrative violations in the measurement and quality of goods, 1997-05
31.

- x 65/2000/TT-BTC, Circular No. 65/2000/TT-BTC of July 5, 2000 guiding the management and use of food quality, hygiene and safety control charges and fees, 2000-07-05.
- x 86/1998/Q§-BNN-BVTV, Decision No. 86/1998/QD-BNN BVTV banning the use of a number of plant protection drugs in Viet Nam's agricultural production, 1998-06-24.
- x 86-CP, Decree No. 86/CP on assignment of State management responsibilities for the quality of goods, 1995 12-08.
- x 90/2000/Q§-BTC, Decision No. 90/2000/QD-BTC of June 1, 2000 promulgating the Tables of fee levels for aquatic product quality, safety and hygiene control, 2000-06-01.
- x 104/2000/Q§-BNN-KHCN, Decision No. 104/2000/QD BNN-KHCN promulgating the Provisional Regulation on the inspection of quality of concrete in irrigation works by the non-destructive method of using ultra-sonic measuring machines and concrete guns, 2000-10-13.
- x 106/Q§-T§C, Promulgating regulation or the seal of verification for state bodies of metrology and other entities which received the authorization of verification, 1991-07-27.
- x 107-T§C/Q§, Promulgating regulation on form of certification of state bodies of metrology and other bases which received the authorization of state verification, 1991 07-20.
- x 116/2000/TT-BTC, Circular guiding the regime of management and use of fees for aquatic product quality safety and hygiene control, 2000-12-19.
- x 117/2000/Q§-BKHCNMT, Decision No. 117/2000/QD BKHCNMT dated 26/01/2000 promulgating the 2000 list of export goods and import goods subject to the State quality inspection, 2000-01-26.
- x 125/2000/Q§-BNN-BVTV, Decision on exceptional registration of a kind of plant protection drug in Viet Nam, 2000-12-06.
- x 143/2001/Q§-TCB§, Decision No. 143/2001/QD-TCBD promulgating the Regulation on control of quality of the post and telecommunications services and networks, 2001-02-28.
- x 171/1999/N§-CP, Decree No. 171/1999/ND-CP dated 07/12/1999 detailing the implementation of the Ordinance on protection of traffic works with regard to riverway traffic works, 1999-12-07.
- x 172/1999/N§-CP, Decree No. 172/1999/ND-CP dated 07/12/1999 detailing the implementation of the Ordinance on protection of traffic works with regard to land road traffic works, 1999-12-07.
- x 228/1999/Q§-TTg, Decision No. 228/1999/QD-TTg dated 15/12/1999 adding the objective of ensuring foodstuff quality, hygiene and safety to the National Target Program for elimination of a number of social diseases and dangerous, 1999-12-15.
- x 380-Q§, Promulgating regulation on state specialized inspection bodies in metrology, 1991-07-01.
- x 540/TTg, Administrative operation on measurement and commodity - quality circulated in market, 1995-09-05.
- x 560/TT-KCM, Guiding the implementation of Decree No 86/CP dated 8 December 1995 of Government relating to assign responsibility of State management in commodity quality, 1996-03-21.

x 650/2000/Q§-BTS, Decision No. 650/2000/QD-BTS dated 04/08/2000 promulgating the Regulation on the State inspection and certification of quality of aquatic goods, 2000-08-04.
x 1010/2000/Q§-BYT, Decision No. 1010/2000/QD-BYT dated 30/3/2000 issuing the list of food commodities subject to quality registration, 2000-03-30.
x 1091/1999/Q§-BKHCNMT, Decision No. 1091/1999/QD BKHCNMT promulgating the Regulation on the State control of import-export goods quality, 1999-06-22.
x 1479/Q§-T§C, Promulgating regulation on accreditation and certification of quality, 1995-08-25.
x 1645/1999/Q§-BKHCNMT, Decision No. 1645/QD BKHCNMT by the Minister of Science Technology and Environment amending the list of export, import goods which were checked the quality 1999 by the State, 1999.
x Law on Foreign Investment in Viet Nam, 1999.
x Order No. 16/1999/PL-UBTVQH10 dated 6 October 1999, Ordinance on metrology.
x Order No. 18/1999/PL-UBTVQH10 dated 24 December 1999, Ordinance on goods quality.
x Decree No. 65/2001/ND-CP dated 28 September 2001, issuing legal system for measuring units of Viet Nam.
x Decree No. 6/2002/ND-CP dated 14 January 2002, concrete guidance on implementation of ordinance on metrology.
x Decision No. 2424/2000/QD-BKHCNMT dated 12 December 2000, temporary guidance on supplier's self declaration of conformity.
x Decision No. 2425/2000/QD-BKHCNMT dated 12 December 2000, temporary guidance on supplier's self declaration of standards development.
x Decision No. 13/2001/QD-BKHCNMT dated 6 January 2001, temporary guidance on safety certification.
x Decision No. 1/2003/QD-BKHCN dated 30 January 2003, decision on management of quality, intellectual property, technology transfer to domestic assembled and imported motorbike, engine and spare parts.

Category:
Standards, testing and inspection body.

INTERNATIONAL CONSULTING AND TRAINING CENTER (ICTC)

Office/postal address:
46 Ngo Quyen Street Hanoi
Phone: (84 4) 8261980 Fax: (84 4) 8261978
E-mail: pthung@fpt.vn
Year established: 1 October 1993 (Pursuant to Decision No. 1096/TM-TCCB by Ministry of Trade, Granted License No. 275 to operate in the scientific and technological field by the Ministry of Science, Technology and Environment on 18 April 1994).
Principle function:
Three main functions: commercial consulting and training in the context of internal and external affairs and research for applying new science technology in Viet Nam.
Services/activities:
x Researches and studies scientific projects for the purpose of promoting cooperation relationships in terms of economics, trade, investment and training;
x Provides services concerning advertisement, trade fairs and exhibitions, science and techniques;
x Holds international seminars and conferences;
x Provides advisory services for the establishment of enterprises and opening of representative offices/branches;
x Organizes tourist and business tours;
x Collects and disseminates information on domestic and foreign trade and economic issues;
x Organizes overseas missions;
x Organizes vocational training for exporting labours.

Publications issued:
x *The results of Uruguay Round conference on trade municipal system, 2000.*
x *Research on making mechanism and policies for producing development of main exports of Vietnam, 2003* (state subject).

x *Research on international treaties of commerce, specially on service-commerce for the integrating process into international economics of Vietnam, 2003.*

x *Research on producing interior equipment from material of fibre glass composite, 2003.*

Membership structure: The International Consulting and Training Centre is a member of the Ministry of Trade of Viet Nam. There are 20 members.

Training:

x Courses on informatic technology; x Courses on foreign languages: English, Chinese, French, etc; x Courses on professional competence of foreign trade and international economic integration; x Courses on long-term and short-term vocational training.

Areas/industries where investment is encouraged:

Services and investment for research, training and cooperation as well as projects of commercial development.

Category:

Investment financing organization, investment promotion authority; trade fair and exhibition authority; trade promotion organization; and training/research institute.

INVESTMENT AND TRADE PROMOTION CENTRE (ITPC)

Office/postal address:
51 Dinh Tien Hoang Street District 1 Ho Chi Minh City
Phone: (84 8) 8236738, 8297426 Fax: (84 8) 8242391
E-mail: itpc@hcm.vnn.vn URL: www.itpc.hochiminhcity.gov.vn

Year established: 1964 (as Export Development Centre; restructured in 1982 as Foreign Trade Development Centre, and renamed Foreign Trade and Investment Development Centre (ITPC) in 1992).

Principal functions:

x To advise municipal authorities on policies and measures to improve business environment and enhance competitiveness of Vietnamese products;
x To provide information on trade and investment;
x To organize trade and investment promotion activities; regular government-business meetings to tackle business-related problems such as taxes, customs, land;
x To promote foreign direct investment and provide one-stop services for foreign investors;
x To support SMEs;
x To offer secretarial and business centre services (package or partial service at the client's request) to local and foreign businesspersons.

Services /activities:

Information:

x Provides economic information on import-export investment and economic laws;
x Prints various publications;
x Provides legal consulting services to domestic and foreign enterprises;
x Maintains databank on domestic and foreign businesspersons and enterprises;
x Provides documents of local and foreign studies specializing in import, export and investment;

Trade promotion: Areas/industries where investment is encouraged:

x Guides and supports foreign businesspersons in searching for business counterparts;
x Undertakes trade brokerage (import-export);
x Organizes business missions, in and out of the country, boosting import-export, exploring new markets;
x Organizes seminars on trade promotion, trade shows; especially annual trade fairs of high quality Vietnamese goods throughout Viet Nam and in the neighboring countries;
x Conducts market studies, marketing surveys for domestic and foreign businesspersons and annual consumer polls;
x Promoting investment;
x Makes introduction of the Ho Chi Minh City investment projects to delegations of foreign investors;
x Supports foreign investors in searching for local counterparts;
x Provides services for domestic and foreign businesspersons;
x Lends office space and provides package (or partial) services for local and foreign companies/businesspersons.

Supporting small- and medium- scale enterprises:

x Undertakes management training courses for SMEs;
x Provides consulting services on obtaining loans, equipment to serve and develop production;
x Provides information for enterprises;
x Provides consulting services on business formalities (accepting to provide regular legal consulting services for individual enterprise);
x Operates a permanent showroom of Vietnamese import-export products.

Publications issued:

x *Export-Import-Investment Directory* (annually, English). x *Vietnam Export-Import Tariff Schedule* (annually, English). x *Transparency on economic performance of Viet Nam and*

Ho Chi Minh City (quarterly and bi-yearly, Vietnamese/English).
x *Trade and Investment Promotion Bulletin* (weekly, Vietnamese).
x Guidebook for investing and doing business in Viet Nam; and booklets on trademark, international business practices, Q&A on taxes.
x *Saigon Tiep Thi* (Saigon Marketing) (weekly,Vietnamese).
x *Saigon Tiep Thi online.*
x *Consumer Guide for Men* (monthly, Vietnamese).
x *Explore* (monthly, Vietnamese).
Local branch:
92-96 Nguyen Hue Street, District 1 Ho Chi Minh City (Showroom)
Office abroad: Viet Nam House in Singapore; other offices to be opened in Japan, Europe and the United States of America.
Membership structure: 76 members.
Training:
Management training courses for SMEs (in cooperation with ESCAP); training courses on trade promotion, export marketing, branding, corporate management skills.
Branches, lines and domains eligible for investment preferences:
x Afforestation, zoning for forest regeneration; planting perennial trees on unused land, bare hills or mountains; land reclamation; salt-making; and aquaculture in unexploited water areas;
x Infrastructure construction, mass-transit development; development of education and training, healthcare and national culture;
x Export goods production and trading;
x Offshore fishing; processing of agricultural, forestry and aquatic products; technical services in direct service of agricultural, forestry and fishery production;
x Scientific research and technological development, scientific and technological services; consultancy on legal matters, investment, business, business administration, intellectual property right protection and technology transfer;
x Other branches and lines.
List of projects with special investment encouragement:
x Production or processing with 80 per cent or more of the products for export;
x Processing of agricultural products, forest products (excluding timber) or aquatic products from domestic raw materials, with 50 per cent of the products for export;
x Production of new breeds with high quality and economic efficiency;
x Agricultural farming, forestation, aquaculture;
x Production of new materials, rare and precious materials, application of new biotechnologies; new technologies for the manufacture of information and telecommunication equipment;
x Hi-tech industries;
x Investment in research and development;
x Manufacture of waste treating equipment;
x Production of antibiotics raw materials;
x Pollution treatment and environmental protection, waste treatment;
x Investment under BOT, BTO or BT contracts.
List of projects with investment encouragement:
x Production or processing with 50 per cent or more of products for export;
x Production or processing with 30 per cent or more of the products for export and with the use of large percentages of domestic raw materials and materials (valued from 30 per cent or more of the production cost).
x With intensive employment of Vietnamese labourers and efficient use of natural resources available in Viet Nam;
x Processing of farm produce, forest products (excluding timber), aquatic products;
x Preservation of food, post-harvest preservation of farm produce;
x Mineral exploration, exploitation and intensive processing;
x Development of petro-chemical industry; construction and operation of oil and gas pipelines, depots, ports;
x Manufacture of equipment, detail groups in oil, gas, mineral or fuel exploitation; manufacture of big lifting and lowering equipment;
x Manufacture of high-quality steel, alloy nonferrous metals, special metals, steel cast, spongy iron for industrial use;
x Manufacture of machine tools for metalworking, metallurgical equipment;
x Manufacture of precision tools, safety check and inspection equipment; manufacture of molds for metal and non-metal products;
x Manufacture of medium- and high-voltage electric equipment;
x Manufacture of diesel engines through advance technologies and techniques; manufacture of dynamic and hydraulic machines and spare parts, compressors;
x Manufacture of automobile and motorbike spare parts; manufacture and assembly of construction equipment, machines and vehicles; manufacture of technical equipment for transport service;
x Shipbuilding, manufacture of equipment and spare parts for freighters, fishing ships;
x Manufacture of information and telecommunications

equipment;

x Manufacture of electronic components and equipment, informatics technology;

x Manufacture of agricultural equipment, spare parts, machines, irrigation and drainage equipment;

x Production of assorted insecticide raw materials;

x Production of base chemicals, pure chemicals, dyes, special-use chemicals;

x Production of cleansing raw materials, chemicals activities;

x Production of special-type content, composite materials, soundproof, electric-insulated and heat-resistant materials, wood substitute composite materials, refractory materials constriction plastic, glass fibers;

x Production of light construction materials;

x Production of paper pulp;

x Production of silk, assorted yarns and special fabric for industrial use;

x Manufacture of high-class raw materials for production of export footwear and garments;

x Manufacture of high-quality packaging for export goods;

x Manufacture of medical equipment in analytical technology and extracting technology in medicine;

x Production of drug raw materials, medicines of GMP international standards.

x Improvement, development of energy sources;

x Mass transit;

x Construction and renovation of bridges, land roads, airports, harbours, railway stations, car terminals, railways;

x Construction of water plants, water supply and drainage systems;

x Construction: commercial operation of infrastructures of industrial parks, export processing zones, hi-tech parks.

List of geographical areas where investment is encouraged:

x Section A: geographical areas facing extremely difficult socio-economic conditions;

x Section B: geographical areas facing difficult socioeconomic conditions.

List of fields with conditional investment:

x Investment only in forms of joint venture or business cooperation contract: -Construction and commercial operation of international telecommunication networks, local telecommunication networks (only in form of business cooperation contract); -Production and processing of oil, gas, rare and precious minerals;

-Consulting services (excluding technical consultancy);

-Air, rail and sea transport: mass transit, construction of harbors and airports (excluding BOT, BTO and BT projects);

-Production of industrial explosives;

-Forestation;

-Tour business;

-Culture;

x Products which must ensure the export percentage requirement:

-The compulsory export percentages for home-made products which have already met the quantitative and qualitative requirements shall be announced for each period by the Ministry of Planning and Investment;

x Processing projects which must be linked to investment in creation of raw material sources:

-Dairy production and processing;

-Vegetal oil and cane sugar production;

-Timber processing;

x Projects for investment in import services, domestic distribution services shall comply with the Prime Minister's regulations.

List of fields not licensed for investment:

x Projects which are detrimental to national security, defense and public interests;

x Projects which cause harm to historical and cultural relics, fine traditions and customs of Viet Nam;

x Projects which cause harm to the ecological environment; projects on treatment of hazardous wastes brought from overseas into Viet Nam;

x Projects for the production of toxic chemicals or use of hazardous agents banned under international treaties.

Titles of laws and regulations on foreign investment:

x Law on Foreign Investment in Viet Nam (1996);

x Law on Amendments and Supplements to a number of articles of the Law on Foreign Investment in Viet Nam in 2000;

x Decision No. 53/1999/QD-TTg dated 26 March 1999 on some measures to encourage FDI;

x Decree No. 24/2000/ND-CP on detailed regulations on the implementation of the Law on Foreign Investment in Viet Nam; 3 / 0 U IA/L

x Circular No. 12/2000/TT-B^H of the Ministry of Planning and Investment providing guidelines for FDI in Vietnam;

x Decree No. 27/2003/ND-CP dated 19 March 2993 on amendments and supplements to a number of articles of Decree No. 24/2000/ND-CP;

x Communique No. 187/pg-QHQT dated 1 April 2003 of the Government Office on correction of Decree No. 27/2003/ND-CP;

x Decision No. 36/2003/QD-TTg of the Prime Minister date 11 March 2003 on foreign investors' contribution of capital to and purchase of shares in Vietnamese enterprises.

Category:

Trade and investment promotion organization.

VIETNAM CHAMBER OF COMMERCE AND INDUSTRY (VCCI)

Office/postal address:

International Trade Centre 9 Dao Duy Anh Street Hanoi

Phone: (84 4) 5742022 Fax: (84 4) 5742020, 5742030

E-mail: vcci@fmail.vnn.vn URL: www.vcci.com.vn

Year established: 1963

Principal functions:

x To promote and assist trade, investment and other business activities in Viet Nam and abroad;

x To represent the Vietnamese business community, Vietnamese employers and business associations for promotion and protection of their interests in domestic and international relations;

x To serve as a forum for the exchange of information and ideas among business enterprises;

x To liaise with the Vietnamese State on matters concerning the economic activity and business environment in Viet Nam;

x To represent the Vietnamese business community for the promotion and protection of the lawful, legitimate interests of the business community and labour users in Viet Nam in domestic and international relations;

x To promote the development of business enterprises, entrepreneurs, the cooperation among business entities and to offer assistance in trade and investment, economic and technological cooperation and other business activities of enterprises in Viet Nam and abroad.

Services/activities:

x Issues publications and provides information about Viet Nam's economy and foreign trade;

x Assists Vietnamese organizations in acquiring information on foreign markets, scientific and technological developments, international laws and regulations on foreign trade;

x Issues Certificate of Origin of Vietnamese export goods and endorses other documents used in international trade;

x Represents foreign parties in application for registration of patents and trade marks;

x Assists foreign businesspersons who contemplate doing business in Viet Nam in such useful services as intermediation, trade information, business consultancy, establishment of their representative offices, arrangement for business tours/ appointments;

x Arranges for Viet Nam's participation in international trade fairs and exhibitions abroad and assists the Vietnamese and foreign parties in the introduction and advertisement of goods and services;

x Arranges seminars and talks with competent organizations both at home and abroad on selected topics such as banking, finance, foreign direct investment, trade, legal and management issues, technologies;

x Organizes various courses on business and investment management, enterprise creation, marketing, trade promotion, foreign business languages;

x Provides services for the settlement of all disputes in foreign trade relations through the Viet Nam International Arbitration Centre, settles all cases of general average at the request of the concerned parties through the Subcommittee of General Average Adjusters (attached to the Chamber);

x Promotes the development of SMEs in Viet Nam through the Small and Medium Enterprises Promotion Centre (SME-PC);

x Helps in the registration and protection of intellectual property and technology transfer in Viet Nam and abroad;

x Collects and studies the views and suggestions of business enterprises for reflection, recommendation and advice to the State on legal matters and economic policies for the improvement of the business environment;

x Participates in the formation and implementation of the strategy for socio-economic development and international economic integration, to participate in the conferences, and missions for economic and trade negotiations in line with State regulation;

x Organizes activities for the promotion and encouragement to business enterprises on the strict observance of laws, improvement of socio accountabilities; good business ethics and culture and sound working relations, protection of the environment and participation in other social activities in line with the Chamber's objectives.

Publications issued:
x *Business Forum Newspaper* (Monday, Wednesday and Friday every week, Vietnamese). x *Business Forum Magazine* (weekly, English*)*. x *Vietnam Business Directory* (annually, Vietnamese). x *Vietnam Info* (CD-ROM). x *Doing business in Vietnam* (guidebook).
Local branches:
171 Vo Thi Sau District 3, Ho Chi Minh City Phone: (84 8) 9329568 Fax: (84 8) 9325472 E-mail: vcci-hcm@hcm.vnn.vn
1 Ho Quy Ly, Ward 2, Vung Tau City Phone: (84 64) 816072 Fax: (84 64) 859651
29 Cach Mang Thang Tan Street Can Tho City Phone: (84 71) 824918 Fax: (84 71) 824169 E-mail: vcci-cantho@hcm.fpt.vn
256 Tran Phu Street, Danang City Phone: (84 511) 821719 Fax: (84 511) 822930 E-mail: vcci.dn@dng.vnn.vn
10 Dinh Tien Hoang Street Haiphong City Phone: (84 31) 842894 Fax: (84 31) 842243 E-mail: vccihp-hv@hn.vnn.vn
68 Yersin Street Nha Trang City Phone: (84 58) 810363
Phone: (84 37) 754640 Fax: (84 37) 754641 E-mail: vccith@hn.vn.vn
155 Tran Phu Street Vinh City, Nghe An Phone: (84 38) 844012 Fax: (84 38) 842026
Members structure: 5,500 membes (as at the end of 2004).
Training:
Regularly organizes training activities in appropriate forms to develop human resources for business enterprises, to help entrepreneurs enhance their knowledge, management skills and business capacity.
Category:
Chamber of commerce.

VIETNAM INSTITUTE FOR TRADE (VIT)

Office/postal address:
46 Ngo Quyen Street Hanoi
Phone: (84 4) 8262722, 8260717 Fax: (84 4) 8248279
E-mail: vit@netnam.org.vn, phanvien@hcm.fpt.vn
Year established: 1996 (merger of the Research Institute for Foreign Economic Relations (RIFER) and the Economic and Technical Research Institute for Trade (ETRIT) under the Ministry of Trade).
Principal functions:

x To conduct research on trade-related issues;
x To provide consulting and advisory service;
x To conduct training of trade personnel at graduate and post graduate levels in various aspects of trade development and techniques.

Services/activities:
x Undertakes studies of scientific foundations for mapping out trade strategies and policies and planning of trade and market development, assess trade performance, practice and policies;
x Provides consulting services; x Provides training courses on foreign economic relation at graduate and postgraduate levels; x Maintains database and disseminates trade information intelligence;
x Cooperates and exchanges information in the field of trade economics with international and local organizations and scientists.
Publication issued:
All results of research work.
Local branches:
Viet Nam Filial Institute for Trade 35-37 Ben Chuong Duong District 1, Ho Chi Minh City Phone: (08 48) 8211961 Fax: (08 48) 8429709 E-mail: phanvien@hcm.fpt.vn
Training:
To conduct training of trade personnel at graduate and post-graduate levels in various aspects of trade economics and trade-related issues.
Category:
Ministry of Trade; state trading organization; and training/research institute.

VIETNAM SUPERINTENDENCE AND INSPECTION JOINT STOCK COMPANY (VINACONTROL)

Office/postal address:
54 Tran Nhan Tong Street
Hanoi Phone: (84 4) 8226021, 9433840, 9436011 Fax: (84 4) 9433844
E-mail: vinacontrolvn@hn.vnn.vn URL: www.vinacontrol.com.vn Year established: 1957 Principal function:
To provide inspection of goods and other related services.
Services/activities:

x Inspects quality, quantity, marking and packing of goods and commodities (including machinery, production line and gemstones);
x Undertakes overall supervision of the goods during production, delivery, preservation, transportation, loading/discharging; supervision of installing and assembling equipments, production line; assessment, consultant and supervision of construction project;

x Produces survey on means of transportation, container; marine survey; gas-free inspection of the ship before repairing or scrap;
x Samples, tests and analyses at labouratory;
x Provides damage survey; acting as the agent for insurance companies in damage survey, adjuster and settling claims;
x Provides fumigation, evaluation, non-destructive test (NDT); welding test; test and calibration of tools and measuring equipment; calibration of tank, lighter; tallying, sealing service; auditing quality management system on request;
x Provides inspection service on request and supplying certificates for managerial purpose of various fields to the Government such as origin of the goods; quality management; safety and hygiene of the goods; balance of investment project; environment protection (industrial hygiene; water treatment; waste water, etc.) and custom clearance service;
x Provides advisory, audit and certification services on international management standards; advisory on quality of goods;
x Carries out entrustment inspection and other services of local and international inspection organizations;
x Provides hotel and office for rent.

Local branches:
255 Le Duan, Danang City Phone: (84 511) 891087, 821031 Fax: (84 511) 830084 E-mail: vinacontroldn@dng.vnn.vn
56 and 80 Pham Minh Duc Haiphong City Phone: (84 31) 760065, 760453-4 Fax: (84 31) 760103 E-mail: vinacontrolhp@hn.vnn.vn
96 Yet Kieu, Hanoi City Phone: (84 4) 9424748, 9421343 Fax: (84 4) 9421002 E-mail: vinacontrolhn@hn.vnn.vn
80 Ba Huyen Thanh Quan District 3, Ho Chi Minh City Phone: (84 8) 8438624, 9316704, 9316323 Fax: (84 8) 9316961, 8437861 E-mail: vinacontrol@hcm.vnn.vn
11 Hoang Long Ha Long City Quang Ninh Province Phone: (84 33) 825535, 826736 Fax: (84 33) 826169 E-mail: vinacontrol-qn@hn.vnn.vn
The International Standard Application Consulting Branch (ISCB VINACONTROL) 54 Tran Nhan Tong, Hanoi City Phone: (84 4) 9435770 Fax: (84 4) 9433603 E-mail: tuvanhtqlcl@hn.vnn.vn
14 Mai Hac De, Vinh City, Nghe An Province Phone: (84 38) 840299 Fax: (84 38) 844819 E-mail: vinacontrolvinh@yahoo.com
Phai Tran T-junction, Hoang Dong ward, Lang Son city, Lang Son province Phone: (84 25) 870080 Fax: (84 25) 870080 E-mail: vinacontrolls@hn.vnn.vn
5 Tang Bat Ho, Qui Nhon city, Binh Dinh province Phone: (84 56) 892565 Fax: (84 56) 892528 E-mail: vinacontrolqnh@dng.vnn.vn
26 Me Llinh, Nha Trang city, Khanh Hoa province Phone: (84 58) 510348 Fax: (84 58) 510347 E-mail: vinacontrolnt@dng.vnn.vn
14/10 A,B Le Hong Phong road, Binh Thuy district Can Tho City Phone: (84 71) 887911 Fax: (84 71) 887944 E-mail: vinacontrolct@hcm.vnn.vn
Phu My town, TanThanh District, Baria Vung Tau province Phone; (84 64) 876563 Fax: (84 64) 893780 E-mail: vinacontrol_pmt@yahoo.com
Membership structure: Over 600 members.
Category:
Inspection institution.

VIETNAM TRADE INFORMATION CENTER (VTIC)

Office/postal address:
46 Ngo Quyen Street Hanoi
Phone: (84 4) 8262316, 8250713 Fax: (84 4) 9349117
E-mail: vtic@bdvn.vnmail.vnd.net
Year established: 1989
Principal functions:
x To collect information on domestic and international economy, trade, marketing, price and investment; x To analyse the above collected information; x To disseminate information domestically and overseas.
Services/activities:
x Publishes various bulletins and books concerning economy, trade, marketing, price, international trade, investment, economic relations and cooperation between Viet Nam and foreign countries;
x Offers advisory services; x Organizes seminars on investment and trade; x Establishes a computerized national trade network known as VINANET with three servers located in Hanoi, Ho Chi Minh City and Danang and connected to various terminals in major markets throughout Viet Nam, being the host of Viet Nam national home page on the ASEMCONNECT network at www.asemconnectvietnam.gov.vn;
x Builds up an economic and trade databank and disseminates information.
Publications issued:

x *Ngoai Thuong* (foreign trade; weekly, Vietnamese). x *Thi truong* (daily market; Vietnamese). x *Thi truong-Gia ca-Vat tu* (market and prices and material; Vietnamese). x *Thon7g tin Thuong mai* (trade information; weekly, Vietnamese). x *Thi ruong-Thuong nghiep Vietnam* (Viet Nam market and commerce; monthly, Vietnamese). x *Thuong mai-Doanh nghiep* (commerce and enterprises; weekly, Vietnamese).
Local branches:
173 Hai Ba Trung Street District 1, Ho Chi Minh City Phone: (84 8) 8237192 Fax: (84 8) 8237192
132 Nguyen Chi Thanh Street Da Nang City Phone: (84 511) 826927 Fax: (84 511) 830125
Category:
Ministry of Trade; trade facilitation body; and trade promotion organization.

FINANCE AND ADMINISTRATION

Vice-President (Finance and Administration)	B. N. Lohani	+632 632 5015

OFFICE OF THE SECRETARY

The Secretary	Robert Dawson	+632 632 4920
Assistant Secretary	Ajay Sagar	+632 632 4921

OFFICE OF THE GENERAL COUNSEL

General Counsel	Jeremy Hovland	+632 632 4890
Deputy General Counsel	Philip Daltrop	+632 632 4906
Assistant General Counsel	Chin Choon Fong	+632 632 4902
Assistant General Counsel	Ashraf Mohammed	+632 632 4913
Assistant General Counsel	Atsuko Hirose	+632 632 6432
Assistant General Counsel		

BUDGET, PERSONNEL, AND MANAGEMENT SYSTEMS DEPARTMENT

Director General	Masayuki Tamagawa	+632 632 4441
Deputy Director General	Hyong-Jong Yu	+632 632 4500
Senior Advisor	Alessandro A. Pio	+632 632 6251
Advisor, BPMSD concurrently Head, Unit for Institutional Coordination	Tomoyuki Kimura	+632 632 6251
Advisor (Human Resources)	Phillip Ash	+632 632 6846
Director, Human Resources Division	Robert Y. Siy, Jr.	+632 632 4216
Director, Staff Development and Benefits Division	Rosario Abad Santos	+632 632 4428
Director, Budget and Management Services Division	Diwesh Sharan	+632 632 4768

OFFICE OF ADMINISTRATIVE SERVICES

Principal Director	C. R. Rajendran	+632 632 4215
Director, Facilities and Asset Management Division	Ken L. Chee	+632 632 4878
Director, Institutional Services Division	Akmal Siddiq	+632 632 6748

CONTROLLER'S DEPARTMENT

Controller	Hong-Sang Jung	+632 632 4540
Assistant Controller, Accounting Division	Chai Sun Kim	+632 632 4782
Assistant Controller, Loan Administration Division	Hiroshi Fukukawa	+632 632 4543

TREASURY DEPARTMENT

Treasurer	Thierry De Longuemar	+632 632 4700
Deputy Treasurer	Jingdong Hua	+632 632 4700
Assistant Treasurer, Financial Policy and Planning Division	Tobias Hoschka	+632 632 4701
Assistant Treasurer, Funding Division	Kazuki Fukunaga	+632 632 4713
Assistant Treasurer, Investments Division	Michael Jordan	+632 632 4712
Assistant Treasurer, Treasury Services Division	Benjamin Lee	+632 632 4730

OFFICE OF INFORMATION SYSTEMS AND TECHNOLOGY

Principal Director	S. Chander	+632 632 4800
Senior Advisor	Rita Nangia	+632 632 6885
Director, Solution Delivery Division	Chan Toong San	+632 632 4117
Director, Technology Division (Officer-in-Charge)	Radhakrishnan Srinivasan	+632 632 4881

OFFICE OF THE VICE-PRESIDENT (OPERATIONS 1) AND SENIOR STAFF

Operations 1		
Vice-President (Operations 1)	Zhao Xiaoyu	+632 632 6015

SOUTH ASIA DEPARTMENT

Director General	Sultan H. Rahman	+632 632 6200
Deputy Director General	Ma. Carmela Locsin	+632 632 6423
Advisor	Sungsup Ra	+632 632 4629
Director, Country Coordination and Regional Cooperation Division	Sekhar Bonu	+632 632 4001
Director, Transport and Communications Division	Sri Widowati	+632 632 6794
Director, Energy Division	Yongping Zhai	+632 632 6301
Director, Agriculture, Natural Resources and Social Services Division	Takashi Matsuo	+632 632 6834
Director, Urban Development Division	M. Teresa Kho	+632 632 6858
Director, Financial Sector, Public Management and Trade Division	Bruno Carrasco	+632 632 6977
Country Director, Bangladesh Resident Mission	Thevakumar Kandiah	+880 2 815 6000-8
Country Director, India Resident Mission	Hun Kim	+91 11 2410 7200
Country Director, Nepal Resident Mission	Barry J. Hitchcock	+977 1 422 7779
Country Director, Sri Lanka Resident Mission	Richard W. A. Vokes	+94 11 2387 055

CENTRAL AND WEST ASIA DEPARTMENT

Director General	Juan Miranda	+632 632 6871
Deputy Director General	Werner Liepach	+632 632 6594
Advisor (based in Turkey Regional Office)	Matthew Westfall	+49 69 2193 6400
Director, Country Coordination and Regional Cooperation Division	Shigeko Hattori	+632 632 6269
Director, Transport and Communications Division	Hong Wang	+632 632 6765
Director, Energy and Natural Resources	Pil-Bae Song	+632 632 6356
Director, Urban Services Division	Ramesh Subramaniam	+632 632 6300
Director, Financial Sector, Public Management and Trade Division	Debra Kertzman	+632 632 6663
Country Director, Afghanistan Resident Mission	Craig Steffensen	+93 20 210 3602

Country Director, Azerbaijan Resident Mission		
Country Director, Kazakhstan Resident Mission	Li Guanghui	+7 3172 325053
Country Director, Kyrgyz Resident Mission	Rie Hiraoka	+996 312 627343
Country Director, Pakistan Resident Mission	Rune Stroem	+92 51 282 5011-16
Country Director, Tajikistan Resident Mission	Joji Tokeshi	+992 372 235 314
Country Director, Uzbekistan Resident Mission	Kazuhiko Higuchi	+998 71 120 7921-22

DEPARTMENT OF EXTERNAL RELATIONS

Quon, Ann
Principal Director
Tel. +63 2 632 5871
Email: aquon@adb.org

Cabrera, Carolyn Dedolph
Head, Publishing, Information and Web Unit
Tel. +63 2 632 5887
Email: cdedolphcabrera@adb.org

Davis, Robert H.
Publishing Specialist
Tel. +63 2 632 6479
Email: rdavis@adb.org

Healy, Eric J.
Public Communications Specialist
Tel. +63 2 632 6805
Email: ehealy@adb.org

Ho, Sophia S.Y.
Principal External Relations Specialist
Tel. +63 2 632 6866
Email: ssyho@adb.org

Hooper, Susan
Communications Specialist
Tel. +63 2 632 5892
Email: shooper@adb.org

Kodama, Harumi
Communications and Planning Specialist
Tel. +63 2 632 5892
Email: hkodama@adb.org

Lane, Karen
Media Relations Specialist
Tel. +63 2 632 6561
Email: klane@adb.org

Lodoen, Sandra
Public Communications Specialist (Speechwriter)
Tel. +63 2 632 5776
Email: slodoen@adb.org

Maekawa, Tsukasa
Principal Media Relations Specialist
Tel. +63 2 632 5875
Email: tmaekawa@adb.org

Nair, Omana
Head, Media and Communications Unit
Tel. +63 2 632 5877
Email: onair@adb.org

Narayanan, Krishnadas
Media Relations Specialist
Tel. +63 2 632 5403

Ordonez, Muriel S.
Publishing Specialist
Tel. +63 2 632 5790
Email: mordonez@adb.org

Perrin, Andrew
Media Relations Specialist
Tel. +63 2 632 5208
Email: aperrin@adb.org

Roch, Delphine
Public Information and Disclosure Specialist
Tel. +63 2 632 5316
Email: droch@adb.org

Rush, Jason
Media Relations Specialist
Tel. +63 2 632 6480
Email: jrush@adb.org

Samson, Maria Cecilia
Communications Specialist
Tel. +63 2 632 5854
Email: csamson@adb.org

Stojanov, Andrea
Web Master
Tel. +63 2 632 5961
Email: astojanov@adb.org

Wood, Philip M.
Media Relations Specialist
Tel. +63 2 632 6654
Email: pwood@adb.org

Angeles, Vicente M.
Design Services Officer

Javellana, Ariel
Multimedia Officer

Tel. +63 2 632 4207
Email: vmangeles@adb.org

Castaneda, Xandro
Associate Web Systems Analyst
Tel. +63 2 632 5818
Email: xcastaneda@adb.org

Dela Cruz, Ramoncito
Senior Media Officer
Tel. +63 2 632 5881
Email: rpdelacruz@adb.org

Deluria, Melissa
Web Site Officer
Tel. +63 2 632 4614
Email: mdeluria@adb.org

Del Rosario, Ma. Priscila P.
Senior Copy Editing Officer
Tel. +63 2 632 5037
Email: mpdelrosario@adb.org

Inciong, Olivia Sylvia O.
External Relations Officer
Tel. +63 2 632 4484
Email: oinciong@adb.org

Tel. +63 2 632 5876
Email: adjavellana@adb.org

Millar, Micheline
Assistant Media Relations Coordinator
Tel. +63 2 632 4541
Email: mmillar@adb.org

Punzalan, Maria Loreto
Publishing Coordination Officer
Tel. +63 2 632 5895
Email: lpunzalan@adb.org

Salazar, Stephanie A.
Communications Officer (Internal)
Tel. +63 2 632 5434
Email: ssalazar@adb.org

Tongson-Rubio, Samantha L.
Multimedia Officer
Tel. +63 2 632 4816
Email: strubio@adb.org

Villaluz, Nick Angelo
Public Information and Disclosure Officer
Tel. +63 2 632 5233
Email: navillaluz@adb.org

TITLE
Congo, Democratic Republic of the Investment, Trade Strategy and Agreements Handbook - Strategic Information and Basic Agreements
Costa Rica Investment, Trade Strategy and Agreements Handbook - Strategic Information and Basic Agreements
Côte d'Ivoire Investment, Trade Strategy and Agreements Handbook - Strategic Information and Basic Agreements
Croatia Investment, Trade Strategy and Agreements Handbook - Strategic Information and Basic Agreements
Cuba Investment, Trade Strategy and Agreements Handbook - Strategic Information and Basic Agreements
Cyprus Investment, Trade Strategy and Agreements Handbook - Strategic Information and Basic Agreements
Czech Republic Investment, Trade Strategy and Agreements Handbook - Strategic Information and Basic Agreements
Denmark Investment, Trade Strategy and Agreements Handbook - Strategic Information and Basic Agreements
Djibouti Investment, Trade Strategy and Agreements Handbook - Strategic Information and Basic Agreements
Dominica Investment, Trade Strategy and Agreements Handbook - Strategic Information and Basic Agreements
Dominican Republic Investment, Trade Strategy and Agreements Handbook - Strategic Information and Basic Agreements
Ecuador Investment, Trade Strategy and Agreements Handbook - Strategic Information and Basic Agreements
Egypt Investment, Trade Strategy and Agreements Handbook - Strategic Information and Basic Agreements
El Salvador Investment, Trade Strategy and Agreements Handbook - Strategic Information and Basic Agreements
Equatorial Guinea Investment, Trade Strategy and Agreements Handbook - Strategic Information and Basic Agreements
Eritrea Investment, Trade Strategy and Agreements Handbook - Strategic Information and Basic Agreements
Estonia Investment, Trade Strategy and Agreements Handbook - Strategic Information and Basic Agreements
Ethiopia Investment, Trade Strategy and Agreements Handbook - Strategic Information and Basic Agreements
Finland Investment, Trade Strategy and Agreements Handbook - Strategic Information and Basic Agreements
France Investment, Trade Strategy and Agreements Handbook - Strategic Information and Basic Agreements
Gabon Investment, Trade Strategy and Agreements Handbook - Strategic Information and Basic Agreements
Gambia Investment, Trade Strategy and Agreements Handbook - Strategic Information and Basic Agreements
Georgia Investment, Trade Strategy and Agreements Handbook - Strategic Information and Basic Agreements
Germany Investment, Trade Strategy and Agreements Handbook - Strategic Information and Basic Agreements
Ghana Investment, Trade Strategy and Agreements Handbook - Strategic Information and Basic Agreements
Greece Investment, Trade Strategy and Agreements Handbook - Strategic Information and Basic Agreements
Grenada Investment, Trade Strategy and Agreements Handbook - Strategic Information and Basic Agreements
Guatemala Investment, Trade Strategy and Agreements Handbook - Strategic Information and Basic Agreements
Guinea Investment, Trade Strategy and Agreements Handbook - Strategic Information and Basic Agreements
Guinea-Bissau Investment, Trade Strategy and Agreements Handbook - Strategic Information and Basic Agreements
Guyana Investment, Trade Strategy and Agreements Handbook - Strategic Information and Basic Agreements
Haiti Investment, Trade Strategy and Agreements Handbook - Strategic Information and Basic Agreements
Honduras Investment, Trade Strategy and Agreements Handbook - Strategic Information and Basic Agreements
Hong Kong, China SAR Investment, Trade Strategy and Agreements Handbook - Strategic Information and Basic Agreements
Hungary Investment, Trade Strategy and Agreements Handbook - Strategic Information and Basic Agreements
Iceland Investment, Trade Strategy and Agreements Handbook - Strategic Information and Basic Agreements
India Investment, Trade Strategy and Agreements Handbook - Strategic Information and Basic Agreements
Indonesia Investment, Trade Strategy and Agreements Handbook - Strategic Information and Basic Agreements
Iran, Islamic Republic of Investment, Trade Strategy and Agreements Handbook - Strategic Information and Basic Agreements
Iraq Investment, Trade Strategy and Agreements Handbook - Strategic Information and Basic Agreements
Israel Investment, Trade Strategy and Agreements Handbook - Strategic Information and Basic Agreements
Italy Investment, Trade Strategy and Agreements Handbook - Strategic Information and Basic Agreements
Jamaica Investment, Trade Strategy and Agreements Handbook - Strategic Information and Basic Agreements
Japan Investment, Trade Strategy and Agreements Handbook - Strategic Information and Basic Agreements
Jordan Investment, Trade Strategy and Agreements Handbook - Strategic Information and Basic Agreements
Kazakhstan Investment, Trade Strategy and Agreements Handbook - Strategic Information and Basic Agreements
Kenya Investment, Trade Strategy and Agreements Handbook - Strategic Information and Basic Agreements
Korea, Dem. People's Rep. of Investment, Trade Strategy and Agreements Handbook - Strategic Information and Basic Agreements
Korea, Republic of Investment, Trade Strategy and Agreements Handbook - Strategic Information and Basic Agreements

TITLE
Kuwait Investment, Trade Strategy and Agreements Handbook - Strategic Information and Basic Agreements
Kyrgyzstan Investment, Trade Strategy and Agreements Handbook - Strategic Information and Basic Agreements
Lao People's Democratic Republic Investment, Trade Strategy and Agreements Handbook - Strategic Information and Basic Agreements
Latvia Investment, Trade Strategy and Agreements Handbook - Strategic Information and Basic Agreements
Lebanon Investment, Trade Strategy and Agreements Handbook - Strategic Information and Basic Agreements
Lesotho Investment, Trade Strategy and Agreements Handbook - Strategic Information and Basic Agreements
Liberia Investment, Trade Strategy and Agreements Handbook - Strategic Information and Basic Agreements
Libya Investment, Trade Strategy and Agreements Handbook - Strategic Information and Basic Agreements
Lithuania Investment, Trade Strategy and Agreements Handbook - Strategic Information and Basic Agreements
Luxembourg Investment, Trade Strategy and Agreements Handbook - Strategic Information and Basic Agreements
Macao, China SAR Investment, Trade Strategy and Agreements Handbook - Strategic Information and Basic Agreements
Macedonia, The former Yugoslav Republic of Investment, Trade Strategy and Agreements Handbook - Strategic Information and Basic Agreements
Madagascar Investment, Trade Strategy and Agreements Handbook - Strategic Information and Basic Agreements
Malawi Investment, Trade Strategy and Agreements Handbook - Strategic Information and Basic Agreements
Malaysia Investment, Trade Strategy and Agreements Handbook - Strategic Information and Basic Agreements
Mali Investment, Trade Strategy and Agreements Handbook - Strategic Information and Basic Agreements
Malta Investment, Trade Strategy and Agreements Handbook - Strategic Information and Basic Agreements
Marshall Islands Investment, Trade Strategy and Agreements Handbook - Strategic Information and Basic Agreements
Mauritania Investment, Trade Strategy and Agreements Handbook - Strategic Information and Basic Agreements
Mauritius Investment, Trade Strategy and Agreements Handbook - Strategic Information and Basic Agreements
Mexico Investment, Trade Strategy and Agreements Handbook - Strategic Information and Basic Agreements
Moldova, Republic of Investment, Trade Strategy and Agreements Handbook - Strategic Information and Basic Agreements
Mongolia Investment, Trade Strategy and Agreements Handbook - Strategic Information and Basic Agreements
Montenegro Investment, Trade Strategy and Agreements Handbook - Strategic Information and Basic Agreements
Morocco Investment, Trade Strategy and Agreements Handbook - Strategic Information and Basic Agreements
Mozambique Investment, Trade Strategy and Agreements Handbook - Strategic Information and Basic Agreements
Myanmar Investment, Trade Strategy and Agreements Handbook - Strategic Information and Basic Agreements
Namibia Investment, Trade Strategy and Agreements Handbook - Strategic Information and Basic Agreements
Nepal Investment, Trade Strategy and Agreements Handbook - Strategic Information and Basic Agreements
Netherlands Investment, Trade Strategy and Agreements Handbook - Strategic Information and Basic Agreements
New Zealand Investment, Trade Strategy and Agreements Handbook - Strategic Information and Basic Agreements
Nicaragua Investment, Trade Strategy and Agreements Handbook - Strategic Information and Basic Agreements
Niger Investment, Trade Strategy and Agreements Handbook - Strategic Information and Basic Agreements
Nigeria Investment, Trade Strategy and Agreements Handbook - Strategic Information and Basic Agreements
Norway Investment, Trade Strategy and Agreements Handbook - Strategic Information and Basic Agreements
Occupied Palestinian territory Investment, Trade Strategy and Agreements Handbook - Strategic Information and Basic Agreements
Oman Investment, Trade Strategy and Agreements Handbook - Strategic Information and Basic Agreements
Pakistan Investment, Trade Strategy and Agreements Handbook - Strategic Information and Basic Agreements
Panama Investment, Trade Strategy and Agreements Handbook - Strategic Information and Basic Agreements
Papua New Guinea Investment, Trade Strategy and Agreements Handbook - Strategic Information and Basic Agreements
Paraguay Investment, Trade Strategy and Agreements Handbook - Strategic Information and Basic Agreements
Peru Investment, Trade Strategy and Agreements Handbook - Strategic Information and Basic Agreements
Philippines Investment, Trade Strategy and Agreements Handbook - Strategic Information and Basic Agreements
Poland Investment, Trade Strategy and Agreements Handbook - Strategic Information and Basic Agreements
Portugal Investment, Trade Strategy and Agreements Handbook - Strategic Information and Basic Agreements
Qatar Investment, Trade Strategy and Agreements Handbook - Strategic Information and Basic Agreements
Romania Investment, Trade Strategy and Agreements Handbook - Strategic Information and Basic Agreements
Russian Federation Investment, Trade Strategy and Agreements Handbook - Strategic Information and Basic Agreements
Rwanda Investment, Trade Strategy and Agreements Handbook - Strategic Information and Basic Agreements
Saint Lucia Investment, Trade Strategy and Agreements Handbook - Strategic Information and Basic Agreements

TITLE
Saint Vincent and the Grenadines Investment, Trade Strategy and Agreements Handbook - Strategic Information and Basic Agreements
San Marino Investment, Trade Strategy and Agreements Handbook - Strategic Information and Basic Agreements
Sao Tome and Principe Investment, Trade Strategy and Agreements Handbook - Strategic Information and Basic Agreements
Saudi Arabia Investment, Trade Strategy and Agreements Handbook - Strategic Information and Basic Agreements
Senegal Investment, Trade Strategy and Agreements Handbook - Strategic Information and Basic Agreements
Serbia Investment, Trade Strategy and Agreements Handbook - Strategic Information and Basic Agreements
Seychelles Investment, Trade Strategy and Agreements Handbook - Strategic Information and Basic Agreements
Sierra Leone Investment, Trade Strategy and Agreements Handbook - Strategic Information and Basic Agreements
Singapore Investment, Trade Strategy and Agreements Handbook - Strategic Information and Basic Agreements
Slovakia Investment, Trade Strategy and Agreements Handbook - Strategic Information and Basic Agreements
Slovenia Investment, Trade Strategy and Agreements Handbook - Strategic Information and Basic Agreements
Somalia Investment, Trade Strategy and Agreements Handbook - Strategic Information and Basic Agreements
South Africa Investment, Trade Strategy and Agreements Handbook - Strategic Information and Basic Agreements
Spain Investment, Trade Strategy and Agreements Handbook - Strategic Information and Basic Agreements
Sri Lanka Investment, Trade Strategy and Agreements Handbook - Strategic Information and Basic Agreements
Sudan Investment, Trade Strategy and Agreements Handbook - Strategic Information and Basic Agreements
Suriname Investment, Trade Strategy and Agreements Handbook - Strategic Information and Basic Agreements
Swaziland Investment, Trade Strategy and Agreements Handbook - Strategic Information and Basic Agreements
Sweden Investment, Trade Strategy and Agreements Handbook - Strategic Information and Basic Agreements
Switzerland Investment, Trade Strategy and Agreements Handbook - Strategic Information and Basic Agreements
Syrian Arab Republic Investment, Trade Strategy and Agreements Handbook - Strategic Information and Basic Agreements
Taiwan Province of China Investment, Trade Strategy and Agreements Handbook - Strategic Information and Basic Agreements
Tajikistan Investment, Trade Strategy and Agreements Handbook - Strategic Information and Basic Agreements
Tanzania, United Republic of Investment, Trade Strategy and Agreements Handbook - Strategic Information and Basic Agreements
Thailand Investment, Trade Strategy and Agreements Handbook - Strategic Information and Basic Agreements
Timor-Leste Investment, Trade Strategy and Agreements Handbook - Strategic Information and Basic Agreements
Togo Investment, Trade Strategy and Agreements Handbook - Strategic Information and Basic Agreements
Tonga Investment, Trade Strategy and Agreements Handbook - Strategic Information and Basic Agreements
Trinidad and Tobago Investment, Trade Strategy and Agreements Handbook - Strategic Information and Basic Agreements
Tunisia Investment, Trade Strategy and Agreements Handbook - Strategic Information and Basic Agreements
Turkey Investment, Trade Strategy and Agreements Handbook - Strategic Information and Basic Agreements
Turkmenistan Investment, Trade Strategy and Agreements Handbook - Strategic Information and Basic Agreements
Uganda Investment, Trade Strategy and Agreements Handbook - Strategic Information and Basic Agreements
Ukraine Investment, Trade Strategy and Agreements Handbook - Strategic Information and Basic Agreements
United Arab Emirates Investment, Trade Strategy and Agreements Handbook - Strategic Information and Basic Agreements
United Kingdom Investment, Trade Strategy and Agreements Handbook - Strategic Information and Basic Agreements
United States of America Investment, Trade Strategy and Agreements Handbook - Strategic Information and Basic Agreements
Uruguay Investment, Trade Strategy and Agreements Handbook - Strategic Information and Basic Agreements
Uzbekistan Investment, Trade Strategy and Agreements Handbook - Strategic Information and Basic Agreements
Vanuatu Investment, Trade Strategy and Agreements Handbook - Strategic Information and Basic Agreements
Venezuela, Bolivarian Republic of Investment, Trade Strategy and Agreements Handbook - Strategic Information and Basic Agreements
Viet Nam Investment, Trade Strategy and Agreements Handbook - Strategic Information and Basic Agreements
Yemen Investment, Trade Strategy and Agreements Handbook - Strategic Information and Basic Agreements
Zambia Investment, Trade Strategy and Agreements Handbook - Strategic Information and Basic Agreements
Zimbabwe Investment, Trade Strategy and Agreements Handbook - Strategic Information and Basic Agreements
ACP (African, Caribbean and Pacific Group of States) Trade and Investment Agreements Handbook - Strategic

TITLE
Information and Basic Agreements
ANCOM (Andean Community) Trade and Investment Agreements Handbook - Strategic Information and Basic Agreements
ASEAN (Association of South-East Asian Nations) Trade and Investment Agreements Handbook - Strategic Information and Basic Agreements
AU (African Union) Trade and Investment Agreements Handbook - Strategic Information and Basic Agreements
BIMSTEC (Bay of Bengal Initiative for Multi-Sector Technical and Economic Cooperation) Trade and Investment Agreements Handbook - Strategic Information and Basic Agreements
BLEU (Belgium-Luxembourg Economic Union) Trade and Investment Agreements Handbook - Strategic Information and Basic Agreements
CACM (Central American Common Market) Trade and Investment Agreements Handbook - Strategic Information and Basic Agreements
CARICOM (Caribbean Community) Trade and Investment Agreements Handbook - Strategic Information and Basic Agreements
CEFTA (Central European Free Trade Agreement) Trade and Investment Agreements Handbook - Strategic Information and Basic Agreements
CEMAC (Economic and Monetary Community of Central Africa) Trade and Investment Agreements Handbook - Strategic Information and Basic Agreements
CEPGL (Economic Community of the Great Lakes Countries) Trade and Investment Agreements Handbook - Strategic Information and Basic Agreements
COMESA (Common Market for Eastern and Southern Africa) Trade and Investment Agreements Handbook - Strategic Information and Basic Agreements
EAC (East African Community) Trade and Investment Agreements Handbook - Strategic Information and Basic Agreements
ECCAS (Economic Community of Central African States) Trade and Investment Agreements Handbook - Strategic Information and Basic Agreements
ECO (Economic Cooperation Organization) Trade and Investment Agreements Handbook - Strategic Information and Basic Agreements
ECOWAS (Economic Community of West African States) Trade and Investment Agreements Handbook - Strategic Information and Basic Agreements
EFTA (European Free Trade Association) Trade and Investment Agreements Handbook - Strategic Information and Basic Agreements
Energy Charter Treaty members Trade and Investment Agreements Handbook - Strategic Information and Basic Agreements
ESA (Eastern and Southern Africa) Trade and Investment Agreements Handbook - Strategic Information and Basic Agreements
EU (European Union) Trade and Investment Agreements Handbook - Strategic Information and Basic Agreements
Eurasian Economic Union Trade and Investment Agreements Handbook - Strategic Information and Basic Agreements
Gulf Cooperation Council Trade and Investment Agreements Handbook - Strategic Information and Basic Agreements
Latin American Integration Association Trade and Investment Agreements Handbook - Strategic Information and Basic Agreements
League of Arab States Trade and Investment Agreements Handbook - Strategic Information and Basic Agreements
Mercado Común Sudamericano (MERCOSUR - Economic Community Consisting of Argentina, Brazil, Paraguay, and Urugua) Trade and Investment Agreements Handbook - Strategic Information and Basic Agreements
OCT (Overseas Countries and Territories) Trade and Investment Agreements Handbook - Strategic Information and Basic Agreements
Organization of the Islamic Conference Trade and Investment Agreements Handbook - Strategic Information and Basic Agreements
Southern African Customs Union Trade and Investment Agreements Handbook - Strategic Information and Basic Agreements
Southern African Development Community Trade and Investment Agreements Handbook - Strategic Information and Basic Agreements
South Asian Free Trade Area Accord Trade and Investment Agreements Handbook - Strategic Information and Basic Agreements
South Pacific Regional Trade and Economic Cooperation Agreement Trade and Investment Agreements Handbook - Strategic Information and Basic Agreements
Arab Maghreb Union Trade and Investment Agreements Handbook - Strategic Information and Basic Agreements
West African Economic and Monetary Union Trade and Investment Agreements Handbook - Strategic Information and

TITLE
Basic Agreements

www.ingramcontent.com/pod-product-compliance
Lightning Source LLC
LaVergne TN
LVHW080012210926
848481LV00011B/3003